WELL GROUNDED

USING LOCAL LAND USE AUTHORITY
TO
ACHIEVE SMART GROWTH

by

John R. Nolon

Professor of Law
Director, Land Use Law Center
Pace University School of Law

Published July 2001, reprinted 2010.

Printed in the United States of America
ISBN 1-58576-024-2

DEDICATION

To the students of Pace University School of Law, particularly the research associates of the Land Use Law Center.

To the thousands of local officials in the nation's villages, towns, and cities who make land use decisions, the professionals who advise them, and the property owners and citizens who find themselves caught up in, bewildered by, and needing to understand local land use law and practice.

To Anne.

Zoning, including its administration and its judicial review, represents the unique American contribution to the solution of disputes over competing demands for the use of private land. When there are conflicting interests, it is patently necessary for someone to determine which of these are valid in a society based upon the belief in private property and the mobility of the individual.

—Richard F. Babcock
The Zoning Game
Municipal Practices and Policies, 1966

ABOUT THE AUTHOR

John R. Nolon is a professor of law at Pace University School of Law, where he teaches property, land use and environmental law and is the Director of the Land Use Law Center. He is an adjunct professor at Yale University where he teaches local environmental law and land use practices. Professor Nolon received a Fulbright Scholarship to develop a framework law for sustainable development in Argentina. He wrote articles on the subjects of regulatory takings and planning and zoning law under a Charles A. Frueauff Research Professorship in 1991-92 and published three books on local land use law and practice in New York under a Frueauff Professorship Award in 1997-98.

Professor Nolon served as a consultant to President Carter's Council on Development Choices for the 1980's, to President Clinton's Council on Sustainable Development, and was a member of Governor George Pataki's Transition Team and New York's Quality Communities Task Force. His writings include over fifty law review and journal articles and practical guidebooks and a book published by McGraw Hill. He is a frequent guest speaker at national, state, and local conferences on the subjects of land use law and sustainable development. Professor Nolon received his J.D. degree from the University of Michigan and his B.A. from the University of Nebraska.

WELL GROUNDED

Using Local Land Use Authority to Achieve Smart Growth

TABLE OF CONTENTS

Chapter 10

INTRODUCTION

Interest in land use law and practice has been stimulated greatly by the unpopularity of urban sprawl and by the excitement over "smart growth"–a new term urging us to use our public resources and legal authority more intelligently to create sustainable communities and landscapes.

The message of smart growth has been articulated in different terms for nearly a half century, reaching a crescendo in the early 1970s when policymakers and scholars combined to warn the nation of the negative consequences of unchecked development patterns and the continued flight of resources from cities. This movement from one millennium to another, however, has witnessed greater popular understanding of the matter and there is now unprecedented interest in the subject of local land use control and environmental protection. It is understood today that land use law and practice directly address the problems associated with sprawl.

This increased awareness and the great tension between the forces of sprawl and smart growth have led to the publication of this new volume. This book puts what was earlier a guidebook to the New York land use system into the national context and adds analysis, perspective, and illustrations for a broader audience interested in these issues in other jurisdictions. This volume contains up-to-date information on the subjects covered in the first edition and adds coverage of a dozen new topics.

Sprawl is defined by the Sierra Club, in a report called *The Dark Side of the American Dream*, as "low-density development beyond the edge of service and employment, which separates where people live from where they shop, work, recreate, and educate – thus requiring cars to move between zones." The most worrisome statistic in the blizzard of negative data regarding sprawl is that, in most metropolitan areas of the country, as the population grows, the amount of land that is developed to meet that demand increases by five to ten times the rate of population growth. In other words, the surface area covered by development in metropolitan areas increases by about 70% to 100% to accommodate a 10% increase in population. The Sierra Club report states that "sprawl contributes to increasing costs for public services, the declining health of central cities, environmental degradation, loss of farmland, and degraded quality of life." In most metropolitan areas, the complaints of mayors, property taxpayers, and environmentalists parallel this general observation.

In defense of current land development patterns, the National Association of Home Builders (NAHB) counters that most Americans want to live in detached single-family houses on the urban fringe; that population growth will increase demand for housing on the fringe because new residential development in cities can only accommodate 10% of housing needs; and that there is plenty of land left for development, noting that only 5% of the land mass in the U.S. is urbanized. Of great moment is the NAHB comment that home builders are building houses and subdivisions in suburban and semi-rural communities that conform to the standards of local land use regulations. In most of metropolitan areas, this observation is correct.

"Smart Growth" has replaced "Growth Management" as the current prescription for the cure of the problems associated with sprawl. Both recommend various means of identifying growth areas and concentrating new commercial, industrial, and residential development in such areas. In most states, land use decisions of this type are made primarily by local governments, and the difficult political issue is how to draw the boundaries of growth and conservation areas and then enact regulations that encourage development in growth areas and limit new development in conservation areas.

In 1994, the Land Use Law Center at Pace University School of Law assembled an Advisory Committee on Sustainable Development in the Hudson River Valley which included a leading scholar on suburbanization, a nationally known expert on neighborhood and community design, a former EPA regional administrator, a Fortune 500 CEO, key environmental leaders and environmental funders, regional planners and developers, inner city leaders, and a variety of other experts. This we did at the request of President Clinton's Council on Sustainable Development, which asked us to project current land use trends 50 years forward, to determine whether they were sustainable, and, if not, to try to identify the key obstacles to sustainability and the most effective strategies to remove those obstacles.

The Hudson River Valley is a breathtaking laboratory and a formidable challenge. It contains 3.5 million acres of land, 10 counties, 242 communities, one of our nation's most beautiful landscapes, and one of its most powerful economic engines. It is in the path of sprawl moving up from New York City and down from Albany.

We did several studies, including one on what we called parcelization–the rate at which large parcels of land were being subdivided into smaller parcels for development. Projecting the rate of parcelization forward revealed that the amount of open land in the region would decline from just under 60% today to around 30% in the year 2050, that there would be a 400% increase in what transportation planners call vehicle hours of delay, and that for every 1% of population added we would urbanize 7% more land.

This is a design issue. This prescription for growth has been designed by 242 local governments. It is found in 242 zoning maps, which are the blueprints that will be used to develop the region. We called the build out of these blueprints the "phantom region" and declared it not sustainable.

The President's Council had asked: What is the most formidable obstacle to the sustainable development of the Hudson River Valley and what is the best strategy you can think of to remove that obstacle? To answer this question, I had to think back over the history of these matters in New York. The state's story involves a tug of war regarding land use control between localism and regionalism–local government and state-created regional agencies. We have a long and complex history in this regard, beginning with the adoption of the first local comprehensive zoning ordinance in the United States in New York City in 1916, followed shortly thereafter by the formation of the Regional Plan Association in the tri-state New York metropolitan area. These are two strong statements: one in the direction of localism, the other in the direction of regionalism.

Every New York governor since that time has made some statement about the importance of having a cogent state policy on land use to guide local decisions. FDR, for example, wrote to the legislature in 1931, "We in this state have progressed to the point where we should formulate a definite, far-reaching land policy for the state." Governor Herbert Lehman commissioned a 1934 report calling for the creation of a permanent state planning office. In 1961, Governor Rockefeller proposed the creation of an Office for Urban Development and received its 1964 report, which was intended to serve as a guide for future planning in the state. In 2000, Governor Pataki signed an executive order calling for a statewide study designed to rationalize state agency programs and plans with locally designated plans for future development.

At the national level, environmental and land use study commissions, courts, and commentators have long bemoaned the parochial effect of local land use decisions and their tendency to exclude affordable housing and to shift environmental impacts to nearby communities. These effects gave rise to what became known as the "quiet revolution in land use control" which was advocated by a 1971 report of the U.S. Council on Environmental Quality. The "revolution" envisioned state legislative efforts to adopt growth management legislation, establish regional land use planning agencies, and tether local decisions to state-adopted land use principles or plans. In 1968, the Douglas Commission, appointed by President Johnson, issued its Report on Urban Problems, Building the American City. The Commission recommended that each state create a state agency for land use planning and prepare state and regional land use plans. For a time, New York led the nation in this direction.

In the early 1970s the state legislature created a model regional land use and planning agency: the Adirondack Park Agency (APA). It governs land use decisions in 12 counties containing 105 local towns and villages. Its jurisdiction contains six million acres of private land, over 20% of the state. It is a classic example of top-down regionalism. The statute creating the APA allows local control over land use only after communities adopt land use plans and regulations that conform to the Agency's plan and regulatory regime.

The early success of the APA and the hortatory language of the Douglas Commission and the Council on Environmental Quality led state planners in New York to think more ambitiously. In 1970, the New York legislature was presented with the Statewide Comprehensive Planning Act, which provided for the creation of state, regional, county, and local plans–all cross-certified and consistent, another classic top-down approach. At the time, this was the nation's most far-reaching attempt to guide and constrain the parochial effects of local land use decision making. The perceived threat to local control was clear, and the political reaction was predictable, swift, and definitive. The bill was withdrawn, and the New York Office of Planning Coordination–the agency that proposed it–was voted out of existence by the state legislature.

Despite this stunning political defeat, the state's highest court, the Court of Appeals, took a remarkably strong position regarding the need for regional mechanisms to make sense out of "insular" land use decisions. In *Golden v. Planning Board of the Town of Ramapo*, 30 N.Y 2d 359, 2 ELR 20296 (1972), the court upheld the town of Ramapo's novel growth management legislation. In so doing, it recognized the limitations of planning a region one community at a time, stating that "only at the regional level can the pitfall of idiosyncratic municipal action be avoided." The court called for a system of "statewide or regional control of land use planning" to "insure that interests broader than that of the municipality underlie various land use policies." It went on to say that "zoning enabling legislation is burdened by the largely antiquated notion which deigns that the regulation of land use and development is uniquely a function of local government." It found that this system suffers from "pronounced insularism" and that "questions of broader public interest have commonly been ignored" by it. In the absence of any regional or statewide planning framework, however, the decision simply sanctioned local growth management, allowing one suburb in the path of metropolitan development to adopt an ordinance in a contextual vacuum.

Since that time, nine voluntary, relatively weak regional councils, funded by local governments, focussing mostly on data gathering, research, grant getting, and technical assistance to local communities, have been New York's approach to regionalism in land use planning in most of the state. These regional councils are not guided by any statewide plan or development and conservation guidelines, paralleling the situation in most states. After a 20-year respite from regional legislation, the state legislature adopted the Hudson River Greenway Act in 1991, creating the Hudson River Greenway Communities Council and providing for a voluntary regional planning process based on local plans and county compacts that adhere to a few greenway planning principles. Now, a decade later, the Greenway is enjoying some success. Over 100 of 242 communities have become participating members.

Strong regionalism has not prevailed in New York for the same reason it has not prevailed in the majority of states. Former Speaker of the House Thomas P. O'Neill Jr. once quipped that "all politics is local." All reform efforts aimed at constraining local control must overcome this political reality. The danger in advocating top-down, statewide land use solutions is that it identifies local control as the problem to be solved, rather than the base on which to build an intermunicipal process, responsive to regional needs. The challenge for advocates of a regional approach to land use planning and control is to identify effective regional processes that respect the critical role that local governments play in land use decisionmaking. To be politically palpable, these solutions must be perceived not as methods of imposing a state or regional body's will on local governments but as means of communicating effectively about regional and local needs, balancing those interests, and arriving at mutually beneficial decisions over time.

Local sovereignty in land use matters has been established and reinforced consistently since the seminal 1926 U.S. Supreme Court decision that declared local zoning constitutional. In *Village of Euclid v. Ambler Realty Co.*, 272 U.S. 365 (1926), the Court recognized the principle of local self-determinism in land use control with these words: "although physically a suburb of Cleveland, Euclid has powers of its own."

In New York, the courts have followed suit. In 1973, in *Bedford v. Mount Kisco*, 33 N.Y.2d 178, 306 N.E.2d 155 (1973), the Court of Appeals heard the town of Bedford's complaint that a rezoning by the village of Mount Kisco from single-family to multi-family use of a parcel bounded on three sides by the town would have an undue impact on the town. The Court of Appeals found for Mount Kisco noting that "the [village] Board of Trustees considered the welfare and economic stability of Mount Kisco, as its first concern.... Bedford understandably differed from the conclusion reached, but that difference must be regarded as the necessary result of conflicting zoning policies that are confronted at the edge of every municipality." *Bedford* represents the settled judicial doctrine that the state courts will not serve as the mediating mechanism for these border disputes in the ordinary circumstance.

New York's legislature has settled into the pattern of codifying and expanding the authority of local governments to control their destinies, individually or intermuncipally. The early 1990s saw significant progress in recodifying state land use law, making better sense out of a full set of land use laws that delegate to local governments the authority to adopt an impressive array of land use strategies. In 1992, the statutes were further amended to provide New York's municipalities extensive authority to enter into intermunicipal agreements in the areas of planning and zoning and to do anything together in this field that they can legally do alone. Since then, an impressive number of intermunicipal compacts have been forged to adopt compatible comprehensive plans and land use regulations, to form joint planning boards, or to enforce land use regulations on an intermunicipal basis. When one generalizes about this experience it is possible to argue that, overall, it constitutes a healthy and successful evolution toward grassroots regionalism. The problem with the generality is that these experiences are highly particular, occurring in all too few locations.

In 1993, we did a comprehensive review of national land use practice at a symposium held that year, the results of which were published in the Fall, 1993 edition of the *Pace Law Review*. Henry Richmond, then Executive Director of 1000 Friends of Oregon, provided a hopeful article about the Oregon Growth Management statute and how critical the citizens' coalition he directed was in getting it adopted and saving it from continual assaults. Doug Porter, the President of the Growth Management Institute, examined the experience of the nine states that had then adopted statewide growth management statutes–noting that most of them were still embryonic and had not yet provided order to the chaos of local land use control. Porter's concerns have been borne out by recent studies of the effectiveness of state-mandated planning in five states, which indicate that the results are highly variable. The jury is still very much out on the much-discussed Maryland Smart Growth Spending Act, where the tension between localism and state-driven planning objectives is high. John Kincaid, then Executive Director of the Advisory Commission on Intergovernmental Relations, surveyed the multiple inefficiencies of decisionmaking by the nation's 87,000 units of local government in the U.S., reviewed the history of consolidation and management ideas, and concluded that such efforts, including regional land use or transportation planning, had enjoyed very limited success nationally, primarily because of local resistance.

This was our experience by the time, in 1995, when the President's Council asked us its provocative question: What is the best strategy for removing the most formidable obstacle to the sustainable development of the Hudson River Valley? The 250 representatives of various groups interested in land development and conservation who testified at our final hearing on the matter kept reminding us of the political reality of land use: local leaders are the gatekeepers of the system. In the continuing absence of national or state-mandated solutions, attention should be paid, they said, to strengthening the system at its foundation. Our response to the Council was that, if such significant control was to be given to local governments in the land use arena, and if the local decisionmaking system is driven primarily by local leaders, most of whom are volunteers with little experience in the field, then we would recommend an aggressive program to train these critical participants in the development of plans for the future of the Hudson River Valley.

We received congressional funding to begin such a program, which is now known as the Community Leadership Alliance Training Program. Over time and with experimentation, we developed a four-day curriculum that trains local leaders in land use strategies, intermunicipal cooperation, and community-based decisionmaking. By the end of this year, we will have trained 350 leaders from 150 communities; we will have created three intermunicipal councils, involving over 30 communities; and we will have in place an aggressive technical assistance program to support the program's graduates and their fellow local leaders. A recent opinion survey of graduates regarding the results of their training indicates satisfaction and success rates of over 90%. We now have over 40 municipal co-sponsors–local governments whose legislatures have adopted resolutions officially co-sponsoring the program.

This represents one approach to combating sprawl and igniting the smart growth movement. Many regionalists and advocates of command and control strategies would call this a "default approach"–one that will do until a higher level of government can impose order on the chaotic palette of local land use decisions. This is not the place to search for silver bullet solutions to such an entrenched and complex problem. This book is not about regionalism, nor is it about national policy. The great confusion caused by the intersection, if not collision, between federal environmental laws and local land use laws is beyond its scope. That said, this book does suggest a strategic path. If local power is so resilient, then perhaps embracing local governments and urging them to collaborate with a national, state, and regional strategy that is designed to honor their concerns and is based on their participation would be a quicker route to a more comprehensive, less cacophonous approach to land use control. As Thomas Jefferson said: "I know of no safe depository of the ultimate power of society but the people themselves, and if we think them not enlightened enough to exercise their control with a wholesome discretion, the remedy is not to take it from them, but to inform their discretion by education."

Jefferson's words have guided the preparation of this book. It is designed to clearly explain many of the techniques that local governments in the 50 states can use to fight sprawl and achieve their visions of a sustainable future. It suggests a different approach to the "quiet revolution," that of investing in the education of local practitioners and decisionmakers and providing incentives for smart land use policies. This may not substitute for more ambitious reform, but, as one of its principal ingredients, surely will enhance its success.

This book could not have been written without the able and enthusiastic assistance of the students of Pace University School of Law. John Turner, Vice-President of the Environmental Law Institute, edited the manuscript. I am also grateful for the contributions of the many practitioners who have debated these matters with me, and the lessons I have learned from dozens of local leaders who have described to me their struggles to understand and employ local land use law and practice.

We are all students of a complex and evolving body of law and practice that is adept at meeting the intricate and controversial land and resource problems arising at the local level. This book attempts to be comprehensive in its coverage, but in a way that provides a ready, easy-to-use, and practical reference to the matter at hand. It is offered for the reader's use with the certain knowledge that the law in general, and this body of law in particular, is capable of resolving the major challenges faced by society in the 21st century.

OVERVIEW

This book is written for two types of readers. It is a practical resource for land use officials, practitioners, and citizens in New York State; it is also a guide to an impressive land use system for students of land use law and practice in other states and countries. As this book goes to print, the United States is struggling to control its sprawling land use patterns and to develop a unifying strategy of smart growth. Most serious scholarship on this subject references the critical role local land use decisions play in contributing to sprawl and understands that local land use practice is a critical building block in developing smart growth agendas for the nation's diverse and challenged regions.

There are over 25,000 officials in New York's 1,600 municipalities who make land use decisions, 5,000 professionals who serve them, and thousands of concerned property owners and citizens who find themselves directly affected by the local regulation of land use. This book is written for them to use in a practical, everyday way. Its objective is to help them understand the process they are involved in, to determine what their options are for effective action, and to plan better how to create sustainable communities.

Common Origin of State Zoning Law
The Standard Zoning Enabling Act — 1926

- Promulgated by an Advisory Committee within the U.S. Department of Commerce.
- Widely adopted by state legislatures.
- Delegated authority to control land use to local governments.
- Required regulations to be made "in accordance with a comprehensive plan."
- Standard components of local land use regimes:
    —Zoning districts
    —Uses permitted
    —Bulk and area regulations
    —Nonconforming uses continued
    —Zoning board of appeals
    —Planning board or commission
    —Zoning administrator

For land use professionals, academics, and citizens in other states, this book explores the details of one state's remarkable land use regime. The New York land use system bears a remarkable resemblance to land use systems in most other states, but, in its great specificity, it offers much to those who are struggling to understand and improve those systems. The New York system, like most, relies heavily on localities to make critical development and conservation decisions. It authorizes localities to use most of the techniques employed in other states; this book's definitions and discussions of those techniques explain and illustrate how they can be employed in other states.

The New York state legislature and courts have provided local officials with a wide variety of innovative methods of pursuing their visions for the future. The local land use system of the Empire State, as this book will explain, can be guided by citizen participation, enabled by authority to use numerous strategies, knitted together by intermunicipal agreements and regional compacts, and influenced and occasionally preempted by the interests of the state and federal governments. Local governments have used this impressive opportunity to create a rapidly evolving field of local environmental law and practice. Its fundamental characteristic, however, is that it is well grounded at the local level, leaving the essential decisions regarding the scale, density, and intensity of development, and the details of environmental conservation, to municipal officials and the interests that influence their land use decisions.

Chapter 1 explains local land use law and practice. All the basic terms, techniques, processes, and decision-making boards are defined and discussed. This provides the basic understanding that is necessary to learn how localities can achieve smarter land use and conservation objectives.

Chapter 2 outlines the basic requirements of smart growth, including the designation of areas for growth and conservation. It compares and contrasts conventional zoning and local smart growth laws and provides a detailed example of how both work. It then discusses and illustrates the use of a number of land use techniques that may be used to achieve smart growth. References to New York cases and statutes, to specific localities where these techniques have been used and illustrations from other states are provided.

Chapter 3 discusses zoning–the principal tool of local land use regulation–and the comprehensive plan upon which zoning is to be based. State law in most states requires that zoning regulations conform to the local comprehensive plan. In New York, this requirement applies to all land use regulations adopted by localities, including environmental protection laws. Since local governments in most states are not required to adopt comprehensive plans, or to keep them up-to-date, judicial rules determine whether land use regulations meet the "in conformance with" requirement when a viable comprehensive plan has not been adopted, or recently updated, by a community. The chapter describes how local governments conduct comprehensive planning and organize their zoning and land use regulations. Checklists for guiding local practice have been constructed from dozens of local comprehensive plans and land use regulations. These checklists can be used to evaluate any locality's comprehensive plan or land use law. They also illustrate the extensive subject matter that is covered by local land use regulation and suggest the immense importance of land use law and practice to the community's quality of life.

Chapter 4 focuses on those aspects of local practice that occupy most of the time of local boards and those who appear before them. It first explains how local boards must conduct their business. Then the process and standards that govern the award or denial of variances, special use permits, and building permits and the approval of subdivision and site plan proposals are discussed in detail. The rules governing the imposition of conditions on these local land use approvals are presented and illustrated. The chapter closes with discussions of the adoption of moratoriums on land development, and the authorization of land uses that frequently cause clashes among neighbors–the continuation or expansion of nonconforming uses, and the attempts of property owners to develop accessory uses or accessory apartments, and to use their residences for home occupations.

Chapter 5 describes the State Environmental Quality Review Act (SEQRA) and its relevance to local land use practice. When the New York legislature adopted SEQRA in the 1970s, few understood how fundamentally it would change local land use practice. Under SEQRA, all local land use bodies are generally deemed "lead agencies" and are required to determine whether the decisions they make might have a significant adverse impact on the environment, which is very broadly defined. This environmental review requirement has greatly extended the review process and expanded the authority of local land use agencies to condition and disapprove of development proposals. Its use is anything but uniform, and the nuances of local practice may determine the outcome of most significant development proposals. SEQRA has provided local governments new tools, as well–in the form of mitigation conditions, cumulative impact studies, generic environmental impact studies, and the designation of critical environmental areas–to protect complete ecosystems and landscapes. New York's environmental review and protection practice is as expansive as any in the nation and serves as an important guide to evaluating or initiating that practice elsewhere.

Chapter 6 notes that, although no state statute delegating authority to local governments uses the term "sustainable development," a number of techniques have been placed in local hands that allow new opportunities to balance land development and conservation for the benefit of current residents and future generations. The chapter describes these creative and flexible techniques, including overlay and floating zoning, cluster and planned unit development, incentive zoning and its complicated cousin, the transfer of development rights, and local waterfront revitalization planning. This chapter demonstrates the extent to which New York's legislature allows and encourages local governments to be creative in harmonizing land uses and guiding the appropriate use of the land.

Chapter 7 discusses the extensive authority local governments have in New York to coordinate their land use policies and practices across municipal lines to achieve sound regional development and conservation objectives. In one form or another, these laws have been on the books for years, but it is only recently that they are being employed in impressive ways by cooperating local governments throughout the state. In this chapter, the several statutes that allow intermunicipal agreements, county and local agreements, and regional cooperation through the Hudson River Greenway Council are discussed, along with dramatic examples of their use to accomplish what local governments cannot achieve working alone.

Chapter 8 presents one of New York's best kept secrets: a body of local environmental law that has evolved quietly over the last several years as localities have used their planning, zoning, and home rule authority to tackle a series of tough environmental issues. The chapter explores the numerous ways that localities have protected natural, aesthetic, historic, and cultural resources using a wide range of delegated powers. These include local initiatives to protect wetlands, trees, landmarks, agricultural lands, viewsheds, integrated landscapes, biodiversity, open space, and recreational resources.

Chapter 9 explains how the tension between state and federal power and local land use authority arises and is resolved, and what local governments have done to retain control while respecting overarching state and federal interests. The chapter notes that some land uses are more difficult for local governments to regulate because their power to do so is limited by statutory or constitutional requirements of the state or federal government. Provisions of a federal telecommunications act constrain local authority to regulate the siting of cellular telephone transmission facilities. The state-adopted Padavan Act requires local governments to allow group homes in their single-family zoning districts except in very limited circumstances. Constitutional protection of speech and religion similarly limits local land use control of adult businesses, signs, and religious institutions. The courts have explained to local governments that their delegated power to control land uses was not intended to allow them to exclude low-income and moderate-income families from their borders, and that they are required to consider the needs of all the residents of the state who are in search of affordable housing.

Chapter 10 concludes with a discussion of protected private property rights and ways of resolving the many types of challenges that are brought by aggrieved property owners or citizens against local land use laws and decisions. The chapter describes these challenges, covering in detail the subjects of regulatory takings and vested rights. It also covers both the role of the courts in reviewing local land use decisions and the role of alternative dispute resolution and preventive methods such as mediation and facilitation.

Over 50 topics are discussed in these 10 chapters. Most of them are covered using a standard format, modeled roughly after the best management practices handbooks produced by the extension service of the United States Department of Agriculture. The topic is first defined. Next the purpose of regulating the subject locally and when localities tend to adopt such regulations are discussed. This is followed by descriptions of the authority local governments have to regulate the subject, the implementation of such regulations, and the legal limitations and concerns that attend local regulation of the subject. In most cases, this is followed by illustrations of local strategies that have been developed. Coverage ends with citations to the relevant statutes, regulations, and constitutional provisions, a case digest of the principal court decisions on the subject, and references to other helpful sources of information. The digests cover the cases that have resolved the essential questions raised since zoning and land use regulations were first adopted by municipalities in New York. The references include website addresses of in-depth articles written by students working with the Land Use Law Center at Pace University School of Law. These final components of each section provide a ready reference to the underlying legal rules in sufficient depth to allow readers to understand the principles at work and apply them to their own circumstances. The book ends with a glossary that defines the recurring technical terms and phrases that appear in these chapters.

Chapter 1

WHAT IS LOCAL LAND USE LAW AND PRACTICE?

This chapter describes the basic elements of local land use law and practice and provides illustrations of how localities can use their legal authority to achieve smart growth. Land use law, broadly defined, encompasses the full range of laws and regulations that influence or affect the development and conservation of the land. This law is intensely intergovernmental and interdisciplinary. In it there are countless intersections among federal, state, regional, and local statutes. Land use law is significantly influenced by other legal regimes, such as environmental, administrative, and municipal law, to name a few.

By dividing their jurisdictions into zoning districts and prescribing how land may be developed within each district, local governments create a blueprint for the future development of each community. When these blueprints are aligned on an intermunicipal basis, the result is a plan for the future development of the region. These patterns evolve as local boards and agencies review, approve, and place conditions on applications for site plans, subdivisions, and special permits. They change as the local legislature rezones discrete areas and as property owners are awarded variances from the strict application of the zoning law.

Many of the intersecting laws and regulations of higher levels of government are adopted, in the first instance, either to influence or to remedy the consequences of local decisions about land use. This is true particularly in the area of environmental law, where state and federal agencies shape and sometimes preempt local decisionmaking in the interest of protecting endangered natural resources such as rivers and aquifers. Nonetheless, it is the decisions made by boards and agencies at the village, town, and city level that are the primary regulatory influence on the land.

A. LOCAL AUTHORITY

State constitutions authorize state legislatures to adopt laws to protect the public health, safety, morals, and general welfare. In the wisdom of the legislatures of most states, significant authority to regulate land use in the public interest has been delegated to the local level. In New York, nearly 1,600 villages, towns, and cities have been authorized to adopt zoning and environmental regulations, to create planning, zoning, and environmental boards, and to provide for their future development using a large number of techniques and strategies.

Under the Town, Village, and General City Law, New York municipalities have specific authority to adopt comprehensive plans and zoning laws and to adopt subdivision and site plan regulations. General authority to legislate with regard to the public health, safety, and welfare and the physical environment is delegated under the Municipal Home Rule Law, which is the source of authority often relied on to adopt natural resource protection regulations. The General Municipal Law provides specific authority to local governments to adopt laws relating to the protection of trees, the preservation of historic districts and landmarks, and the creation of conservation advisory boards, among other matters.

State legislatures often retained authority to regulate certain aspects of land use, delegate some authority to county or regional agencies, and in certain instances share land use authority with local governments. Occasionally, the legislature withdraws this delegated authority by enacting legislation that preempts the local role.

During the past 10 years, the New York State Legislative Commission on Rural Resources and its extraordinarily knowledgeable State Land Use Advisory Committee have recommended numerous amendments of the formerly disparate land use provisions of the Town, Village, and General City Law. The state legislature has enacted most of the commission's recommendations.

**How Local Governments
Get Land Use Authority**

State Constitution
(Police power)

↓

State Legislature
(Power to plan and zone)

↓

Local Governments
(Adopt zoning and land use laws,
create plans,
establish administrative boards)

B. COUNTY AND REGIONAL ACTIONS

For their own purposes, New York counties can create planning boards and adopt comprehensive plans and official maps. They can provide technical assistance to cities, towns, and villages regarding the creation of comprehensive plans and the adoption of land use regulations. Certain local land use actions that affect intermunicipal, county, or state interests must be referred to and commented on by county or regional planning boards before they are taken by cities, towns, and villages. Counties can build roads, establish sewer and water districts that service developed areas, and form or assist a variety of boards that affect land use matters such as soil and water conservation and farmland protection boards.

C. ZONING AND THE COMPREHENSIVE PLAN

Perhaps the most significant land use power that state legislatures delegate to local governments is the authority to adopt zoning laws. These laws divide land within a municipality into zones, or districts, and prescribe the land uses and the intensity of development allowed within each district. In New York, this delegated authority is found in the provisions of the Town, Village, and General City Law known as the zoning and planning enabling acts.

The enabling statutes require land use regulations to be "in accordance with a comprehensive plan" or "in accordance with a well considered plan." Planning "is the essence of zoning" says the judiciary in New York State. Comprehensive planning is society's insurance that the public welfare is served by land use regulation. Where a locality has not adopted a comprehensive plan, or not kept it current, the courts will examine all of the land use policies and actions of

---

How Are Land Uses Regulated?

- Zoning districts are established.
- Uses are permitted "as-of-right."
  —Principal permitted uses (one per lot).
  —Accessory Uses (incidental and subordinate to principal use).
- Uses are permitted by special permit.
  —Declared to be harmonious with principal permitted uses.
  —Can be subject to conditions to protect adjacent properties.
- Nonconforming uses.
  —Allowed to continue unless harmful.
  —Limitations on expansion or reestablishment.
- Other uses not mentioned are prohibited.
  —Unless use variance is obtained.

---

the municipality, including the zoning law itself, for evidence of the comprehensive plan to which zoning and other land use actions must conform.

D. CITIZEN PARTICIPATION

Statutes delegating land use planning and regulatory authority to municipal governments encourage local officials to provide opportunities for citizens to shape and influence the development of comprehensive plans and land use regulations. Public hearings are required or encouraged to be held regarding all local board decisions on development proposals. State regulations governing environmental review of such proposals encourage local agencies to involve all affected parties in developing the content and methodology of the environmental study that is to be conducted. These provisions express a clear policy favoring the early and continual involvement of affected parties at each stage of the local land use process.

E. BALANCING PROPERTY RIGHTS AND THE PUBLIC INTEREST: LIMITING DOCTRINES

The critical role given to local governments in regulating land use involves them in a delicate act of balancing private property rights with the greater public interest. Local land use decisions affect the right of landowners to use their land in the interest of protecting the health, safety, welfare, and morals of the public as a whole. Landowners and citizen groups of all kinds have a coequal interest in what local governments do with regard to land use. Where it serves their interests, they are vigilant in relying on the legal doctrines that limit the government's regulatory authority. These limitations are many.

The first is the doctrine of substantive due process, which requires that land use regulations serve a legitimate public purpose. Second, the administrative process by which regulations are adopted and enforced must follow the procedural requirements of state statutes and meet the fairness requirements of procedural due process. Third, localities may not improperly discriminate among similar parcels or against types of land users in violation of equal protection guarantees of the state or federal constitution. Fourth, since local governments can exercise only those powers delegated to them by the state legislature, land use regulations cannot be ultra vires–i.e., beyond the scope of local authority. The action of the municipality must be undertaken pursuant to legislative power that has been delegated to it. Fifth, local land use regulations must not effect a taking of private property for a public purpose without just compensation in violation of the "takings" provisions of the state and federal constitutions. Sixth, the doctrine of vested rights limits the authority of municipalities in certain cases to impose significant new regulations on existing investments in land, such as completed structures or projects under construction. Seventh, local land use regulations are not permitted to control matters whose regulation has been preempted by the state or federal legislature. Finally, local regulations must not abridge freedoms of speech and religion protected by the state and federal constitutions.

F. PREEMPTION, PARTIAL PREEMPTION, AND EQUITY

Local land use authority is subject to rights created by state and federal statutes and constitutional provisions. A number of these are based in equity. For example, a local zoning law that excludes all growth or types of housing affordable to lower income people is said to be unconstitutionally exclusionary. The police power is to be exercised in the interests of all the people of the state and cannot, by definition, be used for exclusionary purposes–an inherent constitutional principle. In New York, statutes provide that housing for groups of developmentally disabled individuals or substance abusers must be considered single-family housing and allowed in single-family zoning districts. The courts have found either an express or an implied intention in these statutes to preempt local governments' authority to exclude these types of group residences from single-family districts, the predominant residential zoning district in most communities.

Other types of preemptive effects are found in federal statutes that provide for the exclusive licensing of public utilities. Such statutes can preempt or partially preempt local governments' authority to regulate public utilities, which may not be excluded from the municipality or unduly constrained.

G. ZONING PRACTICE

Local governments in most states are not required to adopt zoning laws or other land use regulations. They have the discretion to do so. If a zoning law is adopted, the local legislature must establish a zoning board of appeals, but no other local land use agencies must be created. Most local governments in New York have adopted zoning laws and have established a zoning board of appeals and a planning board to perform various functions necessary for the efficient administration of the zoning regime. Others have adopted a comprehensive plan and have established a variety of other agencies, such as a conservation advisory commission, architectural review board, historic district commission, or wetlands commission.

The roles that these bodies play and the procedures and standards that they must follow are found in the state statutes. These are often supplemented extensively by provisions in the local zoning law and regulations. Local governments have flexible authority to establish standards and procedures that meet their unique needs. It is extremely important to find and interpret the local zoning provisions in order to know how a particular matter is handled in a given community.

Under the typical zoning law, private land use is governed by five basic techniques. Each triggers a different procedure and is governed by different substantive standards:

As-of-Right Uses and Their Accessory Uses: In each zoning district, certain land uses are permitted as the principal and primary uses of land. Accessory uses that are customarily found in association with these principal uses but that are incidental and subordinate to them are also permitted as-of-right. In a single-family zoning district, a single-family home is the principal use and a garage or shed is allowed as an accessory use. In most cases, the owner of an individual lot who proposes an as-of-right use of that lot need only submit construction drawings and secure a permit from the building inspector or department. Typically, no zoning decisions are involved in such an application.

Nonconforming Uses: A use of land that was in existence when a zoning restriction is adopted and which is prohibited by that restriction is called a nonconforming use. Because of the landowner's investment in the use before it was forbidden by law, most zoning laws permit nonconforming uses to continue but not to be expanded or enlarged. Typically, nonconforming uses may not be reestablished after they have been abandoned or may not be reconstructed after serious damage. Where certain nonconforming uses are particularly inconsistent with the as-of-right uses permitted in a district, the zoning law can require the nonconforming uses to be terminated after a specified number of years. Nonconforming uses that are considered threats to public health or safety can be required to cease immediately. The local zoning administrator must decide whether a use is nonconforming or conforming, whether it has been abandoned, or whether proposed improvements constitute a prohibited expansion or enlargement. The administrator's decision on these matters can be appealed to the zoning board of appeals. Occasionally, the owners of nonconforming parcels ask the zoning board of appeals to grant them a use variance that legalizes the nonconforming use and allows it to be expanded or enlarged.

Variances: If a proposed use of property does not conform to applicable zoning restrictions, in certain circumstances it can be authorized by a use or area variance awarded by the zoning board of appeals. Use variances are defined by state statutes as "authorization by the zoning board of appeals for the use of land in a manner or for a purpose which is otherwise not authorized or is prohibited by the applicable zoning regulations." To qualify for such a variance, the petitioning property owner must prove to the zoning board of appeals that the property cannot yield a reasonable return under any use permitted under the zoning law and must meet other burdens of proof required by the state statute. An area variance is defined as "the authorization by the zoning board of appeals for the use of land in a manner which is not allowed by the dimensional or physical requirements of the applicable zoning regulations." In considering a request for an area variance, the zoning board of appeals must balance several statutory factors to determine whether the detriment to the community caused by granting the variance is outweighed by the benefit to the property owner. The statutes require the zoning board of appeals to "grant the minimum variance that it shall deem necessary." The courts have held that the imposition of conditions on variances is proper because they are "corrective measures designed to protect neighboring properties against the possible adverse effects" of the use of the property benefited by the variance.

Special Use Permits: In addition to authorizing certain land uses as-of-right, the zoning law can authorize other uses but only if a special permit is issued by a local administrative agency such as the zoning board of appeals or the planning board. Typically, land uses authorized by special permit include religious institutions, nursing homes, and day-care centers. When such uses are listed as specially permitted uses in the zoning law, they are declared by the local legislature to be harmonious with as-of-right uses in general, although it is recognized that, in a specific location, they might negatively affect adjacent properties and need to be limited or conditioned. If an applicant for a special use permit can demonstrate conclusively that no negative impact will result, or that the proposal effectively mitigates any negative impact, the special use permit will usually be granted.

Rezoning: Finally, where a proposed use is not permitted by one of these devices, the property owner may request that the local government rezone the property, making the proposed activity an as-of-right use under that zoning amendment. In most cases, the local legislature is not required to entertain a single owner's rezoning petition. Alternatively, the local legislature, at its initiative, can act to rezone a parcel or an area in the public interest.

What constitutes a valid zoning regulation? The restrictive view is that zoning is a rigid, district-bound technique and that the locality is constrained by a literal reading of the enabling statutes. This view asserts, additionally, that zoning can regulate only the "use"– not the "user"–of property. The breadth of the statutes delegating zoning authority to local governments, however, and the presumption of validity accorded zoning regulations by the courts, have made it possible for localities to create a variety of zoning mechanisms not referred to in the statutes. These mechanisms have been upheld by the courts as within the localities' implied authority to legislate to achieve the most appropriate use of the land.

H. LOCAL BOARDS

In most municipalities, the most critical land use decisions are made by the local legislature, which adopts the zoning law and other land use regulations, and by the planning board, the zoning enforcement officer, and the zoning board of appeals, which are charged with reviewing development proposals and enforcing the zoning law's provisions. The procedures that must be followed by the legislature in adopting laws and by these administrative agencies in reviewing and approving project proposals are contained in specific enabling statutes adopted by the state legislature as supplemented by the provisions of local law.

When an application for a building permit is submitted to the local building inspector or zoning enforcement officer, the administrator must ascertain before issuing the permit that the proposed construction is in compliance with the zoning law and other land use regulations. If the proposed development is not in compliance with the use and dimensional requirements of the zoning law, the permit must be denied. This denial can be appealed to the zoning board of appeals, which can reverse it or issue a use or area variance in conformance with the standards of state law.

If, on the other hand, the proposed development complies with the zoning provisions but requires subdivision, site plan, special permit, or other approval, the applicant will be referred to the appropriate administrative agency. The local legislature is authorized to designate the planning board, the zoning board of appeals, or another administrative agency to hear and decide upon applications for the approvals. The decisionmaking process must follow prescribed time periods and honor requirements to provide public notice of the matter and to hold public hearings, maintain a record of the agency's deliberations, and file and circulate its final determination. State law requires that local agency meetings be open to the public and that copies of local records be provided to the public upon request.

Only if the standards of local land use regulations are met and the proposal is approved by the administrative agency can a building permit be issued. To qualify for a building permit, the property owner must honor any conditions imposed by the approving agency, and construction plans for the development must conform to the requirements of the state fire protection and building code, as amended by the local legislature.

I. FACILITATION AND MEDIATION

The administrative procedures required by state and local law regarding the review and approval of land development proposals can be supplemented by local procedures providing for the facilitation of land use decisions or the mediation of controversies that arise during the process. In New York, local agencies have the authority in many cases to establish supplemental procedures to which the involved parties may consent. The local legislature has the additional authority to supersede the procedures prescribed by generally applicable state statutes and to establish its own procedures to meet local needs.

Using this authority, local governments can involve the parties that are most affected by land use decisions at an early stage of the decisionmaking process, instead of limiting them to commenting at the public hearing toward the end of the process. Localities can also establish procedures for mediating significant controversies over land use decisions. Through mediation, the parties can recommend actions, supported by relevant and convincing facts, to the administrative body for its consideration. Expert facilitators or mediators can be engaged to manage these processes.

J. JUDICIAL REVIEW

Judicial review of local land use decisions involves the doctrine of separation of powers between the judicial and legislative branches of government. Special statutory provisions limit actions both against governmental bodies in general and against local land use decisions in particular. The applicable rules of judicial review depend on the type of local body that is involved and the type of action that is challenged.

Courts generally defer to local land use decisions–particularly those of local legislatures–affording them a presumption of constitutionality and correctness. This places a heavy burden of proof on challengers to show that local decisions are unreasonable. On the other hand, ambiguities in local land use regulations tend to be resolved in favor of property owners who challenge them. It is said that land use restrictions are in derogation of common law property rights and therefore should be strictly construed.

Judicial review of local land use decisions involves several key issues: What are the procedures that must be used to invoke the jurisdiction of the courts? What standards does the judiciary use to review the decisions of local legislatures, zoning boards of appeals, and planning boards? Who has standing to challenge these decisions? What prerequisites must be met before a challenge is ripe for judicial review? Finally, what remedies are the courts willing to use when local actions are found to be invalid?

K. SUBDIVISION AND SITE PLAN REGULATION: COMMUNITY DEVELOPMENT

Local governments are authorized to adopt regulations governing the subdivision of parcels of land for development, known as subdivision regulations, and the development of individual parcels of land, known as site plan regulations. They do not have to adopt zoning laws before adopting subdivision and site plan regulations, but the normal process is to adopt zoning first. In the typical community, subdivision and site plan regulations supplement the prescriptions of the zoning law by allowing administrative agencies to review and approve specific site design and features for their impact on the neighborhood and community.

According to state statutes, the authority to adopt subdivision regulations serves "the purpose of providing for the future growth and development of the municipality and affording adequate facilities for the housing, transportation, distribution, comfort, convenience, safety, health and welfare of the population." The general purposes of adopting standards and procedures for site plan review and approval are to assure that the development of individual sites does not negatively affect surrounding properties and that the community develops in an orderly and cost-effective fashion.

Local practice in governing land subdivision and site plan development varies widely. Not all subdivisions and site development proposals are required to go through an approval process. The community can limit subdivision and site plan review to major development proposals, as they are defined locally. Some communities subject subdivision proposals first to a preliminary review process and then to final review and approval; others skip the preliminary review step.

Most communities designate their planning board as the body that is authorized to receive and review applications for subdivision and site plan approval. These responsibilities can be delegated to the zoning board of appeals or another administrative agency. Occasionally, the local legislature retains certain types of subdivision or site plan review responsibility.

In their applications, subdividers and site developers can be required to show the location of water, sewer, electrical, sewage, drainage, transportation, landscaping, and other site features on a plat, or map, of the parcel that they then submit for review. By carefully reviewing, modifying, and conditioning the features of the plats, the locality hopes to insure that new development is cost-effective, properly designed, and has a favorable impact on the neighborhood. This authority is central to the local government's ability to control and shape the community's development over time.

L. LOCAL ENVIRONMENTAL REVIEW

Most actions of a local governmental agency that affect the use of the land may not be taken officially until the agency has conducted a thorough review of their potential environmental impact. The state legislature has declared that all state, county, and local agencies "are stewards of the air, water, land and living resources" and "have an obligation to protect the environment for the use and enjoyment of this and all future generations." The state legislatures of over 20 other states have adopted environmental impact review statutes. Few are as extensive and far-reaching as New York's.

The extensive provisions setting forth the procedures and requirements for the environmental review of local land use actions are found in New York's Environmental Conservation Law, Article 8, which is commonly referred to as the State Environmental Quality Review Act, or SEQRA, and in the regulations of the Department of Environmental Conservation. Under SEQRA, a local agency must determine whether an action it is considering may have a significant adverse environmental impact. If an action has such potential, the agency must first prepare an environmental impact statement (EIS), which forces it to consider alternatives and to avoid or mitigate the adverse environmental impacts of a proposed project.

Failure to follow the procedures required by SEQRA will render the action invalid. The procedural steps required by SEQRA and the time periods within which they must be taken have been determined to take precedence over other statutory provisions and deadlines that regulate the land use actions of local governments.

SEQRA requires local agencies to "use all practicable means to realize the policies" of the legislation and to choose alternative actions or impose mitigation conditions, where practicable to "minimize or avoid adverse environmental effects, including effects revealed in the environmental impact statement." The Court of Appeals has held that this language imposes substantive, in addition to procedural, obligations on local decisionmakers that require them to take effective action to protect the environment.

M. SUSTAINABLE DEVELOPMENT AND GRASS ROOTS REGIONALISM

Although land use practice in New York is intensely local in nature, the state legislature has made the tools available to local governments to achieve a cost-effective and balanced land development pattern within the community and among its neighbors. New York law is rich in optional features that allow communities to designate entire landscapes for consistent treatment and thereby create a larger context for zoning and project review decisions.

Incrementally, the courts and the legislature have approved and encouraged the use of a long list of mechanisms that allow thoughtful local leaders to plan for the sustainable development of their communities. This process results in an understanding that certain areas of land are appropriate for development to serve the housing, tax, and commercial needs of the future while others have features that recommend them as conservation areas, set aside to insure the quality of life of future generations. By providing localities with broad authority to enter into agreements with their neighbors, with their counties, and with regional organizations, it is possible to achieve sustainable development patterns across municipal boundaries.

Chapter 2

LOCAL LAND USE CONTROLS THAT ACHIEVE SMART GROWTH

A. DESIGNATING GROWTH DISTRICTS

At a minimum, smart growth requires government to take two related actions. The first is the designation of discrete geographical areas into which private market growth pressures are directed. The second is the designation of other areas for recreation, conservation, and environmental protection.

What is accomplished by directing development to growth areas? Michael Pawlukiewicz, who is the Urban Land Institute's Director of Environmental Land Use Policy, endorses the notion of compact development, by which he means growth that is focused on existing commercial centers, new town centers, and existing or planned transportation facilities. This, he argues, is necessary to create a sense of community, promote economically viable development, insure the ease of movement and safety of residents, and preserve open space, natural resources, and sustainable habitats. In 1979, Portland, to comply with Oregon's innovative growth management law, imposed a growth boundary encompassing the city and 23 surrounding towns. Fifteen miles from city hall, outside the bounded growth area, is the Willamette River Valley, where growth is limited to small-scale development consistent with the predominately agricultural use of the land. Maryland's novel smart growth spending law directs state infrastructure improvements into settled communities and "priority funding areas," which are growth areas designated by county governments. A statewide coalition supporting smart growth in New York has recently released a set of smart growth "themes" which encourage the state to target its infrastructure investments in "locally-designated growth areas."

States That Have Adopted Growth Management Laws That Restrict or Guide Local Land Use Authority:

- Florida
- Georgia
- Hawaii
- Maine
- Maryland
- New Jersey
- Oregon
- Rhode Island
- Vermont
- Washington

Concentrating development in designated growth areas, bounded in some specific way, is a necessary factor in the smart growth equation. Bounded growth, however, is not a novel concept. Local governments have traditionally drawn blueprints for growth in the design of their zoning codes. Zoning's primary characteristic is the creation of hard-edged districts that separate land uses into residential, commercial, and industrial zones. Traditional zoning districts separate land uses to advance a number of public purposes. The architects of zoning thought that this approach to community planning protected children in residential districts from commercial and industrial traffic, for example, and protected residential property values by placing noxious and inconsistent uses in distant locations.

Perhaps we are moving into an era of "smarter growth," one in which public policy encourages more compact and integrated land uses to accomplish a number of contemporary public interests, such as the reduction of car travel and air pollution and the rate of consumption of farmland, natural resources, and environmentally sensitive areas. Smart growth advocates see the designation of areas for more compact, mixed-use development as a present imperative, a necessary change in the zoning blueprint needed to address the concerns expressed by Pawlukiewicz and addressed by the Oregon and Maryland growth management initiatives.

Nationally, there has been much debate as to which level of government should be responsible for drawing the boundaries of designated growth districts. In Oregon, it is the state. In Maryland, it is the county. In New York and most other states, it is the municipality. Drafts of recently proposed smart growth bills in Albany, many ideas circulated by statewide advocates, and the Governor's recent Executive Order 2000-102 all call for local governments to designate growth areas for smart growth planning purposes.

Under the Governor's Executive Order, a Quality Communities Interagency Task Force is to "make recommendations to strengthen the capacity of local governments to develop and implement land use planning and community development strategies through a voluntary program." The bipartisan Hoyt-Rath bill (A. 1969-A; S. 1367-A) declared it to be the policy of the state to "encourage more compact development," and "investment in infrastructure in locally-designated growth areas." Separate bills advanced by other state legislators accept this grassroots approach, adding incentives and penalties geared to creating intermunicipal compacts within which growth area development can be planned on a larger scale. There are no current proposals in New York or in most other states seriously suggesting that growth areas should be designated by county, regional, or state agencies.

AUTHORITY TO DESIGNATE GROWTH AREAS

If local governments are to design the basic blueprint for smart growth, how should they proceed? New York State law provides numerous planning tools for municipalities to use in designating growth and conservation areas. The principal among these, of course, is the comprehensive plan, without which, the Court of Appeals has said, there can be no rational allocation of land use. (*Udell v. Haas*, 21 N.Y.2d 463, 235 N.E.2d 897, 288 N.Y.S.2d 888 (1968)). New York statutes suggest that local comprehensive plans include a statement of goals and objectives regarding the community's physical development and describe the specific actions to be taken to provide for the long-range growth and development of the locality. Town Law §272-a; Village Law §7-722; General City Law §28-a.

Comprehensive plans can, in fact, be quite detailed, incorporating maps, graphs, and studies that can precisely locate designated growth areas and spell out the techniques to be used to encourage development in those areas. This authority is highly elastic, and can be stretched to fit all development contexts, from urban and suburban to rural, where communities wish to control growth. Growth control measures, including goals, objectives, and techniques contained in the comprehensive plan, were validated nearly 30 years ago by the New York Court of Appeals in *Golden v. Planning Bd. of the Town of Ramapo*, 30 N.Y.2d 359, 2 ELR 20296 (1972).

Akin to the authority that local governments have to adopt comprehensive plans is the power to formulate a Local Waterfront Revitalization Plan (LWRP) when the community is located in the state's extensive coastal areas. Under the Waterfront Revitalization and Coastal Resources Act of 1981 (N.Y. Exec. Law §910), a local government may adopt an LWRP covering part or all of the community and devoted to protecting water-related assets while providing for future land uses in the coastal zone affected by the plan. Zoning and other land use regulations are the tools of choice for implementing LWRPs. Under these plans, harbor development districts, riverfront revitalization areas, and waterfront redevelopment zones have been established–all of which may be designated growth areas. Most other coastal and Great Lake states have comparable regimes adopted in response to the federal Coastal Zone Management Act.

State law permits local governments to divide the community into zoning districts and to regulate the density of population, the use of land, and the size, shape, and location of buildings within each district. Town Law §261, Village Law §7-700, and General City Law §20(24). Although this authority has been used in some communities to impose a grid type of development pattern on the land, with residences separated from retail and commercial areas, zoning itself may be used to designate a variety of growth districts to carry out a local smart growth agenda. Municipalities have designated large parcels of land for mixed-use zones, planned unit development districts, planned residential development areas, floating zones, and conservation areas.

DIRECTING GROWTH TO DESIGNATED GROWTH AREAS

Once a growth area has been designated, local governments have a long shopping list of techniques they may chose from to direct development into such areas. One of these is to lower the density of development and to otherwise restrict development permitted outside the growth area. Facilitating development within the area can be accomplished by using the following devices:

Higher Density Districts: In a designated growth zoning district, the density of development can be increased as a matter of right. Municipalities can use their traditional zoning authority to create a mixed-use neighborhood with bulk, area, and use provisions that create the type of compact development pattern envisioned by the smart growth concept. In taking this approach, smart growth advocates argue, the locality needs to create a sufficient density of development to support the transportation and transit services needed to increase pedestrian traffic and reduce car travel.

Bulk and Area Requirements: A designated growth zoning district can contain bulk, area, and parking provisions that encourage types of development that support smart growth principles. By establishing setback lines that require buildings to be brought up to the sidewalk and by requiring parking and garages in the rear, pedestrian use of streets can be encouraged and an attractive neighborhood design created. Access to residential units and offices can be provided through alleys on which garages or parking spaces are located. The number of parking spaces required can be fewer if real prospects of transit services exist. Lot sizes can be reduced and zero lot line requirements can be introduced to create higher residential and mixed-use densities. Design amenities such as front porches and traditional architectural styles can be included in the zoning provisions. Attention to the quality of the design of buildings abutting streets can encourage pedestrian use, which is important in encouraging the use of transit facilities. In some parts of these designed zoning districts, narrower streets can be specified to discourage traffic and ease pedestrian use.

Incentive Zoning: Significant waivers of zoning requirements can be offered to developers, including increasing the density of development allowed, as a method of directing larger-scale development into designated growth areas. Town Law §261-b; Village Law §7-703; General City Law §81-d. Land developers can be required to provide public amenities such as transportation, parks, affordable housing, social service centers, or other infrastructure in exchange for the waivers. In this way, some of the services needed in designated growth areas can be provided by private developers in exchange for the increased density desired in the area.

Special Permits: Larger-scale developments providing for mixed uses may be approved by special permits issued by the planning board or other administrative body. This practice has been followed for decades by municipalities as a method of combining land uses in designated "planned unit" or "planned residential" zoning districts.

Floating Zones: Large-scale developments can be permitted by amending the zoning code to provide for a special use zone, such as a mixed-use development district, that can be affixed to a large area upon the application of all or a majority of the landowners. That application, if successful, results in the amendment of the zoning map to redistrict the subject parcels and permit the new use.

Generic Environmental Impact Statements: When any of these techniques are used to create a designated growth area, a generic environmental impact statement can be prepared that identifies negative environmental impacts and provides for their mitigation. When this happens, it is possible that developers of individual projects will not be required to prepare lengthy and costly environmental impact studies. This alone can provide a powerful incentive for developers to concentrate their projects in designated development areas.

Transfer of Development Rights: State law allows New York municipalities to establish transfer of development rights programs that concentrate development in receiving districts and provide for the transfer of development rights from sending districts. In smart growth terms, the receiving district is the designated growth area and the sending area is a conservation or natural resource protection area. Town Law §261-a; Village Law §7-701; General City Law §20-f.

Intermunicipal Agreements: In New York, local governments have been given liberal legal authority to cooperate in the planning and zoning field. Town Law §284, Village Law §7-741, and General City Law §20-g. Through intermunicipal agreements, they can designate shared or interlocking growth districts that create real market opportunities and a complementary range of housing types, retail services, office buildings, and needed amenities. This is a particularly important technique to consider when several communities share a transportation corridor.

TECHNIQUES FOR PROTECTING THE DESIGNATED GROWTH AREA

One of the more practical limitations to the designation of development areas is the likely opposition of residents in and near the area. They will be concerned about the quality of life in their neighborhoods, the impacts of increased density, and the effect of new development on their property values.

To counter these predictable and reasonable fears, residents will need to be involved in the planning process for the designated growth area. During meetings with these residents a variety of methods of protecting their interests can be discussed. These include adopting landmark protection laws, creating historic district protections, insuring the quality of the design of new and expanded buildings, providing new parks and recreational facilities, establishing cheaper and more convenient transportation alternatives, and explaining the benefits of a properly functioning, pedestrian-oriented neighborhood.

B. SMART GROWTH AND TRADITIONAL ZONING–A COMPARISON

Local zoning can combat sprawl and foster development patterns that limit the land consumed by the housing and commercial development demanded by population growth and shifts. This is evident in reviewing the conventional techniques used in the village of Pawling, New York, which are fairly typical of techniques used on the urban fringe, and an optional set of regulations adopted by the same village to encourage a "smarter" pattern of land use.

The village of Pawling is located in the southeastern corner of Dutchess County on the Connecticut border, about two hours north of New York City by train. Its 2,000 residents live in a community that is located in a vast watershed area known as the Great Swamp. The community is intersected by the north-south Route 22 transportation corridor and the Appalachian Trail, which runs east and west along its northern border. In 1990, the village began a planning process that led to the adoption of a new comprehensive plan and a zoning ordinance. The plan and ordinance contain conventional zoning provisions, as well as incentives and other provisions enacted to concentrate future development in carefully designed, more compact neighborhoods. The differences between these conventional and innovative mechanisms represent two competing paradigms of local land use regulation. The village's conventional approach induces sprawl and illustrates the blueprint for development that the National Association of Home Builders says home builders typically are required to follow. Its innovative devices demonstrate how local governments can regulate land use in line with smart growth principles.

CONVENTIONAL ZONING

Pawling's village board of trustees enacted a zoning ordinance and map that separates the community into seven zoning districts: four residential, two business, and one industrial. Over 70% of the community is zoned R1, which allows single-family residences to be built on lots at least one acre in size. The central business district is zoned B1, which allows mixed use commercial and residential development including multi-family housing. This district is surrounded by relatively small areas that are zoned for single-family residences on lots ranging in size from one-quarter acre to three-quarters of an acre. In B2 zones along the Route 22 corridor, warehouse, manufacturing, and other high-intensity uses are allowed along with more traditional commercial, office, and retail activities. There is one industrial zone, I1, located in the northern part of the village along the railroad tracks.

This conventional zoning pattern is supplemented by a conventional approach to regulating the subdivision of land for residential development. The village board has adopted a standard set of subdivision regulations that regulates subdivisions of more than three lots. Authority to review and approve residential subdivisions is delegated to the village planning board, as it is in most suburban and semi-rural towns and villages. The primary purposes of such subdivision regulations are to insure adequate provisions for vehicular circulation and adequate provision of utilities and other services, and to prevent damage or peril to surrounding properties.

The zoning provisions in the 70% of the village zoned R1 require minimum lot sizes of 40,000 square feet, minimum front lot widths of 150 feet, front yard depths of at least 50 feet, rear yards of 60 feet or more, and side yards totaling at least 70 feet in the aggregate. The subdivision regulations add further "design" standards for residential developments in the village. Collector roads must have 60 foot wide rights of way and 32 feet of pavement, and minor roads must have 50 foot rights of way and 20 feet of pavement. These regulations add that the side lines of each lot must be at right angles to the street lines.

These physical requirements give the planning board, the village board, and land developers very little leeway in subdivision design, lot layouts, or the placement of buildings on the lot. They create a pattern of land development remarkable in its sameness, leading many to call such developments "cookie cutter" subdivisions. Such regulations separate retail and commercial uses from homes so that distances are not walkable; provide wide thoroughfares for the rapid movement of cars, which discourages pedestrian and bicycle movement; create relatively high cost homes on expensive tracts of land; and spread the development allowed over the entire terrain contained in a proposed subdivision.

In these conventional zoning and subdivision regulations can be seen the blueprint for sprawl. Smart growth advocates say that sprawl can be curtailed by concentrating needed new development into designated development districts. Obviously, the low density type of land development created by conventional zoning and subdivision regulations will not satisfy much of the new demand for housing and places to work and shop. A denser blueprint is needed, one that is more cost-effective and environmentally conserving, and that creates a favorable quality of life.

TRADITIONAL NEIGHBORHOOD DISTRICT ZONING

New urbanists, sometimes called neo-traditionalists, advocate zoning and land use regulations that allow traditional urban neighborhoods to be created. They point out that, under conventional zoning and subdivision laws, most traditional neighborhoods found in urban areas can no longer be replicated. The corner drugstore or deli in a residential neighborhood is not allowed, apartments cannot exist above stores, and houses cannot be built close to the sidewalk with cars parked in the rear in garages that front on alleys that kids use as playgrounds. If cookie cutter subdivisions are the result of standards contained in zoning and subdivision ordinances, the new urbanists ask, why can't such regulations be modified to create different, more flexible neighborhoods?

Neo-traditionalists and many smart growth advocates argue that a new type of land development pattern is needed, one that is more concentrated and that creates a quality of neighborhood in which consumers feel comfortable living. One such approach is to create mixed-use neighborhoods where housing types are varied, retail and commercial services are available within walking distance of residences, public green space is provided, visual and recreational amenities exist nearby, and pedestrian and bicycle travel is actively encouraged. Houses in such a neighborhood district can be allowed on smaller lots, retail and commercial uses can be mixed with residential uses, a variety of housing types can be allowed, and accessible open space created and dedicated to the use of all the neighbors.

PAWLING'S OVERLAY ZONING APPROACH

The village of Pawling has adopted a set of "urban regulations" and a number of other mechanisms that encourage some of these aspects of neo-traditional neighborhood design. The village has used statutory authority delegated to it and all other local governments in New York in doing so. It began by amending its comprehensive plan to call for more concentrated land patterns with dedicated open space, a network of trails, a regional green space network, and residential developments that are fitted around a revitalized central business district. The plan also identifies four large tracts of property located in R1 zones and contains conceptual development plans for those tracts, an unusual device to be found in a comprehensive plan. These site-specific conceptual plans increase the number of residential units allowed on each tract, place this greater number of houses allowed on smaller lots, require the dedication of significant amounts of open space to the public, link this open space to trails and other open spaces and parks, and avoid development of the wetlands and steep slopes on the sites. The plans also call for through streets rather than the dead-end cul de sacs typical of new subdivision development in the area. The specific purpose of interconnected streets is to encourage pedestrian and bicycle traffic in the residential neighborhoods created. Only one of the four conceptual plans, with frontage on Route 22, contains any commercial land uses.

For these conceptual plans to be meaningful, the zoning law of the village had to be amended. This was accomplished in 1995 with the adoption of a new zoning code. It contains a schedule of "urban regulations" which provide for six building types allowed in designated zoning districts. (Pawling Zoning Law §98-13 and Schedule B). The urban regulations differ fundamentally from conventional zoning in that they use detailed illustrations to provide for alternative lot layouts, building designs, setbacks, and the location of parking; these give the planning board the type of control over the design of development that is missing in conventional zoning, subdivision, and site plan laws.

"Infill houses" are allowed under the urban regulations, for example, in all four residential districts. Occupancy is limited to residential use, parking is provided on the rear of the lots, space for alleys is provided, front and side yard setbacks are reduced, and balconies, stoops, chimneys, porches, and bay windows are allowed to encroach on the smaller front and side yards adjacent to the street. "Small houses" are allowed under similar provisions in all four residential zones. "Townhouses" are allowed in all residential districts. They are permitted to be built to the lot lines on lots not adjacent to streets and to share party walls, with parking in the rear. Alleyways and stoops are required, and porches and breezeways are allowed.

These provisions allow great flexibility on the part of land developers and the planning board in the village as new development is proposed and reviewed in residential districts. Force is given to the urban regulations by a provision in the zoning law that gives them precedence, when they apply, over the conventional standards of the bulk schedule of the zoning code. Pawling Zoning Law §98-13. They apply, according to the code, to all subdivisions of more than three lots.

With regard to the four large tracts that are conceptually designed in the revised comprehensive plan, the zoning code also implements the objectives of the comprehensive plan. The new zoning provides a density bonus of 30% for any new subdivision proposed on the subject parcels that meets the design guidelines for the tract contained in the comprehensive plan, conforms to the open space configuration and trail system in the comprehensive plan, guarantees the affordability of 15% of the dwelling units, and is connected to the village water and sewer system.

It is the obvious intent of the village board to induce developers of residential property on these four critical sites to follow the detailed design guidelines of the comprehensive plan by providing a significant amount of additional housing by the means of incentive zoning, now allowed under Village Law §7-703, Town Law §261-b, and General City Law §81-d.

An additional incentive to land developers is the streamlining of development proposals that conform with the urban regulations and the conceptual drawings found in the comprehensive plan. Since generic environmental impact statements were completed on the adoption of the plan and the zoning law, it is only necessary for an applicant to prepare and submit a supplemental environmental impact statement. Pawling Zoning Law §98-84. Development proposals that do not follow these regulations and plans will be subject to a more intensive and lengthy review process, which developers are particularly keen to avoid.

In these novel provisions, the village of Pawling has taken an important step toward smart growth and away from sprawl. The comprehensive plan was developed with significant input from all interest groups in the village. It is obvious from the results that greater control of the details of the design of development, more intelligent layouts of subdivisions, more affordability and diversity of housing, and greater coordination of the interconnections of developments in the village were endorsed by the citizenry and their elected leaders. These mechanisms stop short of the creation of growth and conservation boundaries, do not mix land uses to any significant degree, and, of course, have nothing to do with what happens in the critically situated adjacent communities. As an incremental move forward, however, they bear further study and watching.

C. CONSERVATION BOUNDARIES: PRESERVING OPEN LANDS

The other side of the smart growth equation requires local governments to take actions that conserve some of the open lands and natural resources that are threatened by land development pressures.

The preservation of open lands is one of the few land use objectives found in the New York State Constitution. It is the policy of New York State to "conserve and protect [the] natural resources and scenic beauty [of the state] and encourage the development and improvement of . . . agricultural lands for the production of food and other agricultural products." (Article 14, §4). The state legislature has enacted several statutes that delegate to local governments the authority to protect local natural resources and agricultural lands. Under Village Law §7-704, Town Law §263, and General City Law §20(25), zoning regulations may be adopted with reasonable consideration of the character of the zoning district and with a view to encouraging the most appropriate use of the land. Local comprehensive plans can identify and provide for the preservation of "natural resources and sensitive environmental areas." Village Law §7-722(3)(d), Town Law §272-a(3)(d), and General City Law §28-a(4)(d). The Municipal Home Rule Law, §10(1)(ii)(a)(11), authorizes each local government to adopt land use laws "for the protection and enhancement of its physical and visual environment."

Open space serves a variety of purposes, including the conservation of farmland, wetlands, viewsheds, floodplains, coastal areas, habitats, and other natural resources. Open space maintains natural processes of conservation, provides recreational opportunities, promotes aesthetically pleasing landscapes, and maintains community character and the quality of life.

Local governments in New York have extensive authority to limit the development of privately owned land through land use regulations. Using this authority, localities have protected open space through overlay zoning, floating zones, clustering development, environmental review, incentive zoning, transferring development rights, tree preservation, and wetland protection. These techniques enable them to conserve wetlands, habitat, trees, landscape features, soils, floodplains, ridgelines, viewsheds, aquifers, and watersheds.

OVERLAY ZONING

Overlay zoning is a flexible zoning technique that allows a municipality either to encourage or to discourage development in certain areas. An overlay zone is defined as a mapped overlay district superimposed on one or more established zoning districts. It supplements the underlying zoning standards with additional requirements that can be designed to protect the natural features in an important environmental area. A parcel within the overlay zone will thus be simultaneously subject to two sets of zoning regulations: the underlying and the overlay zoning requirements.

The purpose of an overlay zone is to conserve natural resources or realize development objectives without unduly disturbing the expectations created by the existing zoning ordinance. In areas that contain particularly valuable natural resources, zoning might not suffice, and more specific provisions may be needed to preserve the natural environment. Unique natural or aesthetic resource areas, such as a pine barren, wetland resource area, watershed, or tidal basin, can be identified and protected.

To illustrate, an overlay district can be created to protect designated ridgelines in a community. In these areas, landowners would be required to site all structures to avoid occupying or obstructing public views of land within the mapped overlay districts. This generally requires locating buildings away from ridgelines and ridgetops at lower elevations and closer to existing roads. These standards for the placement of buildings are, of course, more stringent and specific than those required by the underlying zoning law.

FLOATING ZONES

The floating zone is a zoning district, created by the local legislature, that is not designated on the municipal zoning map until a landowner or developer applies for rezoning under that district or until some additional condition is met. Alternatively, the floating zone can alight on a parcel proposed for development if the parcel contains critical natural resources.

The town of Washington in Dutchess County, New York, for example, created an environmental floating zone that automatically affixes to a parcel proposed for development when that parcel contains two or more of five designated natural features that the town wishes to protect from the impacts of development.

CLUSTER DEVELOPMENT

Cluster development is a zoning device used to conserve open space. The New York statutes define cluster development as:

> a subdivision . . . in which the applicable zoning ordinance or local law is modified to provide an alternative permitted method for the layout, configuration and design of lots, buildings and structures, roads, utility lines and other infrastructure, parks, and landscaping in order to preserve the natural and scenic qualities of open lands.

Town Law §278; Village Law §7-738; General City Law §37. Normally, land is subdivided and developed in conformance with the dimensional requirements of the local zoning ordinance. Zoning usually requires that the entire parcel be divided into lots that conform to minimum lot sizes and that buildings on subdivided lots conform to rigorous setback, height, and other dimensional requirements. Using its cluster authority, a locality can allow or require allowable development to be placed on a portion of the parcel and the rest to remain undeveloped open space. Clustering can be limited to parcels with particular natural resource characteristics such as wetlands, valuable viewsheds, agricultural soils, or steep slopes.

The Bedford, New York, town board authorized its planning board to use clustering to preserve "a unique or significant natural feature of the site, including but not limited to a vegetative feature, wildlife habitat, surface water supply, underground aquifer, endangered species, rock formation, and steep slopes" and to protect "a unique or significant feature of the man-made environment of the site, including but not limited to a building, structure, or artifact of architectural, historical, or archeological value." The town of Stanford, New York, requires residential structures to be clustered to protect agricultural soils for farming.

STATE ENVIRONMENTAL QUALITY REVIEW ACT

The State Environmental Quality Review Act (SEQRA), Environmental Conservation Law Article 8, plays a vital role in protecting New York State's open space. The essence of SEQRA is the requirement that the impact of all development projects on the environment be considered at the planning stage and that local agencies act effectively to avoid any possible adverse environmental impacts.

SEQRA regulations contain standards that can be used to protect open space. For example, the types of environmental effects that are to be considered and mitigated include potential adverse impacts on land, water, air, plants and animals, agricultural resources, aesthetic resources, historic and archeological resources, growth and character of community or neighborhood, and open space and recreation. SEQRA gives local boards independent authority to impose conditions on project approvals to mitigate negative impacts on open spaces and their associated environmental features.

INCENTIVE ZONING

Under state statutes, local legislatures may allow developers to build at greater densities than allowed under zoning in exchange for public benefits such as the preservation of open space. The town of LaGrange, for example, awards a 40% density bonus when a developer promises to preserve 80% of a site for farming purposes.

The statutes also allow communities to receive cash payments in exchange for the zoning incentives awarded a developer. This allows localities to use the cash to achieve the public benefit directly. Using this authority, it is possible for the community to purchase development rights, or conservation easements, on valuable open space land using the cash contributed by a developer who is granted zoning incentives to build in an appropriate location that can absorb the development impacts. Town Law §261-b; Village Law §7-703; General City Law §81-d.

TRANSFER OF DEVELOPMENT RIGHTS

New York statutes define transfer of development rights as "the process by which development rights are transferred from one lot, parcel, or area of land in a sending district to another lot, parcel, or area of land in one or more receiving districts." Town Law §261-a; Village Law §7-701; General City Law §20-f. A comprehensive plan in the Long Island Pine Barrens allocates development credits to land in the fragile pine barrens aquifer, based on their development yield under local zoning, and greatly restricts development in these "sending districts." The plan establishes receiving districts into which these development credits may be transferred. Developers who own land in these receiving districts may purchase credits from landowners in sending districts. Each purchased credit allows the developer to build one housing unit over that permitted by the receiving district's zoning.

TREE PRESERVATION

Another means of controlling scenic quality and community appearance is the adoption of a tree preservation law. Such a law allows a community to restrict the removal of trees on private property in order to preserve their environmental and aesthetic importance to the community. The purpose clause of one extensive local law explains that the provisions were adopted to reduce tree destruction, which gives rise to barren and unsightly conditions, impairs the stability of real property values, and adversely affects the character of the community. Tree ordinances typically limit their applicability to trees of a certain diameter and height. They establish a permit system, allowing tree removal but only upon a showing of necessity and compliance with certain conditions, such as replacement of all or some of the trees to be removed.

FRESHWATER WETLAND PROTECTION

Under the provisions of the State Freshwater Wetlands Act, local governments in New York State are authorized to adopt a local wetlands law governing all freshwater wetlands within their jurisdiction. Once a local government has filed a wetlands map with the Department of Environmental Conservation (DEC), the municipality may then enact a wetlands law. Most local wetlands laws are adopted pursuant to the Municipal Home Rule Law, which authorizes local governments to adopt laws to protect the "physical environment." Under these local laws, broader definitions of wetlands may be adopted, larger buffer areas regulated, and a more extensive range of activities covered than is possible under state regulations, which govern wetlands 12.4 acres in size or larger.

The New York Freshwater Wetlands Act lists the critical public benefits that wetlands provide. These include flood and storm water control, aquifer protection, groundwater recharge, maintaining stream flow, pollution elimination, erosion control, and the provision of recreational opportunity, open space and habitat for wildlife, including threatened, rare, and endangered species. The purpose of adopting a wetlands law is to preserve these benefits for the public. Generally, landowners who propose to conduct regulated activities must apply to the designated administrative agency for a permit. Where certain standards and conditions can be met, a permit may be granted allowing the regulated activity to proceed. Conditions may be placed on the permit to avoid, minimize or mitigate the loss or degradation of wetlands.

THE ACQUISITION ALTERNATIVE

An alternative to using land use regulations to achieve the conservation objectives of the smart growth agenda is to use local authority to purchase open lands. Local governments in New York are authorized under the General Municipal Law §247 to spend public funds to acquire and maintain open spaces and to limit the future use of open spaces. Open space is defined by this section as land characterized by natural scenic beauty, lands whose condition enhances surrounding developed lands, lands containing valuable natural resources, and lands used for agricultural production. Local governments using public funds to acquire such lands may either purchase the lands outright or purchase some or all of their development rights. To purchase a lesser interest of this type, the local government typically purchases a restrictive covenant or "conservation easement" from the landowner which limits the parcel's development and then pays the landowner the value of the development rights that have been conveyed to the municipality. When public funds are used under §247 to purchase development rights, the local government must reassess the property's value for property tax purposes to reflect the reduced use and value of the land as restricted.

Under the New York Environmental Conservation Law (§§49-0301 – 49-0311), municipalities and not-for-profit conservation organizations are empowered to purchase conservation easements for the purpose of protecting property containing environmental, historical, or cultural assets or agricultural soils. If conservation easements are acquired by local governments under the Environmental Conservation Law, a land conservation organization, or land trust, can be assigned the responsibility of monitoring and enforcing the development restrictions placed on the land.

Using this authority, local governments have established programs that combine the purchase of full title to open lands, the purchase of all development rights not currently used by the landowner, and the lease or purchase of less than all of the development rights, allowing landowners the option of developing part of the land presently or in the future. A variety of local programs can be created to meet the interest of the locality and the financial needs of particular landowners.

METHODS AND EXAMPLES OF ACQUIRING INTERESTS IN OPEN LANDS

Direct Appropriations: Localities may appropriate revenues derived from local property taxes to acquire interests in open lands as part of the local budgeting process. Municipalities may ask their voters to approve a multi-year appropriation of a specified increase in the local property tax rate for the purpose of acquiring interests in open lands. In 1997, for example, voters in Greenburgh approved the creation of a multi-year property tax increase of ½ of 1% to be deposited in a capital reserve fund and used for the acquisition of interests in open lands. The town projected that this tax increase will raise up to $750,000 over its six-year life. The town's plan was to use this resource as a means of leveraging additional county, state, and federal funds for open land acquisition.

Issuance of Municipal Bonds: Municipal bonds may be issued and the proceeds used for the acquisition of interests in open lands. Voters in the town of Pittsford approved a $9.9 million bond issue to purchase development rights to 2,000 acres of mostly agricultural land located so that a wildlife habitat corridor was created linking important ecological resources with the town's remaining historic farms. Since 1974, Suffolk County has issued bonds on three separate occasions, raising over $60 million for the purchase of development rights in farmlands.

Real Estate Transfer Tax: A local government may pass a local law requesting the state legislature to adopt a bill authorizing it to impose a tax on the transfer of title to real property within its jurisdiction. At the request of several towns on the east end of Long Island, the state legislature added a section to the local finance law permitting them to impose a 2% real estate transfer tax to purchase interests in open lands and subjecting them to a variety of requirements regarding the use of the proceeds of the tax. These proceeds supplement funds raised by the communities by other means, including the issuance of municipal bonds.

Reduced Tax Assessment: Local governments may lease development rights from the owners of open lands in exchange for a reduction in property tax assessments during the lease's term. The landowner agrees to a limited-term lease of the land's development rights, a conservation easement is imposed on the land for that term, and during that term a reduced tax assessment is applied lowering the taxes that must be paid by the owner. The town of Perinton in Monroe County uses a tax assessment table that establishes various percentages of tax reduction which are applied in exchange for the town's lease of development rights. The amount of reduction increases when the owner agrees to a longer lease term. A 25-year lease term, for example, earns a 90% tax reduction. Penalties must be paid by owners who default on their lease obligations. These revenues are placed in a capital reserve fund, which is used to purchase development rights on other open lands.

Nationally, local voter initiatives were adopted in many states that dedicate funds to open space acquisition. In Colorado, Aspen and Longmont voters approved a proposal to dedicate a portion of the sales tax increase to open space acquisition. Alachua and Broward county voters in Florida approved bond issues to acquire funds for open space, watershed protection, and recreation. Over 40 communities in New Jersey and 15 in Rhode Island saw voters approve property tax increase proposals for the preservation of open space. Santa Fe and Bernalillio county voters in New Mexico approved large bond resolutions to raise funds for open space acquisition. Several communities in New York, North Carolina, Ohio, Oregon, Pennsylvania, South Carolina, and Washington followed suit.

D. SMART GROWTH APPLICATIONS

What is intelligent about the concept of smart growth is that it marshals growth pressures into cost-effective settlement patterns and leaves large, unfragmented areas of the natural environment open. Recent experience shows that local governments under existing legal authority are capable of accomplishing significant smart growth objectives, both by directing development into designated growth areas and by discouraging development in environmentally significant landscapes.

One of the early lessons of the smart growth era—one inherited from the sustainable development movement—is that both development and conservation objectives should be pursued simultaneously. The two greatly enhance one another. Transfer of development rights requires both a sending and a receiving area. Incentive zoning in one area can provide the resources needed to acquire development rights and achieve conservation in another. Taxpayers can be persuaded to support environmental protection in one part of town when increased net property tax revenues are to be realized from development projected in appropriate places. Communities avoid exclusionary zoning challenges and property rights litigation when their land use policies are balanced and landowner rights are respected.

This balance is hard to legislate. It can evolve locally when all of the stakeholders understand the land use system, feel empowered to become involved, state their interests effectively, and negotiate solutions that respond to the many interests affected by land use decisions. In fact, local decisionmaking processes, if handled collaboratively, can enable smart growth solutions to development controversies and balance planning for the community's future.

SMART GROWTH PROCESSES

When a landowner submits an application for a development permit to a local land use agency, an extended process of negotiation is initiated. The parties to this negotiation are the owner, the members of the local administrative agency with approval authority, other involved public agencies, and those affected by the proposed project: neighbors, taxpayers, and citizens of the community. Unlike commercial and personal negotiations, this process is not viewed by most of its participants as a negotiation in the traditional sense. Local zoning ordinances give the landowner property rights that must be respected. State and local statutes prescribe standards and procedures that the agency members must follow. Affected neighbors and citizens receive notice of their right to attend and speak at one or more public hearings. This process is not organized, in most localities, as a structured negotiation in which the parties meet face-to-face, follow a self-determined process of decisionmaking, and arrive at a mutually acceptable agreement based on facts gathered in the process and give-and-take on all sides.

The local development approval process often costs the applicant significant sums of money, involves only indirect contacts among interested parties, and provides little opportunity to develop better and more creative solutions. For most significant development proposals, the process is lengthy, inflexible, and frustrating. The outcomes are unpredictable and relationships among those involved are more often damaged than strengthened. Nonetheless, during the awkward journey of a development proposal through the local approval process, critical interests of many stakeholders in the matter are expressed, heard, considered, and disposed of by a decision rendered by a voluntary board of local citizens. This is, in the classic sense, a negotiation that resolves, if not satisfies, each participant's interests. When it is seen as such, methods of making it more productive, satisfying, and efficient seem obvious.

Recent efforts have been made to improve the structure of negotiations among affected parties during the course of the approval process. The New York Court of Appeals, for example, sanctioned informal multi-party negotiations during the local environmental review process in *Merson v. McNally*, 90 N.Y.2d 742 (1997). The issue in that case was whether a project that, as originally proposed, involved several potentially large environmental impacts could be mitigated through project changes negotiated in the early environmental review process mandated by the SEQRA process.

The agency involved in *Merson* was the planning board in the town of Philipstown. The owner of a mining site submitted a full environmental assessment form as required by SEQRA along with its application to the board for a special permit to conduct mining operations. In an unusual move, the planning board conducted a series of open meetings with the project sponsor, other involved agencies, and the public. As a direct result of the input received at these meetings, the applicant revised the project to avoid any significant negative impacts. The planning board then issued a negative declaration, finding that the project, as now configured, would not adversely affect the environment.

The Court of Appeals found that the planning board had conducted an "open and deliberative process" characterized by significant "give and take." It described the planning board's actions as "an open process that also involved other interested agencies and the public" rather than "a bilateral negotiation between a developer and lead agency." It found that the changes made in the proposal were not the result of conditions imposed by the planning board but were, instead, "adjustments incorporated by the project sponsor to mitigate the concerns identified by the public and the reviewing agencies…." In short, the planning board had created an effective multi-party negotiating process that met due process requirements.

Another example involves the DEC. The DEC has trained its administrative law judges and other staff in the mediation of disputes that arise during its permitting process. Under Governor Pataki's Executive Order 20, which encourages parties to state regulatory processes to settle disputes through negotiation, the DEC has begun to mediate disputes that arise in permit condition negotiations, for example, as well as after an administrative law judge's decision is rendered and before an appeal to the state courts.

Under a recently adopted statute in Maine, landowners aggrieved by a land use decision of a local decisionmaking body may submit their cases to mediators for resolution. (5 M.R.S.A. §3341). The landowner must have suffered significant harm from the denial of a local land use permit and have pursued all avenues of administrative appeal. If these conditions are met, the landowner may make an application to the Superior Court clerk, who forwards the matter to the Court Mediation Service, which appoints a mediator in the county where the dispute originated. The purpose of providing this alternative to court litigation is "to facilitate . . . a mutually acceptable solution to a conflict between a landowner and a governmental entity regulating land use." The mediation is open to all persons who significantly participated in the underlying governmental land use proceeding. Others who feel their participation is necessary may request to be involved.

Mediation of this type is properly understood as negotiation assisted by a third party who is usually a neutral. Professional mediators can be called in when the parties to a dispute recognize that they have a dispute, understand the importance of mediated resolution, and can agree upon, and have the resources to pay, a neutral mediator. Where these conditions do not exist, someone involved in the local matter may come forward and attempt to structure a process that results in a facilitated decision, using the techniques of the experienced mediator. The alternative to traditional mediation or structured facilitation is to stumble through the local decisionmaking process and to risk litigation by parties not satisfied by it.

Facilitators and mediators are process experts who carefully structure multi-party negotiations. Mediators and facilitators are skilled in effective negotiation and decisionmaking processes. They help by bringing involved parties together, building trust, clearly establishing the interests of those involved, serving as intermediaries, seeing that options to the resolution of the matter are generated, and working toward a settlement that is acceptable to all parties.

Mediated proceedings are usually informal and flexible, allow the parties to structure the decisionmaking process itself, and result in consensus-based settlements that are not binding on the participants or public bodies. When the agreement is based on the consensus of all affected parties, supported by credible facts, and consistent with regulatory standards, it can be highly influential in determining the administrative or policy outcome. In the court-assisted mediation program in Maine, any agreement that requires governmental action is not self-executing. The landowner must submit the written agreement to the governmental agency involved. The Maine statute gives that entity the authority to reconsider its earlier decision as long as no statutory provision regarding the approval process is violated.

Mediation has been used in recent years as a method of building consensus regarding public policies and formulating land use regulations. In this context, mediation techniques assist parties with disparate interests to participate in a productive public decisionmaking process. In the land use and environmental field, this can involve the development of a comprehensive land use plan, the scope of an environmental impact study of a proposed project, determining how to rezone a community, a landscape or a neighborhood, and coming to agreement regarding specific development proposals advanced by a land developer during the permit issuance process.

Illustrations of this use of mediation methods at the federal level include the Negotiated Rulemaking Act (5 U.S.C. §581), the Administrative Dispute Resolution Act (Pub L No. 101-552), and the U.S. Department of Labor's Negotiated Rulemaking Handbook (1992). Several state legislatures have adopted statutes establishing negotiated rulemaking processes. (Fla. Stat. §120.54; Neb. Rev. Stat. §§84-919.01 et.seq.; Idaho Code §§67-5206(3)(c), 67-5220; 1993 Or. Laws 647; 1993 Mont. Laws 400 (H.B. 317); 1993 Tex. Legis. 776 (S.B. 1049)). In New York, Governor Pataki's Executive Order 20 encourages state administrative agencies to use negotiation to prevent and resolve disputes in a wide range of administrative contexts, including permit issuance proceedings.

Increasingly, mediation and facilitation are being used as consensus-building tools for administrative decision and public policy matters at the local level where those affected by the decision or policy are involved in a very early stage in a multi-party negotiation, assisted by a mediator or facilitator. Theoretically, this process stands to benefit the parties the most since, if the outcome is positive, it not only avoids costly future litigation but makes the administrative decisionmaking process much more efficient and beneficial.

The sum of this is that, while smart growth solutions may eventually descend from higher levels of government, they are within the grasp of local officials and the interest groups that shape local land use decisionmaking. Both the substance of local law making and the process of making land use decisions can be smarter and foster smart growth, as the remaining chapters of this book will illustrate.

Chapter 3

PLANNING AND LAND USE REGULATION

A comprehensive plan is a written document formally adopted by the local legislature that contains goals, objectives, and strategies for the future development and conservation of the community. The New York State statutes list 15 separate components that such plans "may" contain, but do not require localities to follow a fixed format in developing their plans for the future. *See* Town Law §272-a (3); Village Law §7-722 (3); General City Law §28-a (4). New York statutes require that zoning, and all other land use regulations, be in conformance with the comprehensive plan. Although these same statutes greatly encourage local governments to adopt comprehensive plans, they do not require villages, towns, or cities to do so. The model zoning and planning enabling acts drafted in the 1920s contained these same provisions and the law in many states is similar to New York's since they are based on the national model.

When the courts have to determine whether a challenged land use regulation conforms to a comprehensive plan where one has not been formally adopted, they will look to "all relevant evidence," including the zoning law itself and all previous studies, policy statements, and land use decisions of the locality, to determine the comprehensive planning objectives that have guided the community in the past. Using that evidence, the court will determine whether or not the challenged regulation meets the requirement that it conform to the comprehensive plan.

States That Require Local Government To Establish Planning Boards and Adopt Comprehensive Plans:

- Alaska
- California
- Florida
- Idaho
- Maine
- Oregon
- Washington

Adopting land regulations that conform to the comprehensive plan provides significant legal protection for such regulations. When a regulation is challenged, the court will inquire whether it significantly advances a legitimate public interest. When judges find that it was enacted to achieve an objective of the comprehensive plan, they generally resolve that issue in the community's favor. When a single parcel or small amount of land is rezoned, the complaint is often heard that such an action constitutes illegal "spot zoning." When it can be shown that the parcel or small area was rezoned to accomplish a specific public objective of the comprehensive plan, and not to benefit the private owner, that complaint is put to rest. Aggrieved persons often allege that zoning regulations are arbitrary and capricious. These assertions, too, are thwarted when it can be shown that the regulation conforms to the comprehensive plan.

Land use regulations are not confined to zoning provisions, which separate the community into zoning districts and specify the land uses and building dimensions that are permitted in each zone. They may include regulations that protect trees, slopes, historic districts, and viewsheds. They may also include regulations that govern the subdivision of land and development of individual sites. Precisely which aspects of land use local governments decide to regulate and how they organize those regulations is a matter of local discretion. Some have adopted a comprehensive land use chapter of their code or a free-standing land use law. Such a chapter or law can include zoning and all other types of land use controls. Other communities may have several chapters of their municipal codes or several free-standing laws that regulate land use, only one of which will be the zoning law.

Land use regulations may be adopted under the authority of local governments to enact zoning laws, under the municipal home rule authority to protect the physical and natural environment, or under other state statutes authorizing localities to accomplish specific objectives. These land use regulations may be contained in a single body of local land use law or enacted as separate, free-standing laws. Some localities include their subdivision and site plan regulations in their zoning law; some do not. Additional land use regulations may be found in the zoning law or adopted separately. These include regulations regarding erosion and sedimentation, wetlands protection, historic district and landmarks protection, sign control, or viewshed protection. In fact, all these provisions regulate land use and constitute the community's land use regulations that are required to conform to the comprehensive plan.

Local governments are encouraged not only to adopt comprehensive plans, but to do so with extensive and effective citizen participation. The requirement that all land use regulations conform to the comprehensive plan reveals the wisdom of the state legislature in urging villages, towns, and cities to adopt comprehensive plans with citizen comment and support. In the absence of a blueprint for the future development of the community, drawn with citizen consensus, individual development or conservation proposals lack the credibility that comes when they carry out the community's vision for itself, as expressed in the comprehensive plan. When communities fail to adopt comprehensive plans, to keep them up to date, and to achieve community consensus for them, the adoption of particular land use regulations or decisions regarding specific proposals can be frustrating, time-consuming, and unsatisfying to proponents and opponents alike.

A. COMPREHENSIVE PLANNING

DEFINITION

The New York State Court of Appeals noted in *Udell v. Haas*, 21 N.Y.2d 463, 235 N.E.2d 897, 288 N.Y.S.2d 888 (1968), that "the comprehensive plan is the essence of zoning. Without it, there can be no rational allocation of land use." Indeed, the statutes require that all land use regulations must be made "in accordance with a comprehensive plan." Therefore, planning should precede any adoption or amendment of a land use regulation.

Various Approaches To Comprehensive Planning

1. The zoning ordinance is the comprehensive plan.

2. The comprehensive plan is one factor cited by courts to determine the validity of land use regulations.

3. The comprehensive plan is used to decide whether a land use regulation is valid.

(New York fits into category 2)

New York statutes define a comprehensive plan as the "materials, written and/or graphic, including but not limited to maps, charts, studies, resolutions, reports, and other descriptive material that identify the goals, objectives, principles, guidelines, policies, standards, devices, and instruments for the immediate and long-range protection, enhancement, growth, and development of the [locality]." Town Law §272-a (2)(a); Village Law §7-722 (2)(a); General City Law §28-a (3)(a).

While there are no required components of a comprehensive plan, the statutes suggest 15 elements for inclusion:

- A general statement of goals, objectives, and standards upon which proposals for the immediate and long-range growth and development of the municipality are based.
- Consideration of the regional needs and official plans of other government units within the region.
- Existing and proposed location and intensity of land uses.
- Consideration of agricultural uses, historic, and cultural resources, coastal and natural resources and sensitive environmental areas.
- Consideration of population, demographics and socio-economic trends, and future projections.
- The location and types of transportation facilities.
- Existing and proposed location of public and private utilities and infrastructure.
- Existing housing and future housing needs, including affordable housing.
- Present and future location of historic sites, educational, cultural, health, and emergency services.
- Existing and proposed recreational facilities and parkland.
- Present and future locations of commercial and industrial facilities.
- Specific policies and strategies for improving the local economy in coordination with other plan topics.

- ◆ Proposed measures, programs, devices, and instruments to implement the goals of the comprehensive plan.
- ◆ All or part of the plan of another public agency.
- ◆ Any and all other items which are consistent with the orderly growth and development of the municipality.

PURPOSE

The comprehensive plan creates a blueprint for the future development and preservation of a community. Often referred to as the "master plan," it is the policy foundation upon which communities are built. A good comprehensive plan both guides the physical and economic development of the municipality and accommodates social, environmental, and regional concerns.

There are several important advantages achieved by communities that engage in comprehensive planning. First, although adoption of a comprehensive plan is not mandatory, the statutes require that "all land use regulations must be in accordance with a comprehensive plan." Town Law §272-a (11); Village Law §7-722 (11); General City Law §28-a (12). Land use regulations are defined to include "zoning, subdivision, special use permit or site plan regulation or other regulation that prescribes the appropriate use of property or the scale, location, and intensity of development." Town Law §272-a (2)(b); Village Law §7-722 (2)(b); General City Law §28-a (3)(b). If the validity of a local land use regulation is challenged, a written, up-to-date comprehensive plan provides the court with the necessary information upon which to base its decision. Second, after a comprehensive plan is adopted, all other governmental agencies planning capital projects within the municipality must first consider the local plan. Additionally, the comprehensive planning process presents an opportunity for a local government to inventory the needs and assets of the community, to develop a shared vision for the future, and to build consensus and support for actions that will implement the comprehensive plan. Finally, with a comprehensive plan in place, strategic land use regulations can be adopted to implement that vision, protecting the locality's natural resources and encouraging economic development where desired.

WHEN

Comprehensive planning may be engaged in at any time, and an adopted plan should be reviewed periodically and amended as necessary. Although many plans contain long-term strategies for community development and conservation, comprehensive plans need to be revisited as change occurs. Planners recommend reviewing the plan every five years and updating it as necessary. The statutes require localities to set forth in the comprehensive plan "the maximum intervals at which the adopted plan shall be reviewed."

If the mechanics of creating and revising the plan are seen as a process that involves citizens and community leaders in developing a collaborative strategy for achieving a municipality's objectives, then frequent attention to the plan will have a positive impact on day-to-day decisionmaking and the practical progress of the community toward its long-range goals.

AUTHORITY

The local legislature is authorized by statute to prepare or amend the comprehensive plan. Alternatively, through resolution, the legislature can direct the planning board or a special board to prepare or amend the plan. A special board is defined as "a board consisting of one or more members of the planning board and such other members as are appointed" by the local legislature. If the plan is prepared by a board other than the local legislature, that board must forward the plan to the local legislature along with its adopted resolution recommending the plan.

IMPLEMENTATION

Good comprehensive planning begins with information gathering. Physical data should be compiled and considered, regarding, for example, roads and transportation, wetlands, water, sewer, utilities, soils, and drainage. Additionally, the community should inventory its assets–natural, historic, cultural, and geographic–and consider to what extent these features should be enhanced or protected. The municipality must also consider its needs. It should ask, for example, whether there are adequate housing resources, parks, economic development, capital infrastructure, and open space in the community. Are there areas that are particularly appropriate for growth and others in need of conservation? The plans of neighboring municipalities should also be examined, as well as regional economic, environmental, and social needs.

Based on this information, the locality can state its objectives in the comprehensive plan. This statement may address both the intermediate and the long-range goals of the municipality. Further, the comprehensive plan may include specific land use techniques by which the municipality can achieve each of its objectives. These include overlay, cluster, incentive, and agricultural zoning, designating critical environmental areas and floating zones, and the transfer of development rights and planned unit developments, among other strategies. Non-regulatory techniques such as land acquisition, tax incentives, infrastructure investment, and streamlined permit review, as well as grant or loan programs, may also be considered.

Local citizens should participate to the greatest extent possible in forming and implementing the comprehensive plan. Surveys and polls, town meetings, charettes and focused workshops are some of the many techniques available to draw citizens into this process. A plan that not only addresses the needs of the community but is developed with citizen participation and through consensus will be more effective in creating a viable work plan for the future.

To assure that the public is given ample opportunity to comment on the components of the plan, the statutes require that one or more public hearings be held during the plan's preparation. *See* Town Law §272-a (6); Village Law §7-722 (6); General City Law §28-a (7). If the plan is prepared by the planning board or a special board, the local legislature must hold a public hearing within 90 days after receiving the proposed plan. Notice of all required public hearings must be published in a newspaper of general circulation at least 10 calendar days before the hearing. During that time, a copy of the proposed plan or amendment must be made available, at the clerk's office, for the public to review.

If the proposed plan is prepared by the special board or the legislature, the planning board can be given an opportunity to review it and make recommendations prior to action by the local legislature. The proposal must, however, be referred to the county for its review and recommendations. Additionally, prior to adoption, a comprehensive plan is subject to the provisions of the State Environmental Quality Review Act, and the impacts of the plan must be considered and, if necessary, mitigated.

ILLUSTRATION

The town of Pittsford, located on the Erie Canal in Monroe County, was concerned with the loss of its farmland, open space, and other natural resources. In 1995, it decided to update its comprehensive plan and create a vision for the town's future. With the help of many individuals and community organizations, the town drafted *A Greenprint for the Future*, "an action plan for protecting important resources . . . It will guide public and private actions to a balanced blend of farmlands, open spaces, and appropriate development."

The plan identifies and recommends specific strategies, including the purchase of conservation easements, incentive zoning, and other land use techniques to protect important resources in the town. In the words of the plan,

> The Greenprint provides a comprehensive solution to the resource protection needs of the developing landscape of the town. When it is finished, the community of Pittsford can reflect on its commitment to the future and look with pride on the balanced blend of open space with development, on the working farmlands and active recreation centers, on the successful commercial areas and quiet preserves.

LIMITATIONS AND CONCERNS

There are many benefits and values to good comprehensive planning. It does, however, take time, cost money, and require effort. Additionally, many good plans are adopted and then lie dormant on a shelf in the clerk's office. This need not be the case. The comprehensive plan can serve as an opportunity for the community to create a shared vision for the future and a strategy to accomplish that vision. It may lead to updating the local zoning law and other land use regulations and incorporating new ideas and techniques to achieve the community's objectives. Since in New York there are few requirements that a comprehensive plan must meet, however, local leaders may devote just the time and resources needed to address their particular planning issues.

Land use regulations are often challenged as being "not in accordance with a comprehensive plan." When there is a written, up-to-date plan, the court is best able to discern whether the regulation is a permissible exercise of local authority. These plans are given great weight, and courts are hesitant to invalidate a regulation adopted to implement such a plan. There is little doubt that a regulation that accomplishes an express objective of the comprehensive plan substantially advances a legitimate public objective, the judicial standard by which challenged regulations are measured.

Difficulty can arise when a locality has no comprehensive plan or the plan is out-of-date. In these cases, the court looks for comprehensiveness of planning by examining all relevant evidence, which can include the municipality's previous land use decisions as well as the zoning law. Based on the information presented, the court will decide whether the challenged action was adopted in conformance with the community's "total planning strategy" or reflects special interest, irrational ad hocery. Obviously, this approach allows the court great discretion. In the absence of a comprehensive plan, a regulation can appear to be arbitrary or capricious–simply a response to the complaints or concerns of neighbors. Insuring that land use regulations advance the objectives of the comprehensive plan has been mentioned in numerous scholarly articles as the community's best insurance against claims that its regulations violate substantive due process guarantees or constitute a taking of property without just compensation.

STATUTES

The definition of a comprehensive plan and the suggested elements that it may contain, as well as all procedural requirements, can be found at New York State Village Law §7-722, Town Law §272-a, and General City Law §28-a.

Village Law §7-704, Town Law §263, and General City Law §20(25) require that zoning laws conform to the comprehensive plan.

CASE DIGEST

The New York Court of Appeals, in *Udell v. Haas*, 21 N.Y.2d 463, 235 N.E.2d 897, 288 N.Y.S.2d 888 (1968), struck down a village zoning amendment because it failed to conform to the comprehensive plan requirement. In 1951, when the plaintiff bought the property, it was zoned Business A, allowing for retail, office, and laboratory uses. Nine years later, the plaintiff's representative presented building plans to the village for a business development. That same night, the planning board recommended that the area in which the plaintiff's property was located be changed from business to residential. The local legislature rezoned the land shortly thereafter but failed to articulate the comprehensive planning objectives achieved by the rezoning.

The court concluded that the "vague desires of a segment of the public were not a proper reason to interfere with the [plaintiff's] right to use his property in a manner which for some 20 odd years was considered perfectly proper. If there is to be any justification for this interference with [plaintiff's] use of his property, it must be found in the needs and goals of the community as articulated in a rational statement of land use control policies known as the comprehensive plan." In the absence of a formally accepted comprehensive plan, the court examined "all relevant evidence," including the zoning map and law, for evidence of comprehensive planning. The court also reviewed a 1958 zoning amendment entitled Development Policy for the Village. This amendment envisioned the village as a low-density, single-family community with commercial development limited to outlying areas. The court noted that the plaintiff's land was located in that commercial area prior to the 1960 rezoning. The court reasoned that a "comprehensive plan requires that the rezoning should not conflict with the fundamental land use policies and development plans of the community" and invalidated the rezoning.

The Second Department has invalidated zoning provisions that established a planned residential district where no principal as-of-right uses were allowed. Instead, the zoning established 12 uses that were permitted only upon issuance of special permits by the zoning board of appeals. *Marshall v. Wappinger Falls*, 28 A.D.2d 542, 279 N.Y.S.2d 654 (2d Dep't 1967). The court held that the establishment of this district was unauthorized by the Village Law and that it "was not zoning in accordance with a comprehensive plan but rather was a device to permit, in effect, lot-by-lot zoning" by the zoning board.

In *Dur-Bar Realty Co. v. City of Utica*, 57 A.D.2d 51, 394 N.Y.S.2d 913 (4th Dep't 1977), the court upheld a planned unit development law that created a land conservation district for land lying in a floodplain which allowed no as-of-right uses but only certain special uses by permit. The court sustained the law because of the "unique use control problems" presented by the environmentally constrained land in the new district. The court distinguished the *Wappinger Falls* decision by stating that "[i]n *Wappinger Falls* . . . it does not appear that the land in the challenged district was in any way unusual in topography or location so as to justify the subjection of all use proposals to case by case decision." However, the creation of the land conservation district in *Dur-Bar* was "a product of an assessment of the character of the land in light of the public health and safety interests in being protected against flooding and other hazards that would result from building in an area unsuitable for intensive development." The court concluded that "the critical difference between *Wappinger Falls* and the present case is that there the special permit device was used as a substitute for comprehensive land use planning, whereas here the device was chosen in furtherance of comprehensive planning."

In *McBride v. Town of Forestburgh*, 54 A.D.2d 396, 388 N.Y.S.2d 940 (3d Dep't 1972), the court wrote that "[i]t would appear that neither a master plan nor even a written plan is necessary." In the court's view, "the requirements of the enabling statute are met if implicit in the law there is the element of planning which is both rational and consistent with the basic land use policies of the community." The court further held that there was a sufficient showing of a comprehensive plan based on the small size of the community and the planning done before the adoption of the law.

The decision in *Golden v. Planning Board of Town of Ramapo*, 30 N.Y.2d 359, 2 ELR 20296 (1972), recognized the authority of local governments to influence the shape and pace of development within their boundaries, provided that the goal is to channel but not exclude development. Here several developers challenged the town's right to adopt a comprehensive plan and zoning law that worked to slow subdivision of property to a pace that the town could support with infrastructure to be provided under its long-term capital plan. "[The town] has utilized its comprehensive plan to implement its timing controls. . . . Considered as a whole, it represents both in its inception and implementation a reasonable attempt to provide for the sequential, orderly development of land in conjunction with the needs of the community, as well as individual parcels of land."

The plaintiffs in *Kraizberg v. Shankey*, 167 A.D.2d 370, 561 N.Y.S.2d 600 (2d Dep't 1990), applied to a town board for a sewer extension and later the formation of a new sewer district. The town board denied this application following public meetings where the community voiced its opposition to the extension. There was no evidence that the town board considered the interests and benefits of the community as a whole or referenced a comprehensive plan. Based on this evidence, the court found the board's actions to be arbitrary and capricious and not supported by substantial evidence. The court held that "the Board's determination denying the establishment of the sewer district was not based upon a determination of the public interest but upon the desire of the town residents and the Board to minimize development," and therefore the decision was invalid.

In *Osiecki v. Town of Huntington*, 170 A.D.2d 490, 565 N.Y.S.2d 564 (2d Dep't 1991), the town maintained that it was "not obliged to slavish servitude to the master plan and that it was free, in 1989, to determine that the master plan should not be followed with regard to [plaintiff's] property." The court determined that the town had failed to articulate a specific rationale for departing from its comprehensive plan in adopting the zoning amendment, and held that to sustain the rezoning without supportive planning rationale "would invite the kind of ad hoc and arbitrary application of zoning power that the comprehensive planning requirement was designed to avoid." The rezoning of the plaintiff's parcel of land was void since it did not comport with the town's comprehensive plan.

REFERENCES

John R. Nolon, *Comprehensive Land Use Planning: Learning How and Where to Grow*, at http://www.pace.edu/lawschool/landuse/nolona.html (visited Feb. 2, 2001).

Cori Fay Traub & David Church, *A Practical Guide to Comprehensive Planning*, New York Planning Federation (1996).

Guide to Planning and Zoning Laws in New York State, New York State Department of State, Division of Local Government; James A. Coon Technical Series.

Zoning and the Comprehensive Plan, New York State Department of State, Division of Local Government; James A. Coon Technical Series.

B. COMPREHENSIVE PLAN DIAGNOSTIC CHECKLIST

In New York, all local land use regulations must be consistent with the community's comprehensive plan. Although state law specifies what may be included in a comprehensive plan, it does little to explain how a community engages in the comprehensive planning process. In the material that follows, a flexible process for developing and amending a local comprehensive plan is discussed. A general planning process is set forth that municipal leaders can follow to insure that the public is properly consulted and supports the plan. Following that description of the process is a checklist of items that a municipality may include in its comprehensive plan. Although the material is based on New York legislation, it is designed for potential use both in New York State and in other jurisdictions.

Because of the great diversity of New York's communities, and for use in communities in other states, it is important that this lengthy listing of steps and components of comprehensive planning be seen only as a checklist, not as a recommendation or prescription. For some communities, excellent comprehensive planning can be done by taking a few steps over a relatively short period to create a brief comprehensive plan that covers just a few key issues that the community faces. The detail of the following material should not give the impression that all communities should take all these steps or that their plans should contain all these components. This checklist, together with the material surrounding it, is simply a listing of topics and considerations for wise minds to apply to local circumstances.

The need for this type of flexibility has been recognized by the New York State legislature. It has found that "[t]he great diversity of resources and conditions that exist within and among [communities] of the state compels the consideration of such diversity in the development of each comprehensive plan." Town Law §272-a (1)(d); Village Law §7-722 (1)(d); General City Law §28-a (2)(d). The following material is intended to suggest a range of options for community leaders to consider.

BASIC STATUTORY PROVISIONS

DEFINITION

A comprehensive plan is a written document that identifies the goals, objectives, and devices for the "immediate and long-range protection, enhancement, growth and development" of the community.

EFFECT

The effect of adopting a comprehensive plan is that all local land development regulations must conform to its provisions. Other governmental agencies, such as state agencies, must consider the local comprehensive plan in planning their capital projects within the locality.

RECOMMENDED COMPONENTS

There are no required components of a comprehensive plan. It "may" contain:

- Statements of goals and objectives
- Identification of existing land uses and population trends
- Consideration of man-made and natural resources
- Location of existing public facilities, utilities and infrastructure
- Existing and future housing needs, including affordable housing
- Existing and future location of public service facilities
- Location of present and future commercial and industrial facilities

- ♦ Policies and strategies for improving the local economy
- ♦ Proposed methods of implementing the plan's objectives and
- ♦ Any other items consistent with orderly growth and development.

OTHER ELEMENTS

The plan must specify the maximum intervals at which the adopted plan will be reviewed. The plan may consider the needs of the region and plans of other relevant public agencies.

PLAN PREPARATION AND ADOPTION

The plan may be prepared by the local legislature, the planning board or a specially constituted board including at least one member of the planning board. Public hearings and other meetings are to be held prior to adoption.

The comprehensive plan must be subjected to environmental review, must be consistent with any agricultural district in the community, and must be submitted to the county or regional planning board for its review and comment. The local legislature must adopt the plan. Following its adoption, the plan must be filed in accordance with the law.

PUBLIC PARTICIPATION IN PLAN PREPARATION

IMPORTANCE

New York State law declares that an open, responsible, and flexible planning process is essential to the preparation of the comprehensive plan. *See* Town Law §272-a (1)(e); Village Law §7-722 (1)(e); General City Law §28-a (2)(e). This invites, but does not require, public participation in all phases of plan development so that public consensus will be reached and the community will support the plan.

PROCESS

New York law allows the board preparing the plan to conduct meetings as it deems necessary to assure full opportunity for citizen participation in the preparation of the plan or in any amendment to an existing plan. At a minimum, the board preparing the plan must hold one public hearing. *See* Town Law §272-a (6); Village Law §7-722 (6); General City Law §28-a (7).

METHODS

To gather all available ideas and secure the support of the entire community, meetings can be conducted on a communitywide basis, in neighborhoods, over long weekends, or in series. Committees and subcommittees can be formed to conduct surveys and prepare reports on public needs and goals. Meetings with representatives of the media can be held, inserts on the process and early drafts can be placed in local papers, and special mailings can be made to all local postal addresses. Special efforts can be made to identify all groups with a stake in the community's future and to involve key representatives in the preparation of the plan. Such representatives can even be appointed to the special board that drafts the plan or can be invited to join an advisory committee to assist the board.

PARTIES INVOLVED

The New York statutory process allows great flexibility in involving citizens and experts in the preparation of the comprehensive plan. A municipality may seek the input of those whose support is necessary for the plan's approval and those who will be affected by the plan's implementation. These groups and individuals may include elected officials, members of the planning board and zoning board of appeals, the administrative enforcement officer, the municipal assessor, the highway superintendent, the park and recreation commissioner, members of the conservation commission, a local historian, the sewer/water superintendent, developers, representatives of local utilities, business groups, civic groups, neighborhood associations, members of the school board, and local environmental organizations. Excluding any of these people from the planning process runs the risk that the plan will not discuss and consider valuable data and views necessary for its effectiveness. In turn, the plan's failure to address important considerations may ultimately generate opposition to its approval.

ORGANIZATION OF THE COMPREHENSIVE PLAN

SUGGESTED PLAN COMPONENTS

As suggested by New York State law, a comprehensive plan may have six major components:

1. **Issue Identification:** sets forth data and community opinion and discusses and analyzes this information to determine the critical land use issues and unique opportunities of the community.

2. **Public Infrastructure:** discusses the adequacy of existing public infrastructure, such as water supply, wastewater treatment facilities, and solid waste disposal, and examines the potential need for increased facilities.

3. **Public Services:** considers the adequacy of existing services such as schools, emergency services, and health-care facilities, and the potential need for increased services.

4. **Resource Protection:** discusses the adequacy of present efforts to preserve both the natural and man-made environments within the community and examines the need for greater protection of these resources.

5. **Economic Development:** identifies present economic development activities, such as tourism and light industry, and sets forth strategies for improving the community's economic base.

6. **Implementation Plan:** establishes how the strategies contained in each component of the plan will be implemented and coordinated with other plan components to achieve the goals of the comprehensive plan.

See Town Law §272-a (3); Village Law §7-722 (3); General City Law §28-a (4).

ORGANIZATION OF COMPONENTS

The components that deal with public infrastructure, public services, resource protection, and economic development are often divided into four additional sub-components or sections:

1. **Background Information:** data and community opinion relevant to the component under discussion.

2. **Goals:** broad statements of ideal future conditions that are desired.

3. **Objectives:** statements of attainable, quantifiable, intermediate-term achievements that help accomplish each goal.

4. **Strategies:** a set of actions to be undertaken to accomplish each objective.

THE PLANNING PROCESS

IDENTIFYING CRITICAL ISSUES

To assess the critical issues and unique opportunities of the community, it is necessary for the board charged with preparation of the plan to consider and evaluate both community opinion and reliable data.

Surveys: Community opinion may be gathered by conducting surveys or holding public meetings where the public presents its views regarding critical issues and unique opportunities.

Data, Information, and Studies: Readily available data may be collected from information sources such as the United States Bureau of the Census, state agencies, and the county government. Studies may be conducted on important local conditions, such as existing land uses, threatened natural resources, and the need for jobs and housing. Important data useful in plan preparation include:

1. History of the community
2. Population trends and demographics
3. Land use and development trends, such as housing, commercial, industrial, and agricultural development
4. Adequacy of existing public facilities, utilities and infrastructure
5. Adequacy of existing public services
6. Present economic trends, such as sales tax information, property tax rates, and employment rates
7. Existing natural resource conditions, such as steep slopes, soil types, wetlands, watercourses, floodplains, aquifers, forests, and rare plant and animal habitats
8. Historic, cultural, and scenic resources
9. Identification of the community's unique strengths and opportunities.

Critical Issues and Unique Opportunities: The purpose of gathering and analyzing community opinion, collecting data, and conducting studies is to identify the critical issues that the community faces as well as its unique opportunities. This information may reveal, for example, that the cost of housing is escalating, the tax base is not expanding, agricultural land is disappearing, or important natural resources are threatened. It will also indicate the unique characteristics, strengths, and opportunities that the community possesses. From this list, the board preparing the comprehensive plan can determine which issues the plan must address in detail and which strategies are the most feasible.

SETTING GOALS

With community participation, the board can set goals that address each critical issue selected in the prior stage of planning and build upon the community's unique strengths, characteristics, and opportunities. The aim in each case is to eliminate the problem identified while strengthening the community's positive attributes. For example, the board's goal might be to provide an adequate supply of housing of various types and prices to meet the needs of the present and future population of the community. Other goals might be to retain existing wetlands and protect them from all sources of pollution, or to preserve and protect the community's unique scenic and historic resources and to base the community's economic development policy on the strategic value of those resources.

ESTABLISHING OBJECTIVES

The board can then identify one or more intermediate-term objectives that will enable the community to reach its goals. An example is to produce 100 units of housing affordable to moderate-income families. Other examples are to amend the zoning law to protect wetlands of a certain size and character, or to adopt a historic district and landmarks preservation law.

To set realistic objectives, the board must carefully assess the resources available to the community in addressing its most critical issues. Including the entire community in the planning process and consulting with outside agencies are important methods of identifying such resources so that critical issues may be dealt with effectively.

DEVELOPING STRATEGIES

Strategies are actions the board recommends to accomplish an objective. In each case, one or more actions may be suggested to attain the objective. For example, the board can recommend that zoning incentives be given to private developers in exchange for the provision of affordable rental and ownership housing for moderate-income families. Similarly, where the community desires to reduce polluted runoff into wetlands, the board can recommend that the zoning law be amended to contain standards to protect wetlands which are as restrictive as those found in the state regulations, that wetlands of one acre or larger be protected, that local permits be obtained before development affecting wetlands is allowed, and that buffer zones of 150 feet be established to protect important wetlands identified by the board. To maintain the existing historic character of the community, the board could also recommend that new housing and commercial development be actively encouraged in specified districts using architectural and site designs that are compatible with the community's historic character. Incentives to attract such development can also be spelled out.

DEVISING AN IMPLEMENTATION PLAN

At the end of the comprehensive plan, the board can recommend how the plan's strategies are to be implemented. An implementation plan designates the agencies or officials responsible for each action, identifies necessary resources, and establishes time periods for completing each action. For example, the planning board might be assigned the task of developing a recommended incentive zoning provision for affordable housing within eight months from the effective date of the comprehensive plan. Similarly, the plan could recommend that the municipal legislature adopt a local law creating a wetlands commission with the authority to issue development permits. The recommendation could stipulate that the local law establish standards that the commission must use to review individual applications.

Drafting the local law could be assigned to the municipal attorney with the aid of the New York State Department of Environmental Conservation (DEC), interested members of the community who are knowledgeable about wetlands and their functions, and developers and landowners who will be affected by the regulations. The implementation plan could then state that the proposed law be circulated by the municipal clerk to the local planning board and county planning agency for their review and recommendations, with adoption of the local law to occur within 12 months of the effective date of the comprehensive plan.

By attempting to assign responsibilities, identify necessary resources, and adopt a time frame to accomplish specific actions, the board will discover whether strategies being explored are realistic. If they seem unrealistic, the board has the opportunity to devise new strategies to achieve the established objectives.

THE COMPREHENSIVE PLAN DIAGNOSTIC CHECKLIST

This checklist illustrates how a comprehensive plan can be organized. It was created by examining New York State law requirements and reviewing the contents of dozens of adopted plans. The checklist is illustrative, not all-inclusive. The amount of detail to be contained in each of the plan's components will depend on the critical issues and unique opportunities found in a particular community and on the resources and time available to prepare a comprehensive plan.

INTRODUCTION

- ♦ Reasons for adopting or amending the comprehensive plan – summary of critical issues and unique opportunities
- ♦ How the comprehensive plan is organized and the purposes it serves
- ♦ Comprehensive planning process
- ♦ How facts were gathered

- How citizen participation was solicited
- How conclusions were drawn
- Municipal history
- Unique characteristics
- Strengths and opportunities
- Weaknesses and critical issues
- Vision for the community's future
- Summary of the goals and objectives of the plan

ISSUE IDENTIFICATION

- Presentation and Evaluation of Data and Information
- Existing land uses
- Residential housing
- Commercial
- Industrial
- Mixed use/planned unit development
- Institutional
- Agricultural
- Conservation/open space
- Affordable housing
- Trends in land use
- Major land uses throughout municipal history
- Projected buildout of community based on existing zoning
- Population and demographics
- Regional population and growth projections
- Recent municipal population and growth projections
- Households
- Age distribution
- Income

FINANCIAL CONDITIONS

- Trends in local revenue raising
- Real property taxes
- Fiscal health
- Resources available by source

COMMUNITY PREFERENCES AND VALUES OBTAINED FROM SURVEYS AND MEETINGS

- Critical issues and problems
- Unique opportunities
- Available resources
- Realistic strategies

STATEMENT OF CRITICAL ISSUES AND UNIQUE OPPORTUNITIES

- ◆ Critical issues
- ◆ Unique opportunities

PUBLIC INFRASTRUCTURE

Background Information: For each of the following types of public infrastructure, this component may contain an analysis of current capacity, future needs, options for meeting those needs, the cost of meeting those needs, and available financial resources.

Transportation Facilities

- ◆ Roads and vehicular traffic
- ◆ Current index of road types and traffic amounts
- ◆ Limited access highways
- ◆ County roads
- ◆ Municipal roads
- ◆ Index of dangerous roads and intersections
- ◆ Travel demand forecasts
- ◆ Level of service standards
- ◆ Public transportation
- ◆ Bus service
- ◆ Commuter and freight railroads
- ◆ Airports
- ◆ Water ferries

Utilities

- ◆ Water supply
  - —Sources–public and private
  - —State and regional protection measures
  - —Wastewater and stormwater collection and treatment
  - —Discharge amounts–public and private
- ◆ Sewage treatment facilities
- ◆ Electricity, gas and other public utilities
- ◆ Telecommunications
  - —Existing facilities
  - —Proposed facilities
  - —Goals
  - —Objectives
  - —Strategies

PUBLIC SERVICES

Background Information: For each of the following types of public services, this component may contain an analysis of current capacity, future needs, options for meeting those needs, the cost of meeting those needs, and available financial resources.

Emergency Services—Fire, Rescue, and Ambulance Operations

- Police protection
- Health-care facilities
- Local hospitals and doctors' offices
- Regional medical facilities

Solid Waste Disposal

- Municipal solid waste
- Hazardous substances
- Recycling programs

Educational Facilities

- Pre-kindergarten
- Elementary–kindergarten through fifth grade
- Junior high school–sixth through eighth grade
- Senior high school–ninth through twelfth grade
- Local and regional higher education facilities

Recreation and Parks

- Municipally owned lands
- Land trust acquired lands
- Active recreational opportunities
- Passive recreational opportunities
  —Goals
  —Objectives
  —Strategies

RESOURCE PROTECTION

Background information: For each of the following types of resource protection, this component may contain an analysis of current capacity, future needs, options for meeting those needs, the cost of meeting those needs, and available financial resources.

Natural and Historic Resources

- Resource type
  —Topography
  —Geology
  —Soils
- Surface water resources
- Scenic environmental areas and open space

- Unique and rare habitats
- Critical environmental areas
- Historical and cultural resources
  —Historic resources
  —Index of present historic sites and landmarks
  —Proposed historic sites and landmarks
  —Current efforts to protect historic sites and landmarks
  —Cultural resources
  —Index of present cultural resources
  —Current protection efforts
- Scenic resources
  —Index of present scenic resources
  —Current protection efforts including design guidelines
  —Goals
  —Objectives
  —Strategies

ECONOMIC DEVELOPMENT

Background Information: For each of the following types of economic development, this component may contain an analysis of current capacity, future needs, options for meeting those needs, the cost of meeting those needs, and available financial resources.

- Employment resources
- Unemployment rate
- Employers
- Industrial Resources
- Commercial Resources
  —Retail
  —Wholesale
- Agricultural Resources
  —Historical agricultural production
  —Current agricultural resources
  —Current efforts to protect existing agricultural lands
- Goals
- Objectives
- Strategies

IMPLEMENTATION PLAN

Summary of planning strategies for implementation: The implementation plan can begin with a list of strategic actions that are to be taken, a description of how various agencies, agents, and groups are to be made responsible for those actions, and a general timetable for completing those actions.

Public Infrastructure

♦ Goals
♦ Objectives
♦ Strategies
♦ Agencies and officials involved in implementation and their responsibilities
♦ Time schedule

Public Services

♦ Goals
♦ Objectives
♦ Strategies
♦ Agencies and officials involved in implementation and their responsibilities
♦ Time schedule

Resource Protection

♦ Goals
♦ Objectives
♦ Strategies
♦ Agencies and officials involved in implementation and their responsibilities
♦ Time schedule

Economic Development

♦ Goals
♦ Objectives
♦ Strategies
♦ Agencies and officials involved in implementation and their responsibilities
♦ Time schedule

REVIEW AND REVISION

Ongoing process by which the plan and its objectives will be reviewed.

Intervals at which the comprehensive plan will be reviewed.

C. THE ZONING LAW AND ITS AMENDMENT

DEFINITION

The local zoning law divides a community into land use districts and establishes building restrictions limiting the height, lot area coverage, and other dimensions of structures that are permitted to be built within each district. At the time that the local legislature adopts a zoning law, it approves a zoning map. On this map, the zoning district lines are overlaid on a street map of the community. By referring to this map, it is possible to identify the use district within which any parcel of land is located. Then, by referring to the text of the zoning law, it is possible to discover the uses that are permitted within that district and the dimensional restrictions that apply to building on that land.

There is no required format for a zoning law in New York. As a result, where municipalities have codified their laws, local codes are organized in a variety of ways. Their provisions range from the relatively simple to the extremely complex. Most zoning chapters of municipal codes contain several articles covering such basic topics as: the purpose of the zoning law, various definitions, the establishment of zoning districts, the uses allowed within those districts, the building and parking restrictions that apply within each district, how preexisting, nonconforming uses are to be treated, uses that are allowed as accessory uses or by special permits within certain districts, the formation and operation of the zoning board of appeals, how amendments can be adopted, and how the code is to be enforced.

A host of additional topics can be included in the zoning law. Among these are standards that must be considered before an owner's application for a subdivision or site plan can be approved; provisions that protect landmarks, historic districts, wetlands, floodplains, or environmentally constrained land; and provisions that regulate the placement of mobile homes or the use of commercial and political signs.

The zoning map, implemented through the text of the law, constitutes a blueprint for the development of the community over time. It is a design for the community's development that is to be created with citizens' participation and that, as it is built out, has far-reaching consequences for those citizens' quality of life.

Once adopted, zoning provisions can be amended by the local legislature. The courts have held that in amending the zoning law local legislatures have a great deal of flexibility to create mechanisms to accomplish the statutory purposes of zoning. Under this implied authority to adopt appropriate mechanisms, local laws have been upheld which, for example, created floating zones that applied to individual parcels of land; allowed mixed uses on parcels in single-use zones; and rezoned individual properties subject to restrictive conditions that insured the appropriate use of the land as rezoned.

PURPOSE

In delegating to local governments the authority to enact zoning regulations, state legislatures are exercising the police power: the authority to adopt legislation "to promote the public health, safety, morals, and general welfare." It is with these words that the grant of authority to regulate land use typically begins, and it is for these purposes that such authority is conveyed to local governments. Originally, zoning was designed to protect private investment in urban land development from unpredictable nearby land uses and to protect urban populations from the perils of fire, unsanitary conditions, unsafe buildings, and uncontrolled traffic. With the migration of urban populations and with increasing suburban and exurban development came additional challenges for zoning to confront, such as revitalizing cities, managing suburban growth, protecting threatened natural resources, and preventing visual blight in the countryside.

Zoning responded to these challenges as courts approved the use of innovative provisions to protect visual assets, conserve environmentally constrained lands, and maintain cultural and historic resources. The New York State statutes make it clear that one of the principal purposes of zoning is to encourage "the most appropriate use of land." Town Law §263; Village Law §7-704; General City Law §20 (24). The courts have supported municipal invention and creativity in adopting zoning provisions designed to accomplish that objective in diverse municipal settings, during rapidly changing times. The hallmark of zoning in New York is its adaptability to local circumstance and its ability to accomplish legitimate public objectives defined by local citizens and their elected leaders.

Against claims that zoning constituted an unwarranted infringement of property rights, the courts initially singled out two purposes of zoning as particularly appropriate reasons to uphold it. First, zoning prevents landowners from using their properties in ways that are injurious to the community. Second, zoning is an appropriate method of creating a balanced and efficient pattern of land development and avoiding the multiple perils of haphazard growth.

WHEN

Local governments are authorized–but not required–to adopt zoning provisions. Deciding when and why to adopt a zoning law is purely a matter of local discretion. According to a 1999 survey by the New York State Legislative Council on Rural Resources, fully 77% of the over 1,600 villages, towns and cities in the state have adopted zoning regulations. Although no survey has been conducted regarding the reasons for adopting zoning, municipalities seem to have done so in areas of the state where there are significant development pressures, serious environmental challenges, or difficult economic circumstances. This suggests that localities adopt zoning to control or manage growth, to promote economic stability and development, and to conserve the environment and enhance the quality of life of their communities.

In the lower 10 counties of the state, where considerable development pressures exist, nearly all communities have adopted zoning. All cities in the state have adopted zoning laws. The 23% of localities that have not adopted zoning tend to be found in rural counties in the southern tier and the north country. There are, however, notable exceptions to this generalization. For example, for reasons that are not well researched, there are several counties in the state where only one or two communities have yet to adopt zoning.

AUTHORITY

Local governments in New York have no inherent authority to regulate land uses and building construction. The power to adopt zoning provisions is delegated to towns, villages, and cities by statutes patterned after a model national act known as the Standard State Zoning Enabling Act, which was promulgated by the United States Department of Commerce in 1922. These provisions empower, but do not require, localities to adopt zoning laws. Specific provisions of the Town, Village, and General City Law grant authority to local governments in New York to divide the community into use districts and to regulate building construction within those districts for purposes set forth in the enabling legislation. *See* Town Law §262; Village Law §7-702; General City Law §20(25).

The state authorizing statutes make it clear that zoning regulations are to be enacted in accordance with a comprehensive plan and to accomplish a number of specific purposes, including conserving the value of buildings, encouraging the appropriate use of land, maintaining the character of zoning districts, facilitating the provision of transportation, water systems, sewage treatment, schools, and parks, lessening traffic congestion, preventing overcrowding, providing adequate light and air, and containing damage from fires, floods, and other dangers. *See* Town Law §263; Village Law §7-704; General City Law §20(24), (25).

To accomplish these purposes, the local legislative body is authorized to divide the community into zoning districts within which it is empowered to regulate the erection, alteration, and use of land and buildings. Within districts, such regulations are to be uniform for each class of building. Regulations can restrict the height and size of buildings, the percentage of building lots that can be occupied, the provision of open space, the density of population, and the location and use of buildings for trade, industry, residence, or other purposes.

IMPLEMENTATION

The power to adopt and amend zoning regulations is legislative, and is exercised by the village trustees, town board, or city council. When a village or town first adopts zoning provisions, a zoning commission must be established to recommend zoning district boundaries and use and dimensional requirements. The commission must hold one or more public hearings on its recommendations, after public notice, before submitting them to the local legislature. Cities, however, do not have to appoint zoning commissions before considering and adopting the initial zoning provisions.

Before the local legislative body adopts the initial zoning regulations, it must hold a public hearing on the proposed regulations, after public notice. The initial adoption of zoning regulations is listed as a Type I action under the State Environmental Quality Review Act (SEQRA), and may require the preparation of a full environmental impact statement.

Amendments to zoning provisions can be adopted only after public notice and hearing on each amendment. Changes in zoning provisions are discretionary legislative acts. The local legislature can amend the zoning law on its own initiative, in its discretion. In villages and towns, when an owner applies for a change in the zoning provisions applicable to his property, the legislative body may simply refuse to consider it, unless the effect of the current zoning provision on the parcel in question is confiscatory. This differs significantly from other local land use applications, such as subdivisions, site plans, variances, and special permits, which must be considered according to procedures and standards established in state and local laws. Only in cities, and there only upon the petition of a requisite number of property owners, must the legislature actively consider an application for rezoning.

Zoning amendments which change the allowable use of 25 or more acres or which have other impacts spelled out in state regulations are Type I actions under SEQRA, and may require the preparation of a full environmental impact statement. Normally, zoning amendments may be adopted by a vote of a majority of the local legislature. Where a petition is submitted by the owners of a certain percentage of the land affected by a proposed zoning change, or where a county or regional agency has review authority and disapproves of the change, more than a simple majority vote is required.

If zoning provisions and their amendments do not conform to the comprehensive plan of the locality or exhibit comprehensiveness of planning, they may be found to be beyond the municipality's power to adopt land use regulations. Amendments of use provisions of the law that apply to particular parcels must be attended by amendments of the zoning map as well. Local laws and regulations may require additional procedures to be followed when zoning amendments are considered: typical provisions require referral to the local planning board for an advisory report, the mailing or service of notice of a public hearing on nearby owners, and the posting of signs on the land subject to the proposed rezoning.

Landowners who wish to develop their parcels in conformance with applicable zoning provisions must apply to the local building inspector or zoning administrator for a building permit. Part of the inspector or administrator's function is to review whether the proposed project and its construction conform to the use and dimensional requirements of zoning. Where they do not, the permit must be denied. Determinations of this sort by the appropriate local official are reviewable by the local zoning board of appeals, which must be formed when the locality first adopts a zoning law.

ILLUSTRATION

The second largest wetland area in New York State is known as the Great Swamp. It contains over 3,000 acres of wetlands and is governed by the land use regulations of five adjacent municipalities in the Putnam and Dutchess County region of the northern New York metropolitan area. The zoning laws of these five communities have all been updated within the last 10 years and all recognize the importance of protecting the Great Swamp, but in a variety of different ways.

In the five communities, land included in the Great Swamp is designated for standard uses: residential, commercial, and industrial. In two of the communities, part of the wetland area is designated a flood hazard zone by the zoning itself. In one community, most of the wetlands is included in this flood hazard zone. In another community, the wetland area is divided among six different use districts, including industrial and highway business. Several of the communities include Great Swamp lands in three or more zoning districts.

Despite this disparate treatment of a critical watershed area in the zoning district provisions, the communities have adopted a number of other provisions to protect the Great Swamp. Three of the communities have adopted wetlands regulations, and one of these has placed the provisions in the zoning law itself. Three of the communities require developers to show watercourses or natural features in their site plan submissions; two of them require that natural resource areas be noted on and protected in subdivision applications. The subdivision and site plan regulations were adopted in most of these communities as separate laws, rather than as a part of the zoning law. Two of the five communities have flood hazard districts in their zoning law, two have separate flood hazard laws, and one has no provisions dealing with flood areas.

LIMITATIONS AND CONCERNS

The requirement in New York State that zoning provisions conform to the comprehensive plan has led to much confusion at the local level and in the courts. This results from the voluntary nature of the local power to adopt zoning provisions and comprehensive plans. Some states require localities to adopt both a zoning law and comprehensive plan and to update them at specified intervals. New York's approach is to empower and enable localities to do what they wish in adopting and updating zoning laws and comprehensive plans.

Where localities have recently adopted a comprehensive plan and conform their land use regulations, including zoning, to that plan, the regulations are greatly insulated from attack. It is very difficult to show that such a regulation fails to substantially advance a legitimate public objective–the judicial standard applied to challenged regulations. For this reason, in adopting land use regulations and zoning amendments, it is critical that the public interest in the regulation and the comprehensive planning objective it achieves be spelled out in the findings of the legislature when it enacts the regulation or amendment.

Vague zoning provisions cause particular problems. The local building inspector or zoning administrator needs specificity and clarity to interpret and apply zoning provisions to particular parcels. The work of the zoning board of appeals is compounded when statutory language is vague. Specific dimensions, standards, and terminology make zoning provisions easier to implement. Although zoning enactments are presumed by the courts to be constitutionally valid, their provisions are interpreted restrictively because they are deemed to be in derogation of the landowner's common law property rights. When courts apply this standard of restrictive interpretation to unclear or general zoning language, they often find in the landowner's favor.

Landowners sometimes claim that a zoning amendment violates their vested rights. This happens when an owner has received a permit under zoning provisions that are changed before construction has been completed. The courts have not established a bright line to determine when, in this process, the owner has vested rights. The New York State judicial rule is that an owner is allowed to continue development under a duly issued permit only where he has undertaken substantial construction and made substantial expenditures prior to the effective date of the amendment. *See Ellington Construction Corp. v. Zoning Bd. of Appeals of the Inc. Village of New Hempstead*, 77 N.Y.2d 114, 122, 56 N.E.2d 128, 132, 564 N.Y.S.2d 1001, 1005 (1990).

STATUTES

New York State Village Law §7-700, Town Law §261, and General City Law §20(24) grant basic land use authority to local governments and allow them to regulate the details of land development and building construction and alteration. This may be done for "the purpose of promoting the health, safety, morals or the general welfare of the community."

Village Law §7-702, Town Law §262, and General City Law §20(25) authorize local governments to divide the community into zoning districts and to regulate the use, construction, and alteration of buildings and land within those districts.

Village Law §7-704, Town Law §263, and General City Law §20(24)-(25) provide that zoning and land use regulations must conform with the locality's comprehensive plan. The purposes of such zoning regulations are to lessen congestion, to secure safety from fire and flood, to prevent overcrowding, to facilitate the provision of infrastructure, and to encourage the most appropriate use of land throughout the municipality.

Section 10(1)(ii)(a)(11) of the Municipal Home Rule Law states that a municipality can adopt local laws for the "protection and enhancement of its physical and visual environment."

Section 10(1)(ii)(a)(14) of the Municipal Home Rule Law states that a municipality can adopt local laws as provided in the Statute of Local Governments. Section 10(6) of the Statute of Local Governments authorizes cities, towns, and villages to adopt zoning regulations.

Village Law §7-706 and §7-710 and Town Law §264 and §266 contain the requirements for adopting and amending zoning provisions.

Village Law §7-708, Town Law §265, and General City Law §83 contain additional requirements for amending zoning provisions.

CASE DIGEST

In *Lincoln Trust Co. v. Williams Bldg. Corp.*, 229 N.Y. 313, 128 N.E. 209 (1920), the Court of Appeals held that zoning was a proper use of a local government's police power. The plaintiff brought an action for specific performance to require the defendant to take title under a private contract for sale. The defendant had purchased land from the plaintiff, "free from all encumbrances." The defendant claimed that the zoning dividing the property into three districts was an encumbrance. He asked that the complaint be dismissed and that the plaintiff return the deposit. The court noted that the separation of land into use districts was a valid exercise of the local police power and was not an encumbrance to title. The court further held that the conduct of an individual and the use of his property may be regulated by laws such as zoning.

A landowner in *Wulfsohn v. Burden*, 241 N.Y. 288, 150 N.E.2d 120 (1925), sought to compel the municipality to approve plans and issue a building permit, claiming that the zoning regulating the property was invalid. The court held that a party attacking a zoning law cannot use the diminution in the value of the land caused by the law as an argument to invalidate the law. The individual attacking the law "must demonstrate that, as a matter of law, these regulations are unconstitutional and that there is no permissible interpretation of all of these facts which justifies their adoption as a reasonable exercise of the broad police power of the state." The court concluded that the requirements of the challenged laws cannot "be said as a matter of law to be so unreasonable that they exceed the limits of discretion reposed in the zoning commission."

In *Euclid v. Ambler Realty*, 272 U.S. 365 (1926), the U.S. Supreme Court first held that the enactment of zoning use districts is a permissible exercise of a local government's police power. Ambler Realty challenged the validity of a law that divided the town into various use districts. The court found that the plaintiff did not carry its burden of proving "that such provisions are clearly arbitrary and unreasonable, having no substantial relationship to the public health, safety, morals, or general welfare." It also found that the zoning law did not violate the plaintiff's equal protection rights and was not a taking of the plaintiff's property without just compensation.

The practice of deferring to the discretion and good judgment of the local legislatures that adopt zoning laws has been followed in New York, where zoning laws are presumed by the courts to be constitutional. This deference places the burden on the challenging individual to show that the legislature acted arbitrarily or that the regulation did not reasonably attain the desired end. In *Town of Islip v. F.E. Summers Coal and Lumber Co.*, 257 N.Y. 167, 177 N.E. 409 (1931), the court concluded that the correct rule to apply when land use regulations are challenged "is to uphold the presumption of constitutionality in the absence of some factual foundation of record for overthrowing it."

The New York Court of Appeals held that a zoning regulation cannot deprive a private property owner of all beneficial use of his property. *Eaton v. Sweeny*, 257 N.Y. 176, 177 N.E. 412 (1931). The court held that zoning benefits the public health, safety, and welfare, and the burdens of acquiring this benefit must be equally distributed. "When, however, the adjustment becomes so one-sided as to be unreasonable and arbitrary, unnecessary to the preservation of the scheme and purpose as a whole, approaching the point where an owner is deprived of any beneficial or profitable use of his property, then the court should step in and afford relief."

The plaintiff has the burden of showing that a zoning law is invalid by establishing that the amendment was not justified under the police power of the state by any reasonable interpretation of the facts. *Shepard v. Village of Skaneateles*, 300 N.Y. 115, 89 N.E.2d 619 (1949).

The Court of Appeals held that "the power of a [local government] to amend its basic zoning law in such a way as reasonably to promote to general welfare cannot be questioned." *Rodgers v. Village of Tarrytown*, 302 N.Y. 115, 96 N.E.2d 731 (1951). The plaintiff challenged a village zoning amendment that allowed construction of multiple dwellings in a single-family zone. The court upheld the amendment, noting that "how various properties shall be classified or reclassified rests with the local legislative body; its judgment and determination will be conclusive, beyond interference from the courts, unless shown to be arbitrary, and the burden of establishing such arbitrariness is imposed upon him who asserts it." The court determined that "[c]hanged or changing conditions call for changed plans, and persons who own property in a particular zone or use district enjoy no eternally vested right to the classification if the public interest demands otherwise."

In order to sustain an amendment to a zoning law, there does not need to "be proof of mistake in the original enactment or a change in the character of the property involved in the reclassification." It is sufficient that the legislature show that conditions in the community have changed since the law was adopted or offer some other rationale that supports the change. *Levitt v. Incorporated Village of Sands Point*, 6 A.D.2d 701, 174 N.Y.S.2d 283 (2d Dep't 1958).

The court in *Udell v. Haas*, 21 N.Y.2d 463, 235 N.E.2d 897, 288 N.Y.S.2d 888 (1968), determined that zoning amendments must be in accordance with a comprehensive plan and must consider the needs of the entire community.

REFERENCES

Land Use Planning & Regulation in New York State Municipalities: A Survey, New York State Legislative Commission on Rural Resources, Albany, N.Y. (Fall, 1999).

Guide to Planning and Zoning Laws in New York State, New York State Department of State, Division of Local Government; James A. Coon Local Government Technical Series.

Zoning Enforcement for Towns and Villages, New York Department of State, Division of Local Government; James A. Coon Local Government Technical Series.

Adopting Zoning Ordinances for the First Time, New York State Department of State, Division of Local Government; James A. Coon Local Government Technical Series.

Zoning and the Comprehensive Plan, New York State Department of State, Division of Local Government; James A. Coon Local Government Technical Series.

D. ORGANIZING LOCAL LAND USE REGULATIONS

DEFINITION

When a municipality has codified its local laws, land use regulations often are found dispersed throughout several chapters of the municipal code. The most familiar of these chapters is zoning. The zoning chapter typically designates use districts and sets forth various regulations for land development within each district. The zoning chapter may or may not include subdivision and site plan regulations. Often it does not contain provisions relating to other land regulations, such as historic preservation, wetlands protection, erosion and sedimentation, tree preservation, sign control, mining, or solid waste management. These provisions may be contained in separate chapters of the code. Alternatively, some communities have included all of their land use regulations in a single chapter of their municipal code that they call the land use chapter. When communities in New York have not codified their local laws, separate land use provisions, such as site plan regulations, may be found in the free-standing zoning law or may be contained in their own law.

There is no required or correct way to organize a community's land use regulations. In a state as diverse as New York, many different approaches are taken to meet local needs. The material that follows discusses the advantages of organizing all land use regulations into a single chapter of the municipal code or into a single free-standing zoning law. It contains a checklist that references a full range of land use regulations. This is not to imply that any particular locality needs all or even most of the regulations included in the checklist or that this format for organizing the regulations into a single law should be followed. Its purpose it to present a complete range of possibilities for consideration at the local level.

PURPOSE

When land use regulations are organized into a single chapter of the local code or into a single free-standing law, the interrelationship among various provisions of the code or law is clarified. By integrating land use regulations in this manner, any changes that may be necessary to make provisions consistent with one another may become evident. Additionally, an integrated land use chapter or law will aid property owners, neighbors, and citizens in determining the regulatory constraints that apply to their land or to land within their neighborhoods.

A single land use chapter or law will also make enforcement and interpretation of land use regulations easier. Planning boards, zoning boards of appeals, and building departments will have an easier time applying land development and protection provisions. Such agencies will be less likely to overlook relevant sections, and the local review and approval procedures can be managed better.

Finally, integrating all land use regulations will aid a community in achieving conformity with its comprehensive plan. Recent revisions to state law require that all land use regulations be in conformance with a municipality's comprehensive plan. This new requirement can be followed more readily if all local land use regulations are contained in a single land use chapter or law.

WHEN

A municipal legislature can reorganize its municipal code or land use laws whenever it believes such reorganization is prudent. It may be best, however, to undertake such reorganization when the municipality is updating its land use provisions to conform to a recently adopted or amended comprehensive plan. Then provisions necessary to achieve the new plan's objectives can be integrated with existing zoning and other land use regulations.

AUTHORITY

The New York state legislature delegated authority to amend zoning provisions to municipalities through the Town, Village, and General City laws. Often, required procedures for amending local laws are contained in the General Provisions section of the municipal zoning chapter or in a free-standing zoning law.

IMPLEMENTATION

The process of reorganizing existing land use regulations requires several steps. First, the local legislature or a special committee designated by the legislature must determine which provisions of the code should be included in the land use chapter or law. Next, to organize these provisions into a single law, a logical arrangement and renumbering of sections within the chapter or law will be necessary. A cross-reference system may be provided after every major section in the chapter or law to direct the reader to other related provisions within it. After redrafting the land use chapter, the municipal code must be changed to reflect the reorganization. Its table of contents and index must be reorganized, as well as any cross-references found in the code. Finally, the local legislature will have to formally amend the code to reflect all of the changes. The same is true for a community that has not codified its laws: the local legislature will have to formally adopt the integrated land use law even though many of the provisions have been previously adopted as components of this new law. Even when a municipality is not enacting new substantive law, reorganization requires the municipal legislature to formally amend the municipal code or law. Such an amendment is subject to all relevant provisions of New York law regarding the adoption and amendment of local laws.

LIMITATIONS AND CONCERNS

Although there are many benefits to including all relevant provisions of the code in a single land use chapter or law, there are also several drawbacks. First, given the extensive nature of their existing laws, it may be difficult for some communities to determine what should be incorporated into the chapter or law. For example, a municipality must determine whether an existing provision as specific as one regulating fuel storage tanks in an aquifer protection zone is a land use regulation that should be placed in the land use chapter or law. Second, when a current code is not particularly complicated or has been used in its present form without amendment for years, the benefits of reorganization must be weighed against the costs of learning a new format. Third, a municipality must consider whether the cost of undertaking code reorganization is merited in its particular circumstances.

The following is a checklist of a model land use chapter or free-standing land use law. It is derived from the land use provisions of a variety of municipalities, and is intended to serve as a guide for municipal officials who are considering a reorganization and integration of the land use provisions of their existing code or laws. The checklist can also be used to inventory and evaluate land use provisions that are dispersed throughout any particular municipal code or set of laws.

LOCAL LAND USE REGULATION CHECKLIST

Article I: General Provisions

A. Title–states the title.

B. Scope–establishes the breadth of issues to be covered by the chapter or law.

C. Statutory Authority–states the legal authority for enacting a land use chapter or law.

D. Purposes–lists the reasons for adopting the land use chapter or law.

Article II: Definitions

A. Definitions–defines words in the chapter that have substantive importance.

B. Word Usage–generally explains that words and terms used in the present tense include the future and that the singular includes the plural and vice versa. Often explains that the normal dictionary definition of words shall be used where the words are not specifically defined.

Article III: Zoning Districts and Map

A. Districts Enumerated–sets forth the various use districts established by the land use chapter. Examples of district types include single-family residential, multi-family residential, commercial, light industrial, conservation, and agricultural. There is no limit to the types and number of districts that a community may establish.

B. Zoning Map–explains that the location and boundaries of the enumerated districts are shown on the zoning map and that the map, together with any amendments to it, if not appended to the chapter itself, is available in the municipal clerk's office.

C. Interpretation of District Boundaries–where there is any uncertainty as to the boundaries between districts, this section provides rules for resolving such ambiguities.

Article IV: District Regulations

A. Application of Regulations–states that no building, structure, or land shall be used and no building, structure or part thereof shall be erected, moved, or altered unless for a use expressly permitted by and in conformance with the regulations for the district in which the building, structure, or land is located.

B. General Regulations–contains regulations that are applicable to all districts, including specifications regarding irregularly shaped lots, building height, minimum lot area, uses of yards, frontage, and driveways, roof structures, and easements.

C. Schedule of Permitted Uses (Schedule A)–lists the types of land uses permitted in particular districts. Where a use is not listed, it is prohibited.

D. Schedule of Area and Bulk Requirements (Schedule B)–defines the area and bulk requirements for each of the enumerated districts. Includes regulations governing minimum lot area, minimum lot width, minimum front and side yard setbacks, minimum rear yard, minimum road frontage, maximum lot coverage, maximum height, parking setback, and floor area ratio.

E. Off-Street Parking and Loading Regulations–sets forth the required number of parking spaces, and their dimensions, for a given use district and particular use.

Article V: Supplementary Regulations–Land Activities

A. Accessory Uses and Structures–establishes regulations governing land uses and structures incidental to the district's primary permitted uses, dwelling units, and structures.

B. Cemeteries–establishes minimum lot size and setback requirements from any street, right-of-way, or property line. May also require site plan approval.

C. Commercial Kennel–regulations can establish minimum lot size and setback requirements.

D. Communications Antenna or Tower; Satellite Dishes–regulates the location, placement and appearance of communication facilities. Under the federal Telecommunications Act of 1996, municipalities are prohibited from excluding such facilities from their jurisdictions.

E. Excavation and Mining–sets forth requirements governing the location or exclusion of mining and excavation operations.

F. Home Occupations–provides for the regulation of home occupations such as professional offices, day-care facilities, and dance studios. May be included under the section on accessory uses.

G. Hotel or Motel–establishes requirements for the location of hotels and motels in particular districts. Sets forth a minimum lot size and required road frontage and side and rear yard setbacks.

H. Landfill or Other Solid Waste Management Facility–may regulate or prohibit the operation of any type of solid waste management facility within the municipality. Where facilities are regulated, provisions may govern the minimum lot size, setback requirements, hours of operation, and number of trucks that either enter or leave the facility. May also require the securing of a special permit and site plan approval. Municipal regulation of a solid waste management facility must be as stringent as state law requirements.

I. Mobile Homes–establishes regulations controlling the location and appearance of individual mobile homes as well as mobile home developments within a community. Also establishes bulk and area requirements for such dwellings.

J. Motor Vehicle Service Stations–may regulate the location of underground storage tanks on the parcel. May prohibit the parking of wrecked or damaged vehicles on the parcel for more than 60 days. May prohibit the siting of a new facility within a certain radius of a pre-existing facility.

K. *Places of Worship*–in addition to regulating the placement of such facilities within particular zones and establishing minimum lot sizes and setbacks, many zoning laws also provide that places of worship are subject to a special permit and site plan approval. Some laws also require a design that is compatible with the existing neighborhood character.

L. *Planned Unit Development*–regulations designed to promote variety and flexibility in land development while stressing the efficient use of open space and public facilities. May provide for the type and number of residential and commercial uses allowed, as well as for bulk and area requirements and design of buildings.

M. *Prohibitions*–general categories of activities or uses that are prohibited in all districts.

N. *Swimming Pools*–establishes requirements for private swimming pools, such as that a pool may only be used as an accessory use to the principally permitted dwelling, that the pool must be enclosed by a security fence at least four feet high, and that the pool must be maintained so as to meet particular bacterial standards.

O. *Uniformity of Design*–especially with new subdivisions, can require that the design of neighboring buildings differs to avoid architectural monotony or adopts a uniform style based on community character.

Article VI: Supplementary Regulations–Resource Protection

A. Natural Resource Protection

Floodplains–regulates the location and construction of buildings and structures in floodplain areas identified on the municipal floodplain maps.

Soil Erosion–establishes regulations to reduce the potential runoff of soil both during and after construction. Many municipalities enact soil erosion provisions under their site plan or subdivision regulations.

Steep Slopes–regulates the development on slopes of a given percentage. Can also prohibit construction on slopes greater than 15 or 20%.

Tree Preservation–regulations adopted to preserve and protect all trees of a certain diameter or larger by creating a tree removal permit process. Where land development requires tree removal, the developer must submit a tree removal plan and receive approval from a tree preservation commission or conservation advisory board.

Wetlands–establishes a permitting scheme for particular activities undertaken in areas defined as wetlands under the local law. May also require setback and buffer requirements from wetland and watercourse areas.

B. Historic Resource Protection

Historic Districts–establishes historic district overlay zones where new development and alterations must be compatible with the architecture of the historic districts. Developer can be required to obtain certificate of appropriateness from a historic preservation commission.

Landmark Preservation–designates particular sites in the community as local landmarks to preserve and protect their integrity for future generations to enjoy. As in historic districts, development adjacent to or near a landmark can be subject to approval from a historic preservation commission.

C. Scenic Resource Protection

Fences and Walls–regulates the height and appearance of fencing or walls.

Landscaping–establishes regulations governing the visual appearance and maintenance of yards, requiring trees, shrubs, and fences to establish visual buffers for particular types of uses.

Signs–regulates the size, illumination, and placement of signs in one or more zoning districts.

Article VII: Nonconforming Uses, Buildings, Structures

A. Continuation–establishes that the lawful use of any building, structure, or land existing at the time of the enactment of the local zoning law or a subsequent amendment can be continued even though such use does not conform to provisions of the land use chapter or amendment.

B. Enlargement or Alteration–generally prohibits the enlargement or expansion of any nonconforming use or structure that does not conform to dimensional requirements.

C. Change in Use–generally prohibits changing one nonconforming use into another nonconforming use, although some communities allow such a change by special permit.

D. Restoration of Damaged Buildings–establishes that a nonconforming use may not be restored if more than a given percentage of the building or structure on the property is destroyed.

E. Discontinuance and Abandonment–specifies that any nonconforming use of land, building, or structure that is discontinued with the intent to abandon may not be resumed; municipalities generally establish a period of discontinuance that evidences an intent to abandon.

F. Amortization–may require the cessation of certain objectionable nonconforming uses, such as a junkyard in a residential zone, within a given time period. Dangerous uses may be terminated.

G. Special Provisions and Limitations for Certain Uses–establishes regulations governing certain nonconforming uses such as signs, soil and stone removal, and mobile homes.

H. Appeals–may provide for administrative appeal to the zoning board of appeals to determine whether a nonconforming use has been abandoned or whether to extend an amortization period for a particular parcel.

Article VIII: Site Plan Regulations

A. Purpose–states that site plan review is enacted to determine whether the proposed use or changes in use of a single parcel of land will exist in harmonious relationship with the existing or permitted use of contiguous land and adjacent neighborhoods. Where a single parcel of land has already been subject to review under subdivision approval authority, such parcel does not undergo site plan review. The chapter or law will designate the planning board or other administrative body as the reviewing board.

B. Submission Requirements–begins with an explanation of which land uses are subject to site plan review such as development on parcels over three acres or any development in a light industrial district. The submission requirements will also establish the elements to be included in a site plan drawing. These may include a given scale (e.g., an inch equals 50 feet); property boundaries; location of all uses, structures, parking lots, and facilities on adjacent property; existing natural resources, such as wetlands and steep slopes; location, dimensions, and height of all proposed structures; provision for pedestrian access; provision for vehicular access; and detailed landscaping plans. Some communities require an initial site plan sketch conference with the planning board or its designated reviewer prior to formal submission so that all necessary site plan elements are included when the plan is submitted to the planning board for review.

C. Board Review–establishes the aspects of the proposed site plan to be considered by the reviewing board, including adequacy and arrangement of vehicular traffic access and circulation; adequacy and arrangement of pedestrian traffic; location, arrangement, and sufficiency of off-street parking and loading facilities; location, arrangement, size, design, and general site compatibility of principal and accessory buildings, lighting, and signage; adequacy of stormwater and drainage facilities; adequacy of water supply and sewage disposal facilities; adequacy and arrangement of landscaping; adequacy of natural resource protection and open space; protection of adjacent or neighboring properties against noise, glare, unsightliness, or other objectionable features; adequacy of fire lanes and other emergency zones; and compatibility of building design with existing characteristics of the neighborhood.

D. Board Action–establishes the timing requirements and required public hearing for site plan approval. May also require that review under the New York State Environmental Quality Review Act (SEQRA) be completed before final approval is granted for the site plan. After completion of SEQRA review and public hearing, may allow for planning board to approve, approve with modifications, or disapprove a proposed site plan by resolution. Will also establish time frame in which applicant must receive stamp and signature of reviewing board chairperson on an approved site plan.

E. Expiration of Approval–states that within a given time period, generally 180 days from the reviewing board resolution granting approval or approval with modifications, the applicant must have the site plan stamped and signed or the approval will expire and applicant will be required to resubmit the site plan for approval.

F. Performance Guarantee–requires that all improvements depicted on the site plan be installed and an as-built drawing be submitted to the zoning enforcement officer prior to the issuance of a certificate of occupancy. Where certain improvements have not yet been completed but the applicant wishes to secure a certificate of occupancy, the applicant must post a performance guarantee.

G. Changed Plans–requires that, where the applicant modifies an approved site plan, the modifications must be approved by the reviewing board, unless they are below minimum threshold levels. In that such a case, the modifications may be approved by the zoning enforcement officer.

H. Waiver of Requirements–provides the reviewing board with the authority to waive certain required elements of the site plan where, because of the particular character or limited nature of the development, the information normally required as part of the site plan is inappropriate or unnecessary or where strict compliance with the requirements of the site plan provision would cause the applicant extraordinary and unnecessary hardship; the findings granting a waiver must be made part of the public record.

Article IX: Subdivision Regulations

A. Purpose–establishes that the objective of subdivision regulation is to provide for the future growth and development of the municipality while affording adequate facilities for housing, transportation, comfort, convenience, safety, health, and welfare of the community. Chapter will designate the planning board or other administrative body as the reviewing board.

B. Definitions–definines various terms found throughout the subdivision regulations, such as "official map", "preliminary plat," "street," and "major and minor subdivision."

C. Policy–establishes that the division of any parcel of land, regardless of use, into two or more lots, plots, blocks, sites, or parcels, with or without the creation of new roads, or any change of existing property lines triggers subdivision review by the board to achieve the objectives set forth above. This section may also state whether the reviewing board is authorized to encourage or require subdivision applicants to cluster their developments. Some localities do not require subdivision approval for smaller subdivisions and lot line adjustments.

D. Major v. Minor Subdivisions–differentiates between major and minor subdivisions, setting forth less rigorous standards for smaller subdivisions. Designation may be based on the number of lots to be subdivided.

E. Procedure–details the procedures to be followed to receive both preliminary and final plat approval from the reviewing board. Some communities may differentiate between major and minor subdivisions, and thus the procedures to be followed may vary somewhat.

General Procedure–requires that whenever any subdivision of land is proposed that comes within the jurisdiction of the reviewing board, the subdivider or his authorized agent must apply for and obtain approval for the proposed plat in accordance with the procedures set forth below.

Initial Consideration–requires the subdivider to meet with the reviewing board to discuss the general aspects of the project as to the character of the site, proposed layout, the subdivision's effect on existing and future development, its effect on public services and infrastructure such as fire protection, roads and water supply, its effect on the natural environment; at the initial meeting the subdivider must also relate other pertinent information such as covenants on the property, restrictions, easements, zoning lines; if a community does create a distinction between major and minor subdivisions, the planning board will make its determination as to which category the proposed project should be reviewed under; some communities may also require the subdivider to submit rough sketches at this time which include an area map at a particular scale, generally one inch equaling 100 feet, the contour of the site, the proposed road layout, uses and structures on contiguous parcels and possibly environmental constraints on the site such as wetlands and steep slopes.

Preliminary Plat Approval–

1. Definition of Preliminary Plat–a preliminary plat is a drawing showing the layout of the proposed subdivision, road and lot alignment, approximate dimensions, topography and drainage, and all proposed structures and roads.

2. Submission of Preliminary Plat–sets forth the required elements of a preliminary plat, including that the plat be clearly marked "preliminary;" the name of the proposed subdivision; the approximate locations and dimensions of the proposed subdivision area; the topography; the names of adjoining property owners; the boundaries and designation of all zoning districts; the location, names, and dimensions of existing streets, easements, property lines, buildings, parks, and public properties; the location of existing sewers and storm drains; the location of natural resource constraints; the location and approximate grade of all proposed streets; the location and dimensions of all proposed easements; the proposed provision of water supply, fire protection, sanitary waste disposal, stormwater drainage, street trees, streetlight fixtures, street signs, and sidewalks; the proposed location and dimensions of all buildings and structures within the subdivision; and the approximate location and dimensions of all property proposed to be reserved for parkland. The submission of the preliminary plat must also be accompanied by proof of ownership interest in the land underlying the subdivision and an environmental assessment form pursuant to SEQRA.

3. Construction Plan–requires that construction plans for all improvements within the subdivision be prepared by a licensed engineer and depict a number of items. The construction plan is submitted along with the preliminary plat.

4. Public Hearing–within 62 days of receipt of a complete preliminary plat application and all accompanying information, the reviewing board must hold a public hearing on the application. The planning board must provide the public with at least five days notice of the hearing in a local newspaper of general circulation and may notify property owners within a locally selected number of linear feet of the perimeter of the proposed subdivision. Within 62 days of the close of the public hearing, the planning board must approve, approve with modification, or disapprove the preliminary plat by resolution. Public hearings may be kept open by the board no longer than 120 days. Preliminary plat approval expires within six months of the planning board resolution if the subdivider has not submitted an application for final plat approval. This approval may be extended by agreement of the planning board and applicant.

Final Plat Approval–

1. Definition–a final plat is a drawing showing the proposed subdivision that includes the elements set forth by the community for final plats. Generally, the elements are those found on the preliminary plat and any parkland that is to be reserved. To complete the application, a

subdivider must also include the application form, the construction plans, a deed to the municipality for all streets and roads that will be dedicated, a detailed statement giving the quantity and cost estimate for all improvements, and evidence that the subdivider has secured all necessary approvals from the county and state.

2. Submission of Final Plat—the final plat must be submitted to the reviewing board within six months of the reviewing board resolution approving the preliminary plat. Failure to do so allows the planning board to revoke the preliminary plat approval.

3. Approval of Final Plat—states that within 62 days of submission of final plat, a public hearing will be held by the planning board. If the planning board finds that the final plat is in substantial agreement with the approved preliminary plat, including modifications, then it may waive the hearing requirement. The planning board is authorized to approve, conditionally approve, or disapprove the final plat within 62 days of the close of the public hearing if held, or within 62 days of its submission if no hearing is held. Timing requirements may be extended by mutual consent of the parties. The final plat must be signed by the chair of the board or its clerk within 180 days of the board's decision on the plat, subject to two possible extensions of 90 days each.

4. Expiration of Final Plat Approval—approval will expire within 62 days of signing if the plat is not filed with the county clerk.

F. Improvements; Bonds; Fees; Agreements—this section lists the improvements that must occur on the subdivision, such as improved roads. Also explains that performance bonds, or other surety, may be used as security so that improvements are constructed.

Article X: Special Use Permits

A. Purpose—sets forth the reasons for allowing special uses in a given district. Generally, because of their characteristics or the unique characteristics of the area in which they are to be located, special uses require careful consideration so that they may be properly located. Chapter will designate the planning board or another administrative body to issue special use permits.

B. Submission of Application—may state that an application for a special use must be submitted to the zoning administrator along with the proper fee.

C. General Standards—establishes requirements applicable to all special uses. To grant a special use permit, the board must find:

1. that the proposed use is in harmony with the general purpose and intent of the land use chapter;

2. that there will be adequate access for fire and police protection;

3. that the streets serving the proposed use are adequate to carry prospective traffic and will not cause a traffic hazard or undue traffic congestion;

4. that the lot on which the use is to be located is of sufficient size and adequate dimension to permit the use in a manner not detrimental to surrounding property;

5. that the buildings, structures, facilities, and site layout will be adequately landscaped and maintained;

6. that the proposed use, buildings and structures will not be detrimental to the public health, and safety, or to property values of the neighborhood.

D. Specific Standards—a community may also establish specific standards for particular uses. Some examples of regulated uses include multi-family dwellings, home occupations, alternate care facilities, cemeteries, and day-care facilities.

E. Revisions and Extensions—states that any revision of an approved special use permit application and any reconstruction, enlargement, extension, relocation, or structural alteration of an approved special use, requires resubmission of a special use permit application for approval.

F. Expiration of Special Use Permit—establishes that a special use permit will expire if the permitted activity is not commenced and diligently pursued within a given time period, generally six months to one year.

G. Revocation—provides the reviewing board with the authority to revoke a special use permit where, after a public hearing, it is determined that there has been a substantial failure to comply with any of the terms, conditions, limitations, or requirements imposed by the special use permit.

Article XI: Planning Board

A. Establishment—authorizes the municipal legislature to create a planning board with at least five members, but no more than seven. May also establish terms of office and eligibility for service.

B. Powers and Duties—sets forth the board's responsibilities, including the review of subdivision, site plan, or special use permit applications.

C. Procedure—establishes the procedure for planning board review of various actions. May also provide procedure for referral of certain land use decisions to the county planning board.

D. Public Notice and Hearing—details the procedure utilized by the planning board to notify the public of hearings, meetings, and other actions.

Article XII: Zoning Board of Appeals

A. Establishment—creates a zoning board of appeals consisting of at least three members, although five is most common. May also establish terms of office and eligibility for service.

B. Powers and Duties—sets forth the board's responsibilities, including hearing and reviewing appeals from any order, requirement, decision, or determination made by the zoning administrator. May provide that the board shall hear and decide applications for subdivision or site plan approval or grant special use permits and variances. Grants the board the authority to interpret the zoning law; many communities also provide the board with the authority to prescribe conditions in the granting of any special use permit or variance to preserve the general purpose and intent of the land use chapter.

C. Procedure–establishes the procedural requirements for actions before the board. Requires that applications be in writing and to refer to the specific provisions of the law involved. Requires referral of applications to the local planning board and in certain instances to the county or regional planning board.

D. Public Notice and Hearing–requires that the zoning board of appeals to provide proper public notice (usually five days notice prior to the hearing, in a newspaper of general circulation). Fixes a reasonable time for a public hearing of any appeal or other matter referred to it.

Article XIII: Other Approving or Advisory Agencies

A. Architectural Review Board–establishes this board to review the proposed development for compliance with legislated architectural standards that are contained in this article.

B. Conservation Advisory Council (CAC) and Conservation Board (CB)–CACs are created to study and protect local open areas by developing an open-space inventory and map that identify such areas and list them in priority order for acquisition or preservation. Once the local legislature has accepted and approved the open space inventory and map, the local legislature may redesignate the CAC as a conservation board, and the open-space inventory and map become the official open-space index for the community. The conservation board now serves as an advisory agency to assist the community with sound open-area planning and to assure the preservation of natural and scenic resources.

C. Historic Preservation or Landmarks Commission–reviews proposed projects within historic districts for compatibility with the district's character and specific landmarks. Sets forth the procedure followed for review of proposed projects. In some communities, the commission may only make recommendations to the planning board. In others, it may issue, condition, or withhold permits.

Article XIV: Administration and Enforcement

A. Zoning Administrator–establishes an administrative officer who has the authority and responsibility to administer and enforce the provisions of the zoning and land use chapter or law. Duties generally include the review and approval of all development permits (building permits, certificates of occupancy, wetland permits, etc.), the issuance of stop-work orders, and the maintenance of records and site inspection. Some communities charge the municipal building inspector with the administration of the zoning and land use chapter or law.

B. Building Permits–establishes that no building or structure in any district shall be erected, reconstructed or restored, structurally altered, or used without a building permit. Requires that the proposed construction conform to the provisions of the zoning and land use chapter before a building permit will be issued. Also establishes the information to be included in the application and application procedure.

C. Certificates of Occupancy–explains that a certificate of occupancy must be received before a structure is used or occupied. Attests to the fact that the actual construction is in conformance with the Uniform Fire Prevention and Building Code and is satisfactory for occupancy or use.

D. Penalties for Offenses–sets forth the penalties that may be levied for violations of the land use chapter or law, including fines and jail sentences.

E. Schedule of Fees–establishes that fees shall be paid on the filing of any application, in accordance with the fee schedule established by the municipal legislature.

Article XV: Amendments

A. Amendment Procedure–sets forth the procedural requirements for amending the land use chapter or law. Generally states that the chapter or law may be amended, changed, modified, or repealed by the local legislature on its own initiative, on recommendation of the planning board, or on petition. Proposed amendments are subject to public notice and hearing requirements and must also be referred to the planning board for its recommendations. Amendments may also have to be submitted to the county or regional planning agency if certain conditions exist. Zoning amendments will also be subject to review under the SEQRA.

Article XVI: Miscellaneous

A. Conflict with Other Laws–states that whenever the requirements of the land use chapter or law are inconsistent with the requirements of any other lawfully enacted law, the more restrictive law governs.

B. Severability–states that if any provision of the land use chapter or law is declared invalid, all other provisions continue to remain valid and fully effective.

C. Effective date–sets forth the date upon which the land use chapter or law becomes legally enforceable.

E. HOME RULE AUTHORITY

DEFINITION

Local governments in New York have "home rule" authority to adopt local laws for a variety of purposes. Normally, zoning and land use regulations are adopted by towns, villages, and cities under the authority delegated to them by the planning and zoning enabling provisions of the Town, Village, and General City laws. Most of the issues in this book assume that local governments have enacted their zoning and other land use regulations under these specifically delegated powers. The Municipal Home Rule Law and the Statute of Local Governments are two separate bodies of law that authorize local governments to adopt regulations relating to land use control. When local legislatures adopt laws under this authority, they are said to be exercising their home rule authority.

PURPOSE

The planning and zoning enabling provisions of the New York State Town Law, Village Law, and General City Law authorize local governments to promote the health, safety, morals, and general welfare of the community by regulating land development. *See* Town Law §261; Village Law §7-700; General City Law §20(24). This includes regulating the size and shape of buildings, the percentage of lots that can be covered by development and the location of buildings for various land uses. In addition, zoning districts are created within which such regulations are to be uniform. Building regulations and zoning districts may be established for a very broad range of public purposes, including the encouragement of the most appropriate use of land throughout the municipality.

Home rule authority in New York is very broad. Under it, local legislatures have created a variety of innovative techniques to control land use, including floating zoning, planned unit development, the transfer of development rights, and incentive zoning, all of which have been sustained as being within the delegated land use planning and zoning authority of local government. Zoning laws sometimes contain provisions regulating wetlands, steep slopes, soil erosion, and tree preservation, all enacted under this same authority.

Occasionally, local officials are unsure whether the land use authority delegated by the Town, Village, and General City laws grants them the power to regulate particular aspects of land use. When this occurs, they turn to the Municipal Home Rule Law and the Statute of Local Governments to determine whether to enact a particular regulation or program as a local law under their home rule authority. Local officials can also use this authority to supersede the provisions of Town, Village, or General City laws and to adopt procedures and substantive rules that are different from those specified under these general state laws.

WHEN

The home rule statutes in New York State give local governments authority to protect the safety, health, and welfare of persons and property and to adopt zoning regulations. The combination in the Municipal Home Rule Law of the authority to adopt zoning regulations and to legislate in the broad public interest provides very general authority to adopt land use regulations and procedures of a variety of types. This authority is broader, in some respects, than that delegated under the planning and zoning provisions of the Town, Village, and General City laws. Home rule authority can be used to fill gaps in the provisions of those laws that focus on the regulation of building size and location, lot coverage, and the uses to which land may be put.

Home rule authority allows the regulation of the physical and visual environment, the protection of game, the prevention of floods, the conservation of soil, and the dumping of waste in watershed areas. Whenever the local legislature wishes to act regarding one of these matters, as well as to enact traditional zoning provisions, it may employ its home rule authority. Local governments have used their home rule authority to adopt laws regarding, for example, noise control, the prevention of soil erosion and sedimentation, the protection of steep slopes, and growth control.

Towns, villages, and cities have used their home rule authority also to supersede general state law when they have wanted to impose substantive requirements on land development not permitted by the Town, Village, and General City laws or to alter procedures prescribed by them. Localities have imposed a parkland dedication fee on site plan developers and have established a second zoning board of appeals using their home rule authority. Neither action was allowed by the Town, Village, and General City statutory provisions that delegate specific zoning and land use authority to municipal governments.

AUTHORITY

In New York State, the Statute of Local Governments gives towns, villages, and cities the authority to adopt zoning regulations. *See* Stat. of Local Governments §10(6). The Municipal Home Rule Law authorizes municipalities to adopt local laws to protect the natural environment in general and to protect several enumerated aspects of the environment. *See* Mun. Home Rule Law §10(1)(ii)(a)(11). Under this authority, localities may act with respect to their property, affairs, and government. This statute also authorizes localities to protect the safety, health, and welfare of persons and property.

The Municipal Home Rule Law also authorizes towns and villages to supersede the provisions of the Town Law, and Village Law to alter prescribed procedures or establish substantive requirements not clearly authorized by these laws. *See* Mun. Home Rule Law §10(1)(ii). The Attorney General has ruled, for example, that a village may enact a local law under its home rule authority to expand the scope of site plan review and to alter the procedure by which site plans are reviewed and approved.

IMPLEMENTATION

Refer to the material in the section on organizing land use regulations for a discussion of the pros and cons of collecting all land use regulations into one free-standing law or chapter of the local code. A single law or chapter makes the land use controls of the community easy to locate and to manage legislatively. Supplemental land use regulations under the municipal home rule authority may be integrated into that law or chapter.

Under recent amendments to the Town, Village, and General City laws, all local land use regulations must be adopted in conformance with the comprehensive plan. This provides another reason to collect all such regulations under the same chapter or law. The comprehensive plan sets the community's land use policy, and land use laws implement the objectives contained in that plan. Organizing the implementation provisions in a single law or chapter makes it easier to monitor the conformance of land use regulations with the comprehensive plan.

In some communities, some land use regulations are adopted by local law under the home rule authority and placed in a remote and separate chapter of the local code or adopted as a separate and distinct free-standing law. This is particularly true of some environmental regulations such as floodplain and wetlands controls. This requires landowners, developers, citizens, and others to review the entire code or body of laws to find all the local regulations related to land use control. Even when the source of authority for a particular land use regulation is the Municipal Home Rule Law, it may be placed for easy reference under the land use chapter of the code or adopted as an amendment to the free-standing land use regulation law of the community.

LIMITATIONS AND CONCERNS

There are four principal limitations on the exercise of home rule authority:

Authority: The subject of the local law must fit within the general or specific authorities conferred by the Municipal Home Rule Law or the Statute of Local Governments.

Consistency: Local home rule laws cannot be inconsistent with the constitution or general state laws. Home rule authority does not allow localities to violate the substantive limits applicable to the regulation of private property. Conditioning a building permit on the developer's agreement to settle a contractual dispute with the village, for example, was an invalid condition relating to matters beyond the scope of land use regulation. The courts have found that fees charged as conditions to the issuance of building permits which have as their purpose raising revenue for the community are illegal taxes, even if enacted under the home rule authority. A village was not able to regulate the form of ownership of multi-family housing under its home rule authority. A zoning law that effectively excludes types of housing that are affordable to low- and moderate-income persons is inconsistent with the principle that the delegated zoning power may not be exercised in a way that is detrimental to the needs of the people of the state as a whole.

Preemption: Localities may not pass home rule laws to regulate a field preempted by the state legislature. For example (*see* case digest hereinbelow), a town was barred from imposing a local licensing requirement on a state-regulated utility–a field preempted by the state legislature. A comprehensive state regime regulating family day-care centers similarly preempted a town's attempt to create performance standards applicable to them as part of its zoning law. The New York State legislature has preempted in part the field of mobile home park regulation. It is not always easy to determine whether the state legislature has preempted a subject; the courts look for evidence that the legislature intended that its regulations should preempt the possibility of varying local regulations. Where the state has adopted a comprehensive set of regulations and has articulated an overriding policy of state wide importance, a court may find an implied intent to preempt local governments from adopting local laws that alter the general state scheme of regulation.

Procedure: The New York Municipal Home Rule Law contains extensive provisions that must be followed for the adoption of a local law, including time periods for local legislators to review the bill, formal introduction, notice of–and holding of–a public hearing, adoption, recordation, and filing. These steps must be followed meticulously for the local law to be effective. Where a local land use regulation is originally adopted by local law, it can be amended or appealed only by local law, not by ordinance or resolution. Villages in New York are not authorized to legislate by the adoption of ordinance. In order to enact zoning provisions of any kind, a village must enact a local law.

STATUTES AND CONSTITUTIONAL PROVISIONS

Article IX of the New York Constitution authorizes the state legislature to adopt legislation to provide home rule authority to local governments.

The Bill of Rights for Local Governments is set forth in §1 of Article IX of the New York Constitution.

Section 10(1)(ii)(a)(11) of the Municipal Home Rule Law states that a municipality may adopt local laws for the "protection and enhancement of its physical and visual environment."

Section 10(1)(ii)(a)(14) of the Municipal Home Rule Law states that a municipality may adopt local laws as provided in the Statute of Local Governments. Section 10(6) of the Statute of Local Governments authorizes cities, towns, and villages to adopt zoning regulations.

The Municipal Home Rule Law §10(1)(ii) provides towns and villages the power to supersede the provisions of the Town and Village Law. Section 37(4) of the Municipal Home Rule Law provides that cities may supersede any inconsistent provision of a state statute that may be amended by local law.

For the procedural requirements that must be followed to adopt a local law under home rule authority, see Municipal Home Rule Law, Article III. Village Law §21-2100 requires that all local laws adopted under powers granted in the Village Law, including zoning regulations, be enacted in accordance with the procedures prescribed by the Municipal Home Rule Law.

CASE DIGEST

"A town can validly enact zoning regulations by local law pursuant to the Municipal Home Rule Law, provided that such regulations are not inconsistent with the provisions of the Constitution or with any general law." *Yoga Society of New York, Inc. v. Incorporated Town of Monroe*, 56 A.D.2d 842, 392 N.Y.S.2d 81 (2d Dep't 1977). The court sustained a town's zoning law that was enacted pursuant to the Municipal Home Rule Law, rather than §264 of the Town Law. It was important to the court that the town provided notice of the proposed adoption of the law through publication in a local newspaper, thereby providing the same procedural safeguards as §264 of the Town Law.

In *Wambat Realty Corp. v. State of New York*, 362 N.E.2d 581, 7 ELR 20363 (1977), the Court of Appeals upheld the Adirondack Park Agency Act, which preempted the land use authority of localities in the Adirondack region to various degrees. The plaintiff claimed that the Act, "which set forth a comprehensive zoning and planning program for all of the public and private lands within the park, together with other restrictions on local land use contained in the act, unconstitutionally deprive[d] the Town of Black Brook of its own zoning and planning powers." The court disagreed, holding that the preservation of the area was a paramount state concern.

The Second Department affirmed that a town board is empowered to adopt zoning regulations by virtue of its Municipal Home Rule Law powers and, in doing so, may supersede the provisions of the Town Law. *Sherman v. Frazier*, 84 A.D.2d 401, 446 N.Y.S.2d 372 (2d Dep't 1982). The plaintiffs challenged a local law that created review board to consider applications for special permits for the conversion of one-family houses to two-family houses. The plaintiffs argued that this local law was beyond the authority of the town since the Town Law provides for the establishment of a single zoning board of appeals. The court sustained the local law, noting that the Municipal Home Rule Law provides authority to towns to supersede the general provisions of the Town Law for the purpose of meeting special local needs such as this.

The Court of Appeals declared invalid a local law that required developers, as a condition of site plan approval, to set aside parkland or pay a fee to the town in lieu thereof. Its decision was based solely on the fact that the local law was not adopted in accordance with the formal requirements of the Municipal Home Rule Law which provide authority to supersede the general provisions of state law. *Kamhi v. Town of Yorktown*, 74 N.Y.2d 423, 547 N.E.2d 346, 548 N.Y.S.2d 144 (1989). The court held that the Municipal Home Rule Law §22(1) "requires a municipality invoking its supersession authority to state its intention with definiteness and explicitness" and to indicate "the particular provision(s) of the Town Law to which it purports to apply."

In *Albany Area Builders Assoc. v. Town of Guilderland*, 74 N.Y.2d 372, 546 N.E.2d 920, 547 N.Y.S.2d 627 (1989), the Court of Appeals held that a local traffic impact fee law was preempted by state legislation. The local law provided that persons applying for permits for development that will generate additional traffic must pay a transportation impact fee. The court held that "the State Legislature has enacted a comprehensive and detailed regulatory scheme in the field of highway funding, preempting local legislation on that subject." The court noted that "[s]uch local laws, 'were they permitted to operate in a field preempted by State law, would tend to inhibit the operation of the State's general law and thereby thwart the operation of the State's overriding policy concerns.'"

"Municipalities have no inherent capacity to mandate the manner in which property may be owned or held." *P.O.K. RSA, Inc. v. Village of New Paltz*, 157 A.D.2d 15, 555 N.Y.S.2d 476 (3d Dep't 1990). The court declared void a local law that prohibited the conversion of multiple-dwelling buildings into condominiums until there had been compliance with numerous requirements. The court held that "the Village does not have the legislative power to regulate the conversion of property ownership which does not involve an alteration in the owner's use of the property."

The Third Department sustained a phased growth law that limited the number of building permits that could be issued in a designated development area. *Albany Area Builders Assoc. v. Town of Clifton Park*, 172 A.D.2d 54, 576 N.Y.S.2d 932 (3d Dep't 1991). The court held that the law was a permissible exercise of home rule authority and not beyond the powers given to the town.

REFERENCES

Joe Stinson, *The Home Rule Authority of New York Municipalities in the Land Use Context*, at http://www.pace.edu/lawschool/landuse/stinso.html (last visited Feb. 2, 2001).

Adopting Local Laws, New York State Department of State, Division of Local Government; James A. Coon Local Government Technical Series.

F. NEW YORK CITY LAND USE LAW

DEFINITION

Under the state constitution, the New York State Legislature has the authority to pass laws to protect the public health, safety, morals, and general welfare of the people. Pursuant to this power, the legislature has delegated significant authority to regulate land use to local governments. Article 5-A of the General City Law delegates authority to cities to enact and enforce their own land use regulations. However, General City Law §81-e specifically excludes cities with more than one million residents from this provision. As the only city in New York State to exceed that threshold, New York City is not required to follow the limitations of authority delegated to other municipalities. It is free to establish a land use decisionmaking process that is responsive to its unique needs. Under its city charter and administrative code, the City has shaped its own regulatory and enforcement structure for land use matters.

New York City's land use system assigns key roles to citywide bodies such as mayor's office, the city council, the city planning commission, and the board of standards and appeals. New York City is divided into five boroughs: Manhattan, Brooklyn, Queens, Staten Island, and the Bronx. Each borough, governed by a borough president and local administrative bodies, is assigned a role in the city's land use control system. While the city has enacted a land use regulatory system similar in several respects to other New York municipalities, its decisionmaking standards and processes for land use are unique in important ways.

PURPOSE

New York City's land use system serves the needs of over seven million residents as well as those of the millions of workers and tourists who visit the city regularly. New York City's system seeks to unify land use regulation in the city through the use of devices such as the Uniform Land Use Review Procedure and other novel administrative and legal procedures. Its land use system allows smaller political units some power over land use down to the neighborhood level. The New York City Charter organizes land use regulation by allocating responsibility for different regulations among the administrative bodies best suited to making appropriate decisions in each case. The New York City land use system therefore has the same goals as the systems in place in smaller municipalities but must effect that purpose in a much more complex context.

WHEN

New York City recognized a need for zoning when it adopted the nation's first comprehensive zoning resolution in 1916, a response to overwhelming development pressures in Lower Manhattan. Before that time, cities in Europe and the United States had adopted nuisance-prevention laws regulating aspects of land use and building construction in some parts of their communities. New York City's effort began in 1910, with the appointment of a study commission, and culminated over six years later, with the adoption of the comprehensive, citywide New York City Zoning Resolution. Since then, the process of zoning has undergone regular and significant transformation as different agencies have become involved in administering a massive system.

New York City continually faces the problems of significant development pressures, serious environmental challenges, and difficult economic circumstances that prompt municipalities throughout the country to adopt and adapt zoning regulations to meet changing circumstances. Among the unique influences that the city has had to absorb was the judicial declaration in 1989 that its legislative board, the Board of Estimate, was unconstitutional and had to be abolished. *See Bd. of Estimate of the City of New York v. Morris*, 489 U.S. 688, 109 S.Ct. 1433, 103 L.Ed.2d 717 (1989). The evolution of the city's regulatory structure in response to these political, demographic, and constitutional pressures has been a process of steady change, which continues with revision of its all-important building bulk requirements that determine the form and scale of development in the city.

AUTHORITY

Since state law does not directly control New York City's land use authority, its power is found instead in its charter and in the provisions of its administrative code and zoning regulations. Under Title 25 of the City's administrative code, in particular §25-110(a)(b) and §25-111(a)(b), the Planning Commission is authorized to regulate buildings, sites, and zoning districts in much the same manner as the state enabling acts empower villages, towns, and other cities to regulate the development of land. The commission is further regulated by §192-d, which makes it responsible for the orderly growth, improvement and future development of the City. The Commission's authority is limited by §§197-c, 200, and 201 of the New York City Charter. Section 197-c requires the commission to adhere to the requirements of the Uniform Land Use Review Procedure (ULURP). Section 200 regulates the adoption and amendment of New York City zoning provisions. Section 201 governs the process for applications for special permits within the jurisdiction of the city planning commission. Sections 197-c and 197-d also authorize the City Council to review many of the Planning Commission's decisions approving land use proposals.

Other municipal bodies and agencies are given authority for special purposes. Under §666 of the City Charter, the Board of Standards and Appeals is granted the power to adjudicate most applications for variances and special permits as set forth in the city zoning resolution. Community and borough boards are authorized by §197-a(a) to propose plans for the development of the City, its boroughs, and its community districts. Section 3020 of the City Charter creates a landmarks preservation commission, charged with protecting the City's architectural, historic, and cultural resources. Finally, the mayor is granted planning authority under §§203 and 204 of the City Charter. This, combined with the authority granted to it under ULURP, makes the mayor's office a powerful force in city land use decisions.

IMPLEMENTATION

Seven city offices or agencies are involved in New York City land use decisions: the Department of City Planning, the City Council, the Board of Standards and Appeals, the Planning Commission, the community and borough boards, the Landmarks Preservation Commission, and the Mayor's office. Though not all are likely to participate in any one decision, each has its own powers and functions. They are most often involved in one of the four major types of land use decisions: subdivision of land, site plan proposals, special permit grants, and environmental quality reviews. To the basic functions of these centralized agencies is added the important role of various neighborhood and borough boards and entities. The integration of the functions of these citywide and decentralized agencies is accomplished by the Uniform Land Use Review Procedure (ULURP). Adopted in 1976 to deal with the increased involvement of community boards in the City's development as well as the growing participation of community members in local government, ULURP acts as the umbrella reviewing process over most important land use decisions.

The Uniform Land Use Review Procedure: New York City Charter §197-c(a) requires land use decisions to be subject to ULURP. The procedures under ULURP are cumbersome and lengthy, but they are so designed to protect neighborhood interests. They encourage and at times mandate the involvement of community and borough boards, borough presidents, and citywide agencies in an effort to achieve a thorough review of land use changes throughout the City.

Most applicants requesting a land use decision must file a standardized land use review application with the New York City Department of City Planning. This requirement applies to alterations in the city map, mapping of subdivisions, platting of land into streets, avenues, or public places, designation or changes of zoning districts, special permits, site selection for capital projects, variances, housing and urban renewal plans, sanitary or waterfront landfills, disposition of city-owned property, or acquisition of real property by the City. The Department of City Planning certifies the application, confirming that all forms, plans, supporting documents, and environmental impact statements, when required, have been included in the application. It then forwards the certified application to the appropriate boards and offices.

The review process then focuses on soliciting neighborhood input. According to §2-03(c) of the ULURP guidelines, the affected community board must notify the public of the application. Subsequently, the board must conduct a public hearing and within 30 days submit a written recommendation or a waiver thereof to the Planning Commission, the applicant, the borough president, and, when appropriate, the borough board. The borough board, in its discretion, may hold its own public hearing and submit an independent recommendation to the city planning commission if the application involves land located in more than one community district. After the community and borough boards have expressed their thoughts on the application, the proposal returns to the Planning Commission for review.

The chair of the Planning Commission and six of its 13 members are appointed by the Mayor, five by the borough presidents, and one by the City Council President. Pursuant to §197-c(h) of the City Charter, the Commission must conduct a public hearing and approve or disapprove land use applications within 60 days of the expiration of the borough president's review period. The Commission may approve a proposal over the objections of an affected borough president with the affirmative vote of nine commissioners. Generally the Commission's disapproval of a proposal is final and terminates the ULURP process.

The City Council has limited review responsibility in the ULURP process. Under §197-d of the City Charter, it must review the Planning Commission's decisions in the following ULURP actions: designation or change of zoning districts, housing and urban renewal plans, and the disposition of residential buildings, unless the buildings are being transferred to non-profit companies for low-income housing. The City Council does have the discretion to review ULURP decisions regarding city map changes and subdivision permits. Finally, an affected borough president may initiate City Council review under special circumstances. The City Council must review the Planning Commission's decision if three conditions are met: the application was approved by the Commission over unfavorable recommendations by an affected community board; the affected borough president opposed the proposal; and the borough president filed a written objection to the Commission's approval of the proposal within five days of receiving written notification of that decision. The City Council must then conduct a public hearing and file its decision with the Mayor within a 50-day review period.

The Mayor retains the ultimate veto authority over any land use decisions by the City Council as long as he vetoes a proposal within five days of the Council's filing of its decision. The Mayor may also veto applications approved by the planning commission which the Council failed to act upon in a timely manner. The Mayor may veto ULURP applications not subject to City Council review by filing a written objection to any decision. However, the City Council, by a two-thirds majority, may override any mayoral veto.

Other provisions of New York City law establish additional procedures for basic land use decisions such as subdivision and site plan approvals, the issuance of special permits and environmental reviews.

Subdivision Proposals: New York City's rules governing the subdivision of land within municipal limits are similar to those of other municipalities in that they require the filing of subdivision proposals with the appropriate authority. The mapping of subdivisions and the platting of land are subject to a public review process under ULURP. Section 25-133 of the New York City Administrative Code provides for the filing of subdivision maps and recording of deeds of subdivided property in much the same manner prescribed by Article III of the New York General City Law.

Site Plan Review and Approval: New York City derives its authority to require site plan drawings and details for most land use applications from §25-110(a) of its Administrative Code. Section 52-110(a) delegates to the Planning Commission the authority to regulate the location and height of buildings as well as designation of open spaces and allowable density of population in any given zoning district. However, neither New York City's charter nor its administrative code contains any formal site plan regulations. The Department of City Planning's "Land Use Review Application" contains a checklist of required filings for land use review under ULURP.

Special Use Permits: New York City divides its special use permit review and approval authority between two administrative agencies: the Board of Standards and Appeals and the Planning Commission. The Board of Standards and Appeals generally has jurisdiction of special permit applications for more localized proposals such as those involving the construction of gas stations, clubs, camps, and public utility installations in residential districts. Its approval process deviates from ULURP by allowing community boards and borough boards to review and recommend applications for special permits. The most important role of the Board in these decisions is to determine whether the proposed project has a negative impact on the neighborhood in question; therefore, input by community boards is essential. The Planning Commission retains the authority to grant special permits for projects that have greater land use impact or involve significant planning issues beyond a local neighborhood's interest. The Commission's role is that of central city planner. Its concerns are focused on projects that have an impact on the City as a whole, or on a significant portion of it. The Commission's process of reviewing and approving special use permits remains subject to the provisions of ULURP.

City Environmental Quality Review: New York City has a two-tiered system of environmental quality review. First, all agencies must abide by the requirements of the State Environmental Quality Review Act (SEQRA). Accordingly, the City has provided for SEQRA compliance in all of its land use regulations. Additionally, the City has established its own process of environmental review, the City Environmental Quality Review (CEQRA). CEQRA identifies lead agencies within the City, sets forth public scoping procedures for lead agencies to follow during the preparation of an environmental impact statement, and provides for an office of environmental coordination to assist lead agencies and other participants in the process.

STATUTES

Zoning Resolution of the City of New York (as amended, 2000):

Article I: general provisions & defined terms (Sections 11-00 to 15-50).

Article II: Residence District Regulations, Inclusionary Housing, Urban Design Guidelines, Quality Housing Program (Sections 21-00 to 28-53).

Article III: Commercial District Regulations (Sections 31-00 to 37-06).

Article IV: Manufacturing District Regulations (Sections 41-00 to 44-585).

Article V: Nonconforming Uses and Non-Complying Buildings (Sections 51-00 to 54-42).

Article VI: Height Regulations Around Major Airports; Waterfront Zoning (Sections 61-00 to 62-87).

Article VII: Administration (Sections 71-00 to 79-44).

Article VIII-XII: Special Purpose Districts (Sections 81-00 to 123-00).

REFERENCES

City Environmental Quality Review, *at* http://www.ci.nyc.ny.us/html/dcp/html/ceqra.html (last visited Feb. 2, 2001).

The Uniform Land Use Review Procedure, *at* http://www.ci.nyc.ny.us/html/dcp/html/ulpro.html (last visited Feb. 2, 2001).

The Unified Bulk Program, *at* http://www.ci.nyc.ny.us/html/dcp/html/bulksum.html (last visited Feb. 2, 2001).

New York City Zoning, *at* http://www.ci.nyc.ny.us/html/dcp/html/zone.html (last visited Feb. 2, 2001).

Edward N. Costikyan & Lexze U. Cornfield, *New York City's New Charter: Land Use Regulations,* N.Y. L.J., Mar. 14, 1990.

Kate Ryan, *New York's Second Land Use System: A Description of New York City Land Use Law & How It Complies*, *at* http://www.pace.edu/lawschool/landuse/nyc.html (last visited Feb. 2, 2001).

Chapter 4
STANDARD LOCAL PRACTICE

Local governments in New York are not required to adopt zoning ordinances or comprehensive plans or to regulate land subdivision or site development. However, once the local legislature adopts a zoning ordinance, it must create a zoning board of appeals to review the zoning administrator's decisions and entertain requests for variances. Local legislatures may also create planning boards to serve in an advisory capacity regarding community planning and the adoption of zoning provisions and to review applications for various land use activities. Other boards–such as a historic district commission, conservation advisory board, architectural review board, or wetlands agency–may be created, depending on local circumstances.

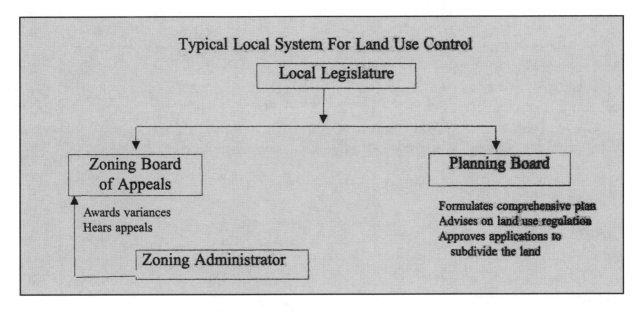

Typical Local System For Land Use Control

Local Legislature

Zoning Board of Appeals

Awards variances
Hears appeals

Zoning Administrator

Planning Board

Formulates comprehensive plan
Advises on land use regulation
Approves applications to
subdivide the land

Of all these boards, typically the three most active are the local legislature, the planning board, and the zoning board of appeals. The roles played by these three land use control bodies are varied. The local legislature–known as the city council, village board of trustees, or town board–adopts and amends the zoning law: a legislative function. It may retain or delegate to the planning or zoning board the authority to review site plan, subdivision, and special use permit applications: an administrative function. When the zoning board of appeals hears appeals from the zoning administrator or grants variances, it is acting in a quasi-judicial capacity.

The procedures that these local bodies must follow are governed, in New York State, not by the State Administrative Procedures Act, but by state statutes that delegate to local governments the power to award variances, approve site plans and subdivisions, or award special use permits. These statutes must be consulted to determine whether a public hearing is required, how notice of the hearing is to be given, the time by which a decision must be rendered, how the decision is to be filed, and who may appeal a local decision to the courts. The local legislature may establish additional procedures that must be followed by local boards.

State statutes define variances, land subdivision, site plan development, and special use permits. They also contain the standards that a local board must consider when reviewing a landowner's application, and they specify what types of conditions may be attached to a board's approval of such an application. Land uses that preexist the adoption of a zoning law or amendment usually are allowed to continue as nonconforming uses, but are not allowed to be expanded or enlarged. The accessory uses that customarily accompany the principal use allowed on the land are also permitted by most zoning laws, as long as they are incidental to the principal permitted use. A variety of home occupations, such as professional offices, may be allowed in residential zones, again if they are incidental to the principal residential use of the property. Some communities have adopted zoning provisions that allow single-family homeowners to establish a second, accessory living unit in their houses, under a variety of conditions.

These subjects consume most of the time of local land use administrative bodies. Local bodies receive applications for variances, site plans, subdivisions, and special permits and determine whether uses are permitted accessory uses or home occupations. Landowners petition them for approvals or favorable rulings, and neighbors and other affected parties become involved in the local process to protect their interests. Occasionally, local legislatures determine that their existing land use controls are incomplete or out-of-date, and they adopt a complete or partial moratorium on the review and approval process of these bodies, until the city council, village board of trustees, or town board can adopt adequate regulations to meet new or unexpected challenges.

A. LOCAL BOARDS AND PRACTICES

DEFINITION

Three boards are principally responsible for making land use decisions in most localities. The first of these is the local legislature, such as the village board of trustees, the town board, or the city council. The second is the zoning board of appeals, which must be created when a zoning law is first adopted by the local legislature. The zoning board performs quasi-judicial functions as a local appeals board and can be delegated administrative functions. The third is the planning board, which may be created to perform a variety of advisory and administrative functions related to community planning and land use decision-making.

The local legislature adopts and amends zoning and land use regulations and sometimes retains the authority to issue certain permits or perform other administrative functions. For example, the legislature may provide in the zoning regulations that certain uses are permitted only upon the issuance of a special permit, and may retain the authority to review and issue those permits instead of delegating that authority either to the planning board or to the zoning board of appeals. Normally, however, the legislature will establish these boards and delegate important administrative functions to them, such as the authority to issue special permits and to review and approve or deny applications for site plan and subdivision approval.

PURPOSE

The New York State Legislature has created these local bodies to provide a framework of local governance regarding the use and conservation of the land and the quality of life as it is affected by land use. This framework includes legislative, judicial, and administrative functions performed by the legislature, zoning board of appeals, and planning board. Observable in the laws governing their operation are a number of familiar legal doctrines, including separation of powers, citizen participation, public notice, access to information and board deliberations, the right to be heard, the right to impartial decision-making, and the right to appeal certain of these decisions. The ultimate purpose is to provide for the public health, safety, and welfare.

The essential function of the zoning board of appeals, and the reason its creation is legally required, is to grant variances from the strict application of zoning regulations in circumstances when they create demonstrable hardships for the owners of properties. One important purpose of the advisory role played by the planning board, which consists of appointed members often with special expertise or training in land use matters, is to provide an impartial and professional perspective on locally controversial decisions based on the long-range needs of the community contained in the comprehensive plan or other local policy documents.

WHEN

There are nearly 1,600 cities, towns, and villages in New York. All of them have local legislatures. All of the cities, approximately 88% of the villages, and approximately 69% of the towns have adopted zoning laws and must, by law, form zoning boards of appeals. All of the cities and approximately 86% of the towns and villages in New York have created planning boards.

AUTHORITY

State statutes require that when a local government adopts zoning regulations it must establish a zoning board of appeals consisting of three or five members. In towns, appointments to the board are made by the legislature; in cities and villages, the mayor or city manager may make appointments.

State law permits the local legislature to establish a planning board consisting of five or seven members. In the case of towns, appointments to the planning board are made by the local legislature; in the case of villages, by the mayor; and in the case of cities, appointments can be made by the mayor or city manager.

State statutes allow the local legislature to retain the authority to review and approve applications for subdivision, site plan, and special permits or to delegate this authority either to the planning board or to the zoning board of appeals. Subdivision review authority can be delegated to the planning board, and site plan authority can be delegated to the planning board or other administrative body, such as the zoning board of appeals. State law requires variances and appeals from the determinations of the official charged with zoning enforcement to be heard by the zoning board of appeals.

City charters may contain special provisions for the functions and procedures of these local bodies, and all local governments may adopt unique provisions under their authority to supersede the provisions of general state law that are otherwise applicable to land use actions.

IMPLEMENTATION

Local Legislature: The central role in the field of local land use control is played by the elected local legislative body. It has the authority to adopt and amend the zoning ordinance, subdivision regulations, site plan controls, and special permit provisions, as well as wetlands ordinances, historic district protections, and open space plans. It may also create other local boards and agencies such as the planning board and zoning board of appeals and decide what authority to delegate to these boards.

The local legislature is responsible for adopting and amending the official map and the comprehensive plan of the community: documents articulating local policy that guides and directs the deliberations and decisions of all three bodies. The local legislature, in summary, is responsible for creating the substantive provisions that affect land use controls, creating the agencies that implement and enforce those controls, and developing many of the procedures and standards that the planning and zoning board of appeals must follow.

Zoning Board of Appeals: The zoning board of appeals is created by the local legislature and may have either three or five members. It is authorized to grant variances and interpret provisions of the zoning law; however, when it acts in this capacity, its jurisdiction is appellate only. Persons aggrieved by the determinations, orders, and decisions of the administrative official charged with the enforcement and interpretation of the zoning law can appeal them to the zoning board of appeals. A majority of the members of the board must vote to reverse any determination, order, or decision.

In hearing an appeal, the zoning board of appeals is operating in a quasi-judicial fashion. The law requires that aggrieved persons appeal within 60 days of the date of a disputed determination, order, or decision. This requires the filing of a notice of appeal, including the grounds for the appeal and the relief that is requested. The board must hold a hearing on the appeal and publish a public notice of the hearing at least five days before it is to be held. At the hearing, board members and parties to the proceedings have the right to cross-examine any witnesses regarding matters that are truly relevant to the issues being decided. The decision of the board must be handed down within 62 days of this hearing, unless the parties mutually agree to an extension. The zoning board of appeals may also be delegated the authority to review applications for permits. In this case, it is exercising original jurisdiction, rather than serving as an appeals board. A person aggrieved by a determination of the zoning board of appeals with regard to the issuance of a permit, interpretation of the law, or award of a variance would appeal directly to the courts through an Article 78 proceeding.

Planning Board: The local planning board is created by the local legislature and may have either five or seven members. It can perform a number of advisory functions and is often delegated the authority to review and approve site plan and subdivision applications and to issue special permits. The legislature can, and in some cases must, delegate a variety of advisory functions to a local planning board, including the preparation of the comprehensive plan, zoning provisions, or site plan and subdivision regulations; reviewing and commenting on requests for specific zone changes or amendments to the comprehensive plan or other regulations being considered by the legislature; and reviewing and commenting on proposed changes in the official map, the adoption of capital budgets, or other matters affecting the development of the community. In some communities, the planning board has been organized as a planning commission. This may have been accomplished under provisions of the General Municipal Law or, in the case of a city, under its charter, which allows the planning board to be organized as a commission. Local differences in practice of this sort must be respected and understood in any given situation.

LIMITATIONS AND CONCERNS

Basic Due Process Requirements: The decisions of local land use bodies must be made in an open and fair manner, by impartial board members, and must be based on reliable evidence that is contained in the record of the board's deliberations. These guarantees are secured by the federal and state constitutions and by a variety of state statutes. Among other mandated procedures, state and local requirements often specify that land use actions can be taken only after a hearing is held following adequate notice and where the public is invited to be heard in a fair and impartial manner. This applies to the adoption and amendment of zoning provisions and decisions on most applications for development permits.

Basing Decisions on Facts in the Record: In making decisions on site plan and subdivision applications and the issuance of variances and special permits, local boards must keep a detailed record of their deliberations. These records can be in narrative form rather than verbatim transcripts. The findings of the board and its decision should be based on reliable evidence contained in this record. The record may be the minutes of the board, if prepared in enough detail to satisfy these requirements.

Keeping and filing a detailed record insures that board decisions are not arbitrary, capricious or an abuse of discretion. Such a record provides the type of information parties need to decide whether to appeal board decisions, and creates the type of record that a court or review board will need to determine the validity of decisions made by land use boards.

Requirement to Provide Information to the Public: Local land use agencies are governed by the state freedom of information law, which provides public access to governmental records. The records that are subject to public access include photos, maps, designs, drawings, rules, regulations, codes, and manuals as well as reports, files, and opinions. Boards may establish reasonable rules regarding access, time to respond, copying, mailing, and paying for the information requested.

Requirement to Hold Open Meetings: Local public bodies, including the legislature and planning board, are required by the state open meetings law to allow the public access to their meetings. Although the open meetings law does not apply to "quasi-judicial proceedings," sessions of the zoning board of appeals and planning board are subject to open meetings requirements under the Town, Village, and General City Law.

All assemblies of these local bodies must be open to the public, including special meetings with applicants or opponents attended by members of the board, and even site visits conducted by the local legislature, planning boards, and zoning boards of appeals. Although closed executive sessions may be held in certain circumstances, courts will scrutinize whether there was a valid reason to hold the meeting in private. Where the deliberations are held in closed session and the public is permitted to know after the fact about decisions that were made in private, both the letter and spirit of the open meetings law are violated.

Requirement to Avoid Conflicts of Interest: State statutes require that every applicant for a variance, zoning amendment, special permit, or site plan or subdivision approval must provide full information regarding any interest of a municipal officer in the matter presented. This disclosure is relevant to the deliberations of land use bodies because state law prohibits municipal officers, including members of any administrative board or other agency, from participating in public matters in which they have a private conflict of interest. Planning and zoning board members have been prevented, under these laws, from deliberating and voting on projects in which they have a private interest or a special connection with the applicant, including a financial investment, a familial relationship, an employment relationship, or any significant contractual relationship.

Limitations on the Actions of the Zoning Board of Appeals: The zoning board of appeals may not hear appeals from the actions of the local legislature, acting in its legislative capacity. The denial of a request for the rezoning of a parcel, for example, may not be appealed to the board. The zoning board of appeals also has no power to review the legal validity of the provisions of the zoning law; it may only interpret provisions of the zoning upon appeal by aggrieved persons from adverse determinations by the responsible administrative official. Zoning boards of appeal may not grant variances that have such an impact as to constitute a rezoning of the land–a function within the province of the legislature. Where a board granted a variance from a two-acre residential development requirement to allow development on lots of one acre, the court held that its action constituted an invalid rezoning, rather than a variance, where the parcel affected was 40 acres in size.

Limitations on the Actions of the Planning Board: A planning board may not consider or issue variances, hear appeals from the official responsible for zoning administration, or issue interpretations of zoning provisions. Planning boards may not act outside their delegated authority or base their decisions on standards not contained in state or local laws and regulations over which they have jurisdiction.

Education of Local Boards: Although municipalities may compensate the members of land use boards, most members serve as volunteers. Often, newly appointed board members have little familiarity with land use law and practice. There is a fair amount of turnover among board members. As a result it is advisable for local governments to provide training for board members. New York State law allows local legislatures to require local board members to complete training and continuing education courses. Under comparable authority contained in local law, the village of Suffern added the following provision to its village code: "All members appointed to the Planning Board and Zoning Board of Appeals are required, as a condition of appointment, to attend a training program related to the function of said board within two years of the date of appointment. Thereafter, each member of the Planning Board and Zoning Board of Appeals shall attend a minimum of two acceptable training sessions each year." Suffern is in Rockland County, whose municipal planning federation provides the training sessions needed by the village board members. Most municipal legislatures in Rockland have adopted similar training requirements. (*See* Suffern Village Code, Chapter 41, Article I).

STATUTES

Under New York State Village Law §7-712(2), Town Law §267(2), and General City Law §81(1), local governments are required to create zoning boards of appeals when they adopt zoning regulations, and to appoint their members, and may delegate additional administrative duties to them.

Under Village Law §7-718(1), Town Law §271(1), and General City Law §27(1), local governments are authorized to create planning boards, to appoint their members, and to refer various matters to planning boards for advisory opinions.

The authority of local governments to supersede general state law can be found at Municipal Home Rule Law §10(1)(ii)(a).

The requirements to provide information to the public are found in the Public Officers Law, Article 6. Section 86(4) requires maps, drawings, regulations, and other documents pertaining to land use decision-making to be provided to the public on request.

The requirements of state law regarding the conduct of open meetings is found in the Public Officers Law, Article 7. Although quasi-judicial proceedings are excluded from this requirement under §108(1), the meetings of the zoning board of appeals must be open under the provisions of the Village Law (§7-712-a(1)), the Town Law (§267-a(1)), and the General City Law (§81-a(1)).

The General Municipal Law, Article 18, governs and prohibits conflicts of interest on the part of municipal officials. Section 809 requires applications for land use decisions to disclose any interest of any municipal officer in the matter presented.

CASE DIGEST

In a case involving the creation of a water district, the court stated that "[i]t is essential to due process that the owners of land affected by the improvement be accorded an opportunity to be heard as to the location of the boundaries and the creation of the district." *Floyd-Jones v. Town*

Board of Town of Oyster Bay, Nassau County, 249 N.Y. 398, 164 N.E. 330 (1928). The court concluded that there was no constitutional violation of due process in this case because all owners of affected property "were given notice and an opportunity to be heard on the question whether their property would be benefited by the improvement."

The trial court in *Gazan v. Corbett,* 304 N.Y. 920, 110 N.E.2d 739 (1953), held that a permit to use land as a refuse dump was rendered void because the notice of hearing was not mailed to residents in the surrounding area, based on the rule articulated in *Mullane v. Central Hanover Bank and Trust,* 339 U.S. 306 (1950). The Appellate Division reversed this decision, holding that the facts of *Mullane* were distinguishable from those in *Gazan. Mullane* held that notice should be "reasonably calculated under all the circumstances to apprise the interested parties of the pendency of the action and afford them an opportunity to present their objections." In *Gazan,* the appellate court concluded that due process was not violated despite the fact that the plaintiffs were not given notice of the hearing by mail. The publication of the notice in the official paper was sufficient to meet due process guarantees and the standard of the *Mullane* case.

Since plaintiffs' property rights were affected by a town board's decision, the plaintiffs were entitled to "some notice and opportunity to be heard before the Town Board." *Calhoun v. Town Board of Saugerties,* 94 Misc. 2d 78, 404 N.Y.S.2d 61 (Sup. Ct. Ulster County 1978). Individuals who were denied trailer permits by a town board challenged the decision because they were not notified that the permit application was being considered and were denied the "opportunity to present facts or argument" regarding the application. They further complained that the town board did not issue a formal written decision as to why their trailer permit application was denied. The court agreed with the challengers, stating that the denial of notice, lack of an opportunity to present evidence, and the board's failure to create a record of decision for court review were in violation of the Town Law.

In *Stein v. Board of Appeals of the Town of Islip,* 100 A.D.2d 590, 473 N.Y.S.2d 535 (2d Dep't 1984), a property owner applied for a permit to alter a legal, nonconforming building. The zoning board of appeals received a notarized letter from an interested party who could not attend the hearing, which produced allegations damaging to the application. The board relied on the letter to deny the applicant's request. In an action brought by the applicant, the court concluded that the letter should not have been considered because the board of appeals did not allow the plaintiff the "opportunity to rebut [the letter's] allegations." The court ordered a new hearing so the plaintiff would be afforded the opportunity to defend himself against the allegations.

The plaintiffs in *Knight v. Amelkin,* 68 N.Y.2d 975, 503 N.E.2d 106, 510 N.Y.S.2d 550 (1986), challenged the denial by the zoning board of appeals of their application for a variance or special exception to alter a building. The court agreed with the plaintiffs' claim that the board's decision was contrary to previous decisions concerning similar applications. It held that the plaintiffs were entitled to an explanation by the board as to why it deviated from its precedent decisions. The court held that "[i]nasmuch as a zoning board of appeals performs a quasi-judicial function when considering applications for variances and special exceptions and completely lacks legislative power, a zoning board of appeals must comply with the rule of the *Field* case."

The rule set forth in *In the Matter of Charles Field Delivery Service*, 66 N.Y.2d 516, 488 N.E.2d 1223, 498 N.Y.S.2d 111 (1985), stated that "[a] decision of an administrative agency which neither adheres to its own prior precedent nor indicates its reason for reaching a different result on essentially the same facts is arbitrary and capricious." The *Knight* court did not conclude that the plaintiffs' application must be granted, but stated that an explanation or, in the alternative, a conforming determination was required.

In *Bowers v. Aron*, 142 A.D.2d 32, 534 N.Y.S.2d 812 (3d Dep't 1988), the plaintiffs challenged the zoning board of appeals' approval of an application to extend a nonconforming use because they were not permitted to speak at a second hearing on the matter. The public notice of the hearing specifically stated that the zoning board would hear all persons in support of or in opposition to the application. The court held that it was "irrational for the Zoning Board to preclude [plaintiffs] from speaking solely on the ground that the prior public hearing had been declared closed."

There must be an indication in the record that a zoning board of appeals acted properly and formally as a body. *McCartney v. Incorporated Village of East Williston*, 149 A.D.2d 597, 540 N.Y.S.2d 456 (2d Dep't 1989). The court held that the plaintiff "may be entitled to seek judicial review of the denial of his variance application" because "there was no indication in the record …that minutes were taken which reflect each member's vote thereon and that the Zoning Board of Appeals formally acted as a body."

A board member who was removed because of a conflict of interest challenged his removal in *Keller v. Morgan*, 149 A.D.2d 801, 539 N.Y.S.2d 589 (3d Dep't 1989). While plaintiff was a member of the planning board for the Town of Schodack, he held an interest in a construction company. The conflict arose when the company entered into a contract with a developer that was waiting for approval of a subdivision by the planning board. The plaintiff voted to approve the subdivision without disclosing his interest in the construction company and the work being performed. Following an investigation into the alleged conflict, the plaintiff was removed as the planning board's chairman. The court upheld plaintiff's dismissal from office because he "neither disqualified himself in this matter nor made any statement concerning the conflict." The dismissal was proper because "[t]he existence of a conflict of interest in such circumstances is patent, and the potential damage to the public welfare in general and the integrity of the planning board in particular is obvious."

"Resolution of questions of conflict of interest requires a case-by-case examination of the relevant facts and circumstances and the mere fact of employment or similar financial interest does not mandate disqualification of the public official involved in every instance." *Parker v. Town of Gardiner Planning Board*, 184 A.D.2d 937, 585 N.Y.S.2d 571 (3d Dep't 1992). The court noted that "the extent of the interest at issue must be considered and where a substantial conflict is inevitable, the public official should not act." The court found that the financial relationship between a planning board member and the applicant was so inconsequential that the member was unlikely to be swayed. The court held that disqualification for conflict of interest was unnecessary.

An executive session of the Solid Waste and Recycling Committee, called because matters that might affect property values were going to be discussed, was found to be improper and in violation of the Open Meetings Law in *Glens Falls Newspapers, Inc. v. Solid Waste and Recycling Committee of the Warren County Board of Supervisors*, 195 A.D.2d 898, 601 N.Y.S.2d 29 (3d Dep't 1993). The court determined that in order to convene an executive session there must be evidence that the value of the property being discussed would be substantially altered by the publicity. Here the court concluded that there was no evidence in the record to support such a claim, and that the claim was pure speculation.

The court in *Anthony v. Town of Brookhaven*, 190 A.D.2d 21, 596 N.Y.S.2d 459 (2d Dep't 1993), had to determine if notice by mail to the address of the property owner as reflected in the town's most recent tax assessment roll was constitutionally sufficient. The town board held a public hearing to discuss the potential rezoning of several parcels of land, including plaintiff's property. The town clerk relied on the tax assessment rolls to send notice of the hearing to surrounding property owners. However, because the plaintiff had recently purchased the property, the notice of public hearing was sent to the previous owner rather than to the plaintiff. Brookhaven's town code defined "property owner" as "the owner as shown on the current Brookhaven town assessment roll." The court concluded that this method of notification was consistent with the requirements of due process. This decision was reached by balancing the governmental interests and the interest of the individual. The court concluded that the administrative burden of determining the actual owner of all affected parcels outweighed that of the harm to the individual. It held that the notice provisions of the city administrative code satisfied the minimum requirements of due process.

REFERENCES

Land Use Planning and Regulation in New York State Municipalities: A Survey, New York State Legislative Commission on Rural Resources, Albany, N.Y. (Fall, 1999).

The Short Course, A Basic Guide for Planning Boards and Zoning Boards of Appeal in New York State, New York Planning Federation (1996).

Zoning Board of Appeals, New York State Department of State, Division of Local Government; James A. Coon Local Government Technical Series.

Record Keeping Tips for Zoning Administration, New York State Department of State, Division of Local Government; James A. Coon Local Government Technical Series.

Conducting Public Meetings and Public Hearings, New York State Department of State, Division of Local Government; James A. Coon Local Government Technical Series.

B. VARIANCES

DEFINITION

A variance allows property to be used in a manner that does not comply with the literal requirements of the zoning ordinance. There are two types of variances: area and use.

A use variance permits "a use of the land for a purpose which is otherwise not allowed or is prohibited by the applicable zoning regulations." Town Law §267(1)(a); Village Law §7-712 (1)(a); General City Law §81-b(1)(a). For example, if a piece of land is zoned for single-family residential use and the owner wishes to operate a retail business, the owner could apply to the zoning board of appeals for a use variance.

An area variance, on the other hand, allows for a "use of land in a manner which is not allowed by the dimensional or physical requirements of the applicable zoning regulation." Town Law §267(1)(b); Village Law §7-712(1)(b); General City Law §81-b(1)(b). An area variance is needed when a building application does not comply with the setback, height, or area requirements of the zoning ordinance. If an owner wants to build a deck on his house that encroaches slightly into a side yard setback area, he could apply to the zoning board of appeals for an area variance.

PURPOSE

Variances provide flexibility in the application of the zoning law and afford the landowner an opportunity to apply for administrative relief from certain provisions of the law. A property owner may seek a use or area variance when an application for a building permit is denied on the grounds that the proposal violates the use or dimensional requirements of the zoning ordinance. Alternatively, the property owner could request the local legislative board to rezone the property so that the requested use is allowed as-of-right.

AUTHORITY

The zoning board of appeals has been delegated the statutory authority to issue use and area variances. The jurisdiction of the zoning board of appeals is appellate only. It is limited to reviewing or hearing appeals from the decisions of an administrative official charged with enforcing the zoning law. In other words, a landowner may not go directly to the zoning board of appeals for an interpretation of the zoning law or for a variance. The zoning enforcement officer must rule on the matter first and that decision must be filed in the enforcement officials office within five days of the decision. That ruling may be appealed to the board. In order to grant a use or area variance, a concurring vote of a majority of the board is necessary. The board is limited to granting the minimum variance necessary that addresses the need for the variance while preserving the character, health, safety, and welfare of the community.

IMPLEMENTATION

When an application for permission to build is made to the local building inspector or department that does not comply with the literal requirements of the zoning law, the proposal must be denied. If the reason for the denial is that the application violates the use or area provisions of the law, the applicant may apply to the zoning board of appeals for a use or area variance.

New York law provides statutory standards for the issuance of use and area variances. The statutes impose upon an applicant a heavy burden of demonstrating that a use variance should be granted, since the applicant is asking that the zoning board of appeals alter the local legislature's determination that a specific use is not appropriate in the zoning district. The legal burden is less stringent when applying for an area variance, since the potential impact on the surrounding area is significantly less.

Statutory Standard for Use Variance: To obtain a use variance, the applicant must demonstrate that the applicable zoning regulations cause an unnecessary hardship. To prove unnecessary hardship, the applicant must establish that the requested variance meets the following four statutory conditions:

1. The owner cannot realize a reasonable return on the property as zoned. The lack of return must be substantial and proved with competent financial evidence. It is insufficient for the applicant to show only that the desired use would be more profitable than the use permitted under the zoning. For example, in *Everhart v. Johnston*, 30 A.D.2d 608, 290 N.Y.S.2d 348 (3d Dep't 1968), the owner of residentially zoned property sought a use variance to construct offices for an insurance agency and a real estate business. The owner testified in support of the application that it would not be economical to renovate the property for residential purposes and that a greater rent could be charged to a commercial lessee. The court held that a showing that "the permitted use may not be the most profitable use is immaterial." What must be established is that "the return from the property would not be reasonable for each and every permitted use under the ordinance."

2. The hardship must be unique to the owner's property and not applicable to a substantial part of the zoning district. If the hardship is common to the whole neighborhood, the remedy is to seek a change in the zoning, not to apply for a use variance. In *Collins v. Carusone*, 126 A.D.2d 847, 510 N.Y.S.2d 917 (3d Dep't 1987), the court held that the applicant had failed to establish that the hardship–being located near a city landfill–was unique to his property. Rather, it was held that the hardship was common to all properties in the area. Thus, the property owner should apply to the local legislature for rezoning.

In *Douglaston Civic Association v. Klein*, 51 N.Y.2d 963, 416 N.E.2d 1040, 435 N.Y.S.2d 705 (1980) the court noted that "uniqueness does not require that only the parcel of land in question and none other be affected by the condition that creates the hardship. What is required is that the hardship condition be not so generally applicable throughout the district as to require the conclusion that if all parcels similarly situated are granted variances the zoning of the district would be materially changed."

3. Granting the variance must not alter the essential character of the neighborhood. In making this determination, the court often considers the intensity of the proposed development as compared to the existing and permitted uses in the neighborhood. For example, a use variance to permit construction of an office building in a single-family neighborhood where several tall commercial structures already exist would not alter the essential character of the neighborhood. Conversely, the court in *Holy Sepulchre Cemetery v. Board of Appeals of the Town of Greece*, 271 A.D. 33, 60 N.Y.S.2d 750 (4th Dep't 1946), held that a cemetery would alter the essential character of a district zoned for residential development, despite the fact that the land in the district was undeveloped at the time of the application.

4. The hardship must not be self-created. In *Clark v. Board of Zoning Appeals of Town of Hempstead*, 301 N.Y. 681, 95 N.E.2d 44 (1950), the Court of Appeals held that "one who . . . knowingly acquires land for a prohibited use, cannot thereafter have a variance on the ground of special hardship." For example, a developer may not acquire land zoned residential at the time of acquisition and successfully petition for a variance to construct office buildings. Whether the purchaser actually knew about the use restriction is not relevant; he is charged with a duty to discover such restrictions.

In issuing a use variance, the board may impose "such reasonable conditions and restrictions as are directly necessary to and incidental to the proposed use of the property. Such conditions shall be . . . imposed for the purpose of minimizing any adverse impact such variance may have on the neighborhood or community."

Statutory Standard for Area Variances: For a zoning board of appeals to grant a variance from the dimensional and area requirements of a zoning ordinance, it must find that the benefits to the applicant of the requested variance outweigh the detriment it will cause to the health, safety, and welfare of the neighborhood. The board must weigh the benefits of the requested variance to the applicant against the five factors set forth in the statute:

1. Will an undesirable change be produced in the character of the neighborhood or a detriment to nearby properties be created by the granting of an area variance?

2. Can the benefit sought by the applicant be achieved by some method that is feasible for the applicant to pursue other than an area variance?

3. Is the requested area variance substantial?

4. Will the proposed variance have an adverse effect or impact on the physical or environmental conditions in the neighborhood or district?

5. Is the alleged difficulty self-created? This consideration shall be relevant to the decision of the board of appeals, but shall not necessarily preclude the granting of the area variance.

In *Sasso v. Osgood*, 86 N.Y.2d 374, 657 N.E.2d 254, 663 N.Y.S.2d 259 (1995), the Court of Appeals interpreted the statutory balancing test for area variances. The case involved an application for an area variance to allow the property owner to build a boathouse on a lot that was smaller than the required minimum lot size. The zoning board of appeals granted the area variance, and several neighbors challenged that decision. In upholding the determination of the zoning board of appeals, the court found that the board had carefully considered the five statutory criteria and made a rational decision. The zoning board had found that construction of the boathouse would not cause a change in the character of the neighborhood since adjacent properties had similar structures. No alternatives other than an area variance existed because the subject parcel was smaller than required and there was no available adjacent land to be purchased so as to meet the minimum requirements. The fact that the hardship was determined to be self-created was not fatal to the granting of the variance. Even though the owner had knowledge that the lot was substandard when purchased, the statute specifically provides that this is just one factor to be considered and "shall not preclude the granting of an area variance." The court found that the zoning board properly weighed the benefit of the variance against the detriment to the community and that the board's findings were amply supported by the record.

LIMITATIONS AND CONCERNS

Use variances involve an inherent contradiction. It is the prerogative of the legislative body to separate one land use from another. This is the essential purpose of dividing the community into zoning districts. The power of a quasi-judicial body, such as the zoning board of appeals, to vary the uses allowed in a district must be limited in order to prevent that body from usurping this essential legislative function. At the same time, the legislature does not want property owners to be denied a reasonable return on their property because of use restrictions where some relief from these restrictions can be afforded without altering the underlying purpose of the zoning district. For this reason, zoning boards have been authorized to grant use variances subject to the requirements of the statute. The statute imposes on the petitioner a burden of proving specific factors. Area variances involve similar tensions, but to a lesser degree. There the zoning board of appeals is charged with the task of balancing the benefit of the variance to the petitioner against its impact on the area.

When making a decision to grant or deny an application for a variance, the zoning board of appeals must rigorously follow the statutory requirements, carefully review the evidence presented, and make a finding based on the record. Particularly in the case of area variances, where the legislature has specified factors that must be considered but has given no guidance as to how to weigh those factors, the record should reveal that all five factors were considered and state the findings of the board with respect to each. Additionally, the board is limited to granting only the minimum variance necessary under the circumstances.

STATUTES

New York State Town Law §267 and §276-b, Village Law §7-712 and §7-712-b, and General City Law §81-b set forth the definitions of use and area variances, establish the authority of the zoning board of appeals to issue use and area variances, and provide the statutory criteria that must be examined.

CASE DIGEST

Use Variance Cases

The plaintiffs in *Kingsley v. Bennett*, 185 A.D.2d 814, 586 N.Y.S.2d 640 (2d Dep't 1992), filed an application with the building department to convert a building in a residential zone to a commercial office use. When that application was denied, the plaintiffs applied to the zoning board of appeals for a use variance, which was also denied. When a use variance is sought, the applicant must meet the stringent requirement of showing unnecessary hardship. The court concluded that the plaintiffs did not meet their burden of establishing the statutory requirements and affirmed the dismissal of the petition. The first requirement must be proved by submitting "dollars and cents evidence" to show that there would not be a reasonable return. The court held that mere "testimony that the land might yield a higher return if the use variance is granted is insufficient."

First National Bank of Downsville v. City of Albany Board of Zoning, 216 A.D.2d 680, 628 N.Y.S.2d 199 (3d Dep't 1995), involved the second requirement for a use variance, which requires the applicant to prove unique circumstances. The bank applied for a use variance for a multi-family dwelling in an area where the maximum use allowed was two-family dwellings. The bank asserted "that the unique circumstances test focuses on the plight of the owner." The court stated that the test instead focused on "whether there are any unique conditions peculiar to and inherent in the property as compared to other properties in the zoning district." The court found that the plaintiff failed to show that the property had any unique conditions that set it apart from other property within the zoning district, and upheld the denial of the use variance.

The third requirement for a use variance is that "the proposed use will not alter the essential character of the neighborhood." In *Supkis v. Town of Sand Lake Zoning Board of Appeals*, 227 A.D.2d 779, 642 N.Y.S.2d 374 (3d Dep't 1996), a landowner's property was rezoned to "residential/recreational." The landowner expanded his use of the property and in doing so violated the new zoning regulations. He applied for and was granted a use variance. The neighboring landowners challenged the variance. The court affirmed the zoning board of appeals' determination that "the use variance would not alter the essential character of the neighborhood because its nature was both residential and industrial." In upholding the zoning board's determination the court noted that "it cannot be said that the proposed use would be 'materially detrimental to the public welfare and injurious to other property in the vicinity.'"

The plaintiffs in *Diana v. City of Amsterdam Zoning Board of Appeals*, 243 A.D.2d 939, 664 N.Y.S.2d 634 (3d Dep't 1997), purchased a former National Guard Armory at a public auction, and planned to convert it into a dormitory for college students. The zoning board of appeals denied their application for a use variance because there was no evidence that the hardship was not self-created. The court determined that "hardship will be considered self-imposed when the applicant for the variance acquired the property subject to the restriction and was aware of the restriction at the time of purchase." The court upheld the zoning board's denial of the application since the plaintiffs were aware of the zoning restriction and were not compelled to purchase the property.

A zoning board's determination denying a variance will be affirmed as long as the board had a rational basis for its decision and there was substantial evidence to support it. When deciding if a zoning board's determination has a rational basis and substantial evidence in use variance cases, the courts have relied on *Cowan v. Kern*, 41 N.Y.2d 591, 363 N.E.2d 305, 394 N.Y.S.2d 579, (1977). There a landowner sought review of the zoning board of appeals' denial of an area variance. The court held that "[a]bsent arbitrariness, it is for locally selected and locally responsible officials to determine where the public interest in zoning lies." Judicial review of local zoning decisions is limited. The court in *Cowan* concluded that "the determination of the responsible officials in the affected community will be sustained if it has a rational basis and is supported by substantial evidence in the record."

In *Conte v. Town of Norfolk Zoning Bd. of Appeals*, 261 A.D.2d 734, 689 N.Y.S.2d 735 (3d Dep't 1999), the plaintiff contested a zoning board's refusal to grant a use variance that would permit him to house a limited number of farm animals on his property. The plaintiff claimed that the refusal imposed an "unnecessary hardship" upon him because the animals were needed for his family's personal consumption. Affirming a zoning board's broad discretion to decide these matters, the court held that a use variance runs with the land and may be granted when there is a hardship relating to that land. However, a variance must not be granted merely to ease the personal difficulties of a current landowner. Furthermore, the court found that the plaintiff had not presented any evidence to show the economic return that the property could yield under the current zoning law. This evidence is required in order to satisfy one prong of the long-standing test for a use variance based on unnecessary hardship. Without this proof, the court found that the zoning board could not grant a use variance and, therefore, did not abuse its discretion in denying petitioner a use variance.

AREA VARIANCE CASES

The court in *Sasso v. Osgood*, 86 N.Y.2d 374, 657 N.E.2d 254, 633 N.Y.S.2d 259 (1995), examined the five factors that must be considered by the zoning board when deciding whether to grant an area variance. The court must look at these five factors and balance the extent to which the area variance will benefit the applicant against the detriment to the health, safety, and welfare of the neighboring community. The board's record supported its conclusion that these factors had been properly considered. The hardship, however, was found to be self-created. In this case, the court held that even though the hardship may have been self-created, the board's "conclusions find ample support from the . . . record, and its determination was not irrational, arbitrary or capricious." *See also Frank v. Scheyer*, 227 A.D.2d 558, 642 N.Y.S.2d 956 (2d Dep't 1996) (granting the plaintiff's petition because the zoning board of appeals' determination "was not supported by substantial evidence" and "the benefit to the petitioner outweighed the detriment to the health, safety, and welfare of the community"); *Stewart v. Ferris*, 236 A.D.2d 767, 653 N.Y.S.2d 973 (3d Dep't 1997) (concluding that the denial of the petition by the zoning board of appeals was supported by substantial evidence because the "area variance would have an effect on the physical condition of the area and result in an undesirable change in the character of the neighborhood").

In *Necker Pottick, Fox Run Woods Builders Corp. v. Duncan*, 673 N.Y.S.2d 740 (2d Dep't 1988), the zoning board of appeals denied the plaintiff's application for a frontage variance. The court found that there was not substantial evidence to support the denial because "the Zoning Board merely reiterated the . . . balancing test without stating the specific facts or reasons that it relied upon in making its determination to deny the [plaintiff's] application." The court granted the application because "the only opposition presented in this case was the generalized grievances of a group of neighboring property owners. . . . [C]ivic opposition was not based on facts, but on the weight of numbers, i.e., how many neighboring property owners were in opposition." *See also Wilson v. Town of Mohawk*, 246 A.D.2d 762, 668 N.Y.S.2d 62 (3d Dep't 1998) (holding that the zoning board of appeals did not use the statutory factors in reaching its determination and therefore did not have substantial evidence to support its denial).

In *Filangeri v. Foster*, 257 A.D.2d 895, 684 N.Y.S.2d 50 (3d Dep't 1999), the Appellate Division reviewed the grant of an area variance to an applicant whose difficulties were self-created. The landowner planned to build a single-family home in the center of a lot that was found to be substandard in size. Following the erroneous issuance of a building permit and partial construction of the home, the owner was required to petition for an area variance, which was granted by the local zoning board of appeals of the town of Gardiner. Town Law §267-b(3)(b) requires a zoning board to consider certain factors, such as whether the granting of the variance will produce an undesirable change in the neighborhood. The board must also weigh the benefit of the variance to the landowner against the detriment to the health, safety, and welfare of the community. The court held that the area variance was properly granted. It was clear that the board used the required balancing test and applied the criteria listed in Town Law §267-b(3)(b). The lot in question was larger in overall area or width than other neighboring properties and therefore the variance would not cause an undesirable change to, or have a detrimental impact on, the neighborhood. Furthermore, the requested variance was not substantial. In light of these considerations, the fact that the difficulty was self-created was relevant but did not, by itself, preclude the grant of the variance.

REFERENCE

Zoning Board of Appeals, New York State Department of State, Division of Local Government; James A. Coon Local Government Technical Series.

C. SUBDIVISION OF LAND

DEFINITION

The subdivision of land involves the legal division of a parcel into a number of lots for the purpose of development and sale. The authority to review and approve subdivisions may be granted to the planning board by the local legislature. The standards to be applied and the procedures to be followed by the planning board are contained in state law and in subdivision regulations that are adopted by the local legislature.

The subdivision and development of individual parcels must conform to the provisions of local zoning which contain use and dimensional requirements for land development. Zoning, however, does not contain specifications regulating many of the details of development which determine, for example, the precise location and specifications for streets, drainage facilities, sanitary sewers, storm drains, and water mains. Subdivision standards go beyond zoning regulations and protect neighborhoods from flooding and erosion, traffic congestion and accidents, unsightly design, noise pollution, and the erosion of neighborhood character.

Under a typical set of subdivision regulations, the landowner must submit a plat of the proposed subdivision showing the layout and approximate dimensions of lots and roads, the topography and drainage, and all proposed facilities at an appropriate scale. A plat is a map, drawing, or rendering of the subdivision that can contain narrative elements.

Local regulations require that the subdivision plat show all streets at sufficient width and suitable grade, sanitary sewers and storm drains, water mains and systems, landscaping, sidewalks, curbs and gutters, fire alarm signal devices, street lighting, signs, and trees. Additional features may be required, such as the location of floodplains, wetlands, building footprints, large trees, archeological sites, and utility easements and lines. Further, the statutes authorize the planning board, under certain circumstances, to require the applicant to reserve land for a park, playground, or other recreational purposes, or to require the payment of a sum of money in lieu of such a reservation.

Where a subdivision application meets the standards contained in the regulations, it must be approved. Where it does not, the planning board may impose conditions to insure that it meets the specifications. Where the subdivision cannot meet the standards, it can be rejected.

PURPOSE

By adopting and applying subdivision regulations, the community seeks to insure that new development is cost-effective, is properly designed, and has a favorable impact on the neighborhood.

Statutes delegating subdivision authority indicate that it is to be used "[f]or the purpose of providing for the future growth and development of the [municipality] and affording adequate facilities for the housing, transportation, distribution, comfort, convenience, safety, health, and welfare of its population." Town Law §276(1); Village Law §7-728 (1); General City Law §32 (1). Localities adopt subdivision regulations to assure that land proposed for development "can be used safely for building purposes without danger to health or peril from fire, flood, drainage, or other menace to neighboring properties or the public health, safety, or welfare." Town Law §277(1); Village Law §7-730(1); General City Law §33(1). The New York Court of Appeals has written that the adoption of subdivision regulation "reflects, in essence, a legislative judgment that the development of unimproved areas be accompanied by provision of essential facilities." *Golden v. Planning Bd. of Town of Ramapo*, 30 N.Y.2d 359, 372, 285 N.E.2d 291, 298, 334 N.Y.S.2d 138,147 (1972).

The regulation of land subdivision is a key element of community planning. When used by communities that have not adopted zoning provisions, subdivision control is the principal method by which the locality insures that land is developed in a beneficial way. When used in conjunction with zoning, subdivision control is an excellent method of insuring that land is developed in accordance with the zoning law and of facilitating the proper layout, design, and development of the community.

WHEN

Normally, communities adopt subdivision regulations to carry out their comprehensive plans and to supplement their zoning provisions. Localities that have not adopted comprehensive plans and zoning provisions may adopt subdivision regulations to regulate the process by which land is subdivided, developed, and sold in the community. Subdivision regulations are typically adopted when communities feel the pressures, and experience the impacts, of land development.

According to a recent survey conducted by the New York State Legislative Commission on Rural Resources, about 70% of the municipalities in the state have adopted subdivision regulations: 92% of cities, 71% of towns, and 66% of villages. Although subdivision regulations have been used in New York for most of the century, most communities did not adopt their subdivision regulations until the 1960s and 1970s.

AUTHORITY

Villages, towns, and cities in New York are authorized by state statutes to adopt and implement subdivision regulations. The adoption of subdivision regulations is permitted – not required – by state law. These statutes authorize localities to impose conditions on subdivision approval; to waive requirements where they are not needed to protect the public; to require the reservation of parkland on the site (if it is to be developed residentially) or to require the payment of a sum of money in lieu thereof; to require the posting of a performance bond or other security to secure the development of improvements on the site; to approve the clustering of permitted density on portions of the parcel to preserve open space; and to require compliance with environmental review provisions when approving subdivision applications.

IMPLEMENTATION

Legislative Role: The local legislature has the authority to adopt subdivision regulations, to decide what standards to include, to determine what types of private land subdivisions are subject to approval, and to appoint the planning board as the local reviewing body.

Filing Certificate: Once the planning board has been authorized to approve subdivisions in the municipality, the municipal clerk shall file a certificate of that fact with the county clerk or register of deeds.

Reviewing Body: The local legislature may retain the authority to review and approve subdivision applications or may delegate that authority to the local planning board. Once the planning board is delegated this authority, it may draft and recommend subdivision control regulations to the legislature for its adoption.

Applicability: The local legislature, in adopting subdivision regulations, can exempt small subdivisions from the approval process, specify whether minor and major subdivisions, as defined locally, are to be treated differently, state whether lot line alterations are controlled by the subdivision regulations, and indicate whether subdivision applicants must go through a preliminary and final approval process or only a final approval process. The locality can specify how detailed subdivision applications must be and how many elements or factors the submitted subdivision map must contain.

Preliminary Submission and Public Hearing: One typical procedure adopted locally is to require the developer of a major subdivision of land to submit both a preliminary plat of the proposed subdivision and a final plat, both of which are subject to review and approval. When this procedure is required, the planning board must hold a hearing within 62 days of the submission of the preliminary plat, subject to public notice at least five days prior to the hearing. The planning board's decision on the preliminary plat must be made within 62 days after the close of the public hearing. The statutes require that public hearings be closed within 120 days of the date they are opened.

Decision on Preliminary Submission: Where the preliminary plat is approved, that decision must be filed with the planning board and municipal clerk within five days of the decision. Where the decision is to approve but modify the preliminary submission, the grounds for modification must be stated upon the record and the board must state in writing any modifications it deems necessary for the final submission.

Submission of Final Subdivision Map/Final Decision: Within six months after an approval of a preliminary subdivision plat, the applicant must submit his final map for review. If he fails to do so, the preliminary approval may be revoked. Where the final plat is in substantial agreement with the approved preliminary plat, the planning board must approve or disapprove the final plat within 62 days of its submission to the planning board clerk. Within five business days of the adoption of the resolution granting approval of the final plat, the plat must be certified by the planning board clerk and filed in that clerk's office, as well as in the office of the municipal clerk.

Default Approval/Expiration of Approval: The failure of the planning board to take action within the established time periods is deemed an approval by default. The approval of the planning board expires 62 days after the date of approval, or the date certified, if not filed by the property owner in the office of the county clerk or register.

Variations: Local authorities may decide not to require a preliminary plat submission and approval process for some or all subdivisions. In such a case, a public hearing, subject to notice, must be held regarding the submission of the final plat. A public hearing, on notice, is also required when the submitted final plat is not in substantial agreement with the approved preliminary plat. In these instances, the final plat submission is subject to the environmental review process as well. Under its power to supersede state law, a local legislature may otherwise vary this process to achieve local objectives.

Environmental Review: Regulations adopted under the State Environmental Quality Review Act (SEQRA) make it clear that a subdivision approval is a discretionary action affecting the environment which is subject to environmental review. The statutes governing subdivision approval attempt to coordinate the procedures required for the review of the subdivision with those required by SEQRA.

The law states that a subdivision plat submission is not deemed complete until the planning board has determined that the subdivision will not have a negative impact on the environment or, if it may have such an impact, until the planning board has completed its review of a draft environmental impact statement. The time periods contained in the subdivision statutes do not begin to run until one of these two events has occurred; further changes in the subdivision process may be required to comply with SEQRA, depending on how the environmental review process is handled and whether the planning board is the lead agency responsible for that process.

The subdivision statutes require a planning board, as lead agency for SEQRA purposes, to hold a single public hearing on the subdivision application in compliance with the hearing provisions under both SEQRA and subdivision regulations. Where the public hearing is held to comply with SEQRA's requirements, 14 days' advance notice of the public hearing is required. SEQRA hearings are optional, not mandatory.

County or Regional Review: The application may also be subject to review by the county or regional planning agency under §239-m of the General Municipal Law. Failure to submit the application to the county in the required circumstance creates a jurisdictional defect in the subsequent local action on the application. In addition, state public health law requires that a landowner who is subdividing a parcel into five or more lots for residential use must obtain a permit from the county or state department of health, which has further legal authority to determine the adequacy of the proposed sewer and water facilities. Metropolitan counties often have more inclusive review provisions, requiring in some cases all subdivision applications to be referred for review.

Parkland Dedication: The state statutes authorize planning boards to insure that the recreational needs of the occupants of residential subdivisions are met by requiring land to be set aside where a municipal study shows that there is now or will be an unmet need for recreational facilities in the municipality. The planning board may require a financial contribution in lieu of a land reservation only where it specifically determines that, in a particular case, the subdivision is not of a sufficient size or adequate character to create a suitable recreational area for the subdivision's occupants.

Provision of Improvements: Site improvements required on approved plats are to be provided directly by the subdivider. Alternatively, their installation can be secured by a performance bond or other security posted by the subdivider. The municipality may elect to provide one or more platted improvements directly or through the creation of an improvement district.

Waiver of Provisions: A planning board may waive certain subdivision requirements where they are unnecessary as applied to the application under review. The statutes provide for such waivers when the planning board finds that the requirements are not "requisite in the interest of the public health, safety, and general welfare."

Area Variance: Where a proposed subdivision contains one or more lots that do not conform to the zoning requirements, an area variance can be requested from the zoning board of appeals without first obtaining a determination of the need for a variance from the official charged with the enforcement of the zoning regulations. The request must be accompanied by a written recommendation of the planning board regarding the proposed variance.

Clustering of Units: The local legislature may authorize the planning board to modify the dimensional provisions of the zoning law to cluster the development of the subdivided parcels. Such modifications allow the subdivision plat to include alternative methods of laying out the lots, buildings, and other improvements in lieu of the layout dictated by the height, setback, parking, landscaping, or other provision of the zoning law. They do not allow the planning board to increase the density of development permitted under all other applicable laws and regulations.

The purpose of authorizing such modifications is to provide flexibility of design in order to preserve the natural and scenic qualities of open lands subjected to subdivision. By clustering the permitted development on the site, the planning board can much more effectively preserve open space and natural resources. The planning board may establish various conditions on the ownership, use, and maintenance of such open lands as necessary to assure the preservation of their natural and scenic quality. The local legislature can require that it approve any such conditions imposed for this purpose.

In its discretion, the legislature may authorize the planning board to require subdividers to cluster the permitted development to preserve open space and natural resources. Typically, however, planning boards are authorized to permit cluster development rather than to require it. This authority can include the power to cluster residential dwellings in any configuration that best accomplishes the purpose of cluster development, including permitting the use of detached, semi-detached, attached, or multi-story structures in any residential zoning district so long as the density permitted under all other provisions of law is not exceeded.

Decision of the Board: The grounds for modification or disapproval of a subdivision plat must be stated in the record of the planning board. A copy of the resolution of the planning board approving a final plat must be sent to the applicant and filed in the office of the municipal clerk within five days of its adoption.

Recording of Plats: The law prohibits the sale of lots in a subdivision until the plat of the subdivision has been filed with the county clerk or register of deeds. In a community where the planning board has been authorized to approve subdivisions, a developer may not file a subdivision plat in the land records office of the county clerk or register of deeds unless the plat has endorsed on it the approval of the planning board.

Judicial Review: Within 30 days of the filing of the decision of the planning board with the municipal clerk, any person aggrieved by that decision may apply to the New York Supreme Court for review under Article 78 of the New York State Civil Practice Law and Rules. The Supreme Court will review the record of the local reviewing board, and, if necessary, take additional evidence, directly or through a referee. Even if the local board is reversed by the court, no legal costs may be assessed against it unless it acted in bad faith, with malice, or with gross negligence in making the decision being appealed.

LIMITATIONS AND CONCERNS

Parkland Reservation: The statutes that allow for the reservation of parkland or money in lieu thereof were adopted to meet the need for recreational facilities of the residents of the subdivision and their guests, not to provide recreational facilities for the public at large. This was clarified by the New York Court of Appeals when it set aside a local requirement that the reserved recreational area be dedicated to the town for park purposes.

The courts and the legislature have made it clear that the authority to require land reservation for recreation or the payment of money in lieu thereof, must be exercised on a case-by-case basis and may not be administered under fixed formulas applicable to all development. In each case, a twostep process must be followed. First, the planning board must make a determination that the subdivision under review will add to the recreational needs of the community. This finding must be based on an evaluation of the present and anticipated future recreational needs of the municipality as determined by estimates of the projected population growth to which the particular subdivision will contribute. Second, based on a review of the particular plat before it, the planning board must determine whether it contains adequate and suitable space for recreational facilities. Only if the board finds that such space does not exist may it require the subdivider to make a cash contribution. All such contributions must be deposited into a trust fund to be used by the municipality exclusively for recreational purposes.

Basing Decisions on Standards in the Regulations and Facts in the Record: Decisions of the reviewing board must be based on the standards contained in the subdivision law and regulations. To be entitled to an approval, the applicant must demonstrate that it has responded to all required elements and met all stipulated standards contained in the regulations. Generalized complaints by local residents are insufficient to justify the denial of a preliminary plat application. Similarly, subdivision approval cannot be withheld based solely on conclusory allegations that the subdivision is not in keeping with the character of the neighborhood, where the plat meets all the applicable requirements of local law.

When the planning board approves a subdivision application, state statutes do not require that the record contain, and that the planning board's decision be based on, evidence supporting its approval. The statutes do require that decisions to modify or disapprove applications be based on evidence found in the record. Keeping a detailed record containing such evidence in all cases, however, insures that board decisions are not arbitrary, capricious, or an abuse of discretion. Such records provide the type of information parties need when deciding whether to appeal board decisions, and create the type of record that is necessary for a court to determine the validity of the board's decisions to approve subdivisions.

Conditions Imposed: State statutes authorize the reviewing board to impose reasonable conditions and restrictions on its approval of subdivision applications when such conditions are directly related and incidental to the proposed plan. The applicant must show that these conditions have been met before the local building inspector can issue a building permit or certificate of occupancy. A planning board, however, is without authority to impose conditions that are unrelated to the legitimate purposes of the laws governing subdivision review and approval. Conditions imposed on subdivision approvals must bear a reasonable relationship to the impact on the community of the subdivision itself.

STATUTES

The New York State statutory provisions authorizing municipalities to adopt subdivision regulations and to provide for the review and approval of subdivisions is found in Village Law §§7-728 through 7-730, Town Law §§276-278, and General City Law §§32-34.

Real Property Law §334 prohibits the sale of subdivided lots to the public until a map of the subdivision has been filed with the county clerk or register of deeds. In municipalities where the planning board has been authorized to approve subdivisions, Village Law §7-732, Town Law §279, and General City Law §34 prohibit the filing of subdivision maps unless the approval of the board is endorsed on the map.

Village Law §7-718(13), Town Law §271(13), and General City Law §17(13) authorize the planning board to recommend subdivision regulations, subject to adoption by the legislature.

Village Law §7-728(10), Town Law §276(10), and General City Law §32(10) require the planning board clerk to submit all applicable plats to the county, if the county has authority to review the matter under §239-m of the General Municipal Law.

The statutory provisions requiring the coordination of environmental and subdivision review processes are found at Village Law §§7-728(5) & (6), Town Law §§276(5) and (6), and General City Law §§32(5) and (6). The environmental requirements of state law are found in the Environmental Conservation Law §§8-0109 through 8-0117 and in NYCRR, Title 6, Part 617.

The provisions governing judicial review of the planning board's decisions are found at Village Law §7-740, Town Law §282, and General City Law §38.

The provisions allowing local legislatures to permit planning boards to cluster development of subdivisions are found at Village Law §7-738, Town Law §278, and General City Law §37.

One of the few statutory provisions specifically permitting a municipality to require the set aside of private land for a specific purpose or to exact money in lieu thereof is found in the law governing subdivisions which allows the planning board to require the dedication of land to parks or recreation or a contribution in lieu thereof to a local trust fund. Village Law §7-730(4), Town Law §277(4), General City Law §33(4).

The authority of local governments to supersede general state law can be found at Municipal Home Rule Law §10(1)(ii)(d)(3). Provisions that must be followed to properly supersede state law are found at Municipal Home Rule Law §22(1).

CASE DIGEST

The court in *Brous v. Smith*, 304 N.Y. 164, 106 N.E.2d 503 (1952), enunciated the policy reasons that support the adoption of subdivision regulations: "'Where subdivision of land is unregulated, lots are sold without paving, water, drainage, or sanitary facilities, and then later the community feels forced to protect the residents and take over the streets and . . . provide for the facilities.' Thus, [subdivision] regulations benefit both the consumer, who is protected 'in purchasing a building site with assurance of its usability for a suitable home,' and the community at large, which naturally gains greatly from the use of 'sound practices in land use and development.'"

In *Golden v. Planning Board of the Town of Ramapo*, 30 N.Y.2d 359, 285 N.E.2d 291, 334 N.Y.S.2d 138 (1972), the Court of Appeals upheld the authority of local governments to regulate and approve the subdivision of land. The court held that this authority was a central function in the adoption of local growth control ordinances. The court also noted that subdivision control "reflects, in essence, a legislative judgment that the development of unimproved areas be accompanied by provision of essential facilities."

The Court of Appeals has affirmed that "a village board of trustees by ordinance or a planning board by regulations can define the term 'subdivision' to include the division of land into two or more lots." *Delaware Midland Corp. v. Incorporated Village of Westhampton Beach*, 79 Misc. 2d 438, 359 N.Y.S.2d 944 (Sup. Ct. Suffolk County 1974), *aff'd*, 48 A.D.2d 681, 369 N.Y.S.2d 378 (2d Dep't 1975), *aff'd,* 39 N.Y.2d 1029, 355 N.E.2d 302, 387 N.Y.S.2d 248 (1976).

A village board of trustees' attempt to reserve final authority to review and approve particular subdivision plats was declared invalid since the trustees had already granted final subdivision approval authority to the village planning board. *Woodhull Associates v. Board of Trustees of the Incorporated Village of Northport*, 63 A.D.2d 677, 404 N.Y.S.2d 670 (2d Dep't 1978).

In *Kamhi v. Planning Board of the Town of Yorktown*, 59 N.Y.2d 385, 452 N.E.2d 1193, 465 N.Y.S.2d 865 (1983), the Court of Appeals held that title to land reserved for parks and recreation on a subdivision map cannot be required to be transferred to the municipality for the use of the public.

"[W]hen [a] planning agency has determined that development of the subdivision might significantly affect the environment, the application for preliminary approval is not complete until a [draft environmental impact statement] has been filed and has been accepted by the agency as satisfactory in scope and content." *Sun Beach Real Estate Development Corp. v. Anderson*, 98 A.D.2d 367, 469 N.Y.S.2d 964 (2d Dep't 1983), *aff'd*, 62 NY2d 965, 468 N.E.2d 296,

479 N.Y.S.2d 341 (1984). The court held that the planning board's action on a subdivision plat application was not untimely since the 45-day limitation in the Town Law does not begin to run until the application is complete. The court accorded priority to environmental review deadlines over subdivision approval deadlines "because the legislative declaration of purpose in the environmental review statute makes it obvious that protection of 'the environment for the use and enjoyment of this and all future generations' far overshadows the rights of developers to obtain prompt action on their proposals." Since Sun Beach was decided, the time limitation in the Town Law has been extended to a 62-day period. *See* Town Law §276(6)(b).

In *Black v. Summers*, 151 A.D.2d 863, 542 N.Y.S.2d 837 (3d Dep't 1989), the court annulled a town board's decision to condition approval of a subdivision application on the requirement that the applicants insure the non-development of specified property owned by the plaintiffs. The court held that "the subject condition is 'not reasonably designed to mitigate any demonstrable defects'" in the proposed subdivision.

In *Bayswater Realty & Capital Corp. v. Planning Board of the Town of Lewisboro*, 76 N.Y.2d 460, 560 N.E.2d 1300, 560 N.Y.S.2d 623 (1990), the court decided that a municipality cannot adopt a general recreational fee schedule and arbitrarily require every subdivider to pay the established fee. The court held that a planning board must make two findings before it may exercise its authority to require a payment in lieu of setting aside park or recreation lands under the Town Law §277(1). First, the planning board must determine whether a "proper case" exists for imposing the requirement by evaluating the present and future needs for park and recreational facilities in the town. Second, the planning board must determine whether the proposed plat contains adequate and suitable space for recreational facilities. Only if it determines that a "proper case" exists and that the plat does not contain such space may the planning board require the subdivider to pay money as a substitute.

Generally, a public hearing, on notice, is required when the submitted final plat is not in substantial agreement with the approved preliminary plat. However, in *Hickey v. Planning Board of the Town of Kent*, 173 A.D.2d 1086, 571 N.Y.S.2d 105 (3d Dep't 1991), the court held that no additional public hearing was necessary since the developer modified its plat as the result of suggestions made by the planning board at the first hearing. The court found that the planning board was authorized to waive the second public hearing pursuant to Town Law §276(4).

"Generally, a planning board is within its power in imposing conditions related to fences, safety devices, landscaping, access roads, and other factors incidental to comfort, peace, enjoyment, health, or safety of the surrounding area." *Koncelik v. Planning Board of the Town of East Hampton*, 188 A.D.2d 469, 590 N.Y.S.2d 900 (2d Dep't 1992). The court held that the planning board had the authority to require an adequate means of access for emergency vehicles, as well as the authority to impose conditions to protect the site's extensive area of undisturbed forest and numerous important plant species.

In *Twin Lakes Farms Associates v. Town of Bedford*, 215 A.D.2d 667, 628 N.Y.S.2d 310 (2d Dep't 1995), the court determined that the plaintiff was entitled to preliminary subdivision plat approval since the application for preliminary approval was complete. The planning board had accepted a draft environmental impact statement from the plaintiff and had conducted a public hearing on the statement pursuant to the State Environmental Quality Review Act (SEQRA). The court held that "the Board's refusal to issue a decision on the application on the ground that the owner had not yet complied with the entire SEQRA process was in violation of the Town Law §276(3) in effect at the time." As a result, the preliminary subdivision application was deemed approved by default. The court found, however, that "the owner was not yet entitled to final subdivision plat approval because complete compliance with SEQRA was required before such approval" could be granted.

In *Penlyn Development Corp. v. Incorporated Village of Lloyd Harbor*, 51 F.Supp.2d 255 (E.D.N.Y. 1999), the court rejected a developer's claim that its federally protected substantive due process rights were denied. The developer claimed that the village planning board had "persistently and irrationally refused to permit" subdivision of a 6.8 acre parcel of its land. Relying on the U.S. Supreme Court's decision in *Board of Regents v. Roth*, 408 U.S. 564 (1972), the district court held that the plaintiff, in order to prove a violation of substantive due process, must first demonstrate a legitimate claim of entitlement to the benefit in question. "The key to determining the existence of a property interest is the extent to which the deciding authority may exercise discretion in reaching its decision, rather than the estimate of the likelihood of a certain decision." Second, to win relief even if there is a demonstrable property interest, Penlyn must demonstrate that the defendants acted in "an outrageously arbitrary or irrational manner in depriving the plaintiff of that interest." Plaintiff argued that the planning board had been divested of its discretion as a result of a prior order of the state Supreme Court which returned the case to the planning board with directions to address certain issues in reference to the subdivision application. Declining to usurp state court jurisdiction over this matter, the federal district court held that the "determination as to whether to approve an application for the partitioning of land is inherently a local concern which can be . . . successfully resolved by a state court." The court further held that the planning board had retained its discretion and, as a result, plaintiff did not have a legitimate claim of entitlement to the subdivision approval and could not pursue its claim of denial of substantive due process in federal court.

In *Aloya v. Planning Bd. of Town of Stony Point*, 93 N.Y.2d 334, 690 N.Y.S.2d 475 (2d Dep't 1999), a developer challenged the town's denial of a subdivision plan. The town planning board first granted "unanimous unconditional preliminary approval" of the builders' plans to subdivide a 45-acre property into 27 lots. Pursuant to General Municipal Law §239-n, this application was then referred to the Rockland County planning department for review. The county recommended disapproval of the application because of insufficient information on drainage impacts. When the proposal was returned to the town, the planning board reheard the issue. Although a majority of the board members present at the meeting voted to approve the application, they failed to meet the requirement of General Municipal Law §239-n, which states that a local planning board cannot override a county planning board's recommendation unless a majority plus one of the members votes to do so. This mechanism exists to prevent "municipalities from disregarding a county agency's known objections." The Court of Appeals held that this failure to override by a supermajority constituted an "action" that terminated the subdivision application, equal in force to a vote to disapprove the application. Plaintiff's argument that it was entitled to "default approval" since there was no majority vote to disapprove the application, would render §239-n meaningless. The court also held that once the plan had been disapproved in this way, the preliminary subdivision approval was revoked. According to the court, this was a necessary conclusion because "the validity of preliminary plat approval is contingent on final approval." Because final approval had been denied in this case, preliminary approval was revoked "by operation of law" when plaintiff filed the final plat application. Any subsequent applications for subdivision approval would have to begin with preliminary approval.

REFERENCE

Land Use Planning and Regulation in New York State Municipalities: A Survey, New York State Legislative Commission on Rural Resources, Albany, NY (Fall, 1999).

D. SITE PLAN

DEFINITION

A "site plan" is defined by state law as a drawing, prepared in accordance with local specifications, that shows the "arrangement, layout, and design of the proposed use of a single parcel of land." Site plan regulations are adopted by the local legislature as part of the zoning law or as a separate set of regulations and contain the specifications that the site plan drawing must include and the standards it must meet.

Local site plan regulations require the developer of an individual parcel of land to file a drawing of that parcel's planned development for review and approval by a local board. Often, site plan regulations apply only to larger-scale commercial developments such as shopping malls and industrial and office parks or to residential developments such as condominium or town house projects. Some communities, however, subject smaller parcels to site plan review.

Parcels subject to site plan review are normally owned by a single individual or entity such as a condominium association, homeowners' association, corporation, or partnership. Since such parcels are not to be subdivided, their development would escape local review if it were not for the locality's site plan regulations. When such regulations have been adopted, individual parcels subject to their terms may not be developed until a site plan has been submitted, reviewed, and approved.

Site plan regulations require that certain elements be shown on the drawing, including access, parking, landscaping and buffering, drainage, utilities, roads, curbs, lighting, and the location and dimensions of the principal and accessory buildings and any other intended improvements. Some communities require site plans, particularly those of larger projects, to show adjacent land uses and to provide a narrative statement of how the site's development will avoid or mitigate adverse impacts on them.

PURPOSE

The purpose of site plan regulations is to insure that the development of individual parcels of land does not have an adverse impact on adjacent properties or the surrounding neighborhood. Such regulations also insure that the parcel's development fits properly into the community and conforms to its planning objectives.

The development of individual parcels must conform to the provisions of local zoning which contain use and dimensional requirements for site development. Zoning, however, does not contain specifications regulating the details of a site's development which protect, for example, the design of vehicular access to the site, the provision of needed landscape features, the location of parking areas, or the architectural features of buildings. Site plan specifications go beyond those of zoning and protect adjacent areas and the community's residents from flooding and erosion, traffic congestion and accidents, unsightly design, noise pollution, and the erosion of neighborhood character. This is their distinct purpose.

WHEN

Normally, communities adopt site plan regulations to carry out their comprehensive plans and supplement their zoning provisions and subdivision regulations. Localities that have not adopted comprehensive plans and zoning provisions may adopt site plan regulations to govern the development of individual sites when development pressures mount.

According to a recent survey by the New York State Legislative Commission on Rural Resources, about 64% of municipalities in the state have adopted site plan regulations: 85% of cities, 62% of towns, and 64% of villages. Although municipalities have enacted site plan regulations since the 1920s under their implied land use authority, relatively few localities adopted them until 1976 when the state legislature specifically delegated site plan authority to them.

AUTHORITY

Since 1976, villages, towns, and cities in New York have been expressly authorized by state statute to adopt and implement site plan regulations. The adoption of site plan regulations is permitted–but not required–by state law. These statutes authorize localities to impose conditions on site plan approval; to waive requirements where they are not needed to protect the public; to require the reservation of park land on the site, if it is to be developed residentially, or require the payment of a sum of money in lieu thereof; to require the posting of a performance bond or other security to secure the development of improvements on the site; and to require compliance with environmental review provisions when approving site plans.

IMPLEMENTATION

Legislative Role: The local legislature has the authority to adopt site plan regulations, to decide what standards and site plan elements must be included, to determine what sites are subject to approval, and to appoint a local site plan review body.

Reviewing Board: The local legislature may retain the authority to review and approve applications or may delegate that authority to the local planning board or other administrative agency, such as the zoning board of appeals.

Applicability: Local site plan regulations may be limited in their application to the development of single parcels of land in specifically designated areas such flood hazard zones, historic districts, coastal zones, or along commercial corridors. Some communities limit the application of site plan regulations to particular zoning districts. Another approach is to require all single parcel development to comply with site plan regulations with certain exceptions, such as one- and two-family residential projects, accessory buildings, or specified low impact uses.

Procedures: The local legislature may provide different procedures for different types of site plan applications. Proposed site development projects may be divided between those considered minor and those whose impacts are major, as defined by type, location, or size. Some communities require major site plan applications to go through two review phases: preliminary and final. Others may allow the reviewing agency to waive certain elements of the site plan regulations for minor or other appropriate projects.

Public Hearings: Under state law, the local legislature may require the board with site plan authority to hold public hearings on site plan applications before taking final action on them. Where a public hearing is not required, the board can conduct a public hearing on particular site plan submissions, in its discretion. Where public hearings are held, they must be conducted within 62 days from the date of application, public notice must be published at least five days before the hearing, and the applicant must be mailed notice of the hearing 10 days in advance. The agency's final decision on the application must be made within 62 days of the close of the public hearing, but this deadline can be extended by mutual consent.

Environmental Review: Site plan approval time periods must be coordinated with those required by the State Environmental Quality Review Act regarding the environmental review of projects which may have a significant adverse impact on the environment. When a site plan applicant is required to submit a draft environmental impact statement, the extensive process and extended timetable contained in the regulations of the Commissioner of the Department of Environmental Conservation must be followed. An application for site plan approval is not deemed to be final until the environmental review process is completed. Any public hearing held during the environmental review process can be used to satisfy any public hearing requirement for the site plan itself.

County/Regional Review: In certain instances, site plan applications must be submitted by the reviewing board to a county or regional planning agency. This must be done where the land subject to approval is within 500 feet of a municipal boundary, an existing or proposed county or state highway or park, an existing or proposed stream channel owned by the county, or county or state land on which a public building is situated. Where such referral is required, it must be submitted 10 days prior to a public hearing held on the matter or if no public hearing is held, before the agency's final action on the application. The time period for the local board's review and decision does not begin until the county or regional planning board has been heard from, or 30 days have elapsed from the date of referral.

Parkland Reservation: Where the residential development of a site will contribute to the need for future recreational facilities and parks in the community, the reviewing board can require the development to contain a park, suitably located on the site. Where one cannot be accommodated, the board can require the applicant to pay a sum of money into a trust fund administered exclusively for recreational purposes.

Area Variances: Where a proposed site plan contains building features that do not conform to the zoning requirements, an area variance can be requested from the zoning board of appeals without first obtaining a determination of the need for a variance from the official charged with the enforcement of the zoning regulations.

Decision of the Board: The planning board or other reviewing board may either approve the site plan application, deny it, or approve it subject to conditions or modifications. If it is denied, the applicant can resubmit a new application with a different site plan for the parcel. Any decision of the reviewing board must be based on evidence found in the record of its proceedings. That decision must be filed in the office of the municipal clerk within five business days of the decision and a copy mailed to the applicant.

Judicial Review: Within 30 days of the filing of the decision of the reviewing board, any aggrieved person may apply to the Supreme Court for review under Article 78 of the Civil Practice Law and Rules. The Supreme Court will consider the record of the reviewing board, and, if necessary, take additional evidence, directly or through a referee, for the proper resolution of the matter. Even if the local board is reversed by the court, no legal costs may be assessed against it unless it acted in bad faith, with malice, or with gross negligence in making the decision being appealed.

LIMITATIONS AND CONCERNS

Standards and Elements: Site plan regulations must contain standards to guide the determinations of the reviewing board and must specify the elements that are to be included on the drawing submitted by the applicant. The delegation of site plan authority to the planning board or other administrative agency is the delegation of legislative authority; the reviewing board must be guided by some specific standards so that its decisions are not wholly discretionary.

Site plan regulations typically contain a series of "elements" that must be included on the drawing and explained in a narrative submission by the applicant. The state statutes contain a number of site plan elements that may be required by the local legislature, including those related to parking, means of access, screening, signs, landscaping, architectural features, location and dimensions of buildings, adjacent land uses, and physical features. Additional elements may be included in the site plan regulations if desired by the local legislature.

Site plan review elements generally contain both qualitative and quantitative measures. For example, they may authorize the responsible agency to preserve certain natural features "insofar as is possible," or to review the adequacy of the arrangement of trees, shrubs, and other landscaping–qualitative standards. They may require that no septic tank be located within 50 feet of any shoreline–a quantitative specification that supplements the requirements of the zoning ordinance. These standards and elements provide guidance to both the reviewing agency and the applicant.

Basing Decisions on Standards in the Regulations and Facts in the Record: Decisions of the reviewing board must be based on the elements contained in the site plan law and regulations. To be entitled to an approval, the applicant must demonstrate that it has responded to all required elements and met all stipulated standards contained in the regulations.

In making decisions on site plan applications, the reviewing board must keep a detailed record of its deliberations. These records can be in narrative form rather than verbatim transcripts. The findings of the board and its decision must be based on reliable evidence contained in this record. The record may be the minutes of the board, if prepared in enough detail to satisfy these requirements.

Keeping a detailed record of this nature insures that board decisions are not arbitrary, capricious, or an abuse of discretion. Such a record provides the type of information parties need when deciding whether to appeal board decisions, and creates the type of record that is necessary for a court to determine the validity of the board's decisions.

Conditions Imposed: State statutes authorize the reviewing board to impose reasonable conditions and restrictions on its approval of site plan applications when such conditions are directly related to incidental to the proposed plan. The applicant must show that these conditions have been met before the local building inspector can issue a building permit or certificate of occupancy. A reviewing board, however, is without authority to impose conditions that are unrelated to the legitimate purposes of the laws governing site plan review and approval.

Acting Beyond the Authority of the Reviewing Board: The board may not base its denial of a site plan on matters that are beyond its authority. For example, a denial based on the failure of the proposed land use to comply with the zoning ordinance is beyond the reviewing board's authority; that determination must be made by the local building inspector and the zoning board of appeals. If the authority to issue special permits has been granted to a different body, the board cannot refuse to approve a site plan application where it finds that a special permit was erroneously granted.

STATUTES

New York Village Law §7-725-a, Town Law §274-a, and General City Law §27-a authorize local governments to adopt and administer site plan regulations.

Village Law §7-725-a(8), Town Law §274-a(8), and General City Law §27-a(8) grant to local legislatures the authority to require public hearings be held before action is taken on site plan applications.

Village Law §7-725-a(2)(a), Town Law §274-a(2)(a), and General City Law §27-a(2)(a) contain the specific elements that the local legislature may require to be included in site plan submissions including any additional elements specified by the legislature.

General Municipal Law §239-m requires that certain applications for site plan review be submitted to the county or regional planning agency for review and comment.

CASE DIGEST

The Second Department declared a section of a town code invalid since it purported to reserve to the town board appellate jurisdiction over site development plans. *Boxer v. Town Board of the Town of Cortlandt*, 60 A.D.2d 913, 401 N.Y.S.2d 570 (2d Dep't 1978). The court held that "a fair reading of subdivision [11] of section 274-a of the Town Law . . . shows the intent to deprive the town board of appellate jurisdiction over site development plans upon which a town planning board has duly acted." *See also Moriarty v. Planning Board of the Village of Sloatsburg*, 119 A.D.2d 188, 506 N.Y.S.2d 184 (2d Dep't 1986) (noting that a town board may not review a planning board's denial of site plan approval); *Spinosa v. Ackerman*, 98 Misc. 2d 1073, 415 N.Y.S.2d 358 (Sup. Ct. Monroe County 1979) (explaining that once a town board has created a planning board and authorized it to grant final site plan approval, the two boards cannot share or divide this power).

In *Gershowitz v. Planning Board of the Town of Brookhaven*, 52 N.Y.2d 763, 417 N.E.2d 1000, 436 N.Y.S.2d 612 (1980), the Court of Appeals held that site plan denial cannot be based on a planning board's determination that a use is not permitted by zoning provisions since that function is within the authority of the official charged with the enforcement of the zoning law and the zoning board of appeals. The zoning board of appeals issued the plaintiff a special use permit to operate an automobile shredder plant after determining that the proposed use was in compliance with the town code. The plaintiff then submitted a site plan to the planning board, which subsequently denied the application on the ground that the proposed use violated the town code. The court held that since the zoning board had approved the use, the planning board was without power to disapprove the site plan on the ground that the use violated the town code.

A town board may reject a site plan where substantial evidence shows that the proposed project would have an adverse impact on public health, safety, and welfare. *Pittsford Plaza Associates v. Spiegel*, 66 N.Y.2d 717, 487 N.E.2d 902, 496 N.Y.S.2d 992 (1985). The plaintiff submitted a site plan for the construction of a seven-screen movie theatre to the town board for its approval. The town board found that the additional traffic would have an adverse impact on public health, safety, and welfare, notwithstanding the zoning board of appeals' conditional approval of a special use permit for the same project. The court held that the town board did not exceed its powers in overruling the zoning board of appeals since it denied the application "under its independent powers expressly provided in the ordinance, namely the 'adequacy and arrangement of vehicular traffic access and circulation.'"

A planning board may not base its denial of a site plan on matters that are beyond its authority. In *Moriarty v. Planning Board of the Village of Sloatsburg*, 119 A.D.2d 188, 506 N.Y.S.2d 184 (2d Dep't 1986), the Second Department reversed the planning board's denial of a site plan application since the denial was based on the inadequacy of water supply for fire protection services. The planning board asserted that it had the power to reject the site plan on that ground pursuant to the Village Law §7-725(1)(a), which authorizes consideration of "such other elements as may reasonably be related to the health, safety and general welfare of the community." The court held that the planning board's authority was limited to the specific elements set forth in the statute and that the health, safety, and general welfare provision delegated no additional site plan review authority to the planning board. The court also held that "the planning board exceeded its powers when it denied site plan approval on a ground that only the building or fire inspector might have invoked."

Since *Moriarty* was decided, the statutory language has been changed, authorizing a planning board to examine "any additional elements specified by the village board of trustees in . . . [the] local law." Thus, a local legislative body may authorize its planning board to consider elements in addition to those specifically enumerated in the state statute so as to insure the adequate review of site plans in accordance with local conditions and concerns. This change in state law applies to villages, towns, and cities. Village Law §7-725-a(2)(a); Town Law §274-a(2)(a); General City Law §30-a(1)(a).

Site plan approval requires compliance with the provisions of the State Environmental Quality Review Act. In *Save the Pine Bush, Inc. v. Albany*, 141 A.D.2d 949, 530 N.Y.S.2d 295 (2d Dep't 1988), the court annulled a planning board's approval of two site plans because the board failed to take a hard look at whether the projects would have a significant adverse environmental effect.

The General Municipal Law §239-m requires certain applications for site plan review be submitted to the county or regional planning agency for review and comment. In *Old Dock Associates v. Sullivan*, 150 A.D.2d 695, 541 N.Y.S.2d 569 (2d Dep't 1989), the planning board's failure to refer a site plan application to the county planning commission before giving final approval rendered its approval void. The court held that because the planning board "failed to comply with this 'legislative mandate' which is 'jurisdictional' in nature," the board's approval was of no effect.

Furthermore, §239-m contemplates that the county review an application in substantially the same format that it was in before the municipal agency. In *Ferrari v. Town of Penfield Planning Board*, 181 A.D.2d 149, 585 N.Y.S.2d 925 (4th Dep't 1992), the court held that where "the revisions are so substantially different from the original proposal, the county or regional board should have the opportunity to review and make recommendations on the new and revised plans." Since the planning board failed to do that in this case, its decision was annulled by the court.

REFERENCES

Land Use Planning and Regulation in New York State Municipalities: A Survey, New York State Legislative Commission on Rural Resources, Albany, NY (Fall, 1999).

Site Development Plan Review Procedure and Guidelines, New York State Department of State; James A. Coon Local Government Technical Series.

E. SPECIAL USE PERMITS

DEFINITION

New York statutes define a special use permit as the "authorization of a particular land use which is permitted in a zoning ordinance or local law, subject to requirements imposed by such zoning ordinance or local law to assure that the proposed use is in harmony with such zoning ordinance or local law and will not adversely affect the neighborhood if such requirements are met." Town Law §274-b(1); Village Law §7-725-b(1); General City Law §27-b(1). An example of a special use is a church in a single-family residential neighborhood. The legislature may conclude that the church should be permitted in a residential district, subject to conditions insuring that the size and layout as well as parking and lighting are carefully designed so that the neighborhood is not adversely affected.

A variety of uses may be permitted in various zones as special uses. These include adult homes, professional offices, group homes, swimming pools, nursing homes, or day-care centers in residential zones, and drive-in establishments, video arcades, marinas, shopping centers, gas stations, and convenience stores in commercial districts. Once a special permit has been issued, it is not personal to the applicant but affixes to, and runs with, the ownership of the land.

The local legislature is empowered to authorize the planning board or other local administrative body to grant special use permits as set forth in the local zoning law. When delegating this authority to an administrative body, the legislature must adopt standards to guide the body in reviewing, conditioning, and approving special uses. These standards will include, for example, requirements that gasoline stations and drive-in establishments provide adequate traffic safety improvements, that professional home offices provide adequate parking and landscape buffering, or that a shopping center provide adequate storm drainage and lighting controls to protect surrounding areas.

Special use permits are referred to by a variety of terms in local practice and in court decisions. These terms include "special exception use," "special permit," "conditional use permit," and "special exception." The statutory term is "special use permit."

PURPOSE

Local legislatures achieve a degree of flexibility by adding special uses to the types of land uses otherwise permitted in zoning districts. At its inception, zoning was justified on the ground that the strict separation of uses was in the public interest and promoted the public health, safety, and welfare. This alone, however, would lead to the creation of single-family districts, residential districts, and neighborhood commercial districts in which relatively few uses are allowed and a variety of uses historically associated with one another–such as church in a residential neighborhood or a gasoline station in a neighborhood retail district–are thereby excluded. By allowing special uses, yet subjecting them to conditions, the legislature achieves needed diversity of uses while insuring compatibility with surrounding properties.

WHEN

When uses that are different from principal, as-of-right uses can be made compatible with those uses by the imposition of conditions, they are often permitted as special uses subject to local administrative review.

AUTHORITY

State statutes define a special use permit; empower the local legislative body to authorize a local agency to grant such permits; allow conditions to be attached to them; authorize the waiver of permit requirements in appropriate circumstances; require public hearings to be held before special permits are granted; require compliance with environmental review provisions of state law; provide for notice to county and regional planning agencies; provide for the filing of decisions on special permits; and allow for their review by the courts.

IMPLEMENTATION

Legislative Role: The local legislature has the inherent power to retain special permit review and approval authority. State statutes empower the legislature to authorize the planning board or other administrative body to grant any special use permits that are allowed in the zoning law.

Reviewing Board: The statutes empower the local legislature to authorize the planning board or other administrative body, such as the zoning board of appeals, to issue special permits.

Standards: The legislature must adopt standards to guide the issuance of special permits by an administrative body, but those standards may be fairly general in scope.

Conditions: The reviewing board has the authority to attach conditions to the issuance of special permits that are directly related to and incidental to the proposed special use. Any such conditions imposed must be met by the landowner before building permits, certificates of occupancy, and other agency permits can be issued.

Public Hearing: The reviewing board must hold a public hearing within 62 days of the date an application for a special permit is received. Public notice of the hearing must be published at least five days before it is held.

County/Regional Planning Agency: In certain instances, special use permits must be submitted by the reviewing board to a county or regional planning agency. Such referral must be sent at least 10 days before the public hearing on the special use permit, accompanied by a full statement of the matter under consideration.

Environmental Review: The provisions of the State Environmental Quality Review Act (SEQRA) which require public agencies to consider the impacts of their decisions on the environment must be complied with by the reviewing board. Where the approval of a special use permit may have a significant adverse impact on the environment, the extensive procedural requirements and the extended timetable of SEQRA must be followed and coordinated with other requirements for the issuance of a special permit.

Waiver of Provisions: The local legislature may empower the reviewing board to waive the application of certain special permit requirements where they are unnecessary as applied to the project under review. The statutes provide for such waivers when the reviewing board finds that the requirements are not "requisite in the interest of the public health, safety, and general welfare." Town Law §274-b(5); Village Law §7-725-b(5); General City Law §27-b(5).

Area Variance: Where a proposed special use permit contains one or more features that do not conform to the zoning requirements, an area variance can be requested from the zoning board of appeals without first obtaining a determination of the need for a variance from the official charged with the enforcement of the zoning regulations.

Decision of the Board: The decision of the reviewing board on the special use permit must be rendered within 62 days of the date of the public hearing. Any decision of the reviewing board must be made on evidence found in the record of its proceedings. That decision must be filed in the office of the municipal clerk within five business days and a copy mailed to the applicant.

Judicial Review: Within 30 days of the filing of the decision of the reviewing board, any aggrieved person may apply to the New York Supreme Court for review under Article 78 of the Civil Practice Law and Rules. The court will consider the record of the reviewing board, and, if necessary, take additional evidence, directly or through a referee, for the proper resolution of the matter. Even if the local board is reversed by the court, no legal costs may be assessed against it unless it acted in bad faith, with malice, or with gross negligence in making the decision being appealed.

ILLUSTRATION

The village of Thomaston created a 25-foot buffer zone between zoning districts to accommodate owners of lots divided by zoning district boundary lines. The zoning law of the village allowed these owners to request a special use permit from the zoning board of appeals to carry the use allowed in either zoning district 25 feet into the other. The owner of a lot occupied by a restaurant which extended into a single-family residential zone applied to the board for a special permit to pave 25 feet of the lot for parking associated with the restaurant. The owner also asked for a use variance in order to extend the parking farther than 25 feet into the single-family zoned portion of its lot.

After a review of the matter, the zoning board of appeals rejected the application for the special permit and variance because they were not in harmony with the general purpose and intent of the zoning plan. In reaching this conclusion, the board cited the same grounds for denying both the special permit and the variance: that the premises were not unique, that the hardship was self-created, and that the use would have an adverse effect on the adjoining property. The New York Court of Appeals reversed the zoning board of appeals' denial of the special use permit and took the occasion to explain the critical difference between a variance and a special permit:

> The denial of the special exception permit, based on factual findings used to support denial of the variance, ignores the fundamental difference between a variance and a special exception permit. A variance is an authority to a property owner to use property in a manner forbidden by the ordinance while a special exception allows the property owner to put his property to a use expressly permitted by the ordinance. The inclusion of the permitted use in the ordinance is tantamount to a legislative finding that the permitted use is in harmony with the general zoning plan and will not adversely affect the neighborhood. Denial of the permit on the ground that the extension of the parking lot 25 feet into the residential zone is not in harmony with the general purpose and intent of the zoning plan is, thus, patently inconsistent.

North Shore Steak House, Inc. v. Bd. of Appeals of Inc. Village of Thomaston, 30 N.Y.2d 238, 243, 282 N.E.2d 606, 331 N.Y.S.2d 645 (1972).

LIMITATIONS AND CONCERNS

Burden of Proof: An applicant's burden of proof in seeking a special use permit is lighter than in seeking a variance. This is due to the fact that the local legislature has declared that the special use requested is compatible with the zoning district if its impacts can be mitigated by compliance with reasonable conditions. The applicant has to offer proof sufficient to show that conditions imposed on the requested permit will amply protect the adjoining properties. Absent a showing in the record as to why the permit should be denied, a reviewing board's refusal to issue the permit is arbitrary and capricious.

Basing Decisions on Standards in the Regulations: Unless the legislative body retains special use permit authority, the zoning ordinance must contain reasonably clear standards to guide the review board in determining whether to grant a special permit. These standards are of critical importance. If they are complied with by an applicant, the permit must be issued. If the permit is to be conditioned or denied, such actions must be taken to enforce the articulated standards.

There are several cases in New York where courts have invalidated the special permit provisions of the zoning law because the standards were too broad and gave the reviewing board unrestricted discretion to approve or reject the permit. Where the special use provisions simply stated, for example, that a permit can be issued for "educational, religious or eleemosynary purposes," with no further standards to guide the review board, the court found them to be too vague. However, where standards are given, even in general terms, courts often uphold them as sufficient. A provision that allowed gasoline stations by special permit was upheld where the standard the review board was to follow was "consideration of the public health, safety, and welfare."

When standards are included in the zoning law, they must serve as the basis for any decision to deny a permit. Where a theater was denied a special permit based on traffic dangers, the denial was reversed because the legislature did not designate traffic as a standard applicable to the special use. In another case, the denial of a special permit because of traffic impacts was reversed where there was no evidence on the record showing that the proposed use would create greater traffic than as-of-right uses allowed in the neighborhood.

Where the legislative body retains the authority to issue special permits, there need not be standards set forth that guide and limit its discretion. As the legislative body, a local council or board can "legislate" standards on a case-by-case basis. Even where standards are included, the legislature is not limited by them. The legislature, however, must not act capriciously. It may not, for example, withhold a permit for reasons not related to the public health, safety, and welfare, for reasons that are contrary to the evidence on the record, or for no reason at all.

Conditions Imposed: Under both the statutes and case law, the reviewing board may impose "reasonable conditions and restrictions as are directly related to and incidental to the proposed special use permit." These conditions cannot be based on considerations that are not in the zoning provisions. Neither can conditions, in most cases, limit the details of operation of a business authorized under a special permit, because these matters are normally unrelated to zoning. In addition, conditions must be stated in a sufficiently clear and definite manner so that the applicant and the neighbors are not left in doubt concerning the extent of the use permitted.

STATUTES

In New York State, local legislatures are empowered to authorize a local administrative body to grant special permits under Village Law §7-725-b, Town Law §274-b, and General City Law §27-b.

General Municipal Law §239-m requires certain special use permits to be submitted to the county or regional planning agency for review and comment.

CASE DIGEST

In *Green Point Savings Bank v. Board of Zoning Appeals of Town of Hempstead*, 281 N.Y. 534, 24 N.E.2d 319 (1939), and in *Larkin Co. v. Schwab*, 242 N.Y. 330, 151 N.E. 637 (1926), the courts held that when the legislature is the permit issuing board, standards need not be contained in the law for the special permit provisions to be valid. *See also Cummings v. Town Board of North Castle*, 62 N.Y.2d 833, 466 N.E.2d 147, 477 N.Y.S.2d 607 (1984) (concurring and also holding that "even if the ordinance sets forth standards, [the legislature] has not divested itself of the power of further regulation unless the standards expressed purport to be so complete or exclusive as to preclude the Board from considering other factors without amendment of the zoning ordinance").

Standards must be developed, however, if another board is the permit issuing authority. For instance, in *Little v. Young*, 274 A.D. 1005, 85 N.Y.S.2d 41 (2d Dep't 1948), *aff'd*, 299 N.Y. 699, 87 N.E.2d 74 (1949), the court held that the failure of the town to prescribe standards for the zoning board of appeals to follow in granting special permits invalidated the board's power to review. *See also Concordia Collegiate Institute v. Miller*, 301 N.Y.189, 93 N.E.2d 632 (1950) (finding an amendment to a zoning law invalid since the review board "was given no standards or guides to exercise its discretion as to what 'educational, religious or eleemosynary purposes' may be permitted").

The Second Department sustained a zoning law that authorized a board of appeals to permit use of premises as a gasoline filling station "after public notice and hearing, and after taking into consideration the public health, safety, and general welfare and subject to appropriate conditions and safeguards." *See Aloe v. Dassler*, 278 A.D. 975, 106 N.Y.S.2d 24 (2d Dep't 1951), *aff'd*, 303 NY 878, 105 N.E.2d 104 (1952). The court held that the delegation of power was proper because "[s]tandards are provided which, though stated in general terms, are capable of a reasonable application and are sufficient to limit and define the Board's discretionary powers." *See also Dur-Bar Realty Co. v. City of Utica*, 57 A.D.2d 51, 394 N.Y.S.2d 913 (4th Dep't 1977) (holding that "the delegation of power from a legislative body to an administrative body is impermissible unless accompanied by adequate standards to guide the administrative body's exercise of discretion").

The New York Court of Appeals discussed the difference between a variance and a special use permit in *North Shore Steak House, Inc. v. Board of Appeals of the Incorporated Village of Thomaston*, 30 N.Y.2d 238, 282 N.E.2d 606, 331 N.Y.S.2d 645 (1972). With respect to special use permits, the court stated that "[t]he inclusion of [a] permitted use in [an] ordinance is tantamount to a legislative finding that the permitted use is in harmony with the general zoning plan and will not adversely affect the neighborhood." A variance, the court pointed out, gives permission to a property owner to use property in a manner forbidden by the general zoning plan.

A zoning board's denial of an application for a special use permit to erect a sign was found to be improper in *Carrol's Development Corp. v. Gibson*, 73 A.D.2d 1050, 425 N.Y.S.2d 420 (4th Dep't 1980), *aff'd,* 53 N.Y.2d 813, 422 N.E.2d 581, 439 N.Y.S.2d 921 (1981). The court held that where "a zoning ordinance authorizes a use permit subject to administrative approval, an applicant need only show that the use is contemplated by the ordinance subject only to the conditions attached to its use to minimize its impact on the surrounding area." Where a special permit is involved, the use must be approved unless the approval body's record of decision discloses reasons for denying the permit. Since the record did not disclose such reasons in this case, the board's denial was overturned.

For a special use permit to be granted, the applicant must put on the record facts showing that it can meet the standards contained in the local law for issuing special use permits. In a case where the applicant had not made such a showing, the Court of Appeals sustained a zoning board of appeal's rejection of an application for a special use permit since a proposed shopping center would create undue traffic congestion and hazard to a nearby school. *Market Square Properties, Ltd. v. Town of Guilderland Zoning Board of Appeals*, 109 A.D.2d 164, 491 N.Y.S.2d 519 (3d Dep't 1985), *aff'd*, 66 N.Y.2d 893, 489 N.E.2d 741, 498 N.Y.S.2d 772 (1985). Because one of the conditions contained in the town's law was that the permitted project create no undue traffic congestion, the board's denial was upheld.

The power to condition special use permits is not unlimited. The conditions must relate to the impact of the development of the land itself and not the manner in which that use will be operated. For example, in *Old Country Burgers v. Town of Oyster Bay*, 160 A.D.2d 805, 553 N.Y.S.2d 843 (2d Dep't 1990), the court annulled conditions that prohibited the use of a drive-through window during breakfast, lunch, and dinner hours to mitigate traffic pressures because that condition related to the details of the business and not the use of the land. There was no showing that the proposed use would have a greater impact than other uses that were unconditionally permitted under the statute.

"While the Town Board is free to consider matters relating to the public welfare in determining whether to grant or deny a special exception or permit, it is impermissible to base the denial solely on the generalized objections and concerns of neighboring community members." *Chernick v. McGowan*, 238 A.D.2d 586, 656 N.Y.S.2d 392 (2d Dep't 1997). *See also Twin County Recycling Corp. v. Yevoli*, 224 A.D.2d 628, 639 N.Y.S.2d 392 (2d Dep't 1996), *aff'd*, 90 N.Y.2d 1000, 688 N.E.2d 978, 665 N.Y.S.2d 627 (1997) (holding that a review board may not base its denial of a special use permit on generalized community objections).

The Court of Appeals declared unconstitutional a municipal zoning ordinance that deprived educational institutions the opportunity to apply for special use permits in a historic residential district. *Trustees of Union College v. Members of the Schenectady City Council*, 91 N.Y.2d 161, 690 N.E.2d 978, 667 N.Y.S.2d 978 (1997). The court noted that "a special permit application 'affords zoning boards an opportunity to weigh the proposed use in relation to neighboring land uses and to cushion any adverse effects by the imposition of conditions designed to mitigate them.' Indeed, if educational uses were included in the category of special permit uses allowed in Schenectady's Historical District, the reviewing body could . . . impose reasonable conditions to mitigate any anticipated negative impacts on the historical character of the area."

In *Sunrise Plaza Associates v. Town Board of the Town of Babylon*, 673 N.Y.S.2d 165 (2d Dep't 1998), the court held that a town board may issue a special use permit for the operation of a proposed restaurant even though the landowner had previously obtained a parking variance from the town zoning ordinance. The plaintiff claimed that the special use permit had been improperly granted because the landowner's proposed use was not in compliance with the requirements of the town ordinance. The court rejected this argument, stating that the town board "properly awarded [the] special use permit inasmuch as the proposed restaurant, operating with a parking variance, was found to be consistent with the surrounding area and would not pose a detriment thereto." The court further noted that "Town Law §274-b(3) expressly provides for the issuance of a special use permit in conjunction with an area variance."

F. BUILDING PERMITS AND CERTIFICATES OF OCCUPANCY

DEFINITION

A building permit is a certificate issued by the official charged with the enforcement of the Uniform Fire Prevention and Building Code (Uniform Code) in the municipality. The Uniform Code contains detailed specifications regulating the design and construction of buildings in New York State. It requires the property owner to obtain a building permit for almost all new construction projects before building begins. Plans to alter existing buildings also require building permits, particularly if they involve any structural parts, safety features, or electrical work.

The building permit certifies that the plans submitted for new construction or alterations conform with the standards and specifications of the Uniform Code. After construction has been completed, before a new or rehabilitated building may be occupied, a certificate of occupancy must be obtained. A certificate of occupancy certifies that the building was completed in accordance with the approved construction plans and meets the provisions of the local zoning law.

PURPOSE

The purpose of the Uniform Code, and of a building permit issued pursuant to it, is to provide a minimum level of protection from the hazards of fire and inadequate building construction. Requiring a building permit before construction begins enables public authorities to determine whether the building will comply with the Uniform Code. Since construction must also conform to the requirements of the zoning law, no building may be built or building permit issued unless the municipality certifies that it complies with the provisions of zoning, as well as with the Uniform Code. Requiring a certificate of occupancy before a building may be occupied after construction is completed provides further assurance that the building has been built in conformance with the Uniform Code and will be used in accordance with the uses permitted under the zoning law.

WHEN

In most major cities, some form of building and fire code was adopted before the advent of comprehensive zoning. As zoning became widely used, the administration of the building and fire code was integrated with its enforcement in most municipalities. By the early 1980s, most developing communities had adopted both zoning laws and fire and building codes and had provided, in some way, for the coordinated enforcement of the provisions of both. Local governments were free to adopt their own codes. This created difficulties for the development and construction industries because of the need to conform to building and fire standards that differed from one community to another.

In 1984, the state legislature adopted the Uniform Fire Prevention and Building Code (Uniform Code) and made it applicable in all cities, towns, and villages in the state, except New York City, giving communities some opportunity to adopt more restrictive provisions and enforcement measures because of unique local circumstances. The legislature stipulated that the Uniform Code is to be enforced by local governments. The legislation made it possible for a municipality to pass a local law indicating that it declines to be responsible for enforcement of the code, in which case its county will be responsible for enforcement. Counties may adopt a local law declining enforcement, which passes enforcement responsibility to the New York State Department of State.

AUTHORITY

The Executive Law places responsibility on all cities, towns, and villages to enforce the Uniform Fire Prevention and Building Code, unless they decline to do so. The Town, Village, and General City Law allows municipal legislatures to provide for the manner in which zoning regulations and restrictions shall be established and enforced.

IMPLEMENTATION

As administered in many communities, an application for a building permit is the first step in the local land use process.

When an application is submitted, the building or zoning official charged with reviewing it determines whether the proposed project must first be reviewed and approved by another administrative body. If, for example, the proposal involves the subdivision of land or development of an individual site that is subject to local subdivision or site plan regulations, the proposal must first be submitted to the planning board or other administrative agency charged with approving site plan and subdivision applications.

Upon the submission of an application for a building permit, the building or zoning enforcement officer must determine whether the proposal conforms to the dimensional and use provisions of the zoning law. If the officer determines that it does not, the application for a building permit must be denied. The applicant may ask the zoning board of appeals to review the building or zoning official's interpretation of the zoning provisions or, if it agrees that the proposal does not comply with zoning, the applicant may ask the zoning board for a use or area variance.

Local practice regarding these determinations varies greatly in a state as diverse as New York. Some cities, villages, and more populous towns have a building inspector and a separate zoning enforcement officer. Most such communities require the local zoning enforcement officer to make all determinations regarding the compliance of proposed construction projects with zoning, subdivision, site plan, and special permit provisions. In these cases, it is the determination of the zoning enforcement officer that is appealed to the zoning board of appeals. Some of these communities have building or development departments within which different officials have been delegated responsibility for Uniform Code and zoning enforcement. In many communities, however, the local building inspector is charged with zoning interpretation and enforcement as well as with fire and building code responsibility.

A building permit may not be required for necessary repairs not affecting structural features or for alterations to existing buildings costing less than a stipulated amount if those repairs do not affect structural conditions, fire safety features, or electrical systems.

The application for a building permit must contain sufficient information to permit a determination that the intended work conforms to the requirements of the Uniform Code. Normally, this includes complete architectural drawings of all proposed building improvements. The building inspector reviews those drawings to determine if they comply with the Uniform Code. Determinations by building officials regarding submitted applications for building permits are to be made expeditiously and are to be based solely on the legisled standards and specifications contained in the relevant codes. The building inspector is, in nearly all instances, a ministerial officer, who is making decisions based not on his discretion but on the specifications contained in relevant codes. In most cases, conditions are not imposed on building permits. The application either meets the provisions of the applicable codes or it does not. If it does, the permit should be issued.

On a statewide basis, the Uniform Code is administered by the New York State Department of State. Its regional services unit provides technical assistance on code issues and administers the code in those municipalities that have declined to enforce the code themselves. Its code interpretation unit provides written interpretations of the Uniform Code upon the request of a permit applicant or a local building inspector. Variances may be requested from the Uniform Code. Depending on the extent of the variance requested, it may be granted administratively by the Department of State or by a regional board of review. Applicants for variances from a regional board must show that the request meets one of several requirements established by the department.

ILLUSTRATIONS

The zoning chapter of the municipal code of the town of Wawayanda stipulates that it "shall be enforced by the Building Inspector, who shall be appointed by the Town Board to serve at the pleasure of the Town Board." Among the duties of the building inspector are "to issue . . . building permits and certificates of occupancy when compliance is made with the provisions of this [zoning] chapter and the New York State Uniform Fire Prevention and Building Code. The zoning chapter also states that "where a building permit is required, no building hereafter erected . . . shall be used or occupied for any purpose until a certificate of occupancy . . . shall have been issued, stating that the building . . . and proposed use thereof comply with the provisions of this [zoning] chapter. Code of the Town of Wawayanda, ch. 185, §§80-82.

In the town of Pawling, the zoning chapter is to be enforced by the Code Enforcement Officer, who is also charged with the issuance of building permits and certificates of occupancy. Pawling Code, ch. 215, §§49-50.

LIMITATIONS AND CONCERNS

Extra caution should be exercised in revoking a building permit. If the developer has incurred substantial expenditures and completed substantial construction in relationship to the project as a whole, rights to the permit may have vested. In such a case, revocation can expose the municipality to significant damages for taking those vested rights without just compensation. Where the permit is revoked by the building inspector without justification following orders from superior municipal officials, the municipality may be held liable for the inspector's acts. If the inspector revokes the permit innocently, based on a mistake of law, or because of the inspector's personal ill will toward the permit holder, the municipality may not be liable for damages caused by the revocation.

When a building inspector denies an application for a permit, the denial must be based on the failure of the application to meet the specific standards established in the Uniform Code or the zoning law of the community. Normally, building permit denials are not discretionary matters. The inspector may not deny a permit based on subjective considerations or fears that the building may be used illegally at some point in the future.

Municipalities are permitted to charge fees for the issuance of building permits and certificates of occupancy. The dollar amount of the fees should be reasonable. The measure of reasonableness is whether they are calculated to recover the cost to the municipality of administering the permit and certificate system. Where those fees are disproportionately large, a court may find them to be an illegal tax and declare the fee structure invalid.

STATUTES AND REGULATIONS

The Uniform Fire Prevention and Building Code Act is found in the Executive Law §§370-383. Section 381 stipulates that enforcement shall be the responsibility of the municipality. It gives the locality the option of electing not to enforce the code, thereby giving the county or state that authority. Section 379 permits local governments to adopt more restrictive construction standards than those required by the Uniform Code where they can demonstrate that these are necessary because of special conditions in the community.

19 NYCRR Part 444 sets forth the minimum standards for administration and enforcement of the Uniform Fire Prevention and Building Code. Section 444.2(a) stipulates that "[e]very city, village, town, and county charged under subdivision 2 of Section 381 of the Executive Law with administration and enforcement of the Uniform Code shall provide for such administration and enforcement of the code by local law, ordinance, or other appropriate regulation."

Village Law §7-700, Town Law §261, and General City Law §20(24) grant basic land use authority to local governments and allow them to regulate the details of land development and building construction and alteration. Village Law §7-704, Town Law §263, and General City Law §§20(24) and (25) grant local legislatures the power to provide for the manner in which zoning regulations and restrictions shall be established and enforced.

The building inspector is a "public officer" under the Public Officers Law §2.

CASE DIGEST

In *Bon Air Estates v. Village of Suffern*, 32 A.D.2d 921, 302 N.Y.S.2d 304 (2d Dep't 1969), an owner of property who paid fees to the village for the issuance of building permits challenged the amount of the fees as constituting an illegal tax. The court held that the amount of a building permit fee should bear a direct relation to the cost of the government service provided. A village does not have the power to impose a tax under the guise of a license or a permit. Where it is shown that receipts from permit fees far exceed the cost of administering the ordinance, the initial conclusion to be drawn is that the fee is in reality a tax. In this case, the owner advanced sufficient proof of excess charges to overcome the presumption of validity attached to the village's law relating to building permits, and a new trial on the matter was ordered.

The refusal of the New York City Department of Buildings to issue a building permit for construction that could be used for an illegal purpose in the future was successfully challenged in *DiMilia v. Bennett*, 149 A.D.2d 592, 540 N.Y.S.2d 274 (2d Dep't 1989). The applicant had amended its earlier application for a building permit seeking permission to add a full bathroom and a private entrance and to divide a large living room on the first floor. The requested amendment was denied on the ground that this would permit the house to be used as an illegal two-family home in a single-family zone. The building department's determination was appealed to the Board of Standards and Appeals, which sustained the denial of the building permit. The court reversed, holding that it was arbitrary and capricious to base a permit denial on a possible future illegal use. As long as the construction meets the specifications of the building code and zoning ordinance, the standard to be applied is the actual use of the building, not its possible future use.

Homeowners in a floodplain brought an action against a village for erroneously issuing a building permit and certificate of occupancy in *Okie v. Village of Hamberg*, 196 A.D.2d 228, 609 N.Y.S.2d 986 (4th Dep't 1994). After the construction of a residence authorized by the permit and certificate, the village determined that the building encroached six feet into an established floodplain area. The village then legalized the encroachment by granting a variance under the floodplain ordinance. The court noted that no liability attaches for the erroneous issuance of a building permit or certificate of occupancy for "a violation of a general duty owed by the town to the public at large." The issuance of a building permit or certificate of occupancy is a governmental function for which a municipality may not be held responsible for damages. The only exception is "when a special relationship exists between the municipality and an individual or class of persons, warranting the imposition of a duty to use reasonable care for those persons' benefit." In this case, the court found that the floodplain ordinance did not create a special duty owed to persons inhabiting a flood-prone area. The intent of the law was to protect the general public from flooding, not just those located within the floodplain.

In *Town of Orangetown v. Magee*, 88 N.Y.2d 41, 665 N.E.2d 1061, 643 N.Y.S.2d 21 (1996), the town brought an action to compel the developer to remove commercial construction that was placed on a site under a validly issued building permit. In response to organized resistance to the construction, the town supervisor instructed the building inspector to revoke the building permit. The town board subsequently amended its zoning law to preclude construction of commercial buildings on the developer's land. The court found that the developer's construction rights had vested under the New York rule which insulates development from zoning amendments when the developer has undertaken substantial construction and incurred substantial expenditures pursuant to a validly issued permit. The court sustained a multimillion damage award to the developer for the taking of its vested rights. It held that the actions of the building inspector were arbitrary and capricious and held the town liable for the inspector's actions. The court noted that where a building inspector acts in good faith, under a mistaken understanding of the law, or acts out of personal ill will toward a permit holder, the town may not be liable for his actions. Here, however, the zoning law gave the inspector sole responsibility for revoking building permits, the inspector was instructed by the supervisor to revoke this permit, and the town demonstrated only political reasons for the revocation. In such a case, a town may be held liable for the inspector's actions.

REFERENCES

Administration and Enforcement of the Uniform Fire Prevention and Building Code, New York State Department of State, Division of Local Government Services; James A. Coon Local Government Technical Series.

Guide to Developing a Local Law for Administration and Enforcement of the New York State Uniform Fire Prevention and Building Code, New York State Department of State, Codes Division.

G. PERMIT CONDITIONS

DEFINITION

Before approving an owner's application for a permit to develop land, local agencies are authorized to impose conditions that are directly related to and incidental to the proposed use of the property. Most applications for local land use approvals are discretionary in nature and conditions can be attached to any development permit to harmonize the proposed land use with surrounding properties and the community. Through the permit condition, the local agency balances the benefit to the owner of the approval and the potential adverse impact of that development on the surrounding area.

Once a condition is imposed on a local land use approval, it must be complied with before a building permit is issued by the local building inspector or department. If the condition is one that is to be met during construction, then its terms must be complied with before the construction is complete and a certificate of occupancy is granted by local authorities.

Among the types of conditions that have been sustained by the courts in the proper circumstances are fences, safety devices, landscaping, screening, access roads, soil erosion prevention, drainage facilities, outdoor lighting, the enclosure of buildings, and restrictive covenants preventing development of land in a floodplain, archeological site, or viewshed, as well as a variety of measures to contain the emission of odors, dust, smoke, noise, and vibrations.

PURPOSE

The purpose of imposing a condition on an owner's application for a land use permit is to balance the owner's interest in developing the land and the community's interest in being protected from any adverse impacts of development. Conditions are imposed to minimize any adverse impact of the proposed use on the neighborhood or community. Conditions on land use approvals add an element of flexibility in decision-making so as to respond to the concerns both of applicants and of those affected by the decisions of local land use agencies.

WHEN

Conditions can be imposed when the local legislature rezones a parcel as well as when local agencies approve subdivision and site plan applications or issue special permits or variances. These local actions all involve discretionary decision-making on the part of a local agency to which permit conditions may be attached. When the agency fears that a project or proposal will have a negative impact on the community, it may deny the application or approve it subject to reasonable conditions that lessen or contain the negative impact.

AUTHORITY

The authority to impose conditions on the approval of a site plan application or on the issuance of a special permit or variance is expressly delegated to local governments by statute. In each case, the statutes state that the conditions must be "reasonable" and "directly related to and incidental to the proposed use of the property."

In the case of variances, conditions must be consistent with the spirit and intent of the zoning ordinance and must be imposed for the purpose of minimizing any adverse impact on the neighborhood. A use that is authorized by special permit has already been declared by the local legislature to be compatible with the surrounding uses in general terms, so conditions attached to special permits are intended to fit that use into a particular neighborhood. Site plan and subdivision conditions must be imposed to implement standards that are contained in the site plan regulations adopted by the local legislature.

State statutes provide authority to approve, deny, or conditionally approve applications for subdivision. Conditions imposed on subdivision approvals must meet the same general standards as conditions imposed on other land use approvals. The statutes provide specific authority to require the developer of a subdivision to set aside suitably located land for recreational purposes or to contribute money in lieu thereof.

The authority to rezone a parcel of land or a portion of a zoning district is part of the express authority of local governments to adopt and amend zoning in the first instance. The authority to amend applicable zoning to provide for a new land use carries with it the implied authority to impose conditions on that use to mitigate its impact on the surrounding area where the permissible uses are not changed. Like conditions imposed in the other contexts, rezoning conditions must be related to and incidental to the use of the property and must be designed to minimize any adverse impact on the surrounding area.

IMPLEMENTATION

Rezoning: Rezoning is a legislative act, taken by the local legislature. In approving a request to rezone property, the legislature is acting to amend the existing provisions of the zoning law and must take all steps required by statute to accomplish this purpose. This requires notice, public hearing, compliance with environmental review provisions, compliance with intermunicipal, county, and regional review requirements, and proper filing of the amendment. Rezoning, like zoning, must conform to the comprehensive plan, and when it does, it is immune from charges that it is illegal spot zoning, even when it affects one relatively small parcel of land.

Variances: Variances are granted by the zoning board of appeals, which must be created locally when zoning is originally adopted. The zoning board of appeals is obligated, in varying the use and area requirements of the zoning law, to grant the minimum variance needed to relieve a unique hardship or practical difficulty created for a particular owner by the zoning law. The zoning board of appeals, in granting a variance, imposes conditions where necessary to minimize its impact on surrounding properties that are being used in compliance with the law's terms.

Other Permits: The standards governing the granting of special permits and the approval of subdivision and site plan applications are contained in the zoning law or other regulations adopted by the local legislature. Typically, the local planning board is authorized to review and approve applications for special permits, subdivisions, and site plans. Alternatively, this authority may be retained by the legislature or delegated to another administrative agency, such as the zoning board of appeals. Before granting its approval of the application, the reviewing board must insure that the standards contained in the law or other regulations are complied with by the proposed development. Frequently, approval is conditioned on the developer's agreeing to modify the design of the development or on the addition of site features to meet the underlying standards adopted by the legislature.

ILLUSTRATIONS

The planning board of the town of Greenville imposed a condition on a landowner's site plan approval for a private hunting preserve which precluded the use of any weapon other than a shotgun in the preserve. Evidence existed on the planning board's record that even the least powerful rifles are capable of firing bullets a distance that exceeded the length and width of the landowner's property. The owner contended that the condition amounted to the rejection by the planning board of a use permitted by the zoning and that it lacked a rational basis. Because of the evidence on the record, the court held that the condition was justified and appropriate under the circumstances.

The zoning board of appeals in the village of Garden City granted an area variance from the minimum lot size to permit the land to be divided into two parcels. The zoning board of appeals conditioned the variance on the relocation of a brick garage on the original parcel to conform to the side yard requirement of the ordinance. At the hearing before the board, the fact that the garage encroached on the side yard setback requirement by two feet was discussed as a secondary issue. The property owners stated on the record that it would be very costly and inconvenient to move the garage as required; they indicated that they would have to destroy and rebuild it. The court held that this condition was unreasonable because its burden was simply too great in proportion to the variance granted. The court stated that "the grant of a variance may not constitutionally labor under a condition which deprives the owner of the effective enjoyment of the variance."

When the town of Gates, as a condition to the rezoning of land to permit retail shopping use, required that the development be conducted by a particular corporation, that condition was struck down. The court stated that "while it is proper for a zoning board to impose appropriate conditions and safeguards in conjunction with a change of zone or a grant of a variance or special permit, such conditions and safeguards must be reasonable and relate only to the real estate involved without regard to the person who owns or occupies it." *Dexter v. Town Bd. of Town of Gates*, 36 N.Y.2d 102, 105, 324 N.E.2d 870, 871, 365 N.Y.S.2d 506, 508 (1975). In a separate matter, a variance for the use of a parcel as an automobile repair shop was inappropriately conditioned on the applicant's discontinuing a second shop in another part of town. This condition, too, was unrelated to the impacts of the proposed land use before the zoning board of appeals.

Often, but not always, conditions that limit the details of operation of a business are set aside as not relating to the proposed use of the land. When a use variance for a real estate office in a residential district was conditioned on the requirement that it be used only in conjunction with the applicant's personal real estate business, that condition was set aside as unrelated to the impacts of the proposed use. When the details of the operation of a nursery school–including the age of students, the hours of school operation, and the number of hours to be worked by a caretaker–were the subjects of a condition imposed on the granting of a variance in the village of Matinecock, the court determined that these details were unrelated to zoning matters and inappropriate. However, a condition limiting the period of operation of the school from September through June was deemed valid because the definition of a private school in the ordinance contained a similar limitation. In another case, a condition that limited an automobile repair shop from keeping more than two non-employee vehicles outside the shop during working hours was sustained as related to the use of the land proposed by the owner's application for a use variance.

LIMITATIONS AND CONCERNS

Although the imposition of conditions is clearly within the authority of local governments, the conditions must comply with several standards or they can be declared invalid. Courts invalidate a condition when there is no rational basis in the record for its imposition, when the condition is unreasonable, when it is not related to the impacts of the proposed development, or when it is vague.

Rational Basis: Courts invalidate conditions that are not supported by evidence on the record of the proceedings that justifies their imposition. Such evidence shows that the administrative agency carefully deliberated the matter, complied with basic due process requirements, and obtained discrete evidence of the need for the condition. In several instances, courts have invalidated conditions that were justified only by neighbors' opposition to the project. Some courts have stated that the administrative agency has a burden of proving the need for the condition; this burden requires, at the least, that the agency consider evidence justifying the imposition of the condition.

Reasonableness: The statutes and cases authorizing the imposition of conditions state that they must be "reasonable." Conditions may be invalidated when, under the circumstances, they impose an undue burden on the landowner. In these instances, it may be that the cost, inconvenience, or other impact on the landowner is too onerous, given the benefit to the public of the condition. This is particularly so when there is a less burdensome alternative to the condition or no indication that the agency considered less burdensome conditions that are adequate to protect the public.

There is some question as to whether an administrative agency can approve an application, but impose a condition that it expire at a particular time. This type of durational condition used to be authorized by statute for variances but was removed by the legislature. This created in some quarters the general impression that durational requirements are invalid conditions. Statements in subsequent cases related to variances call this generalization into question. Because of the heavy burden that durational conditions impose on landowners by terminating the approval at a fixed time, agencies that intend to impose them must be doubly certain that they are reasonable, supported by clear evidence on the record, and related and incidental to the proposed use of the land.

Relatedness: The authority to impose most conditions makes it clear that they must be directly related to and incidental to the proposed land use. This is sometimes described as requiring a nexus between the condition imposed and the impacts of the proposed development. When the condition does not relate to, or lessen, the particular impacts of the development, it is not related to and incidental to the proposed land use as required by law.

The requirement that conditions relate to the impacts of a proposed development has led to several generalizations about requirements that conditions must meet. It is often said, for example, that conditions must relate to the use, not the user, and that conditions cannot regulate the details of the operation of a business. Although these statements have some validity, they are not absolutes. It is true to say, however, that conditions dealing with who uses the land and with the details of business operations are quite often not related to and incidental to the use of the land itself.

Vagueness: Conditions can be struck for vagueness. Agencies imposing conditions must take care to articulate them clearly and definitely so they can be implemented without confusion by the landowner and the local building official. The property owner should not be left in any doubt as to the extent of use that is permitted.

STATUTES

The New York State statutory provisions that authorize conditions to be imposed on local site plan approvals are found at Village Law §7-725-a(4), Town Law §274-a(4), and General City Law §27-a(4): "The authorized board shall have the authority to impose such reasonable conditions and restrictions as are directly related to and incidental to a proposed site plan."

The statutory provisions that authorize conditions to be imposed on the issuance of special permits are found at Village Law §7-725-b(4), Town Law §274-b(4), and General City Law §27-b(4): "The authorized board shall have the authority to impose such reasonable conditions and restrictions as are directly related to and incidental to the proposed special use permit."

The statutory provisions that authorize conditions to be imposed on the issuance of variances are found at Village Law §7-712-b(4), Town Law §267-b(4), and General City Law §81-b(5): "The board of appeals shall, in the granting of both use variances and area variances, have the authority to impose such reasonable conditions and restrictions as are directly related to and incidental to the proposed use of the property. Such conditions shall be consistent with the spirit and intent of the zoning ordinance or local law, and shall be imposed for the purpose of minimizing any adverse impact such variance may have on the neighborhood or community."

CASE DIGEST

In *Church v. Town of Islip*, 8 N.Y.2d 254, 168 N.E.2d 680, 203 N.Y.S.2d 866 (1960), neighboring property owners challenged a legislative zoning change that was granted upon the condition that the defendant owners execute restrictive covenants regarding the maximum area to be occupied by the buildings and regarding the fence and shrubbery. The challengers claimed that the conditional rezoning constituted illegal "contract zoning." The court noted that the rezoning is a legislative act and therefore "is entitled to the strongest possible presumption of validity and must stand if there is any factual basis therefor." It held that the imposition of conditions was constitutional since the conditions were reasonable and were intended to be and were for the benefit of the neighbors.

The court determined the extent of the authority of a zoning board of appeals to impose conditions upon a special exception permit for the operation of a private nursery school in *Bernstein v. Village of Matinecock Board of Appeals*, 60 Misc. 2d 470, 302 N.Y.S.2d 141 (Sup. Ct. Nassau County 1969). The court stated that the conditions imposed "must be directly related to and incidental to the proposed use of the property, and the conditions stated must be sufficiently clear and definite that the permittee and his neighbors are not left in doubt concerning the extent of the use permitted." The court invalidated the conditions which related to the age of the students, the total number of students, and the hours of operation of the school because those conditions applied to the details of the operation of the business and not to the zoning use of the premises.

"While it is proper for a zoning board to impose appropriate conditions and safeguards in conjunction with a change of zone or a grant of a variance or special permit, such conditions and safeguards must be reasonable and relate only to the real estate involved without regard to the person who owns or occupies it." *Dexter v. Town Board of the Town of Gates*, 36 N.Y.2d 102, 324 N.E.2d 870, 365 N.Y.S.2d 506 (1975). The town board had imposed a condition on the rezoning of a residential area that the change of zone shall inure to the benefit of one named corporation. The court held that the condition was improper and unauthorized by the law since it was personal to the applicant and did not relate to the use of the property or the zoning of the property.

In *Janiak v. Planning Board of the Town of Greenville*, 159 A.D.2d 574, 552 N.Y.S.2d 436 (2d Dep't 1990), the planning board conditioned site plan approval for a private hunting reserve on the limitation that only shotguns would be used on the preserve. The court found that there was a rational basis for the board's condition. The record indicated that restrictions were necessary to reduce the danger posed to adjacent landowners from stray bullets.

In *Brous v. Planning Board of the Village of Southampton*, 191 A.D.2d 553, 594 N.Y.S.2d 816 (2d Dep't 1993), the court annulled a condition imposed by the planning board in its approval of a subdivision proposal for an oceanfront parcel. The planning board approved the proposed subdivision on the condition that no second-story addition be made to an existing beach house. The court held that the condition "is unreasonable since it fails to seek to ameliorate any demonstrable adverse effects attributable to the petitioner's proposed use of the land."

REFERENCE

Cozata Solloway, *Local Government Authority to Impose Conditions on Private Development Proposals, at* http://www.pace.edu/lawschool/landuse/permitso.html (last visited Feb. 2, 2001).

H. MORATORIA ON DEVELOPMENT

DEFINITION

A moratorium on development is a local law or ordinance that suspends the right of property owners to obtain development approvals while the community takes time to consider, draft, and adopt land use plans or rules to respond to new or changing circumstances not adequately dealt with by its current laws. A moratorium is sometimes used by a community just prior to adopting its first comprehensive plan and zoning law.

Development moratoriums may be general or specific. A general moratorium imposes a ban on the consideration and approval of all development and building applications in the community. Hardship exemptions may be provided and certain actions exempted; otherwise, all development applications for subdivision, site plan, special permits, wetland permits, and building permits are suspended until new land use regulations are adopted.

A specific moratorium may prevent development approvals in a particular geographic area or of a certain type. Specific moratoriums have been passed, for example, to suspend development approvals on an island owned by one person. Similarly, moratoriums have suspended the right to process proposals for nonresidential or multi-family construction. They have been enacted to affect only the construction of docks, in one instance, or cellular telephone antennas, in another.

PURPOSE

A moratorium on development preserves the status quo for a reasonable time while the municipality develops and adopts a land use strategy to respond to new or recently perceived problems. The moratorium prevents developers and property owners from rushing to develop their land under current land use rules that the community is in the process of changing. By so doing, it helps to accomplish the purpose of the new rules by giving them the broadest possible applicability and preventing development that is inconsistent with them.

In a community with no comprehensive plan or zoning, where development pressures are mounting quickly, a development moratorium serves the same purpose. In this instance, developers are prevented from making land use choices for the community until the new plan and zoning law are put in place.

WHEN

Local legislatures adopt moratoriums in two situations. First, when they decide to adopt their first zoning law or comprehensive plan, or to significantly amend the existing law or plan, they may adopt a moratorium on all development until the new zoning law or plan is enacted. Second, when localities are confronted by a new or recently understood problem that may require an amendment to a particular zoning provision or the addition of new zoning provisions, they may adopt a moratorium on development projects relating to that particular problem.

Moratoriums on development may be used, for example, prior to the adoption of a local overlay zone, a new subdivision law, the designation of a critical environmental area, or the adoption of an environmental constraints ordinance. The moratorium prevents negative impacts of the type of development that the new law or regulation is designed to prevent or mitigate.

AUTHORITY

There is no specific statutory authorization to adopt a moratorium on development. The courts have pointed to two separate sources of authority, while consistently confirming the municipal power to enact moratoriums.

For communities that have adopted a comprehensive plan and a zoning law, the adoption of a moratorium can be considered an implied power. The community is implicitly authorized to take those actions it deems reasonable to encourage the most appropriate use of the land throughout the municipality. In light of new or changing circumstances, a moratorium may be necessary to allow the community to achieve this express purpose of zoning and land use planning.

For communities that have not yet adopted a comprehensive plan and zoning law, the authority to adopt a moratorium is implied either in their delegated authority to adopt zoning or in the municipal police power to protect the community in advance of zoning. Some courts have held that a development moratorium is a form of zoning, implying that it is part of the statutorily delegated power to adopt and amend zoning provisions. Alternatively, a community's authority to adopt a moratorium has been referred to as a police power measure appropriate to prevent conditions that threaten the community's health, safety, welfare, and morals.

IMPLEMENTATION

A moratorium can be seen as the most extreme land use action that a municipality can take, because it suspends completely the rights of owners to use their property. In this light, it is advisable to precede the adoption of a moratorium by findings that confirm the necessity of this action. What are the conditions that mandate the imposition of a moratorium? Are there no available alternatives less burdensome on property rights? Why are the existing land use plans and ordinances not adequate? What recent circumstances have occurred that justify the adoption of the moratorium? How serious and urgent are these circumstances? What hard evidence is there to document the necessity of the moratorium?

When adopting a moratorium, the municipality may set forth how the situation that gave rise to the moratorium is to be dealt with. What local bodies are responsible? What studies are to be done? What resources are being made available to complete those studies? Can deadlines be established for various steps in the process? The more specific and legitimate this plan and timetable are, the more likely it is that the moratorium will be found to be reasonable.

Based on this action plan and timetable, a date can be selected for the expiration of the moratorium. A moratorium can be extended if the timetable cannot be met; however, the reasonableness of the action is enhanced by setting a date for expiration that is legitimate under the circumstances.

A moratorium should be adopted in conformance with all procedures required of any zoning or land use action, including notice, hearing, the formalities of adoption, and filing. While a moratorium does not require an environmental review under the State Environmental Quality Review Act, if it affects adjacent municipalities or county facilities it may be subject to review by the county or regional planning board before it can be formally adopted.

It may be appropriate to exempt certain types of development from the application of the moratorium. These might include construction applications that have been approved and begun but where the developers' rights to proceed have not legally vested. Additionally, actions such as area variances or minor subdivision approvals may be allowed without compromising the integrity of the new strategy being developed.

General state law requires local agencies to follow specific procedures and to adhere to strict timetables in reviewing and approving certain applications. This is so, for example, when approving subdivision and site plan applications. In some instances, projects are deemed to be approved if the agency does not act within the stipulated period. These are known as default provisions. One New York appellate court has held that a moratorium automatically suspends statutory time periods and default provisions. To be certain, however, that these time requirements and default provisions do not apply when a moratorium is adopted, the local legislature may stipulate that each specific time period and all default provisions applicable to the development approvals and permits suspended by the moratorium are superseded by the local law adopting it.

LIMITATIONS AND CONCERNS

Since development moratoriums affect property rights so severely, they must be reasonable or run the risk of being challenged and being voided by the courts, with, perhaps, a damage award resulting against the locality. Reasonableness is best established if the community can document that it is facing a true emergency. Several court decisions sustaining moratoriums refer to the "dire necessity" that justifies them. Such a necessity arises not only when health and safety risks are confronted but also when the community is facing a significant new land use problem that its existing regulations were not designed to handle.

For the same reason, when specific action plans and timetables are established to deal with the necessity or emergency, the reasonableness of the locality's moratorium is demonstrated. Similarly, a community needs to make reasonable progress in carrying out the plan and in adhering to the schedule. Moratoriums that have been extended for up to three years have been sustained by a showing that the community was diligently pursuing its plan and timetable, and shorter moratoriums have been voided because the community was making little or no progress. In the same way, the plan must be calculated to deal directly with the necessity or emergency at hand; otherwise, its reasonableness may be questioned.

Moratoriums do not apply to approved projects where the developer has completed construction or has completed substantial construction in reliance on a development approval or permit. Such developers are said to have vested rights in their permits and are immune from changes in applicable regulations. Other property owners, who have made less progress, are said to have no legitimate or enforceable expectation that the rules applicable to the development of their land might not change in the interest of protecting the public health, safety, or welfare.

ILLUSTRATIONS

While the town of Huntington, New York, was preparing a Local Waterfront Revitalization Plan, it enacted a moratorium prohibiting construction of any docks until 60 days after the plan's adoption. After seven years, however, the plan was still in an "embryonic stage" with "no expectation of one in the indefinite future." A waterfront property owner obtained permits to construct a dock from the Department of Environmental Conservation and the Army Corps of Engineers but was denied a local building permit because of the moratorium. Responding to his challenge to the local law, the court struck down the moratorium as unreasonable under the circumstances.

The court recognized the right of the municipality to act in times of "dire necessity." However, the fact that the town had been "working" on its waterfront plan for seven years was a controlling circumstance in its decision to invalidate the moratorium.

In Tarrytown, a moratorium was adopted to prohibit the construction of cellular telephone antennas. When the moratorium was adopted, the village admitted, in its findings, that there was no hard evidence that cellular telephone transmission facilities are harmful to human health or safety. It found, instead, that citizens perceive that radio frequency emissions may adversely affect their health. When the moratorium was challenged, the court noted that "a municipality may not invoke its police powers solely as a pretext to assuage strident community opposition."

CASE DIGEST

"To justify interference with the beneficial enjoyment of property [as a moratorium does] the municipality must establish that it has acted in response to a dire necessity, that its action is reasonably calculated to alleviate or prevent the crisis condition, and that it is presently taking steps to rectify the problem." *Belle Harbor Realty Corp. v. Kerr*, 35 N.Y.2d 507, 323 N.E.2d 697, 364 N.Y.S.2d 160 (1974).

In *Dune Associates v. Anderson*, 119 A.D.2d 574, 500 N.Y.S.2d 741 (2d Dep't 1986), a town established a moratorium "to temporarily halt development while the town considered comprehensive zoning changes." The plaintiff, who had submitted a subdivision application that was held up by the moratorium beyond the statutory period stipulated for approval, contended that his plat was approved by default. The court held that "[t]he 90-day period of the moratorium . . . should not be counted in determining whether the planning board complied with the statute," and that the plaintiff's plats "are not entitled to approval on default."

In *Pateman v. Marra*, 138 Misc. 2d 807, 525 N.Y.S.2d 533 (Sup. Ct. Westchester County 1988), the plaintiffs claimed that their subdivision plats should be deemed approved because the planning board had to make a determination within 60 days and that period had expired. The court agreed, holding that a temporary moratorium was not applicable to the type of application submitted by the plaintiffs, and that the plaintiffs' application was approved.

"When a local land use decision that is to be referred to the county planning board under Section 239-m of the General Municipal Law is not referred as required, that failure amounts to a jurisdictional defect which renders the local action invalid." *Caruso v. Town of Oyster Bay*, 172 Misc. 2d 93, 656 N.Y.S.2d 809 (Sup. Ct. Nassau County 1997), *aff'd*, 672 N.Y.S.2d 418 (2d Dep't 1998). The town imposed a moratorium in response to a petition signed by the plaintiff's neighbors expressing their concern regarding the division of the plaintiff's property. The court stated that "a moratorium on building has been held a reasonable measure designed to temporarily halt development while the town considered comprehensive zoning changes and therefore a valid stopgap or interim zoning measure." It concluded, however, that the moratorium was invalid for failure to follow the requirements for referral to the county. The court further held that the plaintiff's application "must be processed in the ordinary course of the town's operations now that the moratorium is no longer in effect."

The court in *Duke v. Town of Huntington*, 153 Misc. 2d 521, 581 N.Y.S.2d 978 (Sup. Ct. Suffolk County 1991), held that "the defendant's legislative limitation on plaintiff's right to use his property, now halted for a period extending over three years by virtue of the moratoriums, is considered excessive and unconstitutionally void," because the life of a moratorium "may not exceed a reasonable period of time." The court determined the delay excessive and ordered the town to issue the permit to the plaintiff.

The Town of Pine Plains had "replaced one moratorium law with another and [had] been doing so for nearly five years." The plaintiff in *Mitchell v. Kemp*, 176 A.D.2d 859, 575 N.Y.S.2d 337 (2d Dep't 1991), applied for a variance from the provisions of the moratorium but was denied. The court determined that the controversy was caused "by the Town's unreasonable delay in enacting a zoning ordinance." The court invalidated the moratorium because "[t]he Town here has failed to offer any satisfactory reasons for the nearly five-year delay in enacting a zoning ordinance."

In *Cellular Telephone Co. v. Village of Tarrytown*, 209 A.D.2d 57, 624 N.Y.S.2d 170 (2d Dep't 1995), the Second Department held that the enactment of a temporary moratorium on the installation of antennas was invalid since there was no evidence that the well-being of the community was jeopardized. The court held that the planning board "could not rationally rely upon the speculative and unfounded 'perception' of health risks by some Village residents as a basis to declare a moratorium on the installation of cellular service antennas."

This does not mean, however, that a moratorium on cellular facility applications cannot be imposed for other reasons. In *Cellular Telephone Co. v. Town-Village of Harrison*, N.Y.L.J., Nov. 30, 1995, at 35 (Sup. Ct. Westchester County Nov. 30, 1995), a town's enactment of a 90-day moratorium on the review of cellular antenna facilities was sustained as a proper exercise of municipal power. The court held that the moratorium "constituted a reasonable measure designed to give the Town a short period in which to enact zoning changes to rationally meet the need to address the increasing number of cellular telephone antenna facility applications." This moratorium was adopted not to respond solely to citizen opposition to cellular sites but to develop a rational response in the absence of any provisions in the zoning ordinance to control the siting of cellular facilities.

A moratorium was imposed on property along a creek to determine if the creek should be included in the state's Wild, Scenic, and Recreational Rivers System in *Timber Ridge Homes at Brookhaven, Inc. v. State*, 223 A.D.2d 635, 637 N.Y.S.2d 179 (2d Dep't 1996). The plaintiff argued "that the Legislature's action had been a regulatory taking of the property without just compensation." The court held that since the plaintiff "failed to apply to the New York State Department of Environmental Conservation for a permit exempting it from the moratorium" it had not exhausted all administrative remedies, and was not entitled to relief.

REFERENCE

Land Use Moratoria, New York State Department of State, Division of Local Government Services; James A. Coon Local Government Technical Series.

I. NONCONFORMING USES

DEFINITION

A nonconforming use is created when existing land uses, which were valid when established, are prohibited by a new or amended zoning law. Nonconforming land uses are not defined by state laws but are defined in most local zoning laws. A typical local ordinance may define a nonconforming use as "any use, whether of a building or tract of land or both, existing on the effective date of this chapter, which does not conform to the use regulations of the district in which it is located." Nonconforming use issues arise when the zoning law is first adopted. When a district is zoned residential, for example, all existing nonresidential uses in that district are rendered nonconforming. Later amendments to the zoning ordinance may have the same effect.

When property owners propose an improvement, expansion, rebuilding, or other change in their nonconforming property use, they must be certain to comply with local regulations governing those matters. Normally, these regulations are found in a discrete article of the local zoning law, entitled Nonconforming Uses. That article will prohibit or limit changes in buildings and lot uses that are nonconforming and will provide for the termination of nonconforming uses in a variety of ways, such as limiting their expansion or enlargement, prohibiting the reconstruction of damaged structures, disallowing the reestablishment of nonconforming uses after they have been discontinued for a time, or simply terminating them after the passage of a stipulated amount of time.

PURPOSE

The policy of allowing nonconforming uses to continue originated in concerns that the application of zoning regulations to uses existing prior to the regulations' enactment might be construed as confiscatory and unconstitutional. It was assumed that by limiting the enlargement and reconstruction of nonconforming uses, they would disappear over time. The allowance of nonconforming uses has been characterized by the courts as a "grudging tolerance" of them. The right of municipalities to adopt reasonable measures to eliminate them has been recognized. The ultimate goal of the zoning law is to achieve uniformity of property uses within each zoning district, which can only be accomplished by the elimination of uses that do not conform to the specifications of district regulations.

WHEN

When zoning ordinances are first adopted, they typically contain specific language that allows most nonconforming uses to continue, but not to be abandoned, rebuilt, expanded, or enlarged. When the language of the initial zoning ordinance fails to eliminate nonconforming uses or allows them to be enhanced and perpetuated, it is often amended to contain clearer definitions of important concepts such as abandonment, enlargement, and expansion, or to adopt stricter standards for rebuilding or terminating nonconforming uses.

AUTHORITY

The state statutes that delegate to local governments the authority to adopt zoning regulations implicitly authorize local legislatures to adopt reasonable measures to protect the legitimate investment expectations of owners of developed land. There is no express reference, however, in these authorizing statutes to the authority of local legislatures to allow the continuation of nonconforming uses.

IMPLEMENTATION

There is obvious tension between protecting the investment of the owners of nonconforming uses and achieving uniformity of land use within zoning districts. To achieve this latter goal, a variety of provisions have been added to the typical zoning law to discourage the continuation of nonconforming uses over time. These include provisions that limit an owner's right to expand or enlarge the nonconforming use, to reconstruct the use after substantial damage, to change the property's use to a different nonconforming use, or require the termination of the use after a specified period.

There is significant variety in the way local governments attempt to resolve this tension. This is evident in the different provisions that local zoning laws contain to control, or phase out, nonconforming uses and in the way that courts interpret and apply these provisions.

ILLUSTRATIONS

The variety of nonconforming use provisions is evident in the following review of the provisions that zoning laws contain which attempt to discourage the continuation of nonconforming uses:

Reconstruction and Restoration: The local zoning ordinance may prohibit the restoration of a nonconforming structure that suffers significant physical damage and may require that any such reconstruction be for a use that conforms to the zoning law. Significant physical damage is usually defined as damage that exceeds a certain percentage of the structure's value. Typical standards range from 25% to 50%. These provisions are premised on the theory that owners do not have a right to reconstruct a nonconforming building after damage by fire, weather, natural disaster, or otherwise. In such a case, their property rights were destroyed by the disaster, rather than by the law. The owner is in a situation similar to the owner of a vacant lot, who must comply with the applicable zoning restrictions.

Enlargement, Alteration, or Extension: Similarly, local laws often prohibit the enlargement, alteration, or extension of a nonconforming use. To allow the expansion of nonconforming uses would defeat the zoning law's underlying policy of eliminating them over time. Normally, the law allows the owners of nonconforming land uses to perform property repairs, conduct normal maintenance, and complete internal alterations that do not increase the degree of, or create any new, noncompliance with the locality's zoning regulations.

Courts have upheld prohibitions on the construction of an awning over a courtyard outside a restaurant, on the theory that it would create additional space for patrons to congregate and, in this sense, increase the degree of the nonconforming use. Prohibiting the conversion of seasonal bungalows to year-round residences has also been upheld as an acceptable method of preventing the enlargement of a nonconforming use.

Where the expansion of nonconforming business operations is proposed, the case law is somewhat less clear. Where roads and structures built on a parcel used as a gravel mining operation exhibited the owner's intention to use the entire parcel, the court held that expanding the mining operation to another location on the property was permitted. The addition of a body-toning operation to premises containing a nonconforming beauty parlor, however, was considered a prohibited extension of the prior nonconforming use. The court's interest in protecting the owner's demonstrated investment in the gravel mining operation could explain the difference between these cases.

Nonconforming use provisions in zoning laws vary considerably from one locality to another. A municipality particularly intent on eliminating nonconforming uses may prohibit any physical expansion of a building; another may favor property use by allowing, for example, the construction of an additional story because it does not increase the footprint, or lot coverage, of the structure.

Changing to Another Nonconforming Use: The property owner's right to continue a nonconforming use does not allow the owner to change to a materially different use. The important question here is what constitutes a material change. The consequence of a finding that a material change in use has occurred is that the prior nonconforming use is deemed abandoned and, therefore, terminated. The property owner could argue that the change of a nonconforming use from one commercial use to another, for example, should not be prohibited by the zoning law. The assertion is that to change a building's occupancy from a dairy plant to a business that rents machinery simply shifts the type of nonconformance from one commercial category to another. It has been held, however, that it is not only a change in the volume of business conducted but a change in the character of that business that determines whether one business use is a continuation of another. This is true despite the generic similarity between the old and the new proposed use.

Occasionally, courts hold that changes from one use to another within the same category of use are permitted. In one case, for example, the owner was allowed to establish a storage business in a building that had been occupied as a nursery and florist enterprise. Determinations in these cases depend on the particular facts involved, on the court's interpretation of how material the change will be, and on the specific language of the local ordinance that regulates changes in nonconforming uses.

Abandonment: A property owner's right to continue a nonconforming use may be lost by abandonment. Originally, this required a voluntary, completed act of abandonment by the owner. It was said that there must be the concurrence of an intention to abandon and some act, or failure to act, which implied a lack of interest on the part of the owner to retain the use. Time was considered relevant to the issue of abandonment, but was not enough, alone, to establish it. Furthermore, the mere failure to continue the nonconforming use was not sufficient to establish abandonment.

Today, local zoning laws often stipulate that any discontinuance of the nonconforming use for a specified period constitutes abandonment. Courts hold that such provisions are sufficient to establish the owner's intent to abandon the nonconforming use as a matter of law. Where the established period is reasonable, discontinuance of the use for that time amounts to an abandonment of the use. It has been held that local discontinuance periods apply even when the owner can prove that he did not actually intend to abandon the nonconforming use.

Amortization: Some local ordinances require certain nonconforming uses to be amortized over a specified period at the end of which they must be terminated. The term "amortization" is used to describe these provisions because they allow the owner some time during which to recoup his investment in the nonconforming use. The Court of Appeals has upheld such provisions "where the benefit to the public has been deemed of greater moment than the detriment to the property owner." The courts have said that the test for when an amortization period is reasonable is "a question that must be answered in the light of the facts of each particular case. Certainly, a critical factor is the length of the amortization period in relation to the investment. The critical question, however, is whether the public gain achieved by the exercise of the police power outweighs the private loss suffered by the owners of the nonconforming uses."

Contexts in which amortization provisions are likely to be upheld are:

♦ When the common law of nuisance would allow neighboring property owners to enjoin the continuation of a nonconforming use. For example, a gravel pit, auto wrecking operation, or junkyard, harmful to children in a developing residential area, might be enjoined under a private nuisance action. Likewise, a zoning law can legally require such a nonconforming use to be terminated in an appropriate case. If an amortization provision is challenged, the municipality can show that the owner's property interest is slight because of its vulnerability to a nuisance action. In this context, however, the label "amortization" is inappropriate. The grace period, if any, allowed by the local statute is gratuitous if, in fact, the owner's use may be enjoined as a nuisance.

♦ When the nonconforming use is somewhat noxious and the owner has little investment in it. For example, a provision requiring the owner to cease raising pigeons on the roof or to remove an old outdoor sign might withstand challenge because of the minimal nature of the owner's investment and the significant harm done to the zoning scheme if the owner's activity is allowed to continue. Harder cases are presented when the owner has a demonstrable investment in the use and the public interest in removing it is clear but where the threat to public health and safety is not imminent.

LIMITATIONS AND CONCERNS

The local legislature, in adopting zoning regulations, is most concerned with the separation of incompatible land uses. When a building that preexisted the zoning requirements is out of compliance with setback, area, or height restrictions, it is not a nonconforming use in the technical sense. It is simply out of compliance with the dimensional requirements of zoning: a noncomplying building. Since noncomplying buildings do not offend the legislative policy of separation of incompatible uses, zoning provisions often do not so severely constrain their enlargement or reconstruction. A typical provision may require, for example, that no enlargement or reconstruction of a noncomplying building can increase the degree of noncompliance or create any new noncompliance.

A practice in some municipalities that extends the life of nonconforming uses is that of awarding use variances so that the nonconforming use can be enlarged, expanded, or reconstructed. This can occur when an owner is denied a building permit because the proposed construction would enlarge or reconstruct a nonconforming use. The owner can apply to the zoning board of appeals and, if the owner can show that the statutory criteria for a use variance are satisfied, the board can award the requested variance. Although the board can impose reasonable conditions on the use of the property, the award of a use variance frees the property from the provisions of zoning that limit nonconforming uses. The effect of a variance is to declassify the use as nonconforming.

The property owner asking for a use variance must prove that the variance, if granted, will not alter the essential character of the neighborhood. If it does not, then and to this extent the proposed use is compatible with the surrounding neighborhood. The property owner must also show by competent financial evidence that he cannot realize a reasonable return by using the property under any use allowed in the district or by continuing the nonconforming use in its unaltered condition. This financial requirement makes it very difficult for most owners of existing nonconforming uses to prove that they are entitled to a use variance.

Another local practice that influences the continuation of nonconforming uses is the interpretation of the building inspector as to what types of building improvements are prohibited by the language of the local zoning provisions. Usually, these provisions permit the repair and maintenance of nonconforming uses, or improvements that do not "enlarge or expand" the nonconforming use. Some building inspectors take a broad view of what repair and maintenance are and have a limited view of what constitutes an expansion or enlargement of the nonconforming use. By awarding building permits to improve nonconforming uses, the building inspector indirectly encourages their continuation.

Allowing the expansion and reconstruction of noncomplying buildings, granting variances to allow the expansion of nonconforming uses, or issuing building permits to improve nonconforming uses does not advance the policy of discontinuing nonconforming uses. Such actions do, however, allow the municipality flexibility in accommodating the needs of property owners while mitigating the impacts of the continued presence of these uses on adjacent owners and surrounding neighbors.

CASE DIGEST

The owner has no vested rights to reconstruct a nonconforming building after it has been partly destroyed by fire. The municipality may impose reasonable restrictions on such rebuilding and require substantially destroyed buildings to comply with the zoning regulations when reconstructed. *Bobandal Realties, Inc. v. Worthington*, 21 A.D.2d 784, 250 N.Y.S.2d 575 (2d Dep't 1964), *aff'd*, 15 N.Y.2d 788, 205 N.E.2d 685, 257 N.Y.S.2d 588 (1965).

The Court of Appeals sustained an amortization period in a city zoning law which required the termination of a nonconforming use within three years from the effective date of the ordinance in *Harbison v. City of Buffalo*, 4 N.Y.2d 553, 152 N.E.2d 42, 117 N.Y.S.2d 598 (1958). The petitioners operated a nonconforming use, a junkyard business in a residential zone. Applications by the petitioners for a wholesale junk license and drum-reconditioning license were denied because the terms of the zoning law required the termination of the nonconforming use. The court held that a nonconforming use "may be terminated after a reasonable period, during which the owner may have a fair opportunity to amortize his investment and to make future plans." The court advocated finding a balance between social harm and private injury in order to determine the reasonable period during which an owner of property must be allowed to continue a nonconforming use. The case was remanded for the consideration of several factors: the nature of the surrounding neighborhood, the value and condition of the improvements on the premises, the nearest area to which the petitioners might relocate, the cost of such relocation, and other reasonable costs that the petitioners might sustain. The court noted that if the injury to the petitioners would be substantial, then the ordinance would be unconstitutional as applied to this case.

"One of the prime purposes of restrictive zoning is the phasing out of nonconforming uses by prohibiting any extension thereof. While the benefit to the public of restrictive zoning does not justify immediate destruction of nonconforming uses, the basic principle of zoning embraces the concept of ultimate elimination of nonconforming uses." *Cave v. Zoning Board of Appeals of Village of Fredonia*, 49 A.D.2d 228, 373 N.Y.S.2d 932 (4th Dep't 1975). The court revoked building permits that had been issued to the appellant for the expansion of his trailer park facility, a use that had been declared nonconforming by the village zoning law. The court held that the construction of 14 additional trailer unit locations, "which would more than double the number of locations on appellant's property, would constitute a prohibited extension or enlargement of an existing nonconforming use."

In *Syracuse Aggregate Corp. v. Weise*, 51 N.Y.2d 278, 414 N.E.2d 651, 434 N.Y.S.2d 150 (1980), the Court of Appeals extended the protection afforded a nonconforming quarry to the boundaries of the property even though the principal excavation was limited to a five-acre portion of the property. The court's ruling was based on the fact that "the owner [had] engage[d] in substantial quarrying activities on a distinct parcel of land over a long period of time" and that "these activities clearly manifest[ed] an intent to appropriate the entire parcel to the particular business of quarrying." Cf. *Rudolf Steiner Fellowship Foundation v. Luccia*, 90 N.Y.2d 453, 685 N.E.2d 192, 662 N.Y.S.2d 411 (1997) (holding that "the addition of a second co-worker apartment at a nursing home facility was not a permissible extension of the preexisting nonconforming use").

In *Darcy v. Zoning Board of Appeals of the City of Rochester*, 185 A.D.2d 624, 586 N.Y.S.2d 44 (4th Dep't 1992), the court annulled the zoning board's determination that a nonconforming restaurant use had not been abandoned. The court found that the property had not been used as a restaurant for at least 20 months, and thus the nonconforming use had been discontinued well beyond the six-month period specified in the city ordinance. The court based its decision on the fact that "the ordinance expressly foreclose[d] inquiry into the owner's intent to resume or not to abandon."

The Court of Appeals determined that the cessation of substantially all warehouse operations for 20 months resulted in the discontinuation of the nonconforming use in *Toys 'R' Us v. Silva*, 89 N.Y.2d 411, 676 N.E.2d 862, 654 N.Y.S.2d 100 (1996). Under the New York City Zoning Resolution §52-61, the continuation of a nonconforming use is prohibited if "during a two-year period, 'the active operation of substantially all the nonconforming uses . . . is discontinued.'" In this case, the owner's building permit, which allowed him to maintain a nonconforming use on the premises, was revoked by the court because of the nearly complete cessation of all operations for a period of 20 months. The petitioner pointed to its maintenance of minimal warehouse activity and claimed that "any nonconforming use, however minimal, precludes a finding of abandonment." The court held that "substantial, rather than complete, discontinuation of the active, nonconforming activity forfeits the nonconforming use, and that the good faith of the owner is irrelevant to that determination." The court further concluded that the warehouse operations were "too insignificant to preserve nonconforming use status under §52-61."

J. ACCESSORY USES

DEFINITION

Accessory uses are uses of land that are found on the same lot as the principal use and are subordinate, incidental to, and customarily found in connection with the principal use. For example, a garage may be accessory to a residential use of a property because it is customarily found in connection with and is incidental and subordinate to the principal residential use. Generally, zoning laws state that lot owners may use their land for a permitted principal use and for activities that are accessory to that use.

In order to qualify as accessory, a use must also be incidental and subordinate to the principal use. To be incidental, an accessory use must be reasonably related to the principal use. For instance, a garage or recreational use is reasonably related to the principal residential use and thus is deemed incidental. To be subordinate, the accessory use must be proportionately smaller than the principal use. The garage is generally smaller than the house, for instance.

An accessory use must also be customarily found in conjunction with its principal use. A use is customary if it commonly, habitually, and by long practice has been reasonably associated with a principal use. A most common example of this is vehicle parking for a residence or business. But a municipality need not be limited to specific uses that are customary, so long as the type of use is customary. For instance, a court upheld a zoning board of appeals determination that a skateboard ramp, which is a recreational use, was customary because recreational uses of property that serve the needs of the occupants are customary in a residential district. The test is whether the recreational use is incidental to the residential use, not whether landowners in the town are engaged in similar activities.

PURPOSE

Accessory use provisions in zoning laws allow a range of incidental uses of property that owners expect to engage in when they purchase their property for its principal use. By permitting uses customarily incidental and subordinate to the principal activity, zoning ordinances allow property owners additional beneficial use of their property. Regulations that limit the accessory uses allowed in a district also recognize that some neighborhoods should be protected from accessory uses that are not consistent with the expectations of the property owners. This separation of inconsistent uses into zoning districts is part of the original purpose of zoning.

WHEN

When zoning ordinances are first adopted, they may simply state that customary, incidental, and subordinate uses are permitted along with the principal uses in each zoning district. When the zoning enforcement officer encounters difficulties in determining whether uses are permitted accessory uses under this general definition, the legislature may add specific standards that limit accessory uses and provide greater guidance to that official.

AUTHORITY

While there is no specific delegation of power to municipalities to provide for accessory uses, local governments have authority, under state enabling statutes, to regulate land under the police power. This is a broad authority designed to promote public health, safety, morals, and general welfare. Zoning laws that regulate accessory uses are valid so long as they promote these goals. Since the regulation of accessory uses promotes harmony of land use within regulated districts, it is permissible pursuant to the police power.

IMPLEMENTATION

Local ordinances regulate accessory uses in a variety of ways. Within the local zoning law, language regulating accessory uses may be found in the definitions of "accessory," "lot," or "use," in separate sections, or in the schedule of regulations for individual districts. There are at least five different approaches to regulating accessory uses in a municipality's zoning law.

The municipality may simply permit accessory uses by accepting those uses that meet the qualifications of what is customary and incidental. In this case, the ordinance does not provide guidelines or expressly state what is or is not an accessory use. Rather, the ordinance simply defines accessory uses as customary, incidental, and subordinate in the definition section and then permits these uses in each district.

A zoning law may permit certain accessory uses and prohibit all others. The legislature can do this by listing which accessory uses are allowed in each use district. As a matter of statutory construction, those uses not expressly permitted in the list are prohibited unless clearly stated otherwise. This is the most restrictive means of regulation because it limits what qualifies as an accessory use to the legislature's list. It could result in denial of a use that is otherwise incidental, subordinate, and customary to the principal use.

A more flexible approach is to list and prohibit only problematic accessory uses. This eliminates foreseeable problems with the listed uses while permitting all other accessory uses that are customary, incidental, and subordinate.

The municipality may provide guidelines that can assist the zoning enforcement officer and zoning board of appeals in interpreting what is an accessory use and adopt a nonexclusive, illustrative list of acceptable uses. If this approach is used, it is crucial that the law explicitly state that the list is nonexclusive.

A final regulatory approach is to list some accessory uses that are allowed by special use permit and subject them to certain requirements. This approach can be used by itself or in conjunction with any of the other four approaches.

ILLUSTRATIONS

The town of Southeast's zoning ordinance provides an example of how an accessory use may be defined. It provides that an accessory use is: "A use incidental to the principal use and located on the same lot. In buildings restricted to residential use, the office of a professional, customary home occupations and woodworking and similar workshops not conducted for compensation shall be deemed 'accessory uses.' There may be no uses accessory to an accessory use."

Greenburgh, in Westchester County, has taken the approach of listing permitted accessory uses and prohibiting all others. The zoning ordinance lists the allowed accessory uses in each zoning district. For instance, §285-10, the section regulating the R-40, one-family residence zone, states: "Permitted Uses. No building or premises shall be used and no building shall be erected, altered or added to unless otherwise provided in this chapter, except for the following uses: (1) Permitted uses …(2) Special permit uses …(3) Accessory Uses (a) Off-street parking … (e) private swimming pools and tennis courts, (f) domestic gardens … (i) the keeping of dogs and cats, (j) private garages . . . ."

The town of Yorktown zoning ordinance provides a nonexclusive, illustrative list of accessory uses. A municipality that uses this method should be sure to include a statement that the list is nonexclusive. Section 90-91 of the Yorktown Code governs research and laboratory and offices. It provides: "In any research laboratory and office district, no building or premises shall be used . . . except for one (1) or more of the following uses . . . C. Accessory uses to the laboratory, business and professional offices, including garages for storage and maintenance of company motor vehicles, storage of gasoline and lubricating oils therefor, parking facilities, maintenance and utility shops . . . central heating and power plants . . . water drainage, sewerage, fire protection . . . educational facilities . . . cafeterias, recreation facilities, banks."

LIMITATIONS AND CONCERNS

Permitting accessory uses creates needed flexibility but can also create problems both for landowners and the municipality.

A municipality should be careful when enforcing accessory use regulations against educational institutions and religious organizations. Accessory uses connected to these principal uses are presumed to serve the public interest if they are incidental to the principal use.

A use that violates the zoning law cannot be made legal on the ground that it is merely accessory. This is because, by definition, accessory uses are customarily found in connection with the permitted principal use. Thus it follows that a proper accessory use should not violate the zoning law. Accessory uses must meet all requirements in the zoning law, including setback and lot area requirements. The owner's right to an accessory use cannot be extended into an adjoining district. A use variance may not be granted for an accessory use because the required showing of unnecessary hardship cannot be made for accessory uses.

Although originally intended to permit landowners to use their property fully, the accessory use device is sometimes used to expand greatly the intensity of use, to establish a unique or novel use, to expand a nonconforming use, or to change the use of a property when a variance cannot be obtained. A municipality drafting and enforcing an accessory use provision should be careful to avoid these concerns.

If a municipality denies a property owner's request to construct an accessory use, it should insure that the proposed use was denied is because it was not customary, incidental, or subordinate. A denial based upon the fact that the use is not subordinate should clearly demonstrate that there will be a different impact on the neighborhood from routine accessory uses.

STATUTES

New York State Village Law §7-700, Town Law §261, and General City Law §20 (24) authorize local governments to adopt zoning laws to promote the health, safety, morals, and the general welfare of the community.

The Municipal Home Rule Law authorizes a municipality to adopt and amend local laws relating to powers granted to it in the Statute of Local Governments, which empowers municipalities to adopt zoning regulations.

CASE DIGEST

The zoning board of appeals in *Presnell v. Leslie*, 3 N.Y.2d 384, 144 N.E.2d 381, 165 N.Y.S.2d 488 (1957), denied an application to construct a 44-foot tower as an antenna for a radio station in the petitioner's residence as an accessory use. The court sustained the denial, noting that "it cannot be said as a matter of law that the erection of a 44-foot steel tower in a compact residential area of a suburban community . . . is a customarily incidental use of residential property, or one which might commonly be expected by neighboring property owners." *See also Gray v. Ward*, 74 Misc. 2d 50, 343 N.Y.S.2d 749 (Sup. Ct. Nassau County 1973), *aff'd*, 44 A.D.2d 597, 354 N.Y.S.2d 591 (2d Dep't 1974) (holding that a helipad was not an accessory use because helicopters are not incidental and not customarily found in a commercial area); *Ames v. Palma*, 52 A.D.2d 1078, 384 N.Y.S.2d 587 (4th Dep't 1976) (concluding that a parking lot was too large to be considered a use naturally and normally incidental to the principal use); *Genesee Farms v. Scopano*, 77 A.D.2d 784, 431 N.Y.S.2d 219 (4th Dep't 1980) (holding that a self-serve gas pump at a dairy store is not "customarily incidental and subordinate" to the principal use).

The town of Lewisboro, in *Collins v. Lonergan*, 198 A.D.2d 349, 603 N.Y.S.2d 330 (2d Dep't 1993), granted the appellants a permit to construct a skateboard ramp upon certain conditions. The zoning board of appeals determined that the ramp qualified as a recreational use of the property which was customarily incidental to the permitted principal use of the residence. The test was "not whether other landowners in the municipality are engaged in similar activities, but whether such accessory use can be deemed to be normally incidental to the residential use." The Appellate Division held that the board's "determination that a skateboard ramp is a permitted accessory use because it is customarily incidental to the primary use, had a rational basis, and was not illegal, or arbitrary and capricious." *See also Dellwood Dairy v. City of New Rochelle*, 7 N.Y.2d 374, 165 N.E.2d 566, 197 N.Y.S.2d 719 (1960) (determining that a coin-operated milk vending machine located in the basement of the apartment building did not adversely affect the "character of the residential neighborhood," and was therefore considered an accessory use); *Exxon Corp. v. Board of Standards and Appeals of the City of New York*, 151 A.D.2d 438, 542 N.Y.S.2d 639 (1st Dep't 1989) (holding that a combination convenience store and gas station was a qualified accessory use because it is "commonly and customarily found in connection with, and incidental to, the principal use of an automotive service station"); *Sievers v. City of New York*, 146 A.D.2d 473, 536 N.Y.S.2d 411 (1st Dep't 1989), *aff'd*, 182 A.D.2d 580, 582 N.Y.S.2d 722 (1st Dep't 1992) (finding that a sign advertising Newport cigarettes "cannot be considered accessory to a gasoline service station under the Zoning Resolution").

"[B]ecause educational institutions presumptively serve a beneficial public purpose, local governments may not unreasonably prohibit accessory uses of school premises." *Lawrence School Corporation v. Lewis*, 174 A.D.2d 42, 578 N.Y.S.2d 627 (2d Dep't 1992). In this case, the school was denied a permit to build two swimming pools on its property because the property would be used as "a summer camp rather than an educational program." The court reversed the denial, noting that "educational institutions, like religious institutions enjoy special treatment with respect to residential zoning ordinances" because they "presumptively serve the public's welfare and morals." Given this presumption, the court held that the board's denial of the permit was arbitrary and capricious.

Religious activities that go beyond prayer and worship have been approved as acceptable accessory uses of religious property. *Greentree at Murray Hill Condominium v. Good Shepherd Episcopal Church*, 146 Misc. 2d 500, 550 N.Y.S.2d 981 (Sup. Ct. NY County 1989). The plaintiffs, who owned condominium units in a building adjacent to a church, sought an injunction to stop the church from operating a homeless shelter. The church argued that it is customary for the church to provide for the poor and homeless. The court listed permissible accessory uses of churches as Sunday schools, men's and women's clubs, youth and community centers, day-care centers, and drug programs. The court held that "it is clear that the Church's temporary homeless shelter sanctuary program is, as a matter of law, a permissible 'accessory use' of the Church."

In *Dyno v. Village of Johnson City*, 261 A.D.2d 783, 690 N.Y.S.2d 325 (3rd Dep't 1999), the court was asked to settle a dispute over the placement of a basketball backboard that violated the village's setback requirement for buildings. The court first held that private nuisance claims arising from the use of the backboard were not available to the neighbors in an Article 78 proceeding. The court further held that the backboard did not violate the setback requirements because the requirements applied only to buildings. The backboard was not considered a building, but was an accessory use defined under the Village of Johnson City Code §274-4(B) as one "customarily incidental and subordinate to the principal use." The court pointed out that there were backboards on many other private properties throughout the village, proving that such use is customary.

REFERENCE

Jeffrey Durocher, *Accessory Uses of Land in New York State, at* http://www.pace.edu/lawschool/landuse/accuse.html (last visited Feb. 2, 2001).

K. PERMITTING ACCESSORY APARTMENTS

DEFINITION

An accessory apartment is a second residential unit contained within an existing single-family home. The accessory apartment is designed as a complete housekeeping unit that can function separately from the primary unit. It usually has separate access, kitchen, bedroom, and sanitary facilities. Generally, accessory units are contained within the residential portion of existing single-family homes and are subordinate to the primary unit in size, location, and appearance. Some communities allow owners to apply to create an accessory residential unit in a garage, carriage house, or servants' quarters.

Illustrative Definitions of Accessory Apartments from Zoning Ordinances:

"A dwelling unit which is incidental and subordinate to a permitted principal one-family residence use and located on the same lot therewith, where either unit is occupied by the owner of the premises."

"A dwelling unit in a permitted one-family residence which is subordinate to the principal one-family dwelling unit in terms of size, location and appearance and provides complete housekeeping facilities for one (1) family, including independent cooking, bathroom and sleeping facilities, with physically separate access from any other dwelling unit."

PURPOSE

The policy objectives served by such an ordinance include creating a source of affordable housing for the individuals occupying the units, creating a source of revenue for existing homeowners, providing a more secure living environment for homeowners who are senior citizens, and increasing property tax revenues from existing single-family neighborhoods.

Illustrative Purpose Clauses from Accessory Apartment Ordinances:

"It is the purpose of allowing accessory apartments to provide the opportunity for the development of small, rental housing units designed, in particular, to meet the special housing needs of single persons and couples of low and moderate income, both young and old, and of relatives of families presently living in the town."

"It is the purpose of this ordinance to allow the more efficient use of the Town's existing stock of dwellings, to provide economic support for present resident families of limited income, and to protect and preserve property values."

WHEN

The impetus for the adoption of accessory apartment ordinances has often been the need to control the proliferation of illegal conversions of single-family homes to two-family or even multi-family residences. Illegal conversions are often fueled by a decline in household size in the community, the lack of affordable housing, and the aging of those who own single-family homes.

Illegal conversions of single-family homes can cause multiple problems. They complicate the sale and insurance of the affected property, raise concerns about the safety of the accommodations provided, and cause overcrowding and traffic congestion. Moreover, the property improvements involved are usually not reflected in increased tax assessments. The legalization of such conversions and the adoption of standards for the creation of accessory apartments allow the community to provide a safe and affordable housing choice needed in the market and to add the increased value to the tax assessment rolls.

AUTHORITY

Municipalities base their adoption of accessory apartments either on their delegated zoning authority or on their municipal home rule powers.

Village Law §7-700, Town Law §261, and General City Law §20(24) authorize local governments to adopt zoning laws to promote the health, safety, morals, and general welfare of the community. The authority to regulate building height, bulk, and lot coverage and to separate uses into districts is expressly delegated to local governments. Under Village Law §7-704, Town Law §263, and General City Law §20(24), zoning regulations are to be adopted with reasonable consideration of the character of the zoning district and with a view to conserving the value of buildings and encouraging the most appropriate use of land.

The Municipal Home Rule Law authorizes a city, town, or village to adopt and amend local laws relating to powers granted to it in the Statute of Local Governments. The Statute of Local Governments empowers municipalities to adopt zoning regulations. The Municipal Home Rule Law gives cities, towns, and villages authority to adopt local laws regarding their property, affairs, and government and to protect and enhance their physical and visual environment.

IMPLEMENTATION

Generally, accessory apartment laws authorize property owners to apply for a special permit to create an accessory apartment. They authorize the zoning board of appeals or planning board to approve applications submitted by eligible property owners who demonstrate that they can meet the standards and specifications contained in the accessory apartment ordinance. This allows the local board to review the eligibility of the applicants and occupants and to conduct a review of the design of the unit and of plans for the use of the site. The board is authorized to impose reasonable conditions on each approval to insure that the impact of the apartment on the neighborhood is kept to a minimum. In drafting an accessory apartment law, a community has several choices. The choices it makes are most often guided by the objective, or combination of objectives, that the community is interested in achieving. The principal options are listed below along with other relevant information.

Eligible Applicants: Where the objective of the community is to enable existing owner-occupants to remain in their homes, the community may limit eligibility to homeowners who occupy their single-family homes. This owner-occupant requirement may be justified by a finding that such owners are more likely to maintain their homes and supervise their tenants than absentee owners. Where the objective of the community is to enable senior citizens to continue living in the homes that they own, the eligibility requirements may be narrowed to owner-occupants who are 55, 59, 62, or 65 years of age or older. Where the objectives are to provide affordable housing and to increase tax revenues, communities may make all owners of single-family homes eligible to apply for a special permit for accessory apartments.

Eligible Occupants: The law can stipulate that the occupants of the accessory unit be related to the owner of the home by blood, marriage, or adoption. In general, consanguinity and affinity restrictions of this type should be avoided because of the difficulty of justifying their tendency to discriminate against unrelated persons. If the goal of such restrictions is to limit the number of accessory units, that objective may be achieved by limiting the number of such units allowed in the community or in each neighborhood. Where the goal is to create additional housing opportunities for families with children, the law may authorize the homeowner to occupy the accessory unit and lease the rest of the house to a tenant family.

Size of the Accessory Unit: The size of the accessory apartment may be limited to insure that it is subordinate to the primary unit and that the impact of the occupancy of accessory units on the surrounding neighborhood is minimized. The size of the unit can be limited in one of three ways:

1. Limiting the number of square feet of space in the unit;
2. Limiting the unit to a percentage of the square footage in the single-family home; or
3. A combination of the two.

Laws include maximum sizes ranging from 450 to 800 square feet. Typical percentage limitations are 25% to 40%. Where a home contains 2,000 square feet, a 25% requirement would allow the development of a 500-square-foot accessory apartment. Some laws state that the accessory unit cannot be larger than 600 square feet but cannot exceed 25% of the total floor area.

Location of the Accessory Unit: In urban and small-lot settings, accessory apartment laws often provide that the accessory unit must be created within the existing single-family structure. In larger lot zones, such as one- and two-acre districts and lower density communities, some ordinances provide that accessory units may be located in additions to existing homes or in existing outbuildings, such as garages, barns, and carriage houses that conform to the dimensional requirements of the zoning law.

Design of the Accessory Unit: The impact of accessory units on the neighborhood can be minimized through design standards. The simplest provision states that any exterior alteration to accommodate an accessory unit must conform to the single-family character of the neighborhood. This can be accomplished by requiring the applicant to submit façade renderings as part of the special permit application. The law can also stipulate that any exterior stairways to the accessory unit not be constructed on the side of the residence that fronts on any street.

Duration of Permit: The law can specify that the permit terminates upon, and must be renewed at, certain intervals, such as every one, two, three, or five years and when title to the property is transferred by sale, foreclosure, or the owner's death. A reinspection and recertification of the accessory apartment may be required before a renewal permit may be issued.

Saturation Provisions: To limit the number of accessory apartments and the overall impacts of this additional occupancy on the community, the legislature may consider a variety of provisions. The law can:

- Simply limit the number of applications that may be approved during any period or the total number of accessory units that may exist in the community at any time.

- Limit the number of units that are allowed in any given neighborhood, based on specific findings regarding the need to limit the impacts associated with the development of accessory apartments.

- Limit eligibility to single-family homes existing on the date the law is adopted to prevent developers from adding a second unit in newly constructed homes.

- Restrict eligibility to lots that exceed minimum lot area requirements in the zoning district by 25% to 50%

- Limit to one the number of bedrooms that can be constructed in an accessory apartment.

The law itself can be subject to sunset provisions that limit its existence to a few years' duration and require a thorough revaluation prior to being extended by the legislature for another similar period.

OTHER OPTIONS

Parking: Some communities find that their existing parking requirements for single-family homes are adequate, while others require the provision of one or two parking spaces for the primary unit and an additional space for the accessory unit, or a certain number of parking spaces according to the number of bedrooms created. Stringent parking requirements are another means of limiting the number of accessory units that can be constructed. Another approach to parking is to require that the applicant show that adequate off-street parking will be provided and to leave the matter to the discretion of the approving body. The law may specify that parking should be located, if possible, in appropriate areas, such as side yards, and be screened, where necessary.

Water and Sewage: Applicants can be required to show that adequate water and sewage disposal facilities are available to serve the needs of the occupants of the accessory unit. An overall assessment of the capacity of community water and sewer systems may provide a guide as to whether any accessory apartments should be developed, and, if so, where and to what extent saturation requirements should be adopted. Applications for development on lots served by wells and septic systems should be accompanied by a showing that the groundwater and soils are adequate to handle the increased quantity resulting from the occupancy of the accessory unit and that no pollution of the water supply will occur. Health department approval may also be required where there are concerns.

Additional Health and Safety Provisions: Communities may want to include provisions that require the installation of electric smoke detectors, fire ratings for stairways and hallways between units, and adequate emergency exits.

LIMITATIONS AND CONCERNS

Any provisions contained in an accessory apartment law must be reasonable and supported by specific findings of the local legislature. With regard to any provision of such a law, one must be able to identify the legitimate governmental objective that it achieves and ascertain that the means chosen to achieve that objective are reasonable. Conditions that are designed to lessen the impact of the accessory apartment on traffic, parking, neighborhood aesthetics and property values, and community infrastructure and services are generally valid. Owner-occupancy requirements for eligibility and age restrictions on eligible owners and occupants have also been upheld.

CASE DIGEST

In *Sherman v. Frazier*, 84 A.D.2d 401, 446 N.Y.S.2d 372 (2d Dep't 1982), a homeowner applied for a special use permit to convert his home from one-family to two-family under the town's accessory apartment ordinance. The review board granted this application and the neighbors challenged the approval. They contended that the delegation of the authority to review the applications for accessory apartments to "the Two-Family Review Board instead of to the Zoning Board of Appeals" was a violation of the Town Law, which stipulates that a local government shall establish a zoning board of appeals. The court held that there was nothing in the Town Law that would "preclude a Town Board from delegating special permit powers to a body it creates by ordinance." It concluded, therefore, that the town could exercise its power to supersede the requirements of state law. The court remanded the case to the review board to make findings of fact that were missing on the record under review. The accessory apartment law adopted by the town allows special permits "for premises that 1) are owner occupied; 2) contain a minimum of 500 square feet of habitable space per unit; 3) have two on-site parking spaces; and 4) have a single front entrance with any additional entrances at the side or rear." The characteristics that the board uses to determine if a permit will be issued include: "the character of the area, property values, traffic congestion, safety and welfare, overcrowding of land, unreasonable proximity to churches, schools, theaters, recreational areas and places of public assembly and reasonable development of established uses in the area."

The town of Brookhaven, in *Kasper v. Town of Brookhaven*, 142 A.D.2d 213, 535 N.Y.S.2d 621 (2d Dep't 1988), adopted an accessory apartment law that required applicants for accessory apartments to be owners and residents of the single-family residence in which the apartment is to be created. The plaintiff wanted to establish an accessory apartment but did not reside in the home and was denied a permit. He challenged the owner-occupancy requirement, arguing that it violated constitutional guarantees of equal protection and due process. The court held that the defendant did not exceed its legislative authority by enacting the accessory apartment ordinance. The town had the authority to limit eligibility to owners who occupy their homes. The purpose of the ordinance was to protect "those homeowners who may be of modest means and who will be better able to retain ownership of their residences and to maintain them in aesthetically acceptable conditions by leasing the available, unused living space in their homes."

REFERENCE

A Guide to Accessory Apartment Regulations: The Westchester Experience, Westchester County Department of Planning (March, 1989).

L. HOME OCCUPATIONS

DEFINITION

Historically, single-family homes have been used by their occupants for a variety of occupational uses such as beauty parlors, dressmaking, laundries, and day care. Zoning limits single-family homes to residential uses and to those uses that are customarily associated with residential use and are incidental and subordinate to that residential use. Does this mean that a single-family homeowner can conduct a particular business in a particular neighborhood as an accessory use, or is the occupational use prohibited?

In some communities, this question is answered on a case-by-case basis without benefit of any special regulations. The zoning authorities examine the proposed occupational use and determine whether it is customary, incidental, and subordinate to the residential use. Other municipalities define "home occupations" more specifically in their zoning laws, requiring homeowners to conform their occupational uses to those definitions. Some adopt a list of permitted occupational uses of homes, while others prohibit a specific list of occupations.

PURPOSE

Permitting occupations to be conducted in single-family zoned neighborhoods honors expectations of homeowners that such uses have been permitted historically and are within the bundle of rights purchased with the single-family home. Zoning restrictions limiting the occupational use of homes recognize that residential districts must be protected from home occupations that are out of character with the neighborhood and are not uses that homeowners expect to be affected by when they purchase a home in a single-family area. One of the original purposes of zoning is to separate uses that are inconsistent with one another into distinct zoning districts.

The village of Brewster defines a permitted "home occupation" as:

An occupation, profession, activity or use that is clearly a customary, incidental and secondary use of a residential dwelling unit and which does not alter the exterior of the property or affect the residential character of the neighborhood.

WHEN

Specific definitions of the types of home occupations that are permitted in a community are added in response to complaints from neighbors that occupational uses are altering the residential character of their neighborhoods. The local legislature may add a definition of home occupation when the local zoning enforcement officer encounters difficulties in determining if occupational uses are customary, incidental, or subordinate. In some parts of the state, economic conditions have given rise to a rapid expansion of home occupations, particularly professional offices, leading to the addition of regulatory provisions to the local law.

AUTHORITY

The authority of local governments to balance the right of homeowners to make incidental occupational use of their homes with the expectations of neighbors to enjoy living in a residential environment is part of a municipality's delegated authority to adopt zoning provisions. State statutes make it clear that municipalities may adopt zoning laws for the purpose of encouraging the most appropriate use of land throughout the community.

IMPLEMENTATION

Municipalities may use a variety of techniques to regulate home occupations and professional offices:

They may let their definition of accessory uses govern the matter, leaving it to the zoning enforcement official to determine, in a given instance, whether a proposed occupational use is customary, incidental, and subordinate to the principal permitted use of a parcel as a single-family home.

Local legislatures may adopt a general definition of a home occupation to provide some guidance to enforcement officials to aid their determinations in these matters.

They may supplement their general definition of home occupation with a list of permitted occupations, a list of prohibited occupations, and a definition of permitted professional offices.

The home occupations permitted under these supplemental definitions may be permitted as-of-right or allowed only upon the issuance of a special use permit by a designated reviewing board.

Local legislatures may include specific standards that certain occupational uses must meet, such as limiting the percentage of floor area that may be used, prohibiting the carrying or selling of merchandise, prohibiting any alteration of the exterior of the building, limiting businesses to those conducted by occupants of the residence, and limiting the number of associates, partners, and employees.

ILLUSTRATIONS

A typical accessory use definition reads: "A building or use clearly incidental or subordinate to, and customarily in connection with, the principal building or use on the same lot."

A broad definition of a home occupation is found in the village of Brewster zoning law: "An occupation, profession, activity or use that is clearly a customary, incidental and secondary use of a residential dwelling unit and which does not alter the exterior of the property or affect the residential character of the neighborhood." Art. IV, §170-3B.

A more specific definition of a home occupation, containing a list of excluded uses, was adopted by the village of Hastings-on-Hudson: "Any use customarily conducted entirely within a dwelling . . . which use is clearly incidental and secondary to the use of the dwelling for dwelling purposes . . . The conducting of a clinic, hospital, barber shop, beauty parlor, tea room, tourist home, animal hospital, or raising of animals, or any similar use shall not be deemed to be a home occupation." Art. I, §132.

The town of Carmel's zoning law contains a definition of home occupation listing both included and excluded occupations: "An activity conducted within a dwelling and carried on by an inhabitant thereof, which use is secondary to the use of the dwelling for dwelling purposes as customarily found in the home, and does not change the character thereof. Individuals engaged in music instruction, including voice and instrument lessons, were limited to a single pupil at a time, and the occupations of dressmaker, milliner or seamstress are deemed to be "home occupations." Dance instruction, band instrument instruction in groups, tea rooms, beauty parlors, barber shops, real estate offices or insurance offices shall not be deemed "home occupations." Art. III, §63-7B.

A specific definition of a "home professional office" permitted as a home occupation is contained in the zoning ordinance of the town of Harrison: "The office or studio of a resident physician, surgeon, dentist, or other person licensed by the State of New York to practice a healing art, lawyer, architect, artist, engineer, real estate broker or salesman, insurance broker or agent or teacher." Art. I, §235-4.

LIMITATIONS AND CONCERNS

Whether a particular home occupation is permitted depends entirely on the exact language of the zoning provisions adopted by the local legislature in each community. Most judicial decisions on the subject involve an attempt on the court's part to determine what types of home occupations are permitted by the specific language of the zoning law and whether that language was interpreted reasonably by the local official or board with delegated authority to make decisions on home occupations. Since zoning regulations are deemed by the courts to be in derogation of common law property rights, they are subject to strict interpretation. Local officers and review boards that decide to deny a property owner the right to an occupational use should base their decisions on specific language in the zoning law and on facts that justify those decisions.

Where zoning provisions are very general, great emphasis must be placed on fact finding that justifies a denial in the interest of maintaining the residential character of a neighborhood or that shows an occupational use is not customary, incidental, or subordinate to the principal use of the parcel as a single-family home. For example, the denial of a special use application for an emergency dental office on the grounds that it was not a "true home occupation" was reversed where the ordinance allowed home occupations in general, but did not regulate professional offices as such. In the absence of any fact findings that justified the denial of the proposed occupational use, the board's action was deemed arbitrary and unreasonable.

Where the language of the zoning law is specific, courts typically uphold denials of occupational uses that do not fall within the definitions and standards of the provisions. They have held, for example, that it is reasonable for a law to limit home office use to professionals who fall within a list of licensed or established professions set forth in the law.

STATUTES

New York State Town Law §263, Village Law §7-704, and General City Law §20(25) contain the purposes to be achieved through the adoption of zoning provisions. These include encouraging the most appropriate use of land throughout the municipality.

CASE DIGEST

In *Osborn v. Planning Board of the Town of Colonie*, 146 A.D.2d 838, 536 N.Y.S.2d 244 (3d Dep't 1989), the court concluded that it is not unusual for a home occupation to be operated on a full-time basis as an accessory use of a residence. The town's zoning law permits "any profession or customary home occupation, provided that the same is carried on in the dwelling occupied as the private family residence." The court concluded that the plaintiff's proposal to create a full-time office in her home did not change the character of the residential use of the property and was therefore allowed as an accessory use.

In *Baker v. Polisinelli*, 177 A.D.2d 844, 576 N.Y.S.2d 460 (3d Dep't 1991), the court concluded that the intensity of use involved in a home occupation may determine whether the use is customary and permissible. The court sustained the zoning board's determination that a dance studio for 160 students, operating five days a week, was not a customary use within that district. The court held that "it was [not] irrational for the Board to find that the petitioner's operation was more extensive than what was intended to be permitted under the ordinance as a home occupation."

In *Winnie v. O'Brien*, 171 A.D.2d 997, 567 N.Y.S.2d 943 (3d Dep't 1991), a permit to install a dental chair and equipment in a residence, for occasional emergency treatment, was denied by the zoning board of appeals. The court reversed this determination, holding that the activity the plaintiff proposed fell within the broad definition of home occupation under the town's ordinance and therefore should be granted a special use permit. The fact that any type of professional office was not included in the town's definition of a home occupation could not be used to deny the application where the ordinance's definition of permitted home occupations was broad and general.

In *Criscione v. City of Albany Board of Zoning Appeals*, 185 A.D.2d 420, 585 N.Y.S.2d 821

(3d Dep't 1992), the court determined that the plaintiff's law firm was not a "home occupation" as defined in the zoning law. The court concluded that "[g]iven the fact that the petitioner does not reside in the dwelling unit where his law office is occupied, the law office is clearly not incidental and secondary to the unit's use for dwelling or residential purposes."

In *Simon v. Board of Appeals of Zoning of the City of New Rochelle*, 208 A.D.2d 931, 618 N.Y.S.2d 729 (2d Dep't 1994), the court concluded that "management consulting" did not fall within the permitted home occupations listed in the zoning law. The court held that the plaintiff failed to demonstrate that she was a "professional person" under the zoning law and held that her occupation was not within the "customary home occupations, such as dressmaking or millinery" as set forth in the zoning law.

REFERENCE

Irina Olevsky, *The Regulation of Home Occupations Under Zoning Ordinances, at* http//www.pace.edu/lawschool/landuse/homeoccu.html (last visited Feb. 2, 2001).

M. ENFORCEMENT OF LAND USE REGULATIONS

DEFINITION

Local governments provide for the enforcement of their land use regulations in a variety of ways. Most building construction, building uses, and change in land uses land must comply with the local zoning law and applicable land use regulations. Building permits may not be issued until the responsible local official certifies that the developer has obtained all required land use approvals. Local review bodies, such as the planning board, are authorized to impose conditions on subdivision, site plan, and other required approvals in order to protect the environment, mitigate impacts of development on adjacent properties, and for other public purposes.

Local governments assign responsibility for enforcing land use regulations to local municipal officials or offices, such as a building inspector or the department of buildings. When a local official enforces land use regulations, as opposed to the building code, the official is technically acting as the zoning enforcement officer. In smaller communities, the building inspector may be assigned the duties of the zoning enforcement officer. Larger municipalities generally have officers to enforce land use regulations who are different from the officers who enforce the building code.

The zoning enforcement officer is charged with the duty to inspect construction sites, while construction of approved development is proceeding, and to respond to any complaints that private property is being used in violation of zoning and land use requirements. The officer makes a site inspection and, when a violation is found, notifies the property owner to discontinue a practice that violates local law or to correct the condition that constitutes a violation. When a property owner refuses to comply, the zoning enforcement officer refers the matter to the municipal attorney who may ask a court to issue an injunction requiring compliance or to impose a fine or period of imprisonment as a penalty for the violation. In any court proceeding on a land use matter, the zoning enforcement officer's records and testimony are critical proofs that must be submitted by the municipal attorney to secure a judicial remedy.

PURPOSE

Land use regulations and standards are adopted by local legislatures to protect the public health, safety, welfare, and morals. Where buildings are constructed, or land is used, in violation of those standards, the public interest is compromised. To protect fully the public well-being, local land use regulations must be enforced evenly, fairly, and routinely. The purpose of a competent system of enforcement is to insure that violators are disciplined so that others understand that land use standards are serious and must be met. Where such a system is in place, the public health, safety, and welfare are protected.

WHEN

Any local government that adopts zoning and other land use regulations must provide for the enforcement of their provisions. The need for efficient enforcement is particularly acute where development pressures are great, population pressures are mounting, natural resources are threatened, or the environmental impacts of development are great. Quite often, the enforcement of land use regulations can be of great importance to adjacent property occupants, who can be severely affected by the failure of a neighbor to comply. The same can be said of businesses in the same district who share a mutual interest in the enforcement of land use regulations, such as sign ordinances, sidewalk use, or the elimination of nonconforming uses.

AUTHORITY

The New York State Legislature has delegated the right to enact zoning and other land use laws to the municipalities within its jurisdiction. This authority is a delegation of the state's police power, which allows governments to protect the welfare of the public. With the power to zone and regulate land uses comes the necessity of enforcing those provisions. Municipalities are allowed to take civil action against zoning ordinance offenders. Section 135 of the Town Law, §7-714 of the Village Law, and §20(22) of the General City Law enable the municipalities to enforce zoning ordinances through the use of fines, imprisonment, or both when necessary. They also provide for injunctive relief when appropriate. Town Law §268 and Village Law §20-2006 specify appropriate fines for various zoning violations and provide the respective municipalities with the authority to commence further legal action when necessary.

Criminal actions as a remedy for zoning violations are authorized by the legislature through New York State's criminal procedure law in general, though not specifically in its zoning enabling act. Section 268 of the Town Law explicitly authorizes towns to use criminal sanctions for town code violations. Since the emphasis in zoning enforcement is upon prevention rather than punishment, most municipalities choose to pursue civil rather than criminal remedies. Still, when necessary, use of criminal sanctions to enforce zoning and subdivision restrictions is an appropriate means of enforcement.

IMPLEMENTATION

Generally, a zoning enforcement officer is responsible for administering zoning and land use laws as well as maintaining records of all administrative actions and zoning decisions. The officer is also responsible for enforcing those decisions. Enforcement generally begins when a zoning violation is identified, either by the officer personally or through a citizen's complaint to the municipality. Once an alleged violation is discovered, the zoning enforcement officer is authorized to inspect the premises. Town Law §138 specifically authorizes this inspection; General City Law §20(23) and Village Law §7-714 authorize the officer to take any appropriate action to enforce the zoning law. Towns and villages must specifically empower the officer to enter onto private property, and such entry may take place with the consent of the landowner, after the acquisition of a valid search warrant or in an emergency situation.

If the zoning enforcement officer does confirm a violation, the violator first receives informal notification through a "Notice of Apparent Violation," a document that both indicates that the officer has acted properly and offers the offender an immediate opportunity to correct the violation. If the violation is not corrected, the zoning enforcement officer issues a more formal "Notice of Violation" while at the same time taking affirmative steps to enjoin the violation. The officer may move to revoke the building permit or the certificate of occupancy if construction is already underway. If construction has been completed and the structure is occupied, the officer may refuse to issue new permits with respect to that property until all zoning problems have been corrected. Some communities follow the practice of revoking the building's certificate of occupancy until violations are cured. Alternatively, the municipality may issue a cease and desist order to compel a property owner to correct an existing violation.

Property owners charged with violations have several actions available to them if they do not choose to correct the alleged violation. First, an owner may make an appeal to the local zoning board of appeals. That body has the right to affirm, reverse, or modify the zoning enforcement officer's decision. Second, the owner may apply to the zoning board of appeals for a zoning interpretation or an area or use variance. Lacking interpretive power and the authority to vary the literal language of the zoning code, the zoning enforcement officer is not allowed to make such decisions. Third, the property owner may petition the municipality's legislative body for a zoning amendment. Should the property owner fail in any of the attempts to overturn the zoning enforcement officer's citation and still refuse to correct the violation, the officer and the municipal attorney have the option of bringing a civil, criminal, or injunctive action, or any combination of the three.

Civil proceedings are the most common method of enforcing zoning and land use regulations. State enabling legislation explicitly authorizes municipalities to use injunctive actions to enforce their regulations. A municipality may seek injunctive relief without having to prove public injury caused by the violation; however, it must demonstrate that it is likely to prevail on the merits of its case. By contrast, civil penalties may be assessed only if they are specifically provided for in the zoning code.

New York statutes also give citizens in towns the right to initiate zoning enforcement actions themselves. Private property owners suffering special damages, distinct from those suffered by the community at large, from another property owner's violation of the local zoning code may bring an action for injunctive relief. Town Law §268 allows three aggrieved taxpayers to bring suit to enjoin a violation 10 days after they have notified the municipality and the local government has taken no action. Generally, however, civil actions are brought by the municipality, not by individual citizens.

Criminal actions take another path. The responsibility for bringing a criminal action in zoning enforcement cases is generally delegated by the district attorney to the municipal attorney. An Information and Supporting Deposition formally initiates the criminal complaint by detailing the time and location of the violation, the pertinent facts of the alleged violation, and an affirmation of the zoning enforcement officer as to the document's veracity. Having received this document, the court then summons the violator to appear in court. To expedite this process, some municipalities authorize the zoning enforcement officer to issue appearance tickets to the violator before filing the information and complaint letter with the local justice. If the alleged violator fails to appear, an arrest warrant may be issued by the court. Formal judicial proceedings then progress as they would in any criminal action. Should the violator be found guilty, various criminal fines may be levied, depending on the severity and duration of the violation.

ILLUSTRATIONS

Although municipalities generally have the right to enforce their zoning ordinances, they must do so according to the objective criteria laid out by their ordinances. For example, in 1996, the town of Orangetown sought to terminate the development of an industrial park that had been granted a permit. As work on the large commercial project had progressed, community opposition to the building became organized and political. The resistance was so serious that the town supervisor eventually directed the building inspector to revoke the developer's permit. Although the town presented a series of defenses for its actions, the New York Court of Appeals held that the revocation of the permit was only an effort to satisfy political concerns and therefore not legal. Such an action, taken without a reasonable basis in fact, is arbitrary and capricious and violates the developer's due process rights. The developer in this case was awarded five million dollars, in addition to legal fees and expenses, for the illegal revocation of his building permit. *Town of Orangetown v. Magee*, 88 N.Y.2d 41 (1996). However, should a municipality issue a building permit erroneously, as was the case in *McGannon v. Board of Trustees for Village of Pomona*, 239 A.D.2d 392, 657 N.Y.S.2d 745 (1997), it is not prevented from withdrawing the permit and requiring full compliance with zoning code provisions.

Municipalities must take special care to secure all necessary search warrants when deciding to inspect property for violations of zoning ordinances. Village Law §7-714, Town Law §138, and General City Law §20(23) authorize zoning enforcement officers to inspect for potential zoning violations, but all inspections must meet constitutional safeguards against un-warranted searches and seizures. When a zoning enforcement official for the village of Laurel Hollow suspected a zoning violation, he should have first acquired a search warrant and then entered the premises in questions. *Incorporated Village of Laurel Hollow v. Laverne, Inc.*, 24 A.D.2d 615, 262 N.Y.S.2d 622 (1965). Because he failed to do so, and the zoning violations had not created an emergency situation, any evidence found during the illegal inspection was inadmissible in court, although it did document actual violations. The case against the violator was therefore dismissed.

LIMITATIONS AND CONCERNS

The responsibility for enforcing zoning laws is made difficult by the constitutional limits placed on enforcement procedures. The most prevalent constitutional issues involve the U.S. Constitution's Fourth Amendment's protection against unwarranted searches and seizures. Although search warrants to inspect for potential violations are not always necessary, they are generally required. Courts have not been precise as to when warrants are required for the preparation of a civil rather than a criminal action. However, since a violator's disregard of an injunctive order can lead to criminal contempt proceedings, officers are well advised to acquire search warrants whenever possible. Still, in circumstances where the property owner has applied for a building permit and received one conditionally, the zoning enforcement officer need not apply for a search warrant in order to confirm compliance with the conditions stated in the permit. The landowner, by accepting the conditional approval, is deemed to have consented to the inspections. However, even if an inspection is allowed, the officer's findings must conform to examining the premises for zoning violations as specified. Zoning enforcement officers must be aware that the First Amendment's protection of free speech is a limit placed on zoning regulations and therefore their enforcement. The regulation of signs for property properly zoned for adult use must be within First Amendment bounds.

Municipalities and individuals seeking to enforce or dispute zoning provisions must be aware that specific statutes of limitations apply to many actions. An Article 78 proceeding to review a zoning board of appeals' decision must be commenced within 30 days of the filing of that decision. However, if the petitioner requests a legislative review of the zoning decision, the statute of limitations is extended to four months from the time of the decision. The 30-day limitation also does not apply in the case of a declaratory judgment that challenges the validity of a zoning regulation since such actions are not subject to Article 78 review. They are instead subject to the six-year statute of limitations imposed by New York State's CPLR §213(1). Actions seeking an injunction are also subject to a six-year statute of limitations. Finally, a landowner bringing an action seeking to have the court declare a zoning regulation unconstitutional is not subject to any statute of limitations whatsoever. Criminal actions are also subject to a statute of limitations. Section 30.10(2)(d) of the Criminal Procedure Law sets a one-year statute of limitations for a petty offense or violation. Section 30.10(2)(c) requires that the prosecution of a misdemeanor be commenced within two years of the offense in question.

A property owner may assert a number of defenses against the accusation that he has violated a zoning ordinance. A violator may claim selective enforcement. If a property owner is able to demonstrate that a municipality has consciously and intentionally discriminated against him, the case will be dismissed. An aggrieved property owner may also claim that he has acquired vested rights in the property in question. If the landowner has already completed substantial work while relying upon a valid permit, he may be entitled to proceed with the project even if local zoning regulations have been amended prior to the completion of the project. Finally, a landowner may prevail against a municipality if an ordinance is vague, rendering it unenforceable. However, the courts have interpreted "vague" only to mean language that persons of ordinary intelligence would not understand. Zoning ordinances do not have to specifically define every term within them.

STATUTES

New York State Village Law §7-700, Town Law §261, and General City Law §20 all grant the respective municipalities the authority to enact zoning ordinances and to provide for their enforcement.

Village Law §7-714, Town Law §135, and General City Law §20(22) enable municipalities to enforce zoning ordinances through fines, imprisonment, or injunctive relief.

Village Law §20-2006 and Town Law §268 establish the amounts of fines that may be assessed for various zoning violations.

Village Law §7-712-b, Town Law §267-b, and General City Law §81-b each delegate power to local boards of zoning appeals for the enforcement of local zoning regulations.

Village Law §7-714, Town Law §138, and General City Law §20(23) authorize zoning enforcement officers to inspect premises for potential violations.

CASE DIGEST

In enforcing zoning regulations, a zoning enforcement officer must present substantial evidence to support the claim of a violation. *Kinderhook Equities, Inc. v. Simonsmeier*, 267 A.D.2d 547, 699 N.Y.S.2d 199 (3d Dept. 1999). In 1991, the village of Kinderhook granted a developer a building permit for a commercial structure that was then occupied by CRI. When the village's zoning enforcement officer inspected the premises, he issued a certificate of occupancy allowing the first and second floors to be used as office space. However, at the time of his inspections, it was clear that the basement area was also being used for offices and that the inspector had every reason to know of this. Five years later, the same inspector issued an order to remedy a violation of changed use without a permit, claiming that the use of the basement as office space violated the original certificate of occupancy. The Appellate Division held that the basement's use as office space could not be considered a changed circumstance subsequent to the original issuing of the permit without substantial evidence to support this contention. Since there was abundant evidence that the basement had long been used as office space, there could be no finding of changed circumstances in violation of an issued permit.

Whereas criminal penalties for violations of zoning ordinances are always an option for municipalities under the general provisions of New York State's criminal procedure law, civil penalties are only available if specifically provided for in the zoning ordinances. In *Town of Solon v. Clark*, 97 A.D.2d 602, 468 N.Y.S.2d 201 (1983), the Appellate Division held that Town Law §268 authorized only criminal fines and imprisonment and civil proceedings to prevent further violations, but not civil penalties. The court did hold that a municipality could properly enact provisions in its zoning ordinance authorizing the imposition of monetary penalties in addition to other remedies already available to it. However, unless the town passed an ordinance specifying such a penalty, it could not impose one.

In deciding *Marcus v. Town of Mamaroneck*, 283 N.Y. 325, 28 N.E.2d 856 (1940), the New York Court of Appeals held that citizens as well as municipal officials are permitted to bring an action against a private property owner whose zoning violations impose undue hardship on them. However, in order to prevail in such a suit, the plaintiffs must demonstrate special circumstances that separate their claims from that of the community at large. In this case, a group of private citizens challenged the expansion of a private beach club's facilities, which were located in a district zoned for residential use after the original construction of the club. Since the expenditure involved in the alterations significantly exceeded the amount allowed by one of the town's zoning ordinances, the owners of neighboring properties brought suit. The plaintiffs succeeded on several grounds. First, they were able to demonstrate that they had standing to sue. Their adjoining properties were specially harmed by the expanding beach club facilities. Second, although the beach club owner raised a defense of laches, the Court of Appeals found that the plaintiffs had not delayed their suit in a way that would have encouraged the club owners to continue their building project.

Municipalities must take special care not to violate the equal protection clause of the Fourteenth Amendment in their enforcement of zoning regulations. In *Cedarwood Land Planning v. Town of Schodak*, 954 F. Supp. 513 (N.D.N.Y. 1997), the court held that the Fourteenth Amendment protects landowners' rights to due process and equal protection of the law if they are able to establish a valid property interest at the time of the alleged deprivation of those rights. In this case, a subdivision developer's claims of unconstitutional denial of rights of due process and equal protection were not supported by evidence demonstrating selective enforcement of zoning regulations based on race, religion, or any other protected class.

REFERENCES

Robert M. Anderson, American Law of Zoning, §19.03, 19.05, 31.01, 31.02 (3d Ed. 1986).

Deborah Goldberger, *Zoning Enforcement Law in New York State, at* http://www.pace.edu/lawschool/landuse/enforce/html (last visited Feb. 2, 2001).

New York State Department of State, Zoning Enforcement, June, 1998.

New York State Bar Association, Basics of Administration and Enforcement of Land Use Controls (Spring, 1999).

Photo courtesy of Jay Pendergrass

Chapter 5
ENVIRONMENTAL REVIEW

The New York State Environmental Quality Review Act (SEQRA) applies to all agencies and instrumentalities of the state, which include local agencies such as legislatures, planning boards, and zoning boards of appeals. Local agency decisions on applications for site plan or subdivision approval or the issuance of variances and special permits must be preceded by an assessment of the environmental impact of the proposed project. The adoption of comprehensive plans and zoning ordinances, and their amendment, must also be accompanied by a review of their impact on the environment. SEQRA also applies to proposed plans of local governments to build capital projects or to provide funding for projects of any kind. The essence of SEQRA is the requirement that the impact of all such local actions on the environment be considered in the planning process and that local agencies act effectively to avoid any possible adverse environmental impacts. Most states do not have comparable laws; however, "little NEPA" laws are in place in several jurisdictions, and bills to establish wide-ranging environmental impact reviews have been introduced in a number of states.

States That Have Adopted Generally Applicable Environmental Impact Assessment Requirements:

- California*
- Connecticut
- Hawaii*
- Indiana
- Maryland
- Massachusetts*
- Minnesota*
- Montana
- New York*
- North Carolina
- Puerto Rico
- South Dakota
- Virginia
- Washington*
- Wisconsin

*Local governments in these six states are authorized or required to conduct environmental reviews

Where it has been determined that a proposed project may have a significant adverse impact on the environment, the applicant must submit an environmental impact statement as part of an application for a local land use approval. The local reviewing agency must then take a number of prescribed steps to review the statement under SEQRA's environmental standards. Until the draft environmental impact statement (DEIS) submitted by the applicant is deemed to be complete by the local review agency, the underlying land use application is not complete and the time periods applying to that approval process do not begin to run.

SEQRA gives local land use agencies independent authority to impose conditions on land use approvals to mitigate the potential negative impacts of proposed projects on the environment. The environment is defined very broadly. SEQRA extends local agency authority to impose conditions on land use approvals for the protection of any aspect of the environment. With regard both to these substantive conditions and to the procedures that proposals must follow, SEQRA amounts to a regulatory overlay on the process of reviewing and approving all other applications for land use approvals.

SEQRA amounts to a regulatory overlay on the process of reviewing and approving all other applications for land use approvals.

SEQRA also gives local governments additional authority to study and adopt plans for areas of environmental significance. In certain instances, localities may designate critical environmental areas, conduct cumulative impact analyses, and perform generic environmental impact statements. These environmental review tools expand the techniques available to villages, towns, and cities to anticipate and review future land use impacts in a more comprehensive manner.

A. ENVIRONMENTAL REVIEW TECHNIQUES

DEFINITION

SEQRA requires local agencies, when reviewing development projects, adopting plans, and establishing programs, to prepare an environmental impact statement for actions that may have a significant adverse impact on the environment. SEQRA requires such agencies to use all practicable means to minimize or avoid adverse environmental effects.

In SEQRA terms, the local land use review and approval agency is called the "lead agency" and a development approval, the adoption of a plan, or the enactment of land use regulations, is called an "action." When any local agency is about to undertake an action that is not exempt from review, it must consider the environmental impacts of that action and go through the procedures required by SEQRA.

The case law in New York holds that SEQRA imposes "action forcing" and "substantive" requirements on local land use decisionmakers. Local agencies are required to "use all practicable means to realize" SEQRA's policies and goals and to "act and choose alternatives which, consistent with social, economic and other essential considerations, to the maximum extent practicable, minimize or avoid adverse environmental effects."

PURPOSE

The statutory purposes of the State Environmental Quality Review Act include:

- ♦ To declare a state policy that will encourage productive and enjoyable harmony between man and his environment.
- ♦ To promote efforts that will prevent or eliminate damage to the environment and enhance human and community resources.
- ♦ To enrich the understanding of the ecological systems and the natural, human, and community resources important to the people of the state.

SEQRA declares that all state, county, and local agencies "are stewards of the air, water, land, and living resources" and "have an obligation to protect the environment for the use and enjoyment of this and all future generations." It contains both procedural and substantive requirements for these agencies to follow when discharging this function.

WHEN

SEQRA applies to local land use actions such as approving applications for rezoning, subdivision and site plan review, the issuance of special permits and variances, and the adoption of comprehensive plans and capital projects. Regulations issued under SEQRA list certain actions as Type II actions where no environmental review is required. The Type II list includes, for example, area variances for one-, two-, and three-family houses, the construction of noncommercial structures of less than 4,000 square feet, and the construction or expansion of one-, two-, and three-family homes on improved lots. Ministerial actions, such as the issuance of building permits where no discretion is exercised, are not subject to SEQRA.

With respect to other actions, the local lead agency must take a hard look at the potential environmental impacts and where there may be a significant adverse impact on the environment must prepare an environmental impact statement (EIS) on the proposal or project before granting, conditioning, or denying it. The regulations list certain actions as Type I which are deemed "more likely to require the preparation of an Environmental Impact Statement" than Unlisted Actions, which are simply not listed in the regulations as either Type I or Type II actions. Some examples of Type I actions are the adoption of a comprehensive plan or zoning law, changes in allowable uses in any zoning district affecting 25 acres or more, and the construction of 50 or more homes not to be connected to public water and sewerage systems.

AUTHORITY

The extensive provisions setting forth the procedures and requirements for the environmental review of local land use actions are found in the Environmental Conservation Law, Article 8, commonly referred to as the State Environmental Quality Review Act. Further details regarding these requirements are set forth in the regulations of the Commissioner of the State Department of Environmental Conservation.

IMPLEMENTATION

The following is a checklist of the matters that a local lead agency must consider in complying with the provisions of SEQRA:

- ♦ Is the land use project or proposal an "action" as defined by the law and the regulations?
- ♦ Which agency is principally responsible for approving the action? That agency is the lead agency and has the responsibilities listed here.
- ♦ What type of an action is it? The choices are Type I, Type II, or Unlisted.
- ♦ If the action is a Type II action, no further environmental review is required.
- ♦ If the action is a Type I or Unlisted Action, an assessment of the environmental impact of the action must be conducted.
- ♦ Applicants for Type I and Unlisted Actions must submit an environmental assessment form listing the potential environmental impacts of their projects or proposals.

- If the project or proposal will not have a significant adverse environmental impact, then a negative declaration is issued and no further environmental review need be conducted. The lead agency, however, must take a "hard look" at the possible environmental impacts and set forth in writing a "reasoned elaboration" for its negative declaration.

- If the project or proposal may have a significant adverse environmental impact, then a positive declaration must be issued and a draft environmental impact statement prepared.

- The lead agency may require the preparation of a scope of the contents of the environmental impact statement and may provide for public participation in its preparation.

- The environmental impact statement must consider and examine all relevant environmental impacts, identify possible conditions that can be imposed on the action to mitigate any adverse environmental impacts found and discuss any alternatives to the proposed action that would mitigate or avoid those impacts.

- The applicant must submit a draft environmental impact statement and, when deemed complete, it is filed along with a notice of completion that the lead agency issues.

- If a public hearing on the draft environmental impact statement is to be held, a notice of hearing must be filed and published 14 days prior to the hearing, which must be held within 60 days from the filing of the notice of completion. The regulations give the public a right to comment on the draft and the lead agency a right to respond.

- The lead agency must complete a final environmental impact statement within 45 days of the close of the public hearing, if one is held, or within 60 days of the filing of the draft environmental impact statement, whichever occurs last.

- The lead agency's findings statement, which is based on the final environmental impact statement, is adopted. This statement considers the impacts contained in the environmental impact statement and balances them with social, economic, and other essential considerations, selects mitigation conditions or alternatives to minimize any negative impacts, and determines whether the action, so mitigated, should be approved.

- A positive findings statement demonstrates that the project should be approved and that the action will avoid or minimize environmental impacts to the maximum extent possible. A negative findings statement documents the reasons why the action cannot be approved.

LIMITATIONS AND CONCERNS

The degree of detail required in an environmental review varies with the circumstances and nature of the proposal. Upon review, the court will look to see if the determination of the lead agency was reasonable. With regard to issuing a negative declaration and adopting a findings statement on a final environmental impact statement (FEIS), the court looks to see whether the agency took a hard look at the environmental concerns and made a reasoned elaboration of the basis for its determinations. These standards are difficult to quantify, but they mean, at the least, that local land use agencies must take their environmental review responsibilities seriously and justify their conclusions.

Since the penalty for failure to comply with SEQRA is the invalidation of the action taken by a local land use agency, the procedural requirements of the statute are often followed literally. SEQRA, however, also requires lead agencies to use all practicable means to protect the environment. They must balance environmental ends with economic and social considerations, and the court will not second guess mitigation measures or alternatives chosen, so long as the agency made a reasonable attempt to identify and mitigate the adverse environmental consequences of the action.

STATUTES AND REGULATIONS

The extensive New York State provisions setting forth the procedures and requirements for the environmental review of local land use actions are found in the Environmental Conservation Law (ECL), Article 8, commonly referred to as the State Environmental Quality Review Act, or SEQRA.

The regulations of the Commissioner of the Department of Environmental Conservation are found in Title 6 NYCRR Part 617.

"Agencies" whose "actions" are regulated by Article 8 of the ECL and who are required by it to perform environmental impact assessments of those actions are defined to include "local" agencies. ECL §8-0105(3).

CASE DIGEST

In *Sun Beach Real Estate Development Corp. v. Anderson*, 98 A.D.2d 367, 469 N.Y.S.2d 964 (2d Dep't 1983), *aff'd*, 62 N.Y.2d 965, 468 N.E.2d 296, 479 N.Y.S.2d 341 (1984), the court held that an application for preliminary approval of a subdivision plat was not complete until the procedural steps required under the State Environmental Quality Review Act (SEQRA) have been taken. The town was caught between the conflicting time periods governing the review of a subdivision application and those set forth in SEQRA, which can take considerably more time to complete. The court accorded priority to environmental review deadlines over subdivision approval deadlines "because the legislative declaration of purpose in the statute makes it obvious that protection of 'the environment for the use and enjoyment of this and all future generations' far overshadows the rights of developers to obtain prompt action on their proposals." By implication, this holding applies to the resolution of clashes between the time periods prescribed for other local land use actions and those required by SEQRA.

The Court of Appeals held that the town director of engineering, building, and housing was entitled to require a draft environmental impact statement as a precondition to the issuance of a building permit in *Pius v. Bletsch*, 70 N.Y.2d 920, 519 N.E.2d 306, 524 N.Y.S.2d 395 (1987). The court noted that the issuance of a building permit is not always ministerial. It stated, "In light of the director's specifically delegated site plan approval powers coupled with the authority to make certain case-by-case judgments on site plan design and construction materials issues, the Town of Huntington's subdivision regulations and site improvement specifications vest discretion of a kind which qualifies as an unexempted 'action' in connection with the issuance of a building permit."

Many local land use actions, such as site plan and subdivision approval, require compliance with the provisions of SEQRA. In *Save the Pine Bush, Inc. v. City of Albany*, 141 A.D.2d 949, 530 N.Y.S.2d 295 (3d Dep't 1988), the court annulled a planning board's approval of two site plans because the board failed to take a hard look at whether the projects would have a significant adverse environmental effect. The court found that the planning board's final generic environmental impact statement was inadequate, since it failed to address the issue of the minimum acreage required for the survival of the Pine Bush ecology. Thus, the board's approvals were arbitrary and capricious.

In *Morse v. Town of Gardiner Planning Board*, 164 A.D.2d 336, 563 N.Y.S.2d 922 (3d Dep't 1990), the plaintiffs argued that the lead agency's failure to be sufficiently particular in its environmental review violated SEQRA's requirement that it take a hard look at the environmental consequences of its action, which in this case was a decision to grant final subdivision approval. The court rejected the petitioners' claim that the discussion of alternatives in the environmental impact statement (EIS) was insufficient. Rather, the court found that the EIS complied with SEQRA guidelines, since "a discussion of all reasonable alternatives to the proposed action [is required] and not an exhaustive analysis of every conceivable alternative." The court further noted that the petitioner's disagreement with the board's chosen alternative does not prove that the board did not take the requisite "hard look." Finally, in response to the argument that the board failed to consider the project's impact on the town and county's solid waste management systems, the court held that "[a]n EIS need only address significant environmental impacts which can be reasonably anticipated."

The Court of Appeals has confirmed that scenic concerns may be addressed by local agencies in conducting environmental reviews of project proposals under SEQRA. In *WEOK Broadcasting Corp. v. Planning Board of Town of Lloyd*, 79 N.Y.2d 373, 592 N.E.2d 778, 583 N.Y.S.2d 170 (1992), the owner's application for site plan approval of a radio transmission tower was denied based on aesthetic factors. The planning board determined, after SEQRA review, that the petitioner had failed to adequately minimize or avoid adverse environmental effects to the maximum extent practicable. The court held that "aesthetic considerations are a proper area of concern in [SEQRA] balancing analysis inasmuch as the legislature has declared that the 'maintenance of a quality environment . . . that at all times is healthful and pleasing to the senses' is a matter of Statewide concern." The court noted, however, that aesthetic impact considerations, unsupported by substantial evidence, might not serve as a basis for denying an application regarding a proposed project.

The degree of detail required in a SEQRA review depends on the circumstances involved. In *Valley Realty Devlopment Co., Inc. v. Town of Tully*, 187 A.D.2d 963, 590 N.Y.S.2d 375 (4th Dep't

1992), a town law that rezoned land in a mining district to residential use was upheld as being in compliance with SEQRA. The court stated that "in reviewing an agency's issuance of a negative declaration, a court's inquiry is limited to whether the relevant areas of concern were identified, whether a hard look was given to those areas, and whether a reasoned elaboration was given for the negative declaration." The court noted that "in making such a review, the agency's obligations under SEQRA 'must be viewed in light of a rule of reason'" and that "the degree of detail required will vary with the circumstances and the nature of the zoning proposal." Since there was no evidence that the elimination of the mining district would harm, rather than benefit, the environment, the court sustained the degree of environmental review afforded the zoning change.

In *Save the Pine Bush, Inc. v. Planning Board of Town of Guilderland*, 217 A.D.2d 767, 629 N.Y.S.2d 124 (3d Dep't 1995), the applicant sought approval to subdivide a parcel of land into 65 lots. The planning board did not require the applicant to submit a full EIS even though it had determined that the proposed subdivision constituted a Type I action. A citizens' group challenged the planning board's decision to approve the preliminary plat, claiming that SEQRA had been violated by the planning board's determination that no EIS was required for the project. The court held that "although an EIS is presumptively required for a Type I action, 'an EIS is not a per se requirement of all Type I actions.'" The court concluded that the planning board's review of the reports regarding the potential impacts was sufficient for it to issue a declaration that no adverse environmental impacts were raised by the subdivision application.

The court held that the town board violated SEQRA when it issued a negative declaration instead of proceeding with the preparation of a DEIS in *Eggert v. Town Board of Town of Westfield*, 217 A.D.2d 975, 630 N.Y.S.2d 179 (4th Dep't 1995). The town board classified a zoning amendment as a Type I action, but determined that the amendment "itself" would not have a significant effect on the environment since the rezoning required property owners to apply for special permits before developing under the amendments. The town board acknowledged that there could be adverse environmental impacts if special use permits were granted, but reasoned that such impacts could be adequately considered when applications for special use permits were submitted. The court rejected this argument, stating that to comply with SEQRA, the town board "must consider the environmental concerns that are reasonably likely to result from, or are dependent on, the amendments." The court concluded that the town board "was required to address the potential environmental effects of the amendments, at least on a conceptual basis."

"SEQRA's fundamental policy is to inject environmental considerations directly into governmental decision-making. *" Merson v. McNally*, 90 N.Y.2d 742, 665 N.Y.S.2d 605 (1997). The court allowed the applicant to revise a Type I proposal through open meetings with the planning board, involved agencies, and community members in order to alleviate potentially large environmental impacts of the proposed project. The challengers argued that the planning board's negative declaration was the functional equivalent of a conditioned negative declaration, which is not permitted in a Type I action. However, the court held that "the modifications were not conditions unilaterally imposed by the lead agency, but essentially were adjustments incorporated by the project sponsor to mitigate the concerns identified by the public and the reviewing agencies." The court found that, since the modifications were examined openly and with input from all parties involved, the process was consistent with SEQRA's purposes and the issuance of the negative declaration was proper.

In *West Village Committee, Inc. v. Zagata*, 242 A.D.2d 91, 669 N.Y.S.2d 674 (3d Dep't 1998), the court upheld regulations adopted by the Department of Environmental Conservation (DEC) that were intended to clarify and streamline the EIS process. The regulations provided that if lead agencies or project sponsors initiate scoping prior to the preparation of a draft EIS, then "the project sponsor must submit a draft scope containing certain required information and that, within 60 days of its submission, the lead agency must provide a final written scope to the project sponsor." In addition, the regulations provided that all relevant issues should be raised before the final written scope is issued and that if issues are raised after that time, such information may be incorporated into the draft EIS at the project sponsor's discretion. The petitioners claimed that the DEC's amendments weakened SEQRA since they permitted a project sponsor to determine the content of a draft EIS. The court held that the lead agency has the ultimate authority to determine whether a draft EIS is adequate with respect to its scope and content. It stated that the challenged regulations did not lack a rational basis, "particularly since scoping is a voluntary procedure in which DEC is encouraging participation by project sponsors."

In *Chinese Staff and Workers Association v. City of New York*, 68 N.Y.2d 359, 502 N.E.2d 176, 509 N.Y.S.2d 499 (1986), community residents challenged the approval of a special use permit for the construction of a high-rise luxury condominium. The petitioners argued that the city's environmental review was arbitrary and capricious because it failed to consider the possible displacement of low-income residents. The dispute in this case concerned the breadth of the term "environment." The court held that it is clear from the express terms of the statute and the regulations that the term environment is broadly defined and expressly includes considerations such as "existing patterns of population concentration, distribution, or growth, and existing community or neighborhood characteristics." Therefore, the court stated that the impact that a proposed project may have on population patterns or community character is a relevant concern in an environmental analysis. SEQRA requires the lead agency to consider more than impacts on the physical environment in determining whether to require the preparation of an EIS.

In *H.O.M.E.S v. New York State Urban Development Corp.*, 69 A.D.2d 222, 418 N.Y.S.2d 827 (4th Dep't 1979), the court articulated the standard required to determine whether an EIS must be prepared. The Urban Development Corporation (UDC) determined that the construction and use of a new domed stadium would not significantly affect the environment and issued a negative declaration for the project. The court stated that, for a SEQRA determination to be supported, the record must show that the lead agency identified relevant areas of environmental concern, took a hard look at them, and made a reasoned elaboration of the basis for its determination. The court went on to state that there is a relatively low threshold for requiring the preparation of an EIS, and that one should be required where the action may fairly be said to have a potentially significant adverse impact. The court found that the UDC's issuance of a negative declaration was arbitrary and capricious because it failed to take a hard look at problems and adverse potential effects of the project, such as traffic congestion, parking, and air pollution.

In *Jackson v. New York State Urban Development Corporation*, 67 N.Y.2d 400, 494 N.E.2d 429, 503 N.Y.S.2d 298 (1986), petitioners challenged the approval of a Times Square development project. The petitioners claimed that the FEIS was deficient in that it failed to give sufficient attention to the impact of the project on the elderly citizens of the area or adopt effective measures to mitigate the anticipated displacement of the elderly. The court held that SEQRA does not require an agency to impose every conceivable mitigation measure, or any particular one. Rather, SEQRA only requires mitigation to the maximum extent practicable consistent with social, economic, and other essential considerations. The court stated that when reviewing a SEQRA determination, courts will first review the agency procedures to determine whether they comply with SEQRA's requirements. The court will then review the record to determine whether the agency took a hard look and made a reasoned elaboration of the basis for its decision. It is not the court's job to weigh the desirability of an action or to second-guess an agency's decision.

In *Ferrari v. Town of Penfield Board*, 181 A.D.2d 149, 585 N.Y.S.2d 925 (4th Dep't 1992), the petitioners claimed that a negative declaration that was issued for the development of an office complex should be annulled because, among other things, the respondent failed to notify an involved agency. The court stated that "where an application or an EAF for a Type I action indicates that more than one state or local agency may be an involved agency, the agency which must approve the action is required, as soon as possible, to mail the EAF and application to all involved agencies and to advise those agencies that a lead agency must be agreed upon within thirty days." The respondent failed to notify the DEC during the lead agency designation process or before a negative declaration was issued. Consequently, the respondent was not properly designated the lead agency, and its negative declaration was invalid. The court held that the failure to notify an involved agency in this case was not inconsequential. The participation of the DEC, the state agency with the greatest expertise regarding the issues in question, would have been meaningful. The court remitted the manner to the respondent for de novo commencement of lead agency designation.

In *Sun Company, Inc. v. City of Syracuse Industrial Development Agency*, 209 A.D.2d 34, 625 N.Y.S.2d 371 (4th Dep't 1995), the petitioners claimed that the Syracuse Industrial Development Agency (SIDA) improperly segmented the SEQRA review of a proposed lakefront retail shopping center project from other planned development on the Syracuse lakefront. At the time, the master plan contemplated the creation of a lakefront park, a light industrial trade zone, cluster multi-family housing, a marina, an office park, and mixed commercial and retail uses. SIDA limited its DEIS and other aspects of the environmental review to the retail development project. The court held that this site specific review improperly segmented the impacts of one phase from the other phases included in the long range plan as if they were independent, unrelated activities. The court stated that the plan for redeveloping the entire lakefront area was reasonably related to the retail development project. The court noted that a lead agency may choose, in its discretion, not to examine the cumulative impacts of separate applications within the same geographic area, but the decisive factor is the existence of a larger plan for development. SIDA failed to take into account the existence of a "larger plan" for development. SEQRA defines segmentation as "the division of the environmental review of an action such that various activities or stages are addressed under this part as though they were independent, unrelated activities, needing individual determinations of significance." The court concluded that SIDA improperly segmented the environmental review of the project in light of its cumulative environmental effects. "A lead agency must consider the cumulative effect of other simultaneous or subsequent actions that are included in any long-range plan of which the action under consideration is a part." Furthermore, the court determined that if the circumstances warrant a segmented review it must "clearly state in its determination of significance and any subsequent EIS the supporting reasons and must demonstrate that such review is clearly no less protective of the environment."

In *Glen Head–Glenwood Landing Civic Council, Inc. v. Town of Oyster Bay*, 88 A.D.2d 484, 453 N.Y.S.2d 732 (2d Dep't 1982), the court held that the town board's compliance with SEQRA was fatally defective because the board failed to issue sufficiently explicit SEQRA findings regarding the environmental impacts of the rezoning of certain parcels. The court stated that when an agency decides to carry out or approve an action which has been the subject of an EIS, it shall make an explicit finding that the requirements of SEQRA have been met and that, consistent with social, economic, and other considerations, to the maximum extent practicable, adverse environmental effects revealed in the EIS process will be minimized or avoided. The DEC regulations add that, "No agency, whether lead agency or not, shall make a final decision to approve an action until it has prepared a written statement of facts and conclusions relied on in the EIS, that supports its decision and indicates the social, economic, and other factors and standards which formed the basis for its decision." In this case the town's commission issued findings that simply stated that the applicant complied with SEQRA and that the proposal would avoid adverse environmental effects to the maximum extent practicable. These findings were intended to constitute the findings that a lead agency is required to make in accordance with SEQRA. The town board claimed that it was unnecessary for them to issue any further findings. The court disagreed. It stated that when a lead agency fails to make the required findings, neither the public nor a review court knows what factors were considered and they cannot be satisfied that a hard look was taken.

In *Aldrich v. Pattison*, 486 N.Y.S.2d 23, 107 A.D.2d 258 (2d Dep't 1985), the adequacy of an EIS was challenged for not complying with the procedural and substantive requirements of SEQRA. The court stated that literal compliance with the environmental review procedures set forth in SEQRA and the regulations is required. However, a rule of reason should govern the substantive requirements of SEQRA. Not every conceivable environmental impact, mitigation measure, or alternative must be addressed in order for a FEIS to meet the requirements of SEQRA. The degree of detail that is necessary will vary with the circumstances and nature of the proposed action. Furthermore, the court stated that the hard look standard of review does not authorize the court to conduct a detailed de novo analysis of every environmental impact of a proposed project that was included in or omitted from an FEIS. The court said that a flexible standard of review, allowing for wide latitude of discretion by the administrative agency, is appropriate for the assessment of the environmental consequences of a proposed project. The agency's determination will be annulled only if it was arbitrary, capricious, or unsupported by substantial evidence. This is because the technical and scientific issues addressed are more properly entrusted to an agency than to a court of general jurisdiction.

Several recent New York cases have confirmed that positive declarations that require the preparation of a DEIS not "final agency actions" subject to Article 78 review. In *Rochester Telephone Mobile Communications v. Ober*, 251 A.D.2d 1053, 674 N.Y.S.2d 189 (4th Dep't 1998), the court held that Town of Ogden planning board's issuance of a positive declaration was not a final agency action nor did the declaration cause actual concrete injury to the petitioner. The court reasoned that the positive declaration was a "preliminary step in the [environmental review] process" and merely required the petitioner to prepare a DEIS "analyzing the potential environmental impacts of [the] project." Only when the DEIS has been prepared and reviewed, and certain other steps have been taken, will the planning board approve or disapprove the project. Only then will the issuance of the positive declaration be ripe for review. In *Matter of PVS Chemicals, Inc. v. New York State Department of Environmental Conservation*, 256 A.D.2d 1241, 682 N.Y.S.2d 787 (4th Dep't 1998), the court again held that a positive declaration issued by the DEC, which required the preparation of a DEIS, was a preliminary step in the decision-making process, and was therefore not ripe for review. The issuance of the positive declaration does not constitute a final action because future proceedings in the review process could "render the disputed issue moot or academic." Finally, in *Matter of Sour Mountain Reality, Inc. v. New York State Department of Environmental Conservation*, 260 A.D.2d 920, 688 N.Y.S.2d 842 (3d Dep't 1999), the court held that a developer cannot bring an Article 78 proceeding to challenge the DEC's issuance of a positive declaration and request for a supplemental environmental impact statement (SEIS). The court repeated past warnings that "[a]llowing piecemeal review of each determination . . . would subject [the SEQRA process] to . . . significant delays in what is already a detailed and lengthy process." Hence, a positive declaration by definition can not be considered ripe for adjudication. The court also held that the DEC did not exceed its broad authority to regulate the EIS procedure by requesting the SEIS.

B. ADVANCED ENVIRONMENTAL REVIEW TECHNIQUES

The State Environmental Quality Review Act (SEQRA) requires local agencies, when reviewing development projects, adopting plans, and establishing programs, to prepare an environmental impact statement when those actions may have a significant adverse impact on the environment. SEQRA requires such agencies to use all practicable means to minimize or avoid adverse environmental effects.

In SEQRA terms, the local review and approval agency is called the "lead agency" and a development approval, like the adoption of a plan or a capital project, is called an "action." When any local agency is about to undertake any action, it must consider the environmental impacts of that action and go through the procedures required by SEQRA.

SEQRA applies to local land use actions such as applications for rezoning, subdivision and site plan review, the issuance of special permits and variances, and the adoption of comprehensive plans and capital projects. Case law in New York holds that SEQRA imposes "action forcing" and "substantive" requirements on local land use decision-makers.

This section explores a number of advanced environmental review techniques that supplement and render more effective and extensive the basic requirements of SEQRA, including the authority of local agencies to (1) impose conditions on projects to mitigate their adverse environmental impacts, (2) require an analysis of the cumulative environmental impacts of two or more projects or actions, (3) prepare generic environmental impact statements, and (4) designate critical environmental areas.

MITIGATION CONDITIONS

DEFINITION

Under SEQRA's regulations, "mitigation" is defined as a way to minimize adverse environmental impacts. Lead agencies are required to mitigate any adverse environmental impacts to the maximum extent possible.

PURPOSE

The purpose of imposing mitigation conditions on local land use approvals is to minimize or avoid significant environmental impacts.

WHEN

Mitigation measures are used when any local action, including the approval of development applications, may have a significant adverse impact on the environment. There are two instances in which local agencies may impose such conditions. The first is when an applicant for local approval has been required to prepare a full environmental impact statement, which is required to contain a description of mitigation measures, and the agency has determined that one or more such measures must be adopted to minimize the impacts of the project. The second occurs when an unlisted action is found to have potential adverse impacts and one or more mitigation measures can be identified that will minimize those impacts. In this instance, the lead agency can issue a conditional negative declaration, noting the impact and imposing the mitigation condition, and thereby avoid the cost and time required in the preparation of a full environmental impact statement.

AUTHORITY

Lead agencies are not only authorized but required to use all practicable means, including the imposition of mitigation measures, in order to minimize or avoid adverse environmental impacts.

IMPLEMENTATION

The mitigation of adverse environmental impacts is accomplished by incorporating mitigation measures as conditions placed on the land use action, such as the approval of a subdivision, site plan, special permit, or rezoning application. These mitigation measures are both included in the agency's findings statement, adopted after its review of a final environmental impact statement, and imposed as conditions on the approval of the underlying application being reviewed.

ILLUSTRATION

In the Town of Gardiner, the planning board conditioned its approval of a large residential subdivision on several environmental mitigation measures. These included large lot sizes, restrictions on house colors, required landscaping, the imposition of a conservation easement, and the filing of covenants and restrictions on the land records. These conditions were supported by evidence contained in the environmental impact statement and were used to mitigate environmental impacts identified in the environmental review process.

LIMITATIONS AND CONCERNS

Mitigation conditions must be reasonably related, and roughly proportionate, to the specific impacts of a particular development. If they are not, they risk reversal in the courts. The negative impacts mitigated must be found in the evidence on the record or in the environmental impact statement; conditions may not be imposed solely in response to generalized community objections to the development.

SEQRA does not require a lead agency to impose any particular mitigation condition on a development so long as the lead agency reasonably identifies potential adverse impacts and properly provides for their mitigation in some reasonable fashion.

A lead agency should not issue a conditional negative declaration unless it can certify that a particular mitigation condition will be used and will be effective, or when the environmental impacts of a project are pervasive.

STATUTES AND REGULATIONS

Section 8-0109 of SEQRA (Environmental Conservation Law, Article 8) requires lead agencies to minimize or avoid adverse environmental effects, but only when consistent with social, economic, and other essential considerations; §617.2(x) of the SEQRA regulations (Title 6 NYCRR, Part 617) defines the term "mitigation;" §617.9(b)(5)(iv) requires a draft environmental impact statement to include a description of mitigation conditions.

CUMULATIVE IMPACT ANALYSIS

DEFINITION

A lead agency that is determining the potential environmental impacts of a development proposal may consider that project's impacts in conjunction with those of other projects under review or planned for the area. Although the impacts of any one project or action, when considered alone, may not have a significant adverse environmental impact, the cumulative impacts of these projects or actions may have such an impact.

Where, for example, three or four relatively small residential subdivision applications are pending in an area, the planning board may look at their impacts cumulatively and determine that they may have a significant negative impact whereas, considered alone, they would not. When cumulative impacts are potentially significant, each applicant may be require to complete a full environmental impact statement (EIS) and address the cumulative effects of all the related projects. For projects to be related, they must share common impacts on the environment in a defined area.

Normally, a cumulative impact analysis (CIA) may be conducted in the discretion of the lead agency; occasionally, a lead agency may be required to perform such an analysis. To date, this requirement has been limited to projects or actions that are included in, or undertaken as a result of, an adopted long-range plan of the municipality.

PURPOSE

Under SEQRA, lead agencies usually evaluate the environmental impacts of individual development projects, one at a time. The CIA allows, and occasionally requires, lead agencies to assess the cumulative impacts of projects.

WHEN

Normally, lead agencies consider requiring CIAs when two or more development projects involving moderate or seemingly insignificant impacts are proposed or advanced at about the same time. In that particular environmental context, it may be that a significant environmental impact will result from the projects, when they are considered together. When a municipality has adopted a long-range plan for an area and two or more projects relate to, result from, or depend on that plan, a CIA may be required of these projects.

AUTHORITY

Lead agencies must determine whether a proposed project may have a significant adverse environmental impact and, if it does, require the preparation of a full EIS. In making this determination, the regulations stipulate that the lead agency should consider whether related projects to be approved by the agency, if considered together, would have a significant impact on the environment.

IMPLEMENTATION

As related projects are reviewed by a lead agency under SEQRA, the agency must determine whether each project may have a significant adverse impact on the environment. In making this determination, the agency may consider the impacts of the related projects, as defined here, in a cumulative fashion. If those cumulative impacts constitute a potentially significant impact on the environment, each project may be required to complete a full EIS.

ILLUSTRATION

The city of Albany created a special site plan review process for a commercial district located in the 550 acres of undeveloped land in the Pine Bush area. That process and district were considered a long-range plan for the area. The failure of the city to conduct a CIA on related projects in that area was held to violate SEQRA's cumulative impact analysis requirements. The long-range plan was designed to balance conflicting environmental goals within an area that was ecologically unique. Here the court held that the potential cumulative impacts of other proposed or pending projects had to be considered under SEQRA before a particular application for rezoning could be approved.

LIMITATIONS AND CONCERNS

Where CIAs are conducted in the absence of a comprehensive plan, or a generic environmental impact statement (GEIS), for an area, it may be difficult for applicants to evaluate fully the cumulative impacts of their projects on the area and the area's ability to absorb these impacts over time. A CIA, if required, can be costly, involving redundant and difficult data gathering, analysis, and evaluation. Few "related projects" will be at the same stage in the approval process or be completely designed at the same time. Development projects are subject to change, and data about them are not always easy for others to acquire. If related projects are to be subjected to cumulative analysis by each applicant, the lead agency should be careful to coordinate the environmental studies to avoid excessive costs and delays.

STATUTES AND REGULATIONS

Section 8-0109 of SEQRA requires an EIS to describe the proposed project in its environmental setting and to set forth its short-term and long-term effects. Section 617.7(c)(1)(xii) of the regulations states that, in applying the criteria for determining the environmental significance of a project, the lead agency may consider whether two or more related actions, none of which has a significant impact, would have such an impact when considered cumulatively. Section 617.7(2) states that a lead agency, in determining the significance of a project, must consider reasonably related cumulative impacts, including other simultaneous or subsequent actions included in any long-range plan, likely to be undertaken as a result thereof, or dependent thereon. Section 617.9(b)(5)(iii)(a) states that, where applicable and significant, the draft environmental impact statement must identify and discuss reasonably related cumulative impacts.

GENERIC ENVIRONMENTAL IMPACT STATEMENTS

DEFINITION

A generic environmental impact statement (GEIS) is broader and more general than a site specific environmental impact statement. It is used to identify environmental conditions and to develop standards and review thresholds to insure that future development is compatible with, or protective of, those conditions.

PURPOSE

The preparation of a GEIS may allow for a more efficient and cost-effective review of the environmental consequences of future development projects. The GEIS allows the agency to identify potential problems in advance and to use that information to develop an appropriate way of dealing with those problems. A GEIS can be used to help local officials pay for comprehensive planning in environmentally sensitive and developing areas. The regulations make it clear that a portion of the cost of preparing a GEIS can be charged to the developers of later projects as development applications are submitted. This can be highly cost-effective. The GEIS presents a one-time opportunity to study the environmental needs of an area and to save future applicants the cost of duplicating those studies. Instead, they need only study the unique impacts of their projects or matters that were not fully considered in the GEIS.

WHEN

A local agency can prepare a GEIS in a number of situations: (1) when faced with the prospect of several development proposals in one area; (2) when faced by a large-scale project with several phases and multiple impacts; or (3) when preparing a long-range plan or a program involving a sequence of future actions for an area.

The GEIS is a useful vehicle for conducting comprehensive environmental and development planning for a geographic area that a municipality wishes to protect or an area that it wishes to develop or redevelop carefully. It is also useful when a municipality is preparing its own plan for an area, such as a conservation overlay zone, or is adopting or amending the comprehensive plan with respect to a particular area.

Since subsequent projects that conform to the performance standards and review thresholds contained in a GEIS may be exempt from environmental review or subjected only to limited supplemental environmental impact assessments, the GEIS can be used to streamline the review process of individual development projects. In environmentally sensitive areas, the GEIS can be used to define the type and intensity of development that is suitable for the area and to develop strong mitigation measures that individual projects must adopt to insure compliance with its environmental standards.

AUTHORITY

The SEQRA regulations define a GEIS, detail when it can be used, and explain its possible effects.

IMPLEMENTATION

A GEIS and its findings should set forth specific conditions or criteria under which future actions will be undertaken or approved, including requirements for any subsequent SEQRA compliance. This may include thresholds and criteria for conducting supplemental environmental impact statements on individual projects and their impact on specific topics not fully addressed or analyzed in the GEIS.

In some cases, a GEIS may be general, based on conceptual information, identifying important resources, and discussing the general constraints on and consequences of future options. It may present and analyze, in general terms, a few hypothetical scenarios that could or are likely to occur. In other cases, for the GEIS to truly guide future actions, it may contain detailed data on existing conditions, forecast anticipated development projects and their impacts, project the improvements needed to serve that development and their costs, and establish specific mitigation measures or development thresholds that need to be employed to absorb or limit the impacts of that development. The final GEIS must be formally adopted by the lead agency and filed in accordance with the requirements of the SEQRA regulations.

Illustration

In the town of Colonie, a GEIS was performed on a developing area that contained sensitive environmental resources. It provided for the cumulative environmental analysis of several pending projects and evaluated the potential of the remaining undeveloped land to absorb the impacts of reasonably projected growth. The GEIS included a development mitigation cost schedule for determining and assigning the costs of needed improvements, on an equitable basis, to current and future projects proposed within the area. Under this schedule, developers who received approval from the town for their projects are required to pay established fees to the town which reflect their proportionate share of the costs of water, solid waste, transportation, recreational, and other improvements needed by their developments.

Limitations and Concerns

A GEIS need not contain an exhaustive analysis of every possible environmental impact of future actions in the study area, nor must it contain all the raw data supporting its analysis, as long as there is analysis sufficient to allow reasoned consideration and evaluation of the issues raised. This requires careful consideration, before a GEIS is done, of how large an area to study, how long a period to consider, and what data to gather and analyze. A GEIS may, to a degree, make up for any shortcomings of its data and analysis by requiring later site specific project applicants to conduct supplemental impact studies on specific issues. Even these additional studies may not compensate for an incomplete GEIS where, for example, it fails to take a hard look at the minimum acreage and conditions needed to preserve an ecosystem, water body, or species at risk in a study area.

Regulations

Title 6 NYCRR Part 617.10 of the SEQRA regulations defines a GEIS and explains its potential uses and functions. Section 617.13(a) allows agencies to charge a portion of the lead agency's costs of preparing a GEIS to developers in the study area.

CRITICAL ENVIRONMENTAL AREAS

DEFINITION

The SEQRA regulations define a Critical Environmental Area (CEA) as "a specific geographical area designated by a state or local agency, having exceptional or unique environmental characteristics." The focus of a CEA is on the definition of the critical area and the identification of its unique and exceptional environmental characteristics. Instead of clarifying or streamlining the environmental review of subsequent projects like the generic environmental impact statement, the CEA identifies fragile or threatened areas to insure that their particular characteristics are understood and taken into consideration in the conduct of environmental reviews on subsequent, individual projects.

PURPOSE

An area is normally designated a CEA to require subsequent site specific projects and other actions affecting the geographical area to be reviewed more carefully and fully for their potential negative impacts on the designated area. After an area's designation as a CEA, local, county, and state agencies considering actions that will affect the CEA are required to consider the impact of those actions on the specific environmental characteristics contained in the designation of the CEA. This will frequently justify, if not require, a higher level of environmental review of projects proposed in or near a CEA.

WHEN

Local agencies may designate a CEA when they wish to protect a particular environmental area from adverse environmental impacts. Such an area must have an exceptional or unique character. Characteristics that define such an area include a benefit or threat to human health; a natural setting, such as a fish or wildlife habitat, forest and vegetation, open space, and areas of important aesthetic or scenic quality; agricultural, social, cultural, historic, archaeological, recreational, or educational values; or an inherent ecological, geological, or hydrological sensitivity to change that may be adversely affected by development activity.

AUTHORITY

The Department of Environmental Conservation references §§8-0101, 8-0103, and 8-0113 of SEQRA as authority for the idea that the CEA procedure is an appropriate means of identifying and protecting critical resources. The SEQRA regulations specifically authorize local agencies to designate CEAs and set forth the procedure for such designation.

IMPLEMENTATION

To designate a CEA, a local agency must provide written public notice and hold a public hearing. The notice must identify the boundaries of the CEA and the specific environmental characteristics that justify CEA designation. The DEC suggests that agencies hold an informational meeting with affected landowners, other interested agencies, and the public prior to the required public meeting. After designation, the agency must notify the DEC Commissioner, the regional DEC office, and any other agencies regularly involved in "actions" relating to proposals taking place in the municipality. Designation does not become effective until 30 days after filing the CEA with the commissioner. The designation of an area as a CEA is itself an "action" that is subject to environmental review to determine if the designation will have a significant effect on the environment.

ILLUSTRATION

The town of Wawayanda designated all ridge areas with a natural elevation of 600 feet above mean sea level as a critical environmental area. Although the designation is made pursuant to SEQRA, the law was included in the zoning law as an overlay zone. The law recognizes the value of preserving the ridges from the impacts of wind and soil erosion due to development and breaks in the natural tree line. Any proposed structures are subject to two restrictions: the roof of any structure within the CEA must not be visible from any scenic road designated as such in the town comprehensive plan, and any proposal for development located in the CEA that is likely to be visible from a scenic road at any time must include a sketch of the development and a photograph of the site from the scenic road. Additionally, the planning board is directed to consider a number of guidelines such as the structure's location, height, and color to determine if it is compatible with the preservation of the ridgeline.

LIMITATIONS AND CONCERNS

The designation of a CEA, by itself, may not sufficiently protect the critical environmental characteristics of the designated area. To achieve greater control, localities may adopted land use measures, such as a wetlands law, an overlay conservation zone district, or more stringent subdivision or site plan standards that are applicable to projects affecting an environmentally sensitive area.

A CEA designation does not require agencies to prepare full environmental impact statements on projects or to analyze the cumulative impacts of actions that individually may not significantly impact the environment of the CEA. Local agencies may use their discretion, however, to review the cumulative impacts of projects affecting a CEA. Further, a higher level of environmental review can be insured if the designating agency requires, in its local SEQRA regulations, that actions affecting a CEA are automatically considered Type I actions, which are defined as "more likely to require the preparation of a full Environmental Impact Statement." The DEC regulations stipulate, however, that a local agency may not place on its own Type I list any action designated in the SEQRA regulations as an exempt, excluded, or Type II action.

REGULATION

Section 617.2(i) of the SEQRA regulations contains a definition of a CEA. Section 617.14(g) describes the requirements for CEA designation.

CASE DIGEST

In *Orchard Associates v. Planning Board of the Town of North Salem*, 114 A.D.2d 850, 494 N.Y.S.2d 760 (2d Dep't 1985), the planning board's denial of a conceptual site plan application was upheld because substantial evidence supported its conclusion that the development would have adverse impacts on traffic, sewage, and drainage. The court recognized that "Generic Environmental Impact Statements (GEIS) are held to a lesser degree of specificity than statements prepared for specific site plans and need not address every conceivable alternative to the proposed development." It held that the planning board's requirement that the petitioners obtain commitments for the improvement of the local infrastructure before approval of the plan would be granted was not irrational since this would insure that the adverse impacts of the development were minimized. The court noted, however, that some of the planning board's findings were not supported by the record, and that the provisions of SEQRA "are not to be used as a subterfuge through which commercial development may be totally prohibited."

Under SEQRA, reviewing agencies have the authority to impose conditions on their approvals to mitigate identified adverse impacts. *Jackson v. New York State Urban Development Corp.*, 67 N.Y.2d 400, 494 N.E.2d 429, 503 N.Y.S.2d 298 (1986). The court noted that "in accordance with its balancing philosophy, SEQRA requires the imposition of mitigation measures only 'to the maximum extent practicable' 'consistent with social, economic, and other essential considerations.' Moreover, nothing in the act bars an agency from relying upon mitigation measures it cannot itself guarantee in the future." The court held that since there was substantial evidence that the Urban Development Corporation, as lead agency, had taken a hard look at and considered potential mitigation measures, the court could not overturn its choices.

> "[W]hen an action with potential adverse effects on the environment is part of an integrated project designed to balance conflicting environmental goals within a subsection of a municipality that is ecologically unique, the potential cumulative impact of other proposed or pending projects must be considered pursuant to SEQRA before the action may be approved." *Save the Pine Bush, Inc. v. City of Albany*, 70 N.Y.2d 193, 512 N.E.2d 526, 518 N.Y.S.2d 943 (1987). The Court of Appeals invalidated a zoning law that created a commercial development zoning classification in the Pine Bush, an area containing unusual inland sand dunes and rare plant and animal species. The legislative policy that prompted the zoning change was the desire to reach a balance between commercial development and the maintenance of ecological integrity. The court held that the failure of the city council, as lead agency, "to consider the potential cumulative impact of other pending projects with the [respondent's] application upon the Pine Bush before granting the zoning change constituted a violation of its obligations pursuant to SEQRA."

Pursuant to SEQRA, the types of conditions that may be imposed on a project are extensive because SEQRA's definition of the environment is so broad. *Morse v. Town of Gardiner Planning Board*, 164 A.D.2d 336, 563 N.Y.S.2d 922 (3d Dep't 1990). There, "the Board conditioned [final subdivision] approval on several mitigation measures, including large lot sizes, restrictions on house colors, a mandatory planting program, the filing of covenants and restrictions, and imposition of a conservation easement."

In *Long Island Pine Barrens Society, Inc. v. Brookhaven*, 80 N.Y.2d 500, 606 N.E.2d 1373, 591 N.Y.S.2d 982 (1992), the petitioners argued that 224 development projects in the Central Pine Barrens area, an ecologically sensitive region, would adversely affect the environment by increasing the amount of pollutants that seeped into the area's aquifer system. They claimed that SEQRA was violated since no consideration was given to the cumulative environmental impact of all the pending development projects in the area. The legislature historically recognized the fragility of the aquifer by prohibiting the placement of new landfill sites and prohibiting land uses involving hazardous wastes in certain parts of Long Island. However, the court held that a cumulative impact analysis was not required since the governmental policy to protect the area was not a long-range plan, which must be found before a cumulative impact analysis of all 224 projects would be mandatory.

The court held that the location of a proposed condominium project in a designated critical environmental area (CEA) did not require a town board to consider the cumulative environmental effects of the project with the effects of other proposed projects located within the CEA when performing an environmental review for a special permit application. *North Fork Environmental Council, Inc. v. Janoski*, 196 A.D.2d 590, 601 N.Y.S.2d 178 (2d Dep't 1993). The court found that "the various projects were not 'reasonably related' to each other, and thus, a cumulative impact review was not mandatory."

In *Argyle Conservation League v. Town of Argyle*, 223 A.D.2d 796, 636 N.Y.S.2d 150 (3d Dep't 1996), the court found that the town board took the required hard look at the issues regarding the repeal of a zoning law. As a result, the town board's decision to repeal the law was not arbitrary and capricious or an abuse of discretion. The petitioners claimed that numerous specific areas were not adequately analyzed by the board's final generic environmental impact statement (FGEIS). However, the court rejected this contention, stating that "[t]he degree of detail to which each alternative must be discussed may vary with the nature and circumstances of each proposal, and there is no requirement that the FGEIS contain all the raw data supporting its analysis as is long as the analysis sufficient to allow reasoned consideration and comment on the issues raised."

The court annulled a town board's decision to adopt a negative declaration of environmental significance concerning the construction of a public water storage tank in *Watch Hill Homeowners Ass'n, Inc. v. Town Board of Town of Greenburgh*, 226 A.D.2d 1031, 641 N.Y.S.2d 443 (3d Dep't 1996). The court held that the town board did not make the required "reasoned elaboration" of the basis for its determination and that "one of the factors to be considered in determining if [a significant adverse] impact is likely is the potential for 'impairment of the environmental characteristics' of a CEA."

In *Cathedral Church of Saint John the Divine v. Dormitory Authority of the State of New York*, 224 A.D.2d 95, 645 N.Y.S.2d 637 (1996), the lead agency imposed various conditions on a proposed nursing home expansion project, which was declared a Type I action, in order to protect adjacent property during the construction of the project. The petitioners claimed that the lead agency impermissibly issued a conditioned negative declaration, which may not be issued for a Type I action. The court disagreed, stating that "the conditions which petitioners allege were imposed on [the applicant] were not conditions or mitigation. Rather, they were part of the project plans being reviewed by respondent–plans which had been revised and modified to address problems raised throughout the City's [environmental] review."

"It is clear that segmentation, which is the dividing for environmental review of an action in such a way that the various segments are addressed as though they were independent and unrelated activities, is contrary to the intent of SEQRA and is disfavored. Nevertheless, segmented review is permissible where the lead agency believes that it is warranted under the circumstances, provided that the agency clearly states its reasons therefor and demonstrates that such review is no less protective of the environment." *Concerned Citizens for the Environment v. Zagata*, 243 A.D.2d 20, 672 N.Y.S.2d 956 (3d Dep't 1998). The court held that the Department of Environmental Conservation (DEC) properly conducted segmented environmental review of a proposed solid waste disposal facility, which consisted of an incinerator, a materials recovery station, and a solid waste transfer station. The court upheld the DEC's decision to review separately the permit application for the construction of the transfer station for several reasons: (1) the transfer station is independent of the materials recovery station and the incinerator; (2) the transfer station has utility even if the other two components of the project are never approved and constructed; (3) full environmental review of the transfer station had been submitted; and (4) the related actions had been clearly identified and discussed to the fullest extent possible. Furthermore, the court rejected the petitioner's argument that the DEC failed to consider the cumulative impacts of the transfer station with the integrated project. It stated that "[i]f such were a prerequisite to obtaining a permit for a particular aspect of a project, the lead agency would be required, in every case where segmented review was sought, to conduct a full SEQRA review of the entire project, thus emasculating any concept of segmented review."

In *Town of Henrietta v. Department of Environmental Conservation of the State of New York*, 430 N.Y.S.2d 440, 76 A.D.2d 215 (4th Dep't 1980), the petitioners sought to have set aside the 18 conditions imposed upon permits granted by the DEC. The petitioners claimed that the DEC did not have authority under SEQRA to impose conditions on an approval or a permit when those conditions have no relevance to the approval or permit sought. The court held that SEQRA authorizes the approving agency to impose measures designed to mitigate the adverse environmental impacts identified, so long as these measures are reasonable in scope and are reasonably related to the impacts identified in the EIS. Here, the court upheld all but one of the conditions and stated that each of the imposed conditions represented a relevant concern under SEQRA. According to the court, the SEQRA regulations "make clear that an agency in approving an action must make a written finding that it has imposed whatever conditions are necessary to minimize or avoid all adverse environmental impacts revealed in the EIS." The court went on to state that the EIS is the heart of SEQRA and is meant to be more than just a disclosure statement. Rather, the court stated, "it is an environmental alarm bell whose purpose is to alert responsible public officials to environmental changes before they have reached ecological points of no return."

In *Village of Westbury v. Department of Transportation of the State of New York*, 146 A.D.2d 578, 536 N.Y.S.2d 502 (2d Dep't 1989), a negative declaration that was issued for the completion of a highway interchange project was annulled and the matter was remitted for reconsideration of the project's cumulative impacts. The Department of Transportation (DOT) failed to consider the cumulative impact of the interchange project along with the widening of the Northern State Parkway. The DOT contended that the widening was not a planned project and that it was independent of the interchange project. However, the court found that the DOT's own documents contradicted this contention. The court said the documents actually indicated that the two projects might be dependent on one another. The court found that "the widening project was part of an overall plan by the department, and its cumulative effect, if any, should have been considered prior to the department's issuance of the negative declaration." The court further stated that the failure to consider the cumulative impact prior to issuance of the negative declaration constituted a violation of SEQRA and therefore was arbitrary and capricious.

REFERENCE

Michael Murphy, *Advanced SEQRA Techniques, at* http://www.pace.edu/lawschool/landuse/advseq.html (last visited Feb. 2, 2001).

Photo courtesy of Jay Pendergrass

Chapter 6
BALANCING DEVELOPMENT AND CONSERVATION

New York law provides a variety of ways to encourage land development and conservation in appropriate locations and to avoid the high costs of haphazard development patterns. The local comprehensive plan can be drafted or amended to contain a component on economic development and another on conservation of natural resources. It can identify specific areas within the community where development is desired and large landscape areas where conservation is intended. This development and conservation plan can be implemented by adopting an appropriate combination of implementation techniques as part of the zoning law– techniques that can supplement the operation of the underlying regulation of established zoning districts.

On the development side, economic development districts can be designated as overlay districts, which follow, for example, a major transportation corridor and encompass parts of several underlying zoning districts. Zoning incentives can be provided to developers to build in these districts. In exchange for these incentives, developers can be required to provide needed public services and amenities. Local governments have the authority to increase the number of housing units permitted, or the gross square feet of commercial building allowed, in exchange for the provision of community benefits, such as parks, playgrounds, water, sewerage, and transportation facilities, or even affordable housing and day care. These measures articulate a clear municipal policy that the development district is the appropriate place for higher density development. This policy can be supported further by the local capital budget, which can target development districts for additional or improved infrastructure to service the new development.

Zoning Flexibility Techniques

- Floating zone
- Overlay zone
- Incentive zoning
- Transfer of development rights
- Moratorium
- Cluster zoning
- Planned unit development
- Planned residential development
- Traditional neighborhood development district
- Local waterfront management zoning

Higher density development in appropriate locations also can be achieved through floating zoning. A floating zoning district defines a use–such as an office complex, research laboratory, multi-family housing, or mixed-use development–that the community wants to encourage. The floating zone can be affixed at any time to a qualifying parcel of land, either upon the application of the parcel's owner or upon the initiative of the local legislature. Standards may be adopted for approval of such applications, which guide this type of development into areas where higher density development can be serviced appropriately and can be made harmonious with surrounding land uses. When a floating zoning application is approved, the parcel is rezoned to reflect the new use and becomes a small zoning district; its development is governed by the use, dimensional, and other provisions of the floating zone law.

Even the New York State Environmental Quality Review Act (SEQRA), which was enacted to protect the environment, has features that can be used to encourage economic development. By preparing a generic environmental impact statement on the adoption of an economic development overlay zone, for example, subsequent project proposals whose environmental impacts were included in the generic study can be exempted from further environmental review. This can streamline the review and approval of proposed development projects in such districts, providing another important incentive to developers to buy and improve land where development is favored by local policy.

A technique called transfer of development rights (TDR) can be used not only to encourage development in economic development districts but to compensate for discouraging or disallowing it in environmentally sensitive areas. New York statutes define the transfer of development rights as "the process by which development rights are transferred from one lot, parcel, or area of land in a sending district to another lot, parcel, or area of land in one or more receiving districts." Local governments are allowed great flexibility in designing a TDR program. They can establish conditions that they deem "necessary and appropriate" to achieve the purposes of the TDR program. Where a development overlay district has been established, it can serve as the "receiving district" for a TDR program and provide an important resource for the purchase of development rights, and for discouraging development in conservation districts.

On the conservation side, the comprehensive plan can designate conservation districts: specific landscapes targeted for preservation. To implement this policy, conservation overlay districts can be adopted and generic environmental impact statements can be prepared to identify all the environmental assets located in these districts. As part of these studies, measures that are needed to mitigate the negative effects of development in the conservation districts may be specified. Where the environment is particularly fragile, a district can be designated a "critical environmental area" and more intense mitigation measures can be required of land developers. Environmentally constrained acres can be deducted from density calculations, tight clustering of permitted density can be mandated, larger buffers can be established to protect wetlands, and conservation easements can be imposed on constrained land as a condition of approval for any development proposed. Through the adoption of a TDR program, the remaining allowable density on a parcel can be transferred to a development district and the parcel can be preserved in its entirety. Capital improvement budgets can telegraph the community's intention not to support higher density development in conservation districts.

By combining these techniques in creative ways, local governments can encourage both land development and resource conservation and can create sustainable communities for current and future generations. These are valuable additions to the basic land use techniques that have defined local land use practice over the years.

A. OVERLAY ZONING

DEFINITION

An overlay district is created by the local legislature by identifying a special resource or development area and adopting new provisions that apply in that area in addition to the provisions of the zoning ordinance. The provisions of an overlay district can be more restrictive or more permissive than those contained in the zoning district.

The term "overlay district" refers to the superimposition of the new district's lines on the zoning map's district designations. An overlay district can be coterminous with existing zoning districts or may contain only parts of one or more such districts.

Overlay zones create a framework for conservation or development of special geographical areas. In a special resource overlay district, overlay provisions typically impose greater restrictions on the development of land, but only regarding those parcels whose development, as permitted under the zoning, may threaten the viability of the natural resource. In a development area overlay district, the provisions may impose restrictions as well, but also may provide zoning incentives and waivers to encourage certain types and styles of development. Overlay zone provisions are often complemented by the adoption of other innovative zoning techniques, such as floating zones, special permits, incentive zoning, cluster development, and special site plan or subdivision regulations, to name a few.

PURPOSE

The purpose of an overlay zone is to conserve natural resources or realize development objectives without unduly disturbing the expectations created by the existing zoning ordinance. The existing zoning provisions may properly regulate the relevant district in general, but more specific and targeted provisions may be needed to accomplish pressing land use objectives. Within that context, an overlay zone establishes land use regulations that must be enforced by local authorities under the terms of the law or ordinance adopting the overlay district.

WHEN

An overlay law may be adopted by the local legislature to encourage appropriate development in a specific area or when the zoning law is considered to be inadequate to protect a particular resource area. Instead of changing the provisions of the zoning applicable to all land parcels in the area, the local legislature may want to adopt special provisions applicable to those parcels that have particular development constraints or potential.

The overlay district is most often thought of, and is sometimes defined, as a technique for conserving a fragile natural resource area such as a pine barren, wetland resource area, watershed, or tidal basin. The underlying zoning may permit the subdivision of all land in such an area for residential purposes. If implemented, this might destroy the resource area. To accomplish a more appropriate land use pattern, an overlay district can be adopted that contains special clustering or setback provisions to protect environmentally constrained areas. Other provisions can be added that are not typically found in zoning ordinances, such as grading, landscape restoration, and limitations on the development of steep slopes.

Overlay districts, however, have broad application in a variety of contexts. They can be used, for example, to accomplish the redevelopment or rehabilitation of deteriorated neighborhoods. Within a designated redevelopment overlay district, developers can be given a variety of incentives to redevelop contaminated or substandard properties, to rehabilitate substandard structures, or to provide needed community facilities or affordable housing.

Overlay districts can, at the same time, be used to further the development and conservation objectives of the community. For example, the locality can adopt a conservation area overlay district in one or more environmentally constrained areas and a development area overlay district along a transportation corridor to provide for greater and more cost-effective development patterns. Adopting both overlay districts simultaneously provides needed tax revenue, housing, jobs, and commercial activity while protecting the quality of life and the environment through the conservation of threatened natural resource areas. Various techniques can be employed to accomplish the objectives of both overlay districts. A developer, for example, can be given zoning incentives in the development district in exchange for purchasing a conservation easement on land in the conservation district.

When development and conservation areas overlap municipal borders, communities can enter into intermunicipal agreements to adopt and enforce compatible overlay zones. In this way, the efforts of one community to achieve appropriate land uses along a shared transportation corridor or in an intermunicipal natural resource area can be greatly enhanced.

AUTHORITY

A local government's authority to create an overlay district is implied in the delegation of the power to enact zoning restrictions and create zoning districts. One purpose of zoning is to insure that its provisions consider the character of areas and their suitability for particular uses with a view toward conserving the value of buildings and encouraging the most appropriate use of the land throughout the municipality. New York's highest court has made it clear that "how various properties shall be classified or reclassified rests with the local legislative body; its judgment and determination will be conclusive, beyond interference from the courts, unless shown to be arbitrary."

IMPLEMENTATION

The procedures for adopting an overlay district are the same as for adopting a zoning or rezoning provision. Once relevant studies have been completed, the district has been identified, and its substantive provisions have been drafted, public notice must be given and a public hearing held. The provisions of the overlay district law or ordinance can contain special techniques or procedures for accomplishing its objectives, such as site plan or subdivision standards, clustering permission, or a floating zone. Compliance with environmental review provisions of state law and conformance with the comprehensive plan are also required. Following the adoption of the overlay district, the municipality should make appropriate notations on its zoning map to provide effective notice of its applicability.

The local legislature may want to precede these formal steps with a variety of informal meetings with landowners and citizens who will be affected. This helps the locality to gather needed information, learn more about the impacts of its legislation, and develop support for the proposals. This is always a good idea where land use controls are being amended or adopted in any significant way.

ILLUSTRATIONS

The town of Greenburgh added a Conservation District Zone to its zoning ordinance which, by its terms, operates as "an overlay zone over any other zones allowed in the town." It applies to a particular property upon application by the owner or upon the town board's initiative. All use and dimensional requirements of the underlying zoning district continue to apply after the overlay zone is affixed to a property. The additional provisions of the Conservation District Zone also apply to the property's development. These include criteria for the conservation of particular natural features, how these features are to be protected, including additional setback and buffer areas, prevention of disturbance of natural areas, and the restoration of the landscape of any disturbed areas.

In 1984, the city of Albany adopted an overlay zone to protect 550 acres in the Pine Bush, which contains the only remaining large pine barrens on inland sand dunes in the United States and a number of distinct environmental characteristics including the habitats of endangered wildlife species. The city first provided for the development of low-rise commercial office buildings that could be developed in the district. Then it created a special site plan district in the Pine Bush which delineated a site plan review process with specific criteria to be used in passing upon applications for development within the overlay district.

In 1981, New York City amended its zoning ordinance to create the Special Manhattan Bridge District, encompassing part of Chinatown. It was preceded by a detailed study of the substandard conditions in the area, including the deteriorated condition of much of the housing there. The creation of the overlay district sought to correct these conditions by encouraging the construction of new residential facilities, the rehabilitation of existing structures, and the expansion of community facilities. It authorized the construction of mixed-income housing by special permit and provided a system of density bonus points to developers who donated space for community facilities, constructed low-income housing, or rehabilitated existing substandard housing. In New York City, a variety of other overlay zones have been adopted. They protect special commercial areas such as the Broadway Theater District and the Garment District and a Lower Manhattan Mixed Use District.

LIMITATIONS AND CONCERNS

In adopting an overlay district ordinance or law, the municipality must address several issues:

The local legislature should consider whether its objectives can be met by simply amending the underlying zoning law. It may be that the provisions of the zoning ordinance create a valid baseline for development still applicable to a large number of parcels in the area but that the overlay district is needed for a significant number of special circumstances.

The local legislature must be cautious that the provisions contained in the overlay district are sufficiently specific to provide clear guidance or incentives to the owners of properties and any administrative body involved in approving proposals. The New York Court of Appeals has warned that standards governing the issuance of special permits may not be so general as to allow unchecked discretion on the part of a planning or zoning board. Where the authority to issue special permits and land use approvals is retained by the local legislature, the standards can be less specific, but their application must not be arbitrary and capricious.

The overlay district's burdens must be imposed as uniformly as possible under the circumstances. Recent U.S. Supreme Court decisions warn against singling out particular property owners to bear public burdens unreasonably.

The provisions of the district must be reasonably related to the accomplishment of the law's objectives. If the overlay district prohibits the use of significant portions of a landowner's property, the courts may search for a close relationship between the impacts of the development of the property and the regulation that restricts that development.

STATUTES

In New York State, Town Law §263, Village Law §7-704, and General City Law §20(25) articulate the purposes of zoning, which include those advanced by the creation of an overlay district.

General Municipal Law §96-a authorizes towns, villages, and cities to create historic districts and to enact regulations to protect, enhance, and perpetuate districts, sites, and buildings of special historical interest or value.

Section 10(1)(ii)(a)(11) of the Municipal Home Rule Law states that a municipality may adopt local laws for the "protection and enhancement of its physical and visual environment."

Section 10(1)(ii)(a)(14) of the Municipal Home Rule Law states that a municipality may adopt local laws as provided in the Statute of Local Governments. Section 10(6) of the Statute of Local Governments authorizes cities, towns, and villages to adopt zoning regulations.

CASE DIGEST

Overlay districts have been upheld when created to protect environmental resources. *Save the Pine Bush v. City of Albany*, 70 N.Y.2d 193, 512 N.E.2d 526, 518 N.Y.S.2d 943 (1987). The City of Albany adopted an overlay district to protect inland sand dunes and their rare plant and animal species. The city zoned the area for low-rise commercial office buildings, and then created a site plan review process with specific criteria to be used when reviewing applications for certain uses within the overlay district designed to protect the natural resource. The court held that "there is no constitutional prohibition against the delegation of power, with [such] reasonable safeguards and standards."

The New York Court of Appeals upheld the constitutionality of a special district overlay zone in *Asian Americans for Equality v. Koch*, 72 N.Y.2d 121, 527 N.E.2d 265, 531 N.Y.S.2d 782 (1988). New York City amended its zoning ordinance to create the Special Manhattan Bridge District, which required that new construction be authorized by special permit. The court sustained the ordinance, noting that the district had been created to "protect a badly deteriorated part of the unique area of New York City known as Chinatown" and "to further growth and development of the community."

In *Wal-Mart Stores, Inc. v. Planning Board of the Town of North Elba*, 238 A.D.2d 93, 668 N.Y.S.2d 774 (3d Dep't 1998), the court sustained the planning board's denial of a conditional use permit and site plan application for the development of a large retail store. The court held that it was appropriate for the planning board to place great weight on the visual effect of the development because it would lie partially within an area designated a "Scenic Preservation Overlay," which was established to protect the view of a nearby mountain. The court stated that "despite all efforts to screen the store and parking area from the road, their presence would nevertheless bring about a noticeable change in the visual character of this critical area."

REFERENCE

Matt Bavoso and Timothy Jones, *Overlay Zoning: Application and Implementation in New York State–Part A, at* http://www.pace.edu/lawschool/landuse/overla.htm (last visited Feb. 2, 2001).

B. FLOATING ZONES

DEFINITION

A floating zoning district defines a use–such as an office complex, a research laboratory, or multi-family housing–that the community wants to encourage. The floating zone can be affixed to a qualifying parcel of land, either upon the application of the parcel's owner or upon the initiative of the local legislature. Upon approval, the parcel is rezoned to reflect the new use and becomes a small zoning district; its development is governed by the use, dimensional, and other provisions of the floating zone.

The floating zone law contains a number of provisions intended to mitigate the impact of its development on the surrounding area. Normally, for a parcel to be eligible for rezoning under a floating zone, it must be of a sufficient size to insure that the development can be fitted properly into its surroundings. An owner who requests that the zone be applied to a particular parcel must demonstrate that a variety of impacts will be properly handled, such as traffic and site access; water and sewer service; design continuity; effect on natural resources; visual and noise impact; preservation of open space; and the effect on nearby property values.

PURPOSE

The purpose of adding one or more floating zones to a community's zoning law is to add flexibility to that law, enabling it to accommodate new land uses. As a community's needs change, uses that are not readily accommodated by the adopted zoning law may be desired by local leaders. These uses may be unique and have a relatively significant but manageable impact on their surroundings. Local officials may be unclear as to where such uses should best be accommodated and where developers would prefer to locate them to insure that they are successful economically.

WHEN

Floating zones are usually added to existing zoning laws to define certain uses when the community desires them but, for various reasons, does not know where they should be located. Floating zones allow developers some needed flexibility in locating sites and determining how new land uses can be designed and buffered to fit into their surroundings. In some communities where affordable housing is desired, for example, a multi-family district may be created by the legislature but not located on the zoning map. This allows developers the maximum flexibility to scout out sites and design developments that mix housing types, tenures, and costs to accomplish the municipality's objective of producing affordable housing while requiring the project to fit properly into the neighborhood. Similarly, a community may want to create an office park but may not want to limit its location, in order to give developers ample opportunity to find a site best suited to current market needs.

Since both multi-family housing and office parks can be buffered, serviced, and designed to fit into a variety of contexts, the legislature may be comfortable with the floating zone mechanism to enhance the community's chances of attracting private capital for such developments without unduly impacting adjacent properties.

AUTHORITY

The authority of local governments to adopt floating zones was sustained by the New York Court of Appeals as part of the municipal authority to divide the community into zoning districts. *Rodgers v. Village of Tarrytown*, 302 N.Y. 115, 96 N.E.2d 731 (1951). In that case, Tarrytown's floating zone for garden apartments was attacked as a violation of the requirements that zoning districts be uniform, as invalid spot zoning, and as an impermissible delegation of legislative authority to the planning board.

In sustaining the floating zone, the court wrote:

> Changed or changing conditions call for changed plans, and persons who own property in a particular zone or use district enjoy no eternally vested right to that classification if the public interest demands otherwise. Accordingly, the power of the village to amend its basic zoning ordinance in such a way as to reasonably promote the general welfare cannot be questioned.

302 N.Y. at 121, 96 N.E.2d at 733. The court held that courts must defer to legislative judgment when "the validity of the legislative classification for zoning purposes [is] fairly debatable" and that the burden of showing that an ordinance is not justified under the police power of the state rests with the person attacking the ordinance.

Applying that test to the facts of the case, the court upheld the purposes behind the creation of the new district as following "sound zoning principles" and as being in accordance with a comprehensive plan. Those purposes included providing housing for young families in the area, attracting businesses, and protecting the local tax base. Then, addressing the validity of floating zoning as the method chosen by the village to achieve those goals, the court held that the village's requirement for "separate legislative authorization for each project present[ed] no obstacle or drawback" and that the board of trustees' choice of this procedure was "neither arbitrary nor unreasonable."

The court also noted that the board had not improperly divested itself of its legislative power. It reasoned that even if a property owner met physical standards required for the district, the board could, in the exercise of reasonable discretion, refuse to rezone the property. The court dismissed the allegation of illegal spot zoning, stating that if "an ordinance is enacted in accordance with a comprehensive zoning plan, it is not 'spot zoning,' even though it (1) singles out and affects but one small plot . . . or (2) creates in the center of a large zone small areas or districts devoted to a different use."

Finally, the court held that the law creating the new district was not invalid for its failure to set boundaries for the new district at that time. The court reasoned that the law only set forth the specifications for the new district and there was no need to set the boundaries at that time. The original legislation, the court held, "was merely the first step in a reasoned plan of rezoning, and specifically provided for further action on the part of the board."

In addition to the use of a floating zone to create garden apartments in a single-family zone, the technique has allowed land, otherwise zoned, to be used for laboratories and office parks, gasoline stations, high-rise housing, mixed-use developments, and clustered residential developments.

IMPLEMENTATION

Floating zones are adopted by the local legislature, after public hearing, notice, and environmental review, just as other zoning provisions or amendments are adopted. The law should provide that the designation of parcels to which the floating zone is to apply, and the amendment of the zoning map, shall be commenced upon the application of the landowner or upon the initiative of the municipality.

In determining whether to affix a floating zone to a parcel, the local board must determine whether a proposed development can be harmonized with surrounding uses and conditions. Floating zone laws can require applicants to demonstrate the impacts of proposed development on matters such as traffic, schools, municipal services, and tax base. Review of applications for a floating zone designation may be made by the legislature itself or may be delegated to the local planning or zoning board of appeals, if sufficient standards are established by the legislature to guide the decisionmaking process.

ILLUSTRATIONS

The village of Tarrytown amended its zoning law to create a new zoning district designated Residence B-B. In addition to one- and two-family dwellings, the new district permitted "buildings for multiple occupancy of fifteen or fewer families." However, the boundaries of the new district were not delineated at that time. Instead, the ordinance provided that the boundaries were to be fixed at a later time by amending the village zoning map upon approval of an application by a property owner to have a property rezoned to Residence B-B. To that end, the board of trustees authorized the planning board to approve such amendments but also reserved the right to approve such amendments itself in the event that the planning board withheld approval. The ordinance imposed stringent standards for new zones, including a 10-acre minimum lot size. Other standards dealt with maximum building heights, setback and spacing requirements, and ground area percentages.

The town of Brookhaven's zoning ordinance uses this language regarding its floating zone:

> The Planned Development District (PDD) is hereby established as a floating zone with potential applicability to any property in the Town where its use will serve to further the legislative intent of this Article. The boundaries of each PDD shall be fixed by amendment to the official Zoning Map wherever this District is applied. A metes and bounds description of each such District shall be kept on file in the office of the Town Clerk. Although it is anticipated that the PDD rezoning applications will be submitted on a voluntary basis by applicants, the Town Board may, on its own motion, rezone property to a PDD. This District is intended for sites of at least 50 acres, but the Town Board may consider applications for smaller properties if special circumstances warrant.

Brookhaven Code, Article XXXIIA, 1995.

LIMITATIONS AND CONCERNS

Floating zones often allow for more intensive use of the property than the underlying zoning. This can upset the expectations of nearby property owners. Although the courts have held that property owners have no "eternally vested right to [an existing zoning] classification if the public interest demands otherwise," fairness requires that the expectations of property owners be respected and accommodated without compromising the public interest in proper land use.

For this reason, floating zones should establish specific requirements that properties must meet before they can be rezoned to the new district classification. Critical among these is the size of an eligible lot. These requirements, and any standards applied to a property whose use is reclassified under the application of a floating zone, are essential techniques that allow public objectives to be realized while protecting the character of the community and the expectations of property owners in the vicinity.

Although a property owner may believe that a parcel meets all the stipulated requirements of the floating zone, a thorough review of the proposed redevelopment and its impacts on the surrounding area must be conducted before the parcel's eligibility for the floating zone can be determined. This can create a disincentive for an owner to invest the time and funds needed to apply for the floating zone. It suggests that the local legislature should be as specific as possible about where and when a floating zone application will be approved when designing the floating zone provisions.

STATUTES

New York State Village Law §7-700, Town Law §261, and General City Law §20(24) grant basic land use authority to local governments and allow them to regulate the details of land development and building construction and alteration. This may be done for "the purpose of promoting the health, safety, morals or the general welfare of the community."

Village Law §7-702, Town Law §262, and General City Law §20(25) authorize local governments to divide the community into zoning districts and to regulate the use, construction, and alteration of buildings and land within those districts.

Village Law §7-704, Town Law §263, and General City Law §§20(24) and (25) provide that zoning and land use regulations must be in conformance with the locality's comprehensive plan. The purposes that such zoning regulations are to achieve are to lessen congestion, to secure safety from fire and flood, to prevent overcrowding, to facilitate the provision of infrastructure, and to encourage "the most appropriate use of land throughout such municipality."

Section 10(1)(ii)(a)(11) of the Municipal Home Rule Law states that a municipality may adopt local laws for the "protection and enhancement of its physical and visual environment."

Section 10(1)(ii)(a)(14) of the Municipal Home Rule Law states that a municipality may adopt local laws as provided in the Statute of Local Governments. Section 10(6) of the Statute of Local Governments authorizes cities, towns, and villages to adopt zoning regulations.

CASE DIGEST

The Court of Appeals confirmed the municipality's authority to adopt floating zones in

Rodgers v. Village of Tarrytown, 302 N.Y. 115, 96 N.E.2d 731 (1951). The village board of trustees passed two zoning amendments in 1947 and 1948. The first created a new district for garden apartments with boundaries that were to be fixed by amendment of the official village building zone map when such district was applied to properties in the village. The second ordinance applied the new district to the defendant's property. The plaintiff neighbors claimed that the first ordinance was invalid because it set no boundaries for the new district and made no changes on the building zone map. The court held that "the 1947 amendment was merely the first step in a reasoned plan of rezoning, and specifically provided for further action on the part of the board." The court also stated that the "two amendments, read together as they must be, fully complied with the requirements of the Village Law and accomplished a rezoning of village property in an unexceptional manner." The court noted that "changed or changing conditions call for changed plans, and persons who own property in a particular zone or use district enjoy no eternally vested right to that classification if the public interest demands otherwise. Accordingly, the power of a village to amend its basic zoning ordinance in such a way as reasonably to promote the general welfare cannot be questioned."

In *Chase v. City of Glen Cove*, 41 Misc. 2d 889, 246 N.Y.S.2d 975 (Sup. Ct. Nassau County 1964), the court noted that the city could have utilized the floating zone technique in order to create a Municipal High Rise Housing District. The court found that a zoning ordinance that created a municipal housing district was confiscatory because it rezoned specific property allowing only a single use–municipal housing. This rezoning required the municipality to acquire the land through condemnation and then provide municipal housing. Thus, the owners were deprived of any beneficial use of their property. Furthermore, the city took no steps to condemn the property. The court stated that the city "could have amended the zoning ordinance by creating a floating zone and then specified the property to be brought within that district at or about the time the property was condemned or it could have first condemned the property and then rezoned it. It may not zone to permit only a use in which the owner may not engage unless it takes the property for such use at or about the same time."

The Second Department has affirmed that "the selection of an automobile service station use for floating zone treatment was not unreasonable, arbitrary or discriminatory." *Gordon v. Town of Huntington*, N.Y.L.J., July 29, 1966, at 10 (Sup. Ct. Suffolk County 1966), *aff'd*, 28 A.D.2d 822, 282 N.Y.S.2d 679 (2d Dep't 1967). The court stated that while "floating zone classifications have generally dealt with categories of uses other than gasoline stations . . . there is no great differential between the special exception procedure and the 'floating zone' procedure other than the element of greater discretion vested in the legislative body upon the application for a change of zone. Traditionally, gasoline and service stations have been subject to special treatment, differing from other retail uses."

In *Town of North Hempstead v. Village of North Hills*, 38 N.Y.2d 334, 342 N.E.2d 566, 379 N.Y.S.2d 792 (1975), the Court of Appeals sustained the creation of a cluster residence district (R-CL) as a floating zone that required a minimum plot size of four acres. The petitioners claimed that the part of the zoning ordinance which authorized the creation of this district was exclusionary and unconstitutionally discriminatory because "property owners whose parcels do not meet the four acre requirement are frozen into the R-2 district, whereas owners of larger parcels may apply for the R-CL classification." The court held that the "petitioners' claim that the R-CL classification is unavailable to only seven owners of property presently zoned R-2 serves only to bolster the contrary view that the ordinance is neither impermissibly exclusionary nor unconstitutionally discriminatory." *See also Rodgers*, hereinabove (finding that a minimum plot size requirement of 10 acres was not unfair to the plaintiff or to other owners of smaller parcels and that the "garden apartments would blend more attractively and harmoniously with the community setting [and] would impose less of a burden upon village facilities if placed upon larger tracts of land rather than scattered about in small acres").

The review of a denial of an application to rezone certain property under a floating zone provision "cannot be had in an Article 78 proceeding, for it is of legislative action. The appropriate vehicle for such review is an action for a declaratory judgment." *Amerada Hess Corp. v. Lefkowitz*, 82 A.D.2d 882, 440 N.Y.S.2d 306 (2d Dep't 1981).

In *Beyer v. Burns*, 150 Misc. 2d 10, 567 N.Y.S.2d 599 (Sup. Ct. Albany County 1991), the petitioners asserted that a zoning ordinance that established a senior-citizen housing development by use of a floating zone constituted illegal spot zoning. The court held that the burden of proof was on the petitioners and that they failed to meet this burden. It stated that "the petitioners have not established that the purpose behind the [new district] is to benefit the owners of the proposed location . . . rather than to benefit the community by providing low cost senior citizen housing pursuant to a comprehensive plan."

REFERENCE

Michael Murphy and Joseph Stinson, *Floating Zones, at* http://www.pace.edu/lawschool/landuse/flzone.html (last visited Feb. 2, 2001).

C. CLUSTER DEVELOPMENT

DEFINITION

The New York statutes define cluster development as:

a subdivision . . . in which the applicable zoning ordinance or local law is modified to provide an alternative permitted method for the layout, configuration and design of lots, buildings and structures, roads, utility lines and other infrastructure, parks, and landscaping in order to preserve the natural and scenic qualities of open lands.

Town Law §278(1); Village Law §7-738(1); General City Law §37(1). The statutes state that cluster development may not allow greater density than if the land "were subdivided into lots conforming to the minimum lot size and density requirements . . . of the zoning district in which the property is located."

Normally, land is subdivided and developed in conformance with the dimensional requirements of the local zoning ordinance. Zoning usually requires that the entire parcel be divided into lots that conform to minimum lot sizes and that buildings on subdivided lots conform to rigorous setback, height, and other dimensional requirements. So, for example, in a half-acre residential zone, a property owner will be required to lay out lots of no less than a half acre in size and to place homes on them that are at least 30 feet from the front lot line and no more than 35 feet high.

Under cluster development, the locality permits a land developer to vary these dimensional requirements. This can allow, for example, homes to be placed on quarter-acre lots in a half-acre zone. The land that is saved by this reconfiguration may then be left undeveloped to provide open space and serve the recreational needs of the residents of the development. Often this land is owned and maintained, if necessary, by a homeowners' association.

All municipalities in New York are authorized, but not required, to use this cluster development method. The ability to encourage or require cluster development is linked to the local government's authority to review and approve land subdivision, a function normally delegated to the local planning board. The Town Law delegating cluster authority to town governments, for example, states that "the town board may, by local law or ordinance, authorize the planning board to approve a cluster development simultaneously with the approval of a [subdivision] plat." Town Law §278(2)(a). Parallel provisions exist in the Village and General City Law. *See* Village Law §7-738(2)(a); General City Law §37(2)(a).

The local law exercising a community's cluster development authority can delegate broad or narrow authority to the planning board to cluster permitted development. It can be limited to one project at a time, to one zoning district, to a certain area within the community, to parcels with particular natural resource characteristics such as wetlands or steep slopes, or to the accomplishment of certain stated purposes. The local law can grant the planning board authority to alter all of the dimensional requirements of the zoning law to accomplish its objectives, or to alter only certain of those requirements, such as the required lot size. The uses permitted by the zoning law may not, however, be changed under this authority.

The flexibility that localities enjoy under their authority to cluster development is seldom appreciated. Often, for example, it is assumed that land developers may elect the cluster development method, but may not be required to do so. If the locality wishes, however, it can require development to be clustered to meet local objectives. Under cluster development authority, the planning board may be authorized to permit multi-family housing in a single-family zone–again, however, without increasing the permitted number of houses. Further, clustering can be done in commercial and industrial zoning districts. It is not limited to residential districts, as is often assumed.

PURPOSE

According to the state statutes, the purpose of cluster development is to "enable and encourage flexibility of design and development of land in such a manner as to preserve the natural and scenic qualities of open lands." Clustering also accomplishes other purposes, such as lowering site development costs, preserving on-site resources such as viewsheds, archeological sites, or other significant natural features, reducing the number of access points to adjacent roads, and allowing a wide variety of layouts and design schemes for subdivisions in the community.

New York's highest court stated that "economy, flexibility and scenic beauty are all appropriate reasons for permitting cluster zoning" and that it allows "more efficient use of land containing unusual features . . . for facilitating economical provision of streets and utilities, as well as for preserving the natural and scenic qualities of open lands."

WHEN

The limitations of traditional zoning requirements, including its rigorous lot size and setback provisions, have long been recognized. Their essential function, for most communities, is to establish the maximum density at which land can be developed. By knowing this maximum density, the community can determine its future service and facility needs and otherwise plan its future. As applied to particular parcels and neighborhoods, however, the rigorous dimensional requirements can limit the ability of the planning board to create developments that best meet local needs.

Where, for example, part of the community borders a stream, straddles a ridge, exhibits a certain historical quality, contains productive agricultural soils, or lacks open space and recreational facilities, laying out each new home in the middle of half-acre lots that are distributed evenly throughout the area may not be the best approach to subdividing and developing the land. In these situations, the local legislature may want to give the planning board the flexibility to adjust the dimensional requirements of the zoning ordinance in order to preserve the stream, avoid development of slopes, enhance historical design themes, preserve a viable farm, or obtain open space and recreational amenities.

AUTHORITY

The powers of New York State local governments, described above, are authorized in Town Law §278, Village Law §7-738, and General City Law §37. These sections contain nearly parallel authority for towns, villages, and cities, with the exception that villages can adopt cluster development provisions only by local law, while towns and cities can adopt the provisions by law or ordinance.

The planning board may establish conditions on the ownership, use, and maintenance of the open lands preserved by clustering, if necessary, to assure the preservation of their natural and scenic qualities. The courts have ruled that a developer may not be forced to convey title to the preserved open lands to the locality. Once the local legislature has delegated cluster authority to the planning board, it may not retain authority to review the planning board's decisions. If it wishes, however, the local legislature may retain the authority to approve any conditions imposed on the subdivision by the planning board.

IMPLEMENTATION

The first step in adopting cluster development provisions is for the local legislature to enact a law or ordinance authorizing the planning board to adjust the dimensional requirements of the zoning law in particular circumstances. This legislative act must specify the particular zoning districts in which clustering is to be permitted. The act also must contain the circumstances under which clustering is permitted, the objectives it is to accomplish, whether clustering may be required of a land developer, and which provisions of the zoning law may be altered. These provisions of the act will define how broad the authority and discretion of the planning board will be in applying the cluster technique to subsequent subdivisions.

The developer must submit a conventional subdivision plan, or "plat," so that the planning board can determine the density of development that would be allowed without clustering. The planning board must exercise its judgment to determine the density that would be permitted if a conventional subdivision were approved. Then a clustered subdivision plat may be submitted which places the permitted density on a portion of the site, leaving the remainder as undeveloped open space or as a recreational facility.

All of the requirements of subdivision approval must be met as the clustered subdivision application is reviewed and approved. These include compliance with the provisions of the comprehensive plan, with the environmental review procedures imposed by state and local law, with the public notice, hearing, and other requirements applicable to all subdivision approvals, and with the cluster development law or ordinance adopted by the local legislature.

After the clustered subdivision is approved and formally filed, a copy of the approved plat must be filed with the municipal clerk, who is required to place appropriate notations and references regarding the permitted development on the zoning map of the municipality.

ILLUSTRATIONS

The Town Board of Bedford authorized its planning board to preserve "a unique or significant natural feature of the site, including but not limited to a vegetative feature, wildlife habitat, surface water supply, underground aquifer, endangered species, rock formation, and steep slopes" and to protect "a unique or significant feature of the man-made environment of the site, including but not limited to a building, structure, or artifact of architectural, historical, or archeological value." Bedford's cluster ordinance allows lot sizes in residential zoning districts to be reduced to 10,000 square feet, with widths reduced to no less than 85 feet.

The city of Albany, in authorizing the planning board to cluster development, stated that its purpose was "to provide greater flexibility in the planning of residential subdivisions which will result in:

♦ a choice in the types of environments and living units;
♦ the preservation or creation of open space;

- ◆ a pattern of development which preserves trees, outstanding natural topography and geologic features and prevents soil erosion;
- ◆ an efficient use of land resulting in smaller networks of utilities and streets;
- ◆ an environment in harmony with surrounding development; and
- ◆ the preservation of areas which are physically, aesthetically, historically, and environmentally unique by virtue of their geology, topography, vegetative cover, or previous use."

In Albany, a minimum of four acres is required before clustering of a parcel is authorized, and clusters of attached dwellings of up to five units are permitted.

LIMITATIONS AND CONCERNS

New York State law does not spell out a detailed method of determining the permitted density that can be clustered. It says such density shall not "exceed the number which could be permitted, in the planning board's judgment, if the land were subdivided into lots conforming" to the requirements of the zoning ordinance and "conforming to all other applicable requirements." Town Law §278(3)(b); Village Law §7-738(3)(b); General City Law §37(3)(b).

How, exactly, are planning boards to determine what the density of a conventional subdivision should be if they do not subject it to a complete review under all applicable requirements, including environmental review? If a subdivider is forced to go through a nearly complete review of a conventional subdivision that he does not intend to build, however, a disincentive to clustering has been created. The time and cost of this review will be significant and wasted, from one perspective, because the clustered subdivision itself will have to be fully reviewed at substantial additional expense of time and money. Communities that are attentive to this problem will streamline the determination of how many units can be built conventionally.

The planning board must have sufficient information to make a credible judgment as to the density permitted for a conventional subdivision, but does not need to follow all the formal steps required in the conventional subdivision process. If the applicant fails to submit sufficient information and detailed drawings to allow the planning board to perform this function, the board may deny the application.

When designing their clustering system, localities must be careful to avoid uneven, arbitrary, and discriminatory treatment of applicants for subdivision approval. The act of the local legislature giving the planning board authority to cluster must contain sufficient guidelines to assure that similar situations are treated in a similar fashion. If the local legislature decides to give the planning board cluster authority on a project-by-project basis, there must be careful monitoring to assure even-handed treatment of applicants.

STATUTES

The basic authority to permit the clustering of development in New York State is found at Town Law §278, Village Law §7-738, and General City Law §37.

Municipal authority to review and approve subdivisions is found in Town Law §276, Village Law §7-728, and General City Law §32. These and subsequent sections contain the procedures that must be followed in approving the subdivision of land, including clustering.

CASE DIGEST

In *Town of North Hempstead v. Village of North Hills*, 38 N.Y.2d 334, 342 N.E.2d 566, 379 N.Y.S.2d 792 (1975), the New York Court of Appeals sustained the creation of a cluster residence district (R-CL) as a floating zone that required a minimum lot size of four acres. The petitioners claimed that the part of the zoning ordinance that authorized the creation of this district was exclusionary and unconstitutionally discriminatory because "property owners whose parcels do not meet the four-acre requirement are frozen into the R-2 district, whereas owners of larger parcels may apply for the R-CL classification." The court held that the "petitioners' claim that the R-CL classification is unavailable to only seven owners of property presently zoned R-2 serves only to bolster the contrary view that the ordinance is neither impermissibly exclusionary nor unconstitutionally discriminatory."

In *James L. Garrett Co., Inc. v. Guldenschuh*, 49 A.D.2d 800, 373 N.Y.S.2d 238 (4th Dep't 1975), the court held that a planning board properly denied a cluster plan on the basis that the proposed homes would have a different appearance from the other homes in the neighborhood. The court sustained the board's denial, noting that "[t]he opposition spread on the record of the public hearing by residents of the area opposed to changing the character of their neighborhood together with the charts and photographs [that reveal the difference in appearance] furnished a rational and substantial basis for the decision of the Planning Board."

The Court of Appeals has ruled that a planning board may not impose a condition on clustered subdivision approval that compels a developer to convey title of a portion of the land to the municipality for its use as a park without compensation. *Kamhi v. Yorktown*, 59 N.Y.2d 385, 452 N.E.2d 1193, 465 N.Y.S.2d 865 (1983). The Planning Board had required as a condition of approval that the petitioner convey approximately 40% of his land to the town for development as a public park serving all the people of the community. The petitioner had offered to develop the land as a park for the residents of his development, but he was not willing to open it to the public or to convey it to the town without compensation. The court held that the authorizing statute does "not contain language from which may be implied a legislative grant of power to compel conveyance of land for streets or park purposes without compensation."

In *Friends of Shawangunks, Inc. v. Knowlton*, 64 N.Y.2d 387, 476 N.E.2d 988, 487 N.Y.S.2d 543 (1985), the Court of Appeals held that although "a previously granted conservation easement proscribes erection of residences on part of the land included in a cluster zoning application, the land thus burdened may be counted in determining the number of residential units that may be erected on the unburdened acreage."

"Once a town board chooses to . . . authorize its planning board [to modify applicable provisions of the zoning ordinance], it may not reduce the role of the planning board to that of an advisory body by reserving in itself the right to review the planning board's determination and to approve, approve with modification, or deny an application for cluster zoning." *SRW Associates v. Town Board of Brookhaven*, 121 A.D.2d 713, 503 N.Y.S.2d 896 (2d Dep't 1986).

"Cluster development is an optional planning technique permitting Planning Boards to exercise greater flexibility in subdivision approval for the purpose of achieving more efficient use of land containing unusual features . . . for facilitating economical provision for streets and utilities, as well as for preserving the natural and scenic qualities of open lands." *Bayswater Realty & Capital Corp. v. Planning Board of the Town of Lewisboro*, 76 N.Y.2d 460, 560 N.E.2d 1300, 560 N.Y.S.2d 623 (1990). The court held that a planning board is authorized to require developers to set aside land or money for recreational purposes in addition to the open space already created by the clustering process. The court concluded that the planning board's powers under Town Law §281(d) to cluster development for open-space purposes and under §277(1) to require that a developer set aside land for recreation purposes are not mutually exclusive. It noted that the focus of §277(1) is the preservation of lands needed by the broader community for park and recreational purposes, while the focus of §281(d) is the preservation of open lands within the subdivision itself. The court also held that "in a 'proper case,' where it has made the necessary findings, the Planning Board is not precluded from exercising its powers under both §§277(1) and 281(d) with respect to the same subdivision." If the open space reserved under the cluster development is suitable for recreational use under §277, the developer may receive credit toward his responsibilities under §277 to provide land or pay fees for recreation. (Subsequent to this decision, §281(d) was replaced by §278(3), and §277(1) was replaced by §277(4)).

In *Purchase Environmental Protective Association, Inc. v. Town Board of the Town/Village of Harrison*, 212 A.D.2d 532, 622 N.Y.S.2d 166 (2d Dep't 1995), the court held that the inclusion, in a cluster plan, of a golf course serving residents and nonresidents did not violate the density restrictions of the Town Law because 195 acres of land were devoted to the golf-course lot under both the previous conventional plan and the subsequent cluster plan.

"A planning board's authority is limited to permitting deviation from applicable minimum area, side and rear yard depth, and frontage requirements only after it has determined the number of units that would be permitted if the land were subdivided into lots conforming to zoning requirements." *MacFarlane v. Town of Clayton*, 216 A.D.2d 860, 629 N.Y.S.2d 156 (4th Dep't 1995). The court annulled the planning board's preliminary plat approval because "the alternative subdivision layout submitted by the applicant contained several lots that did not conform to the minimum lot size and other requirements of the town of Clayton's zoning ordinance." The alternative layout submitted for cluster development did not show distances between topographical lines. Therefore, the court could not calculate the actual square footage of the lots, and thus could not determine if all the lots met size requirements.

REFERENCE

Michael Murphy and Joseph Stinson, *Cluster Development, at* http://www.pace.edu/lawschool/landuse/cluste.html (last visited Feb. 2, 2001).

D. PLANNED UNIT DEVELOPMENT

DEFINITION

Planned unit development (PUD) zoning provisions permit large lots to be developed in a more flexible manner than is allowed by the underlying zoning. PUD ordinances may allow developers to mix land uses, such as residential and commercial, on a large parcel and to develop the parcel at greater densities, and with more design flexibility, than is otherwise allowed by the underlying zoning district. PUD provisions often require developers to compensate for the impacts of their projects by setting aside significant and usable open space, providing infrastructure needed to service the development, or offering other community facilities and services.

There is, in New York State, no statutory definition of a PUD. Local governments' use of the technique has established a number of optional methods of designating large lots for more flexible development. PUD ordinances typically leave the underlying zoning in place and offer an alternative to landowners to develop the site in accordance with the PUD provisions.

PURPOSE

Most PUD ordinances utilized in New York provide that their purpose is to achieve greater design flexibility and economies of scale in the development of large lots within the community. The village of Malone, for example, adopted a PUD provision stating that its purpose was "to provide a means of developing those land areas within the community considered appropriate for new residential, recreational, office space, commercial or industrial use, or a satisfactory combination of these uses, in an economic and compatible manner, while encouraging the utilization of innovative planning and design concepts or techniques in these areas."

WHEN

A developing community that anticipates receiving a rezoning or site plan application for the development of a large shopping mall or discount warehouse could use a mixed-use PUD law to negotiate significant design and use changes in the development. Instead of ending up with another faceless commercial strip, the community may use its PUD provisions to provide the leverage, incentives, and process necessary to encourage the development of a better commercial project, reinforced by the addition of some residential uses, community facilities, and attractive landscaping and building design.

The same community, faced with the prospect of one or more large residential developments, could avoid the proliferation of single-lot subdivisions or uniform condominium developments by using PUD provisions to provide for some on-site shopping and services for homeowners. This can be accomplished by adopting a residential PUD provision that allows mixing a variety of housing types and styles with some neighborhood commercial uses. Through design flexibility and control, an appropriate neighborhood can be created, properly serviced by infrastructure, and appropriately landscaped and designed to protect surrounding areas from its impacts.

An urban community could adopt a PUD ordinance as a means of attracting developers of unique large lots. By offering a mix of land uses and flexible design options, developers are free to create a project that is economically and environmentally viable for the site. In a similar way, a rural community could adopt PUD provisions, in advance of development, as its way of indicating the areas that are appropriate for mixed-use and more intense development.

Although PUD development is designed for large-lot development, this does not necessarily mean that its use is limited to communities with one or more large lots that are under single ownership. The PUD provisions can be drafted to present an opportunity to the owners of several medium-sized or smaller lots to work together to combine ownership and take advantage of the PUD development option.

AUTHORITY

There is no separate authorization in New York State statutes for the inclusion of planned unit development provisions in a local zoning law. This authority is, instead, implied in the delegation to local governments of the power to enact zoning restrictions and create zoning districts. One purpose of zoning is to insure that its provisions consider the character of areas and their suitability for particular uses with a view toward conserving the value of buildings and encouraging the most appropriate use of the land throughout the municipality. Several court decisions have considered various applications of PUD ordinances, implicitly upholding their legality.

The New York Court of Appeals has made it clear that "how various properties shall be classified or reclassified rests with the local legislative body; its judgment and determination will be conclusive, beyond interference from the courts, unless shown to be arbitrary." *Rodgers v. Village of Tarrytown*, 302 N.Y. 115, 121, 96 N.E.2d 731 (1951). The court noted that "changed or changing conditions call for changed plans, and persons who own property in a particular zone or use district enjoy no eternally vested right to that classification if the public interest demands otherwise. Accordingly, the power of the [locality] to amend its basic zoning ordinance in such a way as to reasonably promote the general welfare cannot be questioned." A zoning law is not flawed because a district created by its provisions is not affixed to particular land at the time that district is created. It is necessary, however, that PUD provisions be adopted in accordance with the locality's comprehensive plan.

IMPLEMENTATION

The process of adding PUD provisions to the local zoning law is identical to adopting any zoning amendment. The provisions must be drafted, published, subjected to public hearing, adopted, and filed. The challenge of implementation is to choose an appropriate method of designating sites for PUD development, to provide for flexible site and building design, and to determine how PUD developments shall be approved by local authorities.

The PUD law can designate one or more particular sites that the community currently knows it wants developed in a more flexible manner than provided for by the underlying zoning. In this instance, it can leave the underlying zoning provisions in place or require that the site be developed as a PUD. Alternatively, the law can allow PUD development in certain types of situations, generally, and provide for later site designation, upon application by one or more landowners or upon the initiative of the local legislature. This approach allows the locality to use the PUD technique when confronted by a large-scale development whose owner is seeking a rezoning of the land or is applying for as-of-right approval under the existing zoning.

The PUD law must state its purpose, contain standards for site and building development, and describe a process for reviewing and approving individual projects. Care should be taken in drafting these provisions so that landowners, developers, and neighbors are as well informed as possible of the community's objectives and standards.

If the local legislature is to retain the authority to review and approve PUD applications, the standards contained in the law can be more general, legally, although a certain degree of specificity is still helpful in clarifying when and where the community desires PUD development. Where the legislature delegates to the local planning or zoning board the responsibility of reviewing and approving PUD applications, the standards must be more specific.

ILLUSTRATION

The city of Binghamton adopted its PUD provisions "to encourage and promote flexibility, land use efficiency, new development concepts, and quality design in the construction of large-scale projects. These objectives are to be achieved by substituting an approved comprehensive development plan for conventional land use regulations, with such comprehensive development plan to be approved by the planning commission and to become the basis for continuing land use controls in the PUD area."

Binghamton's PUD law was adopted with the primary objective of promoting housing. It allows the planning commission, however, to permit some nonresidential uses in a PUD if the applicant for PUD designation can show that such nonresidential use will promote the objective of the City's comprehensive plan, contribute to the quality of the housing development, and enhance the surrounding neighborhood. These nonresidential uses can occupy no more than 25% of the gross lot area. In this urban context, the PUD provisions require a minimum lot size of three acres. The law allows for a density increase of 30% over the "maximum density normally permitted in the district where the PUD is to be located."

In the town of Bethlehem, PUD provisions of the zoning law were added "to provide for new residential, commercial, or manufacturing uses in which economies of scale or creative architectural or planning concepts may be utilized by the developer." The provisions state that "application for the establishment of a planned development district shall be made to the Town Board by the owners of the lands to be included in the district or by a person or persons holding an option to purchase the lands contingent only upon approval of the application for the change of zone."

In Bethlehem, the application is referred by the town board to the planning board. The applicant is required to submit adequate data, maps, and preliminary plans to allow the planning board to determine the desirability of the proposed project in the proposed location. After reviewing and requiring revisions in the plans, the planning board is to approve, approve with modifications, or disapprove the application and report its findings and decision to the town board. The town board then holds a public hearing, after which it may approve the establishment of the PUD district.

After the district is established in this way, applications for the approval of a building project in the district are made to the town board, which again refers such applications to the planning board. The planning board holds the required public hearing on the building application and may approve, approve with modifications, or disapprove the application and report its decision and findings to the town board. If the planning board denies the building application, the town board may approve the project with any stipulations or conditions it deems necessary to achieve the objectives of the zoning ordinance.

The Bethlehem PUD law contains a schedule governing the use, area, density, and building area ratio and yard dimensions allowed in a PUD district. For residential and commercial districts, five acres or more are required and, subject to certain limitations, commercial and residential uses may be mixed. In a residential PUD, eight multi-family dwelling units per acre are allowed; in a commercial PUD, up to 16 multi-family dwelling units per acre are permitted.

LIMITATIONS AND CONCERNS

When considering the addition of PUD provisions to the zoning law, local officials are presented with several critical questions. Should specific sites be designated for PUD development or should PUD development simply be allowed, with the sites to be designated later upon the application of landowners or developers? Where sites are to be designated at a later time, what technique should be used to identify them and what local body should make that decision? If PUD development is to be allowed but the sites are to be identified later, in which existing zoning districts should the PUD provisions apply? How specific should the criteria be that define the sites that are eligible for PUD designation? What should be the minimum size lot that is eligible? How specific should the standards governing the design of PUD projects be? How can these standards be written to minimize the impact of the PUD development on the surrounding neighborhood?

STATUTES

New York State Village Law §7-700, Town Law §261, and General City Law §20(24) grant basic land use authority to local governments and allow them to regulate the details of land development and building construction and alteration. This may be done for "the purpose of promoting the health, safety, morals or the general welfare of the community."

Village Law §7-702, Town Law §262, and General City Law §20(25) authorize local governments to divide the community into zoning districts and to regulate the use, construction, and alteration of buildings and land within those districts.

Village Law §7-704, Town Law §263, and General City Law §§20(24) and (25) provide that zoning and land use regulations must be in conformance with the locality's comprehensive plan. The purposes that such zoning regulations are to achieve are to lessen congestion, to secure safety from fire and flood, to prevent overcrowding, to facilitate the provision of infrastructure, and to encourage "the most appropriate use of land throughout such municipality."

Section 10(1)(ii)(a)(11) of the Municipal Home Rule Law states that a municipality may adopt local laws for the "protection and enhancement of its physical and visual environment."

Section 10(1)(ii)(a)(14) of the Municipal Home Rule Law states that a municipality may adopt local laws as provided in the Statute of Local Governments. Section 10(6) of the Statute of Local Governments authorizes cities, towns, and villages to adopt zoning regulations.

CASE DIGEST

The Second Department court declared zoning provisions invalid that established a planned residential district in which there were no principal uses as-of-right. Instead, the zoning established 12 uses that were permitted only upon issuance of special permits by the zoning board of appeals. *Marshall v. Wappingers Falls*, 28 A.D.2d 542, 279 N.Y.S.2d 654 (2d Dep't 1967). The court held that the establishment of this district was unauthorized by the Village Law and that it "was not zoning in accordance with a comprehensive plan but rather was a device to permit, in effect, lot-by-lot zoning" by the board.

In *Dur-Bar Realty Co. v. City of Utica*, 57 A.D.2d 51, 394 N.Y.S.2d 913 (4th Dep't 1977), the court upheld a planned unit development ordinance that created a land conservation district for land lying in a floodplain and that allowed no as-of-right use and only certain special uses by permit. The court sustained the ordinance because of the "unique use control problems" presented by the environmentally constrained land in the new district. The court distinguished the *Wappingers Falls* decision by stating, "In *Wappingers Falls* . . . it does not appear that the land in the challenged district was in any way unusual in topography or location so as to justify the subjection of all use proposals to case by case decision." However, the creation of the land conservation district in *Dur-Bar* was "a product of assessment of the character of the land in light of the public health and safety interests in being protected against flooding and other hazards that would result from building in an area unsuitable for intensive development." The court concluded that "the critical difference between *Wappingers Falls* and the present case is that, there, the special permit device was used as a substitute for comprehensive land use planning, whereas here, the device was chosen in furtherance of comprehensive planning."

In *Daum v. Meade*, 65 Misc. 2d 572, 318 N.Y.S.2d 199 (Sup. Ct. Nassau County 1971), the creation of a planned industrial park district by the Town of North Hempstead was challenged as not being in accordance with the comprehensive plan because a new master plan study was underway. The court stated that although there was no master plan adopted at the time the district was created, there was a comprehensive plan consisting of the existing zoning scheme and map and the various documents and studies that pointed to the present and future needs of the town. Consequently, the court held that it was not necessary to wait for the new master plan before enacting the planned unit development ordinance.

The court rejected the landowners' contention that a zoning law that permitted the establishment of planned development districts constituted an invalid delegation of power to the village planning board in *Willey v. Garnsey*, 45 A.D.2d 227, 357 N.Y.S.2d 281 (4th Dep't 1974). The court held that there was "no delegation of legislative authority" to the planning board because the village board had "retain[ed] the power to make the final decision" and the planning board had "act[ed] in an advisory capacity only."

In *Todd Mart, Inc. v. Town Board of Town of Webster*, 49 A.D.2d 12, 370 N.Y.S.2d 683 (4th Dep't 1975), the town provided for the creation of a planned shopping center district upon application by the landowner. A developer challenged the failure of the town board to rezone 20 acres of its land for the construction of a shopping center under those provisions. The court held that the process involved a legislative decision by the town board and, as such, its decision not to rezone because of potential impacts on the community was reasonable. The court noted that "'[t]he planned unit development technique is a legislative response to changing patterns of land development and the demonstrated shortcomings of orthodox zoning regulations.'"

The Second Department declared void a zoning amendment that rezoned property from residential to Planned Development-Extraordinary (PD-E) for the construction of a K-Mart "[s]ince the amendment was not supported by any evidence that it accorded with the City's existing or evolving plans for development of the area." *Hale v. City of Utica*, 61 A.D.2d 885, 403 N.Y.S.2d 374 (4th Dep't 1978). The court listed these reasons for its decision: the property was located in a residential area; the proposed amendment was not approved by the county planning department; and the common council stated primarily economic reasons for rezoning the property. The council "cited the value of the new construction, the number of new jobs, the increase in employment, and the increase in the City's tax base"–matters that the court found "do not relate to sound planning principles."

In *Rye Town/King Civic Association v. Town of Rye*, 82 A.D.2d 474, 442 N.Y.S.2d 67 (2d Dep't 1981), the court held that the town failed to comply with its duties under the State Environmental Quality Review Act (SEQRA) when approving a planned unit development site plan. Although the town had carried out "extensive environmental review procedures in harmony with the spirit of SEQRA," the court concluded that literal compliance with the Act was required. The town did carefully consider numerous environmental factors, such as traffic volume, parking capacity, drainage, soil, vegetation, noise, and aesthetics. However, the court held that the town's failure to prepare an environmental impact statement "was not excusable."

The New York Court of Appeals determined that a town board had no authority to approve a preliminary planned unit development plan since the planning board had previously denied it. *Webster Associates v. Town of Webster*, 59 N.Y.2d 220, 451 N.E.2d 189, 464 N.Y.S.2d 431

(1983). The procedure for planned unit development approval is set forth in the town's zoning law that "expressly conditions Town Board consideration of such plans on prior approval of the Planning Board." The court held that "there is no statutory bar to the establishment of such a condition" and that "the Planning Board's disapproval of . . . [the] proposal foreclosed consideration . . . by the Town Board."

REFERENCE

Michael Murphy and Joseph Stinson, *Planned Unit Development, at* http://www.pace.edu/lawschool/landuse/pud.html (last visited Feb. 2, 2001).

E. INCENTIVE ZONING

DEFINITION

A local legislature can provide a system of zoning incentives to land developers in exchange for the provision of community benefits by those developers. In setting up such a system, the legislature leaves existing zoning provisions in place but permits more intensive development of the land in exchange for certain community benefits. Incentives can be provided to developers of raw land or to those who propose the expansion of existing structures, the adaptive reuse of older buildings, or the redevelopment of brownfield sites and other distressed parcels in older, developed areas.

The incentives that may be offered to developers include adjustments to the density of development—for example, allowing more residential units or a greater building floor area than is otherwise permitted under the zoning law. Incentives can also include adjustments to the height, open space, use, or other requirements of the underlying zoning law.

These incentives are given in exchange for the developer's providing one or more community benefits, including open space or parks, affordable housing, day care or elder care, or "other specific physical, social, or cultural amenity of benefit to the residents of the community." Where the community benefit cannot feasibly or practically be provided directly by individual developers, the system can provide for developers to make cash payments to the locality. Such sums must be held in a trust fund to be used exclusively for the community benefits specified.

Incentive zoning has frequently been used to induce land developers to provide affordable housing for senior citizens, local workers, or low- and moderate-income citizens. The developer is allowed to build a greater number of homes than is otherwise permitted by the zoning law and to sell or rent some of these "bonus units" at market value. In return, the developer is required to use some of that profit to reduce the cost of the affordably constructed residential units. These affordable homes must then be rented or sold to persons or families of low or modest income, or to senior citizens.

PURPOSE

The purpose of incentive zoning is to advance the locality's physical, cultural, and social objectives, in accordance with the comprehensive plan, by having land developers provide specific amenities in exchange for zoning incentives. Development brings with it the need to provide municipal services and facilities to serve and absorb the impacts of additional population, traffic, sewage, water consumption, and the like. One cost-effective way of providing those municipal services and facilities is to concentrate new development in serviceable districts. This can be done by providing density bonuses, or incentives, to developers in such districts on the condition that they provide or pay for the services and facilities needed in the area or in the community as a whole.

WHEN

Generally, community benefits, such as infrastructure and municipal services, are paid for in two ways. Normally, they are covered by the municipality directly out of the revenues derived from taxing real property. Occasionally, they are required to be provided by the developers of specific projects to mitigate the direct impacts of the developments on the community. Developers may be required to pay impact fees, in lieu of providing facilities such as parks, traffic improvements, or water system improvements necessitated by the project. Where authorized by law, requirements for the provision of community benefits or the payment of fees must bear some rough proportionality to the measurable impacts that the specific development will have on the community.

Incentive zoning provides a third alternative: having developers use some of the economic benefits afforded by the incentives to provide or pay for facilities and services. With amendments to the New York State Town, Village, and General City statutes adopted in 1991 and 1992, local authority to create an incentive zoning system is clear. Further, because economic incentives are used to encourage developers to provide needed benefits and because such systems are voluntary, developers tend not to oppose them, although they might often challenge impact fees and mitigation requirements. Finally, because an incentive zoning system can be designed with the needs of an entire district or service area in mind, it can be a more potent system of meeting community facility and service needs than proceeding one development project at a time.

AUTHORITY

Municipalities in New York have long been empowered to adopt incentive zoning systems. Because this authority had been used sparingly, the state legislature amended the Town, Village, and General City statutes to clarify this authority and to provide a specific procedure for creating a system that all municipalities can rely on. Amendments adopted in 1991 and 1992 make it clear that the specific grant of authority for incentive zoning is in addition to "authorization to provide for the granting of incentives, or bonuses, pursuant to other enabling law." Town Law §261-b (2); Village Law §7-703 (2); General City Law §81-d (2). The underlying authority can be found in the zoning enabling statutes of the Town, Village, and General City laws and in the Municipal Home Rule Law. Prior to the 1991 and 1992 amendments, it was held that the general grant of authority in the zoning enabling statutes gave municipalities the authority to adopt incentive zoning systems.

Now that state statutes provide specific procedures for incentive zoning, it is not clear whether local legislatures must use their supersession authority under the Municipal Home Rule Law if they wish to adopt a system in a manner that does not fully comply with the detailed provisions of the new statutes. Any doubt on this subject, however, can be removed if the local government references the incentive zoning provisions of the relevant 1991-1992 statute in its findings, expresses its intent to supersede it, mentions the provisions superseded, and otherwise complies with the requirements for superseding state law.

IMPLEMENTATION

The system of zoning incentives must be adopted by the local legislative body: the town board, village board of trustees, or the city council. Incentive zoning provisions are adopted in the same manner as other zoning ordinances, laws, or amendments. There must be public notice and hearings, conformance with the comprehensive plan, and compliance with environmental review. A number of additional requirements must be met if the local legislature creates the incentive zoning system under authority granted by the 1991-1992 amendments to the Town, Village, and General City laws. These provisions are as follows:

Each existing zoning district in which incentives can be awarded must be designated and incorporated in any zoning map adopted in conjunction with the system.

The legislature must find that each of these districts has the capacity to absorb the additional development authorized by the incentives. Fire, transportation, water, sewer, waste disposal, and community facilities and services must be found to be adequate.

The legislature must find that the development allowed by the zoning incentives will have no significant environmentally damaging consequences, that each affected district contains adequate environmental quality, and that the additional development provided for is compatible with the development otherwise permitted under the underlying zoning ordinance.

Where the legislature finds that the development allowed by the zoning incentives may have a significant effect on the environment, it must prepare a generic environmental impact statement (GEIS) and provide that a proportionate share of the cost of the GEIS shall be paid by each applicant for incentives under the system. This may allow significant streamlining of projects that receive incentives, if they conform with the GEIS and raise no significant environmental impacts not adequately covered by it. In such a case, projects may not be required to include the time-consuming process of preparing a full environmental impact statement.

The legislature must determine whether the system of zoning incentives will have a negative impact on the provision of affordable housing in the community and must take action to compensate for any negative impact.

A procedure for applying the zoning incentives to specific parcels must be established by the local legislature, including:

- The specific incentives that may be granted to an applicant.
- The community benefits that must be provided by an applicant.
- The standards for approving an application for incentives, including how to assess that the benefits received are adequate given the incentives granted.
- The requirements for submitting an application for incentives, and the process for reviewing, approving, and imposing conditions on applications for incentives. (Although the amendments are silent on this subject, it appears that the legislature may delegate the authority to provide incentives to an appropriate review and approval body such as the planning board or zoning board of appeals.)
- Provisions for public notice and hearing prior to the award of incentives, where a hearing is required by the law or ordinance under which the zoning incentive system was adopted.
- Provisions for the receipt of cash in lieu of the direct provision by the developer of the benefits, where the legislature determines that such benefits are not immediately feasible or otherwise practical. In such an instance, the legislature must establish a trust fund into which all cash payments are deposited. This fund is to be used exclusively for the specific benefits authorized by the incentive zoning system.

ILLUSTRATIONS

In the early 1980s, the town of New Castle adopted a system of providing a 100% density bonus to land developers in exchange for the provision of affordable housing, recreational facilities, or specified off-site improvements. This expanded on an incentive zoning system adopted by neighboring Lewisboro nearly a decade earlier. That system provided land developers a percentage increase in residential density in exchange for the construction of housing affordable to moderate-income families earning about the amount paid to town employees.

In the late 1980s, New York City adopted an incentive zoning system that allowed additional floor area to be developed in the Special Manhattan Bridge District in direct proportion to the amount of floor area provided by the developer for senior-citizen centers, day-care facilities, educational facilities, and affordable housing.

LIMITATIONS AND CONCERNS

Although new legislation in New York State has made local authority and procedures for creating incentive zoning systems very clear, there remain many questions to be addressed in the design and execution of any particular incentive program. How, for example, does the municipality insure that the benefit will be provided over time? If the benefit provided is affordable housing, for example, what mechanisms will be used to insure that the units are sold or rented appropriately over time? If the benefit is day care, how does the municipality insure that the space provided by the developer is occupied by a viable day-care provider over a reasonable period?

Residents and property owners in the district where the increased development will occur must be convinced of the advantages to them of the incentive zoning system. Since they will be affected by the additional development, measures to mitigate that impact must be adequate and convincing. The local legislature must find that the area can absorb the additional development, but local residents might argue that the development should be spread throughout the community. The advantages to the developer and the community need to be carefully thought out and articulated to meet this inevitable concern.

STATUTES AND REGULATIONS

In New York State, Town Law §261-b and Village Law §7-703, adopted in 1991, and General City Law §81-d, adopted in 1992, grant parallel authority to towns, villages, and cities to adopt incentive zoning systems and set forth the specific provisions that must be followed.

Title 6 NYCRR Part 617.10 contains the requirements for completing the generic environmental impact statement which may be required before the adoption of a system of zoning incentives.

The authority of local governments to supersede general state law can be found at Municipal Home Rule Law §10(1)(ii)(d)(3). Provisions that must be followed to properly supersede a general state law are found at Municipal Home Rule Law §22(1).

CASE DIGEST

The zoning law challenged in *Blitz v. Town of New Castle*, 94 A.D.2d 92, 463 N.Y.S.2d 832 (2d Dep't 1983), permitted density bonuses of up to 100% in exchange for "senior citizen or low-to-moderate-income housing, units for the handicapped, rental units, energy saving devices, recreational facilities, off-site improvements, and underground parking." The plaintiff challenged the town's zoning ordinance, contending that it was unconstitutionally exclusionary of people in the region who are in search of affordable housing. The court upheld the law, noting that the "zoning ordinances will go no further than determining what may or may not be built; market forces will decide what will actually be built, in the absence of government subsidies." The plaintiff did not carry its burden of proving that the devices included in the town's ordinance were an insufficient response to regional housing needs.

In *Municipal Arts Society of New York v. Koch*, 137 Misc. 2d 832, 522 N.Y.S.2d 800 (Sup. Ct. NY County 1987), the court determined that the cash sale of a zoning bonus was an unacceptable application of incentive zoning. "The Coliseum is located in a zone which permits construction as-of-right of floor space up to a maximum of 15 times the square footage of the lot. This [density] is subject to being increased by up to 20% in exchange for the developer agreeing to 'provide major improvements for the adjacent subway stations' provided that 'the zoning lot for the development . . . which a [density] bonus is requested shall be adjacent to the mezzanine or concourse of the subway station for which the improvement is proposed or an existing connecting passageway to the station.'" Under the development agreement between the city and the developer, the city would be "obtaining not only $35 to $40 million of local subway improvements, but an additional $57 million to be employed for other purposes." The court determined that the sale was inappropriate because the cash payment to be made to the city was to be employed for purposes other than local improvements. The court held that the "government may not place itself in the position of reaping a cash premium because one of its agencies bestows a zoning benefit upon a developer. Zoning benefits are not cash items."

The court in *Asian Americans for Equality v. Koch*, 72 N.Y.2d 121, 527 N.E.2d 265, 531 N.Y.S.2d 782 (1988), upheld a zoning amendment that created a special use district. The new zoning provided that development in the Special Manhattan Bridge District would be "regulated by a system of bonus points permitting increased density in residential buildings for those developers who agree to: 1) donate space for community facilities such as senior citizen or day care centers, educational facilities; 2) construct low-income dwelling units; or 3) rehabilitate existing substandard housing." The plaintiffs argued that the incentive zoning scheme provided greater bonuses for educational and senior citizen facilities than it did for low-income housing. They argued that such housing was necessary to combat the effects of gentrification caused by the creation of the special district and that the zoning discouraged developers from building low-income housing. The court concluded that inducing private developers to provide public benefits involves a complex set of considerations. It held that the plaintiffs had not carried their burden of proving that the bonus scheme was clearly arbitrary or capricious or undertaken for an improper purpose.

REFERENCE

Michael Murphy and Joseph Stinson, *Incentive Zoning, at*
http://www.pace.edu/lawschool/landuse/incent.html (last visited Feb. 2, 2001).

F. TRANSFER OF DEVELOPMENT RIGHTS

DEFINITION

New York statutes define transfer of development rights (TDR) as "the process by which development rights are transferred from one lot, parcel, or area of land in a sending district to another lot, parcel, or area of land in one or more receiving districts." Local governments are allowed great flexibility in designing a TDR program; they can establish conditions that they deem "necessary and appropriate" to achieve the purposes of the TDR program.

To implement a transfer of development rights program, the local legislature identifies a "sending district" where land conservation is sought and a "receiving district" where development of property is desired and can be serviced properly.

In many TDR programs, the zoning provisions applicable to the sending district are amended to reduce the density at which land can be developed. While losing their right to develop their properties at the formerly permitted densities, property owners in the sending district are awarded development rights. These development rights are regarded as severable from the land ownership and transferable by their owners.

TDR programs usually establish some method of valuing the development rights that are to be transferred from the sending to the receiving district. Some communities establish development rights "banks" that purchase development rights from landowners in sending districts and sell them to landowners in receiving districts.

Property owners in the receiving district are eligible to apply for zoning incentives that increase the densities at which their lands may be developed. To qualify for these incentives, the property owners must purchase the development rights from landowners in the sending district or from the development rights bank.

PURPOSE

According to New York statutes, the purpose of a TDR program is "to protect the natural, scenic, or agricultural qualities of open lands, to enhance sites and areas of special character or special historical, cultural, aesthetic, or economic interest or value, and to enable and encourage flexibility of design and careful management of land in recognition of land as a basic and valuable natural resource." Town Law §261-a(2); Village Law §7-701(2); General City Law §20-f(2).

An effective TDR program allows a community whose zoning law creates a hard-to-service, spread-out development pattern, to develop in a more cost-effective manner; likewise, it can increase the tax base while minimizing the costs of servicing land development. It can preserve threatened conservation areas while allowing owners of land in that area to be compensated through the sale of some or all of their former development rights.

WHEN

TDR programs are most often created in response to a perceived crisis in the area that becomes the sending district. That area, for example, may contain a precious resource such as an endangered species, a valuable economic resource such as viable agricultural soils, or a drinking water supply whose existence is threatened by development.

The TDR technique was also designed to combat inefficient land development patterns that can result from the build out of conventional zoning laws. Once the community realizes that its zoning law is creating a high-cost, environmentally questionable pattern of land use, it can create a TDR program to adjust zoning densities. Instead of rezoning to lower densities in the sending areas and increasing densities in the receiving areas (creating a loss of investment expectations in the former and a windfall in the latter), the community can elect to provide for the transfer of development rights as its method of changing its zoning strategy.

AUTHORITY

The authority to create a TDR program is implied from the delegation of authority to local governments to adopt zoning ordinances and create zoning districts. Because this authority had been used sparingly, the state legislature, in 1989, amended the Town, Village, and General City statutes to clarify local TDR authority and to provide a specific procedure for creating and implementing a TDR program.

Although the New York State statutes set out a specific process for establishing a TDR program, they also allow local governments to continue previously created programs and, apparently, to create programs in a different manner from that contained in the statutes. It is not completely clear, however, whether local legislatures must use their supersession authority under the Municipal Home Rule Law if they wish to adopt a TDR program that does not fully comply with the specific provisions of the statute. Any doubt on this subject can be removed by referencing the TDR provisions of the relevant 1989 statute, expressing the intent of the local legislature to supersede them, mentioning the provisions superseded, and otherwise complying with the requirements for superseding state law.

IMPLEMENTATION

In creating a TDR program in New York State, all procedures required for adopting and amending local zoning ordinances or laws, including all provisions for notice and public hearing, must be followed. The local TDR program must be established in accordance with the comprehensive plan.

What constitutes an appropriate sending district is defined by the authorizing statute: it must consist of natural, scenic, recreational, agricultural, forest, or open land or sites of special historical, cultural, aesthetic, or economic value sought to be protected. The statute allows municipalities to establish development rights banks to purchase development credits from landowners in sending districts and to sell them to landowners in receiving districts.

Communities that elect to create their TDR programs under the authorizing statutes must designate sending and receiving districts in a particular fashion, make a variety of detailed findings, and take other specific action.

Before receiving and sending districts are designated, a generic environmental impact statement must be prepared for the receiving district. Subsequently, individual projects developed in the receiving district need to comply with the environmental review procedures of state law only to the extent that their impacts were not reviewed in the generic environmental impact statement.

Receiving districts must be found that contain adequate resources and infrastructure to accommodate the increased development. The board must determine that no significant environmental damage will result from this increase and that the additional development is compatible with that permitted in the underlying zoning ordinance. This finding must be made after evaluating the impacts of the potential increased development permitted by the transfer of development rights to the receiving district.

The locality must evaluate the effect of the TDR program on the potential development of low- or moderate-income housing that might be lost in the sending district or gained in the receiving district. If losses and gains are not roughly equivalent, the locality must take action to compensate for any net loss of such housing.

If the sending and receiving districts are in different taxing districts, the locality must find that the TDR program will not unreasonably transfer the tax burden between the taxpayers of such districts.

A local TDR program must provide for the execution and filing of conservation easements on land in the sending district whose development rights have been purchased under the program. The easement must specify that it is enforceable by the local government.

The program must, in addition, provide for the reassessment, within one year, of the property tax value of any parcel whose development rights have been transferred.

ILLUSTRATIONS

A TDR program was established in the Pinelands area of southern New Jersey under the auspices of a regional pinelands commission created by the state in cooperation with local governments. Under that program, development rights are being transferred from ecologically fragile and agriculturally valuable lands to central receiving districts. These rights are converted to development credits that are created on a per-acre basis. The program awards development credits to landowners in the sending districts by increments of 39 acres. One credit is awarded for every 39 acres of woodlands, two for every 39 acres of productive agricultural land, and 0.2 credits for every 39 acres of wetlands.

Under this New Jersey program, a developer who buys one credit is entitled to build an additional four houses in a residential receiving district. In other words, if a developer owns one acre in a receiving district that is currently zoned for one dwelling unit, he can develop five units on that acre by purchasing one development credit. If a developer wishes to build only one additional home, he would buy one quarter of a credit. A development rights bank has been created to purchase credits from landowners in sending districts and sell them to landowners in receiving districts.

A significant TDR program was recently created in eastern Long Island in the Central Pine Barrens, an environmentally fragile and resource-rich area encompassing over 100,000 acres. Faced by requests for over 220 development projects in the area and stymied by time-consuming and costly litigation over their environmental impacts, the towns, landowners, developers, citizens, and environmentalists joined together to develop a plan, including the use of TDR, to preserve a core area of about 55,000 acres.

The Long Island Pine Barrens TDR program was modeled after the New Jersey Pine Barrens program. The Long Island program was established under state legislation adopted in 1993 and is implemented under a comprehensive land use plan adopted in April, 1995. Several municipalities with jurisdiction over the Pine Barrens area are involved in the program. The comprehensive plan allocates Pine Barrens credits to land in designated sending districts based on their development yield. Land in the sending district may not be developed under the zoning law. Instead, that zoning is used to determine the development rights that may be transferred. The development yield varies according to the number of units the zoning law permits per acre. If zoning permits four units per acre, the development yield factor established is 2.7, yielding that number of credits.

The comprehensive plan establishes overlay districts into which development rights can be transferred. If a developer purchases one credit, he will be able to build one unit above the density allowed in a receiving district. Overall, the receiving areas are structured to provide a demand for credits in the receiving sites that exceeds the number of credits created in the sending sites by a ratio of 2.5 to 1. This ratio was calculated to create sufficient competition to insure an active market for the development credits in the sending districts. The state legislation creating this program established a TDR bank, funded by an allocation of five million dollars to provide an initial market for the credits. The bank is authorized to purchase credits from owners in sending districts and sell them to owners in receiving districts.

LIMITATIONS AND CONCERNS

TDR programs are complex. They require municipalities to engage in a sophisticated analysis of the impacts of the program in both sending and receiving districts. Programs typically raise significant issues that concern residents and owners in both sending and receiving districts. How much development potential is to be lost in the sending districts? How are these development "rights" to be measured and valued? How can a viable market for these rights be created? How many properties in the receiving district must be eligible for more intense development to create a viable market for the development rights created by the program in the sending district? Should a development rights bank be created? How are the administration of the bank and the execution and filing of the required conservation easement documents to be handled? What process should be put in place to review and approve development projects in the receiving district?

A particularly difficult aspect of designing a TDR program is determining how to define and value the development rights that are severed from the land and eligible to be transferred. According to the statute, a formula can be used to quantify the development rights to be transferred based on such factors as the lot area, floor area, floor area ratios, density, height limitations, or any other criteria that effectively quantify an appropriate value. The formula chosen converts development rights into specific development credits. When a development credit is purchased, it carries the right to a certain additional density in the receiving district.

How development rights are valued and how a market for them is created will determine the viability of the TDR program and, perhaps, its legal validity. In recent programs, the agencies

241

created from two to two and a half times the demand for development credits in the receiving district as the number of development credits in the sending district. For this market to work, there must be development pressure in the receiving area resulting in a desire by landowners to purchase development credits from the sending area. Whether such ratios can be established and whether sufficient development pressures exist are factors that must be considered by local leaders who create TDR programs.

ALTERNATIVE APPROACHES

In the description of a TDR program above, it is assumed that the zoning law applicable to the sending district is to be amended to reduce the density at which the land may be developed. This could be called a mandatory TDR program. This definition is based on the way in which TDR programs have most often been structured, not on any limitation in the statutory description of the TDR authority.

However, the statute says nothing about reducing the permissible densities of development in sending zones. Presumably, a TDR program could be set up that leaves the existing zoning in place in the sending district and simply allows the development permitted by that zoning to be severed and transferred to the receiving district. Under such a program, the density incentives in the receiving district could be awarded to property developers in exchange for cash deposits into a dedicated fund that could be used to purchase conservation easements from willing landowners in the sending district. The development rights of the landowners in the receiving district are otherwise unaffected by the program. This could be called a voluntary TDR program.

Further, there is no requirement that any zoning change in the sending district must take all development rights away from properties in that district. Where the sending area can be protected by reducing densities and, for example, clustering the remaining development on unconstrained portions of the land, some development rights can remain attached to the land instead of being severed and made transferable. The owners of land in the sending district could be allowed to develop at a fraction of the previously allowed density and could be awarded fewer development credits as a result. This could be called a partial TDR program.

Whether to adopt a mandatory, voluntary, complete, or partial TDR program depends greatly on the character of the land in the sending district and on its vulnerability to development. Some commentators even suggest that the base densities in the receiving zone be lowered by zoning amendments when the TDR program is created to insure a larger market for the transferable development rights.

Making these choices is one of the more complicated aspects of designing a local TDR program. Most programs have opted for simplicity by proscribing most development in the sending district and providing for the severance and transferability of that development to properties in the receiving district, where the existing zoning is otherwise left in place.

STATUTES

The New York State statutes that authorize local governments to adopt TDR programs are found at Town Law §261-a, Village Law §7-701, and General City Law §20-f.

The authority of local governments to supersede general state law can be found at Municipal Home Rule Law §10(1)(ii). Provisions that must be followed to properly supersede a general state law are found at Municipal Home Rule Law §22(1).

CASE DIGEST

In *Fred F. French Investing Co., Inc. v. City of New York*, 39 N.Y.2d 587, 350 N.E.2d 381, 385 N.Y.S.2d 5 (1976), the New York Court of Appeals declared that the city was unable to use the transfer development rights (TDR) of airspace from the regulated parcel to other receiving areas as a means of validating the rezoning of the petitioner's land as a public park. The court noted that the development rights that were transferred had a "value so uncertain and contingent, as to deprive the property owner of their practical usefulness." Notwithstanding the ineffectiveness of the TDR mechanism in this context, the court held that a TDR provision "may not be disregarded in determining whether the ordinance has destroyed the economic value of the underlying property."

While the court in *French* did not affirmatively sustain the use of transfer of development rights, the following year it did hold the technique to be within the authority of local government. In *Penn Central Transportation Co. v. City of New York*, 438 U.S. 104, 8 ELR 20528 (1978), the Court sustained the City Landmarks Preservation Commission's denial of a permit for the construction of an office building atop historic Grand Central Terminal. The Court stated that "the development rights were made transferable to numerous sites in the vicinity of the terminal, several owned by Penn Central, and at least one or two suitable for construction of office buildings. Since this regulation and substitution was reasonable, no due process violation resulted."

In *Suitum v. Tahoe Regional Planning Agency*, 520 U.S. 725, 27 ELR 21064 (1997), the owner of a single lot that could not be developed because of land use regulations challenged those regulations as a taking of her property rights. The Court held that a property owner, in order to gain standing to challenge land use regulations as a taking, does not have to apply for credits available under a transfer of development rights system to exhaust her administrative remedies. It held that, despite this failure, the owner presented a question of whether the regulation constituted a regulatory taking that was ripe for adjudication. The Court did not decide whether the availability of credits was relevant to the question of whether a regulatory taking had occurred.

REFERENCES

Joseph Stinson, *Transfer of Development Rights, at*
http://www.pace.edu/lawschool/landuse/tdr.html (last visited Feb. 2, 2001).

Maanvi Mitra, *Transfer of Development Rights, at* http://www.pace.edu/lawschool/landuse/tdrpap.html (last visited Feb. 2, 2001).

Richard J. Roddewig and Cheryl A. Inghram, Transferable Development Rights Programs: TDRs and the Real Estate Market Place, American Planning Association Planning Advisory Service Report No. 401 (May, 1987).

G. TRADITIONAL NEIGHBORHOOD DEVELOPMENT

DEFINITION

Traditional Neighborhood Development (TND) is a relatively new alternative to conventional zoning practices. A TND zoning district encourages mixed-used development in compact areas. TND districts provide for efficient land uses, building locations, and transportation systems to create pedestrian-friendly neighborhoods. Conventional zoning districts, in contrast, separate land uses into single-use districts that force residents to depend upon automobiles for travel from home to work or stores. A TND neighborhood contains several well-defined residential areas within walking distance of a mixed-use center, connected by a network of thoroughfares that service cars and pedestrians equitably.

In a TND neighborhood, buildings that face streets are limited by maximum rather than minimum setback restrictions so that buildings are close to sidewalks and become part of the public landscape rather than removed from it. Street design, although able to accommodate automobile traffic, is focused on creating a pedestrian-friendly environment. Diverse types of housing provide affordable residences for people at different income levels and provide for varied building design. By mixing land uses, TND includes many different types of buildings within a relatively small area, offering diversity rather than homogeneity as its objective. TND zoning provisions–often referred to as "urban regulations"–generally contain much more specific design standards than conventional zoning.

PURPOSE

With suburban sprawl being blamed for a host of social, economic, and environmental problems, the issue of how land is developed has emerged as a cornerstone development issue. A TND zoning district aims to create an alternative vision to conventional development patterns. Its proponents argue for the creation of cohesive neighborhoods that differ markedly from the standard, single-use subdivision neighborhood that characterizes urban sprawl. A TND zoning district's purpose is partly social–to actively promote a sense of community through design-oriented regulation rather than regulation of use. The arguments for TND zoning are several: A confined, walkable neighborhood with mixed-use development encourages a sense of belonging in homeowners and local business owners alike. Homes and businesses designed with entrances facing and close to streets foster a sense of being part of the community rather than separate from it. Relatively narrow, interconnected, and multiple-use streets calm traffic, avoid congestion, and provide a balanced transportation system while remaining pedestrian-friendly.

TND districts also provide for the development of efficient systems of central water and sewer delivery, public transportation, and emergency services.

WHEN

TND regulations may be used to provide for newly developed neighborhoods or for the continued development or reuse of existing urban neighborhoods. When significant tracts of open land under single ownership are involved, the TND ordinance can provide for parks, squares, and greenbelts to complement and relieve the generally higher density provided in a TND district. In more developed areas, TND design standards and multiple-use provisions can provide for a neighborhood's gradual transition from its current status to a traditional neighborhood's pattern of land use.

In developing communities, local legislatures may consider adopting a TND district as a method of complementing its smart growth strategy. A TND district can provide for, and accommodate, greater density than most conventional zoning ordinances. It offers a method of providing for water, sewer, transportation, and other services in cost-effective concentrations. A TND zoning district can relieve development pressures on outlying natural resource areas, on farmlands, and on other critical environmental areas.

AUTHORITY

The power to adopt a comprehensive plan and conforming zoning laws has been delegated to towns, villages, and cities by the state legislature. One statutory objective expressed by the state legislature in delegating this authority is to encourage the most appropriate use of land throughout the municipality. The courts have made it clear that as long as this objective is the motivation for a zoning technique created by a local government, the judicial branch will sustain novel devices. The use of planned unit development zoning, which provides for mixed-use, higher density zoning in developing communities, has been sanctioned by the courts and is employed in many communities but is not discretely authorized by state legislation. Under this implied authority, local governments are free to adopt TND zoning districts, including provisions that accomplish the purposes discussed above.

IMPLEMENTATION

Two primary implementation schemes have been used in New York State to incorporate traditional neighborhood development into local land use law. First, municipalities have rezoned conventionally zoned land to create new TND zoning districts. Alternatively, some municipalities have created TND districts in the form of overlay districts that allow, but do not require, new development to conform to their provisions.

A variety of existing mechanisms can be adapted for the implementation of TND:

Municipalities can designate growth districts and rezone them as a TND district to increase density as a matter of right. This mechanism helps insure the viability of a TND district's commercial and retail center as well as its transportation system by providing an adequate supply of consumers in the surrounding neighborhoods.

Alternatively, a TND overlay zone can be created providing for mixed-use, higher density zoning as an alternative to the conventional pattern in place in the area. Incentive zoning can be used in the overlay zone to grant waivers of standard zoning requirements to developers in exchange for their willingness to provide public amenities such as transportation, parks, affordable housing, or social services in the district. Incentive zoning allows the community to offer density bonuses to a developer to construct more residential units or square feet of commercial space per acre in exchange for achieving the more compact development required by TND.

Bulk and area requirements that govern local setbacks, lots sizes, and street configuration can be used to shape public space into a pedestrian-friendly, identifiable community. On a regional level, intermunicipal agreements may be used to establish transit corridors and achieve other regional land use objectives. In this way, the goals of a TND plan can be extended throughout an area while at the same time allowing the local neighborhoods to remain compact.

ILLUSTRATIONS

The zoning code of the City of Austin, Texas includes a traditional neighborhood district. As opposed to its conventional zoning, Austin's TND ordinance:

- Creates neighborhoods that are modest in size and pedestrian-oriented.
- Allows a diversity of housing types, jobs, stores, services, and public facilities within the district.
- Integrates residences, shops, workplaces, and civic buildings within close proximity of each other.
- Designs a neighborhood that respects and preserves unique natural features and open spaces.
- Coordinates a more balanced transportation system with facilities for pedestrians, bicycles, public transit, and cars.
- Creates well-configured squares, plazas, greens, landscaped streets, preserves, greenbelts, and parks woven into a pattern of the neighborhood.
- Provides for civic buildings, open spaces, and other visual features that act as landmarks, symbols, and focal points for community identity.
- Contains design standards to provide for compatible building arrangement, bulk, form, character, and landscaping to establish a livable, harmonious, and diverse environment.
- Forms a distinct edge and defines the border between the public street and the private block interior.
- Provides for architecture and landscape that respond to the unique character of the region.

City of Austin Zoning Code §13-9-2.

Pawling, New York offers another example of a municipality's attempt to reshape its future through the use of TND design regulations. In 1990, the town began a process that led eventually to the adoption of a new comprehensive plan and zoning ordinance that combined features of both conventional and TND zoning practices. While still providing for some traditionally-zoned districts, Pawling's new comprehensive plan called for more concentrated land patterns that incorporated dedicated open space, a network of trails, a regional green-space network, and residential developments placed around a revitalized central business district. The plan also took the unusual step of identifying four large tracts of property in one-acre residential zones and detailing conceptual development plans for those tracts. These parcels are allowed an increased number of residential units per acre, a greater number of houses on smaller lots, and more preserved open space within each tract in an effort to encourage TND development.

To implement these comprehensive plan provisions, Pawling amended its zoning law in 1995. Pawling Zoning Law §98-13 and Schedule B allow six building types in specified zoning districts. The ordinances also include detailed illustrations for alternative lot layouts, building designs, setbacks, and the location of parking, provisions not included in the original zoning ordinance. Furthermore, the zoning code provides a density bonus of 30% for any new subdivision proposed on the parcels identified on the comprehensive plan that meets the TND design guidelines. To qualify for that bonus, the plans must conform to the open space requirements, guarantee the affordability of 15% of the dwelling units, and be connected to the village water and sewer system.

LIMITATIONS AND CONCERNS

As a novel approach to land use planning, TNDs challenge conventional practices. To be successful, however, TND designs must fit into the constitutional and political frameworks already established for accepted zoning practices. Moreover, TND proposals must also take into account issues of scale, transportation needs, environmental impact, and marketing.

Three constitutional limitations on conventional zoning practices apply equally to TNDs. First, to be accepted as a legitimate exercise of the state's police power, TND ordinances must satisfy the constitutional demands of substantive due process. TND ordinances must advance a legitimate government interest. If the goal of the TND regulation is legitimate, the regulation must be a reasonable means of achieving that goal. Otherwise, the ordinance may be found unconstitutional. Second, TND ordinances must not violate the takings clause of the Fourteenth Amendment of the U.S. Constitution. Governments may not take either private property or its value from its owners without just compensation. Therefore, TND ordinances may not impose permit conditions that so severely restrict the use or development of a particular parcel that the owner cannot realize an economic return on investment. Finally, those trying to apply TND ordinances must not change land use allowances simply to benefit one or more property owners rather than to facilitate the goals of a comprehensive zoning plan. Such changes may constitute spot zoning and violate the restrictions placed on land use regulations in general.

Political concerns also limit the potential use of TNDs. Because traditional neighborhood development is a radical departure from conventional zoning and development, some TND projects have encountered significant opposition from residents and municipal administrators alike. Some have raised concerns over the higher density goal of TND proposals. Mixed-use plans are contrary to the current, once idealized conventions of single-use zoning. The flexibility and open-ended nature of TND ordinances may lead to opposition by property owners who are not sure of the development rights they will enjoy under the new approach.

Other concerns may limit the success of TND projects. One critical feature of a TND district is its attempt to integrate commercial uses into residential areas at an appropriate and modest scale. This often runs contrary to forces in the modern marketplace, which favor big-box retail outlets accessible by an integrated highway system used by thousands of customers. Similarly, the small-scale nature of businesses within a neighborhood center, designed so residents can live close to their workplaces, may not provide enough jobs to satisfy local employment demands. These concerns may be answered by providing for these more intense, single-use projects in other parts of the community or nearby region.

Some opponents of the TND concept argue that homes and businesses within these zoning districts will be unmarketable. Mortgage lenders may be cautious about new forms of development, but they can be convinced by sales successes in TND districts elsewhere. The public may associate small lot size with a lower quality of life or a negative impact on property values in the vicinity. In fact, a more realistic criticism of most TND projects is that they do not achieve the affordable housing objectives to which they aspire because of their popularity in the market. Doubts are also expressed about whether TND district residents will be willing to abandon their automobiles for walking, even within the neighborhood centers specifically designed for that purpose. These concerns have been answered by studies demonstrating that people are willing to walk rather than ride if the design is suited to pedestrian transport.

STATUTES

New York State Village Law §7-704, Town Law §263, and General City Law §§20(24), (25) require zoning to conform to the provisions of a comprehensive plan. These statutes also provide for overlay zones, a mechanism regularly used in the development of TNDs.

Village Law §7-703, Town Law §261-b, and General City Law §81-d provide for incentive zoning grants that serve as waivers of conventional zoning mandates and therefore are appropriate mechanisms for TNDs.

Village Law §7-701, Town Law §261-a, and General City Law §20-f provide for the transfer of development rights that are sometimes used by TND developers.

CASE DIGEST

In *Rodgers v. Village of Tarrytown*, 302 N.Y. 115 (1951), the New York Court of Appeals held that a village planning board had the authority to create a new, flexible zoning mechanism: a floating zoning district. The plaintiff argued that the floating zone which allowed multi-family buildings in a single-family zoning district on 15-acre or larger parcels violated the uniformity requirement of zoning districts or constituted illegal spot zoning. The court disagreed and sanctioned the novel concept of first creating a floating zoning district and later affixing it to a specific parcel upon the application of the landowner. In sustaining such techniques as within the locality's implied zoning power, the court noted that a "decision as to how a community shall be zoned or rezoned, as to how various properties shall be classified or reclassified, rests with the local legislative body; its judgment and determination will be conclusive, beyond interference from the courts, unless shown to be arbitrary."

In *W.J.F. Realty Corp. v. State*, 176 Misc.2d 763, 672 N.Y.S.2d 1007 (Sup. Ct. 1998), local landowners brought an action challenging the constitutionality of the Long Island Pine Barrens Protection Act, ECL §57-0103 et seq. (1993), which seeks to protect the local aquifer by limiting construction on lands above it. The court held that the Act promotes a legitimate government interest in a constitutional manner. To administer its provisions, the Act creates a Pine Barrens commission that has the authority to grant building permits to those who can demonstrate hardship in the absence of such permit. The determination of the commission is reviewable by the courts. If the court determines that the refusal to issue a permit constitutes an uncompensated taking, the commission may choose to acquire the land through eminent domain. The property owner must be compensated, and this may be accomplished by awarding development credits to the affected owner under the Pine Barrens transfer of development rights (TDR) program. In this case, the plaintiffs claimed that, even with the award of the credits, an unconstitutional taking had occurred. The court held that the Act's use of development credits as compensation continues a 19th-century governmental tradition of providing new lands in lieu of money in return for land taken by the government. In some cases, a TDR development credit may provide full compensation. In other cases, it might not. The court in *W.J.F.* found that this issue was premature and, therefore, did not address it, but rather held that the Act, including the TDR provisions, was constitutional.

REFERENCES

John R. Nolon, *Smart Growth – A Micro Analysis*, N.Y. L.J., Oct. 20, 1999.

Mark Rielly, *Neo-traditional Neighborhood Development, at*
http://www.pace.edu/lawschool/landuse/tnd.html (last visited Feb. 2, 2001).

H. SENIOR CITIZEN HOUSING ZONING

DEFINITION

The demand for housing for older persons is escalating, and the challenge of providing an appropriate range of housing for seniors is complex because their needs are so variable. Some seniors are fully independent, but need and are willing to pay for a maintenance-free environment. Generally, these types of accommodations can be provided under traditional zoning and private market operations. Condominiums, for example, respond to the needs of this segment of the market. Zoning that allows private market apartments, cooperatives, and condominiums is responsive to this segment of the senior housing market. At the other extreme are seniors with severe health and mobility problems who need skilled nursing care. Typically, they chose to live in nursing homes that are normally allowed to be built in certain zoning districts by special use permit or in designated mixed-use or multi-family zoning districts, as a matter of right.

Between these extremes, older persons have a variety of needs for what is generally called "assisted housing" with special design amenities, such as community rooms and handicap accessibility, and with special services, such as the provision of housekeeping, meals, and limited health care. Frequently, the communal features of such housing require building design and room configurations not permitted by conventional zoning. Seniors in need of semi-independent living quarters of this type also can be accommodated by family members who build cottages on their lots or apartments within their homes and themselves provide the support services needed by their relatives. Limited-income seniors need housing designed and financed to be affordable. Local land use controls that respond to these specific housing needs are called senior citizen housing zoning.

Local governments use a variety of techniques to allow and encourage the private market to create housing responsive to these needs. They may create senior housing zoning districts, authorize local boards to issue special permits for senior housing in designated zoning districts, or create overlay or floating zones for the purpose. They may also allow for the creation of small cottages on single-family lots or separate apartments within single-family homes specifically to accommodate the needs of seniors.

PURPOSE

The objective of local governments in enacting land use controls of this type is to provide housing for this increasing segment of the American population, many of whom have needs that can be met only by specialized housing design and support services. Since most conventional zoning does not allow buildings with these features and does not provide for services to be offered within residential structures, a new type of land use control is needed. At the same time, these new land use devices can bring with them unfamiliar impacts on the surrounding neighborhood: more cars, greater building bulk, higher density of population, the activity created by the providers of needed services, and traffic controls, to name a few. An important additional purpose of zoning for senior housing is to balance the need for housing for older residents with the needs and concerns of the residents of the neighborhoods in which senior housing is located.

WHEN

Local governments become engaged in zoning for senior citizen housing either reactively or proactively. Most often, a developer will petition the local legislature to rezone a particular parcel for multi-family housing with unique design features or services and force the lawmakers' consideration of the proposal. Increasingly, local legislatures are anticipating senior housing needs by adopting one or more zoning provisions of the type mentioned above. In both cases, it is the pressure of the increasing need for a new type of housing that creates the challenge for local lawmakers. Many communities take action because they realize that residents who have lived in the community for much of their lives are being forced to leave when their housing needs change.

AUTHORITY

New York State statutes provide express authority for local legislatures to create special zoning districts and to permit unique forms of housing by special permit. The courts have held that the adoption of innovative zoning techniques such as floating zones, overlay zoning, and planned residential district zoning is within the implied power of local governments. Section 263 of the Town Law, for example, states that zoning regulations may be made "with a view to . . . encouraging the most appropriate use of the land . . ." Comparable provisions in the Village Law and General City Law empower those municipalities. Village Law §7-725-b, Town Law §274-b, and General City Law §27-b authorize local legislatures to allow appropriate administrative bodies to grant special use permits to meet special needs such as senior housing.

IMPLEMENTATION

Three types of housing serve the needs of seniors who can live more or less independently: conventional housing, elderly cottages (ECHO), and accessory apartments:

- ◆ Conventional housing is permitted as of right, such as the single-family home, apartment, or condominium. Seniors may choose to live in any residentially zoned district they can afford.
- ◆ Elder cottages accommodate seniors who are able to live independently but wish to live near potential caregivers, such as family members. An elder cottage is a small, separate unit, usually a temporary structure, that is placed on the same lot as an existing single-family home. As a separate living unit, an elder cottage allows residents the maximum independence while at the same time providing the support of the residents of the lot's primary structure. Typically, elder cottages are allowed by a special use permit granted by the planning board. The legislation authorizing the permit specifies certain setback, volume, landscaping, floor-area, and parking restrictions. In some communities, the number of cottages allowed on any block may be limited, and the unit may be required to be removed when the elderly family member is no longer in occupancy.
- ◆ Accessory apartments can be allowed by special permit within existing single-family homes. The legislation allowing the planning board to issue such permits may restrict their application to owner-occupants, may require that no more than a certain percentage of the house be dedicated to the accessory unit, and many impose on-site parking restrictions and other controls needed to protect surrounding property owners from the impact of the additional unit.

Various types of assisted care facilities can be accommodated by adding provisions for an overlay zone, a floating zone, or a planned residential development district to the zoning ordinance. A senior citizen overlay zone allows an assisted living accommodation to be developed within a community's borders upon the approval of a special permit issued by the planning board. This overlay zone may include more than one existing zoning district, or encompass all districts of a certain type, such as single-family residential zones. A senior housing overlay zone may require proximity to particular facilities and amenities that meet the physical and personal needs of the elderly, such as medical facilities, shopping areas, recreation, and public transit. A wide variety of housing types can be permitted by the overlay zone provisions.

Floating zones can provide for a certain type of senior housing to be built on a parcel meeting certain size and environmental conditions. The floating zone amendment can be highly specific about the type of senior housing allowed, its affordability, and the type of site eligible for that housing. When the floating zone is adopted, no land is designated for the development of senior housing. Later, a landowner or developer can petition the planning board, or local legislature, to apply the floating zone to a parcel meeting the ordinance's standards. Floating zoning provisions can allow the planning board and developer wide discretion in designing senior housing or can be highly prescriptive requiring handicapped accessibility, communal rooms, specific services, and a variety of site improvements and characteristics needed to protect surrounding areas.

Planned residential districts can be added to the zoning ordinance as discrete zones in definite locations or as overlay or floating zones. They typically allow a mix of housing uses to provide different types of housing for various senior housing needs or a combination of housing for elderly and non-elderly households.

Institutional living arrangements, such as nursing homes, can be authorized by special permit or as of right in appropriate zoning districts, such as mixed-use, commercial, and residential districts. To avoid significant neighborhood impacts and opposition, zoning accommodations for nursing homes must have standards for their construction and site planning similar to overlay, floating, and planned residential districts.

ILLUSTRATIONS

New Rochelle, New York, adopted a floating zone for senior housing that it calls a "Single Family Senior Citizen Overlay District." The amendment's purpose is to facilitate "the development of homes that are specifically designed to meet the needs of senior citizens who prefer the single family type home . . . but require certain facilities and amenities to meet their changing physical and social needs." To qualify under this amendment, a parcel must contain at least five contiguous acres. The ordinance contains specific design features, including that the homes provide living primarily on the first floor, with a bedroom accessible by wheelchair and bathroom on the first floor. The homes must be adaptable for the addition of an elevator, and doorways must be wide enough to accommodate wheelchairs. Additionally, there may be no steps leading into the house from the outside. Walks must be designed to prevent slipping and stumbling. Handrails and strategically placed rest areas are required within the development.

The town of Pound Ridge enacted an ordinance designed to encourage the development of senior housing in an effort to offer incentives for its elderly residents to remain in the municipality. The town created a senior citizen housing overlay district within which senior housing is allowed in designated single-family zones by special permit. Instead of specifically establishing required design features, the ordinance generally describes the facilities useful to senior citizens and endorses the accessibility requirements of the American National Standard Institute for the Handicapped. Developers are required to limit the size of the homes to keep them reasonably affordable.

The town of Bedford adopted an ordinance aimed at providing housing to limited-income senior citizens. The ordinance establishes an "EL Housing for Elderly District" which requires that at least 20% of the housing in such a district be affordable to middle-income households. The Bedford law does not set forth any building requirements or standards for services. It assures the provision of housing for seniors by limiting occupancy to households with at least one householder over 62 years of age.

LIMITATIONS AND CONCERNS

Charges of exclusionary zoning accompanied the advent of zoning for senior housing. Opponents of the designation of a district as a "retirement community district" claimed that a town zoning board unconstitutionally created a zone based on an impermissible age-based classification. However, the New York Court of Appeals has held that age considerations are appropriate if they are rationally related to the achievement of a proper governmental objective. Since meeting a community shortage of suitable housing accommodations for a specific population is a proper social objective, the court considered this part of a town's delegated "general welfare" power. On the other hand, when a community imposes a residency requirement in zoning for senior citizen housing, the zoning may be invalidated by the courts as exclusionary. Where there is a need for such housing in the region and a local zoning provision limits occupancy to individuals who have been residents of the locality for a fixed time, such as two years, the provision is vulnerable to attack.

Senior housing zoning has also been challenged as constituting spot zoning. Spot zoning that designates a parcel of land for a use classification distinct from the surrounding area and designed to benefit one landowner to the detriment of his neighbors is impermissible. When senior housing zoning is adopted to meet the objectives of the comprehensive plan, however, it will survive a spot zoning challenge, even if the rezoned parcel is quite small.

Some have challenged senior citizen housing zoning techniques claiming that they are denied equal protection of the law. New York courts have held that rezoning to establish a senior housing district does not violate the equal protection clause of the federal constitution. It would be illogical to hold that it was within the town's power to accommodate the housing needs of the elderly by encouraging construction of senior citizen overlay districts while at the same time prohibiting the town from excluding other segments of the population from residing in such districts. Similar decisions have validated elder cottage and accessory apartment zoning provisions that limit their application to owner-occupants, denying eligibility to absentee owners of single-family homes. A proper nexus between a valid public purpose and the eligibility criteria was found.

STATUTES

New York State Village Law §7-725-b, Town Law §274-b, and General City Law §27-b provide municipalities with the authority to grant special use permits as are necessary in the establishment of senior housing facilities.

Overlay districts floating zones, and planned residential developments are considered to be within the implied authority delegated to local governments under Village Law §7-704, Town Law §263, and General City Law §20(25).

REFERENCES

Stephanie Edelstein, *Assisted Living: Recent Developments and Issues for Older Consumers*, 9 Stan. L. & Policy Rev. 373 (1998).

Patricia Baron Pollak and Alice Nudelman Goreman, Community-Based Housing for the Elderly: A Zoning Guide for Planners and Municipal Officals (American Planning Association, Planning Advisory Service Report Number 420).

Christopher Seeger, *Developing Assisted Living Facilities*, 12 N.Y. Real Estate L. Rev. 10 (Aug. 1998).

I. LOCAL WATERFRONT MANAGEMENT

DEFINITION

Local waterfront management is a process by which a municipality uses applicable local, state, and federal authority to manage and protect its waterfront resources. It does this by adopting a local waterfront management plan, which has significance under local, state, and federal law. A local waterfront management plan can be viewed as an addition to a municipality's comprehensive plan, applicable to coastal areas.

Under New York State law, coastal areas are defined broadly. The state-established waters include Lakes Erie and Ontario, the St. Lawrence and Niagara Rivers, the Hudson River south of the federal dam at Troy, the East River, the Harlem River, the Kell von Kull and Arthur Kill Rivers, Long Island Sound, and the Atlantic Ocean and their connecting waterbodies, bays, harbors, shallows, marshes, and adjacent shorelines. Inland waterways are also included under state law, including rivers, lakes, marshes, and adjacent shorelines.

A local waterfront management plan regulates land uses in a waterfront area and sets forth the policy objectives and implementation procedures for development in that section of a municipality. When done in conjunction with the standards of the state program, it allows the local government to influence and, in some cases, control the capital projects and permits issued by state and federal agencies.

In New York, the state will fund up to 50% of a municipality's activities that lead to the adoption of a local waterfront revitalization plan (LWRP) in coastal areas. New York will also give grants to municipalities to implement their programs to pay the cost of research or design activities and construction projects aimed at protecting, developing, or enhancing a coastal area.

PURPOSE

The coastal areas of the Atlantic Ocean, Long Island Sound, and Lakes Ontario and Erie, combined with a number of smaller water bodies total more than 5,000 miles of shoreline in New York. While these coastal areas make New York rich in natural, cultural, and economic resources, their use and enjoyment has not come without a price. Pollution, erosion, salt intrusion, flooding, habitat degradation, loss of biodiversity, and economic stagnation stress many coastal areas. A local waterfront management plan provides a comprehensive approach to developing the coastline in a responsible manner, preventing irreparable degradation, and protecting the characteristics that have made shorelines so attractive.

WHEN

A local waterfront management plan is appropriate in any community that falls within one of the state-established coastal or inland areas and that wishes to enjoy the benefits of having a formal LWRP. Any coastal municipality that is engaging in comprehensive planning for the first time or is amending its plan may consider drafting a separate waterfront plan in order to receive funding and other benefits under the program. LWRPs are also an appropriate means for revamping a coastal shopping district, or conservation area, or for conducting any specialized planning to solve problems particular to coastal areas.

AUTHORITY

While any community may use its authority to engage in comprehensive planning for its waterfront areas, there is specific federal and state authority to create LWRPs. The federal Coastal Zone Management Act establishes a process for the development of state coastal zone management programs. This Act offers cooperating states federally funded development and administrative grants. States that develop conforming plans and programs also benefit from what is called a federal consistency requirement. This means that any federal agency that proposes to conduct, permit, or fund a project in a coastal area in a state with an approved plan must act consistently with the provisions of the plan. When local governments adopt LWRPs under the state program, this federal consistency requirement applies to the local plans as well.

New York State enacted the Waterfront Revitalization and Coastal Resources Act pursuant to the federal authority. The state developed 44 policies to which all state and federal agencies must adhere. It has delegated authority to local governments to create local waterfront revitalization plans, and provides funding to communities that adopt LWRPs. For such communities, it is the state's responsibility to police and enforce federal consistency requirements.

IMPLEMENTATION

A municipality may develop an LWRP using the same procedure it would to develop a comprehensive plan. This means that a municipality may appoint either its planning board or a special board to develop the LWRP as a component of its comprehensive plan. This provides the LWRP with the legal authority and weight provided a formally adopted comprehensive plan. Alternatively, the locality may adopt an LWRP simply as required by the state under its agreement pursuant to the Waterfront Revitalization and Coastal Resources Act. Once the LWRP has been adopted by the local legislature, the Department of State's Division of Coastal Resources must approve it. Before the state approval, a copy of the LWRP must be submitted to any interested party who may be affected by it. Once approved by the state, the plan is submitted for federal approval to the Office of Coastal Resource Management. If this federal office concurs in the state's approval, the LWRP becomes effective.

An LWRP should include pertinent information that will help to identify coastal problems, provide for implementation, and insure that the programs are properly managed. All LWRPs should identify coastal area boundaries, inventory natural and historic resources in need of protection, state goals and objectives, identify the public and private uses to be accommodated in the waterfront area, and describe proposed means for long-term management of the waterfront area. The plan should also provide organizational structures and delegate management responsibilities. Furthermore, New York's coastal management program, which provides the funding to communities, requires that every LWRP incorporate all of the 44 policies the state is pursuing with this program that are relevant to the local coastal area.

An additional possibility for making an LWRP effective is to adopt it as a critical environmental area (CEA) for purposes of subsequent environmental impact review under the State Environmental Quality Review Act. All future projects would then have to be reviewed for their impact on the environmental features and conditions identified in the LWRP.

ILLUSTRATIONS

Local governments may use traditional land use controls, such as zoning, to carry out an LWRP's goals. For example, the village of Tivoli in northern Dutchess County has established a land conservation district that borders the Hudson River and other major watercourses that flow through the village. No as-of-right uses are permitted in these districts, and only agriculture, wildlife preserves, outdoor recreation facilities, parks, and playgrounds may be established by special permit. The city of North Tonawanda created a waterfront zone that permitted water-dependent uses only. Non-water-dependent uses are allowed by special permit if public access to the waterfront is provided. The town of East Hampton enacted a harbor overlay district that established additional standards to reduce adverse water quality impacts emanating from all permitted uses on parcels adjacent to the shore. The village of Sleepy Hollow established a local law—the Village of

Sleepy Hollow Waterfront Consistency Review Law–that provides a framework for local agencies to follow when acting or reviewing proposed actions in the waterfront area.

In Westchester, two adjacent communities have taken dramatic action using their zoning power to protect their waterfront areas. The village of Larchmont amended its zoning law to create a new waterfront district with R-50 zoning (minimum lot size 50,000 square feet) that encompasses all properties fronting directly on the Long Island Sound and the Larchmont Harbor. The town of Mamaroneck zoned over 400 acres for recreational purposes–an action sustained by the courts because it was consistent with the town's carefully planned LWRP.

Increasingly, communities are using their expansive authority to enter into intermunicipal agreements to manage waterfront areas collaboratively. In the Oyster Bay-Cold Spring Harbor area of Long Island, for example, 14 local governments established a consortium to protect and restore the abundant natural resources and shellfishery in this harbor complex that supplies about 90% of New York's oyster harvest. The communities have cooperated to prepare a detailed management plan for this significant natural area which addresses a variety of needs from reducing pollution from nonpoint sources to revitalization of an abandoned shipyard.

On the north shore of Long Island, in 1995 Nassau County, the towns of North Hempstead and Oyster Bay, the City of Glen Cove, and five villages created the Hempstead Harbor Protection Committee through an intermunicipal agreement. The committee's primary objective was to prepare a watershed management plan to reduce nonpoint source pollution in Hempstead Harbor. The plan was completed in 1997. The committee has continued to collaborate on setting priorities to implement the plan's many recommendations. As a group, the committee members determine what state, federal, and private grants to pursue. The cooperating communities contribute cash and services to match grant program requirements. The committee is cooperating with the neighboring Manhasset Bay Protection Committee on a series of nonpoint source management workshops for local building inspectors and zoning and planning boards.

LIMITATIONS AND CONCERNS

LWRPs are normally adopted to qualify for the benefits of the state Waterfront Revitalization and Coastal Resources Act, and satisfy the formal requirements of that Act and the Federal Coastal Zone Management Act. This gives the LWRP formal status and makes the locality eligible for the benefits of these programs, including funding, the federal consistency requirement, and greater local control of permitting activity in the coastal area. LWRPs can gain additional authority if they are also adopted pursuant to the formal requirements of state law for the adoption of a comprehensive plan. All land use regulations, including those affecting coastal areas, must be adopted in conformance with the comprehensive plan. Coordinating the LWRP with the local comprehensive plan and land use regulations will eliminate legal confusion, prevent legal challenges to land use regulations, and provide for a more orderly planning and regulatory process.

STATUTES AND REGULATIONS

The federal Coastal Zone Management Act can be found at 16 U.S.C. §§1451-1465, ELR STAT. CZMA §§302-319.

The Waterfront Revitalization and Coastal Resources Act is found at NY Exec. Law. §910.

The 44 policies that all LWRPs must fulfill are located in the Act's implementing regulations, 19 NYCRR §600.5. The policies are grouped under the general categories of development, fish and wildlife, flooding and erosion, public access, recreation, historic and scenic resources, agriculture, energy and ice management, and water and air resources.

CASE DIGEST

In 1987, the Supreme Court of Westchester upheld the Village of Mamaroneck's Local Waterfront Revitalization Program and accompanying Final Environmental Impact Statement (FEIS), finding that the village had complied with the State Environmental Quality Review Act's requirements. *Nichols Yacht Yard, Inc. v. Board of Trustees of the Village of Mamaroneck*, No. 19599/84 (Supreme Ct. Westchester, Oct. 28, 1987), *aff'd*, 154 A.D.2d 358, 546 N.Y.S.2d 971 (2d Dep't 1989). The LWRP called for rezoning the village waterfront to create a marine zone. This zone was designed to foster public access, recreation, and water use. Several property owners in the proposed marine zone were opposed to the elimination of uses formally permitted and challenged the sufficiency of the FEIS. The court rejected the claim that the FEIS failed to consider the economic impact on the plaintiffs' properties, finding that the owners had operated profitably for years under the uses allowed in the new marine zone.

A recreational zone created to implement the Town of Mamaroneck's LWRP was sustained against a claim that it was unconstitutional as a taking without just compensation. *Bonnie Briar Syndicate, Inc. v. Town of Mamaroneck*, 216 N.Y.L.J. 34 (1996), *aff'd*, 242 A.D.2d 356, 661 N.Y.S.2d 1005 (2d Dep't 1997). In 1994, the town board adopted a new recreation zone that allowed only private recreational facilities as principal uses and did not permit any residential development. The purpose of the new law was to maintain open space, reduce the potential for substantial flood hazards, and maintain the suburban quality of the community – objectives that were studied and established in the town's LWRP. The plaintiff did not prove that the property could not yield a reasonable economic return under the regulation. The court refused to inquire whether less restrictive means were available to accomplish these objectives, deferring to the local legislature's judgment, which was based on an LWRP that took 10 years to develop.

REFERENCE

Matthew A. Sokol, *Coastal Zone Management in New York, at* http://www.pace.edu/lawschool/landuse/cozoma.html (last visited Feb. 2, 2001).

Chapter 7

INTERMUNICIPAL COORDINATION

Municipalities in New York have extensive authority to cooperate with one another to accomplish their land use objectives. Where villages, towns, and cities share natural resources, transportation corridors, or economic markets, they are authorized to enter into intermunicipal agreements to perform together any municipal function they have power to undertake individually.

The state legislature has made it clear, through enabling legislation, that authority to cooperate includes the power to adopt consistent comprehensive plans, zoning laws, and land use regulations, to combine local land use agencies, and to enter into joint enforcement and monitoring programs. The legislature has also made it clear that county governments may provide technical and advisory services in the land use field to their constituent localities. The Hudson River Greenway Communities Council has been authorized by state statute to provide incentives for localities that adopt local plans and regulations that are in conformance with Greenway planning principles.

Local governments have begun to use this authority in a number of creative ways as they have discovered that it provides them with a new method of expanding their control over the forces that determine their future. As population has grown and natural resources have become more threatened, local governments have embraced the notion that they can control shared wetlands and waterways, floodplains, transportation corridors, and economic markets by entering into compacts with one another, with their counties, and with regional agencies established to help them accomplish their land use objectives.

A. INTERMUNICIPAL AGREEMENTS

DEFINITION

An intermunicipal agreement (IMA) is a cooperative or contractual arrangement between two or more municipalities. Under the Town, Village, and General City statutes, local governments in New York State are specifically authorized to enter into IMAs to adopt compatible comprehensive plans and zoning laws as well as other land use regulations, including wetlands and floodplain laws; aquifer protection, watershed enhancement, and corridor development plans; and historic preservation, cultural resource protection, erosion control, and visual buffering programs. Local governments also may agree to establish joint planning, zoning, historic preservation and conservation advisory boards and to hire joint inspection and enforcement officers. Specifically mentioned in the enabling legislation is the use of IMAs to create an "intermunicipal overlay district for the purpose of protecting, enhancing, or developing community resources that encompass two or more municipalities."

IMAs can be used to provide for more cost-effective and consistent enforcement of existing land use plans and regulations. One municipality may agree to be responsible for hiring and supervising enforcement officers on behalf of itself and one or more others. Two or more municipalities may agree to hire enforcement and administrative personnel for land use purposes and to supervise them jointly and share the costs. Any local administrative agency that handles land use issues can be established as a joint board with one or more nearby communities.

PURPOSE

There are several reasons for municipalities to enter into IMAs. First, IMAs may be adopted to achieve cost-efficiency: to create a more optimal scale of operations for fiscal purposes and administrative efficiency. Second, they can be formed to use citizen board members more capably and efficiently. Third, they can be used to effect control of natural resource or economic market areas that extend beyond municipal borders. Fourth, they may be used to limit the negative impact of projects and activities approved by neighboring municipalities. Fifth, municipalities entering into IMAs may qualify for incentives and funding that would not otherwise be available.

WHEN

Municipalities in rural and sparsely settled regions of the state have used this authority to establish cost-effective and practical approaches to zoning and planning administration. In these instances, volunteers to serve on local administrative bodies are limited and the number of matters coming before local boards are relatively few. There are many examples of communities in such settings establishing joint planning and joint zoning boards and hiring joint land use enforcement officers.

In more densely settled or rapidly developing regions, some municipalities and counties are using IMAs to manage their common waterfront areas, to coordinate their efforts to conserve shared watershed and wetlands areas, to exert control over a larger economic market, and to achieve administrative and fiscal efficiency.

Local officials are often frustrated by the land use actions of their neighbors. Sometimes this is due to the negative intermunicipal impact of a particular development project. Other times it may be because one municipality, acting alone, cannot achieve its objectives. Economic development activities in one community, for example, cannot reverse negative trends in the larger economic market area. Parallel action among localities in the entire market area may be required for any noticeable effect to be had. One community, for example, cannot create enough supply to meet the regional demand for affordable housing. Efforts in one community to protect natural resource areas that are shared with adjacent municipalities frequently do not achieve resource preservation without compatible efforts in all the communities.

Economic development, housing demand, and resource protection are but three examples of issues that often require joint action to be effective. When communities are confronted with such challenges, intermunicipal agreements offer them an opportunity to develop mutually compatible land use plans, regulations, and enforcement programs to accomplish together what they cannot achieve alone.

AUTHORITY

The New York State Legislature has made it abundantly clear that towns, villages, cities, and counties have extensive authority and great flexibility to cooperate in the adoption and enforcement of their land use plans and regulations.

In 1960, the General Municipal Law was amended to give all municipal corporations, including towns, villages, cities, and counties, the authority to enter into intermunicipal agreements for the joint performance of their respective functions. In 1992, provisions were added to the Town, Village, and General City laws to encourage intermunicipal cooperation regarding land use planning and regulation. Finally, in 1993, the General Municipal Law and the Town, Village, and General City statutes were amended to make it clear that local governments may enter into cooperative agreements with county governments, allowing counties to assist localities with the preparation of comprehensive plans and land use regulations, and with the administration and enforcement of local land use plans and regulations.

IMPLEMENTATION

Once the municipalities involved reach an agreement to cooperate on a land use issue, the legal process for proceeding is relatively straightforward. First, the IMA must be adopted by a majority vote of the legislative bodies of each participating municipality. Then the IMA must be carried out according to its terms.

Getting started often presents a stumbling block for interested municipalities. The first step in the process is to determine what land use issues have intermunicipal implications that two or more communities are willing to handle compatibly. Some communities use this step in the process to engage their citizens in the development of an intermunicipal vision for their area and in the development of a clear idea of how each community can help accomplish that vision. The next step is to form an intermunicipal committee or task force to look into the issues identified and determine whether it is practical to develop an intermunicipal strategy to resolve them. Cooperating municipalities may establish a formal "intergovernmental relations council" for this purpose. Such councils may be funded through local revenues.

Once such an approach is deemed potentially fruitful, the committee must develop the details of the agreement that will eventually be drafted by the attorneys for the municipalities and presented to the legislatures for their consideration. Where there are controversial matters to be resolved in this process, it may be helpful to retain an independent mediator to facilitate the resolution of the issues among the members of the intermunicipal committee.

The terms that should be contained in an IMA include, among others:

♦ The responsibilities of each municipality with respect to the adoption or amendment of local regulations.
♦ The commitment of resources to implement or enforce those regulations.
♦ The hiring and termination of joint personnel.
♦ The detailing of their responsibilities and how their time and payment will be divided.
♦ Insurance.
♦ Dispute resolution.
♦ The duration, monitoring, review, amendment, extension, and termination of the agreement.

ILLUSTRATIONS

Early Approaches: During the 1980s and early 1990s, municipal governments used their authority to cooperate in the land use area to establish joint boards and regulatory enforcement efforts.

In 1982, the town of Lowville and the village of Lowville established a joint planning board and a joint zoning board of appeals. Each board has five members: two are appointed by the town, two are appointed by the village, and the fifth is appointed jointly by the town and village. A fiscal agent for each board is appointed by the town. An individual is designated by agreement of both municipalities to serve as the building inspector for both jurisdictions.

The town of Denmark, the village of Castorland, and the village of Copenhagen entered into an intermunicipal agreement to provide for a cooperative enforcement officer who is responsible for the administration and enforcement of the respective land use control laws of the three municipalities. The town is the responsible fiscal agent and handles all finances associated with the agreement. The enforcement officer submits a monthly itemized bill to each of the municipalities for services rendered. When the enforcement officer is acting on behalf of a particular municipality, he or she is considered a public officer of that municipality.

In 1993, the town of Nunda and the village of Nunda created a joint planning board with four members from the town and three members from the village. The two municipalities also have a joint zoning board of appeals with two members from the town and three members from the village.

Recent Efforts: By the mid-1990s, evidence of communities using their intermunicipal authority to adopt consistent plans, regulations, and review processes began to appear. Toward the close of the decade, this authority was being used to coordinate land use planning, regulation, and enforcement over much larger geographical areas and by more complicated means.

In 1994, the town of Castile, the village of Castile, and the village of Perry enacted amendments to their respective zoning regulations to coordinate development and preservation efforts among the three municipalities. The objectives of the amendments included the protection of agricultural uses, the provision for open space, and the prevention of excessive concentration of population.

Ten villages and towns in the Westchester County portion of the Hudson River watershed created the Historic River Towns consortium in 1994. Motivated by an economic recession, they passed joint resolutions to improve local economic activity by promoting tourism through comprehensive marketing, improved transportation, the enhancement of central business districts and tourist sites, and ongoing collaborative planning. The consortium is managed by an executive committee and is administered fiscally by the village of Croton.

In the Oyster Bay-Cold Spring Harbor area, around Huntington, Long Island, 14 municipalities established a consortium, beginning in 1995, to reverse the decline of this shared natural and economic resource area. They entered into a compact agreeing to seek funding, identify priority areas, adopt a harbor management plan, and create model local land use regulations. The collaborative effort is managed by a coastal area advisory committee.

In 1995, 13 localities in the Manhasset Bay area, near Hempstead, Long Island, entered into an agreement to develop a strategy to achieve the economic and environmental well-being of the bay. The localities agreed to seek funding together, to identify priority areas, and to coordinate protection efforts. Their agreement established the Manhasset Bay Protection Committee, with the town of North Hempstead serving as the administrative and fiscal agent of the consortium.

In Monroe County, three towns, the county, and the State Department of Environmental Conservation entered into an agreement in 1997 to protect the Irondequoit Bay, which was threatened by the uncoordinated land use decisions of the participating governments and agencies. They agreed to develop a consistent vision of the bay's future, to educate the public regarding that vision and how it can be realized, to increase public access to the bay, and to develop consistent local regulations affecting the resource. Their intergovernmental agreement establishes the Irondequoit Bay Coordinating Committee.

In 1998, three cities, three towns, and four villages with land use jurisdiction over the watershed of Long Island Sound in Westchester County entered into an intermunicipal agreement to cooperate regarding the prevention of pollution affecting the Sound. They agreed to work toward the development of compatible comprehensive plans, zoning, and land use regulations and to submit a joint funding application to the state to initiate the process. They formed the Long Island Sound Watershed Intermunicipal Council, composed of two representatives of each community, to develop by-laws and recommend additional measures to achieve their mutual objectives.

LIMITATIONS AND CONCERNS

Although IMAs can provide for the adoption of compatible plans and regulations, those legislative actions must be undertaken by each locality separately, in conformance with the IMA. For example, one jurisdiction cannot adopt a zoning law and make it applicable in another. Both jurisdictions must adopt the agreed-upon regulation separately. They can, however, provide for the joint implementation, enforcement, and administration of the separately adopted regulations.

IMAs provide an excellent vehicle for coordinating intermunicipal activity, but they can go only so far in binding the discretion of future local legislative bodies. Like many other agreements, they serve their parties as long as they are useful and agreeable to those involved. Although an IMA can include penalty and termination clauses for failure to comply with its terms, an IMA cannot prevent future legislatures from acting to protect the public health, safety, and welfare simply because that action is inconsistent with the agreement.

STATUTES AND RULINGS

In New York State, General Municipal Law §119-o, adopted in 1960, gives all municipal governments the authority to act together to perform functions each can perform separately.

General City Law §20-g, Town Law §284, and Village Law §7-741, adopted in 1992, authorize towns, villages, and cities to enter into IMAs for land use purposes. These sections are identical to General Municipal Law §119-u, and allow municipalities to enter into intermunicipal agreements with counties to receive professional planning services through county planning agencies.

General Municipal Law §239-n provides authority to local governments to establish inter-governmental-relations councils to promote inter-community planning and develop areas for municipal cooperation.

The costs associated with joint land use planning may be apportioned among the participating municipalities on any equitable basis. 67 St. Comp. 562 (1967).

REFERENCES

Jeff LeJava and Joseph Stinson, *Utilizing Intermunicipal Agreements in Land-Use Decision-Making, at* http://www.pace.edu/lawschool/landuse/imas.html (last visited Feb. 2, 2001).

Intermunicipal Cooperation, New York State Department of State, Division of Local Government; James A. Coon Local Government Technical Series.

B. LOCAL AND COUNTY AGREEMENTS

DEFINITION

Under New York State statutes adopted in 1993, local governments are specifically authorized to enter into agreements with counties that have established planning boards to have the county planning agency and staff "perform and carry out certain ministerial functions on behalf of such [local governments] related to land use planning and zoning." Town Law §284(1); Vil-

clude, but are not limited to, advice and assistance with the preparation of comprehensive plans, land use regulations, and the formation of local agencies such as planning, zoning, and conservation advisory boards.

The types of land use regulations that counties can help localities prepare include any local ordinance or law regarding any aspect of land use and community resource protection. This includes zoning, subdivision, site plan, special permit regulations, and any others that specify the appropriate use of property or the scale, location, and intensity of land development.

Counties can also provide assistance regarding the adoption of comprehensive plans and any type of local community resource planning or regulation. Local community resources are defined broadly to include public facilities and infrastructure systems and geographic areas of special significance to economic development, environmental conservation, or the provision or protection of recreational, open space, natural, historic, scenic, or cultural resources.

The law makes it clear that counties are to provide "ministerial" assistance to localities. Local governments are not authorized to share with counties, or surrender to them, their legislative or administrative prerogatives or duties regarding land use matters.

PURPOSE

Some states, such as Maryland and Ohio, have granted significant land use authority to county governments. *See generally* Md. Code 1957, Art. 66B, §10.01 et seq.; Md. Code 1957; Ohio Rev. Code §713.01 et seq. The county system has certain advantages, such as providing for a broader view of land development and a greater scale of operations. New York has chosen a different approach, emphasizing land control at the municipal level.

With 62 counties and nearly 1,600 towns, villages, and cities in New York, the merits of both systems can be appreciated. Counties typically have jurisdiction over sufficient territory to create workable development patterns to serve the economic, environmental, and quality of life needs of their residents. This can be particularly important when one locality shares areas of special significance with its neighboring communities. Local governments, however, are closer to the people who are affected by the direct impacts of land use decisions. They provide meaningful opportunities for citizen participation in decisions, and have a very real stake in the outcome of each decision.

By authorizing local governments to enter into agreements with their counties regarding land use matters, the state legislature has provided towns, villages, and cities the opportunity to gain some of the advantages of the county system without surrendering local control. If several municipalities ask their county planning staffs for technical advice and support, the county can afford to retain sufficient sophisticated land use professionals to serve local needs. Local governments often lack the resources to do this when acting alone.

WHEN

Whenever localities lack the resources to retain land use staff at the local level, they may want to consider approaching their county governments for assistance. Several localities may have a common land use planning or ministerial need that can be met on a cost-effective basis by having the county retain, train, and supervise permanent staff.

Localities may want to obtain the county's advice to coordinate their actions with those of their municipal neighbors. If the county has a plan for countywide development that is beneficial to a community, it may want to insure that its land use actions conform with that plan. Certain advantages can be realized by such an approach. Economic development activities in one community alone, for example, cannot reverse negative trends in the larger economic market area. Parallel action among localities in the entire market area may be required for any noticeable effect to be had. One community cannot create enough supply to meet the regional demand for affordable housing. Efforts in one community to protect natural resource areas that are shared with adjacent municipalities often cannot work to truly preserve the resource without compatible efforts in all the communities. Joining together and asking for the assistance of the county planning agency is one way of achieving this broader perspective and effect.

In addition to their authority to assist local governments, counties carry out a number of important land use functions. They are empowered to have planning boards; adopt countywide land use plans; render opinions regarding certain local land use actions; participate in regional planning boards and councils; review subdivision applications and septic and sewer projects; establish water and sewer districts; fund and staff soil and water boards; establish and assist environmental management councils; construct roads and bridges and regulate access to them; and operate community development and affordable housing projects.

Where a county has independent authority to carry out an activity, a county/local agreement can also stipulate how these county functions are to be coordinated or shared with the localities involved. These agreements can be effective vehicles not only for arranging the assistance of the county regarding the locality's land use plans and regulations but for coordinating the work of soil and water boards, environmental management councils, county permitting and infrastructure activities, and other county functions.

AUTHORITY

In 1960, the New York State General Municipal Law was amended to give all municipal corporations, including towns, villages, cities, and counties, the authority to enter into intermunicipal agreements for the joint performance of their respective functions. In 1992, provisions were added to the Town, Village, and General City statutes to encourage intermunicipal cooperation regarding land use planning and regulation. Finally, in 1993, the General Municipal Law and the Town, Village, and General City laws were amended to make it clear that local governments may enter into agreements with county governments. Under these agreements, counties can assist localities with the preparation of comprehensive plans, land use regulations, and the administration and enforcement of local land use plans and regulations.

IMPLEMENTATION

An agreement between a county and a municipality must be authorized by a majority vote of the legislative bodies of the county and of each participating municipality. Once adopted, it is carried out according to its terms. The terms of the agreement should specify:

- ♦ The objectives of the agreement.
- ♦ The specific local needs requiring the county's assistance.
- ♦ What technical assistance is to be provided.
- ♦ How it is to be provided.
- ♦ Whether the local government will be charged.
- ♦ How the agreement is to be monitored, reviewed, amended, extended, or terminated.

Where the agreement also covers the coordination of independent county government functions with those of the locality, provisions for such coordination should be included.

ILLUSTRATIONS

Several New York counties now maintain geographical information systems (GIS) that are made available to local governments to assist with land use planning and project review and approval functions. By aggregating the consultant, staff, hardware, and software expenses at the county level, geographical information systems may become cost-effective for local governments that otherwise could not develop such systems on their own. Westchester County, for example, has digitized all the tax parcels of its 45 constituent localities and developed a sophisticated GIS that greatly aids in local land use analysis, planning, and project review.

The town of DeKalb and the village of Richville established a combined planning board in 1991, with the assistance of the St. Lawrence County Planning Office. Three of the five planning board members must be residents of the town but not the village, and the remaining two must reside in the village. The board is authorized to receive applications for site plan review, and to approve, approve with modifications, or disapprove such applications. The board may act as lead agency for review of a proposed site plan under the State Environmental Quality Review Act.

The village of Forestville sought the expertise of Chautauqua County in assessing and developing the village's public water supply. Pursuant to an agreement negotiated between the village and the county, county employees conducted hydrological testing and an evaluation of Walnut Creek to assess the quantity and quality of Forestville's water supply. Forestville, lacking the technical staff to perform this analysis itself, took advantage of the appropriate county resources after experiencing severe water shortages and water quality problems.

Four towns, three cities, one county, and the Niagara Frontier Transportation Authority joined forces to administer a comprehensive waterfront development program along 90 miles of the Lake Erie shoreline. The communities recognized that the only way to properly approach the complicated matter of the redevelopment of the waterfront was through a unified planning and implementation process based on a single plan. To fulfill this goal, the communities established a public benefit corporation, the Horizons Waterfront Commission, and charged it with creating a master plan, directing public and private investment for specific projects along the waterfront, and coordinating the activities of all participating governmental entities. After review and acceptance of the master plan, the municipalities resolved to conform their land use policies and actions to give full force and effect to the master plan. Recently, the commission was dissolved because of the decision of one of the key local participants to withdraw from the agreement.

LIMITATIONS AND CONCERNS

Not all counties have the staff or consultant capacity to meet the technical assistance needs of their constituent local governments. When localities make requests to receive technical assistance, the needs of both the county and the localities must be carefully assessed and coordinated so that appropriate staff may be hired or deployed.

Some local officials are concerned that if such agreements are entered into, the county will attempt to pursue its broader agenda regarding land use at the expense of the locality's objectives. The county's authority under such agreements, with respect to local land use powers and functions, is advisory and ministerial only. Nothing in the agreement can compromise the legislative prerogatives or administrative responsibilities of the local government. Beyond this, local officials must be careful to negotiate agreements that insure that their concerns are paramount in the advice and assistance given by the county.

STATUTES AND RULINGS

New York State General City Law §20-g, Town Law §284, and Village Law §7-741 are identical to General Municipal Law §119-u and allow municipalities to enter into intermunicipal agreements with counties to receive professional planning services through county planning agencies.

The costs associated with joint land use planning may be apportioned among the participating municipalities on any equitable basis. 67 St. Comp. 562 (1967).

General Municipal Law §239-m should be consulted regarding those local land use decisions that must be referred to county governments for review and advisory opinions.

REFERENCES

Intermunicipal Cooperation in Land Use Planning, Technical Memorandum of the Government Law Center, Albany Law School (Oct. 1994).

Intergovernmental Cooperation, New York State Department of State, Division of Local Government; James A. Coon Local Government Technical Series.

C. LOCAL AGREEMENTS WITH THE HUDSON RIVER GREENWAY COUNCIL

DEFINITION

The Hudson River Valley Greenway Communities Council was created by the state legislature in 1991 to develop a cooperative planning approach among localities in the 10-county region that lines the Hudson River from Yonkers to Albany. The goal of the council is to encourage cooperative planning among these localities "which fosters the ability to achieve appropriate economic development consistent with conservation objectives."

Localities in sub-regions of the Hudson River Valley may join together and adopt land use plans that are consistent with the principles contained in the legislation establishing the council. These principles include:

♦ The conservation of open space and natural, cultural, and architectural resources.

♦ Economic development including urban redevelopment, tourism, and protection of unique agricultural lands.

♦ Waterfront reclamation and the promotion of public access to the waterfront.

♦ Establishment of a planning process that uses available information, makes maximum effective use of local planning and zoning authority, and is linked to compatible plans of neighboring communities and of the council.

Participation in the council's planning program is voluntary on the part of individual localities. Matching grants are available to interested municipalities, along with technical assistance, to help them develop an appropriate plan. Once a locality has adopted a plan that is part of a sub-regional plan and is consistent with the council's principles, it is deemed to be a "participating community" and, under state law, it becomes eligible for several benefits. These include matching grants for certain projects, a 5% advantage for funding from state agencies, and state indemnification from legal liability. In addition, such communities benefit from the ability to exempt conforming projects from the State Environmental Quality Review Act and expedite their approval and development. They also receive ongoing assistance from the council, including help with mediating local land use controversies, and the ability to make state agencies operating within the locality consider the local plan and cooperate with it.

Once a local government adopts a plan and is accepted as a participating community, the law gives the council no authority over the locality's actions. If a participating community acts in a way that is deemed to be inconsistent with the council's principles or regional plan, the community may lose the incentives. Beyond this, there is no sanction available to the council to control local action.

PURPOSE

A local government's land use jurisdiction and authority stop at its borders. This geographical limitation often frustrates municipal ability to create workable development patterns to serve the economic, environmental, and quality of life needs of local residents. This can be particularly limiting when one locality shares areas of special significance with its neighboring communities. By authorizing local governments to enter into agreements with their neighbors and the council regarding land use matters, the state legislature has provided towns, villages, and cities the opportunity to gain the advantages of intermunicipal cooperation, as well as the incentives available to participating communities, without surrendering local control.

The legislation creating the Greenway recognizes that "this cooperative planning approach is in the public interest as a necessary and appropriate step to protect the irreplaceable resources of the valley for the benefit of this and future generations."

In its February 1991 report, the Hudson River Valley Greenway Council used these words to reflect on the purpose of local agreements with the Greenway:

> The [land use plans to be created by the Greenway] must provide a mechanism that will enable local, county and state governments to initiate cooperative planning for the Hudson River communities that is voluntary and reflective of the political and fiscal realities of the 1990s, yet visionary enough to enable Greenway communities to deal with the opportunities and problems of the 21st century. Cooperation among the communities of the Hudson River Valley is the only way in which both economic growth and preservation of the region's character can be achieved. The planning for a Hudson River Valley Greenway must originate from local government.

WHEN

Localities may want to coordinate their land use actions with those of their municipal neighbors, within the context of a compatible regional plan for sustainable land development and conservation. Certain advantages may be realized by such an approach. Economic development activities in one community, for example, cannot reverse negative trends in the larger economic market area. Parallel action among localities in the entire market area may be required for any noticeable effect to be had. One community cannot create enough supply to meet the regional demand for affordable housing. Efforts in one community to protect natural resource areas that are shared with adjacent municipalities frequently cannot work to truly preserve the resource without compatible efforts in all the communities.

Without the guarantees of the Greenway statute, localities have little ability to conform state agency actions to their plans. Without participating in the Greenway, they do not enjoy the incentives provided under its statute. Where these benefits would be helpful, and intermunicipal cooperation regarding shared resources and markets seems beneficial, joining together and working with the council provides these benefits and achieves this broader perspective.

AUTHORITY

The Environmental Conservation Law of the State of New York was amended in December, 1991, creating the council, stating its objectives, establishing the processes, and detailing the incentives discussed above. Local governments, by the terms of the statute, are authorized to enter into compact agreements with the council and to become participating communities.

The Greenway statute provides the following definitions:

- ♦ "Greenway Compact" shall mean the overall greenway plan adopted by the Council.
- ♦ "Greenway districts" shall mean areas made up of neighboring communities within the greenway and designated by the council for the purpose of regional planning.
- ♦ "Participating community" shall mean a county, city, town, or village that has adopted the regional plan for its district.

IMPLEMENTATION

The council designates a sub-region for planning purposes and convenes the chief elected officials of the area. The council then provides funding and technical assistance for the development of local and sub-regional plans that meet the council's planning principles and identify projects and areas of regional importance. Following the adoption by the localities of the plan and its implementation procedures, the plan is submitted to the council for review. If it is consistent with the council's principles, the plan is approved. The municipalities then become participating communities and are eligible for the incentives provided by the Greenway statute.

ILLUSTRATIONS

One group of communities in the Hudson Valley which share a critical watershed is negotiating with the council to determine how to develop an intermunicipal plan consistent with Greenway principles. One of the reasons the local officials are pursuing this strategy is to gain some control over state agency permitting activities in their communities. State agencies are issuing permits to a variety of mining, filling, and industrial activities that local officials fear will erode the quality of life in the area. These municipalities are interested in gaining some control over state activities and are impressed by the statutory language that requires state agencies to consider and cooperate with local plans of participating communities.

These same communities also share a threatened drinking water aquifer impacted by developments approved by them all. They are interested in intermunicipal cooperation through the Greenway as a means of coordinating their discussions to preserve the aquifer, while developing a plan for economic development in their market area.

A number of communities have established Greenway committees to develop model comprehensive plans and to demonstrate how to achieve local objectives and meet the council's planning principles. In the town of Stuyvesant, in Columbia County, a plan has been prepared with significant citizen participation and with technical assistance from the council. The plan emphasizes the community's rural nature, preserves agricultural land, promotes tourism, and guides new development into existing hamlets. Its objectives are to maintain a tight-knit community feeling, keep the hamlets as identifiable town centers, minimize sprawl and the conversion of farmland, allow for more effective investment in infrastructure, and generate less traffic.

LIMITATIONS AND CONCERNS

Some local officials are concerned that if such agreements are entered into, the council will attempt to pursue its broader agenda regarding land use at the expense of the locality's objectives. The council, however, has little authority with respect to local land use powers and functions. Nothing in the statute compromises the legislative prerogatives or administrative responsibilities of the local government. Beyond this, local officials must be careful to develop plans that insure their concerns are met and that the implementation of the plans is beneficial to the community.

STATUTE

The New York State Environmental Conservation Law, §§44-0101 et seq., contains provisions regarding the creation, purpose, and administration of the Hudson River Valley Greenway Communities Council.

REFERENCES

A Hudson River Greenway, A Report to the Governor, Hudson River Valley Greenway Communities Council, Albany, NY (Feb. 1991).

Hudson River Valley Greenway, Draft Progress Report (Feb. 1995).

Hudson River Valley Greenway, Opportunities for Economic Development, River Access and Recreation, Summary Projects (Jan. 1996).

D. THE ROLE OF COUNTY GOVERNMENT IN LAND USE

DEFINITION

County governments in New York serve a number of important functions. For some purposes, they are regarded as an instrument of the state and carry out a number of roles in that capacity, including the provision of social services and the protection of public health. For other purposes, counties are regarded as independent units of local government that directly provide a number of governmental functions, such as the development of hospitals, correctional facilities, and county roads, police, and library services. Increasingly, counties serve to coordinate and rationalize the activities of cities, towns, and villages within their jurisdictions and to provide a range of services to them for that purpose.

In all three capacities, county governments carry out a number of activities that influence land use conservation and development. This is true despite the fact that state law delegates primary land use planning and regulatory authority to towns, villages, and cities. Counties, for example, create planning boards and adopt comprehensive plans and official maps. They provide technical assistance to local governments in land use matters and can, upon request, serve as the administrative arm of local governments regarding land use actions.

Counties review applications for the subdivision of land and proposed municipal actions that affect intermunicipal, county, or state interests. They adopt, propose, and create water, sewage, and drainage districts. These districts can finance and construct infrastructure needed to support land development. In addition, counties acquire land for and finance parks, county roads, and facilities for transit or for solid waste disposal, and even affordable housing. County governments create and assist independent soil and water conservation districts, agricultural districts, farmland preservation boards, and environmental management councils. Counties are authorized to act directly to acquire open space and to develop recreational facilities for their populations. This power enables counties to affect significantly the shape of land development patterns through the acquisition of land needed to buffer development trends in the area.

Where local governments fail to act, counties can adopt regulations to control development in wetlands, to prevent coastal erosion, and to administer the Uniform Fire Prevention and Building Code. Counties can apply for and administer a variety of federal programs, including community development block grants. In limited instances, counties veto local land use actions and acquire development rights to farmland. County highway commissioners can control access to county roads.

The populations of counties in New York vary from 5,000 to nearly 1.5 million. The land use issues facing county governments range from the relative tranquility of slow-growth areas to coordinating the land use activities of highly competitive municipal governments in rapidly developing areas. In this diverse environment, counties have used their fairly flexible legal authority in a variety of ways. In general, counties have acted in concert with their municipal constituents, responding to their requests for help, and often coordinating the significant intermunicipal impacts of land development projects. The sum of their actions dramatically illustrates the important and creative impacts they can have on land use matters.

PURPOSE

Counties are called upon to serve a number of purposes in the land use area. They respond to the need of citizens for capital facilities by building roads and other infrastructure necessary to support land development. To protect public health, they review and approve land subdivision proposals to insure that they are adequately serviced by water and sewage facilities. Counties can create a policy and planning framework for local land use decisions that have intermunicipal impacts. They can influence and harmonize the development of the capital projects of federal, state, and local governments. In some cases, counties can provide services more cost-effectively across a broader geographical area than individual municipalities can.

County jurisdictions are more likely to encompass the boundaries of critical natural resources– and they encompass a significantly larger market area–than any individual locality. As a result, their geographical jurisdiction permits them to act effectively to protect and enhance resources and markets. When this geographical jurisdiction is coordinated with the land use authority of municipal governments, the stage is set for an effective system of land conservation and development.

WHEN

There are 57 counties in New York State outside of New York City. All of them are challenged to determine their proper role in land use matters. In sparsely populated areas, local governments acting alone may not have the resources needed to create, monitor, or enforce their local land use regulations and plans. In these regions, counties can help by providing technical and administrative assistance in establishing and staffing review boards, proposing and reviewing needed regulations, and conforming these regulations and the actions of these boards to comprehensive planning. In developing areas, counties can help coordinate the land use decisions of municipalities so that they reinforce rather than compete with one another.

AUTHORITY

General: County governments are organized under the New York County Law and may operate with or without adopting a county charter. State law allows counties to adopt charters to create unique administrative structures and programs and to adopt laws to meet their particular circumstances. Properly adopted charter provisions can provide for the transfer of power between a county and its local governments to meet unique local needs. Charters allow counties to adopt laws inconsistent with general state laws but consistent with the state constitution. Counties have independent authority to adopt local laws and to add provisions to their charters to meet the land conservation and development needs of their citizens.

Land Use Planning and Administration: State law authorizes counties to create and fund county planning boards or, in conjunction with other counties or municipalities in other counties, regional planning councils. Municipalities can play a role in the creation and operation of these boards. County planning boards have the power to conduct planning and research, to draft and propose a comprehensive plan to be adopted by the county legislature, and to recommend to local governments how certain lands should be zoned. They can provide technical services– including the drafting of comprehensive plans and land use regulations–to local governments upon their request. Counties may also enter into intermunicipal agreements with local governments to perform ministerial functions involved in the administration and implementation of land use regulations. Counties can adopt official maps showing present and proposed county roads and rights of way and facilities, and to restrict building on land proposed for future public improvement. The county official map is deemed to be an amendment to the municipal official maps of the communities within the county's jurisdiction, and the county official map serves as the official map of a municipality where a municipality fails to adopt one.

Land Use Referral Requirements: Local governments in New York are required to refer certain land use matters to a county planning board or regional planning council in their area before taking final action on them. These include the adoption of a comprehensive plan, zoning law, or its amendment, and the approval of development applications where the action occurs in or affects land within 500 feet of certain boundaries. These boundaries include county or state roads, parks, streams or drainage channels, governmental buildings, and farms located in an agricultural district. This review requirement extends to proposed land use regulations, such as a townwide moratorium or comprehensive amendments of zoning laws which, by definition, affect boundary areas. The county planning board is to review these matters for intermunicipal or countywide impacts. Where the board disapproves the proposed action or conditionally approves the action, and the referring municipal body chooses to act contrary to the county's recommendation, the municipal body must approve the action by a majority plus one of its members. (Normally, only a majority is required). Under their charters or the General Municipal Law, counties can diminish or expand this authority to review local land use decisions.

Environmental Review: New York State law requiring environmental impact review of land use decisions confers on county agencies that issue development permits the status of an "involved agency" under the State Environmental Quality Review Act. Local governments must refer all proposed projects that may have a significant adverse environmental impact to involved agencies for their review and comments. Even in instances in which actions need not be reviewed by the county, a county agency can become involved in the environmental review process as an "interested" agency.

Infrastructure Development: Counties plan, acquire land for, finance, and build a variety of capital facilities including roads, parks, and governmental buildings. They create water and sewer districts, purchase or condemn land for their projects, and create taxing districts to pay the capital and operating costs of the facilities. County public health departments review and approve the water and sewage facilities of proposed subdivisions within the county. The law prohibits the sale of any subdivided lot until such approval is obtained.

Creation of Soil and Water Districts: Counties may create and assist soil and water conservation districts for the purpose of conserving soil and water resources, improving water quality, and preventing soil erosion and land inundation by floodwaters.

Special Land Use Authority: Counties have some authority to assist in the planning, development, and construction of affordable housing for low- and moderate-income persons. Additionally, counties may adopt, respectively, wetlands and coastal erosion regulations enforceable in municipalities that fail to adopt their own regulations in these areas. Counties may also assist in the organization and planning activities of farmland preservation boards and can establish programs for the protection of farmland, including the purchase of development rights.

IMPLEMENTATION

Intermunicipal Agreements Between Counties and Local Governments: In 1993, the state legislature specifically reiterated the authority of municipalities to enter into intermunicipal agreements with counties to receive professional planning services through county planning agencies. In this way, municipalities lacking the financial and human resources to engage in professional planning activities can receive assistance from county planning agencies to carry out their land use functions. Pursuant to these amendments, a county planning agency can act in an advisory capacity, assist in the preparation of a comprehensive plan, assist in the preparation of land use regulations, and participate in the formation of individual or joint administrative bodies.

County Comprehensive Planning: Westchester County prepared a countywide comprehensive plan entitled "Patterns for Westchester: The Land and Its People," which was adopted by the county's board of legislators in July of 1996. This plan was presented at a number of public hearings throughout the county to allow citizens and municipal officials to voice their support or concerns. It contains a variety of recommendations including:

- the channeling of development to areas where infrastructure can support growth;
- the development of an interconnected system of open space;
- the encouragement of a variety of housing types to meet county housing needs; and
- the enhancement of Westchester's quality of life by protecting the county's educational, cultural, and historical resources.

Other counties that have prepared comprehensive plans include Dutchess County in 1987 ("Directions: The Plan for Dutchess County"), Yates County in 1990, Onondaga County in 1991, and Chenango County in 1992.

Altering General State Land Use Laws: In Westchester County, the county board of legislators changed a requirement of state law regarding the impact of county planning board review of local land use decisions. The county legislature passed a home rule law eliminating a requirement of general state law that local agencies approve projects by a majority plus one of their membership when the action has been disapproved or conditionally approved by a county planning board. With this change, local boards can accept or reject the county planning board's recommendation by a simple majority vote. At the same time, the county board of legislators added a requirement that local governments in Westchester refer such land use actions to one another.

Suffolk County, on the other hand, strengthened the role of its county planning board in reviewing local land use decisions. It used its authority to supersede general state law to provide its planning board with the authority to veto certain municipal land use actions. Now, according to the Suffolk County charter, when two-thirds of the total members of the county planning commission disapprove a proposed local action, the referring municipal body cannot overturn the action. This gives the planning commission veto power over zoning ordinance enactments and amendments. In Nassau County, the county government altered general state law procedures by assuming authority to approve proposals for the subdivision of land outside the jurisdictions of cities and villages.

County Purchase of Development Rights to Protect Farmland: In 1974, Suffolk

County adopted a local law providing the county with the ability to purchase the development rights of agricultural lands. Its purpose is to protect and conserve agricultural lands, open spaces, and open areas, as well as to encourage the improvement of agricultural lands for the production of food. As a result of this program, Suffolk County has protected 6,000 farmland acres from development.

When authorized by the county legislature, the Suffolk County executive may solicit offers from landowners to sell the development rights of agricultural lands. Upon receiving offers for sale, the county executive has the market value of the development rights appraised and then reports the matter to the county legislature. The county legislature then holds a public hearing on the question of acceptance of the offers. Within 30 days of the public hearing, the county legislature must decide whether to purchase the development rights. Although ultimate decisions regarding the purchase of development rights rest with the county legislature, a farmland committee established by the legislature is charged with a variety of duties to insure the success of the program. The committee acts both as an advisory board to the county legislature concerning which lands to consider for purchase and as a review board for the granting of permits dealing with the erection of structures and operation of farmstands on program properties.

ILLUSTRATION

In 1989, one county, three cities, four towns, and the Niagara Frontier Transportation Authority formed the Horizons Waterfront Commission, a public benefit corporation and subsidiary of the New York State Urban Development Corporation. The commission was created to develop and revitalize 90 miles of Erie County shoreline. The communities understood that revitalization of the entire waterfront was essential to the their individual success in providing opportunities for recreation, housing, transportation, and commercial and industrial uses. Parties to the agreement include the towns of Brant, Evans, Hamburg, and Tonawanda, the cities of Buffalo, Tonawanda, and Lackawanna, and Erie County and the Niagara Frontier Transportation Authority. The communities organized the commission to undertake a cooperative, unified planning and implementation process.

The commission was composed of persons from all levels of government. There were 15 voting members and 18 ex-officio members. Voting members were drawn from each level of government, with seven members appointed by the Erie County executive (one from each of the seven municipalities), three members appointed by the Buffalo City mayor, two members appointed by the governor of New York State, and one member each appointed by the Buffalo common council, the Erie county legislature, and the Niagara Frontier Transportation Authority. Non-voting members included representatives from the economic agencies of each of the parties to the agreement as well as other county agencies, business groups, state agencies, and the federal government.

Under the agreement, the commission had the power to develop, adopt, and update a single regional master plan for Erie County's waterfront. The Horizons Waterfront Master Plan (HWMP) was completed between 1991 and 1992. The parties agreed to give full force to the

HWMP, to the extent each deem appropriate, through their individual activities regulating land use and development, the development of infrastructure, and the adoption and implementation of comprehensive plans and their amendments. They agreed to change their official maps, zoning maps, comprehensive plans, and land use regulations as needed.

In addition to its planning authority, the commission had the power to receive and distribute state, federal, and other funds to carry out waterfront development projects. It also had the authority to coordinate the activities of all governmental entities and private investment and development efforts along the waterfront. As a subsidiary of the New York State Urban Development Corporation, the commission had the power of eminent domain and the ability to bypass local zoning laws. These last two powers gave the commission significant authority to carry out projects which could not be effectively and appropriately carried out by a local entity.

Erie County played an important role in the creation and management of the commission. The county executive conceived the idea and initiated the commission's creation. Erie County was also to incorporate the HWMP into a partial county official map. Through this incorporation, the lands set aside for public facilities and other projects devised by the commission would no longer be available for private development unless a use variance was granted by the zoning board of appeals of the appropriate municipality. In exercising its review authority under §§239-l through 239-n of the General Municipal Law, the county insured that local activities coming before the county were in conformity with the HWMP.

LIMITATIONS AND CONCERNS

As the description of the Erie County Horizon Waterfront Commission illustrates, the land use authority of county governments may be used in creative ways to assist local governments to chart and implement intermunicipal land use plans. Such efforts require years of planning and great investment in time and, often, dollars. Interested governments, at all levels, and all interested private sector organizations can be involved in organizations such as the commission, and become committed to its success because of their investment. After initial project successes, the Horizon Waterfront Commission lost its state funding, which caused significant changes in its plans and even in its organizational structure. Intermunicipal agreements with county governments are subject to political change of this type and are, therefore, only as strong as the commitment of their constituent governments. Great energy and creativity are required to obtain, and to keep, that commitment.

STATUTES, REGULATIONS, AND RULINGS

In New York State, County Law §§150 et seq. and Alternative County Government Law §§1 et seq. govern the organization and operations of county governments generally.

Section 33 of the Municipal Home Rule Law allows counties to adopt charters to create unique administrative structures and programs and to adopt regulations to meet their particular circumstances.

Municipal Home Rule Law §10(1)(ii)(a)(12) authorizes counties to adopt local laws concerning the government, protection, order, safety, health, and well-being of persons or property within their jurisdiction.

General Municipal Law §239-c empowers counties to create and fund county planning boards or, in conjunction with other counties or municipalities, regional planning councils. Section 239-c(3) authorizes county planning boards to conduct planning and research activity and to adopt a comprehensive plan. Section 239-c(3) authorizes the county planning board to recommend to local governments how those municipalities should zone certain lands. Section 239-c(3) also authorizes county planning boards to provide technical services, including the drafting of comprehensive plans and land use regulations, to local governments. Additionally, this section provides counties with the authority to enter into intermunicipal agreements with local governments to perform on behalf of a city, town, or village ministerial functions related to land use planning and regulation. Section 239-e delegates to counties the authority to adopt official maps to provide for orderly growth and development and to afford adequate facilities for transportation, flood protection, and other purposes.

General Municipal Law §§239-m and 239–n require local governments to refer certain land use matters to county or regional planning board in their area before taking final action on them.

County Law §§250 et seq. authorize counties to create water and sewer districts, condemn land for their projects, and create taxing districts to pay the capital and operating costs of the facilities.

Public Health Law §1116(1) provides county health departments with binding authority to approve the water facilities of proposed subdivisions within the county. The law prohibits the sale of any subdivided lot until such approval is obtained.

Soil and Water Conservation District Law §5 enables counties to create and assist soil and water conservation districts for the purpose of conserving soil and water resources, improving water quality, and preventing soil erosion and land inundation by floodwaters.

A 1992 Informal Opinion of the Attorney General describes the authority counties have to assist in the planning, development, and construction of affordable housing for low- and moderate-income persons. Using this authority, Westchester County added Chapter 298 to its administrative code to establish standards for the provision of county water and sewer improvements associated with affordable housing development.

Environmental Conservation Law §24-0501(4) and §34-0106 give counties authority to adopt, respectively, wetlands and coastal erosion regulations enforceable in municipalities that fail to adopt their own regulations in these areas.

General Municipal Law §119-o(1) provides municipal corporations, including counties, with express statutory authority to enter into, amend, cancel, and terminate intermunicipal agreements for the performance of their respective functions, powers, and duties.

General Municipal Law §119-u(2)(b), General City Law §20-g(2)(b), Town Law §284(2)(b), Village Law §7-741(2)(b), and County Law §239-d authorize municipalities to enter into intermunicipal agreements with counties to receive professional planning services and administrative assistance from county planning agencies.

NYCRR, Title 6, Part 617, §§2, 11, and 12, defines the environmental review authority of involved and interested agencies, including county governments.

Article 47 of the Environmental Conservation Law authorizes counties to establish environmental management councils that are empowered, among other functions, to maintain an inventory of open space and natural resources, to recommend ecologically sound methods of planning to use the county's resources, and to assist in the review of proposals.

General Municipal Law §239-e authorizes counties to adopt official maps showing present and proposed county roads, rights of way, and facilities, and to restrict private construction on lands proposed for public facilities. The county official map can serve as the official map of a municipality that has failed to adopt one.

CASE DIGEST

In *B&L Development Corp. v. Town of Greenfield*, 146 Misc.2d 638, 551 N.Y.S.2d 734 (Sup. Ct. Saratoga County, 1990), a local law enacted by the Greenfield Town Board, imposing a one-year moratorium on the issuance of building permits, was vacated and annulled owing to the board's failure to submit its moratorium plan to the county planning board pursuant to the General Municipal Law §239-m.

In *Town of Smithtown v. Howell*, 31 N.Y.2d 365, 292 N.E.2d 10, 339 N.Y.S.2d 949 (1972), the New York Court of Appeals held that an amendment to the Suffolk County charter by double referendum validly provided veto power of local land use actions to the Suffolk County planning commission. The commission, composed of 13 appointed members, disapproved a zoning change proposed by the Town of Smithtown. The change would have permitted the construction of an automobile dealership on land within 500 feet of a village boundary. Under §1330 of the county charter, the commission was empowered to veto local land use actions in certain instances. While upholding the charter-provided veto power, the Court of Appeals held that this particular disapproval was ineffective because two-thirds of the entire commission had not voted to disapprove of the local action as required by §1330.

REFERENCES

Jeffery P. LeJava, *The Role of County Government in the New York State Land Use Regime, at* http://www.pace.edu/lawschool/landuse/counta.html (last visited Feb. 2, 2001).

Patricia Salkin, *Regional Planning in New York State: A State Rich in National Models, Yet Weak in Overall Statewide Planning Coordination*, 13 Pace L. Rev. 506 (1993).

Chapter 8

RESOURCE PROTECTION

Local governments have extensive authority to protect their natural resources. This chapter explores that power and the methods localities use to mitigate the impact of development on their resources. It discusses the protection of natural, visual, scenic, and historic resources, open space, watersheds, waterfronts, and agricultural land.

Each of these topics distinguishes itself from the others in some way, but strategically they are closely related. The protection of open vistas, viewsheds, and view corridors and the prevention of visually blighting developments advance aesthetic objectives, an important aspect of the public welfare. In New York, state law authorizes localities to establish conservation advisory councils and architectural review boards as the stewards of these important matters. State law also encourages historic and landmark pres-ervation by empowering localities to estab-

Types of Environmental Resource Protection Laws
• Flood plain control
• Wetlands protection
• Watershed management
• Viewshed protection
• Soil erosion & sedimentation prevention
• Aesthetic assets
• Scenic road protection
• Tree protection
• Stream and watercourse protection
• Steep slope protection
• Vegetation removal

lish commissions or boards dedicated to the preservation of the community's cultural and histor-ical heritage. Local waterfront management and agricultural land protection are encouraged by a variety of additional state statutes adopted to pursue important economic objectives while pre-serving and enhancing the existing character of the community.

Taken together, these topics, beginning with local natural resource protection, constitute a body of local environmental law in New York. Their importance, however, transcends environ-mental protection. As a group, these local strategies can preserve and enhance the man-made and natural environment as a critical component in a comprehensive land use and resource conserva-tion program. These strategies are integral to local efforts to create sustainable, environmentally secure, and economically vital communities.

A. LOCAL NATURAL RESOURCE PROTECTION

DEFINITION

Local legislatures often adopt regulations to minimize the adverse environmental impacts of new development and to protect and enhance the positive environmental features of the com-munity. In fact, basic zoning provisions such as the creation of use districts and setback, minimum lot area, and height requirements serve environmental purposes, among others. They set a context for future development by defining the community's environment and then providing for the alteration of that environment by land uses permitted under the zoning law. By designating zoning districts and specifying the land uses, densities, and dimensions of construction permitted in each one, zoning both permits and limits land development. To a degree, natural resources are permitted to be used and are protected from development by the typical zoning law.

Communities can go further and protect particular environmental resources that they fear will be negatively affected by the development that is permitted under zoning. They can regulate development to protect aquifers, woodlands, wetlands, watersheds, watercourses, lakes, ponds, habitats, floodplains, and open spaces. They can protect steep slopes and woodlands, prevent soil erosion and sedimentation, mitigate pollution from nonpoint sources, control chemical applications, and determine the location of solid waste facilities, junkyards, mines, and quarries. The local laws and ordinances that accomplish these objectives constitute the core of a community's environmental law.

PURPOSE

Local environmental regulations can serve two important purposes. First, they can preserve the quality of life of a community by retaining and protecting existing environmental assets so that a balance between development and environmental protection is achieved. Second, they can prevent the harm to the community caused by pollution related to the development of specific parcels of land.

The first purpose can be achieved by the adoption of the zoning law itself: zoning districts can be designed to achieve a balance between land development and resource protection throughout the community. For example, to the extent that the zoning law distances areas of intense development from natural resources such as watercourses, nonpoint source pollution is prevented and the quality of the community's environment is preserved. Where this balance is not properly created by the underlying zoning law, it can be supplemented by the later adoption of an overlay zone and performance standards that effect such protection. The purpose of such provisions is to "encourage the most appropriate use of land throughout the community," one of the basic purposes of zoning itself.

The second purpose can be achieved by the adoption of local laws and ordinances that protect the public health and safety from pollution related to the development of the land. Physical construction projects can cause environmental pollution during or after construction. Soil erosion and sediment control laws, for example, require land developers to obtain a permit after a thorough review of their construction plans and authorize permits to be conditioned to prevent problems related to erosion, sedimentation, or drainage caused by the excavation, filling, grading, and stripping of the land. Similarly, the removal of mature trees caused by development can be prohibited unless the developer obtains a permit under a local tree preservation law, which is designed to minimize tree removal and require replacement, where possible, of the trees that must be removed. Local subdivision and site plan regulations can prevent pollution both during and after construction by regulating construction activities and insuring that land improvements are designed and located to prevent nonpoint source pollution.

WHEN

The principal objective of most state and federal environmental laws is the prevention or regulation of "point source" pollution, which emanates from, for example, factory smokestacks or drainage pipes of wastewater plants. Generally, these state and federal laws are thought to be successful in curtailing point source pollution from larger developments and the deposit of significant amounts of hazardous substances in specific locations. They have been less effective in preventing air and water pollution caused by broader land development patterns. When local governments wish to address these incremental effects of the development of individual parcels, local environmental laws can be adopted.

Local zoning laws and the issuance of local development permits determine the types of land development that are permitted in specific locations. These decisions, in turn, determine how far commuters drive from home for work, shopping, or recreation, whether public transit is economically feasible, and how much of the land adjacent to sensitive environmental resources is improved with buildings, parking, and roads that can cause nonpoint source pollution. When local governments experience development pressures, they are challenged to adopt or amend their zoning laws to create development patterns that both meet the need for housing, jobs, and public facilities and produce cost-effective and environmentally conserving land use patterns. As local boards review and approve individual development projects, they work to insure that each project is developed and operated in a way that minimizes pollution and degradation of on-site and nearby watercourses, adjacent land parcels, wildlife habitats, and other natural resources.

AUTHORITY

There are five separate sources of authority local governments in New York use to adopt regulations that protect natural resources. Their delegated zoning power enables localities to use zoning provisions to provide for the most appropriate use of the land in accordance with the comprehensive plan, which may accommodate the preservation of natural resources. Under their home rule authority, localities can provide for the protection and enhancement of their physical and visual environment. Special state laws provide localities with authority to preserve trees and wetlands and provide for solid waste management. State laws delegating authority to local governments to adopt regulations for approving site plans, subdivisions, variances, and special use permits authorize land use agencies to impose conditions on approvals to protect the environment. Finally, the State Environmental Quality Review Act requires local land use agencies to use all practicable means to mitigate any adverse environmental impacts of projects that they review and approve.

IMPLEMENTATION

Community Planning: State law requires that all local land use regulations conform to the comprehensive plan. The basis for local environmental laws that regulate land use should be found in the community's comprehensive plan. That plan should contain survey information and data that justify the need for regulation, identify the resources and areas that are in need of special protection, establish environmental goals and objectives, and specify actions that need to be taken to achieve the plan's objectives. A conservation district contained in the city of Utica's zoning law was sustained by the court in part because it was supported by provisions of the comprehensive plan that clearly defined the public interest in being protected against flooding and the other hazards that result from building in an area unsuitable for intensive development.

Community Education: Part of the ongoing community planning process is to educate and involve citizens in identifying the environmental challenges that the community faces and the environmental resources that need to be preserved. The data collected during the comprehensive planning process should be communicated to the residents of the community; their ideas regarding these matters should be gathered and considered in creating the comprehensive plan. Community input regarding the types of regulations and other actions that the locality plans to initiate is particularly important in order to secure community support for these initiatives.

Conservation Advisory Council and Natural Resource Inventory: New York State law encourages localities to form conservation advisory councils (CACs) to develop an inventory of all open areas in the community and to list them in order of priority for acquisition or preservation. Once this inventory is approved by the local legislature, the CAC can become the locality's conservation board, which can be empowered to review and make recommendations regarding development projects that affect listed natural areas or features. These conservation bodies should be involved in the development and implementation of the community's comprehensive plan and in the review of the impact of individual development projects.

Zoning and Overlay Zoning: The community should examine whether the existing zoning law properly considers the impact of development on priority natural areas and other environmental assets of the community. If not, the zoning can be amended, or overlay districts can be created, for the purpose of protecting these areas. The zoning law of the town of Stuyvesant contains a zoning district, called a "conservation district," defined primarily by soil type and existence of steep slopes. Only low-intensity uses are permitted as-of-right in this district for the purpose of preventing inappropriate development and retaining open space.

Using the overlay district approach, the town of Greenburgh created a "conservation district" that can be applied to any site of at least two and a half acres when at least 25% of the site contains specified natural features that the town wants to protect. Provisions in local zoning ordinances against solid waste management facilities and mining as permitted uses have been upheld by New York courts. Zoning laws often contain separate articles regarding subdivision and site plan approvals, and the award of special permits and variances, all of which can be conditioned to protect natural environmental features. Some communities add a separate article to their zoning law to protect wetlands, floodplains, or other natural resource areas.

Regulation Drafting: Localities can adopt laws separate from their zoning laws to protect specific environmental features and to promote specific environmental interests using their home rule authority and authority delegated to them under other state laws. The town of Bedford relied on the authority contained in the State Freshwater Wetlands Act to support its adoption of a separate wetlands protection law. This type of local environmental protection law can be quite extensive. The town of Pawling, using its municipal home rule authority, adopted a Soil Erosion, Sediment Control, and Steep Slopes Protection Law containing numerous findings and establishing a detailed permitting system for development affecting slopes or floodplains and for projects involving tree removal or soil excavation, stripping, clearing, grading, or filling.

Another means of controlling environmental quality is the adoption of a tree preservation ordinance to restrict the removal of trees on private property. The purpose clause of one extensive local tree preservation law explains that the provisions were adopted to reduce tree destruction, which gives rise to barren and unsightly conditions, impairs the stability of real property values, and adversely affects the character of the community. Tree regulations typically apply only to trees of a certain diameter and height, and establish a permit system, allowing tree removal but only upon a showing of necessity and upon compliance with certain conditions, such as the replacement of all or some of the trees to be removed.

Environmental Review Process: Communities can effectively protect environmental quality and prevent environmental degradation by using their authority to review development applications to determine whether they may involve a significant adverse impact on the environment. When a project may have such an effect, the reviewing authority can impose conditions on its approval of the project to mitigate that impact. State regulations conferring this authority on local approval agencies define the environment to include "the physical conditions that will be affected by a proposed action, including land, air, water, minerals, flora, fauna, noise, resources of agricultural, archeological, historic or aesthetic significance . . . existing community or neighborhood character, and human health."

Municipalities can adopt their own environmental review regulations, so long as they are more protective of the environment than the regulations of the commissioner of the State Department of Environmental Conservation (DEC). Many of the objectives sought by the local zoning and home rule laws discussed above which protect the community from the specific adverse effects of significant development projects may be achieved under local environmental review regulations.

Enforcement: To enforce local environmental laws, communities adopt a number of practices. These include hiring environmental inspectors, subjecting development projects to additional permitting processes and criteria, requiring bonds or letters of credit to secure compliance with the environmental conditions imposed on project approvals, subjecting violators to criminal and civil penalties, and issuing stop-work orders.

Intermunicipal Coordination: Increasingly, localities are using their extensive statutory authority to enact land use plans and regulations in conjunction with neighboring municipalities to protect environmental resources that overlap municipal boundaries.

LIMITATIONS AND CONCERNS

Where environmental regulations impose serious burdens on property owners, challengers may claim that the regulations are arbitrary and capricious, and violate constitutional requirements of due process. To withstand such challenges, it is important that communities justify their regulations through advance planning and empirical studies. Studies that define the environmental setting, identify the natural resources to be protected, and document their importance to the community help prove that the public welfare will be protected by regulations adopted to protect and preserve those resources.

The means chosen to protect environmental quality should impose on property use the least burden necessary to achieve the community's objectives.

Local environmental laws that regulate wetlands, solid waste management facilities, and coastal erosion must be adopted in conformance with state statutes regulating these matters.

CONSTITUTIONAL PROVISIONS, STATUTES, AND RULINGS

The New York State Constitution, in Article XIV, §4, declares that "the policy of the State shall be to conserve its natural resources and scenic beauty."

Local Zoning Authority: Village Law §7-700, Town Law §261, and General City Law §20(24) authorize local governments to adopt zoning laws to promote the health, safety, morals, or the general welfare of the community. The authority to regulate building height, bulk, and lot coverage and to separate uses into districts is expressly delegated to local governments. Under Village Law §7-704, Town Law §263, and General City Law §20(25), zoning regulations are to be adopted with reasonable consideration of the character of the zoning district and with a view to encouraging the most appropriate use of land. Zoning and land use regulations in New York must conform to the locality's comprehensive plan pursuant to Village Law §7-704, Town Law §263, and General City Law §20(25). Local comprehensive plans can identify and provide for the preservation of "natural resources and sensitive environmental areas." Village Law §7-722(3)(d), Town Law §272-a(3)(d), and General City Law §28-a(4)(d).

Home Rule Authority: A separate source of authority to protect natural resouces is found in Section 10(1)(ii)(a)(11) of the Municipal Home Rule Law, which states that a municipality may adopt land use laws for the "protection and enhancement of its physical and visual environment."

Additional Delegated Authority: Under §96-b of the General Municipal Law, local governments are authorized to adopt laws for the protection and conservation of trees and related vegetation. The Environmental Conservation Law §24-0501(1) authorizes localities to adopt a wetlands protection law or ordinance, as long as the local regulations are as stringent as state law provisions, including authority over wetlands 12.4 acres or larger, which normally fall under the jurisdiction of the DEC. Sections 34-0101 through 34-0113 of the Environmental Conservation Law require localities to adopt local erosion hazard area ordinances to control coastal erosion if they wish to retain authority over such matters. Under §27-0711 of the Environmental Conservation Law, localities are authorized to adopt regulations of solid waste management facilities that are at least as stringent as state law requirements.

Individual Development Approvals: *Site Plan Approvals*: Village Law §7-725-a(2)(a), Town Law §274-a(2)(a), and General City Law §27-a(2)(a) allow localities to include in their site plan regulations requirements that all site plans show "screening, signs, landscaping, architectural features, location and dimension of buildings, adjacent land uses and physical features meant to protect adjacent land uses as well as any additional elements specified by the [local legislative body.]." *Subdivision Approvals*: Village Law §7-728 and §7-738, Town Law §§276-278, and General City Law §§32-34 and §37 allow local governments to provide for the future development of the municipality by authorizing their planning boards to review and approve subdivision plats that show the lot layout, dimensions, and topography of the subdivision, and to require the permitted development to be clustered on a portion of the land in order "to preserve the natural and scenic qualities of open lands." *Granting Variances*: Village Law §7-712-b, Town Law §267-b, and General City Law §81-b allow local zoning boards of appeals to grant use variances where the applicant can prove that the variance "will not alter the essential character of the neighborhood," and area variances with due consideration given to whether the variance will cause an undesirable change in the character of the neighborhood or a detriment to nearby properties. *Issuing Special Use Permits*: Village Law §7-725-b, Town Law §274-b, and General City Law §27-b allow local governments to issue special use permits subject to requirements that assure the proposed use "will not adversely affect the neighborhood."

Environmental Review: Under the regulations of the commissioner of the DEC, 6 NYCRR Part 617, all local agency approvals of projects that may have a significant adverse impact on the environment must be subjected to a detailed environmental review following the completion of an environmental impact statement. These regulations authorize land use permits to be subject to conditions that mitigate any adverse impact on the physical environment that is identified in the review process.

General Municipal Law §§239-x through 239-y authorizes local governments to create conservation advisory councils and conservation boards.

Title 6 NYCRR Part 617.14(b) authorizes local land use review agencies to adopt environmental review procedures "no less protective of environmental values" than those contained in the state regulations.

CASE DIGEST

In *Landing Estates, Inc. v. Jones*, 67 Misc. 2d 354, 324 N.Y.S.2d 255 (Sup. Ct. Suffolk County 1971), the court held that a planning board's decision limiting a subdivision was not arbitrary and capricious in light of a serious risk of pollution to a unique saltwater pond outside the confines of the subdivision. The planning board limited the plaintiff's proposed subdivision to eight lots, even though the ordinance setting the minimum lot area requirement would have authorized 13 lots. The court held that the board could require the plaintiff to give up five lots, noting that "[i]t may consider . . . the 'safety' and 'general welfare' of the county, including adjacent areas." The court also determined that the "proposed subdivision was a threat to the survival" of the pond, which sustained much aquatic life and other wildlife.

Local governments may enact sign regulations to protect aesthetics. A village sign control law prohibiting commercial signs exceeding four square feet was sustained by the Court of Appeals in *People v. Goodman*, 31 N.Y.2d 262, 290 N.E.2d 139, 338 N.Y.S.2d 97 (1972). The law was enacted in recognition of the unique cultural character and natural resources of the small summer resort community. The court held that "aesthetics is a valid subject of legislative concern" and that "reasonable legislation designed to promote the governmental interest in preserving the appearance of the community represents a valid and permissible exercise of the police power . . . Under the police power, billboards and signs may be regulated for aesthetic purposes."

The Fourth Department affirmed a town board's denial of an excavation permit for a portion of land in an environmentally sensitive area in *Pecora v. Gossin*, 78 Misc. 2d 698, 356 N.Y.S.2d 505 (Sup. Ct. Monroe County 1974), *aff'd*, 49 A.D.2d 668, 370 N.Y.S.2d 281 (4th Dep't 1975). The petitioner applied to the board for a permit to excavate and remove soil from a part of his land in preparation for residential use, which was the only permitted use of the land. The board subsequently denied the application, recognizing the danger of development in the area because of its extremely erosive soil characteristics and steep slopes. The court sustained the denial, stating that "the fact that [the petitioner] is not permitted to excavate on a portion of his property does not mean he cannot make a reasonable return upon the property as a whole."

The Fourth Department sustained a conservation district for lands lying within a floodplain of a river in *Dur-Bar Realty Co. v. City of Utica*, 57 A.D.2d 51, 394 N.Y.S.2d 913 (4th Dep't 1977). It held that the zoning law, which allowed no use as-of-right and only certain special uses by permit, was supported by findings in the city's comprehensive plan. The court stated that "the designation is a product of assessment of the character of the land in light of the public health and safety interests in being protected against flooding and other hazards that would result from building in an area unsuitable for intensive development."

Overlay districts have been upheld when they were created to protect environmental resources. *Save the Pine Bush v. City of Albany*, 70 N.Y.2d 193, 512 N.E.2d 526, 518 N.Y.S.2d 943 (1987). The City of Albany adopted an overlay district to protect inland sand dunes and their rare plant and animal species. The city zoned the area for low-rise commercial office buildings, and then created a site plan review process with specific criteria designed to protect the natural resources which were to be used when reviewing applications within the overlay district.

A municipal tree preservation ordinance was found to be a proper exercise of a town's authority to protect the community's health and general welfare. *SeaBoard Contracting & Material, Inc. v. Smithtown*, 147 A.D.2d 4, 541 N.Y.S.2d 216 (2d Dep't 1989). The court stated that "an examination of the legislative purpose underlying the ordinance indicates that the town determined that the indiscriminate and unregulated cutting of trees had caused unnecessary problems of erosion, loss of top soil, sedimentation on roadways, and a diminution in the production of oxygen, cover for wildlife and wind and noise insulation."

"Cluster development is an optional planning technique permitting planning boards to exercise greater flexibility in subdivision approval for the purpose of achieving more efficient use of land containing unusual features . . . for facilitating economical provision for streets and utilities, as well as for preserving the natural and scenic qualities of open lands." *Bayswater Realty & Capital Corp. v. Planning Board of the Town of Lewisboro*, 76 N.Y.2d 460, 560 N.E.2d 1300, 560 N.Y.S.2d 623 (1990). The court held that a planning board is authorized to require developers to set aside land or money for recreational purposes.

In *Eastbrook Construction Co., Inc. v. Armstrong*, 205 A.D.2d 971, 613 N.Y.S.2d 776 (3d Dep't 1994), the court sustained a planning board's denial of an application for a wetlands activity permit for the construction of a house near wetlands. The court held that the board's findings "that the proposed construction would lower the water table which would possibly result in the elimination of wetlands" provided sufficient support for denial.

Primary zoning districts have been used to prohibit environmentally damaging uses. In *Gernatt Asphalt Products, Inc. v. Town of Sardinia*, 87 N.Y.2d 668, 664 N.E.2d 1226, 642 N.Y.S.2d 164 (1996), the Court of Appeals sustained a zoning provision that prohibited the siting of new mines in the community. The court stated that "[a] municipality is not obliged to permit the exploitation of any and all natural resources within the town as a permitted use if limiting that use is a reasonable exercise of its police powers to prevent damage to the rights of others and to promote the interests of the community as a whole."

In *Wal-Mart Stores, Inc. v. Planning Board of the Town of North Elba*, 238 A.D.2d 93, 668 N.Y.S.2d 774 (3d Dep't 1998), the court sustained the planning board's denial of a conditional use permit and site plan application for the development of a large retail store. The court held that it was appropriate for the planning board to place great weight on the visual effect of the development because it would lie partially within an area designated a "Scenic Preservation Overlay," which was established to protect the view of a nearby mountain. It noted that "despite all efforts to screen the store and parking area from the road, their presence would nevertheless bring about a noticeable change in the visual character of this critical area."

REFERENCES

Jeffrey P. LeJava, *Local Regulation of Natural Resources, at* http://www.pace.edu/lawschool/landuse/locreg.htm (last visited Feb. 2, 2001).

Land Resource Protection, New York State Department of State; James A. Coon Local Government Technical Series. This document contains model tree preservation, soil and sediment control, and subdivision regulations.

B. CONSERVATION ADVISORY COUNCILS AND OPEN SPACE PRESERVATION

DEFINITION

Conservation advisory councils (CACs) are created by local legislatures to advise on the development, management, and protection of local natural resources. The CAC is to cooperate with other official municipal bodies active in the area of community planning and development approvals.

CACs are created to study and protect local open areas, including those areas characterized by natural scenic beauty which, if preserved, would enhance the value of surrounding development, establish a desirable pattern of development, achieve objectives of the comprehensive plan, or enhance the conservation of natural or scenic resources. CACs are directed to keep an inventory and map of all local open areas and obtain information pertinent to their proper use. The inventory should identify open areas and list them in order of priority for acquisition or preservation. The map is to identify open areas designated for preservation, including those having conservation, historic or scenic significance.

Once the local legislative body has received and approved the CAC's open area inventory and map, it may redesignate the CAC as a conservation board. At this juncture, the inventory and map become the official open-space index of the municipality and the conservation board can be assigned additional duties to assist the community with its open-area planning and to assure the preservation of its natural and scenic resources. These duties include:

- the review of applications made to other local bodies that seek approval to use or develop any area on the open-space index; and

- the submission of a report on such requests for approval regarding the impact of the proposal on the listed open area and on the open area objectives of the locality.

Both CACs and conservation boards are authorized to perform other duties assigned to them by resolution of the local legislative body as long as they are consistent with their general statutory advisory role regarding the development, management, and protection of local natural resources.

PURPOSE

The formation of a CAC provides an opportunity for the legislature to appoint local experts in this subject matter to an official advisory body that can assist, guide, and encourage other local bodies in protecting and preserving open areas and natural resources. An effective CAC identifies and collects needed data regarding the community's natural resources, open areas, and historic and scenic assets. Once accepted by the local legislature, a CAC's open-area inventory and map becomes the official index of these assets and expresses the community's commitment to their responsible management and protection.

CACs and conservation boards may also assist the planning board, special board, or local legislature in preparing or amending the comprehensive plan with respect to open-area information, policy, and protection. CACs and conservation boards can help prioritize the importance of open areas and advise their legislatures regarding effective strategies for protecting open areas, including acquisition, cluster development, overlay zoning, and critical environmental area designation. They can also assist local lead agencies in assessing and mitigating the adverse environmental impacts of development approvals and other local actions.

WHEN

Most communities can benefit from the work of an effective CAC. In rural areas where development pressure is less, advance planning can help preserve agricultural lands, maintain scenic beauty, and protect priority natural areas from the impacts of development. In developed communities, the conservation, enhancement, and increase of available open space and natural features can be a significant method of maintaining the quality of life and property values of local residents. The conservation board can also assist with the review and modification of development proposals that might affect priority open areas.

AUTHORITY

In New York State, the General Municipal Law contains provisions that authorize local legislatures to form CACs, redesignate them as conservation boards upon the completion of an open-space inventory and map, and grant them duties related to their statutory role of advising local bodies regarding the development, management, and protection of natural resources.

IMPLEMENTATION

To establish a CAC, the local legislature must pass a local law or ordinance. According to the New York General Municipal Law, a CAC shall be made up of not less than three but not more than nine members. They are appointed by the legislature for a term of not more than two years. Up to two appointees may be between the ages of 16 and 21. The chair of the CAC is also designated by the legislature from among the CAC membership. Members of the CAC may be removed by the legislature for cause and after a public hearing. CACs must keep records of their meetings and file an annual report with the legislature by the end of each year.

Upon the submission and acceptance of its open-space inventory and map, the CAC can be redesignated by the legislature as a conservation board. This designation gives the conservation board the authority to review development and other land use proposals that affect any of the listed open areas. Upon the receipt of such a referral, the conservation board must submit a written report to the referral body within 45 days. Its report must evaluate the proposed use or development in light of the open-area planning objectives of the municipality and must include an analysis of the effect of the development on open areas listed in the local open-space index.

If the local legislature decides to create the CAC by local law, a public hearing must be held. This presents an opportunity for the local legislature to receive citizen input, as well as to generate interest in and support for the CAC's activities.

ILLUSTRATIONS

The conservation board of the city of White Plains commented on the amendment of the city's comprehensive plan at the outset of the amendment process. It analyzed and stated the importance of the preservation of three large contiguous open properties in the city, taking note of various issues such as steep slopes, woodlands, and site contours, the adequacy of the proposed preservation of a greenprint edge, and the possibility of acquiring some or all of the properties. Similar input was offered regarding the city's proposed amendments to its zoning law, emphasizing the need for regulations that preserve wetlands and other environmentally sensitive features.

The town board of the town of Clarence took the first step toward linking hundreds of homes with schools, parks, stores, and offices when it authorized its CAC to apply for funding for a pathway project under the federal Intermodal Surface Transportation Efficiency Act.

Issues under consideration by the town of Amherst's CAC included the acquisition by the town of title or an easement to a secluded 22-acre body of water, the impact of rezoning a property on the town's open space, the prospect of adopting a tree preservation plan, the use of pesticides under a local mosquito control program, the conduct of a public educational event regarding chemical pollution, seeking park designation of a 1,300-acre tract along Tonawanda Creek, and preventing vandalism in a local nature preserve.

The resolution of the town of North Castle establishing its CAC expressed the intent of the town board with this declaration:

> The preservation and improvement of the quality of the natural environment within the Town of North Castle, in the face of population growth, urbanization, and technological change with their accompanying demands on natural resources, are found to be of increasing and vital importance to the health, welfare and economic well-being of present and future inhabitants and require forthright action by the governing body of the Town of North Castle. It is recognized that the biological integrity of the natural environment on which man is dependent for survival and the natural beauty of our surroundings, which condition the quality of our life experience, cannot be protected without the full cooperation and participation of all the people of the Town of North Castle working in partnership with local and state officials and with various public and private institu-

tions, agencies and organizations. Establishment of a board for conservation of the environment is a necessary step in fostering unified action on environmental problems.

LIMITATIONS AND CONCERNS

The role of the CAC and the conservation board is advisory only. Other local boards create and amend the comprehensive plan, including its open-areas component; review and approve development proposals; and determine the capital spending priorities of the locality. To be effective, a CAC or a conservation board must coordinate carefully with these approval bodies, avoid duplication and confusion of local processes, and focus on its role as the body that is most knowledgeable about the open areas and natural resources of the community.

Fulfilling that important role requires time, energy, and resources. If the identification of open areas and natural resources is to serve as an effective index and aid in decision-making, it must be accompanied by data gathering. When the CAC or conservation board renders advisory opinions—which the New York State attorney general has pointed out are not binding on other local boards—they are persuasive and compelling only to the extent that they are backed by competent information. In communities in which resources for data gathering are limited and in the absence of help from outside agencies, the CAC or conservation board will be challenged to gather, evaluate, and order scientific and other hard data needed for its advisory role to be effectively discharged. In this regard, the local CAC or conservation board can be greatly assisted by an effective countywide or regional environmental management council charged with identifying and studying open space in the area.

STATUTES AND RULINGS

In New York State, General Municipal Law §239-x confers authority on local legislatures of all towns, villages, and cities to create conservation advisory councils.

General Municipal Law §239-y confers authority on the local legislature of a town, village, or city to designate its conservation advisory council (CAC) as a conservation board when the CAC has prepared a conservation open-area inventory and map that has been accepted by the local legislative body as the open-space index of the municipality.

General Municipal Law §239-x(6) authorizes local CACs to request the assistance of the state Department of Environmental Conservation to conduct research, provide technical and research assistance, and describe local natural resource areas. The Local Environmental Assistance Program under which this type of assistance was provided and under which up to 50% of certain expenses of CACs could be reimbursed has not been funded by the state legislature in recent years.

Environmental Conservation Law §47-0105 authorizes the governing bodies of counties to establish a county environmental management council (EMC), whose membership shall include one representative of every CAC in the county.

Under Environmental Conservation Law §47-0107, an EMC is required to keep an index of all open areas within the county, keep an index of open marshlands, swamps, and other wetlands, and develop an inventory of natural resources in the county. EMCs are permitted by this section to assist other governmental boards such as local CACs in the preparation of plans and reports and the review of development proposals.

Informal opinions of the attorney general of the State of New York have clarified some additional matters involving CACs. Local governments may use their home rule authority to establish procedures and standards for their CACs to follow other than those contained in the General Municipal Law. Op. Att'y Gen. (Inf. 83-28). Members of CACs are not public officers since councils are not authorized to exercise sovereign power of government. Their role is purely advisory. Op. Att'y Gen. (Inf. 90-54). A local open-space inventory map cannot be amended without first being approved by the CAC. Op. Att'y Gen. (Inf. 91-73).

CASE DIGEST

The court in *Carpenter v. City of Ithaca Planning Board*, 190 A.D.2d 934, 593 N.Y.S.2d 582 (3d Dep't 1993), relied on the observations of the conservation advisory council of Ithaca to conclude that the planning board had "failed to take the requisite hard look" expected of lead agencies in discharging their environmental review responsibilities under the State Environmental Quality Review Act (SEQRA). When there is evidence in a land use application that the planning board's approval of a proposal might have significant adverse environmental impacts, the planning board must make a positive declaration of environmental impact and require the applicant to prepare an environmental impact statement. In this case, the board made a negative declaration, finding that the proposal would not have adverse environmental impacts of any significance. The conservation advisory council "suggested that based on the lack of site and soil analysis and testing, a positive declaration should be adopted." The court concluded that the subdivision proposal might have a significant impact on the environment. It annulled the planning board's determination because the record revealed that there were "potential drainage and runoff concerns." Where a lead agency under SEQRA fails to make a proper determination of environmental impact, as in this case, the proper remedy is invalidation of the board's approval.

The court in *Darlington v. City of Ithaca Board of Zoning Appeals*, 202 A.D.2d 831, 609 N.Y.S.2d 378 (3d Dep't 1994), upheld the New York Supreme Court's dismissal of the case for lack of standing. The plaintiff was acting as chair of the city of Ithaca's conservation advisory council (CAC). The court had to determine if the plaintiff in that capacity had standing to bring an action to annul a ruling made by the defendant zoning board. The court stated that the CAC "was created by the City of Ithaca Common Council to perform monitoring, inventory, coordination and advisory functions." The court concluded that the CAC "lack[ed] the express legislative authority to initiate legal actions." The court held that the plaintiff lacked standing because the "CAC is prohibited from exercising any duties other than those authorized unless assigned by Common Council," and filing an action of this type was not authorized to the CAC.

C. CONSERVATION EASEMENTS AND LAND TRUSTS

DEFINITION

A conservation easement is a voluntary agreement between a private landowner and a municipal agency or a qualified not-for-profit corporation to restrict the development, management, or use of the land. The owner of the real property deeds an interest in the land–a conservation easement –to a qualified public or private agency. That agency holds the interest and enforces its restrictions against the transferring owner and all subsequent owners of the land.

The conservation easement restricts the use of the property in such a way that its natural or man-made features are not altered or developed in a manner that is inconsistent with their conservation or preservation. Existing uses on the property and expansions of uses not inconsistent with the preservation or conservation of these features are allowed on the restricted parcel.

Conservation easements may be donated, sold at full-market value, or sold at below-market value by the owner of the land. If the easement is donated or is sold at below-market value, the landowner may qualify for an income tax deduction in the year of the donation or bargain sale. Subject to a conservation easement, the land may qualify for a lower estate tax valuation on the death of the owner, thereby reducing the tax burden on the beneficiaries of the owner's estate. Similarly, the local property tax assessments may be lowered, benefiting the landowner on an annual basis thereafter.

A land trust is a local or regional not-for-profit organization, private in nature, organized to preserve and protect the natural and man-made environment by, among other techniques, holding conservation easements that restrict the use of real property. Land trusts usually pursue their own organizational agendas. However, under contract with a local government, a land trust may agree to serve as a vehicle for the negotiation, acquisition, holding, and enforcement of conservation easements agreed to by, or imposed on, landowners as part of the local development review and approval process.

PURPOSE

The purpose of a conservation easement is to preserve or conserve the scenic, open, historic, archaeological, architectural, or natural condition of real property. The easement is used to preserve scenic viewsheds, wildlife habitats, ecosystems, forest land or farmland, historic buildings or districts, and open space as such. In addition to restricting land use, conservation easements may permit public access, such as hiking over a trail on the property or biking along a designated path.

The purpose of involving a private land trust in a municipal conservation program is to save the local government the expense and inconvenience of holding, monitoring, and enforcing conservation easements and to take advantage of the land trust's expertise in these matters.

WHEN

Conservation easements are appropriate when either a local government or a land trust believes that natural or man-made features of real property need protection, in addition to that afforded by zoning and other land use regulations. By purchasing the development rights on agriculturally productive farmlands and subjecting them to a conservation easement, the community or land trust can perpetuate and allow the reasonable expansion of the current agricultural use of the land, while providing compensation to the farmers for forgoing the right to develop their land.

A municipality can contract with a private land trust to hold and enforce conservation easements in order to take advantage of the land trust's funding, staff, expertise, and ability to act more quickly and decisively than a public body.

AUTHORITY

Title 3 of Article 49 of the New York Environmental Conservation Law provides for the creation and enforcement of conservation easements, eliminating several questions about the legal viability of conservation easements created under the general property law of the state.

IMPLEMENTATION

A conservation easement must be embodied in a written instrument, recorded on the county land records and filed with the New York DEC. The property encumbered by the easement must be described by adequate legal description. By statute, the holder of a conservation easement may enter and inspect the burdened property in a reasonable manner and at reasonable times to assure compliance.

Conservation easements are assumed to be created in perpetuity. However, the term of any specific easement may be limited to a fixed period or ended upon the happening of a specific event, such as the extinction of a species for which the protected land serves as a habitat. The easement may give the parties the authority to modify its terms by mutual agreement. Where modifications are permitted and occur, the modified agreement must be in writing, filed, and recorded.

Conservation easements can be enforced by the original grantor of the easement, the land trust or public agency to whom the easement is granted, or a third party specifically named in the agreement. Where a not-for-profit land trust holds the easement and is unable to enforce its terms, the state's attorney general may bring an enforcement action. If an action for enforcement is granted, the judge may issue an injunction requiring compliance or may require that money damages be paid.

To hold a conservation easement under New York law, a land trust must be organized for the conservation or preservation of real property, have the power to acquire interests in real property, and be qualified as exempt for federal tax purposes pursuant to §501(c)(3) of the Internal Revenue Code.

In order to record the document creating a conservation easement, the parties must complete and file forms published by the Office of Real Property Services. Where five hundred dollars or more is paid for the easement, a transfer tax may have to be paid unless the grantee is a public body. County deed stamp and recording fees may also be imposed.

ILLUSTRATIONS

A homeowner in East Hampton, Long Island, applied to the town's zoning board of appeals for a permit for an addition to his home. The board conditioned the approval on the granting of a scenic and conservation easement to the town. The easement would bar any subsequent development on part of the property in the interest of protecting wetlands and other environmentally significant areas.

The owner challenged the board's determination. On appeal, the court found that the preparation by the town of an environmental assessment form addressing the specific environmental impacts of the homeowner's proposal satisfied the zoning board's burden of showing the essential nexus between the condition and the legitimate conservation interests of the town. This environmental assessment also demonstrated rough proportionality between the easement and the projected environmental impacts of the proposed construction.

The Olana State Historic Site, located in the Hudson River Valley's Columbia County, was constructed in the late 19th century by Frederic Church, a student of the landscape painter Thomas Cole. Olana is a picturesque Persian-style villa famous for its sweeping views of the Hudson, the Catskill Mountains, and the pastoral landscape of Columbia County. Church painted many of his landscapes from that perch, inspired by the vistas spread out before him. Despite the fact that Olana is now owned by the State of New York, the fate of those vistas has been uncertain, given modern development trends.

Since 1986, Scenic Hudson, Inc., a not-for-profit conservation organization, has been working to protect the Olana viewshed. By procuring conservation easements from willing landowners, Scenic Hudson has protected over 400 acres, including an orchard, a vineyard, and several largely wooded residential properties. In each case, a limited amount of development is permitted, carefully sited, with design considerations and size and scale limitations.

The following standards, contained in the cluster subdivision regulations of the Town of Clinton, New York, illustrate how conservation easements can be used to protect open space and natural resources. These standards give the local planning board the authority to require applicants to impose conservation easements as part of the approval by the Board of a proposed subdivision of land in which the development is clustered on a portion of the land owned. In Clinton, the C and AR5 districts referred to in the standards are in more environmentally sensitive areas of town than the other districts mentioned. Consider how the imposition of the easement strengthens the town's hand if enforcement of the conservation restrictions is required in the future. Remember, by then the developer/applicant will no longer own the land which will be in the hands of individual lot owners and, perhaps, their homeowners' association.

1. Common open space totaling not less than sixty percent (60%) of the total cluster development site in the C and AR5 districts, or forty percent (40%) of the total cluster development site in the AR3, MR1, CR1, RH and H districts, shall be provided in perpetuity as part of the cluster development. A plan for maintenance or landscaping of the common open space shall be reviewed and approved by the Planning Board. No portion of this minimum required open space shall be utilized for roads, driveways, utility structures, or similar features.

2. Open space land may be owned in common by a homeowner's association, held in private ownership subject to a permanent conservation easement or dedicated to the Town if such agreement is approved by the Town Board. If owned by a homeowner's association, the common open space land shall be protected by conservation easement from future subdivision and development. The Planning Board shall assure that proper provision has been made for ownership and maintenance of open space land, roadways and other improvements. Ownership shall be structured in such a manner that real property taxing authorities may satisfy property tax claims against the open space lands by proceeding against all individual owners in the homeowner's association and the dwelling they each own. Ongoing maintenance standards shall be established, enforceable by the Town against an owner of open space land as a condition of subdivision approval, to assure that the open space land does not detract from the character of the neighborhood. Maintenance standards may include the obligation to mow open fields to maintain their scenic character or agricultural potential.

3. A perpetual conservation easement leaving the open space land forever wild or limiting the use of such land to agricultural, managed forest land, passive recreational or open space us, or to the residential use specified as part of the plan, and prohibiting institutional, industrial, or commercial use of such open space, pursuant to Section 347 of the General Municipal Law and/or Sections 49-0301 through 49-0311 of the Environmental Conservation Law, may be granted to the Town, with the approval of the Town Board, or to a qualified not-for-profit conservation organization acceptable to the Planning Board. Such conservation easement shall be reviewed and approved by the Planning Board and shall be required as a condition of plat approval under the Town's Subdivision Regulations. The conservation easement shall not be amendable to permit commercial, industrial, institutional or further residential development, and shall be recorded in the Dutchess County Clerk's office simultaneously with the filing of an approved cluster subdivision plat.

4. The open space shall be shown on the plat map and shall be labeled in a manner to indicate that such land is not to be further subdivided for building lots and is permanently reserved for open space purposes. Residential structures and buildings accessory to

non-commercial recreation, conservation, or agriculture may be erected on this land, subject to the cluster development plan.

LIMITATIONS AND CONCERNS

It is unclear under New York law if the terms of a conservation easement that impose affirmative obligations on landowners are enforceable. An affirmative obligation is one that requires the landowner to maintain the property in a specific manner, such as maintaining the condition or color of the exterior surfaces of existing buildings. Under the common law of conservation easements in New York, such provisions were not enforceable, and the statute seems to be ambiguous in this respect.

Although a conservation easement may, by its terms, establish that it is subject to modification by future agreement, the advisability of providing for such change is questionable. Where change is allowed, the conditions under which amendments may be made should be as objective and clear as possible. Changes may have tax consequences when real property tax exemptions or income tax deductions have been claimed.

Conservation easements may be extinguished by the foreclosure of liens on the property that preexisted the easement. In order to prevent such an occurrence, the municipality or land trust must secure a title report before acquiring an easement, discover all existing mortgages and liens, and negotiate subordination agreements from all lien holders.

Landowners who are considering granting conservation easements to public bodies or land trusts should investigate and comply with the provisions of those bodies of law that determine whether the easement qualifies them for favorable income, estate, or property tax treatment. The Internal Revenue Service will issue letter rulings regarding the deductibility of a conservation easement but will not determine the appropriate amount of that deduction in advance.

The appraisal that determines the value of the easement for tax deduction purposes must meet federal standards, which may be stricter than the state statutory standards that define conservation easements. For example, to qualify for deductibility under the federal tax code, an easement must be granted in perpetuity, not for a term of years. The grant of a conservation easement does not automatically qualify the property owner for a local real property tax assessment reduction; a petition for reassessment may have to be filed. In New York, the decision on reassessment rests with the local assessor.

It is a common misconception that conservation easements grant to the public the right to cross or use the restricted land. More often than not, they do not grant such a right. To conserve a natural feature or preserve a man-made feature, a use restriction is often sufficient. When a public access easement is required as a condition for local land use approval, the locality must show that there is a close nexus between a legitimate public objective and the end achieved by imposing the easement on the applicant's property. Further, the locality must show that the burden of the easement on the land is roughly proportionate to the impact of the proposed development on the community.

For example, if a pedestrian and bicycle easement (a public access easement) is imposed as a permit condition, the locality should have a study documenting that the impact of the project on increasing traffic is roughly proportional to the extent to which the easement will alleviate that traffic.

STATUTES

The New York Environmental Conservation Law, §§49-0301 et seq., defines and regulates the creation of conservation easements in New York State.

Although affirmative obligations in conservation easements were not enforceable at common law in New York, Environmental Conservation Law §49-0305(5)(e) states that "[i]t is not a defense in any action to enforce a conservation easement that . . . [the easement] imposes affirmative obligations upon the owner of any interest in the burdened property, or upon the holder."

CASE DIGEST

A conservation easement was found to not diminish the value of the property for property tax assessment purposes in *Adirondack Mountain Reserve v. Board of Assessors of the Town of North Hudson*, 99 A.D.2d 600, 471 N.Y.S.2d 703 (3d Dep't 1984), *aff'd,* 64 N.Y.2d 727, 475 N.E.2d 115, 485 N.Y.S.2d 744 (1984). The Adirondack Mountain Reserve (AMR) owned 16,000 acres of land in the towns of Keene and North Hudson. In 1978, AMR sold 9,000 acres to the state on the condition that the land remain in its natural condition and open for public use. The AMR was required in turn to grant a conservation easement to the state allowing its land to be used for trails, paths, and roadways. Following this sale, the town of Keene reassessed AMR's remaining land and increased its property tax. The AMR challenged the tax assessment. The court upheld the assessment, holding that "the value of the dominant estate owned by the State … has been minimally benefited and the value of the servient estate retained by [AMR] has suffered little or no burden" affecting its current value.

In *Friends of the Shawangunks v. Knowlton*, 64 N.Y.2d 387, 476 N.E.2d 988, 487 N.Y.S.2d 543 (1985), Mountain Houses sold a conservation easement to the Palisades Interstate Park Commission. The easement permitted Mountain Houses to use the 240-acre parcel for one single-family residence, a potable water storage pond, an existing golf course, and various accessory uses. Any other development was prohibited. The issue was whether the 240 acres burdened by the conservation easement could be included in determining the number of residential units permitted under the town's cluster zoning resolution. Under state statutes, local boards may not allow a landowner to cluster any greater density of development than is allowed under applicable requirements of law. The court found that the land burdened by the easement could be included, holding that "a conservation easement is not an 'applicable requirement' and nothing in the Town Law or the Environmental Conservation Law forecloses the owner of the land thus burdened from using it as open area required under the cluster zoning ordinance." The court distinguished limitations on land uses that are created under zoning laws from conservation easements, noting that zoning is a "legislative enactment" while the easement is a private agreement between parties.

In *Grogan v. Zoning Board of Appeals of the Town of East Hampton*, 221 A.D.2d 441, 633 N.Y.S.2d 809 (2d Dep't 1995), plaintiffs challenged a scenic and conservation easement imposed as a condition to the zoning board of appeals' grant of a variance allowing them to build an addition to their home. The plaintiffs challenged the easement condition as arbitrary and capricious. The easement prevented development on a portion of land designated as a wetland, but did not permit public access. The court concluded that the town adequately sustained its burden of proof by "demonstrating a rough proportionality between the easement and the projected environmental impacts of the [plaintiffs'] construction proposal." In the environmental assessment form submitted with the application, the town had concrete evidence to persuade the court that the determination was reasonable. The court stated that "the easement is an appropriate measure to address the specific environmental impacts of the [plaintiffs'] proposal, "that the decision was a "valid [and] individualized" determination, and that the easement "substantially advance[d]" the governmental interest of preserving wetlands and "environmentally significant areas" and was not arbitrary and capricious.

REFERENCES

Joseph Stinson and Liane Wilson, *Preserving Open Space with Land Trusts and Conservation Easements, at* http://www.pace.edu/lawschool/landuse/lndtrs.html (last visited Feb. 2, 2001).

John C. Partigan, *New York's Conservation Easement Statute: The Property Interest and Its Real Property and Federal Income Tax Consequences*, 49 Alb. L. Rev. 430 (1985).

D. WATERSHED PROTECTION/NEW YORK CITY WATERSHED PROTECTION

DEFINITION

Watershed management is much like the traditional planning and regulating that is done within a municipality except that, instead of being confined to a locality's borders, the plans and regulations are applicable to an area defined by an aquatic resource. It is a broad concept that incorporates all currently available programs, resources, and regulatory tools to protect aquatic ecosystems and human health.

A watershed management program involves several phases. These include:

- identifying a stream, river, lake, or other water body in need of protection;
- drawing the boundaries of the land that drains into that water body;
- knowing the agency or agencies that will assume responsibility for the quality of water in that land area;
- understanding the causes of the deterioration of the quality of that water; and

A typical watershed management plan will include a physical description of the watershed area and a clear description of the land uses that threaten its future quality. It will also prioritize the features and areas of the watershed that must be preserved and improved to insure its vitality as a habitat, source of drinking water, or recreational resource.

PURPOSE

Watersheds are not usually confined to one set of political boundaries. Thus, watershed areas are often governed by the uncoordinated regulations of authorized local, county, state, and federal agencies. Often these various regulations, taken together, do not constitute an effective program for protecting and preserving aquatic resources. The purpose of an effective watershed management program is to coordinate these existing provisions into a cohesive program for appropriate land use within the designated area. This will insure more comprehensive and effective protection of watershed resources.

WHEN

Most local governments, whether rural, developed, or developing, should consider identifying their principal watersheds. They should also be interested in assessing watershed quality and in examining the existing and future land uses and changes that might negatively affect the water bodies. Watershed management is initiated both to reclaim lost natural functions and attributes essential to the health of the community and to prevent their future deterioration. It is particularly needed when habitat is limited, biodiversity is threatened, recreational uses are impacted, drinking water quality is eroded, and the scenic quality of the community is implicated.

AUTHORITY

The following is a summary of the existing intergovernmental statutory framework within which local governments act to regulate resources or land uses on a watershed basis.

FEDERAL LAWS:

The Watershed Protection and Flood Prevention Act authorizes the Secretary of Agriculture, in cooperation with federal, state, and local agencies, to survey watersheds and other waterways to develop coordinated management programs.

The Coastal Zone Management Act provides for state environmental planning, protection, and restoration programs in coastal areas. It provides federal grants to states to develop and implement management programs to address the effects of land uses on the resources of the coastal zone. In New York, incentives are given to local governments to adopt and enforce local waterfront revitalization plans independently or with one or more adjacent communities in the coastal zone.

The Endangered Species Act allows for the creation of critical habitats for each endangered species. The destruction or substantial modification of critical habitats is prohibited if it will result in a reduction in numbers or distribution of a species.

NEW YORK STATE:

Under a variety of statutes, state agencies are authorized to take actions that can have a positive impact on maintaining the quality of the state's critical watershed areas:

Interstate Pollution Control Compacts: New York State participates in four interstate water pollution control compacts that require planning on a watershed basis: the Delaware River Basin Compact, the Great Lakes Basin Compact, the Champlain Basin Compact, and the Susquehanna River Basin Compact. These compacts offer an example of express authority to manage water resources on an interstate watershed basis. They apply, however, to only a few of New York's many watersheds.

Local and Regional Water Resources Planning and Development: Under Title 11 of the Water Resources Law, the Department of Environmental Conservation (DEC) is authorized to undertake comprehensive planning for the protection, control, conservation, development, and beneficial utilization of the water resources of the state. Any county, city, town, or village may submit a proposal for survey and study of regional water resources by the DEC and receive comprehensive planning assistance.

Freshwater Wetlands Act: Article 24 of the Environmental Conservation Law grants authority to the state to regulate wetlands 12.4 acres or larger and their 100-foot buffers, or wetlands that are deemed to be of unusual local importance. Local governments may regulate these and smaller sized wetlands by adopting freshwater wetland laws that are as strict as or stricter than the state's regulations. These authorities allow state and local agencies to issue, deny, or condition permits for land use activities proposed in the regulated wetland areas.

Waterfront Revitalization and Coastal Resources Act: Article 42 of the Executive Law authorizes the Department of State to assist local governments in developing comprehensive plans for their coastal areas. One or more local governments can develop Local Waterfront Revitalization Plans, implement those plans using their local land use authority, and require state and federal actions to consider and to conform to those plans.

Wild, Scenic, and Recreational River Designation: Title 27 of the Water Resources Law provides for the management, protection, and enhancement of certain wild, scenic, and recreational rivers. Under the statute, rivers can be designated wild, scenic, or recreational and then managed according to established management standards. There are specified management directives for each type of designation. Local governments and citizen groups are permitted to conduct studies and write proposals concerning the designation of rivers as wild, scenic, and recreational.

Coastal Erosion Hazard Ordinances: Article 34 of the Environmental Conservation Law encourages localities to use all applicable authority to minimize erosion hazards caused by development in the coastlines of the state. The statute allows municipalities to enact local erosion hazard area laws in conformance with the DEC regulations.

Intermunicipal Agreements: Ample authority exists for the regulation of watersheds through the use of intermunicipal agreements. The state legislature has provided express authority for municipalities to enter into cooperative agreements in order to prepare a comprehensive plan and enact and administer land use regulations. This could be done on a watershed basis.

WATERSHED PLANNING AT THE COUNTY LEVEL:

County Small Watershed Protection Districts: Article 5-D of the County Law was enacted to encourage cooperation between federal agencies and counties of the state to prevent flood damage and to protect the state's land and water resources. The board of legislators of a county is authorized to delegate to its soil and water conservation district board the authority to submit watershed work plans to the commissioner of the DEC for approval. The work plans have the purpose of undertaking, constructing, and maintaining projects for flood prevention, land treatment, and the conservation of water. The commissioner may approve the plan after a public hearing. The soil and water conservation district board is then required to petition the board of legislators, known in some counties as the board of supervisors, to delineate areas of the county as watershed districts.

County Lake Protection and Rehabilitation Districts: Article 5-A of the County Law provides that a county board of legislators may establish county districts for lake protection and rehabilitation. Upon petition by the affected municipalities, or at least 25 owners of real property in the district, the board may direct that maps and plans be prepared for the establishment of certain areas as county lake protection and rehabilitation districts.

Soil and Water Conservation Districts: The counties can create soil and water conservation districts to implement the Soil and Water Conservation Districts Law. Conservation district boards are established under this law to prevent soil erosion, flooding, and sediment damage, to control and abate nonpoint sources of water pollution, and to provide for agriculture water management.

WATERSHED PLANNING AT THE MUNICIPAL LEVEL:

Most local land use controls are not designed to protect watersheds, although they can be. The basic land use control is the zoning map. It divides the municipality into use districts and typically allows every conforming parcel to be developed for that use. In most communities, zoning district lines are not drawn with watershed boundaries in mind. Areas that contain unusual environmental features such as wetlands, floodplains, or woodlands can be zoned for large-lot residential development. This lessens developmental density, traffic, impervious coverage, and population impacts but still allows the critical areas of watersheds to be developed. In addition, the location of buildings and improvements may be affected by subdivision standards or wetlands regulations. The standards in these regulations can protect natural features on individual parcels. Such protections are limited, however, by the boundaries of zoning districts, which typically are not drawn around watershed boundaries.

A few municipalities have enacted natural resource ordinances to further protect environmental features. These may take the form of sedimentation and erosion controls, floodplain regulations, or coastal zone protection provisions. Municipalities may also amend their comprehensive plans to designate watershed areas in need of protection and formally establish those areas as conservation overlay districts. Within those districts, detailed standards for the protection of the watershed can be adopted to control development, and other techniques, such as conservation easements, can be used to achieve the district's conservation.

IMPLEMENTATION

The U.S. Environmental Protection Agency (EPA) suggests that there are three phases to enacting a watershed protection approach to land conservation: assessment; planning; and implementation and evaluation.

Assessment: EPA recommends that the community identify the primary threats to human and ecosystem health within the watershed and then involve the leaders of involved or affected constituent groups in the watershed planning and management process.

Watershed Planning: It then recommends the development of a comprehensive management plan that confronts the key issues and results in a vision for the entire watershed. Planning on a watershed basis is similar to land use planning for a municipality, except that the plan focuses principally on watershed issues and develops strategies to protect the entire watershed. This may require intermunicipal cooperation where two or more communities share the watershed.

Implementation and Evaluation of the Watershed Plan: Once the plan is developed, it can be implemented by measures such as the redesign of zoning districts or the creation of an overlay district that is coterminous with the watershed. Then the involved municipalities may adopt regulatory standards to protect the watershed and enforce them in all their local project review, conditioning, and approval processes.

LIMITATIONS AND CONCERNS

Water quality can be negatively affected by contamination from solid and hazardous waste deposits and by a wide variety of point and nonpoint sources of pollution. Any of these sources can contribute pathogens, nutrients, metals, toxic substances, and synthetic organic compounds to a receiving water body. To be effective, watershed planning must identify and effectively deal with all these sources of pollution. This can be an extensive and time-consuming undertaking.

Politics also affect watersheds. The primary political issue is that few watershed boundaries correspond to political boundaries. If there is some overlap of these boundaries, local groups are unlikely to use their own resources to protect part of the watershed that neighboring communities are not willing to protect. Additionally, control over watersheds is divided among federal, state, and local governments, whose actions may not be coordinated with one another. Efforts must be made to coordinate watershed planning intermunicipally and intergovernmentally so that individual municipal efforts can succeed.

Tax, economic, and property rights issues compel watershed planners to consider where development can be accommodated in and around watersheds. The needs of communities for efficient tax bases, of people for jobs and housing, and of property owners for economical use of their land must be respected and accommodated in community planning and land use regulation of all kinds. Often, the political will that is needed to support watershed preservation cannot exist unless a viable plan for land development in appropriate locations is also advanced.

STATUTES

In New York State, Village Law §7-700, Town Law §261, and General City Law §20(24) grant basic land use authority to local governments and allow them to regulate the details of land development and building construction and alteration. Village Law §7-702, Town Law §262, and General City Law §20(25) authorize local governments to divide the community into zoning districts.

Village Law §7-725-a, Town Law §274-a, and General City Law §27-a authorize local governments to adopt and administer site plan regulations.

Village Law §§7-728–7-730, Town Law §§276–278 and General City Law §§32–34 authorize municipalities to adopt subdivision regulations and to provide for the review and approval of subdivisions.

The state provisions that give authority to local governments to enter into intermunicipal agreements are General Municipal Law §§119-o, 199-u, General City Law §20-g, Town Law §284, and Village Law §7-741. These sections also provide for intergovernmental planning and land use regulation.

The Watershed Protection and Flood Prevention Act is found at 16 U.S.C. §§1001-1011.

The Coastal Zone Management Act is found at 16 U.S.C. §§1451-1464, ELR STAT. CZMA §§302-319.

The conservation of endangered and threatened species and their habitats is governed by the Endangered Species Act, 16 U.S.C. §§1531-1544, ELR STAT. ESA §§2-18.

New York State has several interstate water pollution control compacts. The Delaware River Basin Compact is found at Environmental Conservation Law §21-0701. The Great Lakes Basin Compact is found at §§21-0901 et seq. Sections 21-1101 et seq. govern the Champlain Basin Compact. The Susquehanna River Basis Compact is governed by §§21-1301 et seq.

A local government has authority to regulate freshwater wetlands under the Freshwater

Wetlands Act. Environmental Conservation Law §§24-0101 et seq. and the Municipal Home Rule Act §10.

Local waterfront revitalization planning is supported and encouraged by Executive Law §910.

Rivers and water bodies can be designated wild, scenic, and recreational under the Environmental Law §§15-2701 et seq. Section 15-2715 states that "[t]his section is not intended to preclude or discourage studies and proposals by other agencies or by citizen groups." County Law §§299-l to 299-y.

Threatened coastal areas are identified and protected under Article 34 of the Environmental Conservation Law at §§34-0101 et seq.

The County Small Watershed Protection District Law was enacted to encourage state cooperation with county governments to prevent flood damage. County Law §§299-l to 299-y.

County Lake Protection and Rehabilitation Districts can be created for lake conservation under County Law §§250 et seq.

County legislators are authorized to create soil and water conservation districts by the Soil and Water Conservation Districts Law §2.

ILLUSTRATION-REGULATIONS TO PROTECT THE NEW YORK CITY WATERSHED

One example of blanket regulations used to protect a watershed is the New York City Department of Environmental Protection (DEP) Watershed Regulations, which were enacted in 1997. The term "New York City Watershed" is a misnomer, because what is involved is actually a collection of watersheds from which the City draws its drinking water. The boundaries of the watershed encompass areas east of the Hudson River in Westchester, Putnam, and Dutchess Counties and west of the Hudson in Delaware, Schoharie, Green, Sullivan, and Ulster Counties. The regulations were promulgated by New York City to avoid filtration of the city's water supply and to prevent its contamination, degradation, and pollution.

These regulations were designed differently from the process discussed above. They were developed at the initiative of one municipality, New York City, which worked in conjunction with the affected communities. What developed was a memorandum of agreement (MOA) under which participating municipalities agreed to act in good faith to effect and comply with the watershed regulations. In return, the city agreed to make funds available to assist local governments in complying with many of the provisions of the regulations.

While protecting the drinking water for the city, the regulations impose significant limitations on local land use control because they prohibit and restrict activities necessary for development within the watershed. Three provisions in particular limit a municipality's ability to choose where and how to develop in its jurisdiction.

Regulation of Wastewater Treatment Plants: The regulation of wastewater treatment plants (WWTP) prevents large-scale developments in certain portions of the watershed. A WWTP is defined as any facility that treats sewage and discharges treated effluent in the watershed and that requires a permit under Titles 7 or 8 of Article 17 of the Environmental Conservation Law. The design of all new WWTPs requires the approval of the DEP. No part of any absorption field for subsurface discharge from a plant shall be within a buffer zone of 100 feet of a watercourse or wetland or within 500 feet of a reservoir, reservoir stem, or controlled lake. In addition, WWTPs with surface discharge are prohibited anywhere in three types of areas in the watershed: 60-day travel time zones, coliform basins, and phosphorous restricted basins. A 60-day travel time zone is an area from which it takes 60 days or less for the water to travel to intake points in the New York City water supply which are located prior to the point of disinfection where the water is no longer subject to surface runoff. Coliform restricted basins are drainage basins of a reservoir or controlled lake in which the established coliform standards are currently exceeded. Phosphorus restricted basins are drainage basins in which the phosphorus load to a reservoir or controlled lake exceeds established phosphorus restrictions.

These prohibitions severely limit large development projects from being built within these restricted areas. Typically, larger developments must be serviced by surface discharge WWTPs because of the physical limitations of subsurface discharge plants. There are, however, limited opportunities for construction of new surface plants within restricted basins. One example of this is the provision regarding the creation of a "Croton Plan" in the watershed counties east of the Hudson. This plan can allow for the placement of new surface WWTPs in phosphorus and 60-day travel time basins if specific criteria are met.

Regulation of Subsurface Sewage Treatment Systems: Restrictions on subsurface sewage treatment systems (SSTS) further limit land development in watershed areas. A SSTS is defined as any underground system used for collecting, treating, and disposing of sewage into the ground. The design and construction of a new or altered SSTS requires the approval of the DEP. In addition, no part of any absorption field shall be located within the buffer zone of 100 feet of a watercourse or wetland or 300 feet of a reservoir, reservoir stem, or controlled lake. Since these buffer zones may be located in locally designated development districts, these provisions can limit currently planned land development in watershed areas.

Impervious Surface Regulations: Finally, the regulations contain restrictions on the construction of impervious surfaces that will restrict development within the watershed. Impervious surfaces are defined as those that are resistant to penetration by moisture and include, for example, paving, concrete, asphalt, and roofs–in other words, most development. The construction of these surfaces is not allowed within a buffer zone of 100 feet from a watercourse or wetland or within 300 feet of a reservoir, reservoir stem, or controlled lake.

While there are exceptions for certain areas within a watershed and for individual residences, permits for such construction may not be awarded unless a stormwater pollution prevention plan is submitted and approved by the DEP in order to protect against polluted run-off. These plans may require review and approval by a stormwater project review committee and the

DEP. Stormwater pollution prevention plans are also required for projects such as the construction of a residential subdivision, for projects that will create an impervious surface totaling over 40,000 square feet, and for new roads within limiting distances from watercourses.

These regulations can be problematic for municipalities, many of which have zoning ordinances that permit commercial and industrial projects in established travel corridors, which often run along watercourses. Therefore, cities, towns, and villages within the watershed must rethink their development plans and take into account the DEP's new authority to review and approve plans for development.

REFERENCES

Matt Bavoso, *Watershed Management in New York State Under Current Law: An Approach and Authority,* at http://www.pace.edu/lawschool/landuse/bavoa.html (last visited Feb. 2, 2001).

Heather Andrade, *The Effect of the New York City Department of Environmental Protection Watershed Regulations on Land Use,* at http://www.pace.edu/lawschool/landuse/watshe.html (last visited Feb. 2, 2001).

E. PROTECTING AESTHETIC AND SCENIC RESOURCES

DEFINITION

Local legislatures often adopt regulations to minimize the negative aesthetic impacts of new development and to protect and enhance the positive aesthetic features of the community. In fact, basic zoning provisions such as setback, minimum lot area, and height requirements serve aesthetic purposes, among others. They set a context for future development by defining the neighborhood environment and establishing scenic quality. The same can be said of the separation of land uses into zoning districts, which creates a physical environment that enhances property values and the quality of life. These zoning provisions protect and enhance community appearance as well as advance a variety of public health and safety objectives.

Communities protect local aesthetic and scenic resources in a variety of other ways. They regulate the size and placement of signs, limit the location—or require the removal—of billboards, and establish architectural review boards to enforce design standards in new construction. In addition, they adopt tree preservation ordinances and other natural resource protection laws, protect historic districts

Aesthetic Regulations
States are divided on whether aesthetics may serve as a basis of land use regulations.
1. Aesthetics may be the sole objective of a regulation.
2. Aesthetics may be one, but not the only, objective of a regulation.
3. Aesthetics may not be an objective of land use regulation.
(New York fits into category 1)

rezoning approvals and variances to protect the aesthetic quality of the affected neighborhood or of an identified viewshed or view corridor.

PURPOSE

Local aesthetic regulations can serve two important purposes: to prevent bad design and to preserve existing visual assets. The negative impact that some developments, such as junkyards or billboards, can have on the community is mitigated or eliminated by aesthetic regulation. In addition, positive visual assets, such as historic buildings and landmarks or a nearby landscape, can be preserved through such regulations.

All land use regulations must protect the public health, safety, welfare, or morals. Aesthetic regulations are justified principally as a method of protecting the public welfare. Stabilizing and enhancing the aesthetic values of the community increases civic pride, protects property values, and promotes economic development. Vibrant communities generally contain natural and man-made features that provide visual quality and distinction, and these features, in turn, enhance the reputation of the community as a desirable place to work, visit, and live. Regulations that protect important visual features from erosion and that prevent visual blight further the public welfare and constitute a valid exercise of the police power.

WHEN

Visual blight can occur in a community in a variety of ways. It can occur when billboards and signs with no design integrity or consistency proliferate in a downtown area or along a commercial road. Similarly, the development of strip malls and retail stores in a commercial center or corridor can create visual confusion that repels shoppers, tourists, and additional investment. In some communities, unattractive land uses such as junkyards, repair shops, solid waste disposal sites, and mining operations can create an environment that prevents the development of the commercial or mixed-use neighborhoods envisioned by the zoning ordinance.

There are a variety of visual resources that a community may want to protect from the potential negative effects of new development. These may include a historic district, a distinctive landmark building, a corridor of distinctive architecture, views of outlying hills, mountains, or rivers, a dramatic visual entry into the community, or a cultural or historic landscape. When this type of visual asset enhances a locality's reputation and character, regulations that preserve it for the benefit of the community may be needed.

Where there are remaining undeveloped areas within a community, the local legislature may want to use its zoning law and other police power laws to create neighborhoods of distinctive architecture and attractive scenic qualities. In these situations, local lawmakers can protect and enhance the visual quality of the community by using their power to:

+ Adopt comprehensive plans and zoning laws.
+ Enact tree preservation ordinances.
+ Condition variances and development approvals.

♦ Review the environmental impacts of all official local actions.
♦ Establish design standards and create architectural review boards.
♦ Eliminate public nuisances.

AUTHORITY

Authority for local governments to protect local aesthetic and scenic assets comes from many sources. These include the power to adopt zoning provisions to accomplish the most appropriate use of the land and to adopt a comprehensive plan to provide for the preservation of historic and cultural resources. Under their home rule authority, localities may provide for the "protection and enhancement of its physical and visual environment." Special state laws provide localities with authority to preserve trees, landmarks, and historic districts. State laws delegating authority to local governments to adopt regulations and procedures for approving site plans, subdivisions, variances, and special use permits recognize that such regulations may be drafted to protect the visual environment. As lead agencies under the State Environmental Quality Review Act, local reviewing bodies must take all practical steps to avoid significant adverse environmental impacts on environmental resources of "historic or aesthetic significance."

IMPLEMENTATION

Comprehensive Planning: If a community wishes to adopt local laws that regulate aesthetics, it can create a basis for those regulations in its comprehensive plan. In adopting or amending the comprehensive plan, there can be findings that identify the aesthetic problems that the community wishes to eliminate or prevent and the aesthetic resources that it wishes to preserve. Since all land use regulations are to conform to the comprehensive plan, such provisions will help to sustain aesthetic regulations that are challenged by affected property owners.

Zoning: Zoning laws can establish neighborhood character and aesthetic quality through the judicious use of zoning districts within which certain uses are prohibited and certain height, lot area, and setback provisions are required for new developments. These laws, in addition, can contain specific "nuisance prevention" provisions, such as specifications for signs in commercial areas, as well as requirements that eliminate nonconforming uses, such as billboards or junkyards, over a reasonable time.

Identification and Study of Unique Aesthetic Resources: Where aesthetic assets of the community need to be protected, they should be identified and their importance to the community should be documented by studies and community surveys. This can be reflected in the comprehensive plan, the zoning law or other local enactment such as the adoption of an overlay zone, a separate law establishing design standards and creating an architectural review board, or by the adoption of a historic district or landmark law.

Overlay Zones: Unique aesthetic resource areas or sites can be identified and protected through the use of overlay zoning. Overlay zones, in general, do not disturb the underlying zoning requirements; they specify other considerations and requirements to protect and enhance identified areas in need of additional protection. In this way, the adoption of an overlay zone for aesthetic purposes provides an opportunity for the community to recognize and protect an existing viewshed or view corridor or a series of local landmarks or landscapes in need of preservation.

Sign Control Ordinances: Provisions can be added to the zoning law or can be separately enacted to control the location, size, and aesthetics of signs and billboards. In addition to advancing aesthetic purposes, such provisions can protect public safety, stabilize property values, and foster sound economic development. The First Amendment to the U.S. Constitution protects the content of signs, which may not be regulated except to achieve a compelling state interest. But this constraint does not affect the authority of local governments to regulate the time, place, and manner by which signs and billboards communicate their messages. Some municipalities in New York have adopted extensive provisions that regulate the type of construction, size, location, color, illumination, design, texture, and other aspects of signs and that apply different standards in selected zoning districts.

Design Review Laws: Localities can adopt design review laws for the purpose of controlling community appearance. Under such a law, an architectural review board can be created with advisory authority only or with the authority to review, approve, disapprove, or conditionally approve proposed new construction and building improvements before the building inspector is authorized to issue a building permit. The authority of the architectural review board can be limited to a certain type of construction, to particular zoning districts, or to areas of special scenic, architectural, and aesthetic importance, as defined by the law.

The chief concern of the board is whether the exterior design and treatment of the proposed construction conforms with the design review standards contained in the regulation. Generally, two standards of review are included in such laws:

- First, whether the proposed construction is "excessively dissimilar" to an established pattern of design.
- Second, whether the proposed project is "excessively similar" to existing buildings where the objective is to prevent the monotonous visual impact of new development in the area.

Some design laws authorize review boards to eliminate "visual offensiveness" or to conform design in discrete areas to the character of specific landmarks or architecture of distinction.

Tree Preservation Laws: Another means of controlling scenic quality and community appearance is the adoption of a tree preservation law. Such a law allows a community to restrict the removal of trees on private property in order to preserve their environmental and aesthetic importance to designated districts or to the community as a whole. The purpose clause of one extensive local law explains that the provisions were adopted to reduce tree destruction, which gives rise to barren and unsightly conditions, impairs the stability of real property values, and adversely affects the character of the community. Tree ordinances typically limit their applicability to trees of a certain diameter and height. They establish a permit system, which allows tree removal, but only upon a showing of necessity and upon compliance with certain conditions, such as replacement of all or some of the trees to be removed.

Local Development Approvals: Local action on applications for site plan, subdivision, special permit, or rezoning approval and variances can be conditioned to respect aesthetic matters. This can be accomplished in a variety of ways. Site plan and subdivision regulations adopted by the local legislature can require that aesthetic impacts be revealed in maps, plats, and drawings submitted for review. These regulations can authorize the reviewing body to condition any approval on design and layout changes that are reasonably related to the prevention of aesthetic damage or to the preservation of nearby aesthetic resources. In the same way, the award of special use permits and variances can be granted upon conditions that prevent aesthetic damage or preserve aesthetic assets. When a project may have a substantial adverse impact on aesthetic or historic resources, the local approval agency may condition its approval by requiring the applicant to take steps that mitigate those impacts under the agency's environmental review authority.

LIMITATIONS AND CONCERNS

Where design and aesthetic standards impose serious burdens on property owners, challengers may claim that the regulations are arbitrary and capricious, and violate constitutional requirements of due process. To withstand such challenges, it is important that communities justify their regulations through advance planning and empirical studies. Studies that define the aesthetic setting, identify the scenic resource, and document its importance to the community help prove that the public welfare will be protected by regulations adopted to protect and preserve aesthetic values.

When regulations to protect aesthetic values achieve additional community objectives, those objectives should be stated to provide a firmer base for the regulations' validity. These might include stabilizing property values, in the case of a design review law; public safety, in the case of sign control laws; and advancing economic development and tourism, in the case of the adoption of an aesthetic overlay district or of viewshed or view corridor regulations.

The means chosen to protect aesthetic values should impose on property use the least burden necessary to achieve the community objectives.

The aesthetic or design standards established by the local legislative body should be as specific as possible to withstand challenges claiming that the administrative agencies charged with implementing them have too much discretion or that they have been delegated authority that is overbroad.

The legislature, additionally, might require the administrative agency to find "clear and convincing evidence" that a proposal fails to meet established standards before denying or conditioning any land use approval on aesthetic grounds.

CONSTITUTIONAL PROVISIONS, STATUTES, AND RULINGS

The New York State Constitution, in Article XIV, §4, declares that "the policy of the State shall be to conserve its natural resources and scenic beauty."

Zoning for Aesthetic Purposes: Village Law §7-700, Town Law §261, and General City Law §20(24) authorize local governments to adopt zoning laws to promote the health, safety, morals, and the general welfare of the community. The authority to regulate building height, bulk, and lot coverage and to separate uses into districts is expressly delegated to local governments. Under Village Law §7-704, Town Law §263, and General City Law §20(24), zoning regulations are to be adopted with reasonable consideration of the character of the zoning district and with a view to conserving the value of buildings and encouraging the most appropriate use of land. Courts have approved zoning provisions based on their understanding of the relationship between such provisions and the public interest in the present character, appearance, and environment of the community.

Comprehensive Planning and Aesthetics: Zoning and land use regulations in New York must conform to the locality's comprehensive plan pursuant to Village Law §7-704, Town Law §263, and General City Law §20(25). Local comprehensive plans can identify and provide for the preservation of historic and cultural resources, natural resources, and sensitive environmental areas. Village Law §7-722(3)(d), Town Law §272-a(3)(d), and General City Law §28-a(4)(d).

Home Rule Authority: A separate source of authority to regulate aesthetics is found in §10(1)(ii)(a)(11) of the Municipal Home Rule Law, which states that a municipality may adopt land use laws for the "protection and enhancement of its physical and visual environment."

Design Standards: The General Municipal Law §96-a authorizes local governments to regulate districts, sites, and buildings having any "aesthetic interest or value" which "may include appropriate and reasonable control of the use or appearance of neighboring property within public view or both." Village Law §7-702 and Town Law §262 grant villages and towns the power to "regulate and restrict the erection, construction, reconstruction, alteration, or use of buildings, structures or land." It is under these statutes that local governments have adopted design review ordinances and created architectural review boards to review compliance of new development.

Tree Preservation: General Municipal Law §96-b authorizes local governments to adopt tree preservation laws based on aesthetic as well as other grounds.

Historic District and Landmark Preservation: General Municipal Law §119-aa-dd authorizes local governments to establish a landmark or historic preservation board or commission with powers "to carry out all or any of the authority possessed by the municipality for a historic preservation program."

Aesthetic Conditions on Site Plan Approvals: Village Law §7-725-a(2)(a), Town Law §274-a(2)(a), and General City Law §27-a(2)(a) allow localities to include in their site plan regulations requirements that all site plans show "screening, signs, landscaping, architectural features, location and dimension of buildings, adjacent land uses, and physical features meant to protect adjacent land uses as well as any additional elements specified by the [local legislative body]."

Aesthetic Conditions on Subdivision Approvals: Village Law §§7-728 and 7-730, Town Law §§276-278, and General City Law §§32-34 and 37 allow local governments to provide for the future development of the municipality by authorizing their planning boards to review and approve subdivision plats that show the lot layout, dimensions, and topography of the subdivision. They also allow localities to permit or require the development to be clustered on a portion of the land in order "to preserve the natural and scenic qualities of open lands."

Aesthetic Considerations in Granting Variances: Village Law §7-712-b, Town Law §267-b, and General City Law §81-b allow local zoning boards of appeals to grant use variances where the applicant can prove that the variance "will not alter the essential character of the neighborhood," and area variances with due consideration given to whether the variance will cause an undesirable change in the character of the neighborhood or a detriment to nearby properties.

Aesthetic Considerations in Issuing Special Use Permits: Village Law §7-725-b, Town Law §274-b, and General City Law §27-b allow local governments to issue special use permits subject to requirements that assure the proposed use "will not adversely affect the neighborhood."

Aesthetics and Environmental Review: Under the regulations of the Commissioner of the State Department of Environmental Conservation (DEC), 6 NYCRR Part 617, all local agency approvals of projects that may have a significant adverse impact on the environment must be subjected to a detailed environmental review following the completion of an environmental impact statement. All such reviews must state whether the action or approval will have a negative impact on resources of "historic or aesthetic significance." Conditions may be imposed on the project's approval to mitigate any negative impact.

CASE DIGEST

In *Berman v. Parker*, 348 U.S. 26 (1954), the U.S. Supreme Court established that the police power, on which local land use regulation rests, is to protect the public welfare, which is broad and inclusive. "The values it represents," Justice Douglas wrote, "are spiritual as well as physical, aesthetic as well as monetary. It is within the power of the legislature to determine that the community should be beautiful as well as healthy, spacious as well as clean, well-balanced as well as carefully patrolled."

In *People v. Stover*, 12 N.Y.2d 462, 191 N.E.2d 272, 240 N.Y.S.2d 734 (1963), the New York Court of Appeals upheld a local law that prohibited clotheslines in yards abutting certain streets unless a special use permit is obtained. The court held that "it is settled that conduct which is . . . offensive to the senses of hearing and smell may be a valid subject of regulation under the police power . . . and we perceive no basis for a different result merely because the sense of sight is involved."

The Court of Appeals, in *Old Farm Road, Inc. v. Town of New Castle*, 26 N.Y.2d 462, 259 N.E.2d 920, 311 N.Y.S.2d 500 (1970), sustained the creation of a local architectural review board and its authority to issue or deny permits based on design considerations to those who seek to erect signs and buildings in the community.

A village sign control law prohibiting commercial signs exceeding four square feet was sustained by the Court of Appeals in *People v. Goodman*, 31 N.Y.2d 262, 290 N.E.2d 139, 338 N.Y.S.2d 97 (1972).

In *Suffolk Outdoor Advertising Co., Inc. v. Hulse*, 43 N.Y.2d 483, 373 N.E.2d 263, 402 N.Y.S.2d 368 (1977), the Court of Appeals upheld a local law prohibiting the erection of non-accessory billboards and providing for the removal of all nonconforming billboards in the community. The case echoes the fundamental principle that "aesthetics constitutes a valid basis for the exercise of the police power."

A municipal tree preservation law was found to be a proper exercise of town's authority to protect the community's health and general welfare. *SeaBoard Contracting & Material, Inc. v. Smithtown*, 147 A.D.2d 4, 541 N.Y.S.2d 216 (2d Dep't 1989).

The Court of Appeals has confirmed that scenic concerns may be considered by local agencies in conducting environmental reviews of project proposals under the State Environmental Quality Review Act (SEQRA). In *WEOK Broadcasting Corp. v. Planning Board of the Town of Lloyd*, 79 N.Y.2d 373, 592 N.E.2d 778, 583 N.Y.S.2d 170 (1992), the court held that "aesthetic considerations are a proper area of concern in SEQRA balancing analysis." It noted, however, that aesthetic impact considerations, unsupported by substantial evidence, might not serve as a basis for denying an application regarding a proposed project. The planning board's aesthetic reasons for denial were inadequate because they were not based on substantial evidence; the court found the planning board's determination that the project "might" have a negative visual impact "hopelessly conclusory."

The Third Department sustained a planning board's denial of an application to build a large Wal-Mart store located in a designated scenic preservation overlay district. *Wal-Mart Stores, Inc. v. Planning Board of the Town of North Elba*, 238 A.D.2d 93, 668 N.Y.S.2d 774 (3d Dep't 1998). The town's land use code required applicants for such permits to show that the proposed project "will not result in a clearly adverse aesthetic impact." The proposed project was to be constructed within the viewshed of a critical portion of the "western gateway" to the community. After reviewing computer simulations of the proposed development, including efforts to screen the store and parking from the road, the planning board found that the project would cause a noticeable change in the visual character of the viewshed and denied the application. The Appellate Division's review of the record did not persuade it that there was no rational basis to support the planning board's denial of the project.

REFERENCES

Patrick Morrell, *Municipal Regulation of Aesthetics, at* http://www.pace.edu/lawschool/landuse/areg.html (last visited Feb. 2, 2001).

Sign Control, New York State Department of State, Division of Local Government Services; James A. Coon Local Government Technical Series.

F. REGULATING SIGNS AND OUTDOOR ADVERTISING

DEFINITION

Local governments regulate signs and outdoor advertising to enhance the appearance of the community and to promote traffic safety. Sign control regulations restrict the size of signs and their placement on lots and buildings. They also regulate the illumination, color, movement, or construction material of signs, among other matters. These regulations are often contained in the zoning chapter or law of the community. They may be contained as a separate chapter of the code or adopted as a freestanding regulation in a community that has not codified its laws and regulations. Property owners are required under most sign control laws to obtain a permit before erecting any sign. They must demonstrate that the proposed sign conforms to the provisions of the law before a permit may be issued.

PURPOSE

The New York Court of Appeals has held that the authority to regulate signs is based on the legitimate interest of local governments in protecting aesthetic values and community appearance. *Suffolk Outdoor Advertising Co., Inc. v. Hulse*, 43 N.Y.2d 483, 373 N.E.2d 263, 402 N.Y.S.2d 368 (1977). Valid sign and outdoor advertising regulations have as their central purpose the creation and maintenance of an attractive, high-quality visual environment in a neighborhood selected for sign regulation. They may also serve to prevent traffic hazards and accidents. The sign control law of the city of Ogdensburg states:

> The purpose of the sign regulations is to promote and protect the public health, welfare, and safety by regulating advertising visible from public roads and other outdoor graphics for commercial gain. These regulations are intended to protect property values, maintain an attractive business climate and protect the physical appearance of the community. The regulations are further intended to reduce distractions and obstructions that may contribute to traffic accidents or safety hazards.

Ogdensburg Code §221-42.

The sign control section of the Code of the town of Southeast states: "The appearance, character and quality of a community are affected by the location, size, construction, and graphic design of its signs. Therefore, such signs should convey their messages clearly and simply to enhance their surroundings."

317

WHEN

Sign control provisions often are contained in the original zoning law adopted by the community. They may be added as a zoning amendment when the visual disturbance of signs and outdoor advertising causes community and local legislative concern. When roadside vistas, critical gateways to the community, residential neighborhoods, or main street commercial districts are disturbed by the visual clutter of unregulated signs, local legislatures can enact sign control provisions to preserve the aesthetics of the community.

AUTHORITY

The law is well settled in New York that a municipality may impose sign restrictions in order to regulate aesthetics. The Court of Appeals has stated that the "State and its political subdivisions may regulate the erection and maintenance of outdoor advertising under the police power . . ." *People v. Goodman*, 31 N.Y.2d 262, 290 N.E.2d 139, 338 N.Y.S.2d 97 (1972). It stated further that "aesthetics is a valid subject of legislative concern and that reasonable legislation designed to promote the governmental interest in preserving the appearance of the community represents a valid and permissible exercise of the police power . . . Under the police power, billboards and signs may be regulated for aesthetic purposes." Typically, communities adopt sign control laws under the authority delegated to them by the state legislature to enact zoning regulations. Alternatively, sign control laws may be enacted under municipal home rule authority to protect the physical or visual environment.

IMPLEMENTATION

In New York State, most sign control provisions are found in the municipal zoning law, but they can be adopted separately as a free-standing land use regulation or separate chapter in a municipal code. Regulations may limit signs in a variety of ways, such as restricting their size, placement on lots and buildings, illumination, color, movement, construction material, or information about off-premise commercial matters.

After a sign control law has been adopted, property owners wishing to erect a sign on their premises normally are required to apply to the building inspector or zoning enforcement officer for a sign permit. The owners of properties on which signs existed prior to the adoption of the law also may be required to obtain permits within a prescribed period. Drawings of proposed signs may be required as part of the owner's application, including the visual message, text, copy, or content of the sign. The application may require the owner to state the proposed location, method of erection, height, projection and other details of placement, and the specifics of any proposed illumination or movement. If the application conforms to the requirements of the sign control law, a permit is issued and the sign may be erected in compliance with the permit. After a permit is secured and a sign is erected, a permit is generally unnecessary to change its message or to repaint or repair the sign.

Sign control laws may require the removal of certain preexisting signs that do not conform to their provisions. Billboards are sometimes subject to such removal requirements. Generally, owners of such signs are allowed to maintain them for a fixed period to insure that their investment is recouped, at least to a reasonable degree. Laws usually provide for such owners to get an extension of time for removal if they can prove financial hardship caused by the provisions. These amortization provisions insulate the law from claims that it constitutes a regulatory taking of property without just compensation.

ILLUSTRATIONS

The sign control provisions in the village of Chester are found in the zoning chapter of the village code in the article entitled "Specific Regulations." The provisions state that "all signs not specifically permitted are prohibited." For each zoning district, the provisions include numerous types of regulations. Certain types of signs are permitted, including signs advertising the sale, rental, or lease of the premises on which they are located. These signs are not to exceed six square feet in area. The regulations permit one nameplate or professional or announcement sign not exceeding two square feet in area. They allow identification signs not exceeding 16 square feet in area for a place of worship, hospital, nursing home, private school, or apartment building. Identification signs can only refer to operations on the premises upon which the sign is located. In business districts, more imposing signs may be erected, but these are limited to identity signs and wall signs. The provisions establish a maximum number of square feet of signage that may be placed on a single façade and on the building as a whole. Height projections, extensions from the building, and distance from the street are regulated. Similar regulations apply to industrial districts, but in these areas billboards not visible from any village street are allowed. The law allows but limits in certain ways signs in all zoning districts that contain information regarding construction in progress, political campaigns, or traffic directions. The village's sign provisions state that "notwithstanding any other provisions of this section, any sign authorized herein is allowed to contain noncommercial copy in lieu of any other copy. Any provision authorizing commercial copy may be read so as to authorize noncommercial copy in lieu thereof." Village of Chester Code §19.

In the town of Greenburgh, the sign control law allows only those signs permitted and stipulates that signs are accessory uses, permitted only in conjunction with a primary permitted use under the zoning law, and "shall relate solely to the business or profession conducted on the premises and advertise only the name of the owner or lessee, the name of the establishment, the type of establishment and goods or services or the trade name of the establishment and the goods manufactured or sold or services rendered, except for traffic and public convenience signs." Town of Greenburgh Code §43A-3.

Certain signs are exempt from the town's sign control law in the town of Southeast. These include historical markers, tablets, and statues; memorial signs and plaques; names of buildings and dates of erection meeting certain specifications; emblems not exceeding 12 square feet installed by government agencies, religious, or non-profit organizations; flags and insignia of any government; on-premise directional signs of a certain size; and non-illuminated warning and no-trespassing signs of a certain size. Town of Southeast Code §138-75.

LIMITATIONS AND CONCERNS

Sign control laws have been subjected to a number of legal challenges. Courts, which normally defer to the judgment of local legislatures in adopting land use regulations, show less deference when the constitutionally created freedom of expression is regulated. In these cases, judges tend to place a burden on the government to demonstrate the clear public interest that justifies the regulation. Sign control regulations do not violate the constitutional protection of free speech when they are limited to time, place, and manner restrictions and are not aimed at the content of the signs. Courts are particularly sensitive about laws prohibiting signs with political or ideological content. For this reason, many laws specifically permit such signs and regulate only their size and location. To avoid free-speech challenges, some sign laws make it clear that noncommercial material may be contained in any sign permitted on a commercial establishment. Exceptions to the prohibition of signs should not be content-based, because they may violate free-expression guarantees.

Property owners may challenge restrictions on the types of signs that are permitted when the signs they wish to erect are prohibited but others are allowed. The owners may claim that such distinctions violate their equal protection rights. Why should an owner be prohibited from placing a portable sign on the property when attached signs are permitted? Is there a legitimate public interest basis for this different treatment of portable signs? Are they more offensive aesthetically or more dangerous as a group than signs that are affixed to buildings or attached permanently to the ground? Similarly, can real estate signs be prohibited in a residential zoning district while political signs are permitted? What is the justification for the difference in treatment other than the fact that commercial messages enjoy less constitutional protection than political messages? Is that justification sufficient?

Sign control provisions requiring changes in commercial trademarks placed on outdoor signs have been challenged as a violation of the federal Lanham Act, which preempts state and local laws requiring trademark alteration. Some sign control laws limit the number of colors that can be used in certain settings. These restrictions may require the alteration of a trademark appearing on an exterior sign. Although the federal appellate courts are split on the issue, a federal district court in New York determined that Congress did not intend to limit zoning regulations of signs, including trademarked colors, when it adopted the Lanham Act.

Provisions requiring the removal of billboards may be attacked as a violation of federal or state constitutional prohibitions on the taking of private property without just compensation. The issues in such a case are whether the amortization period provided for the owner to recoup its investment is fair and reasonable; how significant the public's interest is in removing the billboard; whether an extension is allowed where a hardship is demonstrated; and whether the owner applied for and was denied an extension.

CONSTITUTIONAL PROVISIONS AND STATUTES

The New York State Constitution, Article XIV, §4, declares that "the policy of the State shall be to conserve its natural resources and scenic beauty."

Village Law §7-700, Town Law §261, and General City Law §20(24) authorize local governments to adopt zoning laws to promote the health, safety, morals, or the general welfare of the community. The authority to regulate building height, bulk, and lot coverage, and to separate uses into districts is expressly delegated to local governments under Village Law §7-704, Town Law §263, and General City Law §20(24).

Village Law §7-704, Town Law §263, and General City Law §20(25) require that zoning and land use regulations must conform to the locality's comprehensive plan. Under Village Law §7-722(4)(d), Town Law §272-a(3)(d), and General City Law §28-a(4)(d), local comprehensive plans can identify and provide for the preservation of community aesthetics, historic and cultural resources, natural resources, and sensitive environmental areas.

Home Rule Authority: A separate source of authority to regulate signs and outdoor advertising is found in §10(1)(ii)(a)(11) of the Municipal Home Rule Law, which states that a municipality can adopt land use laws for the "protection and enhancement of its physical and visual environment."

CASE DIGEST

In *Mid-State Advertising Corp. v. Bond*, 274 N.Y.2d, 8 N.E.2d 286 (1937), the plaintiffs challenged a Troy law that prohibited the erection of billboards unless they were on the same property as the business they were advertising. The court found the law invalid, noting that it was "not an attempt by zoning to exclude billboards or other advertising signs from localities where such devices might mar the beauty of natural scenery or distract travelers on congested city streets." The court affirmed the Special Term's holding directing the city to issue the permit to the plaintiff for the erection of the billboard. In his dissent, Judge Finch noted that "[i]t is not unreasonable for a municipality or a state to desire to beautify its streets or highways."

A billboard at issue in *New York State Thruway Authority v. Ashley Motor Court, Inc.*, 10 N.Y.2d 151, 176 N.E.2d 566, 218 N.Y.S.2d 640 (1961), was within 500 feet of the Thruway in violation of the Authority's sign law. The defendant challenged the law as "a taking of property rights without compensation." The court held that the legislature was acting within its police power in creating the law and ordered the sign removed. It found that the legislation was enacted to render "the Thruway safe for the traveling public by providing for maximum visibility and by preventing unreasonable distractions."

The question of whether a village sign law violates the constitutional protection of free speech when used to prohibit the erection of a large political sign was addressed in *Gibbons v. O'Reilly*, 44 Misc. 2d 353, 253 N.Y.S.2d 731 (Sup. Ct. Westchester County 1964). A political campaign erected a 22-foot-wide sign in a residential district, violating a village law that prohibited signs of this size and character. The court upheld the regulation, stating that "[i]f the guarantee of the First Amendment can be used to justify the erection of signs and billboards of unlimited size in an area restricted to one-family homes, then it would seem that zoning is a mere delusion." The court based its decision on *People v. Stover*, 12 N.Y.2d 462, 191 N.E.2d 272, 240 N.Y.S.2d 734, (1963), in which the Court of Appeals concluded that "it is perfectly clear that, since [First Amendment] rights are neither absolute nor unlimited, they are subject to such reasonable regulation as is provided by the ordinance before us."

The court in *Cromwell v. Ferrier*, 19 N.Y.2d 263, 225 N.E.2d 749, 279 N.Y.S.2d 22 (1967), overruled in part the restrictive holding of Mid-State Advertising. This court found the laws in these cases to be indistinguishable. It wrote that since the decision in Mid-State, "outdoor advertising had become a less and less important facet of the advertising business while, at the same time, its deleterious effects have substantially increased." The court found the law to be constitutional because the local legislature's police power extends to "those esthetic considerations which bear substantially on the economic, social, and cultural patterns of a community or district."

The defendant in *People v. Goodman*, 31 N.Y.2d 262, 290 N.E.2d 139, 338 N.Y.S.2d 97 (1972), had four signs on his drugstore, each exceeding four square feet in area. He was found guilty of violating the sign law of Ocean Beach, which prohibited signs that exceeded four square feet in size and allowed signs to be "placed only on the property on which the commercial or business use occurs." The court examined the law and concluded that it "represent[ed] a valid and permissible exercise of the police power," which includes the regulation of the erection of outdoor advertising.

The sign and zoning law of Brighton, which required billboards to be removed within 34 months of its enactment, was upheld. *Rochester Poster Advertising Co., Inc. v. Town of Brighton*, 49 A.D.2d 273, 374 N.Y.S.2d 510 (4th Dep't 1975). The 34-month amortization period, in the court's words, "represented a reasonable reconciliation of the public and private interests and an adequate time for amortization of plaintiff's investment."

The Irondequoit zoning board of appeals' decision to deny a variance to permit an existing trademark roof sign to remain on certain property was upheld in *Silverman v. Keating*, 52 A.D.2d 1076, 384 N.Y.S.2d 336 (4th Dep't 1976). The court, citing *Goodman*, noted that "[i]t is well settled that the state and its political subdivisions have power to regulate the erection and maintenance of outdoor advertising signs under the police power." The court found that the plaintiff failed to show that the board's denial was arbitrary or capricious.

In *Suffolk Outdoor Advertising Co. v. Hulse*, 43 N.Y.2d 483, 373 N.E.2d 263, 402 N.Y.S.2d 368 (1977), a law was challenged that prohibited all non-accessory signs after 1972 and provided a three-year amortization period for the removal of nonconforming signs already erected. The law's purpose was to protect the aesthetic values of the community. The court found that "aesthetics constitutes a valid basis for the exercise of the police power and that the Southampton law prohibiting nonaccessory billboards is substantially related to the effectuation of this objective."

The New York Court of Appeals, in *Modjeska Sign Studios, Inc. v. Berle*, 43 N.Y.2d 468, 373 N.E.2d 255, 402 N.Y.S.2d 359 (1977), upheld a six-and-a-half-year amortization period for the removal of nonconforming signs. It reversed the lower court's determination that the law constituted a taking, and held that the amortization period was reasonable and allowed the offenders ample time to correct or obtain some monetary benefit from the sign before it had to be removed.

The plaintiff in *Sarrds, Inc. v. City of White Plains*, 68 A.D.2d 905, 414 N.Y.S.2d 209 (2d Dep't 1979), challenged the city's sign law as invalid because it "served to confiscate its property without just compensation." The court compared this case to Modjeska, since the amortization periods in both cases could not be extended. It concluded that the plaintiff was "entitled to an immediate hearing as to whether the amortization period provided in the law herein is unreasonable as applied" and denied the defendant's motion to dismiss.

Storeowners challenged a town sign control law in *Payless Shoesource, Inc. v. Town of Penfield*, 934 F. Supp. 540 (W.D.N.Y. 1996). Their federally regulated trademark "Payless ShoeSource" was distinctively lettered and displayed in yellow, except for the two "o"s, which were orange. The town's sign law required signs to be displayed in other colors. The plaintiff ignored and then challenged that law. The plaintiff's claim was that the town violated §1121(b) of the Lanham Act, which provides: "No State ... or any political subdivision ... may require alteration of a registered mark." The question addressed by the court was whether an aesthetic regulation constitutes the type of alteration referred to in §1121(b). After reviewing the legislative history of the Act, the court found that the congressional committee hearings had examined this issue and concluded that the Act would not affect local zoning regulations but was drafted to preempt state legislative action requiring trademark alteration. The court held that if the plaintiff "chooses to display an outdoor sign, it must comply, like all other stores in the plazas, with the Town's sign restrictions—restrictions that allow plaintiff and the other tenants to display the distinctive lettering of their marks, but merely regulate their color ... Stated simply, plaintiff has confused its sign with its trademark." *See also Lisa's Party City, Inc. v. Town of Henrietta*, 2 F. Supp. 2d 378 (W.D.N.Y. 1998) (holding that the sign law "limits the permissible aesthetic characteristics of exterior signs in shopping centers but, in doing so, does not affect the marks themselves"). *But see Blockbuster Videos, Inc. v. City of Tempe*, 141 F.3d 1295 (9th Cir. 1998) (holding that validating zoning laws such as Tempe's would defeat the Lanham Act's purpose of protecting goodwill and enhancing consumers' ability to distinguish among competitors).

REFERENCE

Municipal Regulation of Signs, New York State Department of State, Division of Local Government Services; James A. Coon Local Government Technical Series.

G. AGRICULTURAL LAND PROTECTION

DEFINITION

The law of the State of New York provides dozens of mechanisms to protect agricultural land. These include authorizing and funding county agricultural and farmland protection boards and funding for the purchase of development rights on agricultural land. Within agricultural districts established by such boards, state law provides property tax relief, freedom from nuisance suits, and protection from public actions, including those of local governments that might threaten the viability of farming. In addition, state law offers an income tax credit to some farmers, provides some relief from wetlands regulation for farm operations, and helps farmers comply with other environmental regulations.

Although these provisions reflect the strong commitment of the state to protecting agricultural land, the land use decisions of local governments greatly influence whether farmland in any community will remain viable. State law provides a number of tools to local officials who wish to protect their working farms and viable agricultural soils. These include providing for agricultural land protection in comprehensive planning, the power to adopt zoning provisions that allow, encourage, and protect farming, and the authority to condition non-farm development projects so that they can co-exist with nearby farming. State law authorizes local governments to use transfer of development rights programs, incentive zoning, conservation easements, and land acquisition programs for the specific purpose of protecting existing farm areas and operations.

Other than requiring the consideration of the impact of certain local land use actions on agricultural lands and operations, however, New York State law does not mandate that local governments act effectively to protect agriculture. For this to happen there must be interest, willingness, and effective initiative on the part of locally elected and appointed land use officials.

PURPOSE

The New York State Constitution declares that "the policy of the State shall be to conserve its natural resources and scenic beauty and encourage the development and improvement of its agricultural lands for the production of food and other agricultural products." New York State Constitution, Article XIV, §4. This constitutional policy recognizes a number of important contributions of agriculture to the people of the state. They include the provision of an affordable supply of food, the contribution of agriculture to the state's economy (including the provision of jobs, demand for goods and services, and payment of local and state taxes), and the unique role that agricultural lands play in preserving a community's character, promoting tourism, and stabilizing property values.

Local actions taken to protect existing farms and agricultural lands attempt to retain these contributions to an individual community. There are many areas in the state where farmland pays more in local property taxes than it requires in municipal services. Agricultural lands in some communities are essential to the vitality of a flourishing or developing tourist industry.

Consciously or not, local citizens remain in or are attracted to some communities because of the character of the community provided by its agrarian land uses. In many cases, these land uses are a fundamental part of the history and culture of the community.

WHEN

Effective local action to protect farmland is needed in at least two instances:

First, farming in some communities struggles to compete and survive when property taxes are uncompetitively high or when the costs of doing business are increased by the demands of neighbors inconvenienced by farm operations. Since farmers in any given community compete with farmers in a much larger region, local competitive disadvantages can lead to the disappearance of economically and environmentally valuable farmland. Local action can lower or stabilize property taxes assessed against farmland and immunize farmers from the demands of their neighbors.

Second, farmland in developing communities can be lost to residential subdivision or other land uses that could be located in other parts of the community where they would be more cost-effective to service and more profitable to their developers. When market forces demand land for development, localities may want to channel that demand into zoning districts where development can be more cost-effective and where viable agricultural lands do not exist.

AUTHORITY

The citations below reference a variety of state statutes authorizing local governments to develop a farmland protection policy, to make farming more profitable, and to channel land development to nonagricultural districts in the community.

Local Farmland Policy: A proper context for municipal actions that protect farmland can be set by appointing an agricultural representative to the local planning board, considering existing agricultural uses in the comprehensive plan, and adopting a strategy to protect farmland in that plan.

Eliminating Competitive Disadvantages: To make farming competitive, municipalities are authorized by law to lower property tax assessments for farmlands in certain cases, to adopt "right to farm" laws that protect approved farming operations from neighbors' nuisance suits, and to protect farming from adjacent or nearby non-farm developments by, among other techniques, mitigating the negative impact of any project on agricultural land uses.

Channeling Land Development to Nonagricultural Districts: Localities are authorized to adopt zoning provisions that make all farm-related land uses permitted uses in zoning districts, to create agricultural zoning districts, to transfer development rights from agricultural lands to development districts, to offer incentives for developments to locate in non-farm areas, and to purchase the development rights of farmland. Municipalities are also authorized to enter into agreements with their neighboring communities to adopt consistent approaches to the protection of farmland resources that they share.

IMPLEMENTATION

Appointment to Planning Board: Local planning boards are often involved in the preparation or amendment of the comprehensive plan, in advising the local legislature on zoning matters, and in the review and approval of subdivision and site plan applications and the award of special use permits. Appointing authorities in towns and villages located in an agricultural district are authorized to appoint a farming representative as a member of their planning board to protect and promote agricultural interests.

Comprehensive Planning: The land use policy of the community is established by the comprehensive plan, and all municipal land use regulations must conform with that plan. State law makes it clear that the comprehensive plan may consider agricultural land uses as an important component of the community's policy. State law provides that a newly adopted or amended comprehensive plan "shall take into consideration applicable county agricultural and farmland protection plans" created by the county agricultural and farmland protection board. Comprehensive plans typically include fact-based findings supporting their policy commitment to matters such as the protection of farmland and outline a strategy and implementation plan to accomplish such objectives.

Zoning: The local zoning law can identify agricultural areas as primary zoning districts and provide for the continuation and expansion of agricultural land uses in those zones. Even where no agricultural district exists, zoning laws can designate agricultural land uses as permitted uses in certain districts and thereby encourage farming and its expansion.

Where the zoning law designates farmland for residential development without listing agricultural uses as permitted uses, a variety of problems beset farmers. Their farm buildings and operations are considered nonconforming uses, which are discouraged in a variety of ways in many zoning laws. To expand or change their operations farmers may be required to get variances or special use permits – a process that can be time consuming, unpredictable, and unsuccessful.

Other innovative zoning provisions can be added to the local law to encourage agricultural uses. These include transfer of development rights provisions or incentive zoning, supplemented by the use of conservation easements, which are explained in Chapters 5 and 7.

Acquisition of Development Rights: Localities can establish a trust fund for the purchase of the development rights of agricultural lands by offering incentives to developers to build in growth or development districts in exchange for cash contributions by the developers to the municipality. Municipalities and county governments can also use operating revenue, municipal bond proceeds, and state and federal program funds to purchase the development rights of agricultural lands. Suffolk County, on Long Island, and Pittsford, a Rochester suburb, have used municipal financial resources and leveraged additional dollars for this purpose.

Coordinating Project Approvals in Agricultural Areas: New York State law requires that local governments are prohibited from unreasonably regulating or restricting farm operations in an agricultural district unless [it] bears a direct relationship to the maintenance of public health or safety. All towns and village agencies must require the preparation of an agricultural data statement before issuing a special use permit, site plan approval, use variance, or subdivision approval. This requirement applies to the development of properties in an established agricultural district. Such a statement requires, among other things, the submission of a map showing the site of the proposed project relative to the location of farm operations. Owners of farmland in proximity to the project must be notified of the pending action, giving them an opportunity to become involved and to influence the agency's decision. Provisions similar to these could be adopted by a municipality that is not in an established agricultural district, using its delegated zoning authority or its home rule power.

Environmental Review: New York State law requiring environmental review of local actions that may have a significant adverse impact on the environment favors agricultural uses in two ways. First, a variety of farm management practices and farm construction activities are listed as Type II actions, which do not require environmental reviews. Second, one of the considerations in determining whether a proposed project must complete an environmental impact statement (EIS) is whether it involves a substantial change in the use of agricultural land. State environmental regulations list proposed nonagricultural land uses in an agricultural district as the type of action that is likely to require the preparation of an EIS and significantly lower the thresholds for such determinations.

Section 239-m Referrals: New York legislation requires that, except for the granting of an area variance, any municipal action that applies to real property located within 500 feet of the boundary of a farm located in an agricultural district must be referred to the county planning agency for its review. If the county planning agency recommends modification or denial of the proposed municipal action, such as a subdivision or site plan approval or rezoning, the local approving agency can act inconsistently with the recommendation only by a vote of a majority plus one of its members.

Intermunicipal Agreements: Increasingly, localities are using their extensive statutory authority to enact land use plans and regulations in conjunction with neighboring municipalities to protect resources, such as farming areas, that overlap municipal boundaries.

Other Actions: State law provides the owners of farmland with two additional sources of relief if they dedicate their land to farming for a minimum of eight years or if their land is located in an agricultural district. The first of these is relief from real property taxes: a qualified farm is required to be assessed as land used for agriculture even if it is zoned for non-farm development and has a significantly higher market value because of its non-farm development potential. The second is relief from nuisance suits brought by neighbors of such farmland to enjoin allegedly offensive farming activity if that activity is deemed to be a sound agricultural practice by the state commissioner of agriculture. Local assessors have some discretion as to how they reassess land under these provisions and can assist farmers by taking seriously the intent of the law to reduce property tax assessments in recognition of the land's true value as a farm.

CONSTITUTIONAL PROVISIONS, STATUTES, AND RULINGS

The New York State Constitution, Article XIV, §4, sets forth the state's policy favoring the preservation of agricultural land.

Village Law §7-718(11) and Town Law §271(11) provide for the appointment of a representative of agriculture to the local planning board.

Village Law §7-722(3)(d), Town Law §272-a(3)(d), and General City Law §28-a(4)(d) provide that the comprehensive plan may include "consideration of agricultural uses."

Village Law §7-739 and Town Law §283-a require that applications for subdivision and site plan approvals and for the issuance of special use permits and use variances regarding land in an agricultural district must include an agricultural assessment statement and must give notice of the matter to affected landowners.

Title 6 NYCRR, Part 617.7(c)(viii), regulating the environmental review of development proposals, includes as a criterion for requiring an environmental impact statement (EIS) consideration of whether a project involves a substantial change in the use of agricultural land.

Title 6 NYCRR, Part 617.4(b)(8) lists a proposed non-agricultural land use in an agricultural district as the type of action that is likely to require the preparation of an EIS if it exceeds 25% of the thresholds applicable to determining whether other actions require preparation of an EIS.

Section 239-m of the General Municipal Law requires that, except for the granting of an area variance, any municipal action that applies to real property within 500 feet of the boundary of a farm located in an agricultural district must be referred to the county or regional agency for its review.

The Agricultural and Markets Law §304-a through §308 provides reduced property tax assessments and relief from nuisance suits to the owners of farmland that is located in an agricultural district or that is dedicated to agriculture for a minimum of eight years.

"The activities of farmers in . . . engaging in the use of wetlands . . . for growing agricultural products shall be excluded from regulated activities and shall not require a permit." Freshwater Wetlands Act, New York Environmental Conservation Law, §24-0701(4).

REFERENCES

Michael N. Morea, *New York State Laws that Provide for the Protection of Agricultural Lands, at* http://www.pace.edu/lawschool/landuse/morea.html (last visited Feb. 2, 2001).

Sean F. Nolon and Cozata Solloway, *Preserving Our Heritage: Tools to Cultivate Agricultural Preservation in New York State, at* http://www.pace.edu/lawschool/landuse/aga.html (last visited Feb. 2, 2001).

H. AGRICULTURAL ZONING

DEFINITION

Agricultural zoning designates a portion of the municipality as an agricultural district subject to specific regulation under the locality's zoning law. In an agricultural district, agricultural uses are permitted as-of-right and non-farm land uses either are prohibited or are allowed subject to limitations or conditions. Permitted uses in an agricultural zone typically include all forms of agriculture, forestry, nurseries, and fisheries. Various accessory uses may also be permitted as-of-right, such as garages, machine sheds, barns and other farm buildings, beekeeping, and composting.

Other land uses can be allowed by special permit in an agricultural zone, subject to appropriate conditions. These can include tourism activities such as roadside stands, signs, and bed and breakfast inns; farm-related housing and businesses; accessory residential units for family members; day-care or family-care enterprises; or other small-scale, compatible commercial uses.

Agricultural zoning frequently allows permitted and accessory uses to be carried out on relatively large lots, ranging from 25 to over 100 acres. Limited subdivision of these lots may be allowed subject to setback, landscape buffers, design, and lot placement specifications, and other requirements designed to promote and protect continued agricultural uses in the district.

The primary objective of agricultural zoning is to minimize the subdivision of existing land parcels into smaller sized lots. This insures that the area retains its agricultural character and that parcels in the zoning district are large enough to be used reasonably for agricultural purposes.

The owners of non-farm lots in agricultural zoning districts may be allowed certain flexibility in the use of their land. A non-farm lot includes one not used for agricultural purposes on the date the zoning law is adopted or a lot that is smaller than the minimum lot size required for an agricultural use. Dwellings may be allowed on such non-farm lots subject to conditions, including being located on the least productive farmland or as far away from adjacent farming operations as possible.

PURPOSE

The purpose of agricultural zoning is to protect and promote the continuation of farming in areas with prime soils and where farming is a viable component of the local economy. The advantages of agricultural zoning are that it preserves large tracts of land for farming purposes; creates stability within the district, thereby promoting investment in farmland and farm facilities; prevents the pressures that threaten farming in developing regions; and limits local property tax assessments by establishing agriculture as the primary and permitted use of land in the zoning district.

Many municipalities accommodate current or anticipated land development pressures by zoning the entire community, including viable agricultural land, for commercial, industrial, or residential uses. Typically, such laws establish minimum residential lot sizes of two to five acres as the permitted use of agricultural land.

In these areas, farmers complain that they have to seek variances or special use permits to expand or construct new buildings or to engage in new farm-related activities and that such procedures are difficult, costly, and often unsuccessful. Further, local property tax assessments tend to escalate under such zoning, making it more difficult for farming to be profitable and providing a reason for farmers to sell agricultural land for non-agricultural uses.

In contrast to this approach, agricultural zoning establishes agricultural and accessory uses as permitted uses. Landowners are not required to apply for permits, variances, or permission to carry out farm-related land uses. Their land values and property and estate taxes are based on the allowed agricultural uses.

A number of studies in rural communities show that agricultural lands pay more in taxes than they require in services from their municipalities. When compared to the cost/benefit impact of residential development in these same communities, the fiscal impact of agriculture on municipal budgets often is particularly beneficial. Although these studies vary greatly and are extremely sensitive to a community's location and stage of development, they show that agricultural land use often costs the local government in services about 20%-50% of the tax revenue it contributes, compared to 110%-130% for residential development in these same communities.

Rural communities that are experiencing development pressures may also find that agricultural zoning complements their long-range plans. Zoning viable agricultural land throughout the community for large-lot residential uses is seldom cost-effective and often serves as a disincentive to continued agricultural activity and investment. Random suburbanization of developing communities creates great pressure for increased public services and infrastructure. Local citizens often want to encourage continued farming in viable agricultural districts because agricultural uses perpetuate the character of the community, retain desired open space, enhance tourism, maintain cost-effective land uses, and contain development pressures in serviceable districts.

Agricultural zoning is consistent with a fundamental change that is occurring in local zoning practice. Where once the entire community was divided into relatively uniform zoning districts, today's local land use laws tend to differentiate among parcels of land and parts of the community. They protect steep slopes, viewsheds, cultural and historical assets, drinking water, wetlands, flood-prone areas, aquifers, stream quality, and other natural features that are needed to protect the public health and to maintain and promote community values and character.

Similarly, communities are becoming aware of the costs of servicing various projects and are rethinking permitted densities and uses, particularly in outlying areas, to create more cost-effective land development patterns. They are allowing higher density development in hamlets and serviceable corridors and at busy crossroads. Agricultural zoning complements such actions. It not only maintains a valuable economic use of the land but can bring additional benefits to the community by allowing carefully sited housing, cottage industries, or small-scale businesses as uses subject to special permits. These conditional uses both enhance the cost-efficiency of the community in general and, potentially, increase the profitability of farmland ownership by offering farmers a variety of economic options while maintaining reasonable tax assessments and stabilizing agricultural investments.

WHEN

When communities are interested in accomplishing the purposes listed above, they should consider creating an agricultural zoning district. Such zoning can complement redevelopment and expansion plans in hamlet centers and along transportation corridors and can reinforce the community's economic plans to promote recreational land uses and tourism.

Large-lot zoning in New York has been upheld when it is enacted in accordance with the locality's comprehensive plan. When agricultural zoning is based on the locality's plan to maintain its agricultural economy and lands, to preserve open space, or to protect the community from the ill effects of urbanization, it will be presumed valid and be upheld unless a challenger can show that the zoning was arbitrary or unreasonable.

AUTHORITY

There is no separate authorization under the New York Town, Village, and General City laws for adopting an agricultural zone. The protection of land for agricultural purposes is a legitimate zoning objective under the state zoning enabling acts. Towns, villages, and cities may include an agricultural district in their zoning laws just as they include industrial, commercial, and residential zones. One of the few land use objectives found in New York's constitution is to "encourage the development and improvement of its agricultural lands for the production of food and other agricultural products." New York State Constitution, Article XIV, §4.

IMPLEMENTATION

Agricultural zoning is adopted and implemented just as other zoning provisions are: by the local legislature, after public notice and hearing and the advice of the local planning board. Because of the many interests affected by agricultural zoning, communities may want to hold a variety of meetings with landowners and citizens to explore the many kinds of agricultural zoning that have been adopted in other communities. Based on these meetings, a system can be designed that is best suited to the particular needs of farmers, farm businesses, and local taxpayers and citizens.

ILLUSTRATION

In 1975, the comprehensive plan for Lancaster County, Pennsylvania, identified 278,000 acres of productive farmland that merited protection. In 1978, the county promulgated a model law for the consideration of the county's 41 localities. The plan identified agriculture as "the single most important component of the local economy." By 1988, 33 local legislatures had adopted agricultural zoning provisions, encompassing 242,000 acres. By 1994, all but two localities had adopted agricultural zoning, covering 320,000 acres. The model law of Lancaster County allows relatively little subdivision of land for residential purposes and provides for only a few tightly controlled conditional uses.

LIMITATIONS AND CONCERNS

The adoption of an agricultural zoning district can be controversial. Farmers, particularly, want to know what the full economic effects of the zoning will be. Will their property taxes be maintained at a reasonable level, consistent with the land's agricultural use? Are they offered all reasonable economic uses of their land consistent with the maintenance of the district as an agricultural area? Is the zoning sufficiently flexible to allow them to respond to changes in agricultural markets? Are their family and personal land use needs taken into account?

Other municipal residents have equally serious concerns. Why shouldn't the agricultural area gradually become residential? Wouldn't residential development of farmland bring in more tax revenue? Is it true that in this community the residential development of farmland can cost more in municipal services than it will generate in increased tax revenue? Will agricultural zoning truly protect the community's historic character and add to its future quality of life?

For these questions to be answered and for residents to conclude that agricultural zoning is in everyone's best interest, the local legislature should hold numerous meetings with farmers and citizens and provide them with sufficient data on these issues.

There is clear tension between allowing flexibility for landowners in an agricultural district to use their land for some non-farm uses and simply prohibiting most non-farm uses. Special permits for non-farm land uses may be granted in a large number of cases sufficient to gradually erode the primary agricultural nature of the area and thus fail to achieve the underlying purpose of agricultural zoning. This argues for restricting the conditional and accessory uses allowed in an agricultural district and for requiring review of flexibility provisions every few years.

Finally, to be effective, agricultural zoning may need to be implemented on an intermunicipal basis to protect a farming area large enough to achieve overall agricultural viability. Municipalities have ample authority under existing state law to enter into agreements to adopt and enforce compatible agricultural zoning provisions.

CONSTITUTIONAL PROVISIONS AND STATUTES

The New York State Constitution, Article XIV, §4, provides that "[t]he policy of the State shall be to conserve and protect its natural resources and scenic beauty and encourage the development and improvement of its agricultural lands for the production of food and other agricultural products."

Under Village Law §7-704, Town Law §263, and General City Law §20(24), zoning regulations are to be adopted with reasonable consideration of the character of the zoning district and with a view to encouraging the most appropriate use of land.

Zoning and land use regulations in New York must be in conformance with the locality's comprehensive plan pursuant to Village Law §7-704, Town Law §263, and General City Law §20(25). Local comprehensive plans can identify and provide for the preservation of agricultural lands. Village Law §7-722, Town Law §272-a, and General City Law §28-a.

REFERENCES

Sean F. Nolon and Cozata Solloway, *Preserving Our Heritage: Tools to Cultivate Agricultural Preservation in New York State, at* http://www.pace.edu/lawschool/landuse/aga (last visited Feb. 2, 2001).

Protection of Rural Character and Natural Resources, Albany Law School Government Law Center (Dec. 1990).

Agricultural and Farmland Protection for New York, American Farmland Trust, Saratoga Springs, N.Y. (Aug. 1993).

Cost of Community Services Study; Towns of Beekman and Northeast, Cornell Cooperative Extension of Dutchess County (June 1989).

Promoting Partnerships for Agricultural Industry Growth and Farmland Protection in New York State, New York State Legislative Commission on Rural Resources, American Farmland Trust, New York Farm Bureau, New York Department of Agriculture and Markets, Scenic Hudson (Sept. 1998).

I. RECREATIONAL ZONING

DEFINITION

The creation of a recreational zoning district is a novel concept. It involves the establishment of a zoning district where the permitted uses are limited exclusively to private clubs, golf courses, fitness centers, riding stables, tennis and swimming clubs, and other similar uses. Creating a zoning district in which permitted uses are limited to private recreational uses is analogous to creating a neighborhood commercial district in which only neighborhood retail and service uses are permitted. Both serve the need for commercial services that develop as a community's population grows.

Local governments can provide for the recreational needs of their citizens in other ways that are not discussed in detail in this section. Local governments can acquire land directly for public parks and recreational facilities or use their regulatory power to provide for or to limit recreational uses in a variety of ways. The zoning law, for example, may allow certain commercial recreational uses, such as a skating rink or miniature golf course, either as a matter of right in another zoning district or by special permit in designated areas. Local zoning laws also may allow or restrict the recreational use of property as an accessory use to another principal permitted use, such as a swimming pool or tennis court in a single-family residential district. Zoning boards of appeals may be asked to grant a use variance to allow a recreational use where one is not otherwise permitted under the local law.

PURPOSE

A recreational zoning district, where uses are limited exclusively to private recreational activities, can be created to serve a number of public purposes. It can respond to a public demand for private recreational services and facilities. It can also achieve a variety of environmental objectives, such as preserving open space and protecting floodplains. For instance, the town of Mamaroneck enacted a recreational zone to prevent siltation, pollution, and flooding, to preserve the suburban quality of the community as a whole, and to meet the private recreational needs of its residents. All of these reasons were articulated by the local legislature in establishing an exclusively recreational zoning district that included the lands owned by three existing private golf clubs operating on over 400 acres in the town. This recreational district was adopted to implement the town's Local Waterfront Revitalization Plan, which it took over a decade to develop.

WHEN

Several conditions existed in the town of Mamaroneck that led to the creation of its private recreational district. First, the comprehensive plan called for the preservation of the open-space character of the community and the prevention of development activity that would increase flooding, erosion, and pollution. The lands regulated contained certain environmental features such as wetlands, scenic vistas, and rock outcroppings that merited preservation under existing local policies. The residential development of these properties would have affected the limited remaining open character of the community in a variety of ways. Second, there existed in the community a robust and unmet demand for private recreational activities. Mamaroneck was developed heavily as an affluent residential community, whose citizens needed and could afford a variety of private recreational services and facilities that were lacking in the area. Finally, the 400 acres that were included in the recreational zoning district were currently and historically used for private recreational use and operated at a profit.

AUTHORITY

There is no specific delegation of power from the New York State legislature to municipalities that allows them to create recreational districts. This authority is implied in the delegation of the power to enact zoning restrictions and create zoning districts. The Town, Village, and General City statutes stipulate that zoning regulations shall consider the character of the district and its peculiar suitability for particular uses, and shall be made with a view to encouraging the most appropriate use of the land throughout the municipality. Preserving the suburban or open character of the community, scenic vistas, and natural resource features such as wetlands, and preventing flooding and water pollution are legitimate police power objectives that municipalities are allowed to pursue through zoning. The courts have typically deferred to the means chosen by local governments to accomplish the objectives of their comprehensive plans. This deference has been exhibited toward a variety of innovative zoning mechanisms, including floating zones and overlay zones as well as recreational zoning, particularly where they can be shown to conform with the adopted comprehensive plan of the community.

IMPLEMENTATION

In New York State, the adoption of a recreational zone, in which principal permitted uses are limited to private recreational uses, requires an amendment to the zoning law and map by the local legislature, after public hearing, notice, and environmental review. Local laws and regulations may require additional procedures to be followed when zoning amendments are adopted. Typical provisions require referral to the local planning board for an advisory report and the mailing or service of notice of the public hearing on nearby owners. The law must designate the specific properties that the district will encompass and must provide for the amendment of the zoning map. The legislature must indicate how the new recreational zoning district conforms to language contained in the comprehensive plan or, in the alternative, how the creation of the district advances comprehensive planning in the community.

LIMITATIONS AND CONCERNS

There are a number of possible challenges that a municipality may face when it creates a recreational zoning district. These challenges suggest that there are meaningful limitations to the use of recreational zoning, and several concerns that must be addressed if it is to be adopted.

First, the authority of the local government to create such a district may be challenged. To withstand an allegation that it has exceeded its authority in enacting the law, a local government must show that the district achieves objectives of the adopted comprehensive plan or must articulate the specific comprehensive planning rationale that supports the creation of the district. This will also avoid challenges that the zoning unduly singles out one or a few property owners to bear the burden of the regulation. For instance, because its objectives were closely tied to its comprehensive plan the town of Mamaroneck avoided a claim that it did not possess the legal authority to create a recreational zoning district. The town showed that its recreational zone served to preserve open space and to prevent siltation and flooding–important objectives of its recently adopted Local Waterfront Revitalization Plan.

Second, a municipality should protect itself against an equal protection challenge. It may be vulnerable to such claims if there are similarly situated properties that are not zoned recreationally. Faced with such a claim, the courts look to the propriety of the treatment of the plaintiff's property compared to neighboring properties. Differences must exist that explain why certain properties are zoned recreational and other, similar properties are not. For example, if exempted properties do not contain significant environmental features, have not been used for private recreational uses, or are simply not needed to meet the demand for recreational facilities in the community, the locality may survive an equal protection challenge.

Third, a municipality must also insure that its actions are reasonable and cannot be found arbitrary and capricious. Such a charge can be avoided by carefully describing the public objectives that are achieved by recreational zoning and insuring that the law is designed to accomplish those objectives. For example, an arbitrary and unreasonable exercise of a city's police power to adopt zoning regulations was determined to have occurred when a zoning law restricted to public recreational use property that had been used as private recreational lands by tenants of the property owner. The effect of the regulation was to allow public use of land that had been maintained as private recreational space for residents of the plaintiff's privately owned apartment buildings. The fact that the city's zoning allowed the owner to transfer its development rights to other properties and that the zoning conformed to the comprehensive plan did not save it from being invalidated by the court as being arbitrary and unreasonable under the circumstances. A showing that there was not a demand in the market for private recreational uses or that there are no community benefits to be derived from the recreational zoning would also render it unconstitutionally arbitrary and unreasonable.

Finally, a property owner may challenge a recreational zoning district as a regulatory taking. In *Bonnie Briar Syndicate v. Town of Mamaroneck*, 216 N.Y.L.J. 34 (1996), *aff'd*, 242 A.D.2d 356, 661 N.Y.S.2d 1005 (2d Dep't 1997), the court held that a recreational zoning district, limiting the private owner's uses to private recreational facilities and services, was not a regulatory taking. The plaintiff could not show, through competent dollars-and-cents proof, that the regulation destroyed all but a bare residue of economic value. In fact, the property had been used profitably as a golf club and, there was evidence of demand for recreational uses in the market areas.

STATUTE

The New York statutory authority to divide the municipality into districts and the purposes that are to be achieved by zoning regulations are found at §§261-263 of the Town Law, §§7-700 through 7-704 of the Village Law, and §§20(24) and (25) of the General City Law.

CASE DIGEST

In *Fred F. French Investing Co. v. City of New York*, 39 N.Y.2d 587, 350 N.E.2d 381, 385 N.Y.S.2d 5 (1976), the court found that a zoning law that restricted formerly private parklands to public recreational uses was an arbitrary and unreasonable exercise of the city's police power to adopt zoning regulations. The fact that the city's zoning conformed to the comprehensive plan did not save it from being unreasonable under the circumstances. The effect of the regulation would have been to allow public use of land that had been maintained as private recreational space for residents of the plaintiff's privately owned apartment buildings.

In 1990, the New York Appellate Division, Fourth Department, upheld the zoning law of the Village of Valley Stream, which restricted the use of property to uses in effect at the time of the adoption of the law and to park and recreational uses. *Shukovsky v. Clavin*, 163 A.D.2d 919, 558 N.Y.S.2d 431 (4th Dep't 1990). The plaintiff alleged that the law was confiscatory because it, together with a deed restriction on the property, precluded his use of the property. Since the plaintiff did not plead or prove that the property could not yield a reasonable return, the court held that the law was valid.

In *Clearwater Holding, Inc. v. Town of Hempstead*, 237 A.D.2d 400, 655 N.Y.S.2d 768 (2d Dep't 1997), the Second Department held that the creation of a marine recreation district did not amount to a taking of property. The court held that since the property owner did not carry the heavy burden of proving that the property was not capable of producing a reasonable return, no taking had been established.

Five months later, the Second Department had another occasion to review the constitutionality of a recreational zone, in *Bonnie Briar Syndicate v. Town of Mamaroneck*, 216 N.Y.L.J. 34 (1996), *aff'd*, 242 A.D.2d 356, 661 N.Y.S.2d 1005 (2d Dep't 1997). The recreational zoning district at issue limited the private owner's uses to private recreational facilities and services. The court sustained the local zoning law since the plaintiff did not show that the property could not yield a reasonable economic return under the regulation. The court held that it would not second-guess the discretionary judgments of the local legislature by finding that less restrictive means were available to accomplish the objectives sought. It also held that this land was not unduly singled out to bear a burden that should be borne by the public as a whole. The court found that the law was not being used to carry out a government enterprise which should be achieved through eminent domain, that the regulated properties were adaptable to private recreational use, and that the regulation accomplished the purposes of the community's comprehensive plan.

REFERENCES

John R. Nolon, *Recreational Zoning, Concept Used in Inappropriate Context Raises Troubling Issues*, N.Y. L.J., Dec. 17, 1997.

Patrick J. Rohan, Zoning and Land Use Controls, Chp.10 (Matthew Bender 1997).

J. FRESHWATER WETLANDS REGULATION

DEFINITION

Nearly all types of construction and development activities that are regulated by local land use laws may also be regulated under applicable federal, state, or municipal wetlands laws. There are a number of land use activities that may not proceed unless the landowner receives a wetlands permit if the activity affects a regulated wetland or buffer area. These include the construction of a home or residential subdivision, the development of a commercial store or strip mall, the extension of a driveway or road, the addition of a room, garage or tennis court, or the placing of any impervious surface on the land. In addition to this permit, the landowner must also receive approval under any applicable local regulations, such as those governing land subdivision, site plan development, and the award of special permits or variances.

Other activities not typically regulated by local land use laws may be governed by wetlands laws. These include agricultural activities such as animal grazing, harvesting wetlands vegetation, draining or filling of any wetland, fence construction, fertilizer and chemical applications, and other personal or business activity on the land that could pollute a wetland or diminish its viability.

Wetlands laws typically contain a list of activities that are exempt from wetlands regulation. Examples of exempt activities include certain agricultural operations such as irrigation ditch construction and non-intensive recreational uses. Particularly harmful activities, such as the deposit of hazardous chemicals, may be prohibited altogether. Generally, landowners who propose to conduct regulated activities must apply to the designated administrative agency for a permit. Where certain standards and conditions can be met, a permit may be granted allowing the regulated activity to proceed. Conditions may be placed on the permit to avoid, minimize, or mitigate the loss or degradation of wetlands.

PURPOSE

The New York Freshwater Wetlands Act lists the critical public benefits that wetlands provide. These include flood and storm water control, aquifer protection, groundwater recharge, maintaining stream flow, pollution elimination, erosion control, and the provision of recreational opportunity, open space, and habitat for wildlife, including threatened, rare, and endangered species. The purpose of adopting a wetlands law is to preserve these benefits for the public.

WHEN

The federal and state legislatures passed wetlands laws when they concluded that wetlands provide important benefits to the public and were rapidly disappearing or deteriorating because of land use activities on or near them. Land development activities cause the loss of wetlands at a current national rate of around 100,000 acres annually. The federal and state governments adopted wetlands protections beginning in the 1970s to fight the even more rapid disappearance of wetlands that was occurring then.

It is when local governments perceive that the extent of protection afforded by the federal and state regimes is not sufficient that they adopt their own regulations, either to bring more wetland areas under control or to achieve more local control of wetlands protection.

AUTHORITY

Three levels of government have legal authority to regulate wetlands on privately owned property:

Federal Role: The federal Clean Water Act gives the U.S. Army Corps of Engineers and the U.S. Environmental Protection Agency (EPA) the authority to promulgate rules regulating wetlands throughout the nation. The federal definition of wetlands is a broad one, based on the presence of water saturation, wetlands vegetation, and certain types of soils. If a wetland's health may affect the viability of navigable waters or harbor migratory birds, it may be subject to federal regulation. Federal law regulates the wetlands themselves, not buffer areas around the wetlands unless a proposed activity in an adjacent area directly affects dedicated wetlands.

State Role: The Freshwater Wetlands Act, adopted by the New York State Legislature, gives the Department of Environmental Conservation (DEC) authority to regulate wetlands that are 12.4 acres or larger and to regulate smaller wetlands that are of unusual local significance. Smaller wetlands qualify for regulation by the DEC if they provide habitat for endangered or threatened species, protect developed areas from flooding, or are connected to a public water supply. The Freshwater Wetlands Act and the DEC commissioner's regulations define wetlands mainly by the presence of types of vegetation that are typically found on wetlands and adjacent areas within 100 feet of the wetlands' boundary.

Local Role: Local governments have authority to regulate wetlands in a variety of ways. Under the Freshwater Wetlands Act, they can adopt wetlands regulations at least as restrictive as the state's, demonstrate their competence to administer their regulations, and then replace the DEC as the regulator of wetlands within their jurisdiction. When this happens, only the local government regulates wetlands within its borders. Very few localities in New York have elected this option. Most local wetlands laws are adopted pursuant to the Municipal Home Rule Law, which authorizes local governments to adopt laws to protect the "physical environment." Under these local laws, broader definitions of wetlands may be adopted, larger buffer areas regulated, and a more extensive range of activities covered. When localities use their home rule authority to regulate local wetlands, they typically regulate smaller sized wetlands than the DEC. If they wish, they also may regulate wetlands 12.4 acres in size or larger but only if their regulations are at least as protective of wetlands as the state program. When localities choose to regulate wetlands under their home rule authority, their regulations are concurrent with those of the DEC, and landowners must comply with both sets of standards separately.

Local planning and zoning boards may also regulate activities that affect wetlands as they review and approve development applications. This happens, for example, when the local legislature adopts standards to protect wetlands in subdivision, site plan, and special permit regulations. Localities may also add such standards to their procedures for issuing variances and for conducting environmental reviews of all development applications. If such standards are added, then local administrative bodies may take the impact of proposed projects on wetlands into consideration and impose conditions, or deny applications, to protect the wetlands' functions as a routine part of their development review and approval process. Some localities also protect wetlands by adopting floodplain, erosion and sedimentation, and clearing and grading regulations or by designating specific sensitive areas for extra protection.

IMPLEMENTATION

In adopting or amending a local wetlands law there are several decisions that a municipality must make:

Definition of Wetlands: The first is how to define what constitutes a wetland. Municipalities tend to adopt federal or state definitions and reference federal or state manuals that define either soil conditions or vegetative cover characteristic of functioning wetlands. The choices made here can significantly increase or decrease the acres of land that are subject to regulation.

Size of Wetlands: Local wetlands laws regulate wetlands ranging in size from 5,000 square feet to in excess of 10 acres. Some local laws specify no minimum size, subjecting all wetlands to regulation.

Regulation of Adjacent Areas: Local wetlands permits can be required for regulated activities taking place not only on identified wetlands but also in buffer areas around these wetlands. The prevalent measurement of these buffer areas is 100 feet measured horizontally from the wetlands' boundary. A larger or smaller buffer area can be established.

Regulated Activities: The range of activities regulated by a local wetlands law is determined in several ways. Some activities are simply prohibited in wetlands and their buffers, such as the deposit of hazardous chemicals. Other activities are listed as regulated activities, such as the construction or enlargement of any structure or road. In order to conduct such activities on a wetland or buffer, a local permit must be secured. Additional activities may be permitted as-of-right, such as the repair of walkways or walls or landscaping and planting in buffers.

Mapping of Local Wetlands: Some municipalities prepare a map of the wetlands and buffer areas subject to their regulation to guide property owners. Others perform site visits when applications for other permits are made to determine if wetlands are involved in proposed construction activities. Site visits are also conducted when local officials receive reports that regulated activities are proceeding without a permit in wetland areas.

Approval Agency: Local wetlands laws vary greatly in delegating wetlands permit issuance authority to local administrative agencies. Some create a local wetlands control commission or water control commission to review and approve wetlands permits. Others delegate permitting authority to one or more existing administrative agencies, such as the planning or zoning board, and assign advisory functions to a wetlands commission, conservation advisory board, or environmental board. Occasionally, the local legislative body retains permit authority. Other localities use wetlands inspectors in an advisory role, during the review and approval process, or allow the inspector to make permit decisions in cases where minimal wetlands disturbance is anticipated. Some municipalities allow planning and zoning boards to review wetlands applications where the proposed project requires that board's approval under other land use controls, such as subdivision or site plan regulations.

Administrative Processes: Local wetlands laws may specify the information needed in an application, whether a public hearing and notice are required, or discretionary time limits for reviews and decisions and for referrals to other bodies for advisory opinions.

Avoidance, Minimization and Mitigation Plans: Where a regulated activity will cause unavoidable and necessary loss of wetlands or wetlands functions, local laws may require that applicants submit a plan demonstrating that wetlands loss has been avoided where possible, has been minimized by specific measures that will be followed, or will be compensated by the creation of equivalent wetlands in proximity to lost or diminished wetlands.

Comprehensive Strategies: Some localities protect wetlands in a more comprehensive manner than by simply defining wetlands, requiring regulated activities to be by permit, and avoiding wetlands losses to the extent possible. One such technique is to identify a critical environmental or conservation area that contains wetlands and other fragile resources including habitats, slopes, and wooded areas. Such areas may be designated a critical environmental area and be subjected to heightened review under the State Environmental Quality Review Act procedure. They may also be denominated an overlay district where development and land use activities are subjected to higher review standards, including wetlands controls.

ILLUSTRATIONS

The town of Kent, in Putnam County, adopted its Freshwater Wetlands law in 1988 as Chapter 103 of its municipal code. It was adopted "to preserve, protect and conserve freshwater wetlands and the benefits derived therefrom, to prevent the despoliation and destruction of freshwater wetlands and to regulate the development of such wetlands in order to secure the natural benefits of freshwater wetlands, consistent with the general welfare and beneficial economic, social and agricultural development of the town." The town's law regulates contiguous wetlands covering at least 40,000 square feet–about one acre–that are identified by water saturation during at least three consecutive months or by the presence of aquatic or semiaquatic vegetation of the type listed in §24-0107 of the state Freshwater Wetlands Act or certain listed soils types as defined by the United States Department of Agriculture Natural Resource Conservation Service.

Kent's wetlands law regulates a number of listed activities, including erecting or enlarging any structure of any kind, road construction, digging wells, installation of septic tanks, sewage treatment effluent discharge, draining, dredging, excavation, any form of deposit or storage of any material, use of off-road vehicles, tree and brush cutting, and "any other activity which substantially impairs any of the several functions served by wetlands." Certain activities are permitted as-of-right on wetlands within limits. These include gardening, removal of natural products of wetlands, outdoor recreation, grazing and farming, and dam operation and maintenance.

Under this local law, any person proposing a regulated activity must file an application for a permit. The law provides for split jurisdiction regarding the review of an application for a permit. When a regulated activity also requires an application to the town board, planning board, or zoning board of appeals, that body is given jurisdiction over the wetlands application and issues or denies the wetlands permit. These approving authorities must refer the matter to the local wetlands inspector and conservation commission for their review and written report on the matter. This referral can take no longer than 30 days, and inaction by the inspector and commission during this period is deemed to indicate no objection to the application. Where no application and approval other than the wetlands permit is required, the town engineer is designated the approving authority regarding wetlands protection. Public hearings on the wetlands permit application are held in conjunction with any public hearing required for any other land use approval that the regulated activity requires.

Where the activity is subject to other land use approval, a decision on the wetlands permit is to be made simultaneously with the determination on that other approval. Otherwise, the authority considering the application must approve, deny, or approve with modifications within 60 days of its receipt. The Kent law contains a list of standards to be used in determining whether to approve, condition, or deny a permit application. These include the environmental impact of the proposed activity, alternatives to it, the suitability of the activity in the area, alternatives to the activity, and "the extent to which the exercise of property rights and the public benefit derived from [the activity] may outweigh or justify the possible degradation of the wetland." Enforcement of the provisions of the town's wetlands law is delegated to the wetlands inspector.

The provisions of the wetlands law of the town of Bedford, in Westchester County, differ from those of the town of Kent in several ways. Under the Bedford law, a map of locally regulated wetlands is to be prepared and maintained. Wetlands are defined primarily by the presence of hydric soils and/or lands that are saturated by water in a way that is sufficient to support a prevalence of hydrophytic vegetation, which is extensively defined. The town regulates wetlands of all sizes and buffer areas within 100 feet of their boundaries. All permit applications are submitted to a wetlands control commission consisting of five resident members with qualifications in wetlands-related matters. All decisions on wetlands permit applications are made by this commission, and all environmental reviews required by the State Environmental Quality Review Act are conducted by it, whether or not the regulated activity is subject to review by other local administrative agencies. Public hearings may be held by the commission, in its discretion.

The applicant for a wetlands permit in Bedford has the burden of proving that "the proposed activity is not adverse to the general health, safety, or economic and general welfare of the residents of Bedford or its neighboring communities, that it will not degrade the environment or result in any of the adverse impacts stated in [§ 2 of the local wetlands law]." The law indicates that applicants also have the responsibility of obtaining all other "approval or permits required by any other agencies prior to construction in accordance with the wetlands permit." Obtaining such approvals is the responsibility of the applicant, and no activity may be started until all required approvals are obtained.

The town of Somers, in Westchester County, regulates wetlands that are 5,000 square feet in size or larger and buffer areas within 100 feet of such wetlands. Applications for wetlands permits are made to the town engineering department and are reviewed by the planning board, which is required to hold a public hearing on each application. The town's wetlands law requires each applicant to develop a wetlands mitigation plan specifying measures that provide for "replacement wetlands that recreate as nearly as possible the original wetlands in terms of type, function, geographic location and setting."

LIMITATIONS AND CONCERNS

Decisions of local wetlands permitting bodies to deny a permit or impose significant conditions on a permit must not be arbitrary or capricious. They should be based not on unsupported opinion but on facts and studies. Under some local wetlands laws, the factors that are to be used to identify regulated wetlands are complicated and numerous. Wetlands regulators must be sure that their decisions identifying lands as regulated wetlands are based on facts that support the identification under the standards contained in the local law. This is particularly important when the applicant provides concrete evidence indicating that the subject parcel does not contain the type of wetlands defined by the local wetlands law.

Conditions imposed on wetlands permits should be clearly calculated to avoid, minimize, or mitigate the loss of wetlands functions directly attributable to the proposed activity that is being permitted.

Because wetlands may be subject to regulation by three separate levels of government and two or more administrative agencies at the local level, efforts to coordinate, simplify, and streamline the review and permit process are important. For activities that affect state regulated wetlands, for example, the Army Corps of Engineers has agreed to receive a copy of the application to the DEC as the application it requires. Since almost all local wetlands laws are adopted pursuant to municipal home rule authority, they create a concurrent set of regulations with which a property owner must comply. Local and state regulations may have different wetlands definitions, exemptions, prohibitions, and waiver and variance procedures. This can result in situations in which, after a long and complex process, a landowner can secure a state wetlands permit with no assurance that the regulated activity will be permitted locally and vice versa. Similarly, what may be permitted by the DEC may not be authorized under other local land use controls, and vice versa. Similar situations can be created at the local level, for example, where an activity requiring a local wetland permits also requires an additional approval by a local agency. Some local governments have coordinated the review and approval process by delegating wetlands permit authority to the local board that has authority over the separate application.

In deciding whether to deny a wetlands permit, the approving agency should be attentive to whether the regulations allow the property owner to realize a reasonable return on his property. If the wetlands regulations destroy all but a bare residue of the economic value of the regulated parcel, its owner may succeed in bringing an action against the local government claiming that its property has been taken for a public purpose without just compensation.

STATUTES

Article 24, §24-0501, of the New York Environmental Conservation Law permits localities to assume from the DEC the responsibility for freshwater wetlands regulation.

Article 24, §24-0509, of the Environmental Conservation Law makes it clear that local governments may regulate wetlands within their jurisdiction "whether such wetlands are under the jurisdiction of the Department of Environmental Conservation . . . provided, however, that any such regulation by a local government shall be at least as protective of freshwater wetlands" as the state program.

Subsections 10(1)(ii)(a)(11) and (12) of the Municipal Home Rule Law state that any county, city, town, or village may adopt laws for the "protection and enhancement of its physical and visual environment" and for the "safety, health, and well-being of persons or property" within its jurisdiction. This includes the authority to protect the quality and benefits of local wetlands on behalf of the public.

CASE DIGEST

Wetlands that are adjacent to waters that bear on interstate commerce, or their tributaries, are within the reach of the Clean Water Act (CWA) and, therefore, of federal wetlands regulation. *National Resource Defense Council, Inc. v. Callaway*, 392 F.Supp. 685 (D.D.C. 1975); but see *Solid Waste Agency of Northern Cook County v. U.S. Army Corps of Engineers (SWANCC)*, 121 S. Ct. 675 (2001) ("isolated" wetlands not adjacent to or hydrologically connected to navigable waters are not subject to federal regulation under the CWA; application of the statute to those wetlands would pose "significant constitutional questions"). The *Callaway* court had declared that Congress' definition of navigable waters as the waters of the United States, including territorial seas, does not limit the term "wetlands" as used in the CWA to the traditional tests of navigability. For discussions of *SWANCC*, see Christy H. Dral & Jerry J. Phillips, *Commerce by Another Name:* Lopez, Morrison, SWANCC, *and* Gibbs, 31 ELR 10413 (Apr. 2001); Stephen R. McAllister & Robert L. Glicksman, *Federal Environmental Law in the "New Federalism" Era*, 30 ELR 11122 (Dec. 2000); Michael J. Gerhardt, *Federal Environmental Regulation in a Post-*Lopez *World: Some Questions and Answers*, 30 ELR 10980 (Nov. 2000); Charles Tiefer, *After* Morrison, *Can Congress Preserve Environmental Laws From Commerce Clause Challenge?*, 30 ELR 10888 (Oct. 2000); Philip Weinberg, *Does that Line in the Sand Include Wetlands? Congressional Power and Environmental Protection*, 30 ELR 10894 (Oct. 2000).

New York statutes give the Department of Environmental Conservation (DEC) authority to regulate wetlands that are 12.4 acres in size or larger. Smaller wetlands may qualify for protection if the DEC determines that they are of "unusual local importance." *Tilles v. Williams*, 119 A.D.2d 233, 506 N.Y.S.2d 193 (2d Dep't 1986). A wetland meets this test if it provides habitat for a threatened or endangered species, provides flood control that protects a neighboring developed area, or is hydraulically connected to a source of public drinking water. In this case, the court reversed a wetlands designation made by the DEC that had hinged on the role the property played as a critical habitat for the endangered Eastern Tiger Salamander and as a source of hydraulic recharge for an area aquifer. The landowner offered evidence showing the absence of a proven salamander population and indicating soil conditions that made it impossible for the wetlands to serve as a source of freshwater recharge. The evidence supporting the wetland designation had not been supplemented by further field research that rebutted the plaintiff's claims. The court held that DEC's assertion of jurisdiction over the property was "clearly without a rational basis."

Landowners in *Eastbrook Construction Co., Inc. v. Armstrong*, 205 A.D.2d. 971, 613 N.Y.S.2d 776 (3d Dep't 1994), obtained septic tank approval for their single-family house from the Westchester County Department of Health and a building permit from the Town of Lewisboro's building inspector. After construction began, the permits were suspended pending the issuance of a wetlands permit. Following the denial of the wetlands permit, the plaintiffs claimed that through the issuance of the building permit they had gained vested rights. The court held that "the issuance of a building permit in contravention of the Town's Freshwater Wetlands Protection Law did not confer vested rights." The plaintiffs could not claim that a mistaken or erroneous building permit created such rights. The court concluded that the town was required to enforce correctly the wetlands law, which dictated the denial of the building permit.

Under state judicial standards, as long as a wetland permitting decision is rationally supported by substantial evidence, a court will not substitute its judgment for that of the local wetlands authority. *Fawn Builders, Inc. v. Planning Board of the Town of Lewisboro*, 223 A.D.2d 996, 636 N.Y.S.2d 873 (3d Dep't 1996). The court upheld the town's denial of an application to build on environmentally sensitive wetlands despite the plaintiff's proposal to mitigate the impact of the project. The court held that a municipal agency can use its discretion in reviewing permit applications, so long as its decision is supported by a rational interpretation of the available evidence.

In *Purchase Environmental Protective Association v. Strati*, 163 A.D.2d 596, 559 N.Y.S.2d 356 (2d Dep't 1990), a planning board approved a project for a development on a wetlands site, despite finding that not all of the wetlands on the site had been properly delineated as required by the local wetlands law. The planning board had relied on expert consultants who "properly excluded from consideration certain wetlands present on the site as a matter of their 'subjective determination.'" The court held that the planning board's "determination to issue the permit to conduct regulated activities on the wetlands was based on an erroneous interpretation of the law and must be annulled."

The court in *Drexler v. Town of New Castle*, 62 N.Y.2d 413, 465 N.E.2d 836, 477 N.Y.S.2d

116 (1984), held that "non-qualifying wetlands fall outside the mandates of the statutory scheme and are subject only to local regulations." The plaintiffs claimed that the Town was barred from regulating activities on wetlands unless it first filed a map identifying local wetlands. The wetland in this case was not a state designated wetland and the local law regulating the use of the wetland did not require its designation on an official map. The court held that "the clear language of the statutory provisions . . . establishe[d] that nonstatutorily qualifying wetlands are excluded from the mapping requirements of [the Act]." The court further concluded that the wetlands were "subject to the exclusive authority of the local government."

In *Ardizzone v. Elliott*, 75 N.Y.2d 150, 550 N.E.2d 906, 551 N.Y.S.2d 457 (1989), the Court of Appeals invalidated a wetlands protection law adopted by the Town of Yorktown that did not conform to the requirements of the Freshwater Wetlands Act. The court held that the DEC had "exclusive authority to regulate state-mapped wetlands under the Freshwater Wetlands Act unless a local government has expressly assumed jurisdiction over such wetlands," as provided in the state statute. The court concluded that the language of the section did not give "any indication that the Legislature intended to provide for concurrent [s]tate and local jurisdiction over all freshwater wetlands." The court voided all local freshwater wetlands laws or laws that had not been adopted in compliance with the procedures outlined in Article 24. However, this holding has been reversed by state legislative action. In 1990, §24-0509 was amended to allow concurrent jurisdiction over wetlands between the DEC and local governments.

The court in *Honore De St. Aubin v. Flacke*, 68 N.Y.2d 66, 496 N.E.2d 879, 505 N.Y.S.2d 859 (1986), referenced the standard that landowners must meet to prove that a wetlands regulation constitutes a taking of property. The court noted that a landowner must also show "dollars and cents evidence that under no use permitted by the regulation under attack would the properties be capable of producing a reasonable return; the economic value, or all but a bare residue of the economic value, of the parcels must have been destroyed by the regulations at issue." In order to demonstrate deprivation of constitutional rights, the landowner must do more than show a reduction in the value of the property. "[A] property owner does not prove a taking solely by evidence that the value has been reduced by the regulation, even if it has been substantially reduced."

In *Basile v. Town of Southampton*, 89 N.Y.2d 974, 678 N.E.2d 489, 655 N.Y.S.2d 877 (1997), the court denied a takings claim made by a landowner who took possession of the property with the knowledge that it was subject to the town's local wetlands law. The property was being taken by eminent domain authority, and the condemning authority claimed that the value of the property in the hands of the owner was its value subject to the preexisting wetlands regulation. The court agreed, noting that "[g]enerally, upon condemnation, property value should be calculated with due consideration paid to the applicable restrictions upon use. . . . Whatever taking claim the prior owner may have had against the environmental regulation of the subject parcel, any property interest that might serve as the foundation for such a claim was not owned by claimant here who took title after the redefinition of the relevant property interests."

REFERENCE

John R. Nolon, *Wetlands Controls*, N.Y. L.J., Aug. 19, 1998.

K. OPEN SPACE ACQUISITION

DEFINITION

Municipalities provide for the acquisition of open space in a variety of ways. They may purchase private lands outright and dedicate those lands to public use. In appropriate cases, they may use public funds to purchase the development rights to private lands. This involves the purchase of a conservation easement with public funds. The easement gives the public the right to restrict the future development of private lands to their current use or stipulated limited future uses. Alternatively, local governments may work with land trusts that may purchase title to, or conservation easements on, private lands or accept donations of title or easements from landowners.

Local governments secure the funds necessary for the purchase of open space in a variety of ways:

- ♦ Some localities have appropriated a portion of their local revenues derived from property taxes for this purpose, either annually or through multi-year appropriations.
- ♦ Others have floated municipal bonds, the proceeds from which are dedicated to acquisition of open lands.
- ♦ Similarly, some local governments may decide to use the income from transfer of title taxes for this purpose.
- ♦ Reduced tax assessments in exchange for conservation easements that preserve open space are becoming more common as are land purchase installment arrangements that allow a municipality to purchase desired lots over time.

Municipalities have these options available to them to fund their open land acquisition programs. They may use any one or any combination of them to advance their particular reasons for preserving open land.

PURPOSE

As development pressures mount, local governments search for methods of retaining the open character of their communities. When the search is simply for "openness," then the preservation of any open space that will retain the community's historic open character will suffice. In most communities, however, other critical objectives motivate the search for methods of retaining open lands. Some communities seek to preserve specific scenic vistas that are uniquely important to their historic character. In farming communities, there is often a desire to retain viable agricultural lands and the economic vitality and tax revenues that those farms generate. Maintaining the farms themselves often bears a crucial relationship to the historic nature of the community that many current residents value. In many communities, there is a profound concern for maintaining sufficient open lands to provide shelter and a hospitable environment for valued animal and plant species that are rapidly disappearing because of increased land development. Other communities combine these objectives and seek, for example, to preserve viable farmlands while protecting habitats, wetlands, and other natural resources on those lands.

WHEN

Local governments may seek to protect their remaining open lands when the preservation of such properties becomes critical to the community's future. Open space includes any area that is characterized by natural scenic beauty or whose condition or quality is such that it will enhance the present or potential value of surrounding developed lands or enhance the conservation of natural or scenic resources or preserve the community's historic character. When faced with increased development pressures, residents and municipal officials may wish to preserve a general sense of openness, to insure the continuation of farming in rural areas, to protect lands that harbor wetlands, habitats, valued species, and other natural resources, to maintain critical viewsheds, or some combination of these objectives.

AUTHORITY

Municipalities in New York have broad authority to acquire land for public purposes. The state legislature has provided specific authority for municipalities to purchase open lands or a lesser interest in them through the General Municipal Law §247 and the Environmental Conservation Law §§49-0301 et seq. These laws allow local governments to acquire title to land, to purchase a lesser interest in the land, such as a conservation easement, or to lease development rights.

Most municipalities rely upon General Municipal Law §247 for authority to implement an open lands purchase program. When this law was enacted in 1960, the legislature recognized that rapid development was threatening lands with significant scenic, aesthetic, or physical value. As a means of conserving these important resources, the legislature declared that it is in the public interest for any county, city, town, or village to expend public funds "to acquire, maintain, improve, protect, or limit the future use of or otherwise conserve open spaces." Under §247, municipalities may "acquire, by purchase, gift, grant, bequest, devise, lease or otherwise, the fee or any lesser interest, development right, easement, covenant, or other contractual right" in lands defined as "open space." ("Fee" is a legal term used to refer to the full legal title to a parcel of land.)

When a municipality acquires a lesser interest in a parcel of land, such as its development rights, the General Municipal Law §247 directs municipalities to reassess the property value for local tax purposes to reflect the limitation placed on the future use of that land. This reassessment will reduce an owner's property tax burden as an additional incentive to preserve the land. Section 247 also provides that any such interest acquired by a municipality is enforceable not only against the original landowner but also against anyone who acquires the land in the future, so long as the municipality's interest is filed properly on the county land records. The development rights validly purchased by a municipality may never be used by the landowner or anyone who acquires a legal interest in the land from that owner.

Sections 49-0301 through 49-0311 of the Environmental Conservation Law provide additional authority for municipalities to purchase the development rights of open lands. These statutes permit municipalities to acquire conservation easements for the purpose of conserving, preserving, and protecting the environmental, historical, and cultural resources of the state, including the preservation, development, and improvement of agricultural lands. The law defines a conservation easement as "an easement, covenant, restriction or other interest in real property . . . which limits or restricts the development, management or use of real property . . ."

When the title to the land is purchased by a municipality, the landowner receives a cash payment and the local government assumes the obligation of managing the property, which is then removed from the tax rolls. When the municipality purchases development rights to private land, the owner retains the land's title and the property remains on the tax rolls. The landowner receives the difference between the value of the land with the development restriction and the value of the land without the development restriction. The landowner may also receive tax benefits in the form of reduced property taxes and reduced estate taxes. There may be additional income tax advantages when the landowner has donated some or all of the land's development rights to the municipality or to a qualified land trust.

There are two differences between acquisitions made under the conservation easement provisions of the Environmental Conservation Law and lesser interests in land acquired under §247 of the General Municipal Law. A conservation easement may be enforced by a third party named in the instrument creating the easement. This allows a municipality to delegate monitoring and enforcement responsibilities under the conservation easement to a land trust or other not-for-profit corporation with the legal authority and capacity to do so. No such flexibility exists under §247. Also, under the conservation easement statute, not-for-profit land trusts and conservation organizations may purchase easements directly.

IMPLEMENTATION

Acquisition of Open Space: Under the authority granted to them by the state legislature, municipalities are able to develop specific programs to acquire open space. Programs fall into one of four categories: purchase of title to land, purchase of development rights, lease of development rights, or a combination of these approaches.

Municipalities may acquire full legal title to a parcel of open land. To do so, they must pay the landowner the full market value of the property and make this payment at the time of acquisition. The municipality also assumes full legal responsibility for the property, as well as all costs of maintaining it. Such acquired open lands are assets on the books of the local government and are removed fully from the property tax rolls. This is a particularly attractive option when the locality wishes to acquire lands for active or passive recreational purposes.

Because of the significant direct and indirect costs of such a program, municipalities may wish to consider a purchase of development rights program which leaves title to open lands in the hands of private owners, allows current land uses to continue, and earns property tax revenues for those uses. Under a purchase of developments rights (PDR) program, a municipality pays a landowner for restricting the future use of the land forever. The restriction usually takes the form of a conservation easement under which the landowner retains title to the land and the municipality gains the right to enforce the restriction that the easement imposes on the land's development. The cost of the development rights is the difference between the value of the land with the development restriction on it and the value of the land for its "highest and best use," usually commercial or residential development. In exchange for placing the development restriction on the property, the owner benefits from reduced property and estate taxes.

A lease of development rights (LDR) program is one in which a municipality acquires the development rights of a parcel through a conservation easement for a period of years rather than in perpetuity. In exchange for restricting the property's development, the landowner receives preferential tax treatment in the form of reduced property taxes and an annual rental payment. The benefit to the municipality of such a program is that it is able to spread the cost of the easement over a number of years rather than pay for the development rights completely in the first year. An additional benefit to the landowner is that the owner retains the possibility of developing the land in the future and thus maintains the property's long-term equity value. The most significant problem with a LDR program, however, is that the land still has the potential to be developed at some future date.

Funding Mechanisms: Having provided that municipalities may expend public funds for the acquisition of open lands under the General Municipal Law §247(2) and allowed them to establish various methods of expending these funds, state law provides several methods that municipalities can use to raise funds for this purpose. They may raise funds through real property taxes, bonds, real estate transfer taxes, or sales and use taxes. They may use the funds immediately or set aside a portion of the revenues received in a capital reserve fund. Since 1996, municipalities may also enter into land installment purchase obligations for the purpose of acquiring interest in or title to open space.

Municipalities have the authority to assess and collect real property taxes. They may spend those funds in a number of ways. Funds collected from property taxes may be used for any public purpose, including the acquisition of land or development rights. Under their budget authority, local legislatures may allocate a fixed amount in a given year to purchase title to land or development rights. They may also designate funds for this purpose in a multi-year plan. No referendum of the voters is required for the local legislature to allocate the current year's property and other tax revenues for public purposes such as this. Referenda are usually used to authorize the dedication of tax funds to an open space purchase program over a period of years.

Municipalities are also authorized to contract indebtedness for public purposes such as the acquisition of land or development rights. Under the state's local finance law, indebtedness may take the form of bonds or notes. When bonds or notes are sold, their proceeds are required to be held in a special fund and must be used for the exact purpose for which the bonds were issued.

The issuance of municipal bonds may be subject to a voter referendum, depending on the amount of the bond issue, the length of the repayment period, and the purpose for which they are used. To pay the principal and interest on the sums borrowed from the bondholders, a steady stream of revenue over the bonds' repayment period is necessary. Normally, municipalities use the revenues derived from property taxes to pay the principal and interest due on municipal bonds that were issued for the purchase of open lands or their development rights.

Funding may also be procured by levying a tax on the sale of real estate in the community. Because there is no general state enabling legislation that permits municipalities to impose such a tax, a municipality must first seek passage of specific enabling legislation from the state legislature pursuant to the Municipal Home Rule Law §40. Under this provision, either the chief executive officer of a municipality who has the concurrence of a majority of the local legislature or the local legislature itself by a two-thirds vote may request that the state legislature pass a bill authorizing the imposition of a real estate transfer tax in that specific municipality. The request must state that a necessity exists for the revenues to be derived by the transfer tax and must recite the facts demonstrating that necessity. Once approved by the state legislature, the transfer tax must then be approved in a local referendum.

Counties may assess and collect local sales and use taxes pursuant to Article 29 of the Tax Law. Taxes may be placed on a number of items including the sale of tangible personal property, utility services, food and drink, hotel room occupancy, and amusement charges. The net revenues from these taxes may be used for the acquisition of open lands under certain circumstances. All of the net revenues derived from a county sales or use tax may be set aside for county purposes or distributed to constituent municipalities. Since a county is permitted to expend county funds for the acquisition of open lands, it may set aside a portion of the net tax proceeds from sales taxes for the acquisition of such land.

Long-Term Financing Options: Municipalities have the authority to use techniques to defer the payments on open land purchases until a future date. These techniques allow a community to make long-term financial plans, purchase lands at current prices, and preserve open space.

The first of these techniques is to issue municipal bonds that are sold to bond holders as described above. The proceeds of the sale of bonds to the bondholders are then held in a capital reserve fund. Principal and interest payments are made by the municipality on an annual basis. These payments come from annual property tax revenues assessed on and collected from real property owners over the life of the bonds, which is generally thirty years. Because the bonds represent the obligation of a governmental entity, interest payments to the bondholders are tax-exempt.

Under Article II, §6-c of the General Municipal Law, a local legislature may create a capital reserve fund and designate certain moneys for the purchase of open lands. When established for this purpose, the fund may be subject to public referendum before it is established. Moneys placed into this fund may then be used to purchase title to land or development rights. The importance of such a capital reserve fund is that once moneys are placed into the fund, they can only be used for the designated purpose and may not be diverted to other purposes by future local leaders with different objectives. A capital fund of this type is used to hold the proceeds of bonds or funds derived from a multi-year dedication of property taxes until they are needed to purchase open space.

Under a New York law enacted in 1996, municipalities may enter into land installment purchase obligations for the purpose of financing the acquisition of interests or rights in real property under §247 of the General Municipal Law. A municipality is allowed to pass a bond resolution authorizing it to purchase land or development rights on an installment sales contract basis from the individuals who own such land. These individuals become creditors of the municipality, similar to bond holders who purchase municipally issued bonds. The value of the land or development rights acquired can be repaid to the landowners under an installment sales contract lasting up to 30 years. Using this authority, a municipality may acquire either title to land or the land's development rights in the present while spreading the cost of the acquisition over as many as 30 years.

The installment purchase obligation has roughly the same financial impact on the community as issuing long-term bonds for the purchase of interests in open lands. In fact, the process is initiated by the adoption of a bond resolution by the local government. With both the issuance of bonds and the purchase of land through the installment method, the locality is able to obtain land at present value while paying for that purchase over a longer term, usually 30 years. Payments to the land owners are made from each year's property tax revenues.

ILLUSTRATIONS

Creation of a Capital Reserve Fund Through a Multi-Year Property Tax Increase: In 1997, voters in the town of Greenburgh, in Westchester County, approved a capital reserve fund from which moneys are used to acquire and protect the town's remaining natural areas, wetlands, trails and greenway corridors. This fund was established pursuant to General Municipal Law §6-c for the purposes set forth in §247.

The town "Greenways Fund" is financed by an increase of one half of one percent (0.5%) of the prevailing tax rate levied on the assessed value of property in the town. At the time of passage, it was estimated that the increase of 0.5% would cost the average homeowner about $10 a year. This increase of 0.5% continues until 2004, at which time the fund can be continued. If, however, no properties are acquired by that time, the money in the fund will revert to town's general fund.

Lease of Development Rights: In 1976, the town of Perinton, Monroe County, enacted a conservation easement law to acquire interests in land for preservation of open space. These conservation easements must restrict development for a minimum of five years. The conservation easement law also establishes conservation easements for farming purposes where, in addition to agreeing not to develop the land for the period of the easement, the landowner agrees that the lands under the easement will be used for agricultural purposes.

Unlike other communities, the town does not pay for the conservation easements it acquires. Instead, the town provides reduced tax assessments to landowners in exchange for restricting development on their property as directed by the General Municipal Law §247(3). The town assessor's office utilizes a tax assessment table that establishes the percent of property's pre-assessment value that remains taxable. For instance, where a landowner agrees to a five-year conservation easement, 75% of the pre-assessment value of the property remains taxable. If a landowner agrees to a conservation easement for a period of 25 years, only 10% of the property's pre-assessment value remains taxable.

The process for creating a conservation easement begins with the property owner who is permitted to submit an application to the town's conservation board. The conservation board then determines whether the proposal to grant the town a conservation easement would benefit the town. If the conservation board finds that the easement will be beneficial, it recommends that the town board hold a public hearing to determine whether the town should acquire the easement. After the hearing, the town board makes its decision. If it agrees to accept the easement, the easement is then recorded in the Monroe county clerk's office.

The town's conservation easement law also provides Perinton with a means to raise funds for the purchase of open space lands. A provision of the law requires landowners who cancel their easement before its period has expired, or who substantially violate the easement, to pay a penalty and back taxes on the land under easement. This money is then placed into a capital reserve fund established by the town board called the "Open Space Retention Reserve Fund." Moneys placed into this fund are used to acquire interests in open lands. Recent acquisitions with fund money have totaled nearly 400 acres.

Use of Municipal Bonds to Purchase Development Rights: By 1990, only 12 family farms remained in the town of Pittsford, Monroe County. Recognizing the importance of farmland and open space to the community, the town commissioned a fiscal impact study in 1993. The study illustrated that it would cost Pittsford less to issue bonds to purchase the town's remaining open space than if the land were developed for single-family housing as permitted under the town's zoning code. With this in mind, Pittsford inventoried the town's open space based on criteria established by the town board. Open space lands were prioritized, and in 1996, Pittsford identified 2,000 acres for preservation in the town's Greenprint for the Future. Lands to be preserved included wildlife habitat corridors that linked important ecological resources and the town's remaining historic farms.

Using its bonding authority, the town board approved the issuance of $9.9 million in municipal bonds to purchase the development rights to seven farms totaling 1,100 acres. Each landowner entered into a conservation easement with the town. These easements divide each farm into three areas–homestead, farmstead, and farm area–and set forth permissible activities in each area. The easements also provide the town with the right to visual access to the property in its scenic and open state, and permit public access in certain designated areas of each farm.

LIMITATIONS AND CONCERNS

New York's laws on the subject of issuing bonds for the purchase of open space and the requirements for permissive or mandatory referenda are complex. They require competent counsel to interpret them in order to establish local land purchase programs.

There are many constituencies in most localities that support open space preservation. Their preservation interests range from farming, recreation, or wildlife habitats to scenic vistas. In establishing open lands acquisition programs, the interests of these groups must be meshed and prioritized. This task may be difficult and time-consuming.

Once the specific purposes of a local open lands program are established, local leaders must establish specific criteria for the expenditure of public funds. These are necessary to avoid the appearance of favoritism and to carry out the priorities established for the program.

In developing communities, open lands are expensive to purchase. It is difficult to raise sufficient funds from real property taxes to acquire the open lands that are desired. This leads to efforts to leverage funds raised locally with funds available through state, federal, and private sources. Communities often find that having established a local revenue source for open space acquisition makes them more competitive in securing funds from these other sources.

STATUTES

The New York State Constitution, at Article XIV, §4, articulates the state's desire to conserve and protect its natural resources and scenic beauty.

General Municipal Law §247 grants municipalities the authority to implement an open lands purchase program. Subsection (2) specifically authorizes the acquisition of lands to be preserved as open space and allows municipalities to expend public funds in doing so. Subsection (3) authorizes the reassessment of these lands when appropriate.

Environmental Conservation Law §§49-0301 through 49-0311 further authorize municipalities to purchase development rights for open land through the use of conservation easements.

Municipal Home Rule Law §40 provides the structure for authorizing a municipality to impose a real estates transfer tax which may be used to fund open land acquisition.

General Municipal Law §6-c allows local legislatures to create capital reserve funds, which may be used for the purchase of open lands.

REFERENCES

Jeffrey LeJava, Mark Rielly & John R. Nolon, Open Lands Acquisition: Local Financing Techniques Under New York Law, Metropolitan Conservation Alliance Technical Series Paper No. 2 (Mar. 2000).

Joseph Stinson & Liane Wilson, *Preserving Open Space with Land Trusts and Conservation Easements,* at http://www.pace.edu/lawschool/landuse/lndtrs.html (last visited Feb. 2, 2001).

Chapter 9

LIMITATIONS ON LOCAL LAND USE AUTHORITY

Although the New York State legislature has delegated significant land use authority to local governments, it has limited that authority where necessary to accomplish paramount state objectives. In areas where it is competent to regulate, the federal government has limited the scope of local land use authority as well. Federal and state constitutional provisions constrain local land use regulations that affect freedom of religious practice or free speech and expression.

The topics in this chapter make it clear that planning, zoning, and land use regulations are not the exclusive domain of local governments. Constitutionally, the authority to control land uses is vested in the state government and is delegated to villages, towns, and cities as instrumentalities of the state. A corollary of that notion is the principle that zoning laws cannot be exclusionary, since they must be adopted in consideration of the needs of all the people of the state. Neither growth itself, nor a particular class of people, such as those of low and moderate income, may be excluded under this principle.

The state legislature has directed local governments to accept group homes for the developmentally disabled as single-family housing permitted as-of-right in their single-family zoning districts. Unless the locality can find an acceptable alternative site or prove over-concentration of such housing in the area, it must allow the group home to be established in its single-family neighborhood. Other forms of state-assisted housing have been found to preempt local zoning controls in this way.

At the federal level, telecommunications statutes have restricted the range of local control over the siting of cellular transmission facilities. Those facilities have been determined by federal law to have no negative effect on public health, and any attempt to regulate their location to prevent public health injuries has been preempted by federal law. The impact of federal environmental statutes on local land use regulation is not covered in this book. Generally, federal environmental laws encourage state governments to adopt statutes to protect air, water, and other natural resources that do not preempt local regulatory authority. Instead, the resulting state environmental laws establish concurrent standards and permit requirements for certain developments that are subject to local land use regulations as well. Developers, in these situations, must receive permits from local and state agencies and comply with both sets of regulations.

Zoning and land use regulations that restrict the location of religious institutions are limited under both the federal and the state constitutions, which protect the exercise of religion from unreasonable governmental interference. Local governments must also be cognizant of federal and state constitutional protection of free speech and expression in light of recent attacks on local efforts to restrict the location of billboards, signs, and adult businesses.

Local governments have learned to accommodate these limitations on their land use authority by using a number of creative techniques both to honor the state and federal purposes and to legislate in the interest of their residents. Their efforts in this regard continue to present interesting issues to the courts, which are called on to balance federal, state, and local prerogatives.

A. AFFORDABLE HOUSING AND EXCLUSIONARY ZONING

DEFINITION

When local zoning laws prevent lower income households from living in the community, those laws are called exclusionary zoning and can be declared unconstitutional by the courts. Zoning laws and other municipal actions that are aimed at providing housing for persons of limited income are called inclusionary zoning. State statutes provide municipalities with a variety of mechanisms that can be used to encourage and provide desired affordable housing. The topic of affordable housing covers both exclusionary and inclusionary zoning.

Exclusionary Zoning: In New York, the obligation not to exclude households in need of affordable housing means that communities may not exclude from their residential zoning districts types of accommodations, such as multi-family housing, that generally are more affordable than single-family homes on individual lots. Developers are given standing to challenge zoning laws that exclude more affordable types of housing since their rights cannot "realistically be separated from the rights of . . . nonresidents, in search of a comfortable place to live." A locality that has been found zoned in an exclusionary fashion can be required by the court to amend its zoning laws to accommodate more affordable types of housing. This is one of the few instances in New York when the courts will direct a local legislature to take a particular action such as rezoning to accommodate a specific amount of affordable housing.

Inclusionary Zoning: State statutes, in New York State and frequently in other jurisdictions, encourage local governments to adopt inclusionary programs regarding affordable housing. Localities have specific authority to provide zoning incentives, such as additional development density, to encourage private developers to set aside a percentage of residential units in a proposed development for affordable housing. Municipalities may abate local taxes, provide mortgage financing, acquire and dispose of property, and subsidize and provide infrastructure for affordable housing built by private and non-profit corporations organized under state housing laws. Cities, towns, and villages are authorized to establish municipal housing authorities that can issue bonds and make land available, provide infrastructure, and subsidize the costs of operating the projects of their municipal housing authorities.

Most discussions of affordable housing refer to state and federal subsidy programs that define affordable housing as synonymous with "low-income housing." The public housing programs and housing subsidy programs administered by the U.S. Department of Housing and Development and various state agencies have largely defined affordable housing in the public mind as high-rise rental housing for low-income families or publicly subsidized rural housing of a particular architectural design. There is, however, no standard definition of affordable housing to direct or bind a municipality that wishes to establish an inclusionary program or avoid a successful exclusionary zoning challenge. Localities may wish to encourage or assist either rental housing or housing that is for sale. Municipally encouraged or assisted affordable housing may be multi-family townhouses, garden apartments, attached low-rise units, single-family modular units, or any other housing type that can be affordably constructed. Local affordable housing initiatives can aim to serve any income group that is priced out of the local housing market.

PURPOSE

By encouraging the development of housing for those in need of affordable homes a local government provides housing for individuals and families that it wishes to accommodate to create a more efficient, workable, and equitable community. Local governments are encouraged to include in their comprehensive plans the consideration of regional needs, including housing, and to respond to the present and future housing needs of the community, including affordable housing. The comprehensive planning studies of the community may identify a particular housing need for senior citizens, young families, or other special population groups. Local governments in New York have used their zoning authority to encourage the development of housing for all types of households: senior citizens, middle-income families, homeless families, employees of the municipality, volunteer firemen, farm workers, and first-time homebuyers. Another purpose of providing affordable housing is to avoid costly litigation attacking the community for exclusionary zoning practices, which can result in court orders to rezone private land to accommodate a developer's affordable housing proposal.

WHEN

When local legislators discover that municipal employees or volunteers, senior citizens, young families, or other groups of households are having trouble finding affordable housing in the community, they may wish to take some action to encourage its development. Localities may want teachers in the local school system, municipal employees, police officers, and firefighters to live in the community for a variety of reasons related to the public interest. In high-cost areas, older residents who have lived in the community for decades and young adults who grew up in the community may not be able to find affordable housing and may be forced to move elsewhere. When communities in a region do not zone to include affordable housing, businesses can suffer from a lack of workers or be required to pay higher salaries to subsidize their commuting costs.

AUTHORITY

Local governments receive from the state their power to adopt zoning laws. Under the state constitution, powers delegated to local governments are to be exercised in the interests of all the people of the state, not just those who reside in the community. Local governments are not authorized to exercise the delegated power to adopt zoning laws that exclude large segments of the population who may not be able to afford single-family homes on individual lots or other high-cost forms of housing permitted under the local zoning law.

It is considered an implied power of local governments to exercise their zoning authority in a way that encourages the provision of affordable housing. In addition, a state statute specifically authorizes cities, towns, and villages to provide zoning incentives – such as additional development density or waivers of specific zoning requirements – to developers in exchange for the provision of affordable housing. Both the Private Housing Finance Law and the Public Housing Law authorize localities to subsidize and facilitate the provision of low- and moderate-income housing in a variety of ways, including the provision of land, operating subsidies, mortgage financing, and tax exemption.

IMPLEMENTATION

Localities can amend their zoning laws to include more affordable types of housing as permitted land uses in their zoning districts. These can include multi-family housing of a variety of types, factory constructed and modular homes, and clustered housing on smaller lots, with party walls and with other cost efficiencies.

Alternatively, communities can adopt an incentive zoning provision to achieve the housing objectives of the local comprehensive plan following the normal steps required for amending the zoning law. The particular zoning districts in which such incentives may be granted shall be designated by the amendments. A finding must be made that the additional development authorized by such incentives can be accommodated in those districts by the infrastructure and services available and without environmentally damaging consequences. The incentives can include waivers of all zoning requirements including "density, area, height, open space, use, or other provisions." These waivers may be awarded in exchange for the provision of "community benefits," including "housing for persons of low or moderate income." The zoning amendment must also set forth the procedure by which the incentives will be awarded, including the review and approval process, the incentives that may be awarded, and the type of affordable housing to be provided in exchange for these incentives.

The New York Public Housing Law, adopted in 1926, was the first statute of its kind in the nation. The law established that the expenditure of public funds for the provision of housing for lower income households was a public purpose to which public funds could be dedicated. It authorized the formation of municipal housing authorities and empowered them to issue bonds to finance their projects, to acquire land by condemnation, and abate local property taxes to reduce the operating costs of their housing. Municipal housing authorities have been able to provide truly affordable housing for lower income households by entering into contracts with federal and state agencies to issue tax-exempt bonds and subsidize the costs of operation. The Public Housing Law specifically authorizes local governments to make land available to municipal housing authorities and to provide infrastructure and operating subsidies to their projects.

Private developers and non-profit organizations are authorized to organize state-regulated housing companies under various articles of the Private Housing Finance Law, adopted originally in 1955. As amended, this law allows a variety of such companies to be created and allows municipalities to assist their projects by abating property taxes, acquiring and disposing of real property, and providing direct financial subsidies and supportive infrastructure.

LIMITATIONS AND CONCERNS

Local officials sometimes resist taking action to provide affordable housing because of the great demand for it in their regions. They fear that if their community sponsors or encourages affordable housing they will be inundated with households excluded from other communities that do not provide affordable housing. Statutes in New York encourage local governments to enter into intermunicipal agreements or to work with their county governments to insure that the provision of affordable housing is equitable, so that each community provides its fair share of the area's housing need.

Plaintiffs attacking exclusionary zoning have a difficult burden of proof in showing that a municipality's zoning law does not meet its fair share of regional housing needs. When the town of Cortlandt's zoning law was attacked as exclusionary, the court referenced the Westchester County Fair Share Housing Plan, one of the few relatively complete county housing plans in the state. The plan includes an allocation to each locality of its share of 5,000 units of affordable housing that the county found were needed by the year 2000. Because of this allocation plan, the court was able to determine that the town's actions failed to consider regional housing needs.

In the absence of a governmentally sanctioned study of the area's housing needs, plaintiffs must prove that there is an unmet regional housing need and that the defendant municipality has not accommodated its fair share of that need. This imposes an onerous burden on plaintiffs. What is the region for the purpose of establishing housing need? What housing need exists? How accurate and credible are the data used to prove that need? What percentage of this need is that of lower income people? How does one prove that other municipalities in the region have not zoned to meet the housing needs of these lower income families? What number of lower income residences represents the municipality's fair share of the regional need? How can the plaintiff demonstrate that the local zoning does not accommodate that number of lower income people?

Until the challenger has borne the burden of proving that the local zoning has failed to consider regional needs, defined in this way, and that it has an exclusionary effect, the municipality needs to prove nothing. The traditional policy of the judiciary of deferring to the legislative acts of municipal governments effectively immunizes localities from exclusionary zoning attacks until the challenger affirmatively proves that the local zoning has an exclusionary effect.

In both New Jersey and Connecticut, statutory mechanisms have been created by the state legislature to remove this serious burden of proof barrier to exclusionary zoning challenges. In New Jersey, the legislature adopted the Fair Housing Act of 1985 to provide for the development of low- and moderate-income housing under local zoning (N.J. Stat. Ann §§52:27 D-301-329). It established the Council on Affordable Housing (COAH) to implement the statute's fair share plan, based on an extensive statewide housing study and allocation formula. The COAH determines the fair share of each locality and reviews and certifies local fair share housing plans. Such plans are prepared and submitted by municipalities throughout the state. If a local government fails to submit such a plan, or if the plan does not merit COAH certification, the locality is particularly vulnerable to developer challenges. If a developer of affordable housing is denied approval to build in a locality without a certified plan, the court is likely to mandate the rezoning of the developer's land to a higher density allowing the construction of affordable housing.

In Connecticut, the state legislature adopted the Affordable Housing Land Use Appeals Act of 1990, which expressly reverses the burden of proof when a municipality denies a developer's application to construct affordable housing (Conn. Gen. Stat. §8-30g). Under the Act, a municipality that denies a developer's application to construct affordable housing carries the burden of proving that its action is justified by showing that it was "necessary to protect substantial public interests in health, safety . . . and such public interests clearly outweigh the need for affordable housing." Connecticut communities in which at least 10% of the housing stock is affordable to low- and moderate-income families are exempt from the application of this burden-shifting statute.

STATUTES

The authority of localities to provide zoning incentives to developers in exchange for housing for low- and moderate-income households is found in Town Law §261-b, Village Law §7-703, and General City Law §81-d.

The authority of municipal housing authorities, and of local governments to assist their projects, is contained in the various articles of the New York Public Housing Law.

The authority of private and non-profit developers to form state-regulated housing companies, and of local governments to assist their projects, is found in several articles of the New York Private Housing Finance Law.

CASE DIGEST

The courts in New York have exhibited a forceful judicial policy regarding affordable housing: "What we will not countenance, then, under any guise, is community efforts at immunization or exclusion." *Golden v. Planning Board of the Town of Ramapo*, 30 N.Y.2d 359, 285 N.E.2d 291, 334 N.Y.S.2d 138 (1972).

In *Berenson v. Town of New Castle*, 38 N.Y.2d 102, 341 N.E.2d 236, 378 N.Y.S.2d 672 (1975), a landowner attacked as exclusionary a suburban town's zoning law that contained no provision for the development of multi-family housing in any zoning district in the jurisdiction. The Court of Appeals found the town's law to be exclusionary, stating that "[t]he primary goal of a zoning law must be to provide for the development of a balanced, cohesive community which will make efficient use of the town's available land." The court held that "in enacting a zoning law, consideration must be given to regional [housing] needs and requirements" and that "[t]here must be a balancing of the local desire to maintain the [s]tatus quo within the community and the greater public interest that regional needs be met." The court also appealed to the state legislature for help on this matter, noting that zoning "is essentially a legislative act. Thus, it is quite anomalous that a court should be required to perform the tasks of a regional planner. To that end, we look to the Legislature to make appropriate changes in order to foster the development of programs designed to achieve sound regional planning."

Developers are given standing to challenge zoning laws that exclude more affordable types of housing since their rights cannot "realistically be separated from the rights of . . . nonresidents, 'in search of a comfortable place to live.'" *Berenson v. Town of New Castle*, 67 A.D.2d 506, 415 N.Y.S.2d 669 (2d Dep't 1979).

The *Berenson* issue returned to the Court of Appeals in *Robert E. Kurzius, Inc. v. Incorporated Village of Upper Brookville*, 51 N.Y.2d 338, 414 N.E.2d 680, 434 N.Y.S.2d 180 (1980). The Village of Upper Brookville appealed a lower court ruling that its five-acre minimum lot size for single-family residences was invalid under *Berenson*. The Court of Appeals sustained the zoning in the absence of any showing that the village had failed to consider regional housing needs and that such needs were unsatisfied. The court held that there was no evidence that the zoning law was enacted with an "exclusionary purpose," implying that a showing of such a purpose would be an additional rationale for finding a zoning law unconstitutionally exclusionary.

In *Blitz v. Town of New Castle*, 94 A.D.2d 92, 463 N.Y.S.2d 832 (2d Dep't 1983), the court held that Westchester County's legislatively adopted Residential Development Policy "is presumptively valid and the evidence at trial clearly established the rationality and soundness of that legislative finding." The existence of this legislative housing plan, in other words, created a presumptively valid definition of regional housing need that relieved the burden of proof that had crippled developer challenges in the past. The decision articulated yet another standard by which allegedly exclusionary zoning laws are judged. It established the "expected proportionate share" doctrine, under which the judicial inquiry should be "whether [a town's] provisions for housing are at all commensurate with some general notion of its expected contribution to the regional housing need."

In *Allen v. Town of North Hempstead*, 103 A.D.2d 144, 478 N.Y.S.2d 919 (2d Dep't 1984), a durational residence requirement imposed as a condition for qualifying to live in housing developed in a Golden Age Residency zoning district was found to violate the *Berenson* tests. The court determined that the requirement was enacted with an exclusionary purpose and that the town had failed to consider regional housing needs. The court wrote that "[t]he durational residence requirement at bar has a more direct exclusionary effect on nonresidents like plaintiffs than the almost total exclusion of multi-family housing held to be unconstitutional by this court [in *Berenson*]." Here, ample proof of the need for affordable housing of senior citizens in surrounding communities was placed on the record.

An amendment to New York City's zoning resolution, which sought to reverse Chinatown's badly deteriorated state, was found to be valid under *Berensen* in *Asian Americans for Equality v. Koch*, 72 N.Y.2d 121, 527 N.E.2d 265, 531 N.Y.S.2d 782 (1988). The amendment allowed construction at greater than usual densities on the condition that the developer provide certain amenities to the community such as community facilities, subsidized units for low-income families, or the rehabilitation of some existing substandard residential structures. The plaintiffs claimed that the amendment's incentives failed to provide sufficient low-income housing to satisfy the region's needs and thus amounted to unconstitutional exclusionary zoning.

Defining "community" as New York City in its entirety, the Court of Appeals in *Asian Americans* noted that *Berenson* did not require that each zone within a community be balanced. The court further noted that it is constitutional to exclude specific uses in a particular area so long as the regional and community needs are provided for elsewhere. The court reasoned that New York City had no affirmative duty to provide for an array of uses on a neighbor-hood-by-neighborhood basis because its residential stock contained much low-income housing. The court explained that "[i]n our prior decisions we have not compelled the City to facilitate the development of housing specifically affordable to lower income households; a zoning plan is valid if the municipality provides an array of opportunities for housing facilities."

In *Continental Building Co. v. North Salem*, 211 A.D.2d 88, 625 N.Y.S.2d 700 (3d Dep't 1995), the Appellate Division affirmed that North Salem's zoning law was unconstitutionally exclusionary under the *Berenson* requirement that local zoning "must adequately consider re-gional [housing] needs and requirements." The court held that a zoning law, challenged as exclusionary, "will be invalidated only if it is demonstrated that it actually was enacted for an im-proper purpose or if it was enacted without giving proper regard to local and regional housing needs and has an exclusionary effect. Once an exclusionary effect coupled with a failure to bal-ance the local desires with housing needs has been proved, then the burden of otherwise justify-ing the law shifts to the defendant [municipality]."

The *North Salem* decision expressed what had been implied by the Court of Appeals in its 1975 *Berenson* decision: the New York exclusionary zoning cases are concerned with the exclu-sion of a particular socioeconomic group–low-and moderate-income families–and it is their rights that the developer represents when attacking the exclusion of an adequate supply of multi-family housing from the local zoning law. Clearly, local zoning authority delegated by the state legislature may not be used to exclude a significant percentage of the population of the state, i.e., low- and moderate-income citizens. The health, safety, and welfare of the people of the state, not of the indi-vidual locality, justify the exercise of local police power authority such as zoning.

A developer challenged a town's zoning law as exclusionary in *Triglia v. Town of Cortlandt*, N.Y.L.J., Jan. 21, 1998, at 31 (Sup. Ct. Weschester County Jan. 8, 1998). In 1993, the town amended its zoning law to eliminate all multi-family housing as-of-right in the community. The plaintiff had applied to build 120 two-story multi-family units, 10 of which would be affordable to lower income families. The town board had approved this proposal, but after the 1993 amend-ments it refused to take any further action regarding the plaintiff's application.

The court, in ruling the town's actions unconstitutionally exclusionary, noted that the town "has completely failed to allow feasible provision for affordable (high density) housing con-struction in the most likely manner calculated to achieve that goal (i.e. multi-family housing). By passing a zoning law that completely omits any affordable multi-family housing of any sort of more than four units, the Town has either acted 'for an exclusionary purpose' or its actions have 'had an exclusionary effect' under *Berenson*." The court ordered the defendant municipality to present to it within four months of the decision "such amendments to the Zoning Law as may allow for multi-housing zones in the Town of Cortlandt for the Court's inspection upon failure of which the Zoning Ordinance shall be deemed annulled and set aside."

REFERENCES

John R. Nolon, *Shattering the Myth of Municipal Impotence: The Authority of Local Government to Create Affordable Housing*, Fordham Urb. L.J. (1989).

Julie Solinski, *Affordable Housing Law in New York, New Jersey, and Connecticut*, at http://www.pace.edu/lawschool/landuse/afford.html (last visited Feb. 2, 2001).

B. REGULATION OF CELLULAR FACILITIES

DEFINITION

In 1981, the Federal Communication Commission (FCC) established rules for developing a wireless cellular telephone system. It created over 700 cellular markets in the nation and licensed cellular telephone companies to operate within each market, assigning each one a designated frequency band for the transmission of telephone signals. Antennae used to transmit these signals emit radiofrequency radiation. This type of radiation has a relatively long wavelength and is not considered to be capable of damaging atomic structures in humans, animals, or other organisms. Other common sources of this type of radiofrequency emissions include radio and television antennae, computers, and radar.

A cellular transmission system is made up of contiguous cells, each of which can cover up to several square miles. Each cell has its own base station, which includes antennae, and associated electronic equipment that sends and receives signals to and from mobile phones. Base station antennae may be supported by towers of a variety of designs or may be mounted on tall structures such as water towers or rooftops. Height is a crucial factor in constructing these facilities, since wireless communication requires a clear line-of-sight for effective transmission and reception. As a mobile phone user drives from one cell area to another, the signal between the phone and the current base station weakens, and the call is automatically switched to a nearer station to maintain a clear signal. Each cell is electronically connected to a switching office, which, in turn, is connected to the regular telephone lines that are part of the traditional public telephone network. This network is a public-utility system that serves the public's interest in having an efficient communication network.

As a public-utility system, the cellular transmission network and its individual carriers are subject to federal and state regulation. Private cellular companies are also subject to local zoning regulations that control the construction of structures such as cellular base stations and transmission towers and antennae. Wireless communication facilities are land uses, much like other land uses; for this reason, local discretion in siting wireless communication infrastructure was initially unrestricted. As consumer demand for wireless services grew, however, Congress and the courts stepped in to limit local control in certain instances. As a result, the siting of wireless communication infrastructure remains a local land use decision, subject to the limitations of federal law.

PURPOSE

Local governments create special regulations for the siting of cellular transmission facilities in order to mitigate the negative impact that these often-imposing structures can have on the surrounding area. It is a legitimate objective of local land use authority to protect the scenic and aesthetic quality of the community. Regulations designed to carry out that purpose have been sustained in a variety of contexts, including the regulation of cellular facilities.

WHEN

As the demand for cellular transmission services grows, local governments are presented with an increasing number of requests to approve cellular transmission facilities in various locations in the community. In the mid-1990s, many communities discovered that their local land use regulations did not provide a mechanism for balancing the public's need for a complete cellular transmission network with the need to protect neighborhoods and landscapes from the potential negative aesthetic impacts of these facilities. Normally, to resolve this tension, municipal officials create special local regulations for cellular transmission facility siting.

AUTHORITY

Local governments in New York derive their legal authority to regulate the siting of cellular transmission facilities from the state statutes that delegate to them the authority to adopt comprehensive plans and zoning laws. Such laws may be adopted to conserve the value of buildings and to encourage the most appropriate use of land throughout the municipality. This authority includes the power to regulate the height and bulk of buildings.

Local comprehensive plans can identify and provide for the preservation of historic and cultural resources, natural resources, and sensitive environmental areas, including viewsheds and the aesthetic resources of the community. A separate source of authority to regulate aesthetics is found in the Municipal Home Rule Law, which states that a municipality may adopt land use laws for the "protection and enhancement of its physical and visual environment." Municipal Home Rule Law §10(1)(ii)(a)(11).

Local board determinations on cellular carrier applications for variances, site plans, and special permits are actions that require an analysis of the potential adverse environmental impacts of the proposed projects. Included in all such reviews must be whether the approval will have a negative impact on resources of "aesthetic significance" and, if so, what conditions may be imposed on the project's approval to mitigate that impact.

IMPLEMENTATION

Generally, cellular companies desiring to construct cellular transmission facilities must submit an application for a building permit to the local building inspector or department. If the proposed construction does not comply with the zoning law's use or dimensional requirements, the permit must be denied. This denial may be appealed to the zoning board of appeals, which may grant a variance in conformance with state law. A site plan may then have to be submitted and approved before a building permit may be issued for the cellular facilities. Alternatively, local zoning regulations may permit cellular transmission facilities but require cellular companies to apply for site plan approval or a special permit, in which case the applicant must be referred to the appropriate administrative agency for its review.

Mitigation requirements are routinely imposed as reasonable conditions for the granting of a variance or the approval of an application for a site plan or special permit. Local board determinations regarding variances, site plans, and special permits are subject to environmental review under the State Environmental Quality Review Act (SEQRA). This statute requires local agencies to assess the potential environmental impacts of their actions and to disapprove applications that would result in adverse environmental impacts, or to condition their approval upon the implementation of mitigation measures designed to prevent such negative impact. A negative effect on resources of aesthetic importance is considered the type of impact that may be mitigated under SEQRA or may justify the denial of an application.

LIMITATIONS AND CONCERNS

Local boards may not adopt moratoriums on applications for approval of cellular transmission facilities or restrict or deny such applications simply because of significant citizen opposition. All such decisions must be based on facts that are on the record of the proceedings of the board so that they are not unconstitutionally arbitrary or capricious.

Localities must not prohibit the location of cellular transmission facilities within their jurisdiction, but must accommodate them subject to reasonable restrictions. Where cellular facilities are not listed as a permitted use in the zoning law, the denial of a use variance may be vulnerable to attack; if the denial will result in a gap in the cellular service network, a variance may have to be granted under federal telecommunications law.

Local regulation of such facilities may not be based on concerns for human health. Protecting citizens from the health hazards of the radiofrequency emissions from cellular transmission facilities has been prohibited by the Federal Telecommunications Act of 1996.

The Act also requires that localities not discriminate among providers of functionally equivalent services, or fail to respond to applications from wireless carriers within a reasonable period. Federal law also requires that denials of applications must be in writing and must be supported by substantial written evidence found in the record of the proceedings.

Local regulations that establish a preference system for the siting of cellular facilities must be careful not to discriminate against types of properties without giving a valid reason for denying preferences for siting. Where a local law gave preference to siting on town-owned land, the court found no rational basis for preferring town-owned land, in general, over other types of properties on aesthetic grounds.

ILLUSTRATION

The town of Greenburgh's law governing the siting of wireless facilities was the result of a cooperative effort between town residents, local officials, and a cellular telephone company. The town initially instituted a moratorium on approvals of cellular facilities. This created a period that all sides used to negotiate an acceptable approach. The resulting law utilizes a tiered approach, imposing "placement conditions" on the siting of all wireless facilities. Wireless providers are required, first, to attempt to place facilities near major thoroughfares and other specified preferred locations, then to consider other nonresidential areas, and then to look at residential locations. As a last resort, they may locate wireless infrastructure within 350 feet of schools, parks, playgrounds, day-care centers, and health-care facilities. Each step requires proof that the previous option would not be sufficient to provide adequate service.

The law classifies wireless infrastructure as a special permitted use in most cases. It does allow wireless facilities to be sited as-of-right in specified preferred areas, but only if a tower is not needed and if maximum height requirements are satisfied. All antenna towers and monopoles, except when permitted as-of-right, require special permits and are subject to further conditions, including those designed to minimize the negative aesthetic impact on the neighborhood. Additionally, co-location is encouraged by requiring that the carrier prove that a reasonable attempt to locate the antennae on another carrier's tower was unsuccessful owing to enumerated technological, structural, or engineering limitations, or to an inability to secure a lease agreement at a reasonable cost.

The law also provides for periodic review of its provisions by an antenna advisory board, whose members are appointed by the town board. Antenna advisory board members must be "knowledgeable of [FCC] rulings, communications law, and Townwide planning objectives," since their job is to "review ongoing advancements in antenna technology, zoning law compliance with [FCC] rulings, and to offer recommendations to the Town Board regarding subsequent amendments and enforcement."

STATUTES

Village Law §7-700, Town Law §261, and General City Law §20(24) authorize local governments to adopt zoning laws to promote the health, safety, morals, and general welfare of the community. The authority to regulate building height, bulk, lot coverage, and to separate uses into districts is expressly delegated to local governments.

Under Village Law §7-704, Town Law §263, and General City Law §20(24), zoning regulations are to be adopted with reasonable consideration of the character of the zoning district and with a view to conserving the value of buildings and encouraging the most appropriate use of land.

Zoning and land use regulations in New York conform with the locality's comprehensive plan pursuant to Village Law §7-704, Town Law §263, and General City Law §20(25). Local comprehensive plans can identify and provide for the preservation of historic and cultural resources, natural resources, and sensitive environmental areas. Village Law §7-722(4)(d), Town Law §272-a(3)(d), and General City Law §28-a(4)(d).

Home Rule Authority: A separate source of authority to regulate aesthetics is found in Section 10(1)(ii)(a)(11) of the Municipal Home Rule Law, which states that a municipality may adopt land use laws for the "protection and enhancement of its physical and visual environment."

Under the regulations of the Commissioner of the State Department of Environmental Conservation, 6 NYCRR Part 617, local agencies must take a hard look at the potential adverse environmental impact of projects they are asked to review. Included in all such reviews must be whether the action or approval will have a negative impact on resources of "aesthetic significance" and, if so, what conditions may be imposed on the project's approval to mitigate that impact. The project may be denied if mitigation is not deemed effective.

The Telecommunications Act of 1996, Pub. L. No. 104-104, 110 Stat. 56 (1996) (amending Communications Act of 1934, codified at 47 U.S.C. §§151 et seq.), provides for the creation of an efficient nationwide cellular communications system. Section 704 preserves local zoning authority over the placement, construction, and modification of wireless service facilities subject to limitations. That section provides, however, that local governments may not regulate such facilities on the basis of the health effects of radiofrequency emissions, discriminate among providers of functionally equivalent services, or fail to respond to applications from wireless carriers within a reasonable time. Denials of applications must be in writing and must be supported by substantial written evidence found in the record of the proceedings.

CASE DIGEST

The factors normally applicable to the review of a requested variance are not applied in the same way when the entity requesting the variance is a public utility rather than a private property owner. *Consolidated Edison Co. of New York, Inc. v. Hoffman*, 43 N.Y.2d 598, 374 N.E.2d 105, 403 N.Y.S.2d 193 (1978). The court held that the utility, to qualify for a variance, must show that the variance is related to its mandate to render safe and adequate utility service and that the variance requested is reasonably necessary to provide that service to the public. The court noted that "where the intrusion or burden on the community is minimal, the showing required by the utility should be correspondingly reduced."

In 1993, the New York Court of Appeals held that a cellular telephone company is a public utility and that the construction of the antenna tower is a public utility building. *Cellular Telephone Co. v. Rosenburg*, 82 N.Y.2d 364, 624 N.E.2d 990, 604 N.Y.S.2d 895 (1993). The court reversed the zoning board's denial of an application for a use variance to establish a cellular site at

Children's Village in Dobbs Ferry, noting that the standard set forth in *Consolidated Edison* applies to all public utilities. The court found that the utility had made the requisite showing that the installation was necessary to provide cellular service, that it would have a negligible impact on the surrounding neighborhood, and that it would not affect humans, animals, or other organisms. The court held that the erection of the cellular site would enable the plaintiff to remedy gaps in its existing service in the Dobbs Ferry area and that there was no rational basis to support the zoning board's denial of the variance.

The Second Department reversed a planning board's denial of a site plan application to install a cellular communication facility on land owned by a country club. *Cellular Telephone Co. v. Meyer*, 200 A.D.2d 743, 607 N.Y.S.2d 81 (2d Dep't 1994). The court held that the proposed cell site "presented a minimal intrusion into the community," and thus, the planning board's denial was arbitrary and capricious.

In *Cellular Telephone Co. v. Village of Tarrytown*, 209 A.D.2d 57, 624 N.Y.S.2d 170 (2d Dep't 1995), the Second Department held that the enactment of a temporary moratorium on the installation of antennas was invalid since there was no evidence that the well-being of the community was jeopardized. The court held that the village "could not rationally rely upon the speculative and unfounded 'perception' of health risks by some Village residents as a basis to declare a moratorium on the installation of cellular service antennas."

In *Cellular Telephone Co. v. Town-Village of Harrison*, N.Y.L.J., Nov. 30, 1995, at 35 (Sup. Ct. Westchester County Nov. 28, 1995), a town's enactment of a 90-day moratorium on the review of cellular antenna facilities was sustained as a proper exercise of municipal power. The court held that "the moratorium . . . constituted a reasonable measure designed to give the Town a short period of time in which to enact zoning changes to rationally meet the need to address the increasing number of cellular telephone antenna facility applications." This moratorium was adopted not to respond solely to citizen opposition to cellular sites but to develop a rational response in the absence of any provisions in the zoning law to control the siting of cellular facilities.

In *Countryman v. Schmitt*, 176 Misc.2d 736, 673 N.Y.S.2d 521 (Sup. Ct. 1998), the owner of a residential lot sued the town of Rush challenging a town law that established a priority list for the siting of cellular facilities. The law required cellular providers to obtain a special permit, which was more likely to be granted if the facility was located on town property or on fire department properties than in a residential district. The property owner claimed that the town ordinance unconstitutionally denied him the right to sell rights to his property to a cellular tower provider. Although the court refused to find a taking of plaintiff's property, the court did hold that the town ordinance was unconstitutional. While the professed objective of protecting the aesthetic nature of the community is a valid exercise of local police power, the priority list developed by the town "relates solely to the fortuitous circumstances of ownership," not the actual aesthetic impact of the towers. Because the means used to achieve the objective of the ordinance were not rationally related to its objective, to protect the community's aesthetic character, the law was an invalid and arbitrary exercise of the town's zoning power and therefore unconstitutional. Furthermore, the court found the ordinance unconstitutional on equal protection grounds.

The court found that, under the ordinance, there was "preference according to ownership." Like plaintiff's property, much of the town-owned property, eligible for cellular facility development under the local law, was located in residential zones and was, therefore, similarly situated to the plaintiff's property. Under the ordinance, however, the two types of property were treated differently, to the plaintiff's disadvantage. Because the court had already found that a rational basis was lacking, the plaintiff's equal protection claim was successful.

REFERENCE

Laurie Dichiara, *Wireless Communication Facilities: Siting for Sore Eyes, at* http://www.pace.edu/lawschool/landuse/cell.html (last visited Feb. 2, 2001).

C. REGULATION OF ADULT BUSINESSES

DEFINITION

The regulation of adult uses occurs when local governments adopt special land use laws aimed at controlling businesses that provide sexual entertainment or services to their customers. Adult uses include X-rated video shops and bookstores, live or video peep shows, topless or fully nude dancing establishments, combination book/video and "marital aid" stores, non-medical massage parlors, hot oil salons, nude modeling studios, hourly motels, body painting studios, swingers clubs, X-rated movie theaters, escort service clubs, and combinations thereof.

Adult entertainment businesses have thrived in marginal urban centers over the last 25 years. In recent years, these businesses have been moving into higher quality urban areas and into surburban and rural areas. Some adult businesses are characterized by blacked-out windows or large and gaudy signs. These businesses may harbor illegal sex- or drug-related activities, and may attract loiterers and petty criminals. The primary concern of municipal officials is the tendency of adult uses to concentrate. Clustering of adult uses impacts the surrounding neighborhoods in a variety of negative ways.

One approach to regulating adult uses is to require their dispersal throughout non-residential areas in an effort to avoid the deleterious secondary effects of concentration. Dispersal zoning generally requires 250 to 2500 linear feet between adult uses and sensitive uses such as churches, schools, residences, and parks. Local laws often require that adult businesses must be 250 to 2500 linear feet from one another. Another approach—concentration zoning—limits adult uses to relatively small districts where the negative impacts can be better controlled and isolated. Some municipalities use licensing to supplement their zoning controls. Others define adult uses as special uses, limiting them to specific zoning districts and requiring a careful review prior to the issuance of a conditional permit.

PURPOSE

The public purpose justifying adult use zoning is to prevent or contain the increased crime, diminished property values, and blight that can occur when adult businesses operate in a neighborhood. Studies prepared prior to the adoption of local adult use regulations in New York have identified the "secondary effects" of these uses. These include increased sex-related crimes, drug dealing, and petty street crime, a reduction in property values, long-term economic decay, adverse effects on surrounding businesses, and the perception of urban decay.

Hyde Park, New York, prepared a report relying on studies conducted in municipalities across the country and assessing the impacts of adult uses on its rich history and tourist trade. In 1996, following this report, Hyde Park enacted adult use regulations. The purpose of the town's law is

> to preserve the integrity and character of residential neighborhoods and important natural and human resources of the town, to deter the spread of blight and to protect minors from the objectionable characteristics of these adult uses by restricting their proximity to churches, schools, nursery schools, day care centers, educational institutions, parks, historic and scenic resources, civic and cultural facilities and residential areas.

WHEN

Communities are moved to action when they experience or fear the negative secondary effects of adult establishments and sense a need to adopt special regulations to control those effects. New York City adopted an aggressive dispersal zoning law after adult business uses expanded greatly over a 25-year period. Before any adult uses came to Hyde Park, the town adopted a dispersal zoning law. Other communities adopted regulations immediately after the first few adult uses opened for business.

AUTHORITY

The public interest in controlling the secondary effects of adult uses provides the legal, factual, and political justification for their regulation. The U.S. Supreme Court has held that secondary effects studies are the factual backbone supporting the substantial government interest necessary for controlling adult uses through land use regulations. On the basis of these studies, communities use the authority delegated to them by the state to adopt zoning provisions to protect the public safety and welfare "with a view to conserving the value of buildings, and encouraging the most appropriate use of land throughout the municipality."

IMPLEMENTATION

Municipalities can adopt adult use zoning regulations based on impact studies conducted by them or by other jurisdictions that are relevant to their particular circumstances. Courts have held that government regulation of adult uses must be supported by evidence such as that gathered through public hearings, law enforcement memoranda, affidavits from planners and real estate experts, and statistical and empirical evidence. Information collected in secondary effects studies becomes the factual and evidentiary basis justifying restrictions on adult uses.

Adult use laws should not be adopted simply in response to community opposition. The use of empirical and anecdotal evidence has been approved by courts to show the negative impacts of existing adult businesses in communities. The evidence can be provided by business owners and community leaders at public hearings held prior to the law's adoption. Whenever possible, this type of evidence should be supported by factual information such as crime statistics, real estate sales, or rental data.

Regulations should be limited to regulating the time, place, or manner of the location and operation of adult businesses and should avoid constraining the content of any particular type of expression that amounts to constitutionally protected free speech.

If the dispersal approach is chosen and adult uses within proscribed distances from sensitive or other adult uses must be relocated, studies should be conducted to indicate that there are adequate sites and buildings to permit relocation. If relocation is challenged, the court will examine the physical and legal availability of alternative sites, including their accessibility to the general public, the existence of supportive infrastructure, the likelihood of a site's becoming available for relocation, and its suitability for commercial business operation.

Where communities need time to study how best to regulate adult businesses, they are authorized to adopt a moratorium on the issuance of permits to adult businesses. Reasonable progress toward studying the situation and drafting zoning controls should be made following the adoption of a moratorium or before one is extended.

LIMITATIONS AND CONCERNS

Basing Regulation on Moral Objections: References to moral objections to adult uses in local laws may be enough to spark a constitutional challenge. Regulations concerning themselves with the "objectionable" nature of adult businesses or requiring that applicants for adult use permits be of "good moral character" are particularly vulnerable to attack. These factors may not provide sufficient basis for the adoption of police power regulations.

Regulating Obscenity: Laws regulating adult uses, particularly bans on "obscene" adult uses, are vulnerable to attack because the courts have confined obscenity to the "most explicit, thoroughly hardcore materials that lack any redeeming value whatsoever." This does not prevent regulations limiting adult businesses to serving only adults, because laws that prevent the sale of pornographic materials to children are constitutional.

Confiscation of Investments: Some adult use businesses involve significant financial investments that must be respected by regulations requiring their relocation or cessation. Amortization periods that allow the owners of such businesses time to recoup their investments are often found in laws regulating adult uses.

Regulating Forms of Expression: Municipalities must be careful not to aim their prohibitions and restrictions at the content of the expression found in adult business services but to limit their laws to regulating the secondary negative effects of adult use businesses.

Selective Regulation: Laws regulating select types of adult businesses must be careful to avoid violating equal protection guarantees that public regulations must not discriminate against similarly situated properties without justification based in the public interest.

Adequate Standards: When adult use businesses are required to obtain licenses or special use permits, the local legislature must be careful to specify fair standards that must be applied in reviewing and acting on applications. If it appears that the reviewing agency has unguided discretion to deny applications it finds objectionable, the law may violate rules regarding the delegation of legislative authority or guaranteeing that the regulation of such activities not be based on the content of expression or on the moral character of the applicants.

ILLUSTRATIONS

New York City's dispersal zoning has been upheld by both state and federal courts. It regulates any "adult establishment" defined as "a commercial establishment where a substantial portion of the establishment includes an adult bookstore, adult eating or drinking establishment, adult theater, or other adult commercial establishment, or any combination thereof." The law creates four categories of adult uses, depending on whether "specified anatomical areas" or "specified sexual activities" are depicted and whether the business excludes minors by reason of age. These definitions help to distinguish regulated adult uses from other businesses, such as video stores, that may offer adult content only as a small part of their business activity. Standards are provided to help determine whether an adult bookstore devotes a "substantial portion of its stock-in-trade" to regulated adult materials.

The New York City law contains a number of dispersal requirements and anti-clustering provisions. In addition to being barred from all residential districts, both new and existing adult uses are barred from certain manufacturing and commercial districts that also permit residential development. Where adult uses are allowed in manufacturing and commercial districts, they must be located at least 500 feet from a number of "sensitive receptors," defined as churches, schools, residence districts, low-density commercial districts, and manufacturing districts, where new residential development is allowed. Adult establishments must also be located at least 500 linear feet from another adult use. The law does allow for adult uses to remain if a church or school is established within 500 feet after the effective date of its adoption.

Other provisions limit one adult establishment per zoning lot and place a 10,000-square-foot limit on usable floor area and cellar space. The law imposes special restrictions on accessory business signs which partially supersede otherwise applicable commercial sign provisions. Adult establishment accessory business signs must not exceed 150 square feet per establishment, and may have no more than 50 square feet of illuminated non-flashing signage.

Adult establishments that violate the dispersal requirements become nonconforming uses and are subject to an amortization period of one year. The Board of Standards and Appeals (the City's zoning board of appeals) may grant limited extensions beyond the one-year period where the applicant has made substantial financial expenditures, has not recovered substantially all of those expenditures related to the nonconformity, and where the extension period is the minimum period sufficient for the applicant to recover substantially all of those expenditures.

The law adopted by the town of Islip does not define adult businesses using terms such as "specified anatomical areas" or "specified sexual activities" but, rather, defines adult businesses as those that exclude young patrons by reason of their age. The Islip law allows adult uses that existed prior to its adoption to be amortized over periods ranging from one and a half to five and a half years, based on the amount expended in establishing the business.

Hyde Park, like other municipalities adopting dispersal zoning, provides limited exceptions to its restrictions. The town zoning board of appeals may waive the dispersal provisions if:

♦ The proposed use will not be contrary to the public interest or injurious to nearby properties.
♦ An adult use will not be contrary to any program of neighborhood conservation or improvement in either a residential or nonresidential neighborhood.
♦ 51% or more of the people residing, owning, or operating a business within the anti-concentration areas sign a petition stating they have no objection to an adult use in a proposed location.

The city of Buffalo incorporates operational requirements. Adult businesses that offer private viewing of "movies, tapes, slides, pictures or live performances of any kind," for example, must allow the vestibule or booth to be totally unobstructed and accessible from the aisle side, while insuring that the remaining walls are free of openings. A lighting minimum of ten foot candles is also required.

The village of Nyack's law establishes these standards as the conditions for obtaining a special permit:

♦ No more than one adult use on a lot.
♦ No adult uses in a residential building.
♦ No residences in a building in which an adult use is established.
♦ A 500-foot buffer between the lot lines of adult businesses.
♦ A 200-foot buffer between the lot lines of an adult use and any zoning district that permits residential use.
♦ A 200-foot buffer between the lot lines of an adult use and any "church, community center, funeral home, school, day-care center, hospital, alcoholism center or drug treatment center, counseling or psychiatric treatment facility or public park."

CONSTITUTIONAL AND STATUTORY CITATIONS

The New York State Constitution states that "[e]very citizen may freely speak, write and publish his sentiments on all subjects, being responsible for the abuse of that right, and no law shall be passed to restrain or abridge the liberty of speech or of the press." Article I, §8.

The authority of local governments to adopt zoning provisions to protect the public safety and welfare "with a view to conserving the value of buildings and encouraging the most appropriate use of land throughout [the] municipality" is found in Village Law §7-704, Town Law §263, and General City Law §§20(24) and (25).

CASE DIGEST

Certain types of conduct relevant to adult uses are not protected by the First Amendment of the U.S. Constitution. For example, recreational dancing, because it lacks a communicative element between audience and performer, is not a protected form of speech when performed for exercise or personal pleasure. *Doran v. Salem Inn, Inc.*, 422 U.S. 922 (1975). The Court found that customary "barroom" types of nude dancing may involve the "barest minimum" First Amendment protection. *See also Kent's Lounge, Inc. v. City of New York*, 104 A.D.2d 397, 478 N.Y.S.2d 928 (2d Dep't 1984) (holding that "recreational dancing is not a form of speech protected by the First Amendment").

The first U.S. Supreme Court case to address the tension between the local regulation of adult uses and the First Amendment was *Young v. American Mini Theaters*, 427 U.S. 50 (1976). The Court held that adult uses may be identified by their content and regulated by time, place, and manner restrictions where there was no purposeful suppression of speech. The Court countered the adult use business owners' argument that the regulations created a prior restraint on free expression by holding that the locational requirements were valid time, place, and manner restrictions. The Court held that, although total suppression will not be tolerated, a "line may be drawn on the basis of content without violating the government's paramount obligation of neutrality." The Court also concluded that drawing such a line was justified by the community's interest in ameliorating negative secondary effects to preserve neighborhood character. The Court held that, while the constitutional interest in protecting messages communicated by adult books and films is of a "wholly different, and lesser, magnitude than the interest in untrammeled political debate," erotic messages conveyed by adult books and films may not be totally suppressed. *See also Nakatomi Investments, Inc. v. Schenectady*, 949 F. Supp. 988 (N.D.N.Y. 1997) (holding that banning topless dancing based on a "distasteful erotic message" was unconstitutional).

The Court upheld a local zoning law requiring adult motion picture theaters to locate 1,000 feet from any residential zone, family dwelling, church, park, or school in *Renton v. Playtime Theatres, Inc.*, 475 U.S. 41 (1986). Following *American Mini Theaters*, the *Renton* Court allowed the adult use regulation to impose time, place and manner restrictions. The Court reinforced *American Mini Theaters'* holding that "preserv[ing] the quality of urban life" is a substantial government interest—an interest that may be justified by factual studies documenting the negative secondary effects associated with adult businesses. Significantly, this case held that local governments may rely on studies conducted by other cities describing the negative secondary effects of adult uses as long as the evidence the city relies upon is reasonably believed to be relevant to the problem that the city addresses. The court found further that the law was narrowly tailored to affect only the group of uses producing the unwanted secondary effects. It also held that the availability of 5% of the entire land area of the town for relocation was reasonable and that adult-business owners must "fend for themselves in the real estate market" because economic impact is not a viable First Amendment argument.

In *People ex rel. Arcara v. Cloud Books, Inc.*, 68 N.Y.2d 553, 503 N.E.2d 492, 510 N.Y.S.2d 844 (1986), the Court of Appeals declared that "New York has a long history and tradition of fostering freedom of expression, often tolerating and supporting works which in other states would be found offensive to the community." This case and subsequent cases make it clear that New York uses a higher standard to protect expression in the arts than that bestowed by the federal constitution.

The case of *Town of Islip v. Caviglia*, 73 N.Y.2d 544, 540 N.E.2d 215, 542 N.Y.S.2d 139 (1989), reviewed the town of Islip's adult use law, which required a 500-foot buffer zone between adult uses and residentially-zoned uses, schools, churches and other places of religious worship, parks, playgrounds, and playing fields. The law also required a one-half-mile distance between adult uses. Using the test articulated in *Renton*, the Court of Appeals upheld the law as a valid time, place, and manner restriction.

In *Barnes v. Glen Theater, Inc.*, 501 U.S. 560 (1991) the Court held nude dancing to be a protected form of free expression. The court has repeatedly held that, like adult books and films, topless and nude dancing are types of expression that must be afforded at least a minimum of First Amendment protection.

The Court of Appeals upheld New York City's extensive dispersal zoning law in *Stringfellow's v. City of New York*, 91 N.Y.2d 382, 694 N.E.2d 407, 671 N.Y.S.2d 406 (1998). The court's primary concern under state constitutional analysis was whether the law struck the proper balance between "community needs and free expression." The court noted that a purposeful attempt at controlling the expressive content of adult businesses would fail constitutional scrutiny. The lower court had concluded both that the law was "justified by concerns unrelated to speech" and that it was "no broader than needed to achieve its purpose" as required under the state constitution. In New York, a municipality may have a far stronger case if it prepares independent studies directly relating to the secondary effects of adult uses. The court noted that "anecdotal evidence and reported experience can be as telling as statistical data and can serve as a legitimate basis for finding negative secondary effects particularly where, as here, the non-empirical information is extensive and indicative of a clear relationship between adult uses and urban decay." The court found New York City's law to be content-neutral because its predominant purpose was to remove the negative secondary effects caused by adult uses; it was not a "purposeful attempt to regulate speech."

In 1999, the Appellate Division decided another case between Stringfellow's and the City of New York. *City of New York v. Stringfellow's of New York, Ltd.*, 253 A.D.2d 110, 684 N.Y.S.2d 544 (1st Dep't 1999). The court asked whether an "adult eating and drinking establishment" could remove itself "from restrictive zoning regulations by the simple expedient of admitting previously banned minors when accompanied by a parent or guardian." In examining the intent of the city's zoning resolution, the court held that there was no question that New York City Zoning Resolution §12-10(b) intended to prohibit eating or drinking establishments offering adult entertainment in residential districts. Even when minors are admitted to a place of entertainment that customarily permits "live performances which are characterized by an emphasis on 'specified anatomical areas,'" the establishment is still primarily an adult establishment.

In *801 Conklin Street Ltd. v. Town of Babylon*, 38 F. Supp. 2d 228 (E.D.N.Y. 1999), the plaintiff attacked the town of Babylon's effort to regulate the spread of adult businesses by requiring a special permit instead of limiting them to adult business zones. The federal district court held that the town's approach violated the First Amendment. The court noted that "a permit scheme qualifies as a prior restraint (on the constitutionally protected freedom of expression) because it essentially requires the permittee to obtain the government's permission or approval" prior to engaging in an act of protected speech. Babylon's special use permit provision, therefore, left open the possibility of content-based discrimination by the town board. The court held that the "open-ended nebulous requirements, which clearly bestow unlimited discretion to the Town Board" were heightened by an additional provision that allowed the board to "impose any additional requirement to assure that standards . . . will be met." Once an activity is constitutionally protected, a municipality may not discriminate in its zoning regulations based on the content of such expression.

REFERENCE

Steve McMillen, *Adult Uses and the First Amendment; Zoning and Non-Zoning Controls on the Use of Land for Adult Businesses, at* http://www.pace.edu/lawschool/landuse/adult.html (last visited Feb. 2, 2001).

D. GROUP HOMES, DISABILITIES, AND ZONING

DEFINITION

Group homes include residences for a variety of special population groups in need of supervised living facilities. Individuals residing in group homes may be mentally or physically disabled, recovering substance abusers, teenaged mothers, or victims of domestic violence. Able-bodied elderly persons, college students, young professionals, and other people not related by blood, marriage, or adoption also form groups that may wish to live together. When such groups of unrelated persons seek housing in a single-family home, the question arises as to whether they are a "family" entitled to live in a residential unit in a single-family zoning district.

Some local governments have prevented such groups from living in single-family districts by narrowly defining the "family" permitted to live in a single-family home. A typical provision defines a family as comprising any number of persons related by blood, marriage, adoption, or a fixed number of persons not so related. These definitions have raised questions about whether treating "traditional" families differently from "nontraditional" families is legal, particularly where the nontraditional group functions like a traditional household.

Local zoning laws may accommodate residential facilities for nontraditional groups of people by allowing them upon the issuance of a special permit. In some communities, such groups are effectively excluded because of a restrictive definition of family and the absence of a special use provision.

PURPOSE

There are many legitimate purposes for limiting the number of individuals who may occupy single-family homes. These purposes may include controlling the municipal services that may be needed, limiting congestion and overcrowding, and preventing noise, traffic, and parking problems. In addition, some local governments have limited the number of nontraditional household members permitted in single-family zoning districts to preserve "family, youth or property values."

These municipal purposes may conflict with the overriding legal purposes of the state constitution or statutes adopted by the state legislature. For example, one purpose of the due process clause in the state constitution is to insure that zoning provisions are designed to accomplish legitimate public purposes and that the means chosen are rationally related to the achievement of those purposes. The equal protection clause of the U.S. Constitution insures that regulations treating groups of people differently are justified by legitimate public objectives. Some legal definitions of family for zoning purposes have been invalidated for violating these constitutional norms.

In New York State, the Padavan Act limits the ability of municipalities to define who constitutes a family for zoning purposes. The Act aims to promote and encourage the placement of mentally disabled individuals in community settings to provide the least restrictive environment consistent with the needs of such individuals. This law allows mentally disabled individuals to live in single-family homes in order to enable them to be as fully integrated and productive as possible. Local zoning provisions that frustrate the purpose of the Padavan Act are seldom upheld.

The federal Fair Housing Act and Amendments prohibits housing discrimination on the basis of color, race, religion, national origin, gender, or handicap, including physical or mental impairment. The federal Americans with Disabilities Act implements a comprehensive approach to eliminating discrimination against the disabled. Local zoning provisions that violate these protections risk invalidation.

WHEN

Local zoning laws generally include a definition of the type of family permitted to occupy a residence in a single-family zoning district. They also set forth types of residential facilities that are allowed by special permit in various zoning districts. When local zoning boards of appeal are presented with an application for a residential facility not permitted by the use provisions of the law, the board must determine whether the applicant meets state law requirements for the issuance of a use variance.

AUTHORITY

Local governments in New York derive from the state legislature their legal authority to define the family that may reside in single-family homes and the types of residential facilities permitted by zoning. Under this delegated authority, local laws may be adopted to prevent the overcrowding of the land, to conserve the value of buildings, and to encourage the most appropriate use of land throughout the municipality.

Under the due process clause of the New York Constitution, local zoning regulations may not restrict occupancy of single-family homes to four or fewer "unrelated individuals" living and cooking together as a single housekeeping unit. The New York Court of Appeals has ruled that "restricting occupancy of single-family housing based generally on the biological or legal relationships between its inhabitants bears no reasonable relationship to the goals of reducing parking and traffic problems, controlling population density and preventing noise and disturbance."

A state statute, known as the Padavan Act, provides that community residences and family-care homes for the mentally disabled, licensed by the state, are deemed family units for the purposes of local land use regulation. The state legislature preempted the matter by declaring that groups of mentally disabled persons living in licensed facilities are "families" for the purpose of local zoning and may live in "single-family" homes. Unless a municipality can find an alternative site or provide clear and convincing evidence that the location of a licensed group home under the Padavan Act will alter the character of the area or that the area is saturated with group homes, it must allow the proposed group home to exist.

Local authority to adopt zoning laws may be limited by the protections afforded disabled individuals under the federal Fair Housing Act and Amendments and the Americans with Disabilities Act.

IMPLEMENTATION

The local legislature adopts and amends local zoning laws subject to the preemption of its authority by state law and the protections afforded individuals by state and federal law.

The Padavan Act applies to residences licensed by the New York State Office of Mental Health or the Office of Mental Retardation and Developmental Disabilities that provide housing for up to 14 individuals. Residences covered by the Padavan Act include those provided under the family-care program, which involve the provision of a home to the mentally ill by private individuals in their homes, and under the community residence program, where project sponsors acquire or construct homes for a number of mentally disabled individuals.

Under the Padavan Act, the project sponsor of the community residence program must notify the chief executive officer of the community of its intent to locate a residential facility in a particular home. The sponsor must identify the proposed site, the type of community residence, and the anticipated number of residents. The municipality has 40 days to analyze the proposal, approve or reject the site, or suggest one or more suitable sites. The municipality may object to the establishment of a facility because it would result in over-concentration of community residential facilities for the mentally disabled in the municipality or in the area in proximity to the site.

If a municipality claims over-concentration, the question is whether the nature and character of the area in which the facility is to be based would be substantially altered as a result of establishment of the facility. Over-concentration is determined by identifying the number of similar facilities located in proximity to the area of the proposed facility.

LIMITATIONS AND CONCERNS

New York cases limit, but do not prevent, localities from imposing requirements on the occupancy of single-family homes. Drafting and enforcement problems exist, but the courts' decisions allow limitations clearly directed at achieving stability and limiting congestion in single-family neighborhoods by regulations affecting all households equally. When the local law discriminates against a group of persons that operates like a traditional family, however, it may violate basic due process guarantees.

Localities must be careful not to regulate residential facilities where state law has preempted the subject matter. Local regulation of residential facilities provided under some sections of the Social Service Law, the County Law, and the Padavan Act has been preempted and is beyond the reach of local governments. State laws supporting shelters for foster care and substance abusers have been found not to preempt local regulation. If, however, the effect of local zoning is to block the provision of state licensed and supported shelters within the community, such zoning is vulnerable to attack.

Local zoning laws that fail to accommodate group homes for persons deemed to be disabled under federal law, including the mentally disabled, may be invalid under the federal Fair Housing Act and Amendments or the Americans with Disabilities Act. Some federal courts have held that local zoning requirements are not exempt from the application of these statutes. The regulations of the Department of Justice under the Americans with Disabilities Act require local governments to "make reasonable modifications in policies . . . to avoid discrimination on the basis of disability" unless it can be shown that such modifications would fundamentally alter the nature of the local service, program, or activity.

These federal and state laws make it very difficult for local governments to adopt special zoning provisions that single out housing for disabled individuals for special regulation or prohibitions. Some local zoning laws, for example, require residential facilities for special population groups to be located a certain number of linear feet from one another, or specify that special permits for such facilities, not be awarded if a certain number of them exist in a defined area. At a minimum, such local regulations should be justified by a careful showing that they promote legitimate public purposes and that the special requirements are rationally related to accomplishing these purposes. Mandatory guidelines or permit conditions regarding housing for the disabled are particularly susceptible to challenge under recently adopted federal statutes.

ILLUSTRATIONS

Definition of Family: The Zoning Code of the City of Mount Vernon, New York, defines family as "[o]ne or more persons having a common domestic bond who live together in one dwelling unit as a traditional family or its functional equivalent, headed by one or more resident persons who have the authority over the care, functioning or management of their common household." A "dwelling unit" is defined as "[a] building or portion thereof providing complete housekeeping facilities for one family, including independent cooking, sanitary and sleeping facilities." Single-family dwellings are a permitted principal use in all residential zoning districts. If the group occupying a single-family home is the functional equivalent of a traditional family, it will be allowed as a principal permitted use in every residential zoning district.

In contrast, the town of Ossining's Zoning Code defines family as "[o]ne or more persons occupying a dwelling unit as a single nonprofit housekeeping unit. More than five persons not related by blood marriage or adoption, shall not be considered to constitute a family." The vast majority of the town's zoning districts are one-family residential districts with permitted uses restricted to "[o]ne-family detached dwellings, not to exceed one dwelling on each lot." The code definition of "dwelling unit" is "[a] building, or entirely self-contained portion thereof, containing complete housekeeping facilities for only one family." A group home consisting of six unrelated individuals would effectively be excluded as a permitted use.

Special Permit: The city of Mount Vernon permits "domiciliary care facilities" as a special permitted use in most residential zoning districts. A "domiciliary care facility" is defined in the zoning law as "[a] private proprietary nursing home, convalescent home, or home for adults, a home for the aged, a group residence or other residential care facility for adults as defined in the New York Social Services Law or regulations promulgated thereunder, and any similar facilities operated under the supervision of federal departments and agencies." A project sponsor proposing a group home not meeting the zoning law's "traditional family standard" may apply for a special permit.

The Mount Vernon code's general conditions for approving special permits include a showing that the structure and intensity of use are such that the proposed use will be in harmony with the appropriate and orderly development of the area where it is located; that the development of the permitted use will not hinder or discourage the appropriate development and use of adjacent land and buildings; and that operations in connection with the specially permitted use will not be more objectionable to nearby properties by reason of noise, traffic, fumes, vibration, or other such characteristics than would be the operations of permitted uses not requiring a special permit.

The zoning law of the town of Ossining allows, by special permit, "rest homes or sanitaria for general medical care and treatment of the mentally ill, but excluding facilities for the permanent confinement of the mentally ill, drug addicts, and chronic alcoholics."

Use Variances: Where a proposed group home residence is excluded by the definition of family and not allowed by special permit, its sponsor must apply to the local zoning board of appeals for a variance from the use provisions of the zoning law. This requires the sponsor to demonstrate to the zoning board of appeals that:

♦ it cannot realize a reasonable return under any use permitted by the law;
♦ the hardship suffered by the sponsor is unique and not a general condition applying to much of the district;
♦ The project will not alter the essential character of the neighborhood; and
♦ the hardship has not been self-created.

STATUTES

The authority of local governments to adopt zoning provisions to promote health and general welfare and to prevent the overcrowding of land, "with a view to conserving the value of buildings and encouraging the most appropriate use of land throughout [the] municipality," is found in Village Law §7-704, Town Law §263, and General City Law §§20(24) and (25).

Section 41.34 of the Mental Hygiene Law, known as the Padavan Act, defines a group of individuals ranging from four to 14 individuals as a single family for local zoning purposes if their home is licensed by the New York State Office of Mental Health or Office of Mental Retardation and Developmental Disabilities. The law requires notice to the affected community, and subjects such homes to certain dispersal guidelines to avoid saturation in any particular neighborhood.

42 U. S.C. §3604 [the federal Fair Housing Act and Amendments] states that it is unlawful "to discriminate in the sale or rental, or to otherwise make unavailable or deny a dwelling to any buyer or renter because of a handicap." This provision protects a handicapped potential resident of a group home and any person associated with that resident. This section also requires local governments to "make reasonable accommodation in rules, policies, practices or services, when accommodations may be necessary to afford such [handicapped] persons equal opportunity to use and enjoy a dwelling."

42 U.S.C. §12132 [the American with Disabilities Act] prohibits discrimination against the disabled by public entities including local government. "Subject to the provisions of this subchapter, no qualified individual with a disability shall, by reason of such a disability, be excluded from participation in or be denied the benefits of the services, programs, or activities of a public entity, or be subjected to discrimination by any such entity."

CASE DIGEST

In *City of White Plains v. Ferraioli*, 34 N.Y.2d 300, 313 N.E.2d 756, 357 N.Y.S.2d 449

(1974), the New York Court of Appeals held that a zoning law requiring a "family" to consist of genetically or legally related individuals was too restrictive. The White Plains zoning law defined family as "one or more persons limited to the spouse, parents, grandparents, grandchildren, sons, daughters, brothers or sisters of the owner or the tenant or of the owner's spouse or tenant's spouse living together as a single housekeeping unit with kitchen facilities." The court held that the Ferraioli family, consisting of an adult couple, their two children, and 10 foster children, was the functional equivalent of a family and was permitted to occupy a single-family home despite the city's family definition.

In 1974, the U.S. Supreme Court upheld a village zoning provision defining family as any number of related persons, but only two unrelated persons, living and cooking together, for the purpose of defining who may occupy single-family housing in the village. In *Village of Belle Terre v. Boraas*, 416 U.S. 1 (1974), the Court held that "a quiet place where yards are wide, people few, and motor vehicles restricted are legitimate guidelines in a land-use project addressed to family needs." The Court wrote that the police power "is not confined to the elimination of filth, stench, and unhealthy places." It held that the local authority to zone "is ample to lay out zones where family values, youth values, and the blessings of quiet seclusion and clean air make . . . a sanctuary for people."

The Court of Appeals has held that operation of an unsecured detention home established pursuant to County Law §218-a was exempt from local zoning regulation. *People v. St. Agatha Home for Children*, 47 N.Y.2d 46, 389 N.E.2d 1098, 416 N.Y.S.2d 577 (1979). The Town of Pound Ridge charged a private child-care organization, licensed by the county, with violating the provisions of its single-family zoning district. The court held that Westchester County was authorized and required to provide non-secure detention facilities pursuant to the County Law §218-a. Thus, the local zoning laws could not overrule the county's decision to establish the privately operated children's home.

The state laws regulating residential facilities for substance abusers, in contrast to the Padavan Act and County Law §218-a, have not been held to preempt local zoning regulation. In *Incorporated Village of Nyack v. Daytop Village, Inc.*, 78 N.Y.2d 500, 583 N.E.2d 928, 577 N.Y.S.2d 215 (1991), the Court of Appeals found that Article 19 of the Mental Hygiene Law represented "a sweeping effort to address the . . . problems that have flowed from the scourge of substance abuse in this State." Nevertheless, it held that this does not lead "to the conclusion that the State's commitment to fighting substance abuse preempts all local laws that may have an impact, however tangential, upon the siting of substance abuse facilities." The court distinguished Article 19 from Padavan by stating that Padavan expressly withdrew the zoning authority of local government, and further found that there was no implied preemption evident from the wording of Article 19, its legislative intent, or promulgated regulations. However, the court left open the possibility that local zoning regulations that effectively "block the placement of substance [abuse] facilities within its borders" might warrant a finding of preemption.

Courts have also been reluctant to find that the state has preempted local zoning regulations pertaining to the siting of group homes for foster care. In *Group House of Port Washington, Inc.*

v. Board of Zoning and Appeals, 45 N.Y.2d 266, 380 N.E.2d 207, 408 N.Y.S.2d 377 (1978), the Court of Appeals held that a town may not use its zoning regulation's definition of family to exclude a small group home for foster care of children, but carefully narrowed its holding by stating that "[w]e need not, and accordingly we do not reach the broader question whether the State has pre-empted this area to the extent that a municipality may not forbid the establishment of a 'group home' authorized under State law." *But see People v. Town of Clarkstown*, 160 A.D.2d 17, 559 N.Y.S.2d 736 (2d Dep't 1990) (holding that provisions of a town zoning law regulating family day-care homes were preempted by the Social Services Law).

In *McMinn v. Town of Oyster Bay*, 66 N.Y.2d 544, 488 N.E.2d 1240, 498 N.Y.S.2d 128 (1985), the Court of Appeals invalidated a zoning law that interpreted family as "any number of persons related by blood, marriage, or legal adoption, living and cooking on the premises together as a single, non-profit housekeeping unit" or "any two (2) persons not related by blood, marriage or legal adoption, living and cooking on the premises together as a single, nonprofit housekeeping unit, both of whom are sixty-two (62) years of age or over, and residing on the premises." According to the court, "Manifestly, restricting occupancy of single-family housing based on the biological or legal relationships between its inhabitants bears no reasonable relationship to the goals of reducing parking and traffic problems, controlling population density, and preventing noise and disturbance." These legitimate goals, including the goal of preserving the character of a single-family zone cannot be achieved through such a narrow definition of family.

In *Children's Village v. Holbrook*, 171 A.D.2d 298, 576 N.Y.S.2d 405 (3d Dep't 1991), the court held that the definition of family included in a town zoning law was facially invalid under the state due process clause, notwithstanding the fact that the same zoning law did include a provision allowing group homes in a single-family zoning district by special permit. The Town of Clarkstown's zoning law defined family as "any number of individuals related by blood, marriage or adoption [or not more than five individuals who are not so related], living together as a single housekeeping unit." The conditions for a special permit did not distinguish between family style group homes and institutional group homes. According to the court, "without a constitutionally valid definition of family in the zoning law, its specific regulation of group homes is also objectionable in that it may be applied to 'exclude [from the class of occupancies not requiring a special permit] households that due process requires be included.'"

In 1994, the Second Department declared valid a zoning provision that included a rebuttable presumption that four or more unrelated persons living in a single dwelling did not constitute the functional equivalent of a traditional family. *Unification Theological Seminary v. City of Poughkeepsie*, 201 A.D.2d 484, 607 N.Y.S.2d 383 (2d Dep't 1994). The city's zoning law provided "broad criteria" to rebut the presumption "including whether the group shares the entire house, lives and cooks together as a single housekeeping unit, shares expenses for food, rent, utilities, or other household expenses, and is permanent and stable." The court held that there was a fair opportunity for a party to show that a proposed group home was indeed a functional equivalent of a single family; thus there was no violation of the state constitution's due process clause.

In *Jennings v. New York State Office of Mental Health*, 90 N.Y.2d 227, 682 N.E.2d 953, 660 N.Y.S.2d 352 (1997), the Court of Appeals interpreted the facility siting criteria of the Padavan Act. A community residence to be licensed by the New York State Office of Mental Health was proposed to be sited in an Albany neighborhood. The mayor objected, and a hearing was held. The court noted that "while over concentration is certainly relevant, whether the nature and character of an area will be substantially altered by the establishment of the proposed facility is the dispositive inquiry."

In 1997, the Second Circuit held that the Americans with Disabilities Act applies to local zoning decisions. *Innovative Health Systems, Inc. v. City of White Plains*, 931 F. Supp. 222 (S.D.N.Y. 1996), *aff'd,* 117 F.3d 37 (2d Cir. 1997). The plaintiff was a licensed provider of out-patient treatment services for alcoholics and substance abusers. It leased the first floor of an apartment building in the city's downtown area and city officials initially ruled that the plaintiff's use was a permitted office use under the zoning regulations. After a series of well-attended public hearings, the zoning board interpreted the proposed use as a clinic or "hospital or sanitoria" use, an impermissible use in the zoning district. There was evidence that the city had permitted office use in the district by psychiatrists and social workers who offered outpatient services comparable to the plaintiff's. The district court concluded that "the evidence supports plaintiff's claim that defendants bowed to political pressure." In affirming the district court injunction against the city, the Second Circuit held that the Americans with Disabilities Act clearly encompasses zoning decisions by the city "because making such decisions is a normal function of a government entity." Furthermore, consonant with the District Court's approach, the Second Circuit found that the Act clearly encompasses "all discrimination by a public entity, regardless of the context."

REFERENCE

Anna L. Georgiou, *Regulating Group Homes–A New York Model, at* http://www.pace.edu/lawschool/landuse/grphme.html (last visited Feb. 2, 2001).

E. RELIGION AND ZONING

DEFINITION

The regulation of land uses proposed by religious institutions is subject to greater constraints than the regulation of secular land uses. New York courts have declared that religious uses of real property promote the public welfare and are inherently beneficial to the public. Municipalities must make serious efforts to accommodate the development of houses of worship and related, or accessory, religious uses. Religious uses of property include bible studies, homeless shelters, day-care centers, community service centers, soup kitchens, and other activities related to the spiritual calling of a congregation when those activities are accessory to a house of worship located on the property.

PURPOSE

The purpose of judicial rules restricting the authority of local governments to limit religious land uses is to encourage the beneficial purposes served by churches, synagogues, and other houses of worship and their related activities. Religious land uses advance the public interest in the same way that police power regulations, such as zoning provisions, are intended to do. Further, the First Amendment to the United States Constitution, applicable to the states and local governments through the Fourteenth Amendment, protects the freedom of religious expression. One New York court characterized the matter in this way:

> Human experience teaches us that public officials, when faced with pressure to bar church uses by those residing in a residential neighborhood, tend to avoid any appearance of an anti-religious stance and temper their decision by carefully couching their grounds for refusal to permit such a use in terms of traffic dangers, fire hazards and noise and disturbance, rather than on such crasser grounds as lessening of property values or loss of open space or entry of strangers into the neighborhood or undue crowding of the area. Under such circumstances, it is necessary to most carefully scrutinize the reasons advanced for a denial to insure that they are real and not merely pretexts used to preclude the exercise of constitutionally protected privileges.

WHEN

The issue of how a local government regulates religious land uses arises when the locality adopts or amends its zoning law in ways that limit and control those uses. The issue also arises when a religious institution proposes a religious land use by applying to a local land use approval agency for a special use permit, subdivision or site plan approval, variance, or other permission to build. Often such proposals give rise to objections from neighbors who fear that the religious institution and the uses it will bring to the area will diminish the quality of life in the neighborhood and their property values.

AUTHORITY

The authority of local governments to regulate land uses is based on their police power to regulate in the interest of public health, safety, morals, and the general welfare. Since religious land uses have been held by the courts specifically to promote these interests, local laws or land use decisions that exclude or severely limit religious uses may not constitute a valid exercise of the police power authority of local governments. Land use regulations that are aimed directly at activities that constitute the exercise of religious beliefs are particularly suspect because of the constitutional protection afforded religious expression.

IMPLEMENTATION

Under most local zoning laws, religious land uses are allowed in residential and other compatible zoning districts under a special use permit that may be issued by the planning board or zoning board of appeals. This amounts to a declaration by the local legislature that religious land uses are in harmony with the other uses allowed in these districts but that reasonable conditions may need to be imposed on the proposed use to avoid particular negative impacts on the neighborhood. These conditions must be reasonable and calculated to protect legitimate interests and may not be aimed at preventing or obstructing the exercise of religious expression.

Proposed religious development projects may be required to obtain subdivision or site plan approval and may be subject to other land use controls such as sign laws and landmark protections. Occasionally, religious institutions apply for area variances allowing them relief from the dimensional requirements of zoning. Here, too, any conditions imposed on religious land uses must be clearly reasonable and carefully calculated to promote legitimate interests.

When laws are adopted that regulate religious land uses, the legitimate community interests that are to be protected should be identified and explained in the law. A law that does not specify the objectives for its enactment, or the standards to be applied by the reviewing body, may result in decisions that are invalidated by the judiciary as being arbitrary and capricious.

The Adoption of the Zoning Law: Municipalities may not totally exclude places of worship from the community because such an act could not be justified as achieving legitimate public interests.

The Application of Subdivision and Site Plan Regulations: The denial of a religious institution's application based on traffic, safety, sewerage, and property values is not permissible when there is evidence that the religious use can be accommodated while mitigating the adverse effects on the community.

Issuance of Variances: Greater flexibility is required of a zoning board of appeals in reviewing an application for an area variance submitted by a religious institution than by a secular applicant. The board must make every effort to accommodate the proposed use by imposing reasonable conditions instead of denying the application. If the zoning law totally excludes religious land uses, an aggrieved religious group would be likely to attack the law as facially exclusionary rather than to seek a use variance.

Landmark and Historic District Regulations: These land use controls are applicable to proposed religious development projects that are required to obtain certificates of appropriateness prior to any activity that will alter the landmark or historic nature of an existing structure. Where the religious institution's proposed project is for secular purposes unrelated to the religious activities of the institution–such as the construction of private offices or residences – it is afforded little additional deference. Landmark and historic district controls are adopted for legitimate public purposes and are neutral with respect to their impact on the free exercise of religion.

Sign Laws: The rejection of a church's proposal to construct a sign was upheld because it was a reasonable restriction on the religious use and was directly related to the valid community interest in preserving its appearance.

Accessory Uses: Uses of property that are customarily and incidentally associated with a house of worship on the same property are also permitted under most zoning laws. This includes the use of space as a homeless shelter, day-care center, food kitchen, sports field, playground, or retreat center. Most of these activities are associated either with worship services, such as Sunday school, or with the religious understanding that such activities are relevant to the spiritual life of the institution's members.

Principal Uses: The flexibility of interpretation applied to accessory religious uses does not necessarily extend to principal uses. A principal use of land such as the creation of a center to study the Holocaust was found not to be a religious use under a local zoning law. It was held that affiliation with or supervision by religious organizations does not, per se, transform institutions to religious ones.

ILLUSTRATIONS

Local governments in New York tend to permit religious land uses by defining the term "place of worship" and allowing it and its accessory uses as a matter of right or as a specially permitted use in certain zoning districts.

Definitions: In the definitions section of its zoning law, the town of Milan defines a place of worship as: "A building or structure which, by design and construction, is primarily intended for religious services or instruction, including social and administrative rooms accessory thereto." Town of Milan Zoning Code, §200-5 (1996). The town of Red Hook defines a place of religious worship in this way: "Any building, together with its accessory buildings and uses, where persons regularly assemble for religious worship and/or related education, social, cultural and fundraising activities, and which building is maintained and controlled by a recognized religious body organized to sustain public worship." Town of Red Hook Zoning Code, §143-4 (1993).

As-of-Right Uses: The zoning law of the town of Fishkill provides that in all residential districts, the Restricted Business District, the Planned Business District and the General Business District, "[p]laces of worship, including parish houses and religious schools" are permitted as-of-right. Town of Fishkill Zoning Code, §150 (Table I) (1997). In the town of Milan, the zoning law allows places of religious worship to exist as-of-right in all residential and agricultural districts, the Hamlet District, and the Highway Business District. Town of Milan Zoning Code, §200 (Table A) (1996). In New Rochelle, in most residential districts, the following are permitted as-of-right: "churches and other places of worship, including exterior bulletin boards not exceeding six (6) square feet in area; parish houses and Sunday school buildings; and nonresidential uses on church property that are endorsed by the governing body of churches or other houses of worship, are not primarily commercial in nature and are traditional religious uses or celebrations or which have the purpose of providing charitable, educational, cultural, or civic benefits provided that the same comply with the relevant provisions of title 9 of the New York State Code of Rules and Regulations." City of New Rochelle Zoning Code, §331-16 (1996).

Special Permit Uses: In the village of Brewster, within all residential districts, the Professional and Office district, and the Neighborhood Business District, "institutional uses, including churches/places of worship, schools, libraries, nursing homes, alternative care nursery schools, and day-care facilities" are allowed by special permit. Village of Brewster Zoning Code,

§170-6(C)(2) (1991). In the town of Red Hook, in all residential districts, the Hamlet District and the Institutional District, "places of religious worship, including meeting halls, parish houses and similar facilities" are allowed by special permit. Town of Red Hook Zoning Code, §143 (District Table of Uses) (1993). In the special permit uses section of the Red Hook Code, religious uses are further regulated by the following language: "Churches or other places or worship shall be allowed by special permit in [residential districts] provided that:

- Minimum lot area shall be three (3) acres, except in the RD5 District where minimum lot area of five (5) acres shall be required.
- Access shall be provided either directly from a state or county highway or by a through town roadway other than a residential subdivision street.
- No building shall be erected or parking area located closer than fifty (50) feet to any public right-of-way or property line or such greater minimum distance as required for the zoning district in the District Schedule of Area and Bulk Regulations."

Town of Red Hook Zoning Code, §143-78.

LIMITATIONS AND CONCERNS

The exclusion of places of public worship from the zoning law of a community is not permitted in New York because such a law does not promote the health, safety, morals, or general welfare of the community.

The exclusion of churches from a particular residential zoning district based on the adverse effect on property values, the loss of potential tax revenues, the decreased enjoyment of neighboring property, or the potential traffic hazards is an arbitrary and capricious exercise of the locality's police power.

An application for a land use permit for a religious land use cannot be denied unless it can be demonstrated that the reviewing body attempted to accommodate the use. It is presumed that religious uses will have a beneficial effect on a residential area. That presumption, however, may be rebutted if evidence is presented that there will be a significant impact on the public health or safety that cannot be mitigated by the imposition of conditions on the religious land use. In such cases, the denial of a permit for a religious land use may be sustained.

The First and Fourteenth Amendments of the U.S. Constitution prohibit local governments from adopting laws that inhibit or prevent the exercise of religion. When laws are adopted that are facially neutral and of general applicability, the government need not show a compelling interest for their adoption if the effect they have on religious expression is incidental. A local law such as one preventing the ritual sacrifice of animals lacks neutrality because it is aimed at impeding a specific religious practice and fails to advance a legitimate state interest.

CONSTITUTIONAL PROVISION

"Congress shall make no law respecting the establishment of religion or prohibiting the free exercise thereof." U.S. Const. Amend. I. This language was held applicable to state and local governments under the Fourteenth Amendment in *Cantwell v. Connecticut*, 310 U.S. 296 (1940).

CASE DIGEST

A zoning amendment that prohibited the building of churches or places of public worship within a village was invalidated in *North Shore Unitarian Society v. Village of Plandome*, 200 Misc. 524, 109 N.Y.S.2d 803 (Sup. Ct. Nassau County 1951). It was held that no "municipality in the State of New York may, by enactment of a zoning law, wholly exclude from within its borders, churches and places of public worship" because "such an law would not substantially promote the health, safety, morals, or general welfare of the community." *See also Cornell University v. Bagnardi*, 68 N.Y.2d 583, 503 N.E.2d 509, 510 N.Y.S.2d 861 (1986) (stating that "because of the inherently beneficial nature of churches and schools to the public . . . the total exclusion of such institutions from a residential district serves no end that is reasonably related to the morals, health, welfare and safety of the community").

In *Diocese of Rochester v. Planning Board of Town of Brighton*, 1 N.Y.2d 508, 136 N.E.2d 827, 154 N.Y.S.2d 849 (1956), the court held that "churches and schools occupy a different status from mere commercial enterprises and, when the church enters the picture, different considerations apply." The court concluded that the application of a zoning law was unconstitutional where the exclusion of a church from a residential area was based upon the adverse effect upon property values, the loss of potential tax revenue, the decreased enjoyment of neighboring property, and potential traffic hazards. It was determined that the local board's decisions to deny the plaintiff's application for a permit to construct a church and school were arbitrary and capricious and that the above considerations were insufficient to warrant the exclusion of such structures.

The New York Court of Appeals has extended its preferential treatment of houses of public worship to a wide variety of accessory uses in which churches and other religious institutions engage. *Community Synagogue v. Bates*, 1 N.Y.2d 445, 136 N.E.2d 488, 154 N.Y.S.2d 15 (1956). There, the court annulled a village board of appeals' denial of an application for a permit to use premises for a church for public worship and other strictly religious uses. The petitioner's goal was to create a permanent place for religious worship, religious teaching and training, fellowship, guidance, community activities, and indoor and outdoor activities for youth. The board determined that the petitioner's use was for purposes other than a church for public worship and other strictly religious uses. The court reversed, holding that "[a] church is more than merely an edifice affording people the opportunity to worship God. Strictly religious uses and activities are more than prayer and sacrifice and all churches recognize that the area of their responsibility is broader than leading the congregation in prayer." The court further stated that "[t]o limit a church to being merely a house of prayer and sacrifice would, in a large degree, be depriving the church of the opportunity of enlarging, perpetuating, and strengthening itself and the congregation."

In *American Friends of the Society of St. Puis, Inc. v. Schwab*, 69 A.D.2d 646, 417 N.Y.S.2d

991 (2d Dep't 1979), the court annulled a village board of trustees' denial of site plan approval for the proposed construction of a church in a residentially zoned area. The board claimed that the proposed construction would depreciate property values, create fire and traffic hazards, and "adversely affect the health, safety, and welfare of residents of the village." The court held that the denial of the application was premature because the applicant had offered to comply with all appropriate safety requirements. The court remitted the matter to the board for the purpose of fashioning "such reasonable conditions as will permit establishment of petitioner's Church while mitigating the detrimental or adverse effects of such use upon the community." It was also noted that the zoning power may not be used "to deny the constitutional right to the free exercise of religion by a chilling application of zoning laws" and that "it is necessary to most carefully scrutinize the reasons advanced for a denial to insure that they are real and not merely pretexts used to preclude the exercise of constitutionally protected privileges."

In *Society for Ethical Culture in the City of New York v. Spatt*, 51 N.Y.2d 449, 415 N.E.2d 922, 434 N.Y.S.2d 932 (1980), the Court of Appeals held that the Landmarks Preservation Commission's designation of a religious organization's property as a landmark did not interfere with the free exercise of the organization's religious activities. The landmark designation subjects the organization to substantial restriction in its use of the property. However, the organization did not claim that it wanted to modify the structure for religious purposes; instead, it implied that it wanted to develop the property to rent to non-religious tenants. The court stated that "[a]lthough the Society is concededly entitled to First Amendment protection as a religious organization, this does not entitle it to immunity from reasonable government regulation when it acts in purely secular matters."

The Fourth Department held that "[i]t is wholly appropriate to impose limitations on a church property and its accessory uses when reasonably related to the general welfare of the community, including the community's interest in preserving its appearance." *LakeShore Assembly of God Church v. Village Board of the Village of Westfield*, 124 A.D.2d 972, 508 N.Y.S.2d 819 (4th Dep't 1986). The church argued that the zoning board of appeals violated its First Amendment right to the free exercise of religion by imposing restrictions on the size of a sign it sought to erect. The court held that the limitations imposed were not arbitrary and capricious and "such determination reflects a reasonable accommodation of the church's request with the concerns of the neighbors as to aesthetic and safety considerations."

In *Yeshiva & Mesivta Toras Chaim v. Rose*, 136 A.D.2d 710, 523 N.Y.S.2d 907 (2d Dep't 1988), the court sustained a zoning board of appeals' denial of a building permit because the proposed center for the study of the Holocaust was not a religious use under the town zoning law. The court stated that "while recognizing that the courts of this State have been very flexible in their interpretation of religious uses under local zoning laws, the flexibility has been directed to ancillary or accessory functions of religious institutions whose principal use is a place of worship. Affiliation with or supervision by religious organizations does not, per se, transform institutions into religious ones."

The U.S. Court of Appeals upheld a landmarks law against a First Amendment claim in *St.*

Bartholomew's Church v. City of New York, 914 F.2d 348 (2d Cir. 1990). The Landmarks Preservation Commission had designated the church and its auxiliary building as landmarks, thus prohibiting the church from demolishing or altering the buildings without prior approval by the commission. Subsequently, the commission denied three applications by the church to replace the auxiliary building with an office tower. The church instituted an action, claiming that the Landmarks Law unconstitutionally burdened its free exercise of religion by "impair[ing] the church's ability to carry on and expand the ministerial and charitable activities that are central to its religious mission." The Court sustained the Landmarks Law as constitutional, holding that it "is a facially neutral regulation of general applicability" that had an incidental effect on a religious activity.

"It is well settled that, while religious institutions are not exempt from local zoning laws, greater flexibility is required in evaluating an application for a religious use than an application for another use and every effort to accommodate the religious use must be made." *Genesis Assembly of God v. Davies*, 208 A.D.2d 627, 617 N.Y.S.2d 202 (2d Dep't 1994). The court annulled a determination of a zoning board of appeals denying the petitioner's application for a variance for the construction of a church. The board's denial was based on the shortage of off-street parking spaces. The court held that "the proposed religious use could have been accomodated by granting the variance subject to conditions limiting, inter alia, the number of persons attending services and the number of services or meetings per week." *See also Harrison Orthodox Minyan, Inc. v. Town Board of Harrison*, 159 A.D.2d 572, 552 N.Y.S.2d 434 (2d Dep't 1990) (holding that the town board abused its discretion in denying the petitioner's application for a special use permit without making any attempt to accommodate the proposed religious use).

The U.S. Supreme Court sustained a zoning law that required city approval of any construction affecting historic buildings within a historic district, even though it involved the denial of a building permit to expand the size of a church, in *City of Boerne v. Flores*, 521 U.S. 507 (1997). The Catholic Archbishop of San Antonio challenged the local law under the Religious Freedom Restoration Act (RFRA) of 1993, which prevented federal, state, and local governments from substantially burdening the exercise of religion even if the burden resulted from a rule of general application. The plaintiff claimed that the local historic preservation law violated the federal statute since the building expansion was necessary to accommodate the church's growing membership. The Court invalidated the RFRA, determining that the Act was "a considerable congressional intrusion into the states' traditional prerogatives and general authority to regulate for the health and welfare of their citizens."

REFERENCE

Helen M. Maher, *Religious Freedom and Zoning, at*
http://www.pace.edu/lawschool/landuse/religiop.html (last visited Feb. 2, 2001).

Photo courtesy of Jay Pendergrass

Chapter 10

PROPERTY RIGHTS, JUDICIAL REVIEW, AND CONFLICT RESOLUTION

A key reason for the development of zoning was to protect investments in privately owned land. At hearings held in the early 1920s regarding the development of the Standard Zoning Enabling Act, developers whose property values were diminished or destroyed by the incompatible development of nearby properties strongly encouraged the promulgation of a model zoning act. Although many of the plaintiffs who challenged zoning were landowners who complained that it had diminished the value of their land, the courts upheld this land use technique, in part, because its effect was to stabilize property values throughout the community and to provide security for investments in the land.

Another critical reason for the creation of zoning in these early years was to coordinate land development with the provision of supportive physical infrastructure by the government. Often early comprehensive zoning laws were developed in tandem with official maps and long-term capital plans necessary for the growth and development of residential, commercial, and industrial districts. Because local governments were to provide and maintain infrastructure to serve developed land, it made sense to allow municipalities to enact a blueprint for their future development in the form of a zoning law.

In the early days of the operation of this land use system, once land was zoned a developer could examine the law and determine which land uses were permitted. Within a matter of weeks or months, he could file an application for permission to build, go through a brief project review process, and secure a building permit.

The great demand for land development precipitated by the end of World War II and by the relatively robust economies of the 1950s and 1960s encouraged the rapid development of prime land in urban and suburban America. Gradually, as development progressed further into the countryside, the local regulatory environment changed. Some land uses were reclassified from as-of-right, permitted uses to specially permitted uses, and developers were forced to subject their proposals to agency review and the imposition of conditions to protect surrounding properties from the impacts of the proposed development. The development of some individual parcels of land required site plan approval, again subject to conditions. In New York, in the early 1970s, most significant development proposals were subjected to environmental review under the State Environmental Quality Review Act (SEQRA). The approval process grew with the addition of permits to preserve wetlands, guard against sedimentation and erosion, and protect the quality of drinking water supplies, among other objectives.

Today, developers know that in many communities the review and approval process for a project—which had taken only a few months to navigate in the 1960s—can take years and cost significant sums of money to complete. Subdivision, site plan, and special use approvals are subject to increasingly demanding standards and to the imposition of more numerous conditions. SEQRA gives local reviewing agencies discretionary authority to impose conditions on land use approvals in the interest of protecting environmental interests, which are defined very broadly. Moreover, citizen groups have learned that by speaking at public hearings, documenting the adverse environmental impacts of proposed developments, and urging a project's disapproval or reduction in scope, they can influence the way local officials exercise their discretion and can slow down and scale down many development projects.

In response to the complexity and discretionary nature of local land use regulations, landowners and developers frequently challenge in court what they regard as overly costly regulations, arbitrary project denials, and unreasonably restrictive conditions. Neighbors, citizens, and environmentalists just as frequently contest in the courts the approval of development proposals that they believe will have a significant negative impact on their properties and environment.

A wide variety of legal challenges may be brought to the courts by those who support and oppose land development. Increasingly, project proponents, opponents, and review boards are exploring the idea of submitting controversies about land development proposals to mediation. They are also experimenting with new ways to facilitate collaborative decision-making regarding such proposals in order to avoid disputes and expedite the agency review process.

A. CHALLENGES BROUGHT AGAINST LOCAL REGULATIONS

DEFINITION

Local land use regulations can be challenged in a variety of ways. They can be alleged to violate substantive due process guarantees, procedural due process requirements, or the equal protection clause of the federal or state constitution, or to be beyond the legal authority of the local regulatory body.

These challenges may be brought by the owner of the affected property or by the owners of affected nearby properties as well as by others who can show that they are affected in some special way by the regulation. Even organizations or associations of individuals may sue when they can show that their members are directly affected by the regulation and that the association is open and representative. As a result, local governments are vulnerable to legal challenges from various affected parties who may chose among these approaches to attack local land use regulations.

AUTHORITY

Land use regulations are enacted under the police power delegated by the state to the local legislature. The police power is the authority of government to enact regulations to protect the public health, safety, welfare, and morals. The United States Supreme Court has called police power regulation "one of the most essential powers of government."

Broad authority to regulate land uses is delegated to local governments through enabling acts that empower them to enact zoning regulations, create zoning districts, and adopt comprehensive plans. This broad grant of authority carries with it the implied authority to choose the means necessary to accomplish the purposes of conserving the value of buildings and property and encouraging the most appropriate use of the land throughout the community. Specific authority has been granted to local governments to regulate a variety of aspects of land use, including historic districts, aesthetic impacts, building design, wetlands, and environmental impacts of land development.

Because of the importance of police power regulations and the doctrine of separation of powers, the courts have adopted rules of self-restraint when presented with challenges to police power regulations. These rules presume the constitutionality of the regulation, impose a heavy burden of proof on the challenger, resolve doubts in favor of the regulator, and, in most cases, result in a low level of judicial scrutiny.

WHEN

Substantive due process challenges allege that the local regulation does not advance a legitimate public purpose. Sometimes this challenge asserts that the regulation is arbitrary and capricious, such as a regulation that is adopted simply in reaction to citizen opposition and not on the basis of information, studies, and deliberate analysis.

Procedural due process challenges are brought when a community fails to follow a statutorily prescribed process or rushes to judgment on a land use decision, thereby violating the rights of involved parties to receive notice, to be given an opportunity to be heard, or to enjoy the benefits of a deliberate and thoughtful process on the part of the decisionmaker.

Equal protection claims assert that a land use classification or decision treats one parcel, or a few parcels of land, differently from similarly situated parcels with no apparent justification for the different treatment.

Ultra vires claims allege that the municipality did not have the legal authority to take the challenged action. They assert that the regulatory body acted beyond the scope of its delegated or implied authority and that its action therefore is invalid because it is an unauthorized action of government.

AVOIDING CHALLENGES TO LOCAL LAND USE REGULATIONS

When presented with a challenge to a land use regulation, courts generally exercise judicial restraint. The regulation is presumed valid, and the challenger bears a heavy burden of proof. However, where local regulations are set aside by the courts, their invalidation can be traced to several common errors:

- The reasons for the regulations are not stated clearly.
- No comprehensive plan has been adopted or it has not been kept up to date.

- The plan has not been followed.
- The local action is not justified by clear evidence but, rather, is primarily a response to the opposition of neighbors.

There are a number of precautions that a local government can take to avoid having their regulations set aside:

- Adopt a comprehensive plan, keep it up to date, and back it up by studies. Be sure that all land use regulations conform to the plan. A regulation that is adopted specifically to further an objective of a comprehensive plan is likely to be found to have a substantive connection to a legitimate public objective and to satisfy the demands of substantive due process.
- Where a comprehensive plan has not been adopted or is out of date, the local legislature should specify the public purpose advanced by the land use law and explain how the law advances that objective.
- The community should follow a deliberate and understandable process of adopting and amending local land use regulations. All citizens and affected parties should be provided effective advance notice and given an ample opportunity to be heard in a forum that is conducted fairly.
- Land use regulations must treat all similarly situated properties equally. Such regulations are not likely to be declared unconstitutional. The local agency should be careful to act consistently when imposing standards on landowners or interpreting the zoning law.
- In drafting and applying local laws such as site plan, subdivision, or wetlands regulations, local officials must specify the standards that applications must meet and must apply them uniformly and carefully.
- Local bodies must be certain that the actions they take and the conditions they impose are within their legal authority to act.
- Engaging the community and affected parties in meaningful discussions regarding the adoption or application of land use regulations reduces the tendency of affected parties to challenge decisions.

CONSTITUTIONAL PROVISION

The New York State Constitution, Article I, §6, requires that no person shall be deprived of life, liberty, or property without due process of law.

CASE DIGEST

SUBSTANTIVE DUE PROCESS

In the seminal zoning case *Village of Euclid v. Ambler Realty Co.*, 272 U.S. 365 (1926), the plaintiff landowners challenged the village's zoning law, which divided its property into three separate use zones. Their claim was that the law served no legitimate public purpose and was constitutionally invalid on its face. In this case, the U.S. Supreme Court established the standard of review to be used by the courts when a zoning law is challenged on substantive due process grounds: "[T]he reasons [must be] sufficiently cogent to preclude us from saying, as it must be said before the law can be declared unconstitutional, that such provisions are clearly arbitrary and unreasonable, having no substantial relation to the public health, safety, morals, or general welfare."

In *Walus v. Millington*, 49 Misc. 2d 104, 266 N.Y.S.2d 833 (Sup. Ct. Oneida County 1966), *aff'd*, 31 A.D. 2d 777, 297 N.Y.S.2d 894 (4th Dep't 1969), the plaintiffs challenged the validity of a zoning law reclassifying the defendant's parcel from single-family residential to general business. Other than a few nonconforming uses within the general vicinity, the area was primarily developed as a single-family residential neighborhood. The municipal legislature's failure to show reasons for deviating from the comprehensive plan was found to be spot zoning and to be fatal to the rezoning of the individual parcel.

The rezoning was held to be invalid because it was not in accordance with the "comprehensive plan" of the community. The court stated that "an underlying purpose [of comprehensive planning is] to control land uses for the benefit of the whole community based upon consideration of the community's problems and . . . a general policy to obtain a uniform result." In addition, "it requires a consideration of the individual parcel's relationship to the community as a whole. [T]he requirement is that a plan be implicit in the zoning regulation as a whole and that the amendments be consistent with such [a] plan and not be enacted on a piecemeal or haphazard basis." In the absence of a showing that the regulation conformed with the comprehensive plan or achieved some stated and valid public objective, the court found no substantive basis for the rezoning.

In *McMinn v. Town of Oyster Bay*, 66 N.Y.2d 544, 488 N.E.2d 1240, 498 N.Y.S.2d 128 (1985), the substantive due process tests used to determine the validity of a land use regulation were reviewed by the New York Court of Appeals. The court applied a two-part test that such regulations must meet to satisfy substantive due process requirements. First, the zoning law "must have been enacted in furtherance of a legitimate governmental purpose." Second, "there must be a reasonable relation between the end sought to be achieved by the regulation and the means used to achieve that end." The town's zoning law allowed any number of persons related by blood, marriage, or adoption to occupy a home in a single-family zoning district but limited occupancy among those not so related to two persons 62 years of age or older. The plaintiffs had rented their house to four unrelated young men and argued that the means used to limit occupancy were unreasonable. The court found that there was a legitimate governmental purpose in preserving the "character of traditional single-family neighborhoods, reduction of parking and traffic problems, control of population density, and prevention of noise and disturbance." It held, however, that the means of achieving this purpose were not reasonably related to that end. Restrictions based on the size of the household would be reasonably related to the achievement of the town's legitimate purpose. The means chosen by the town, however, imposed this limitation only on unrelated households, which failed the test of rationality and was characterized as a violation of the plaintiffs' due process rights.

In *Penlyn Development Corp. v. Incorporated Village of Lloyd Harbor*, 51 F. Supp. 2d 255

(E.D.N.Y. 1999), the court rejected a developer's claim that its federally protected, substantive due process rights were denied. The developer claimed that the village planning board had "persistently and irrationally refused to permit" subdivision of a 6.8 acre parcel of its land. Relying on the U.S. Supreme Court's decision in *Board of Regents v. Roth*, 408 U.S. 564 (1972), the district court held that the plaintiff, in order to prove a violation of substantive due process, must first demonstrate a legitimate claim of entitlement to the benefit in question. "The key to determining the existence of a property interest is the extent to which the deciding authority may exercise discretion in reaching its decision, rather than the estimate of the likelihood of a certain decision." Second, to win relief even if there is a demonstrable property interest, Penlyn must demonstrate that the defendants acted in "an outrageously arbitrary or irrational manner in depriving the plaintiff of that interest." Plaintiff argued that the planning board had been divested of its discretion as a result of a prior order of the state Supreme Court which returned the case to the planning board with directions to address certain issues in reference to the subdivision application. Declining to usurp state court jurisdiction over this matter, the district court held that the "determination as to whether to approve an application for the partitioning of land is inherently a local concern which can be . . . successfully resolved by a state court." The court further held that the planning board had retained its discretion and, as a result, plaintiff did not have a legitimate claim of entitlement to the subdivision approval and therefore could not pursue its claim of denial of substantive due process in federal court.

PROCEDURAL DUE PROCESS

In *Pokoik v. Silsdorf*, 40 N.Y.2d 769, 358 N.E.2d 874, 390 N.Y.S.2d 49 (1976), the municipality's unreasonable delaying tactics resulted in the invalidation of the rezoning of plaintiff's property. The property owner's application for a building permit to construct two additional bedrooms was originally rejected because of previous zoning violations. The owner revised the building plans, but the building inspector did not act on them. A court order compelling the building inspector to act on the application was granted, yet, in spite of this order, three months later the application was denied. The owner appealed to the zoning board of appeals, but was forced to reschedule the hearing because no one appeared on behalf of the municipality. Meanwhile, the local legislature amended the zoning law, limiting the number of bedrooms permitted.

This new law became effective prior to the zoning board's hearing, and resulted in the denial of the building permit. The Court of Appeals held that the amended law could not apply, and found that the municipality's delaying tactics were improper. The general rule that zoning amendments can be made at any time was not applied to this town's actions. Its irregular and dilatory tactics constituted a "special facts exception" to that rule. Under these circumstances, the owner's compliance with the zoning requirements at the time of the revised application created a right to the permit. The court held that the owner had been denied his right to begin construction before the effective date of the amendment because of the "abuse of administrative procedure" by municipal officials.

Local agencies must follow the procedural steps that are required of them under state statutes governing their actions. New York's State Environmental Quality Review Act (SEQRA) is an example of such a statute. In *Eggert v. Town Board of Town of Westfield*, 217 A.D.2d 975, 630 N.Y.S.2d 179 (4th Dep't 1995), the court held that the town board violated the procedural aspects of SEQRA when it issued a negative declaration instead of proceeding with the preparation of an environmental impact statement. The town board classified a zoning amendment as a Type I action, but determined that the amendment itself would not have a significant effect on the environment since the rezoning required property owners to apply for special permits before developing under the amendments. The town board acknowledged that there could be adverse environmental impacts if special use permits were granted, but reasoned that such impacts could be adequately considered when applications for special use permits were submitted. The court rejected this argument, stating that "[t]o comply with SEQRA, the Town Board must consider the environmental concerns that are reasonably likely to result from, or are dependent on, the amendments." The court concluded that "the Town Board was required to address the potential environmental effects of the amendments, at least on a conceptual basis." Its failure to take this step resulted in the invalidation of its action.

EQUAL PROTECTION

In *Udell v. Haas*, 21 N.Y.2d 463, 235 N.E.2d 897, 288 N.Y.S.2d 888 (1968), a property owner complained that the reclassification of his land from business use to residential was discriminatory and violated his right to equal protection of the law. The court identified the issue as being "the propriety of the treatment of the subject parcel as compared to neighboring properties." The property owner provided evidence that other similarly situated properties in the same neighborhood were allowed to be used for business uses. The court agreed that this local action was discriminatory and invalidated the village's zoning classification.

BEYOND DELEGATED AUTHORITY

In *Moriarty v. Planning Board*, 119 A.D.2d 188, 506 N.Y.S.2d 184 (2nd Dep't 1986), the property owner proposed to build a metal fabricating plant on a vacant parcel of industrially zoned property. The zoning law required the owner to obtain site plan approval from the village planning board before any building permit could be issued. After submitting an application, the site plan approval was denied by the board because of inadequate fire protection mechanisms. The question was whether the planning board was empowered to deny site plan approval because of fire protection concerns. The court found that it was not, since that power was delegated to another official, the local building inspector. The court stated that "[z]oning laws are . . . in derogation of common-law property rights and thus are subject to the long-standing rule requiring their strict construction." Because the state legislature did not authorize the board to assume the powers of local fire inspectors to deny building permits because of inadequate fire protection, the court annulled the board's denial of the application.

Since *Moriarty* was decided, the statutory language has been changed, authorizing a planning board to examine "any additional elements specified by the village board of trustees in . . . [the] local law." Thus, a local legislative body may authorize its planning board to consider elements in addition to those specifically enumerated in the state statute so as to insure the adequate review of site plans in accordance with local conditions and concerns. This change in state law applies to villages, towns, and cities. Village Law §7-725-a(2)(a), Town Law §274-a(2)(a), and General City Law §30-a(1)(a).

REFERENCE

John R. Nolon, *Challenges to Local Land Use Regulations, at* http://www.pace.edu/lawschool/landuse/challe.html (last visited Feb. 2, 2001).

B. VESTED RIGHTS

DEFINITION

The doctrine of vested rights protects property owners from changes in zoning when they have received a valid building permit and have completed substantial construction and made substantial expenditures in reliance on the permit. When a court finds that a property owner has vested rights to a validly issued permit, the effect is to immunize the approved project from all changes in zoning or other land use regulations. This judicially created doctrine is called "common law" vested rights. There is also a more limited "statutory" vested rights rule in New York, adopted by the state legislature, which immunizes approved subdivision plats from changes in the dimensional or area requirements of zoning for a period of one to three years, depending on the circumstances.

In order to vest rights to the permit, the amount spent or the construction completed must be substantial in relation to the entire project. The cost of the land, the demolition of existing structures, processing and consultant fees, or excavation work in preparation for construction is not enough to vest rights. A court will not consider a particular expenditure unless there is a "special connection" between the expenditure and the approved use. For example, in considering whether there had been substantial expenditures to entitle the completion of a mall, a court would not consider the expenditure of $120,000 to widen a road where the road would have had to be constructed to serve the residential development that was allowed under the amended law.

PURPOSE

There are dual purposes for the doctrine of vested rights. One is to protect the investment of landowners who have made significant expenditures and completed significant construction in reliance on a valid land use permit. When landowners have undertaken substantial construction and expenditure, they are no longer subject to zoning changes; this protects the owner's investment from confiscation. The second is to preserve municipal authority to protect the health, safety, and welfare of the community. The New York vested rights rule gives local governments some flexibility to change the rules to protect the public from the time a permit has been issued until a substantial investment under that permit has been made.

WHEN

The doctrine of vested rights applies when a municipality amends its zoning law, rendering a progressing development project in violation of the new regulation. If the municipality seeks to revoke the building permit and stop the project, the property owner can claim vested rights and seek a court order enjoining the locality from enforcing the new regulations against this property.

AUTHORITY

There are two sources of the doctrine of vested rights. The first is the common-law principle created by the courts to protect property rights from being confiscated by changes in land use regulations. The state legislature has also enacted a statutory scheme, which allows for vested rights of approved residential subdivisions. The New York Town, Village, and General City laws all provide that where a subdivision plat for a residential development has been approved by a local board and properly filed, any subsequent increase in minimum lot areas, lot dimensions, yard, or setback requirements in excess of those shown on the approved subdivision plat shall not affect any of the lots delineated on the plat for a period established in the statute.

IMPLEMENTATION

First, a property owner must secure a validly issued land use approval and building permit from the relevant local authorities. If the approval or permit was granted erroneously, in violation of any legal requirement, it can be revoked even after substantial expenditure and construction have taken place. Second, the local legislature must change the zoning or land use regulations applicable to the permitted project in a way that prevents that project from being completed. Third, the owner must be able to prove to the court that substantial expenses and construction have occurred that serve the approved project and not the land use allowed under the amended zoning. Expenses and construction that contribute to the substantiality test must be over and above those needed to serve the reduced or different development allowed by the changed regulations. Finally, the landowner must not have committed some overt act indicating his intent to abandon his vested rights.

Under the statutory protection provided to approved residential subdivisions, the landowner need not complete the entire subdivision during the prescribed period. The entire project will be vested if the landowner has met the common-law standard of substantial expenditure and investment during the period.

LIMITATIONS AND CONCERNS

A landowner's rights will never vest under an invalidly issued permit. The doctrine of vested rights assumes that the property owner acted in justifiable reliance on a validly issued permit. Property owners should insure that they have a valid permit before claiming vested rights.

Where a developer completes one or more phases of a development, vested rights to the entire project may accrue. Where the later stages of the project have not been substantially constructed but the developer has made substantial project improvements in earlier project stages that support and benefit later stages, a court may find that rights to the entire development have vested.

Property owners may lose vested rights by abandonment. The court may find that a landowner has abandoned his vested rights if the completion of the project is delayed for a long period and there is some overt act implying that the developer has abandoned the vested rights.

A community may encounter difficulties if an owner is prevented by arbitrary delaying tactics from obtaining a valid building permit and vesting his rights under it. In such a case, the municipality may be prevented from applying the changed regulations and denying an owner a permit under the previous regulations.

STATUTES

In New York State, Town Law §265-a, Village Law §7-709, and General City Law §83-a prohibit a community from changing the dimensional requirements of zoning applicable to an approved subdivision plat for a specific period.

CASE DIGEST

THE GENERAL RULE

The court in *Ellington Construction Corp. v. Zoning Board of Appeals of the Incorporated Village of New Hempstead*, 77 N.Y.2d 114, 566 N.E.2d 128, 564 N.Y.S.2d 1001 (1990), determined that the New York rule for vested rights is "where a more restrictive zoning law is enacted, an owner will be permitted to complete a structure or development which an amendment has rendered nonconforming only where the owner has undertaken substantial construction and made substantial expenditures prior to the effective date of the amendment." The property owner must also have incurred expenditures and made improvements in reliance on the validly issued permit. The rights must also vest after the issuance of the permit but before the zoning amendment becomes effective. *See also Town of Lloyd v. Kart Wheelers Raceway, Inc.*, 28 A.D.2d 1015, 283 N.Y.S.2d 756 (3d Dep't 1967) (holding that vested rights were not established even though the new owner claimed that it had expended over $33,000 on new facilities); *Smith v. Spiegel & Sons Oil Corp.*, 31 A.D.2d 819, 298 N.Y.S.2d 47 (2d Dep't 1969), *aff'd*, 24 N.Y.2d 920, 249 N.E.2d 763, 301 N.Y.S.2d 984 (1969) (holding that "the purchase of property, the demolition of structures thereon, and the retaining of architects to prepare plans was not work of a substantial character").

The court ruled against a property owner who failed to show that the extent of completion of the excavation and the foundation constituted a substantial part of the entire project. *Riverdale Community Planning Ass'n v. Crinnion*, 133 N.Y.S.2d 706 (Sup. Ct. Bronx County 1954), *aff'd,* 285 A.D. 1047, 141 N.Y.S.2d 510 (1st Dep't 1955). In *Glenel Realty Corp. v. Worthington*, 4 A.D.2d 702, 165 N.Y.S.2d 635 (2d Dep't 1957), the court held that the developer had acquired a vested right to complete a retail shopping center where it had almost completed the foundation work.

In *Reichenbach v. Windward at Southampton*, 80 Misc. 2d 1031, 364 N.Y.S.2d 283 (Sup. Ct. Suffolk County 1975), *aff'd*, 48 A.D.2d 909, 372 N.Y.S.2d 985 (2d Dep't 1975), the court held that the property owner had not made substantial expenditures so as to vest rights to construct a motel prior to a zoning amendment that precluded motels. The owner had spent $3,150 on footing and foundation work and $3,345 on plans and surveys for the project, but the total estimated cost of the motel project was $600,000. Thus, expenditures amounted to just over 1% of the estimated cost of the entire project–not enough to support a vested rights claim.

The court in *Town of Hempstead v. Lynne*, 32 Misc. 2d 312, 222 N.Y.S.2d 526 (Sup. Ct. Nassau County 1961), in holding that there had not been substantial expenditures entitling the owner to finish a mall development, refused to consider $120,000 spent by the developer to widen a road to the site where the road, as widened, would also serve the residential development that was allowed under the amended law.

RIGHTS WILL NEVER VEST UNDER AN INVALID PERMIT

In *Parkview Associates v. City of New York*, 71 N.Y.2d 274, 519 N.E.2d 1372, 525 N.Y.S.2d 176 (1988), the developer was issued a building permit to construct a 31-story building. The applicable zoning, which allowed a maximum of 19 stories, was misinterpreted by the builder and the City Department of Buildings. When the mistake was realized, construction was nearly complete. The court sustained the city's order to demolish 12 stories because the "original permit in this case was invalid inasmuch as it authorized construction . . . in violation of [the] New York City Zoning Resolution." The property owner's argument that the City should be estopped from enforcing the law because of the department's mistake and the nearly completed construction was not successful.

THE SINGLE INTEGRATED PROJECT THEORY

In *Telimar Homes, Inc. v. Miller*, 14 A.D.2d 586, 218 N.Y.S.2d 175 (2d Dep't 1961), the court held that a zoning law amendment that required a minimum lot size of one half acre as opposed to a quarter acre did not apply to the plaintiff. The builder had been granted approval to subdivide the land into quarter-acre lots. Following this approval, construction of roads began, "plans were prepared and model homes were built . . . all on the basis that it was a single over-all project." The court concluded that because substantial construction had commenced and substantial expenditures had been made, the builder had "acquired a vested right to a nonconforming use as to the entire tract."

In *Schoonamaker Homes v. Village of Maybrook*, 178 A.D.2d 722, 576 N.Y.S.2d 954 (3d Dep't 1991), a planning board granted subdivision approval for property that was to be divided into separate sections for apartments, townhouses, and single-family residences. The townhouse and single-family sections of the project were developed. Twenty years later, when the developer applied for building permits to construct the apartments, the village amended its zoning law to decrease the density permitted for apartments and denied the permits because the application did not meet these new requirements. The developer challenged the denial based on the single integrated project theory. Under this theory, a developer who seeks approval for a project to be constructed in several stages has vested rights to the entire project even if the later stages of the construction have not been started where substantial infrastructure construction on the first phases serves the later stage. The court held that the developer had acquired vested rights to develop all apartment units, but that the developer had abandoned those rights during the 20-year delay. Overt acts of abandonment by the developer were shown.

THE OVER AND ABOVE RULE

The court in *Padwee v. Lustenberger*, 226 A.D.2d 897, 641 N.Y.S.2d 159 (3d Dep't 1996), held that a plaintiff must establish a strong factual basis showing that most of the improvements or expenditures made prior to a zoning amendment would not be "equally useful" for the reduced development allowed under an amended zoning law. The plaintiff was granted subdivision approval to divide its parcel into five lots. Two years after the approval, the village amended its zoning law to increase the minimum lot size. Subsequently, the developer was denied a building permit for one of the lots because the lot did not meet the minimum size. The court focused on two related factual issues: whether the improvements made would be equally useful in a development that conformed with the new zoning requirements, and whether the cost of improvements made under the amended law would have been "significantly less than" what the developer expended under the original law. The court agreed with the municipality that "a majority of the improvements made by the petitioner would be 'equally useful' in a . . . development that would conform to the [amended] zoning requirements and the cost . . . would not have been significantly less that the amount the [plaintiff] expended."

APPLICATION OF STATUTORY VESTING RULE

The statutory grace period merely grants the developer a specified time in which to vest his rights. If the developer fails to acquire vested rights within the prescribed time, then subsequent zoning requirements will apply to his property. *Freundlich v. Town Board of Southampton*, 73 A.D.2d 684, 422 N.Y.S.2d 215 (2d Dep't 1979), *aff'd*, 52 N.Y.2d 921, 419 N.E.2d 342, 437 N.Y.S.2d 664 (1981).

In *Ellington Construction Corp. v. Zoning Board of Appeals of the Incorporated Village of New Hempstead*, 77 N.Y.2d 114, 566 N.E.2d 128, 564 N.Y.S.2d 1001 (1990), the zoning board of appeals argued that the statute afforded "protection only for those lots in a filed subdivision that an owner has completed or for which it has actually obtained a building permit during the exemption period." The court disagreed, holding that the statute "was intended to permit a developer to secure the right to complete a subdivision in accordance with existing zoning requirements by manifesting a commitment to the execution of the subdivision plan through completing improvements and incurring expenditures in connection therewith, during the exemption period, sufficient to constitute vesting under common-law rules."

LOSING VESTED RIGHTS BY ABANDONMENT

For abandonment of vested rights, there must be an intent to abandon and an overt act implying that the developer is abandoning his vested rights. *Putnam Armonk, Inc. v. Town of Southeast*, 52 A.D.2d 10, 382 N.Y.S.2d 538 (2d Dep't 1976).

In *202 Developers, Inc. v. Town of Haverstraw*, 175 A.D.2d 473, 573 N.Y.S.2d 517 (3d Dep't 1991), the court rejected the town's argument that the developer had lost its right to develop certain property because it "did nothing to develop the property for eleven years after it gained site approval." There was no overt act or other evidence of an intent to abandon other than the passage of time.

To determine if a zoning board's conclusion that vested rights have been abandoned is valid, the court must consider whether the conclusion was based on "substantial evidence." *Schoonamaker Homes v. Village of Maybrook*, 178 A.D.2d 722, 576 N.Y.S.2d 954 (3d Dep't 1991). Even though the court found that the plaintiff had vested rights, it concluded "that there was substantial evidence to support a finding of abandonment." Witnesses testified that the plaintiff had told them the site would be used for parkland or commercial use. Advertisements for the overall development had specifically mentioned single-family homes and townhouses but made no reference to apartments. This evidence demonstrated the intent of the plaintiff to abandon its vested rights in the property.

EQUITABLE ESTOPPEL RULE

The issue in *Pokoik v. Silsdorf*, 40 N.Y.2d 769, 358 N.E.2d 874, 390 N.Y.S.2d 49 (1976), was whether, because of improper actions of municipal officials, the petitioner was entitled to an order directing the issuance of a permit. Plaintiff had wanted to build a two-bedroom addition to his four-bedroom house. The application was denied and he appealed. While the appeal was in process, the local legislature amended its zoning law to limit one-family homes to four bedrooms. The final denial was based on this amendment. The court found repeated abuses by certain municipal officials in their treatment of the plaintiff's application and that the reasons for denying the earlier permit applications were meritless. It held that it was "abundantly clear that at all times prior to the effective date of the amendment the petitioner was entitled to a permit." The court concluded that the delay in this case was a "special facts exception" to the rule that "a case must be decided upon the law as it exists at the time of the decision," and therefore "the zoning law as amended, [did] not apply and the arbitrary action of the board may not prevail."

REFERENCE

Michael Murphy, *Closing the Bookends on Vested Rights, at* http://www.pace.edu/lawschool/landuse/vest.html (last visited Feb. 2, 2001).

C. REGULATORY TAKINGS

DEFINITION

Occasionally, courts will find that the impact of a regulation on private property rights is so burdensome that it violates the constitutional guarantee that property shall not be taken for a public use without just compensation. What courts do not allow is the singling out of a few property owners to bear a burden that, in the interest of fairness and justice, the public as a whole should bear. In select situations, a land use regulation can be invalidated as a "regulatory taking" and compensation can be awarded to the regulated property owner for the damages caused.

Regulatory takings are sometimes referred to as inverse condemnations or de facto takings. Both these terms reference the government's power of eminent domain, the authority to condemn title to land needed for a public purpose. Under both the U.S. and the New York State Constitutions, such takings are allowed but the validity of the public purpose must be demonstrated and just compensation must be paid to the owner of the condemned property. When a government regulation has the practical effect of a public condemnation, the owner may allege that the regulation is a regulatory taking, a de facto taking, or the inverse condemnation of the affected parcel.

When land use regulations, such as zoning provisions, are challenged as regulatory takings, the courts presume that they are constitutional. This means that challengers must carry a heavy burden of proof that the regulations violate the constitutional guarantee; all reasonable doubts are resolved in favor of the regulator. To carry their burden of proof, property owners must produce dollars and cents evidence that all but a bare residue of the property's value has been destroyed by the regulation.

Two tests are applied by courts to determine whether a regulation is a taking. First, does it "substantially advance a legitimate state interest." Second, does it "deny the owner economically viable use of his land"? If the challenger can bear the heavy burden of proving that either of these standards is violated, a regulatory takings claim may succeed.

Courts take a more aggressive approach where a condition imposed on a land use approval gives the public a right to enter the landowner's property. In this situation, it is the public agency that must satisfy the court that there is sufficient relationship between the impact of the proposed development and the public benefit achieved by the condition imposed.

AUTHORITY

Broad authority to regulate land use is delegated to local governments through enabling acts that authorize them to enact zoning regulations, create zoning districts, adopt comprehensive plans, and pass laws to protect the physical environment. This broad grant of authority carries with it the implied authority to choose the means necessary to accomplish the purposes of conserving the value of buildings and property and encouraging the most appropriate use of the land throughout the community. Specific authority has been granted to local governments to regulate a variety of aspects of land use, including historic districts, aesthetic impacts building design, wetlands, and environmental impacts of land development.

Land use regulations are enacted under the police power delegated by the state to the local legislature. The police power is the authority of government to regulate private affairs to protect the public health, safety, welfare, and morals. The U.S. Supreme Court has called police power regulation "one of the most essential powers of government, one that is least limitable. There must be progress, and if in its march private interests are in the way, they must yield to the good of the community." *Hadacheck v. Sebastian*, 239 U.S. 394, 410, 36 S.Ct. 143, 60 L.Ed. 348 (1915).

Because of the importance of police power regulations and the doctrine of separation of powers, the courts have adopted rules of self-restraint when confronted with a challenge to a land use regulation. These rules presume the constitutionality of the regulation, impose a heavy burden of proof on the challenger, resolve doubts in favor of the regulator, and, in most cases, result in a low level of judicial scrutiny.

The authority to regulate property is not without its limitations, however. The courts review regulations to determine whether a few property owners are being singled out to bear a burden that, in fairness, should be borne by the public as a whole. When regulations force landowners to allow the public access to their private lands, courts use stricter standards to review the validity of the regulations. If the effect of a regulation is to leave the owner with only a bare residue of the parcel's value, courts require a showing that such a limit on the land's use was inherent in its title or in the background principles of property law in the state.

WHEN

Broadly Applicable Regulations: The police power allows local governments to distribute the burdens and benefits of generally applicable laws, such as zoning, among the owners of property in the community for the benefit of the public. Zoning provisions, such as use restrictions, height limitations, and setback requirements, are said to benefit and burden all property owners in a roughly equal manner. While a parcel's use is limited by these restrictions, its value is enhanced by similar restrictions on all other properties in the community.

Regulations that are broadly applicable in this way are very seldom held by the courts to be regulatory takings. If the owner can carry the heavy burden of proving that, as applied to his property, such regulations leave no economically viable use of the land, the court may declare it to be a regulatory taking. The U.S. Supreme Court mandated the rezoning of one plaintiff's property when he was able to prove through reliable experts that there was no market for the residential use of his land that had been zoned exclusively for residential use in a developed industrial area. As a matter of practice in most localities, owners who find themselves in this situation would be granted a use variance by the zoning board of appeals, if the problem is somewhat unique to the owner.

Particularized Regulations: Sometimes the burden of police power regulations falls on the owners of a relatively few parcels of land in the community. This happens, for example, when the land use regulation applies only to historic properties or to land that contains freshwater or tidal wetlands, steep slopes, or artifacts. While relatively few landowners in the community are burdened, the public as a whole is benefited by the regulation.

Although the general rules of judicial restraint apply with respect to these regulations, the judicial analysis of such regulations may be more elaborate. In these instances, the court will examine the character of the regulation, the public purpose it serves, the legitimate investment-backed expectations of the property owner, and the extent to which the regulation distributes its burdens as evenly and fairly as possible. The judicial tests, and the deference shown by the court to the regulator, are the same as with generally applicable regulations. Applying these standards, New York courts routinely uphold complex, special purpose regulations like wetland controls and historic district restrictions as long as they permit some economically viable use of the land.

Forced Conveyances: When the regulation requires a property owner to allow public access to his land, the courts apply a heightened degree of judicial scrutiny. Such regulations often require the property owner to convey an easement to the community allowing public access to the land as a condition of receiving the approval of a local agency.

The right to exclude others from one's property is considered a fundamental right of land ownership. When a land use condition implicates that right, it is not necessarily a taking, but the court senses that the basic guarantee of the Constitution may be violated and applies tougher judicial tests of validity. In these instances, the regulator must show that there is an essential nexus between the condition imposed and the public purpose that is to be achieved by the condition. Courts also look for specialized studies showing that public benefits obtained by the condition imposed on the property are roughly proportional to the adverse impacts of the development on the community.

Where a property owner was required to grant an easement to the community for a bicycle path as a condition for the approval of a site plan application, the court set aside the condition because the city had made no individualized determination—conducted no separate study—to determine the extent to which the condition would mitigate the specific project's contribution to traffic congestion.

Total Takings: Courts also apply a heightened degree of scrutiny when reviewing a regulation that allows an owner no viable use of his property. Such regulations may be said to constitute a "total taking" and to implicate the constitutional guarantee that property will not be confiscated for public use without just compensation. The U.S. Supreme Court has said that in the "extraordinary circumstance when no productive or economically beneficial use of land is permitted, it is less realistic to indulge our usual assumption that the legislature is simply adjusting the benefits and burdens of economic life." *Lucas v. South Carolina Coastal Council,* 505 U.S. 1003, 1017, 22 ELR 21104, 21108 (1992). In such cases, there is a "heightened risk that private property is being pressed into some form of public service under the guise of mitigating serious public harm."

Unless the regulator can show that the use prohibited by the regulation would not be allowed under nuisance law or "background principles of property law," or is inherent in the title to the land, a regulation that prohibits all beneficial use will be considered a regulatory taking.

Preexisting Regulations: New York courts have held that when an individual purchases property that is subject to land use regulations that affect its value, the purchaser may not challenge the regulation as a taking of its property rights. Such a regulation, the courts say, forms part of the title to the property as a preexisting rule of state law. While the title to the regulated parcel may be conveyed by the landowner, the purchaser's title is necessarily limited to the rights to use the property under the law at the time of the purchase. This rule does not, of course, affect a purchaser's right to challenge the constitutionality of a preexisting regulation on some other ground, such as equal protection or ultra vires.

The New York position on this point on is different from that adopted by the U.S. Supreme Court. In June of 2001, the Supreme Court held that a blanket rule that purchasers who take title with notice of an adopted land use regulation have no right to compensation "is too blunt an instrument to accord with the duty to compensate for what is taken." The Court held that a pre-existing regulation affecting a parcel is not necessarily inherent in the title taken by a purchaser or heir and cannot be used as a *per se* device to deny the right to compensation.

AVOIDING A REGULATORY TAKINGS CHALLENGE:

There are a number of precautions that local governments can take to avoid successful regulatory takings challenges:

- ♦ Adopt a comprehensive plan, keep it up to date, and back it up by studies. Be sure that local land use regulations conform to the plan. A regulation that is adopted specifically to further an objective of a comprehensive plan is likely to be found by a court to substantially advance a legitimate public interest.
- ♦ When adopting land use regulations, be sure that all similarly situated properties are similarly regulated. A regulation that limits the use of all properties that are historic or that contain wetlands of a certain type will likely be found to distribute the benefits and burdens of the regulation as fairly and broadly as possible. Such regulations conform to the "principle of generality," which puts courts at ease and tends to reduce fears that individual owners are being singled out.
- ♦ Where land use regulations might prevent all economically beneficial use of land owned by a particular individual, be sure that there is a readily available mechanism for the owner to prove that no reasonable use of the land is allowed and to obtain a hardship exemption from the strict application of the regulations. If the local government awards an exemption that allows some reasonable use of the property, an owner will not be able to claim that the regulatory regime destroys all but a bare residue of value.
- ♦ When government imposes conditions on the approval of development projects

which require owners to allow public access to their properties, individual studies must be conducted to show that the condition is both necessary to mitigate the project's impact on the community and roughly proportionate to that impact.

♦ In New York, projects that are likely to have a substantial adverse impact on the environment are subjected to the requirement that an environmental impact statement be filed. When such studies are done carefully and conditions are later imposed by a local agency to mitigate demonstrated adverse impacts, judicial standards applicable to the review of regulatory takings challenges are likely to be met. This is particularly so if the environmental review process is conducted correctly, because conditions imposed to mitigate environmental impacts are to be consistent with social, economic, and other essential considerations. Properly conducted environmental review studies are likely to meet the essential nexus and rough proportionality tests applied in certain types of regulatory takings challenges.

♦ Instead of greatly limiting land uses through regulations, the community should explore the many innovative tools and techniques that local governments are encouraged to use under statutes adopted by the state legislature. Where the public objective can be accomplished, for example, by clustering development, by transferring development rights, by incentive zoning, or by purchasing conservation easements, burdens on landowners can be minimized and the chances of facing regulatory takings challenges reduced.

LIMITATIONS AND CONCERNS

Courts have held that property owners who win regulatory takings suits may be awarded monetary damages for the injury done to them from the time the regulation was imposed until it is invalidated by the court. The risk of suffering a damage claim has made regulators more cautious in imposing restraints and conditions on the use of property.

The justices of the U.S. Supreme Court have warned against generalizing about when a regulatory taking occurs. They have stated that there is no "set formula" for determining when a regulation has gone so far as to constitute a taking and that they prefer to engage in ad hoc, factual inquiries to make such determinations. It is incorrect to say, as a general matter, for example, that a land use condition that imposes a public access easement on the subject land is a regulatory taking. The principal case striking down a challenged public access easement held that a different public access easement—one that bore an essential nexus to the public objective to be achieved—would have been approved.

Similarly, it is incorrect to state that a regulation prohibiting all beneficial uses of the land is always a taking. If the regulator can show that background principles of property law, such as nuisance principles, would prohibit the use, then the regulation will not be held to be a taking. In New York, if the court finds that the regulation existed prior to the plaintiff's purchase of the affected property, no taking will be found.

For most land use regulations, the courts defer greatly to local determinations and seldom find regulations to be takings. It is where individual property owners are forced to allow the public on the land, where all uses are prohibited, or where single property owners are forced to bear particular public burdens that the courts will take a more careful look at the regulation. They inquire whether the regulation truly accomplishes a legitimate public purpose or whether the total prohibition of use is justified, and they shift the burden of proving the matter to the regulator.

CONSTITUTIONAL PROVISIONS AND STATUTES

The Fifth Amendment of the U.S. Constitution, which applies to state and local governmental action through the Fourteenth Amendment, prohibits the deprivation of property without due process of law and the taking of property for a public use without just compensation.

Section 1 of the Fourteenth Amendment states: "No State shall make or enforce any law which shall abridge the privileges or immunities of the citizens of the United States; nor shall any State deprive any person of life, liberty, or property, without due process of law; nor deny any person within its jurisdiction the equal protection of the laws."

The New York State Constitution, Article I, §7, states that "private property shall not be taken without just compensation."

Village Law §7-700, Town Law §261, and General City Law §20(24) authorize local governments to adopt zoning laws to promote the health, safety, morals, or the general welfare of the community. The authority to regulate building height, bulk, and lot coverage and to separate uses into districts is expressly delegated to local governments.

The statutory authority to divide the municipality into districts is found at §262 of the Town Law, §7-702 of the Village Law, and §§20(24) and (25) of the General City Law.

Under Village Law §7-704, Town Law §263, and General City Law §20(24), zoning regulations are to be adopted with reasonable consideration of the character of the zoning district and with a view to conserving the value of buildings and encouraging the most appropriate use of land.

The Municipal Home Rule Law, §10(2)(ii)(a)(11) authorized all local governments in New York to adopt laws to protect and enhance the physical and visual environment.

CASE DIGEST

The general principle on which many regulatory takings cases are based was articulated in *Armstrong v. United States*, 364 U.S. 40 (1960): "The Fifth Amendment's guarantee that private property shall not be taken for a public use without just compensation was designed to bar Government from forcing some people alone to bear public burdens which, in all fairness and justice, should be borne by the public as a whole." In this case, the Court reviewed and invalidated a government action that made the enforcement of certain property liens impossible, effecting a total taking of them. The case involved the illusive task of drawing the line between what adverse impacts on property by lawful governmental actions are compensable "takings" and what impacts are "consequential" and therefore not takings. The Court noted that "[t]he total destruction by the Government of all value of these liens, which constitute compensable property, has every possible element of a Fifth Amendment 'taking' and is not a mere 'consequential incidence' of a valid regulatory measure."

Regulations burdening relatively few landowners may receive more extensive judicial analysis when challenged as regulatory takings. This is perhaps because such regulations run the risk of unfairly singling out a few property owners to bear a burden beneficial to the public as a whole. In *Penn Central Transportation Co. v. City of New York*, 438 U.S. 104, 8 ELR 20528 (1978), the Court adopted a multifactor balancing approach to reviewing New York City's landmarks preservation law and regulations. It examined the character of the government action, its economic impact, and its interference with the landowner's reasonable investment-backed expectations before declaring the law valid. In New York City, a landmarks preservation law singled out 31 districts containing over 400 landmark buildings for regulation. These buildings represented less than one-tenth of one percent of the buildings in the city. The owners of designated properties were required to obtain a certificate of appropriateness before altering the exteriors of their buildings. Penn Central, which owned Grand Central Terminal, applied for a certificate to allow it to build a 50 story tower over the station. When permission was denied by the Landmarks Commission, Penn Central claimed that the application of the law constituted a taking of property. Since Penn Central did not prove that the regulation interfered with present profitable uses of the property or denied it a reasonable return on its investment, no taking was found.

In *Spears v. Berle*, 48 N.Y.2d 254, 397 N.E.2d 1304, 422 N.Y.S.2d 636 (1979), the New York Court of Appeals cited the standard applicable in New York to most regulatory taking claims. The landowner in this case was denied a permit to conduct mining operations because the proposed activity would virtually destroy all wetlands on the site. The court noted that "a land use regulation, be it a universally applicable zoning law or a more circumscribed measure governing only certain designated properties, is deemed too onerous when it renders the property unsuitable for any reasonable income productive or other private use for which it is adapted and thus destroys its economic value, or all but a bare residue of its value." The court explained further that a landowner "who challenges land regulations must sustain a heavy burden of proof, demonstrating that under no permissible use would the parcel as a whole be capable of producing a reasonable return or be adaptable to other suitable private use . . . To carry this burden the landowner should produce dollar and cents evidence as to the economic return that could be realized under each permitted use . . . Only when evidence shows that the economic value, or all but a bare residue of the value, of the parcel has been destroyed has a taking been established."

The two-part test often used to determine whether a land use regulation is an invalid taking was set forth in *Agins v. Tiburon*, 447 U.S. 255, 10 ELR 30361 (1980): "The application of a general zoning law to particular property effects a taking if the law does not substantially advance legitimate state interests . . . or denies an owner economically viable use of his land." The U.S. Supreme Court held that the rezoning of plaintiff's land to five acre single-family and open-space uses did not effect the inverse condemnation of the plaintiff's land. Inverse condemnation was defined by the Court as "a shorthand description of the manner in which a landowner recovers just compensation for a taking of his property when condemnation proceedings have not been instituted." Zoning regulations that protect the community's residents from the ill effects of urbanization "long have been recognized as legitimate." In this case, the landowners "will share with other owners the benefits and burdens of the city's exercise of its police power. In assessing the fairness of the zoning laws, these benefits must be considered along with any diminution in market value that the [landowners] might suffer."

The U.S. Supreme Court has held that a municipal ordinance must be substantially related to the public health, safety, morals, or general welfare. In *Nectow v. City of Cambridge*, 48 S. Ct. 447 (1928), the city's zoning was found to be unconstitutional as applied to plaintiff's property. The ordinance divided the city into three districts: residential, business, and unrestricted. Under this ordinance, part of plaintiff's property was zoned residentially. As a result of this restriction, plaintiff's deal to sell the property fell through. The plaintiff claimed that the ordinance as applied to him "deprived him of his property without due process of law in contravention of the Fourteenth Amendment." Plaintiff alleged that, as currently zoned, his property had no value because the surrounding area precluded its residential use. The Court agreed, finding that the factories and railroad tracks in the unrestricted zone surrounding plaintiff's property rendered the property valueless if confined to residential use. Since the residential zoning of the plaintiff's land could not be implemented it was not substantially related to achieving the public health, safety, morals, or general welfare.

In *Arverne Bay Construction Co. v. Thatcher*, 278 N.Y. 222 (1938), the New York Court of Appeals held that an ordinance which rezoned the plaintiff's property in Brooklyn from "unrestricted" to "residential" was unconstitutional. The court first addressed the issue of whether, having sought a variance from the applicable ordinance, plaintiff was then barred from attacking the validity of the ordinance when the application was denied. It was held that, while an application for a variance "necessarily assumes the validity of the ordinance," the denial of such variance cannot serve as binding adjudication as to whether or not a taking has occurred. The court then went on to consider the takings claim. The plaintiff, under the current zoning law, was unable to build a gasoline service station on his premises as desired and was limited to only residential uses. However, plaintiff's property surrounded by an incinerator and sewer which gave off odors not conducive to residential development. As justification for the rezoning, the City claimed that they intended to "aid the development of the new district in accordance with plans calculated to advance the public welfare of the city in the future." The court found that such planning is permitted under the police power, but that it is limited. A temporary restriction on the use of land is permissible "in order to promote the public good." At the time of this case, nine years had elapsed since the defendant had enacted the new ordinance, during which time the land had become no more suitable for residential development. That it would become suitable in the future was a hope, but not a certainty. Therefore, the court found that this was a permanent restriction on plaintiff's use of the property. Such a permanent restriction must be recognized as a taking. The court noted that "[t]he only substantial difference . . . between restriction and actual taking, is that the restriction leaves the owner subject to the burden of payment of payment of taxation, while outright confiscation would relieve him of that burden."

The New York Court of Appeals, in *Northern Westchester Professional Park Assoc. v. Town of Bedford*, 458 N.E.2d 809, 60 N.Y.2d 492 (1983), addressed the level of proof required to substantiate a confiscation claim. The plaintiff had requested a rezoning of his property from a residential to a business-office park district. When the Town denied the request, the plaintiff brought an action claiming that the denial deprived him of his due process because his property could not be used for any purpose under the applicable residential regulations. The court denied his claim, holding that he had not offered sufficient proof. In so holding, the court stated that the burden of proof was on the party challenging the ordinance to show that "no reasonable return may be obtained from the property under the existing zoning . . . ." Furthermore, the court held that this burden remained with the plaintiff throughout the case. Mere evidence of economic injury would not be sufficient to shift the burden to the Town. Nor would it be sufficient to allege significant economic injury, in the absence of other proof. Rather, the court set forth a formula to follow in order to determine whether the ordinance permits a reasonable return. First, the owner's total investment in the property, including taxes and expenses, must be computed. It must be shown that "the purchase price did not include a premium over fair market price at time of purchase in the expectation that the property would be downzoned." Second, the owner's investment must then by multiplied by the rate of return. The rate of return is determined by reference to similar property in the community. This figure is then measured against the rate of return that is likely under the current zoning regulations. This will provide a basis for the assertion that all value has been destroyed. If the rate of return is not reasonable solely because of the zoning regulation, it is confiscatory. The court, in this case, held that the property owner had failed to provide sufficient evidence because he did not consider various possible uses and he did not sufficiently establish his investment in the property.

A New York City law that required a landowner to permit a cable television company to install its equipment upon his property was found to be a regulatory taking in *Loretto v. Teleprompter Manhattan CATV Corp.*, 458 U.S. 419 (1982). The landowner had not applied to the city for any land use permit. She simply was required by the law to allow the cable company access to her site and to allow equipment that occupied one-eighth of a cubic foot of space to be permanently attached to her building. The court noted that, in this context, "[past] cases uniformly have found a taking to the extent of the [physical] occupation, without regard to whether the action achieves an important public benefit or has only minimal economic impact on the owner."

A Los Angeles County interim flood control law was challenged as a regulatory taking in *First English Evangelical Lutheran Church of Glendale v. County of Los Angeles*, 482 U.S. 304, 17 ELR 20787 (1987). The Court assumed as true the landowner's allegation that the law effected a total taking of its property value and was therefore invalid as a regulatory taking. This allowed it to consider the question of whether a landowner is entitled to damages for a temporary taking. Such a holding would allow an owner compensation for the period running from the enactment of a regulation that constitutes a taking to the time it is invalidated by the courts. Previously, the rule had been that compensation must be paid for the period beginning with the date a regulation is declared invalid as a taking and only if the government insists on enforcing it. This prior rule allowed the government to amend the offensive regulation and avoid compensating the landowner for the taking even when the regulation had been in effect for many years, as it had been in this case. The Court held "that where the government's activities have already worked a taking of all use of property, no subsequent action by the government can relieve it of the duty to provide compensation for the period during which the taking was effective." It went on to say that this holding does "not deal with the quite different questions that would arise in the case of normal delays in obtaining building permits, changes in zoning laws, variances, and the like which are not before us." On remand, the California courts determined that the flood control law in this case did not constitute a taking. The "temporary takings rule" of the *First English* case, however, endures.

A local law that regulated the use of single-room occupancy buildings in New York City was found to be a regulatory taking in *Seawall Associates v. New York*, 74 N.Y.2d 92, 542 L.E.2d 1059, 544 N.Y.S.2d 542 (1989). The property owner purchased one such building with plans to demolish it and construct a new commercial structure. The regulation, adopted subsequent to the purchase, prohibited the demolition and conversion of the building, required its rehabilitation as a single-room residential facility, and mandated that the owner lease the units to certain types of tenants as defined by the law. The Court of Appeals was particularly concerned by the requirements of the law that coerced an owner, who was not in the business of leasing apartments, to rent to particular tenants. The court noted that a private "owner suffers a special kind of injury when a stranger invades and occupies the owner's property, and property law has long protected an owner's expectation that he will be relatively undisturbed at least in the possession of his property." The court pointed out that "the right to exclude others has traditionally been considered one of the most treasured strands in an owner's bundle of property rights."

In *Lucas v. South Carolina Coastal Council*, 505 U.S. 1003, 22 ELR 21104 (1992), the trial court had found that the state's Beachfront Management Act rendered the landowner's two beachfront lots valueless. Regulations under the Act prohibited development within a setback line established to prevent erosion along the beach. The regulations did not permit landowners any variance for hardship caused by the prohibition. The Court referenced Justice Holmes' admonition in *Pennsylvania Coal Co. v. Mahon*, 260 U.S. 393 (1922), that "while property may be regulated to a certain extent, if regulation goes too far it will be recognized as a taking." The Court recognized that "government hardly could go on if to some extent values incident to property could not be diminished without paying for every such change in the general law." It stated, however, that "regulations that leave the owner of land without economically beneficial or productive options for its use–typically, as here, by requiring land to be left substantially in its natural state–carry with them a heightened risk that private property is being pressed into some form of public service under the guise of mitigating serious public harm." Relying on the trial court's determination, the Court found that "all economically beneficial or productive use" (*see Agins*, above) of the plaintiff's land had been taken. It went on to hold that the state must compensate the plaintiff for this value unless, upon remand, it can "identify background principles of nuisance and property law that prohibit the uses he now intends in the circumstances in which the property is presently found." In other words, if the restriction imposed on the land by the regulation is "inherent in the title to the land," it is valid, even where all economically beneficial use is taken. Upon remand, no such principles were found, and the state was required to pay the plaintiff full value for his land.

The Court examined the validity of an easement imposed as a condition to a site plan approval in *Dolan v. City of Tigard*, 512 U.S. 374, 24 ELR 21083 (1994). The city required the landowner to dedicate a portion of her property lying within a 100-year floodplain for the improvement of a storm drainage system along a nearby creek and that she dedicate an additional 15-foot strip of land adjacent to the floodplain as a pedestrian/bicycle pathway. The conditions required the owner to convey an easement to the city allowing it and the public access to her land. The landowner objected, claiming that these land dedication requirements were not related to the proposed development and, therefore, constituted an uncompensated taking. The Court stated that "[w]ithout question, had the city simply required petitioner to dedicate a strip of land along Fanno Creek for public use, rather than conditioning the grant of her permit to redevelop her property on such a dedication, a taking would have occurred."

Citing *Nollan v. California Coastal Commission*, 483 U.S. 825, 17 ELR 20918 (1987), the Court stated that when dedication conditions are imposed on a land use permit, they must bear an "essential nexus" to a legitimate public objective. In view of clear findings regarding the seriousness of the flooding and traffic problems in the city and along the creek, such a nexus was found. The Court went on to establish, for the first time, a test that is to be used to determine "the required degree of connection between the [dedication conditions] and the projected impact of the proposed development." For this purpose, the Court wrote that "we think a term such as 'rough proportionality' best encapsulates what we hold to be the requirement of the Fifth Amendment. No precise mathematical calculation is required, but the city must make some sort of individualized determination that the required dedication is related both in nature and extent to the impact of the proposed development." It found that the city had not shown why a dedicated public greenway, rather than a private one, was required in the interest of flood control. In regard to the pedestrian/bicycle path dedication, the Court held that the city's finding that the path "could offset some of the traffic demand" was too general. The city did not "meet its burden of demonstrating that the additional number of vehicle and bicycle trips generated by the petitioner's development reasonably relate to the city's requirement for a dedication of the pedestrian/bicycle pathway easement." The Court required the city to "make some effort to quantify its findings in support of the dedication . . . beyond the conclusory statement that it could offset some of the traffic demand generated."

The U.S. Supreme Court, in *Monterey v. Del Monte Dunes at Monterey*, 526 U.S. 687, 29 ELR 21133 (1999), held that the "rough proportionality" test set forth in the *Dolan* case was limited to exaction cases. It declined to extend it to cases in which the plaintiff challenges a denial of a development permit. In this case, the plaintiff brought an action against the city for repeatedly rejecting its development proposals and imposing new standards with each rejection. After five years, the plaintiff brought a Section 1983 action alleging a violation of due process and equal protection and a taking. The jury was instructed that it should find for the plaintiff if it found that plaintiff had been denied all economically viable use of its property or that the city's decision to reject the plaintiff's proposal did not substantially advance a legitimate public purpose. The jury found for the plaintiff and the city appealed. The Ninth Circuit Court of Appeals, in affirming, stated that "[e]ven if the City had a legitimate interest in denying Del Monte's development application, its action must be 'roughly proportional' to furthering that interest." The Supreme

Court found that this was inaccurate because this standard had not been extended beyond exaction cases, where private property is required to be dedicated to public use. The Court held that this rule was not designed to address issues present in the current case where the plaintiff's proposal was denied rather than conditioned on dedication to public use. For discussions of *Del Monte Dunes*, see Steven J. Eagle, Del Monte Dunes, *Good Faith, and Land Use Regulation*, 30 ELR 10100 (Feb. 2000); John D. Echeverria, *Revving the Engines in Neutral:* City of Monterey v. Del Monte Dunes at Monterey, Ltd., 29 ELR 10682 (Nov. 1999).

The New York Court of Appeals considered the "essential nexus" test in *Bonnie Briar Syndicate, Inc. v. Town of Mamaroneck*, 94 N.Y.2d 96 (1999). In affirming the decision of the Appellate Division, the court held that the *Agins* test remained the proper test for a regulatory taking: a regulatory taking occurs when the ordinance does not substantially advance a legitimate state interest or when it deprives the owner of the economically viable use of his land. In *Bonnie Briar*, the plaintiff alleged that the rezoning of its property from residential to recreational use constituted a taking. As a result of the rezoning, plaintiff's plan to construct a number of homes was denied by the town. However, the town had conducted years of studies and had documented its need to preserve open space, create recreational opportunities, and provide for flood control. The plaintiff, nonetheless, argued that under the *Nollan* test, "there is an insufficiently 'close causal nexus' between the rezoning measures and the legitimate public interests defendants sought to achieve." Although the plaintiff conceded that the Supreme Court, in *Del Monte Dunes*, limited the *Dolan* "rough proportionality" test to exaction cases, the plaintiff maintained that the court must consider the "essential nexus" test since the Supreme Court did not expressly state that it was also inapplicable to takings cases. The Court of Appeals disagreed and held that, in limiting the "rough proportionality" test to exaction cases, the Supreme Court "necessarily rejected the applicability of the 'essential nexus' inquiry to general zoning regulations as well."

In *Grogan v. Zoning Board of Appeals of the Town of East Hampton*, 221 A.D.2d 441, 633 N.Y.S.2d 809 (2d Dep't 1995), plaintiffs challenged a scenic and conservation easement imposed as a condition to the zoning board of appeals' grant of a variance allowing them to build an addition to their home. The plaintiffs challenged the easement condition as arbitrary and capricious. The easement prevented development on a portion of land designated as a wetland, but did not permit public access. The court concluded that the town had adequately sustained its burden of proof by "demonstrating a rough proportionality between the easement and the projected environmental impacts of the [plaintiffs'] construction proposal." The town had concrete evidence in the environmental assessment form submitted with the application that persuaded the court that the determination was reasonable. "[T]he easement is an appropriate measure to address the specific environmental impacts of the [plaintiffs'] proposal" and is a valid and individualized determination. The court held that the easement substantially advanced the governmental interest of preserving wetlands and environmentally significant areas and was not arbitrary and capricious.

The denial of a variance from a setback requirement that prevented the landowner from building on its one-acre lot was challenged in *Gazza v. DEC*, 89 N.Y.2d 603, 679 N.E.2d 1035, 657 N.Y.S.2d 555 (1997). The landowner purchased the parcel for $100,000 knowing it was subject to wetland regulations from which a variance from the State Department of Environmental Conservation (DEC) would have to be obtained to allow its development as a single-family parcel. The landowner estimated that, if the variances were granted, the land would be worth $396,000. Because the owner could not demonstrate that the variances would have no adverse impact on the tidal wetlands contained on the property, the request was denied. The effect of the denial was to limit the use of the site to a catwalk, dock, and parking lot–activities that would have required variances from the village's zoning board. Rather than pursue these local variances, the landowner challenged the denials as a regulatory taking. The court noted that "[o]ur courts have long recognized that a property interest must exist before it may be taken." A taking claim may not "be based upon property rights that have already been taken away from a landowner in favor of the public." "[R]egulatory limitations that inhere in the title itself will bind a purchaser" (citing *Lucas*, above).

The court's holding that "a promulgated regulation forms part of the title to property as a preexisting rule of state law" was used to deny takings claims in three other cases decided by the New York Court of Appeals on the same day as *Gazza*. In *Anello v. ZBA*, 89 N.Y.2d 535, 678 N.E.2d 870, 656 N.Y.S.2d 184 (1997), the Court of Appeals denied a takings claim where the village's steep slope law prevented an owner who purchased a lot after the law was adopted from building a single-family house on her lot. In *Kim v. City of New York*, 90 N.Y.2d 1, 681 N.E.2d 312, 659 N.Y.S.2d 145 (1997), no taking was found where the landowner had constructive notice when he bought the land of a city charter provision allowing the city to enter the site and place fill on it to provide lateral support for the elevation of a public road that was below legal grade. In *Basile v. Town of Southhampton*, 89 N.Y.2d 974, 678 N.E.2d 489, 655 N.Y.S.2d 877 (1997), the court denied a landowner's claim that the value of its land taken in condemnation proceedings should be assessed as if wetland regulations did not apply to the site. The court held that wetland regulations "do not effect a taking when a purchaser acquires property subject to such regulations."

Four years following the New York Court of Appeals rulings in these four cases, the U.S. Supreme Court handed down a decision that substantially modified the New York rule. In *Palazzolo v. Rhode Island,* 2001 WL 721005, the Court reversed a determination by the Rhode Island Supreme Court that a landowner had no right to challenge a regulation as a regulatory taking when the regulation was in place when title to the land was acquired. The Court first held that Palazzolo's case was ripe for adjudication after having submitted applications for permits to fill tidal wetlands for development as a private beach club.

Palazzolo owned a 20 acre parcel, most of which was salt marsh subject to tidal flooding. Development would have required significant fill, up to six feet in some places, to support any development. Under the Rhode Island coastal wetland regulations, development on the tidal wetlands portion of this site was prohibited unless the owner secured a special exception permit for an activity that serves a compelling public purpose which benefits the public as a whole. Since the responsible state agency, in denying Palazzolo's application to fill 11 of 18 tidal wetland acres for a private beach club, made a determination that this type of private development of tidal lands was not eligible for a special use permit, the Court held that the matter was ripe. In this unusual context, no further applications by Palazzolo were necessary to determine how the land could be developed privately under the regulations. An application for a permit to fill fewer acres would not change the determination that the requisite "public interest" was being served. This constituted a final determination that there can be no filling of this class of wetlands for any ordinary land use and, therefore, the case was ripe for judicial review.

This ripeness issue bears on the court's holding regarding the effect of a preexisting regulation on the existence of a takings claim. The Court stated that it would be illogical and unfair to bar a regulatory takings claim because of the transfer of land after a regulation was adopted where the steps necessary to make the claim ripe were not taken by the previous owner. Here, Palazzolo's claim ripened after applications were submitted and denied, became ripe at that moment, and accrued to his benefit as owner. A majority of the Court could not agree on whether the existence of a regulation at the time of purchase should be considered in determining whether the regulation interfers with the purchaser's investment-backed expectations, one of several factors used to determine if a taking has occurred. The Supreme Court remanded the case to the Rhode Island courts for a determination as to whether a taking had in fact occurred. Palazzolo's property contained two upland acres and it was agreed that a substantial residence could be built on that land. The Supreme Court upheld the Rhode Island Supreme Court's determination that the coastal regulations did not constitute a total taking under *Lucas v. South Carolina Coastal Council,* 505 U.S. 1003 (1992). The Court noted that the development rights on the upland area did not constitute a token interest and that, therefore, the regulations did not leave the land economically idle as must be the case for the *Lucas* total taking rule to apply.

The plaintiff, in *Good v. United States*, 189 F.3d 1355, 30 ELR 20102 (Fed. Cir. 1999), claimed that an unconstitutional taking had occurred when he was denied a permit by the Army Corps of Engineers. The plaintiff purchased the land in 1973 and had obtained permits from the Corps in 1983, 1984, and 1988. Each of these expired and, because construction had not begun, the plaintiff was required to obtain a new permit. In 1990, the permit was denied because the development constituted a threat to animals protected by the federal Endangered Species Act (ESA). The ESA had not been in effect at the time that the plaintiff purchased the land in 1973. The plaintiff alleged that the denial constituted a taking. The court found that a taking had not occurred because in order to find a taking the plaintiff must show that the denial "interfered with his investment-backed expectations." The plaintiff must show that the property was acquired in "reliance on the non-existence of the challenged regulation." There was evidence that, at the time of the purchase, the plaintiff was aware that he might have some difficulty obtaining the necessary permits. Furthermore, even though the ESA was not in existence when the plaintiff purchased the property, the "regulatory climate" suggested that it was forthcoming and that environmental factors were becoming significant in the permit issuance process. The court held that "[i]n view of the regulatory climate that existed when Appellant acquired the subject property, Appellant could not have had a reasonable expectation that he would obtain approval to fill ten acres of wetlands in order to develop the land." For a discussion of *Good*, see Robert Meltz, *Wetlands Regulation and the Law of Regulatory Takings*, 30 ELR 10468 (2000).

REFERENCE

John R. Nolon, *Footprints on the Shifting Sands of the Isle of Palms: A Practical Analysis of Regulatory Takings Cases,* 8 J. Land Use & Envtl. L. 1 (1992).

D. JUDICIAL REVIEW

DEFINITION

When zoning provisions are adopted and land use determinations are made by local legislative or administrative bodies, they are subject to review by the courts. There are a variety of rules that govern access to the courts, the timing of applications for judicial review, the standards used by courts to review such actions, and the remedies that courts will employ to resolve disputes brought before them.

The courts in New York, relative to courts in other states, have adopted fairly liberal rules of access, typically allowing adjacent and nearby property owners and associations of residents to challenge land use decisions that affect them in some special way. On the other hand, the New York courts defer to the legislative and administrative judgments of municipal bodies by presuming the validity of their actions and imposing a fairly heavy burden of proof on those who challenge them. The state legislature has further protected municipal actions by requiring that challengers bring their challenge, in most cases, within 30 days or four months of the municipal action.

Courts are reluctant to order local legislatures to take specific actions; they are more comfortable issuing judgments that declare legislative actions valid or invalid, and simply enjoining legislatures from enforcing invalid regulations or decisions. This reluctance to order legislatures to act is part of the important doctrine of separation of powers between the judicial and legislative branches of government. The judiciary is not so inhibited, however, when reviewing the actions of a planning board or zoning board of appeals, which is an administrative agency or performs quasi-judicial functions for the locality. With respect to the decisions and actions of these bodies and officials, courts will require specific actions to be taken, such as the award or revocation of a building permit or subdivision approval.

PURPOSE

The state legislature and the judiciary, in establishing the rules of access to the courts, recognize that the purpose of land use regulations–to protect the public health, safety, and welfare–is enhanced by allowing a broad range of affected parties to challenge their adoption and enforcement. At the same time, the importance of allowing local legislatures and boards to function efficiently and to exercise their discretion without undue judicial interference is recognized in the court's deference to local actions. In most cases, judges will allow any reasonable interpretation of the evidence presented to justify and protect that local action from invalidation.

These rules and standards present a dilemma to those who consider the significant expense and time involved in contesting local land use actions. While challenges are permitted, there are significant obstacles to succeeding, except in those instances where it can be proved that the local action is clearly arbitrary or capricious, unsupported by any valid evidentiary findings, or clearly in violation of required procedures.

WHEN

Challengers are allowed to seek judicial review of local land use decisions when they are affected by the action in some special way, different from the general public. Although land use actions are required to benefit the general public, not all local residents have "standing" to sue. However, the judicial policy on land use issues is that it is desirable to resolve disputes on their merits rather than by preclusive and restrictive standing rules.

The owners of properties that are the direct subject of a land use action are given standing to challenge the action when it directly restricts the use or enjoyment of their property. Additionally, standing is afforded to nearby property owners who can demonstrate that they will be adversely impacted as a result of the challenged action. For example, the owner of a parcel a half-mile away from a development project approved by a local agency does not have standing to challenge its approval based on proximity alone, but may have standing if he can show that hydrogeologic formations and drainage patterns beneath the site indicate that his drinking water would be adversely affected by the development.

Certain associations of affected individuals may also bring actions on behalf of their members. To be awarded standing to challenge land use actions, associations must be fairly representative of the community, have open membership, have the capacity and authority to maintain judicial actions, and be organized to protect the interest allegedly affected by the land use action.

Property owners cannot challenge a land use action solely because they will suffer economic competition from a newly permitted development or business. Limiting economic competition has been held by the courts as not within the "zone of interest" of zoning and land use regulation; parties whose only injury is increased competition, therefore, are not allowed to challenge a project's approval.

Given the expense of litigation and the deference of judges to official local land use actions, potential litigants may want to pursue other methods of conflict resolution when allowed to do so by local procedures. Recent interest in the mediation of controversial land use proposals at the local level suggests that there are, at times, alternatives to litigation that can be considered before invoking the jurisdiction of the courts.

AUTHORITY AND IMPLEMENTATION

In New York State, those who are "aggrieved" by a decision of a zoning board of appeals, building official, planning board, or other local body are given the legal authority to apply to the

Supreme Court of the state for relief under Article 78 of the Civil Practice Law and Rules. Such persons are permitted to ask the court to review the decisions of these boards and officials. When an action is found to be invalid, the court may order the local board or official to conform the action to the requirements of the substantive law. This may be done either by enjoining the enforcement of an invalid action or by mandating affirmative action, such as the issuance of a permit illegally denied. These remedies are available against a local legislative body when it is acting in an administrative capacity, such as issuing or denying a special permit or approving or denying a site plan.

Where the discretionary actions of a legislative body acting in its legislative capacity are challenged, courts rarely require the legislature to take specific and affirmative action. Rather, the court will issue a judgment declaring the action to be invalid and enjoin its enforcement. Such an action can be brought to declare a zoning provision unconstitutional. Declaratory judgment actions can be brought to determine whether a rezoning conforms with the comprehensive plan or constitutes illegal spot zoning, to determine the validity of a refusal to rezone a parcel of land, to determine the constitutionality of conditions attached to a rezoning, or to determine the authority of a municipality to adopt a particular zoning provision.

The courts may require the local legislature to exercise its zoning authority in a particular fashion in the rare event that it has found that the zoning law is discriminatory or exclusionary. In an exclusionary zoning case, where the court mandated the rezoning of the plaintiff's property to multi-family zoning, the court noted that "with the single exception of discriminatory zoning of similarly situated parcels . . . a judicial declaration that a zoning law was invalid was never accompanied by a declaration which actually rezoned that property or placed it within a particular use classification."

LIMITATIONS AND CONCERNS

In addition to the standing rules that limit access to the courts, a variety of other factors affect parties who seek judicial review of local land use actions.

Strict Standards of Judicial Review: Courts apply fairly restrictive standards when reviewing challenges to local land use actions. In a sweeping and decisive statement on this issue, the New York Court of Appeals said:

> The crux of the matter is that the responsibility for making zoning decisions has been committed primarily to quasi-legislative, quasi-administrative boards composed of representatives of the local community. Local officials, generally, possess the familiarity with local conditions necessary to make the often sensitive planning decisions which affect the development of the community. Absent arbitrariness, it is for locally selected and locally responsible officials to determine where the public interest in zoning lies. Judicial review of local zoning decisions is limited; not only in our court but in all courts. Where there is a rational basis for the local decision, that decision should be sustained. It matters not whether, in close cases, a court would have, or should have, decided the matter differently. The judicial responsibility is to review zoning decisions but not, absent proof of arbitrary and unreasonable action, to make them.

Cowan v. Kern, 41 N.Y.2d 591, 599, 363 N.E.2d 305, 310, 394 N.Y.S.2d 579, 584 (1977). With regard to the adoption and amendment of zoning and land use regulations by local legislatures, the New York courts have stated that such actions enjoy a strong presumption of constitutionality. If there is a reasonable relationship between the end sought to be achieved and the measure adopted to achieve it, the regulation in question will be upheld.

Where the decisions of local land use agencies are not supported by credible evidence on the record of their proceedings, and particularly where the record shows that the land use action was taken solely in response to local citizen opposition, local land use actions will be invalidated as arbitrary or an abuse of discretion.

Statute of Limitations: In New York State, challenges to decisions of the zoning board of appeals and planning board must be brought within 30 days of the date of their filing. The same period applies to determinations by the building inspector and for most decisions on applications submitted to any local body, including the local legislature when it is acting in a permit issuing capacity. Challenges based on procedural defects in local land use proceedings must be brought within the same 30-day period. Where the challenge is to a discretionary legislative decision, such as the adoption of a zoning amendment, it must be brought within four months.

Exhaustion and Finality: Before a decision of a New York local zoning board of appeals, planning board, or zoning official can be challenged, it must be a final decision and impose direct and immediate impacts or injury on the challenger. Similarly, a challenge may not be brought when available administrative remedies have not been sought. Where the challenger can appeal the matter to another body, such as a zoning board of appeals, or where a rehearing on the matter complained of can be had, the jurisdiction of the court cannot be invoked. Where an applicant for a building permit fails to appeal the denial to the zoning board of appeals, for example, he cannot appeal the denial to the courts. Where the only question is a legal one, or the challenge is to the constitutionality of the regulation on its face, administrative appeals need not be exhausted, because the local administrative agency does not decide such issues.

STATUTES

In New York State, Village Law §7-712-c, Town Law §267-c, and General City Law §81-c provide that a person aggrieved by any decision of the zoning board of appeals or any officer, department, board, or bureau of the municipality may apply to the New York Supreme Court for review by a proceeding under Article 78 of the Civil Practice Law and Rules (CPLR).

CPLR §§3001 and 3017(b) authorize aggrieved parties to test the validity of zoning and land use regulations by bringing an action for a declaratory judgment.

Local decisions regarding site plan and subdivision applications and the issuance of variances and special permits are subject to a 30-day statute of limitations for bringing an Article 78 proceeding. This requirement is found in Village Law §§7-712-c, 7-725-a and b, and 7-740; Town Law §§267-c, 274-a and b, and 282; and General City Law §§27-a and b, 38, and 81-c.

CASE DIGEST

LEGISLATIVE ACTIONS

The New York Court of Appeals has held that "the power of a [local government] to amend its basic zoning law in such a way as reasonably to promote the general welfare cannot be questioned." *Rodgers v. Village of Tarrytown*, 302 N.Y. 115, 96 N.E.2d 731 (1951). In *Rodgers*, the plaintiff challenged a village zoning amendment that allowed construction of multiple dwellings in a single-family zone. The court upheld the amendment, noting that "how various properties shall be classified or reclassified rests with the local legislative body; its judgment and determination will be conclusive, beyond interference from the courts, unless shown to be arbitrary, and the burden of establishing such arbitrariness is imposed upon him who asserts it." The court determined that "[c]hanged or changing conditions call for changed plans, and persons who own property in a particular zone or use district enjoy no eternally vested right to the classification if the public interest demands otherwise."

"A zoning change is a legislative act and is presumed to be constitutional and valid." *Coutant v. Town of Poughkeepsie*, 69 A.D.2d 506, 419 N.Y.S.2d 148 (2d Dep't 1979). The case demonstrates again that the plaintiffs have the burden of proving the zoning law invalid.

The court in *Vezza v. Bauman*, 192 A.D.2d 712, 597 N.Y.S.2d 418 (2d Dep't 1993), held that an Article 78 proceeding is not an appropriate vehicle for challenging the constitutionality of zoning laws. *Cf. Save the Pine Bush, Inc. v. City of Albany*, 70 N.Y.2d 193, 512 N.E.2d 526, 518 N.Y.S.2d 943 (1987) (holding that "the general rule is that an Article 78 proceeding is unavailable to challenge the validity of a legislative act such as a zoning law . . . [unless] the challenge is directed not at the substance of the law but at the procedures followed in its enactment . . .") The proper action in these cases is one for a declaratory judgment.

A property owner in *Janiak v. Town of Greenville*, 203 A.D.2d 329, 610 N.Y.S.2d 286 (2d Dep't 1994), challenged the validity of a local law amending the town's zoning law regarding the requirements that must be met by site plan applications. The court concluded that "the challenged action is clearly legislative in nature, as evinced by its general applicability, indefinite duration and formal adoption." The court held that to challenge the validity of a legislative enactment, a declaratory action should be used, and not an Article 78 proceeding.

The court in *Esselte Pendaflex Corp. v. Incorporated Village of Garden City*, 216 A.D.2d 519, 629 N.Y.S.2d 59 (2d Dep't 1995), held that "the role of the courts is limited to determining whether the law bears at least a minimal relationship to a legitimate, governmental objective."

PLANNING BOARD ACTIONS

The failure of a planning board to provide a factual basis for its decision precludes judicial review. The conclusory statements in this case "fail[ed] to provide the factual basis for the Board's decision and foreclose[d] intelligent judicial review." As a result of this failure, the board's decision was invalidated. *Leibring v. Planning Board of Town of Newfane*, 144 A.D.2d 903, 534 N.Y.S.2d 236 (4th Dep't 1988), as amended, 147 A.D.2d 984 (4th Dep't 1989).

The applicants for subdivision approval in *King v. Chmielewski*, 76 N.Y.2d 182, 556 N.E.2d 435, 556 N.Y.S.2d 996 (1990), filed an Article 78 proceeding to compel the Town Clerk to issue a certificate of approval or to nullify the town planning board's determination denying the subdivision application. "The statute places on the petitioners–and not the planning board– responsibility for following up on their application by determining when a board's decision has been filed in its office." "The petitioners' challenge to the Town Clerk's refusal to issue a default certificate is not governed by the time constraints delineated in [the] Town Law . . . but by the CPLR . . . which imposes a four-month statute of limitations period."

"[I]t is the function of the [Planning] Board, not the court, to weigh and reconcile . . . conflicting evidence." *Thomas v. Brookins*, 175 A.D.2d 619, 572 N.Y.S.2d 557 (4th Dep't 1991). *See also Hess Realty v. Planning Commission of Town of Rotterdam*, 198 A.D.2d 588, 603 N.Y.S.2d 95 (3d Dep't 1993) (holding that the planning board has no authority to interpret zoning laws); *Wal-Mart Stores, Inc. v. Planning Board of the Town of North Elba*, 238 A.D.2d 93, 668 N.Y.S.2d 774 (3d Dep't 1998) (stating that planning board determinations are not "true adjudicatory hearings" and therefore the standard of review is "one of rationality, not substantial evidence").

ZONING BOARD OF APPEALS ACTIONS

A landowner sought review of a zoning board of appeals' denial of an area variance in *Cowan v. Kern*, 41 N.Y.2d 591, 363 N.E.2d 305, 394 N.Y.S.2d 579 (1977). The court held that "[a]bsent arbitrariness, it is for locally selected and locally responsible officials to determine where the public interest in zoning lies. Judicial review of local zoning decisions is limited. Where there is a rational basis for the local decision, that decision should be sustained." *See also Fuhst v. Foley*, 45 N.Y.2d 441, 382 N.E.2d 756, 410 N.Y.S.2d 56 (1978) (holding that "[a] zoning board determination should not be set aside unless there is a showing of illegality, arbitrariness or abuse of discretion"); *Smith v. Town of Islip*, 202 A.D.2d 674, 609 N.Y.S.2d 912 (2d Dep't 1994) (limiting the court's review of the board's decision to "whether that determination has a rational basis and is supported by substantial evidence").

A restaurant chain sought review of a denial of a special exception permit and area variance in *McDonald's Corp. v. Rose*, 111 A.D.2d 850, 490 N.Y.S.2d 588 (2d Dep't 1985). The court held that "the findings of the [zoning board of appeals] are without factual support in the record . . . and represent an arbitrary and capricious exercise of respondent's authority." Rather than remand the decision, the Appellate Division reviewed the record and decided that the restaurant owner had proved its right to the special exception permit and had met the requirements for the area variance.

In *Greene v. Johnson*, 121 A.D.2d 632, 503 N.Y.S.2d 656 (2d Dep't 1986), the court refused to review the decision of a zoning board of appeals because it had made no findings of fact and remanded the matter to the board to make a determination based on additional fact finding. *See also Masten v. Baldauf*, 147 A.D.2d 566, 537 N.Y.S.2d 860 (2d Dep't 1989) (holding that "a zoning board of appeals" set forth its findings in its resolution . . . and they were sufficient to show the actual grounds for its decision and to 'permit adequate judicial review'"); *Berka v. Seltzer*, 170 A.D.2d 450, 565 N.Y.S.2d 234 (2d Dep't 1991) (holding that a zoning board of appeals' findings on the record "relieved the Supreme Court of having to remit the matter to the Board for the purpose of issuing a decision that included its reasons for the denial").

In an action to review the granting of a permit for construction of a car wash in *Sun-Brite Car Wash, Inc. v. Board of Zoning and Appeals of Town of North Hempstead*, 69 N.Y.2d 406, 508 N.E.2d 130, 515 N.Y.S.2d 418 (1987), the court held that "[a]ggrievement warranting judicial review requires a threshold showing that a person has been adversely affected by the activities of defendants." The court discussed standing, noting that "[s]tanding principles, which are in the end matters of policy, should not be heavy handed; in zoning litigation in particular, it is desirable that land use disputes be resolved on their own merits rather than by preclusive, restrictive standing rules. . . . The petitioning party must have a legally cognizable interest that is or will be affected by the zoning determination; proof of special damage or in-fact injury is not required in every instance to establish that the value or enjoyment of one's property is adversely affected."

The court in *Kemp v. Zoning Board of Appeals of Village of Wappingers Falls*, 216 A.D.2d 466, 628 N.Y.S.2d 187 (2d Dep't 1995), held that the plaintiffs did not have standing because they "failed to establish that the variance in question caused them injury within the zone of interests protected by zoning regulations, inasmuch as the only potential injury suggested in the record is an increase in business competition."

In *Town of Clinton v. Dumias*, 69 A.D.2d 836, 415 N.Y.S.2d 81 (2d Dep't 1979), the zoning board of appeals filed a letter decision with the town clerk. The letter was also sent to interested parties informing them of the board's decision. The court concluded that since the letter contained the required information and was filed with the town clerk prior to the filing of the minutes, it was sufficient to start the running of the statute of limitations. *Cf. DeBellis v. Luney*, 128 A.D.2d 778, 513 N.Y.S.2d 478 (2d Dep't 1987) (holding that "the filing with the Village Clerk of the minutes of a board meeting which contained the decision and resolution of the board, reflecting each member's vote and a formal procedure in which the board acted as a body, was sufficient to start the running of the statute of limitations").

In *Cohen v. Hahn*, 155 A.D.2d 969, 547 N.Y.S.2d 780 (4th Dep't 1989), the court concluded that "it was error for the court to order a hearing de novo in Supreme Court on petitioner's application for a use variance. The determination whether to grant a variance lies within the discretion of the zoning authorities and a reviewing court may not conduct a trial de novo." *See also St. Onge v. Donovan*, 71 N.Y.2d 507, 522 N.E.2d 1019, 527 N.Y.S.2d 721 (1988) (holding that a decision based on substantial evidence by the zoning board of appeals may not be heard by the reviewing court under a trial de novo unless the decision was made illegally, arbitrarily, or as an abuse of discretion).

If the defense of failure to file the petition within the prescribed period (30 days) is not raised before the New York Supreme Court, it is waived and may not be raised on appeal from that court. *Hoffay v. Tifft*, 164 A.D.2d 94, 562 N.Y.S.2d 995 (3d Dep't 1990).

"An entity seeking to institute litigation must have the capacity to do so. Such capacity can only be granted expressly or by necessary implication by the legislative body that created the entity. . . ."The conservation advisory council was created" to perform monitoring, inventory, coordination and advisory functions and lacks the express legislative authority to initiate legal actions." *Darlington v. City of Ithaca Board of Zoning Appeals*, 202 A.D.2d 831, 609 N.Y.S.2d 378 (3d Dep't 1994).

E. USING MEDIATION TO RESOLVE LAND USE DISPUTES

DEFINITION

Mediation is a voluntary process of dispute resolution. A neutral third party is engaged to assist the interested parties in arriving at a mutually acceptable solution to a controversy. The mediator has no authority to resolve the dispute or to impose a settlement. Rather, the mediator's role is to facilitate discussions among the participants, assisting the parties in identifying the issues at hand, and helping to find alternative solutions to the problem.

Mediation is one method of resolving disputes regarding land use actions pending before a municipal body such as a planning board, zoning board of appeals, or local legislature.

A local mediation law can be adopted by the local legislature. It encourages parties interested in land use disputes to participate in a mediated settlement of those disputes. A model mediation law is included in this chapter. The model law authorizes, but does not require, the parties to retain a mediator and to participate in good faith in the mediation process. The law authorizes local land use review and approval boards to suspend applicable time periods to allow mediation to occur. The interested parties and the municipality may share the costs of mediation.

Neither the parties in interest nor the local board is bound by the results of the mediation under this model law. If the parties resolve the dispute, they may submit their agreement, along with the facts on which it is based, to the local board for its consideration. If the board finds that the facts are accurate, it may concur with the agreement, but it must exercise independent judgment based on a review of the matter that is open to the public.

According to a 1999 nationwide study by the Lincoln Land Institute and the Consensus Building Institute, participants in mediated land use dispute resolution process rated them highly. Eighty-six percent of those participating reported that their reaction to mediation was either favorable (40%) or very favorable (46%). In addition, 85% thought the mediator played a critical role in contributing to the success of the process. Nearly two-thirds of the disputes were settled, but even in unsettled cases, fully 64% of the participants felt that mediation had helped the parties make significant progress.

PURPOSE

The primary purpose of a local law encouraging the mediation of such disputes is to provide a more flexible process that allows the interests of all parties to the dispute to be considered in resolving the dispute. Mediators are trained to build trust among parties unaccustomed to collaborating with one another and to encourage all sides to search for solutions that all interested parties can accept.

Local boards are often frustrated and obstructed by the controversy that accompanies land use proposals. Mediation can unite parties behind a negotiated proposal and facilitate the board's review and approval of it. At a minimum, mediation can narrow the range of issues in dispute and create a more collaborative method of discussing remaining disagreements.

WHEN

Early in the Process, to Prevent Disputes: Although mediation is described as a dispute resolution technique, it is also an effective means of avoiding disputes in the land use area. Often, when a developer seeks approval of a project from a local board, the public may not become involved in the process until the public hearing stage. By this time, the developer may have invested substantial time, money, and energy in the proposal and have become highly invested in it. Because of this investment, the developer may resist suggested changes, more than if those suggestions had been made earlier. Public hearings and public comment periods, which occur in the later stages of project review, often result in requests to significantly modify the proposal. Mediation may be employed to bring the interested parties together much earlier in the process, so that a project's design accommodates the concerns of as many of the interested parties as possible. In this way, mediation can influence the developer's application, resulting in early amendments to plans based on the results achieved in mediation.

Later in the Process, to Resolve Disputes: Disputes that arise later in the land use approval process may be resolved through mediation. The usual process of reviewing the proposal may not provide as effective a means for proponents and opponents of projects to resolve their differences. When the local government allows the parties to mediate these differences, they are provided with an opportunity to explore a variety of ways of realizing the objectives of all interested parties.

AUTHORITY

In New York State, the Municipal Home Rule Law authorizes a city, town, or village to adopt and amend local laws relating to powers granted to it in the Statute of Local Governments. The Statute of Local Governments empowers municipalities to adopt zoning regulations. The Municipal Home Rule Law gives cities, towns, and villages authority to adopt local laws regarding their property, affairs, and government and to protect and enhance their physical and visual environment.

Local laws must be consistent with general state laws. There is no general New York State law that expressly permits or preempts the adoption of a local land use mediation law. There are, however, general state laws that require local land use agencies to follow specific procedures and to respect discrete timetables. A local mediation law modifies these procedures and timetables to accommodate effective mediation of disputes. The Municipal Home Rule Law allows local governments to alter, or supersede, these procedures and the time requirements contained in state law.

IMPLEMENTATION

Although mediation can be encouraged and enabled by the local government, the local land use decision-making board normally will not participate in the mediation process as a party in interest. Land use review agencies must maintain their objectivity and make their decisions based on facts that are placed on the public record created in an open and public manner. Local agencies may appoint a representative to attend mediation sessions, to provide information, and to observe the process and understand the results.

Under a local mediation law, the members of local land use bodies are authorized to encourage the parties interested in and affected by a proposal to mediate their differences. If they agree to proceed, a mediator acceptable to the parties must be identified and retained. The mediator then facilitates the gathering and dissemination of relevant information, establishes rapport among the parties, and encourages them to identify their interests and to understand those of the other side. During the course of several meetings, with the mediator communicating with the parties between meetings, the parties arrive at an agreement that represents an acceptable compromise of their interests. The agreement is drafted, refined, and settled and is then presented to the local board for consideration.

When the parties in interest submit a mediated agreement to the local land use board, that agreement does not bind the public decision-making board. The legal decisionmaking authority of a public body cannot be delegated to private parties, nor may the decision be based solely on private agreements. However, when an agreement is designed to protect the critical concerns of the stakeholders, it will carry significant weight in the official decisionmaking process. Part of the mediator's assignment will be to be certain that all relevant facts are considered in arriving at the agreement, that all interested parties are involved in the process, and that any agreement is supported by the facts.

ILLUSTRATION

In one case, the owner and developer of a small shopping center applied for a variance to add a car wash, convenience store, and gas station at the site. Community resistance to the proposal was great, with residents voicing fears that the traffic and noise generated by the new facilities would negatively affect their property values and quality of life. The town's planning director suggested that the parties engage a mediator.

Although all parties were apprehensive about the process from the start, the alternative—litigation—was less appealing. With the help of a mediator, the four key interest groups were identified, alternatives were developed and evaluated, and a negotiated settlement was created. In a joint presentation, the four parties proposed their final agreement to the planning commission and town board, which unanimously ratified the project.

After this successful venture, the owner again sought a variance to allow a tenant at the shopping center to extend operating hours in one of the businesses. Instead of approaching his local board first, the owner went to the neighbors, told them about his needs, worked out an agreement, and later received the requested permit.

LIMITATIONS AND CONCERNS

There are two limitations to using mediation early in the local review and approval process. The first is that the interested parties may not identify themselves until later in the process, after the project has been discussed at board meetings. The second is that the parties may not believe that there is a sufficient dispute to justify the time, expense, and risk of subjecting the matter to mediation.

A limitation to mediating a genuine dispute later in the process is that the positions may have hardened, distrust among the parties may have developed, and the parties may wish to litigate the matter, as an alternative to resolving their interests through mediation.

There is no legal requirement that binds the decisionmaking body to the terms of the agreement, save its independent, fact-based assessment of the reasonableness of the agreement.

Parties to mediated disputes usually prefer that the proceedings be confidential. This preference is at odds with the general policy that the discussion of land use matters should be open to the public. Since the mediation sessions are not considered official meetings of the local review board, they are not subject to the Open Meetings Law. Legally, mediation meetings can be held as closed sessions. Politically, this may be difficult to accomplish.

Mediation should not prolong the process or delay decisionmaking. If done correctly, it can create a receptive atmosphere for decisionmaking. Potential parties to mediation are unlikely to participate unless the process has integrity and moves expeditiously. Similarly, they will need assurances that any agreement reached will be considered seriously by the reviewing board.

STATUTES

The New York Municipal Home Rule Law, §10(1)(ii)(a)(14), authorizes a city, town, or village to adopt and amend local laws relating to "[t]he powers granted to it in the statute of local governments."

Section 10(6) of the Statute of Local Governments empowers municipalities to "adopt, amend, and repeal zoning regulations."

The Municipal Home Rule Law, §10(1)(ii)(a)(11), gives cities, towns, and villages authority to adopt local laws for "the protection and enhancement of [their] physical and visual environment."

The Municipal Home Rule Law, §10(1)(i), gives cities, towns, and villages authority to adopt local laws not inconsistent with provisions of the constitution relating to their local property, affairs, or government.

To exercise its supersession authority, a town or village must follow the procedures outlined in the Municipal Home Rule Law. Section 22 requires that a local law that supersedes a state law "shall specify the chapter . . . number and year of enactment, section, subsection or subdivision, which it is intended to change or supersede."

REFERENCES

Edith M. Netter, *Using Mediation to Resolve Land Use Disputes*, Zoning & Planning Law Handbook §7.01 (Apr. 1992).

Barbara McAdoo & Larry Bakken, *Local Government Use of Mediation for Resolution of Public Disputes*, 22 Urb. Law. 179 (1990).

Joseph Tomain, *Land Use Mediation for Planners*, 7 Mediation Quarterly 164 (1990).

New York State Legislative Commission on Rural Resources, A Model Local Law for Mediation of Land Use Disputes, Albany, N.Y. (Jan. 1998).

MODEL LOCAL LAND USE MEDIATION LAW

This model local land use mediation law:

- Contains a declaration of policy that identifies the purpose of mediation and preserves the decision-making authority of municipal boards, agencies, and officers.
- Provides for the costs of mediation to be shared by the participants in the mediation and the municipality.
- Lists the minimum qualifications required for mediators and excludes the municipality itself from being a "party in interest."
- Identifies mediation as a voluntary process, vests the local review board with authority to suspend time limits on land use reviews, and outlines procedures for suspending those time limits.
- Recognizes the need for confidentiality in mediation proceedings.
- Mandates compliance with accepted mediation practices.
- Encourages parties to give fact-based reasons for supporting the agreement and to place those reasons on the public record.
- References illustrative provisions of general state statutes that the local law is intended to supersede.

LOCAL LAW NO. 1 OF 200-

Providing for the use of mediation in land use disputes in the Town, Village, or City of
_____.

Be it enacted by the [name of local legislature] of the [name of community] as follows:

Chapter ___ (Zoning) of the Local Laws of the [name of community] is hereby amended by adding a new article as follows:

ARTICLE ___

Section 1: Short Title and Applicability

A. This local law shall be known as the "[name of community] Land Use Mediation Law."

B. This law shall apply within the jurisdiction of the [town, village, or city of _____].

Section 2: Declaration of Policy

A. The [name of local legislature] recognizes that disputes often occur between proponents of, and parties affected by, proposals for developments pending before planning, zoning, and land use agencies and boards in [name of community]. Often these disputes result in litigation that is costly and time-consuming for all concerned. To provide an alternative to litigation for resolving such disputes, the [name of local legislature] encourages the use of voluntary mediation as set forth in this local law.

B. This local law shall be liberally construed so as to effectuate the purposes described herein. No provision of this law shall be construed to abridge the powers or decision-making authority of the [name of local legislature] or any other board, office, committee, or official to which the [name of local legislature] has delegated the responsibility for issuing permits, granting approvals, or otherwise advising the [name of local legislature].

Section 3. Fiscal Implications

All costs associated with voluntary mediation conducted pursuant to this local law shall be allocated among the parties in interest in a manner to be determined by them. The [name of local legislature] of the [town, village or city of _____] is hereby authorized to allocate public funds to pay the costs of mediation and to enter into agreements for sharing those costs.

Section 4. Definitions

"LOCAL BOARD" shall mean the local legislature, zoning board of appeals, planning board, or other local board or agency charged with reviewing and approving proposals that affect the development or conservation of land within the jurisdiction of [name of community].

"MEDIATOR" shall mean an individual who has been certified as a mediator under the guidelines of the unified court system community dispute center program or a person who, prior to January first, nineteen hundred and ninety-seven, has served as a mediator in two or more separate disputes involving municipal planning and zoning.

"PARTY IN INTEREST" shall mean individuals or agents identified by the mediator as having a substantive concern or role in the outcome of a given planning or zoning proceeding conducted by the [name of community], provided however, that the [name of community] shall not be deemed a party in interest for the purposes of this article.

Section 5. Procedures

A. Mediation shall supplement, not replace, planning and zoning practices (including public hearings) otherwise applicable in the [name of community]. The use of mediation shall be voluntary and shall be available in any dispute in which two or more parties in interest agree to voluntary mediation.

B. Any party in interest regarding a proposal pending before a local board may request that the matter be mediated and that the local board suspend time limits contained in the state law or the local laws of the [name of community], relevant to such proposal for a period of 60 days.

C. The decision of a local board to consent to the suspension of time limits is entirely within the discretion of that board. Any such consent shall be conditioned, at a minimum, on the following:

1. Public notice of the proposed voluntary mediation shall be given in the official newspaper, by one or more parties of interest, at least 10 days and not more than 60 days prior to the granting of such consent by the local legislature or body. An affidavit of service of public notice shall be filed with the municipal clerk. Such notice shall include, at a minimum, the basis of the dispute and the permit or approval being sought; the name of the interested party seeking the permit or approval; and directions for contacting someone who will be responsible for providing information regarding the mediation and the procedure for joining the mediation.

2. The suspension of time limits shall not exceed 60 days. Upon expiration of the 60 days, the mediator, on behalf of parties to the mediation, may request an additional suspension period, not to exceed 60 days. There is no limit to the number of additional suspension periods to which the local legislature or body may consent. The legislature or body may receive evidence at a public hearing from any party in interest with regard to the progress of the mediation to determine whether consent to an extension of the suspension of time limits would be appropriate. Public notice of the hearing shall be published at least 10 days prior to the hearing in the official newspaper.

3. Nothing in this section shall be construed to limit the authority of the legislature or body to impose additional or more restrictive conditions upon its consent to the suspension of time limits.

Section 6. Confidentiality

Unless otherwise required by law, the parties in interest may agree that the proceedings of the mediation shall remain confidential.

Section 7. Accepted Practices

Any mediation undertaken pursuant to the provisions of this local law shall be conducted in accordance with accepted mediation practices including, but not limited to, those contained in Appendix A of this local law, and those developed by the New York State Dispute Resolution Association, Inc., for use by community dispute centers established pursuant to Article 21-A of the Judiciary Law.

Section 8. Effect of Agreement

The [town, village or city of _____] shall not be bound by the terms or conditions of any agreement resulting from voluntary mediation conducted pursuant to this local law. Terms or conditions of such an agreement may be presented at a public hearing on the requested permit or approval or appeal of their denial. The [name of local legislature], zoning board of appeals, planning board, or other reviewing authority may refuse to consider such terms or conditions presented if the parties in interest fail to provide factual justification for them on the record.

Section 9. Legislative Intent: Supersession of the Town Law

This Article is hereby adopted pursuant to Municipal Home Rule Law §10(1)(i) and §10(1)(ii)(a)(14) and Statute of Local Governments §10(6) of the State of New York. It is the intent of the Legislature, pursuant to Municipal Home Rule Law §10(1)(ii)(d)(3), to supersede the provisions of the Town Law, Chapter 16 §§264(1), 265(1), 267-a(5),(8),(11), 274-a(8),(10),-b(6),(8), 276(5),(6),(8), [and specific reference to any local laws incorporating relevant time limits] relating to time limits in connection zoning and planning determinations. [If this local law is adopted by a village or city, insert parallel provisions of the Village Law or General City Law.]

Section 10. Severability

If any provision of this Local Law is held to be unconstitutional or otherwise invalid by any court of competent jurisdiction, the remaining provisions of the Local Law shall remain in effect.

Section 11. Effective Date

This local law shall become effective upon filing with the Secretary of State.

F. FACILITATION OF LOCAL LAND USE DECISIONS

DEFINITION

Litigation and mediation assume the presence of a land use dispute and the need for a third party, such as a court or mediator, to help resolve that controversy. Facilitation is a technique that may be used to manage the community decision-making process so that controversies are minimized or avoided. Facilitation uses the same strategic approach as mediation. It involves the identification of all the parties who have an important interest in the matter, the convening of the parties, and discussions among them that identify their true interests, leading to decisions that are based upon those interests.

Facilitation may be used at any stage in the land use planning and decision-making process, including the preparation of a comprehensive plan, amendment of the zoning law, formulation of supplemental land use regulations, and review of significant development proposals. Experiences of local leaders indicate that this process is extremely flexible and can be led, or guided, by any number of participants in the normal land use process. The impetus for proper facilitation can come from the chair of a land use agency, one of its members, an applicant, a locally elected leader or staff member, or any number of potential opponents of the matter before the board.

With the proper training and orientation, some of these individuals may be able to serve as the facilitator of the process. Alternatively, persons not normally involved in the process can be trained and called on to facilitate land use decisionmaking processes, or outside, experienced facilitators can be used.

PURPOSE

Facilitation changes the normal land use decisionmaking process so that it involves the parties affected by those decisions in a more effective manner, typically much earlier in the process. It is intended to secure needed input early in the process, to create understanding in the community about the issues involved, to build support for the decision ultimately made, and to avoid delays later on. In this way, facilitation can head off controversies and avoid the need for litigation or mediation. If used over time, facilitation can create a stronger democratic tradition in a community and can help the community adapt to the complex challenges of the future.

A facilitator can supplement the traditional leadership roles played by elected and appointed leaders of local land use bodies, such as the legislative body, planning board and zoning board of appeals. These leaders are expected to assume responsibility for decision-making on substantive matters, to possess expertise relevant to the decision, and to control the process by which decisions are made. Facilitators are process experts who collaborate with board chairs or mayors to design and implement effective procedures that enable those affected by a pending decision to become productively involved, to express their true interests, and to see decisions made that consider those interests. This frees the decisionmaker to focus on the substantive issues under discussion and to maintain the broader perspective needed for effective community leadership.

Experts on modern leadership styles claim that the traditional model of leadership places unrealistic expectations and pressures on elected and appointed officials. That model has the leader in the trenches, with hands on every aspect of the problem, responsible for the conduct of the overall campaign as well as for the location, depth, and length of each trench. This approach calls attention to the leader and puts on that person the responsibility for all aspects of decision-making. When decisions work, the public is quiet, if not apathetic. When decisions fail, or are unpopular, the response is "throw the rascals out!" In neither case is the public involved, invested, and contributing as effectively as possible to the solution. Members of the commonwealth are not taking collective responsibility for decisions in line with this country's democratic traditions and expectations.

Involving the community in productive ways through the work of facilitators draws on the collective energy, skill, and wisdom of those affected by community decisions. Leadership experts suggest that today's complex quality of life problems—jobs, tax base, housing, environmental protection, and sustainable development—require not just solutions to individual problems but changes in the attitudes and behavior of citizens and the leaders of private sector and civic organizations. Over time, a community that takes a facilitated approach to problem solving is adapting to change in a powerful way that positions it to handle the complexities of tomorrow.

WHEN

The development of a comprehensive plan, the amendment of the zoning law, and the adoption of significant new land use regulations are opportunities that call for broad community participation. Decisions on applications for subdivision, site plan, and special permit approval can raise significant land use issues that affect numerous interests groups, which need to be involved in the process. In all of these cases, elected or appointed leaders of the community must design processes, establish agendas, respond to questions, run meetings, and follow up on those meetings. Calling on a facilitator to assist with this process can improve the process, ease pressures on the ultimate decisionmakers, and free them to concentrate on the substantive outcome rather than on the process itself.

AUTHORITY

New York law encourages citizen participation in comprehensive planning, zoning, and land use regulation decisionmaking, and in the project approval process. The state legislature has expressly and forcefully set forth its policy on this matter: "The participation of citizens in an open, responsible and flexible planning process is essential to the designing of the optimum comprehensive plan." Since all land use regulations are to conform to the comprehensive plan and all land use decisions to be based on the adopted regulations of the community, this policy should inform and guide all major land use decisions are made by local boards. It is reflected in the public hearing requirements for most land use permits and in the encouragement given to local agencies conducting environmental reviews to provide for public comment and participation in creating the scope of review for project proposals that may have a significant impact on the environment.

IMPLEMENTATION

Effective facilitation of land use decision-making can be initiated in either of two ways. It can be a deliberate effort on the part of elected or appointed leaders to establish a regular system of facilitated meetings. Facilitators can be identified within the community and trained, or an experienced outside facilitator can be retained to assist on a regular basis. Alternatively, any citizen or local leader can decide to function as a facilitator if that person is willing to assume the posture and develop the necessary skills. There are many examples of effective facilitation, from variance procedures being facilitated regularly by the chair of a zoning board of appeals to a member of a conservation advisory board facilitating an entire community planning process to revitalize a village's waterfront.

Experience indicates that training is integral to a facilitator's success. Facilitators need to know how effective decision-making processes are conducted, the roles of the facilitator, decision-maker, and other participants, and how the facilitator confronts and solves the problems that arise. The facilitator must learn how to prepare for meetings, begin a meeting, set agendas, express interests, define problems, generate optional solutions, assess solutions, reach agreements, and implement and monitor agreements.

To play an effective role in the decision-making process, the facilitator should have a neutral relationship with the participants and an impartial attitude toward the issues under discussion. This reality makes it more difficult, though not impossible, for an elected or appointed official to play the facilitator's role. In addition, the facilitator should complement the decisionmaker's role in the process–a fact that makes it even more difficult for an involved board member to be the process facilitator.

A facilitator should have several discrete attitudes and skills. Chief among these are a respect for the participants and their interests, an ability to listen to statements and help participants state their true interests clearly, an understanding of how to synthesize discussions and summarize conclusions, an openness to new ideas, and patience with dissenters, foot draggers, and alienated participants.

ILLUSTRATIONS

After returning from a course on facilitation, a member of a coastal zone management commission got involved in the preapplication stage of a residential subdivision proposal. She knew that some aspects of the proposal were bound to inflame community opposition and suggested to the applicant that he meet with the likely opponents to consider redesigning the proposal to meet their interests. After several meetings, the applicant redesigned the subdivision, created a significant buffer around protected wetlands and unprotected habitat, and then submitted his proposal. The subdivision application was determined by the planning board to be unlikely to have any significant negative impact on the environment, and it moved through the regular subdivision approval process relatively quickly and without opposition.

The chairman of a city planning commission who was trained in facilitation knew that over the course of the coming year his commission would receive three applications for development proposals that would affect a historic village green. After consultation with the city council and his board members, he invited all three potential applicants to come to an informal meeting to discuss their interests in the green and their proposals. Because of the positive, informal, and collaborative atmosphere he created, the participants were able to discuss and agree on the essential contributions the green made to their individual interests and to rethink their proposals to protect, and to enhance, those contributions. The development of guidelines for each proposal emerged organically from the well-managed meeting and influenced the proposals that were ultimately received by the commission.

The founder of a communitywide activist group spent a year building bridges with the significant interest groups in a rural community whose comprehensive plan designated the remaining farmland for preservation. This objective of the plan was not being achieved because the local legislature had not adopted land use regulations recommended in the comprehensive plan. The reasons for this resistance on the part of the legislature were not clear. By inviting a skilled facilitator into the process and carefully planning an informal meeting involving local legislators and all those interested in land use issues in the community, a discussion was held that revealed the legislators' concern with the adequacy of the tax base if residential subdivision development was discouraged on farmland. This issue was elevated as the central matter to be addressed, and an effective strategy was created to determine the impact of farmland preservation on the financial bottom line of the town. This receptivity to the legislators' interests resulted in their pledge to proceed with the strategy recommended in the comprehensive plan, pending receipt of the study.

A member of a local conservation advisory board returned from facilitation training with a renewed interest in addressing the serious failure of the community to plan for the revitalization of its extensive Hudson River waterfront. The need to develop a strategy for the waterfront's future had been apparent for over two decades, but repeated efforts to move in a positive direction had failed. After a round of negotiations with village trustees and planning and conservation board members, she began a series of discussions with local commercial, civic, and environmental leaders to host an event to unite the community in support of positive planning for their land at the river's edge. Together they developed plans for a waterfront festival and conference that engaged, quite literally, the entire community in planning for and carrying out the event. The festival elevated their interest, and the conference heightened their understanding of effective strategies available to them. The direct result was a resolution by the board of trustees to prepare a comprehensive plan for the riverfront, the appointment of a representative board to prepare that plan, the scheduling of a series of meetings with all interested groups, and the submission of an application for funding to prepare needed studies.

LIMITATIONS AND CONCERNS

Like mediation, the establishment of a formal approach to facilitated land use decision-making faces a number of obstacles. Facilitators must be identified and trained. The community must be educated about the benefits of this new and different approach that will change the status quo. There is a general lack of awareness of and support for collaborative processes of this kind. If a facilitator is an established community leader, her objectivity may be questioned, and, if not, her credibility may be suspect. The job of identifying and involving credible representatives of all involved interest groups in the community is a difficult one because of these groups' varying states of organization and effectiveness.

STATUTES AND REGULATIONS

New York State Town Law §272-a(1)(e), Village Law §7-722(1)(e), and General City Law §28-a(2)(e) contain the policy statement of the state legislature encouraging citizen participation in comprehensive planning.

Title 6 NYCRR Part 617.8(e) mandates the participation of the public in the process of developing a scope for the environmental review of projects and actions that may have a significant impact on the environment.

CASE DIGEST

In a somewhat controversial decision, the New York Court of Appeals breathed significant flexibility into the State Environmental Quality Review Act (SEQRA) review process. *Merson v. McNally*, 90 N.Y.2d 742, 688 N.E.2d 479, 665 N.Y.S.2d 605 (1997). The issue in that case was whether a project that, as originally proposed, involved several potentially large environmental impacts could be redesigned in the early SEQRA process to avoid negative impacts. If so, this would end the environmental review process and save the time and cost involved in preparing and reviewing an environmental impact statement.

The agency involved in the *Merson* case was the planning board of the Town of Philipstown. The owner of a mining site submitted a full environmental assessment form as required by SEQRA along with its application to the board for a special permit to conduct mining operations. In an unusual move, the planning board conducted a series of open meetings with the project sponsor, other involved agencies, and the public. As a direct result of the input received at these meetings, the applicant revised the project to avoid any significant negative impacts. The planning board then issued a negative declaration, finding that the project, as now configured, would not negatively affect the environment. The plaintiffs, a group of community residents, claimed that the board's action constituted a conditional negative declaration that, under SEQRA regulations, cannot be issued for the type of action involved here to avoid going the next step and preparing an environmental impact statement.

The Court of Appeals disagreed, finding that the planning board had conducted an "open and deliberative process" characterized by significant "give and take." It described the planning board's actions as "an open process that also involved other interested agencies and the public" rather than "a bilateral negotiation between a developer and lead agency." It found that the changes made in the proposal were not the result of conditions imposed by the planning board but, instead, were "adjustments incorporated by the project sponsor to mitigate the concerns identified by the public and the reviewing agencies . . ." As one source of authority for this degree of flexibility in the early environmental review process, the court pointed to the SEQRA regulations that describe the purpose of requiring an applicant to file a full environmental assessment form: "[The form is] intended to provide a method whereby applicants and agencies can be assured that the determination process has been orderly, comprehensive in nature, yet flexible enough to allow introduction of information to fit a project or action."

The Philipstown planning board is somewhat typical of the volunteer boards in New York that are charged with environmental review responsibility as they consider applications for subdivision and site plan approval and for the issuance of special permits and variances. There are approximately 25,000 volunteer board members in the state. As *Merson* illustrates, they are the ones who must design and conduct the orderly, "open and deliberative process" that was essential to the court's decision to uphold the negative declaration issued by the planning board in that matter.

Chapter 11

Conclusion

Three decades ago, Richard Babcock, the distinguished land use practitioner, prefaced his book *The Zoning Game* with the observation that zoning represents "the unique American contribution to the solution of disputes over competing demands for the use of private land. When there are conflicting interests, it is patently necessary for someone to determine which of these are valid." His complete statement is found on the dedication page of this book, and is referenced in this conclusion to emphasize that land use decisionmaking fundamentally concerns itself with conflict resolution.

For over 30 years, we have been struggling to define who Babcock's "someone" is and to determine where land use authority should be grounded. Throughout the 1970s and 1980s, we relied increasingly on the federal government to establish standards for natural resource protection, while local governments continued to make the decisions that dictated the pace and shape of development within the broad market and demographic forces that swept the country. The emphasis in the 1990s on the devolution of power and decisionmaking to the grassroots level heightens our understanding of the important role that local governments have played in determining land and natural resource use for most of this century. Although federal and state influences are powerful, it is inescapable that Babcock's "someone" is now, as in the 1960s, the officials who make local land use decisions.

Perhaps the greatest potential strength of the land use system in New York State, and one of the reasons why this book chose to examine the New York process in depth, is its extraordinary reliance on officials and leaders who serve on and appear before local decisionmaking boards. This potential is evidenced throughout this book. We have seen how local officials are beginning to use mediation and facilitation to involve interested parties in land use decision-making to improve those decisions and avoid costly litigation. Meaningful citizen participation is taking place in comprehensive planning and in the adoption of land use regulations to create a common vision and policy base to build support for subsequent land use actions. There are recent and dynamic examples of the use of the authority that local governments have to enter into intermunicipal agreements to gain control over shared natural resources and market areas.

This book, as a whole, highlights the great flexibility that the New York legislature has given to its municipalities to employ land use strategies capable of guiding development to areas where it is desired and of achieving effective conservation of critical natural landscapes. This said, there is much still to be done. Having constructed many critical intersections of influence at the local and intermunicipal level, additional connections need to be established. A gubernatorial task force is studying how to use the resources of state agencies to provide incentives for local smart growth initiatives and intermunicipal compacts. We are still searching for ways of aligning federal, state, and local land use plans, regulations, and programs. The New York experience suggests, however, that reform movements be respectful of the historic role assigned to local government in land use.

The local base of the land use system provides some the connections needed to resolve critical land use conflicts and work toward mutually beneficial results. The increasing use of mediation, facilitation, citizen participation, and intermunicipal compacts establishes a dialogue about how the destiny of the Empire State should be shaped. Contemporary theories about the efficient behavior of systems suggests that such a dialogue, effectively conducted, will lead to fair and balanced results, respectful of private property rights and the needs of the public at large. More needs to be done to strengthen this dialogue, horizontally, within communities and among local governments and to extend it, vertically, to include regional, state, and federal agencies.

Through their recent use of the full scope of the authority delegated to them, New York's municipal leaders are demonstrating that, as those charged with the resolution of conflicts over the use of private land, this unique land use system is well grounded at the community level with its still firm hold on the American democratic tradition. This is a firm base on which to build a land use system competent to handle the challenges of the 21st century.

Appendix A: Glossary of Terms and Phrases

Accessory Apartment. A second residential unit that may be contained within an existing single-family home, garage, or carriage house. An accessory apartment is usually required to be a complete housekeeping unit that can function independently, with separate access, kitchen, bedroom, and sanitary facilities.

Accessory Use. The use of land that is subordinate, incidental to, and customarily found in connection with the principal use allowed on a lot by the zoning law. A garage is incidental to the principal use of a lot as a single-family residence and is customarily found on a single-family parcel.

Action. Under the New York State Environmental Quality Review Act, any project or physical activity that is directly undertaken, funded, or approved by a state or local agency that may affect the environment. Actions include planning and policy-making activities and the adoption of rules and regulations that may affect the environment.

Administrative Body. A body created by local legislatures to undertake administrative functions such as the review of applications for site plans, subdivisions, and special use permits. *See* "Reviewing Board."

Adult Use. A business that provides sexual entertainment or services to customers. Adult uses include: X-rated video shops and bookstores, live or video peep shows, topless or fully nude dancing establishments, combination book/video and "marital aid" stores, non-medical massage parlors, hot oil salons, nude modeling studios, hourly motels, body painting studios, swingers clubs, X-rated movie theaters, escort service clubs, and combinations thereof.

Advisory Opinion. A report by a local administrative body, which does not have the authority to issue permits or adopt laws and regulations, prepared for the consideration by a local body that does.

Aesthetic Resources. Natural resources such as open vistas, woods, scenic viewsheds, and attractive man-made settings whose appearance is an important ingredient in the quality of life of a community.

Affordable Housing. Housing developed through some combination of zoning incentives, cost-effective construction techniques, and governmental subsidies which can be rented or purchased by households who cannot afford market-rate housing in the community.

Agency. Under the State Environmental Quality Review Act (SEQRA), any state or local agency–including zoning boards of appeals, local legislatures, planning boards, and, under certain circumstances, even building inspectors–that makes discretionary decisions that may affect the environment. These agencies are subject to SEQRA regulations whenever taking an "action."

Aggrieved Party. Only aggrieved parties may appeal a reviewing body or local legislature's land use decision to the courts. The decision must result in some demonstrable harm to the party that is different from the impact of the decision on the community as a whole.

Agricultural Land Protection. Any law, regulation, board, or process that has as its objective the preservation of farming on land dedicated to agricultural use. Examples include agricultural zoning, farmland preservation boards, property tax relief for farmers, and anti-nuisance laws.

Agricultural Zoning District. A designated portion of the municipality where agricultural uses are permitted as-of-right and non-farm land uses either are prohibited or are allowed subject to limitations or conditions imposed to protect the business of agriculture.

Amortization of Nonconforming Uses. Nonconforming uses that are particularly inconsistent with zoning districts within which they exist and are not immediately dangerous to public health or safety may be terminated or amortized within a prescribed number of years. This amortization period allows the landowner to recoup some or all of his investment in the offensive nonconforming use.

Appellate Jurisdiction. A zoning board of appeals has appellate jurisdiction to review determinations of the zoning enforcement officer. Denials of building permits and determinations that proposed land uses do not meet the zoning law's standards may be appealed to the zoning board of appeals. Land use decisions of the zoning board of appeals, planning board, and local legislature may be appealed to the courts, which exercise appellate jurisdiction over them.

Approval. A discretionary decision made by a local agency to issue a permit, certificate, license, lease, or other entitlement or to otherwise authorize a proposed project or activity.

Architectural Review Board. A body that reviews proposed developments for their architectural congruity with surrounding developments and either renders an advisory opinion on the matter or is authorized to issue or deny a permit. Its review is based upon design criteria or standards adopted by the local legislature.

Area Variance. A variance that allows for the use of land in a way that is not permitted by the dimensional or physical requirements of the zoning law. This type of variance is needed when a building application does not comply with the setback, height, lot, or area requirements of the zoning law. For example, if an owner wants to build an addition to a house that encroaches into the side-yard setback area, that owner must apply to the zoning board of appeals for an area variance.

Article 78 Proceeding. Article 78 of the Civil Practice Law and Rules allows aggrieved persons to bring an action against a government body or officer. This device allows review of state and local administrative proceedings in court.

As-of-Right Use. A use of land that is permitted as a principal use in a zoning district. In a single-family district, the construction of a single-family home is an as-of-right use of the lot.

Buffer. A designated area of land that is controlled by local regulations to protect an adjacent area from the impacts of development.

Building Area. The total square footage of a parcel of land which is allowed by the regulations to be covered by buildings and other physical improvements.

Building Code. The Uniform Fire Prevention and Building Code, as modified by local amendments. This code governs the construction details of buildings and other structures in the interests of the safety of the occupants and the public. A local building inspector may not issue a building permit unless the applicant's construction drawings comply with the provisions of the building code.

Building Height. The vertical distance from the average elevation of the proposed finished grade along the wall of a building or structure to the highest point of the roof, for flat roofs, or to the mean height between eaves and ridge, for gable, hip, and gambrel roofs.

Building Inspector. The local administrative official charged with the responsibility of administering and enforcing the provisions of the building code. In some communities, the building inspector may also be the zoning enforcement officer.

Building Permit. A permit that must be issued by a municipal agency or officer before activities such as construction, alteration, or expansion of buildings or improvements on the land may legally commence.

Bulk Regulations. The controls in a zoning district governing the size, location, and dimensions of buildings and improvements on a parcel of land.

Bulk Variance. *See* "Area Variance."

Capital Budget. The municipal budget that provides for the construction of capital projects in the community.

Capital Project. Construction projects including public buildings, roads, street improvements, lighting, parks, and their improvement or rehabilitation paid for under the community's capital budget.

Cellular Facility. An individual cell of a cellular transmission system that includes a base station, antennae, and associated electronic equipment that sends to and receives signals from mobile phones.

Central Business District (CBD). The traditional business core of a community, characterized by a relatively high concentration of business activity within a relatively small area. The CBD is usually the retail and service center of a community. Because of its compactness, there is usually an emphasis on pedestrian traffic in the CBD.

Certificate of Occupancy. A permit that allows a building to be occupied after its construction or improvement. It certifies that the construction conforms to the building code and is satisfactory for occupancy.

City Council. *See* "Local Legislature."

Cluster Subdivision. The modification of the arrangement of lots, buildings, and infrastructure permitted by the zoning law to be placed on a parcel of land to be subdivided. This modification results in the placement of buildings and improvements on a part of the land to be subdivided in order to preserve the natural and scenic quality of the remainder of the land.

Components. Elements of a comprehensive plan that are suggested by state law.

Comprehensive Plan. A written document that identifies the goals, objectives, principles, guidelines, policies, standards, and strategies for the growth and development of the community.

Condition. A requirement or qualification that is attached to a reviewing board's approval of a proposed development project. A condition must be complied with before the local building inspector or department can issue a building permit or certificate of occupancy.

Conditional Use Permit. *See* "Special Use Permit."

Conditioned Negative Declaration (CND). Under the New York State Environmental Quality Review Act, a CND is a negative declaration issued by a "lead agency" for an "unlisted action." This involves an action that, as initially proposed, may result in one or more significant adverse environmental impacts but that, when modified by mitigation measures required by the lead agency, will result in no significant adverse environmental impacts.

Conservation Advisory Council (CAC). A body created by the local legislature to advise in the development, management, and protection of the community's natural resources and to prepare an inventory and map of open spaces.

Conservation Board. Once the local legislature has reviewed and approved an open-space inventory and map, it may designate the conservation advisory council as a conservation board and authorize it to review and comment on land use applications that affect community open space.

Conservation Easement. A voluntary agreement between a private landowner and a municipal agency or qualified not-for-profit corporation to restrict the development, management, or use of the land. The agency holds the interest and is empowered to enforce its restrictions against the current landowner and all subsequent owners of the land.

Conservation Overlay Zones. In conservation overlay zones, the legislature adopts more stringent standards than those contained in the underlying zoning districts as necessary to preserve identified resources and features in need of conservation or preservation.

Critical Environmental Area (CEA). A specific geographic area designated by a state or local agency as having exceptional or unique environmental characteristics. In establishing a CEA, the fragile or threatened environmental conditions in the area are identified so that they will be taken into consideration in the site-specific environmental review under the New York State Environmental Quality Review Act.

Cumulative Impact Analysis. In conducting an environmental review of a proposed project, its negative impacts on the environment may be considered in conjunction with those of nearby or related projects to determine whether, cumulatively, the adverse impacts are significant and require the preparation of an environmental impact statement.

Decision. The final determination of a local reviewing body or administrative agency or officer regarding an application for a permit or approval.

Deed Restrictions. A covenant or restriction placed in a deed that restricts the use of the land in some way. These are often used to insure that the owner complies with a condition imposed by a land use body.

Density Bonus. *See* "Incentive Zoning."

Density. The amount of development permitted per acre on a parcel under the zoning law. The density allowed could be, for example, four dwelling units per acre or 40,000 square feet of commercial building floor per acre.

Determination. A decision rendered by an officer or administrative body on an application or a request for a ruling.

Development Overlay Zones. In development overlay zones, the legislature may provide incentives, such as density bonuses or waivers of certain zoning requirements, for developers who build the type of development desired.

District. A portion of a community identified on the locality's zoning map within which one or more principal land uses are permitted along with their accessory uses and any special land uses permitted by the zoning provisions for the district.

Dwelling Unit. A unit of housing with full housekeeping facilities for a family.

Easement. An easement involves the right to use a parcel of land to benefit an adjacent parcel of land, such as to provide vehicular or pedestrian access to a road or sidewalk. Technically known as an easement appurtenant.

Eminent Domain. The government's right to take title to private property for a public use upon the payment of just compensation to the landowner.

Enabling Act. Legislation passed by the New York State Legislature authorizing counties, cities, towns, and villages to carry out functions in the public interest. The power to adopt comprehensive plans, zoning ordinances, and land use regulations is delegated to towns, villages, and cities under the Town Law, Village Law, General City Law, and Municipal Home Rule Law.

Environment. The environment is defined broadly under the New York State Environmental Quality Review Act to include the physical conditions that will be affected by a proposed action, including land, air, water, minerals, flora, fauna, noise, resources of agricultural, archeological, historic or aesthetic significance, existing patterns of population concentration, distribution, or growth, existing community or neighborhood character, and human health.

Environmental Assessment Form (EAF). As used in the New York State Environmental Quality Review Act process, this is a form completed by an applicant to assist an agency in determining the environmental significance of a proposed action. A properly completed EAF must contain enough information to describe the proposed action and its location, purpose, and potential impacts on the environment.

Environmental Impact Statements (EIS). A written "draft" or "final" document prepared in accordance with the New York State Environmental Quality Review Act. An EIS provides a means for agencies, project sponsors, and the public to systematically consider significant adverse environmental impacts, alternatives, and mitigation strategies. An EIS facilitates the weighing of social, economic, and environmental factors in the planning and decision-making process. A draft EIS (DEIS) is the initial statement prepared by either the project sponsor or the lead agency and circulated for review and comment before a final EIS (FEIS) is prepared.

Environmental Quality Review. The process that reviewing boards must conduct to determine whether proposed projects may have a significant adverse impact on the environment and, if they do, to study these impacts and identify alternatives and mitigation conditions that protect the environment to the maximum extent practicable.

Environmental Review. The New York State Environmental Quality Review Act requires local agencies that review applications for land use approvals to take a hard look at the environmental impact of proposed projects. Where the proposed project may have a significant adverse impact on the environment, the agency must prepare an environmental impact statement before approving the project. The adoption of comprehensive plans, zoning amendments, and other land use regulations is also subject to environmental review.

Exclusionary Zoning. When a community fails to accommodate, through its zoning law, the provision of affordable types of housing to meet proven regional housing needs, that community is said to practice exclusionary zoning.

Executive Session. A meeting, or part of a meeting, that is closed to the public because the topics to be discussed involve real estate, litigation, or sensitive personnel matters.

Facilitation. A process of decisionmaking guided by a facilitator who insures that all affected individuals and groups are involved in a meaningful way and that the decisions are based on their input and made to achieve their mutual interests. Facilitators may be neutral outside third parties or community leaders trained or experienced in the process.

Family. One or more persons occupying a dwelling as a single housekeeping unit.

Final Plat Approval. The approval by the authorized local reviewing body of a final subdivision drawing or plat that shows the subdivision, proposed improvements, and conditions as specified in the locality's subdivision regulations and as required by that body in its approval of the preliminary plat.

Floating Zone. A zoning district that is added to the zoning law but "floats" until an application is made to apply the new district to a certain parcel. Upon the approval of the application, the zoning map is amended to apply the floating district to that parcel of land.

Floodplain. The area on the sides of a stream, river, or watercourse that is subject to periodic flooding. The extent of the floodplain is dependent on soil type, topography, and water flow characteristics.

Floor Area Ratio (FAR). The gross floor area of all buildings permitted on a lot divided by the area of the lot. In zoning, the permitted building floor area is calculated by multiplying the maximum FAR specified for the zoning district by the total area of the parcel. A permitted FAR of 2 would allow the construction of 80,000 square feet of floor space on 40,000 square feet of land (40,000 x 2 = 80,000).

Freedom of Information Law. The New York State Freedom of Information Law requires that the public be provided access to governmental records, including local land use documents, such as photos, maps, designs, drawings, rules, regulations, codes, manuals, reports, files, and opinions. Public access may be denied if it would constitute an invasion of privacy.

Freshwater Wetlands Regulation. Laws passed by federal, state, and local governments to protect wetlands by limiting the types and extent of activities permitted within wetlands. These laws require landowners to secure permits before conducting many activities, such as draining, filling, or constructing buildings.

Frontage. Zoning laws typically require that developable lots have a specified number of linear feet that front on a dedicated street. A 100-foot frontage requirement means that a lot must have 100 linear feet on the side of the parcel that fronts on a street.

Goals. Broad statements of ideal future conditions that are desired by the community and that are contained in the comprehensive plan. For example, a community may have a goal of "providing an ample stock of affordable housing."

Group Home. Residences for a variety of special populations in need of supervized living facilities. Individuals residing in group homes may be mentally or physically disabled, recovering substance abusers, teenaged mothers, or victims of domestic violence. Able-bodied elderly persons, college students, young professionals, and other people not related by blood, marriage, or adoption might also form groups that wish to live together. When such groups of unrelated persons seek housing in a single-family home, the question arises as to whether they are a "family" entitled to live in a residential unit in a single-family zoning district.

Historic District. A regulatory overlay zone within which new developments must be compatible with the architecture of the district's historic structures. Alterations and improvements of historic structures must involve minimum interference with the historic features of the buildings. The local legislature establishes standards that a historic preservation commission uses to permit, condition, or deny projects proposed in historic districts.

Historic Preservation Commission. A commission established to review proposed projects within historic districts for compliance with standards established for new development or alteration or improvement of historic buildings and landmarks.

Home Occupation. A business conducted in a residential dwelling unit that is incidental and subordinate to the primary residential use. Regulations of home occupations usually restrict the percentage of the unit that can be used for the occupation, the exterior evidence of the business, and the amount of parking allowed and traffic generated.

Home Rule Authority. Home rule authority gives local governments the power to adopt laws relating to their local property, affairs, and government, in addition to the powers specifically delegated to them by the legislature. In New York State, the Municipal Home Rule Law gives a municipality the authority to regulate for the "protection and enhancement of its physical and visual environment" as well as for the "government, protection, order, conduct, safety, health, and well being of persons or property therein." Zoning laws may also be adopted under home rule authority.

Implementation Plan or Measures. Implementation plans coordinate all the related strategies that are to be carried out to achieve the objectives contained in the comprehensive plan. An implementation plan answers the questions: who, what, where, and how.

Incentive Zoning. A system by which zoning incentives are provided to developers on the condition that specific physical, social, or cultural benefits are provided to the community. Incentives include increases in the permissible number of residential units or gross square footage of development, or waivers of the height, setback, use, or area provisions of the zoning ordinance. The benefits to be provided in exchange may include affordable housing, recreational facilities, open space, day-care facilities, infrastructure, or cash in lieu thereof.

Infrastructure. Infrastructure includes utilities and improvements needed to support development in a community. Among these are water and sewage systems, lighting, drainage, parks, public buildings, roads and transportation facilities, and utilities.

Intermunicipal Agreements. Compacts among municipalities to perform functions together that they are authorized to perform independently. In the land use area, localities may agree to adopt compatible comprehensive plans and ordinances, as well as other land use regulations, and to establish joint planning, zoning, historic preservation, and conservation advisory boards or to hire joint inspection and enforcement officers.

Involved Agency. An agency that has jurisdiction by law to fund, approve, or directly undertake an action, but does not have the primary responsibility for the action as does the lead agency under the New York State Quality Environmental Review Act.

Judicial Review. The oversight by the courts of the decisions and processes of local land use agencies. It is governed by special statutory provisions that limit both actions against governmental bodies in general and actions against local land use decisions in particular. The applicable rules of judicial review depend on the type of local body that is involved and the type of action that is challenged. The courts in New York have adopted fairly liberal rules of access, typically allowing adjacent and nearby property owners and associations of residents to challenge land use decisions that affect them in some special way.

Jurisdictional Defect. When a legislative action or a land use determination is taken without following a mandated procedure, such as referral to a county planning agency or the conduct of environmental review, the action or determination suffers from a jurisdictional defect and is void. Without following mandated procedures, public bodies do not have jurisdiction to act.

Land Trust. A not-for-profit organization, private in nature, organized to preserve and protect the natural and man-made environment by, among other techniques, holding conservation easements that restrict the use of real property.

Land Use Law. Land use law encompasses the full range of laws and regulations that influence or affect the development and conservation of the land. This law is intensely intergovernmental and interdisciplinary. In land use law there are countless intersections among federal, state, regional, and local statutes. It is significantly influenced by other legal regimes such as environmental, administrative, and municipal law.

Land Use Regulation [Local]. Laws enacted by the local legislature for the regulation of any aspect of land use and community resource protection, including zoning, subdivision, special use permit or site plan regulation, or any other regulation that prescribes the appropriate use of property or the scale, location, or intensity of development.

Landmark Preservation Law. A law designating individual historic or cultural landmarks and sites for protection. It controls the alteration of landmarks and regulates some aspects of adjacent development to preserve the landmarks' integrity.

Lead Agency. The "involved agency" under the New York State Environmental Quality Review Act that is principally responsible for undertaking, funding, or approving an action. The lead agency is responsible for determining whether an environmental impact statement is required in connection with the action and for the preparation and filing of the statement if one is required.

Local Board. *See* "Reviewing Body."

Local Law. The highest form of local legislation. The power to enact local laws is granted by the state constitution to local governments. Local laws, in this sense, have the same quality as acts of the state legislature, both being authorized by the constitution. They must be adopted by the formalities required for the adoption of local laws.

Local Legislature. The local legislature adopts and amends the comprehensive plan, zoning, and land use regulations, and sometimes retains the authority to issue certain permits or perform other administrative functions. The local legislature of a city is typically called the city council; of a village, the village board of trustees; and of a town, the town board.

Lot Area. The total square footage of horizontal area included within the property lines. Zoning laws typically set a minimum required lot area for building in each zoning district.

Lot. A portion of a subdivision, plat, tract, or other parcel of land considered as a unit for the purpose of transferring legal title from one person or entity to another.

Master Plan. A term used synonymously by many to refer to the comprehensive plan. The statutory, official name for the community's written plan for the future is the comprehensive plan.

Mediation. A voluntary process of negotiation, conducted by a trained mediator who works with all involved parties to identify their true interests and to achieve a resolution that responds effectively and fully to those interests.

Minutes. The minutes typically cover the important discussions, facts found, and actions taken at a meeting. The Open Meetings Law requires that the minutes provide a record of motions, proposals, and actions.

Mitigation Conditions. Conditions imposed by a reviewing body on a proposed development project or other action to mitigate its adverse impact on the environment.

Mixed Use. In some zoning districts, multiple principal uses are permitted to coexist on a single parcel of land. Such uses may be permitted, for example, in neighborhood commercial districts, where apartments may be developed over retail space.

Moratorium. A moratorium suspends the right of property owners to obtain development approvals while the local legislature takes time to consider, draft, and adopt land use regulations or rules to respond to new or changing circumstances not adequately dealt with by its current laws. A moratorium is sometimes used by a community just prior to adopting a comprehensive plan or zoning law, or a major amendment thereto.

Multi-Family Housing. Most zoning maps contain districts where multi-family housing is permitted by the zoning law. Under the district regulations, buildings with three or more dwelling units are permitted to be constructed, such as garden apartments or multi-story apartment buildings.

Municipal Clerk. The public official authorized by the local legislature to keep official records of the legislative and administrative bodies of the locality. Final determinations of reviewing boards ordinarily must be filed with the municipal clerk.

Negative Declaration ("neg dec"). A written determination by a lead agency, under the New York State Environmental Quality Review Act, that the implementation of the action as proposed will not result in any significant adverse environmental impacts. A "neg dec" concludes the environmental review process for an action.

Nonconforming Building. A building constructed prior to the adoption of the zoning law or zoning amendment which is not in accordance with the dimensional provisions, such as building height or setback requirements, of that law or amendment.

Nonconforming Use. A land use that is not permitted by a zoning law but that already existed at the time the zoning law or its amendment was enacted. Most nonconforming uses are allowed to continue but may not be expanded or enlarged.

Notice. Notice requirements are contained in state and local statutes. They spell out the number of days in advance of a public hearing that public notice must be given and the precise means that must be used.

These means may include publication in the official local newspaper and mailing or posting notices in prescribed ways. Failure to provide public notice is a jurisdictional defect and may nullify the proceedings.

Objectives. Statements of attainable, quantifiable, intermediate-term achievements that help accomplish goals contained in the comprehensive plan. For example, an objective would be to achieve "the construction of 50 units of affordable housing annually until the year ____."

Official Map. The adopted map of a municipality showing streets, highways, parks, drainage, and other physical features. The official map is final and conclusive with respect to the location and width of streets, highways, drainage systems, and parks shown thereon and is established to conserve and protect the public health, safety, and welfare.

Open Meetings Law. The Town, Village, and General City Law requires local legislative, administrative, and quasi-judicial bodies to open all their meetings to members of the public. This law applies to all meetings where a majority of the board members are present, except those meetings that are held as executive sessions.

Ordinance. An act of a local legislature taken pursuant to authority specifically delegated to local governments by the state legislature. The power of villages to adopt ordinances was eliminated in 1974. Technically, therefore, villages do not adopt, amend, or enforce zoning ordinances. Zoning provisions in villages are properly called zoning laws.

Original Jurisdiction. When an aggrieved party must appeal a determination to a quasi-judicial or judicial body in the first instance, that body has original jurisdiction over that matter. The zoning board of appeals, for example, has original jurisdiction to hear appeals of the determinations of the zoning enforcement officer.

Overlay Zone. A zone or district created by the local legislature for the purpose of conserving natural resources or promoting certain types of development. Overlay zones are imposed over existing zoning districts and contain provisions that are applicable in addition to those contained in the zoning law.

Parcel. A piece of property. *See* "Lot."

Planned Unit Development. An overlay zoning district that permits land developments on several parcels to be planned as single units and to contain both residential dwellings and commercial uses. It is usually available to landowners as a mixed-use option to single uses permitted as-of-right by the zoning ordinance.

Planning Board/Commission. Planning boards must consist of five to seven members. Planning boards may be delegated reviewing board functions and a variety of advisory functions, including the preparation of the comprehensive plan, drafting zoning provisions, or suggesting site plan and subdivision regulations, in addition to other functions. One important purpose of the planning board's advisory role is to provide an impartial and professional perspective on land use issues based on the long-range needs of the community contained in the comprehensive plan or other local policy documents.

Plat. A site plan or subdivision map that depicts the arrangements of buildings, roads, and other services for a development.

Police Power. The power that is held by the state to legislate for the purpose of preserving the public health, safety, morals, and general welfare of the people of the state. The authority that localities have to adopt comprehensive plans and zoning and land use regulations is derived from the state's police power and is delegated by the state legislature to its towns, villages, and cities.

Positive Declaration ("pos dec"). A written determination by a lead agency, under the New York State Environmental Quality Review Act, that the implementation of the action as proposed is likely to have a significant adverse impact on the environment and that an environmental impact statement will be required.

Preliminary Plat Approval. The approval by the authorized local administrative body of a preliminary subdivision drawing or plat that shows the site conditions, subdivision lines, and proposed improvements as specified in the locality's subdivision regulations.

Principal Use. The primary use of a lot that is permitted under the district regulations in a zoning law. These regulations may allow one or more principal uses in any given district. Unless the district regulations allow mixed uses, only one principal use may be made of a single lot, along with uses that are accessory to that principal use.

Public Hearing. A hearing that affords citizens affected by a reviewing board's decision an opportunity to have their views heard before decisions are made. New York State statutes require that public hearings be held regarding the application for a variance or a subdivision approval. Public hearings regarding site plan applications and draft environmental impact statements may be required as a matter of local practice.

Public Services. Services provided by the municipal government for the benefit of the community, such as fire and police protection, education, solid waste disposal, street cleaning, and snow removal.

Quasi-Judicial. A term applied to some local administrative bodies that have the power to investigate facts, hold hearings, weigh evidence, draw conclusions, and use this information as a basis for their official decisions. These bodies adjudicate the rights of the parties appearing before the body. The zoning board of appeals serves in a quasi-judicial capacity when it hears appeals from the determination of the local zoning enforcement officer.

Record. Local boards must keep a detailed record of their deliberations in making decisions on site plan and subdivision applications and the issuance of variances and special permits. These records may be kept in narrative form rather than in verbatim transcript form. A clerk or secretary hired by the municipality often manages these records. The records should include the application and reports, studies, documents, and minutes of the board meetings.

Recreational Zoning. The establishment of a zoning district in which private recreational uses are the principal permitted uses. The types of recreational uses permitted include swimming, horseback riding, golf, tennis, and exercise clubs open to private members who pay dues and user fees or to the public on a fee basis.

Recusal. A term used when a board member has a conflict of interest and must abstain from voting on any issues relating to that private interest. The board member is said to be recusing himself from all deliberations on the matter.

Redaction. The practice of striking or otherwise taking out of a public record sensitive, private, or confidential information, in a way that does not disturb the meaning of the record.

Regulatory Taking. A regulation that is so intrusive that it is found to take private property for a public purpose without providing the landowner with just compensation.

Resolution. A means by which a local legislature or other board expresses its policy or position on a subject.

Restrictive Covenant. An agreement in writing and signed by the owner of a parcel of land that restricts the use of the parcel in a way that benefits the owners of adjacent or nearby parcels. *See* "Conservation Easement."

Reviewing Board. The administrative body charged with responsibility for reviewing, approving, conditioning, or denying applications for a specific type of land use such as a variance, special use permit, or site plan or subdivision approval.

Rezoning. An act of the local legislature that changes the principal uses permitted on one or more parcels of land or throughout one or more zoning districts. Rezoning includes the amendment of the zoning map, and of the use provisions in the district regulations applicable to the land that is rezoned.

Role of County Government. Functions carried out by county government that affect land use include the adoption of land use plans, public health reviews of plans for water supply and sewage disposal, planning reviews of certain local land use decisions, the development of county roads and projects including parks, the creation of environmental management councils, farmland protection boards, soil and water district boards, and other entities, and the provision of technical and coordination sources in the land use area.

Scoping. A process under the New York State Quality Environmental Review Act by which the lead agency identifies the potentially significant adverse impacts related to a proposed use and how they are to be addressed in an environmental impact statement (EIS). This process defines the scope of issues to be addressed in the draft EIS, including the content and level of detail of the analysis, the range of alternatives, and the mitigation measures needed, as well as issues that do not need to be studied. Scoping provides a project sponsor with guidance on matters that must be considered and provides an opportunity for early participation by involved agencies and the public in the review of the proposal.

Screening. The act of placing landscape features, such as trees, and shrubs, or man-made screens, such as fences or berms, to reduce the impact of development on nearby properties.

SEQRA. The New York State Environmental Quality Review Act requires local legislatures and land use agencies to consider, avoid, and mitigate significant environmental impacts of the projects that they approve, the plans or regulations they adopt, and the projects they undertake directly.

Setback. A setback restriction requires that no building or structure be located within a specified number of feet from a front, side, or rear lot line.

Sign Regulation. Local laws that regulate the erection and maintenance of signs and outdoor advertising with respect to their size, color, appearance, movement, and illumination, and their placement on structures or their location on the ground.

Site Plan. A site plan, consisting of a map and all necessary supporting material, shows the proposed development and use of a single parcel of land.

Special Exception Permit. *See* "Special Use Permit."

Special Use Permit. Special uses are allowed in zoning districts, but only upon the issuance of a special use permit subject to conditions designed to protect surrounding properties and the neighborhood from the negative impacts of the permitted use. Also called conditional use permit, special exception permit, and special permit.

Spot Zoning. The rezoning of a single parcel or a small area to benefit one or more property owners rather than to carry out an objective of the comprehensive plan.

Statute of Limitations. A law that requires that an aggrieved party file a legal action in a quasi-judicial or judicial forum within a specified period or lose the right to file that action. Regarding many land use determinations, the period begins from the date the determination is filed with the municipal clerk.

Strategies. A set of actions to be undertaken to accomplish each objective contained in a comprehensive plan. To obtain the objective of "50 units of affordable housing" the plan may include as strategies: (1) Form a housing trust fund, and (2) Allow for accessory apartments in residential units.

Subdivision Plat. *See* "Plat."

Subdivision. The subdivision of land involves the legal division of a parcel into a number of lots for the purpose of development and sale. The subdivision and development of individual parcels must conform to the provisions of local zoning which contain use and dimensional requirements for land development.

Taking. *See* "Regulatory Taking."

Town Board. *See* "Local Legislature."

Transfer of Development Rights. Provisions in a zoning law that allow for the purchase of the right to develop land located in a sending area and the transfer of those rights to land located in a receiving area.

Type I Action. Under the New York State Environmental Quality Review Act, an action that is more likely to have a significant adverse impact on the environment than unlisted actions. Type I Actions are listed in the regulations of the state Department of Environmental Conservation (DEC) commissioner. *See also* "Action."

Type II Action. An action that is not subject to environmental review under the New York State Environmental Quality Review Act. Type II Actions are listed in the regulations of the DEC commissioner. These actions have been determined not to have a significant impact on the environment or to be exempt from environmental review for other reasons. *See also* "Action."

Unlisted Actions. These are all of the actions that are not listed as Type I or Type II actions for the purposes of the New York State Environmental Quality Review Act process. These actions are subject to review by the lead agency to determine whether they may cause significant adverse environmental impacts.

Use District. *See* "Zoning District."

Use Variance. A variance that allows a landowner to put his land to a use that is not permitted under the zoning law. For example, if a parcel of land is zoned for single-family residential use and the owner wishes to operate a retail business, the owner must apply to the zoning board of appeals for a use variance. A use variance may be granted only in cases of unnecessary hardship. To prove unnecessary hardship, the owner must establish that the requested variance meets four statutorily prescribed conditions.

Variance. This is a form of administrative relief that allows property to be used in a way that does not comply with the literal requirements of the zoning ordinance. There are two basic types of variances: use variances and area variances.

Vested Rights. Vested rights are found when a landowner has received approval of a project and has undertaken substantial construction and made substantial expenditures in reliance on that approval. If the landowner's right to develop has vested, it cannot be taken away by a zoning change by the legislature.

Village Board of Trustees. *See* "Local Legislature."

Watershed. A geographical area within which rainwater and other liquid effluents seep and run into common surface or subsurface water bodies such as streams, rivers, lakes, or aquifers.

Wetlands. Wetlands may be either freshwater or tidal. They are typically marked by waterlogged or submerged soils or support a range of vegetation peculiar to wetlands. They provide numerous benefits for human health and property as well as critical habitat for wildlife, and are generally regulated by federal, state, or local laws.

Zoning Board of Appeals. Under state statutes, a zoning board of appeals must be formed when a local legislature adopts its zoning law. It must consist of three to five members. The essential function of the zoning board of appeals is to grant variances. In this capacity, it protects landowners from the unfair application of the laws in particular circumstances. The zoning board of appeals also hears appeals from the decisions of the zoning enforcement officer or building inspector when interpretations of the zoning ordinance are involved.

Zoning District. A part of the community designated by the local zoning law for certain kinds of land uses, such as for single-family homes on lots no smaller than one acre or for neighborhood commercial uses. Only these primary permitted land uses, their accessory uses, and any special uses permitted in the zoning district may be placed on the land in that part of the community.

Zoning Enforcement Officer. The local administrative official who is responsible for enforcing and interpreting the zoning law. The local building inspector may be designated as the zoning enforcement officer. Land use applications are submitted to the zoning enforcement officer, who determines whether proposals are in conformance with the use and dimensional requirements of the zoning law.

Zoning Law or Ordinance. New York State law allows city councils and town boards to adopt zoning regulations by local law or ordinance. Since 1974, village boards of trustees have not had the authority to adopt legislation by ordinance; they may adopt legislation only by local law. Technically, zoning regulations adopted by villages are zoning laws. Only city and town legislatures may adopt zoning ordinances. Zoning regulations, however, are often referred to as zoning ordinances regardless of these technical distinctions.

Zoning Map. This map is approved at the time that the local legislature adopts a zoning ordinance. On this map, the zoning district lines are overlaid on a street map of the community. The map divides the community into districts. Each district will carry a designation that refers to the zoning code regulations for that district. By referring to the map, it is possible to identify the use district within which any parcel of land is located. Then, by referring to the text of the zoning code, it is possible to discover the uses that are permitted within that district and the dimensional restrictions that apply to building on that land. The zoning map, implemented through the text of the zoning law, constitutes a blueprint for the development of the community over time.

APPENDIX B: TABLE OF STATUTES

This table was created by the NYS Legislative Commission on Rural Resources as a reference to the major statutes relevant to the practice of land use law. The first column lists sections from the General City Law, the second from the Town Law, the third from Village Law, and the last column lists other applicable laws.

SUBJECT	CITY	TOWN	VILLAGE	OTHER
Acquisition of open space and areas				NY Gen. Mun. §247
Adirondack Park Act				NY Exec. §§800–820
Ag. and farmland protection programs				NY Agric. & Mkts. §§321–326
Agricultural data statement		283-a	7-739	
Agricultural districts program				NY Agric. & Mkts. §§300–310
Appropriations		261		
Business Improvement Districts				NY Gen. Mun. §§980–980-p
Canal system				NY Canal §§138-a–138-c.
Capital Program				NY Gen. Mun. §99-g
Co-generation/small hydro/ alt. energy production				NY Energy §21-106
Community gardens				NY Agric. & Mkts. §§31-g–31-i
Community residential facilities				NY Mental Hyg. §41.34
Comprehensive plan	28-a	272-a	7-722	
Conflict with other laws		269	7-716	
Conservation Easements				NY Envtl. Conserv. §§49-0311–49-0311
Construction of solid waste facilities				NY Pub. Health §§1380–1383
Control of outdoor advertising				NY High. §88
County, metropolitan, regional planning boards				NY Gen. Mun. §§239-b-f, l-n

SUBJECT	CITY	TOWN	VILLAGE	OTHER
Delaware River Basin Compact				NY Envtl. Conserv. §§21-1701–21-1707
Driveways		130		
Dumping and litter	20	64 130	4-412	
Economic development zones				NY Gen. Mun. §§955–969
Entry by town engineer on private lands		32-A		
Factory manufactured homes				NY Real Property §233, NY Veh. & Traf. §122-c
Fine Arts and particular structure				NY Pub. Bldgs. §§40–44
Flood plain regulations		263		NY Envtl. Conserv. §§36-0101–36-0113
Grant of power	20 (25)	261	7-700	
Historic Preservation				NY Gen. Mun. §§119-aa–dd
Housing		138		
Hudson River Greenway Act				NY Envtl. Conserv. §§44-0101–44-0121
Intermunicipal Cooperation	20-g	284	7-739	NY Gen. Mun. §§5-G, 119-u
Junk yards				NY Gen. Mun. §136 (automobile), NY High §89
Land fill sitings				NY County §226-B
Licenses and permits		283		
Long Island Pine Barrens Protection Act				NY Envtl. Conserv. §§57-0101–57-0137
Long Island South Shore Estuary Reserve				NY Exec. §§960–970-a
Mined land reclamation				NY Envtl. Conserv. §§23-2701–23-2723
Municipal improvements in streets	36	280	7-736	
Official map	26 29	270 273	7-724	
Permits for work within the state highway right of way				NY High §52
Permits for buildings in bed of mapped streets	35 35-a	280	7-734	
Permits for buildings not on improved mapped streets	36	280-a	7-736	
Planning board/commission	27	271	7-718	NY Gen. Mun. §§235–237
Planning board; judicial review	38	282	7-740	

SUBJECT	CITY	TOWN	VILLAGE	OTHER
Private streets				NY Gen. Mun. §238
Public streets; encroachment	38-a	130 281	6-632	
Purpose	20	263	7-704	
Right to Farm Act				NY Agric. & Mkts. §308
Scenic byways program				NY High §§349-aa–dd
Scenic rivers program				NY Envtl. Conserv. §§15-2701–15-2723
Separability clause	39	285	7-742	
Signs		130	4-412	NY Gen. Mun. §74-c
Site plan review	27-a	274-a	7-725-a	
Site selection of community residential facilities				NY Mental Hyg. §41.34
Special use permits	27-b	274-b	7-725-b	
State Energy Plan				NY Energy §6-104
State Energy Conservation Construction Code Act				NY Energy §§11-101–11-110
Subdivision review	32 33	276 277	7-728 7-730	
Subdivision; realty				NY Pub. Health §§1115–1120 (water supply), NY Envtl. Conserv. §§17-1501–17-1515
Subdivision; record of plats	34	279	7-732	
Subdivision; cluster development	37	278	7-738	
Subdivision; Suffolk County sewage		277	7-730	
Subdivision; filing of maps				NY Real Prop. §334
Transfer of development rights	20-f	261-a	7-701	
Tree conservation				NY Gen. Mun. §96-B
Uniform fire prevention and building codes				NY Exec. §§370–383
Urban revitalization				NY Exec. §§894–907
Voting on law		63		
Waterfront revitalization of coastal areas and inland waterways				NY Exec. §§910–923
ZBA; enforcement		268 138	7-714 20-2010	
ZBA; permitted action	81-b	267-b	7-712-b	
ZBA; judicial review	82	267-c	7-712-c	
ZBA; procedure	81-a	267-a	7-712-a	

SUBJECT	CITY	TOWN	VILLAGE	OTHER
Zoning board of appeals	81	267	7-712	
Zoning districts	20	262 262-a	7-702	
Zoning; changes	83	265	7-708	
Zoning; incentive	81-d	261-b	7-703	
Zoning; first adoption, commission		266	7-710	
Zoning; exemptions	83-a	265-a	7-709	
Zoning; method of adoption of regulations	81 133	264	7-706	

APPENDIX C: TABLE OF CASES

Note: "ELR" citations are to *The Environmental Law Reporter®*,
Environmental Law Institute®